Eva Anderson Lawton

CATALOGUE OR BIBLIOGRAPHY

OF THE

LIBRARY

OF THE

HUGUENOT SOCIETY

OF

AMERICA

[SECOND EDITION]

––––––

COMPILED BY

JULIA P. M. MORAND

––––––

GENEALOGICAL PUBLISHING CO., INC.

BALTIMORE

Originally Published
Second Edition
Limited to 100 Copies
New York, 1920

Reprinted
Genealogical Publishing Company
Baltimore, 1971

Library of Congress Catalog Card Number 72-141421
International Standard Book Number 0-8063-0475-8

Made in the United States of America

This Second Edition of a Bibliography of Their Library Is

Dedicated and Presented

to

The Huguenot Society of America

by

Mrs. James Marsland Lawton

As a Memento of Her XXIX Years' Interest and Efforts as

Chairman of The Library Committee.

LIBRARY COMMITTEE

MRS. QUINCY O'M. GILLMORE
MISS ELSIE SCHUYLER CRANE
MRS. JAMES M. LAWTON, *Chairman*

INTRODUCTION

THE Second Edition of this Catalogue of the Library of the Huguenot Society of America gives evidence of remarkable growth and improvement since the publication of the First Edition, made about twenty-nine years ago.

The desire of the Society is assuredly fulfilled: There is now established in New York City a special Library of the History and Literature of the Huguenots!

This Collection has been classified with particular reference to the emigrations and various settlements of the Huguenots, and with regard to their influence upon the commercial, religious, and social life of the various countries in which they found a refuge.

There are many other books in this Library that treat more or less upon Huguenot history and times: These are placed in classes distinct from Huguenot literature, in order to make them more accessible and useful.

Under each class the books are arranged alphabetically by the author's name, excepting in the classes of Individual Biography and Genealogy. These sub-divisions follow their respective classes, under the name of the person or the family name. Anonymous books are entered under the title and also under the author's name, if the name be found.

The letters and number at the right of every entry in the Catalogue correspond to the letters and numbers that appear on the back of every book. It is necessary to give these when a book is called for.

All pamphlets are catalogued, classified, and shelved in pamphlet boxes until bound into volumes for their respective classes.

"It is well known that the history of these Huguenot people is replete with phases and facts of the most interesting character. . . . Its scope is almost limitless in variety. It touches, in its course through decades and centuries, not only religion, politics, invention, the arts and sciences, statesmanship and families, but it embraces nearly every branch of learning known to the province of letters. It is colored with romance; it is rich in acts of heroism; it is picturesque in its side lights. Every descendant of the Huguenots in this country has doubtless some tradition, document, or fragmentary record; and, while these alone may seem of little worth, when brought into connection with others they may prove important links in the chain of priceless information. It is fully expected that every Huguenot family in America, from the Atlantic to the Pacific, will sooner or later be represented in the membership of this Society by some of its representative descendants, and it is desirable that every one should awaken to the importance of aiding in the discovery and preservation of family records, church records, genealogical tables, public documents, entries in ancient Bibles, prayer-books, and Huguenot publications, manuscripts, autographs, and personal memoranda, as far as practicable."

For almost two years past work upon this Library was pursued continuously. At the outset it was impossible to decide or calculate the extent of the undertaking, and as it progressed it increased at every step!

Minute particulars of the work involved would hardly be of interest outside of the fellowship of those professionally interested in the art of cataloging and library economics.

Suffice it to say that in this labor of (in one word) *rejuvenization* of the Libary of your Society, not only every branch of that art has been employed, but necessity demanded ingenuity born of practical conception to contribute to the plainest, easiest, and quickest means to the underlying motive of the work: namely, that this valuable and interesting Library might no longer remain dormant, unknown, unsought, unread, and unappreciated!

To perform this work, and simultaneously to adhere to the plan exemplified by the Compiler of the earlier edition of this Catalogue, has been difficult to accomplish.

This introduction is in part compiled from the former edition of this Bibliography, the compiler desiring to link the present with the past, to color to-day's practical requirements with the sentiment of yesterday, and to point toward the needs and ambition of the morrow of this particular object and work of the Society.

The Compiler desires to add that her efforts are based upon many years' acquaintance with this Library and her work thereupon periodically.

May the ability to fulfill the dearest desire of your Chairman of the Library Committee redound to the pleasure of her beloved Society!

J. P. M. M.

April 1st, 1919.

CONTENTS

FRONTISPIECE AND DEDICATION
INTRODUCTION ix

PART I

Subjects   Class Page

HISTORY OF HUGUENOTS IN FRANCE . . . . HA   1
HISTORY OF HUGUENOTS IN OTHER COUNTRIES . . . . . HB   20
CHURCH HISTORY . . . . HC   31
FRENCH HISTORY . . . . HD   37
AMERICAN HISTORY . . . . HE   41
OTHER HISTORY . . . . HF   67
BIOGRAPHY . . . . HG   71
BIOGRAPHY, INDIVIDUAL . . . . HG   89
GENEALOGY . . . . HH 107
GENEALOGY FAMILY NAMES . . . . HH 133
DESCRIPTION AND TRAVEL . . . . HI 159
MANUSCRIPTS . . . . HJ 161
AUTOGRAPH LETTERS . . . . HJ 164
SOCIETIES (WORKS PUBLISHED BY) . . . . HK 165
PERIODICALS . . . . HL 194
THEOLOGY . . . . HM 195
LITERATURE . . . . HN 201
MISCELLANEOUS . . . . HO 205

PART II

DICTIONARY CATALOGUE 207
ADDENDA TO DICTIONARY 345
GEOGRAPHICAL REFERENCE 347

CATALOGUE OF THE LIBRARY

PART I

Arranged according to Classification

PLAN OF CLASSIFICATION

Class A.
History of Huguenots in France

Class B.
History of Huguenots in other countries

Class C.
Church history

Class D.
French history

Class E.
American history

Class F.
Other history.

Class G.
Biography

Class H.
Genealogy

Class I.
Description and travel

Class J.
Manuscripts

Class K.
Societies

Class L.
Periodicals

Class M.
Theology

Class N.
Literature

Class O.
Miscellaneous

CATALOGUE OF THE LIBRARY

AGUESSE, Laurent. Histoire de l'établissement du protestantisme en France, contenant l'histoire politique et religieuse de la nation depuis François Ier jusqu'à l'Edit de Nantes. Paris, 1882-86. 4 vols. O.
HA—Ag9

ALBY, Ernest. Les Camisards (1702-11). Paris [1857]. 241 pp. D.
HA—All

ANQUEZ, Léonce. Histoire des assemblées politiques des réformés de France (1573-1622). Paris, 1859. 519 pp. map. O.
HA—An7

—— Same.
HD—An6

APOLOGIE de Louis XIV et de son conseil, sur la Révocation de l'Edit de Nantes pour Servir de Réponse à la Lettre d'un Patriote sur la tolérance civile des Protestants de France. Avec une dissertation sur la Journée de la S. Barthelemi. VI, 566 pp., I-LXIII. n.p., 1758. D. par, [Caseirac, Jean Hovi de].
HA—C337

APOLOGIE pour les reformez. 1683. par, Paul Fetizon.
HA—F43

ARNAUD, Eugène. Histoire de l'académie protestante de Die en Dauphiné au XVIIe siècle. Paris, 1872. 116 pp. O.
HA—Ar62
Gift of Dr. Abram Du Bois.

—— Histoire des églises réformées de la vallée de Bourdeaux en Dauphiné. Paris, 1876. 50 pp. O.
HA—Ar6
Gift of Dr. Abram Du Bois.

—— Histoire des Protestants de Crest en Dauphiné pendant les trois derniers siècle. 102 pp. Q. Paris, 1893.
HA—Ar6
Bound with his: "Memoires historiques."

—— Histoire des protestants de Provence du Comtat Venaissin et de la principauté d'Orange. Paris, 1884. 2 vols. map. O.
HA—Ar61
Gift of Dr. Abram Du Bois.

—— Histoire des Protestants de Vivarais et du Valay pays de Languedoc de la Réforme a la Révolution. 2 vols. Q. Paris, 1888.
HA—Ar66
Vol. I: 1st, 2d, and 3d periods.
Vol. II: 4th period.
Gift of the Author, with (his) marginal notes.

—— Mémoires historiques sur l'origine les moeurs, les souffrances et la conversion au Protestantisme des Vaudois de Dauphiné. 90-126; 17-40; 1-70 pp. O. 1896.
HA——Ar6
Gift of the Author.

ARNAUD, Eugène. Notice historique et bibliographique sur les controverses religieuses en Dauphiné pendant la période de l'Edit de Nantes. 64 pp. O. Grenoble, 1872.　　　　HA—Ar6
Bound with his: "Memoires historiques."

—— Notice historique sue les deux Cathéchisme officiels de l'Eglise reformée de France, Calvin & Ostervald. 38 pp. O. Paris, 1885.　　　　HA—Ar6
Bound with his "Memoires Historiques."

—— Supplément aux Synodes du désert, de Edmond Hugues. Renfermant vingt-un synodes ou colloques inédits du Désert de Dauphiné. 60 pp. Sq. Q. Paris, 1892.　　　　HA—H871A

BABUT, Charles, pasteur. Inauguration du Musée du Désert . . . 24 Sept. 1911. Allocutions de F. Praux, E. Hugues, et C. Babut. Cevennes, 1912. O. (pp. 45-55.)　　　　HA—M986

BAIRD, Henry Martyn. History of the rise of the Huguenots. London, 1880. 2 vols. map. O.　　　　HA—B16
Vol. I. From beginning of the French reformation to Edict of January (1562).
Vol. II. From Edict of January (1562) to death of Charles the Ninth (1574).

BARRAU, J. J., and DARRAGON, B. Montford et les Albigeois. Bruxelles, 1840. 2 vols. S.　　　　HA—B27

BAUM, [Jean] Guillaume, Editor. Histoire ecclesiastique des églises reformées au royaume de France. . . . 1883-'89.　　　　HA—B46

—— Mémoires de Pierre Carrière dit Corteis. . . . 1871.　　HA—C812

BEARD, Augustus F. Churches of the Huguenots and the religious condition of France. 1884. O.　　　　HB—H12
From the *Andover Review*. 1884. Vol. I.
Presented by the publisher.

BEAUJOUR, Sophronyme. Essai sur l'histoire de l'église réformée de Caen. Caen, 1877. 597 pp. O.　　　　HA—B38
Gift of Dr. Abram Du Bois.

BELLEROCHE, E[dward]. Edit (l') de Nantes et les évènements successifs qui en ont amené la promulgation. Conférence, 13 Avril 1898, à New York. (The Huguenot Soc. of America.) 50 pp. D. Liège, 1898.　　　　HA—N19
Autograph gift of the Author.

[BENOIT, Elie.] HISTOIRE DE L'EDIT DE NANTES. Contenant Les choses les plus remarquables qui se sontpassées en France avant & après sa publication, à l'occasion de la diversité des Religions: *Et principalement les Contraventions, In executions, Chicanes, Artifices,* Violences & autres *Injustices, que les Reforme se plaignent d'y avoir souffertes, jusques à* L'Edit de Revocation, en Octobre, 1685. A Delft, Chez Adrien Beman, 1693. Q. pp. 3470. Five volumes.
Gift of The Hon. John Jay.

[BENOIT, Elie.] Histoire de l'Edit de Nantes. Delft, 1693-95. 5 vols. plates. Q. HA—B44

BERARD, Alexandre. Les Vaudois: leur histoire sur les deux versants des Alpes du IVe siècle au XVIIIe. 328 pp., 1 pl. O. Lyon, 1892. HA—B461
Gift of the French Société.

[BEZE, Théodore de.] Histoire ecclésiastique des églises réformées au royaume de France. Edition nouvelle avec commentaire, notice bibliographique. Par G. Baum et par Ed. Cunitz. Paris, 1883-89. 3 vols. O. HA—B46
Vol. III, contenant la préface, l'introduction et la table alphabétique par R. Reuss.

BIANQUIS, Jean. La révocation de l'Edit de Nantes à Rouen; essai historique suivi de notes sur les protestants de Rouen, par Emile Lesens. Rouen, 1885. 103 pp. O. HA—B47
Gift of Dr. Abram Du Bois.

BION, Jean. Relation des tourments qu'on fait souffrir aux protestants qui sont sur les galères de France; réimprimée sur la seconde édition avec une préface par O. Douen. Paris, 1881. 53 pp. O. HA—B52

BONNET, Jules. Derniers récits du seizième siècle. Paris, 1876. 350 pp. D. HA—B64

——— Nouveaux récits du seizième siècle. Paris, 1870. 361 pp. D. HA—B641

——— Récits du seizième siècle. Paris, 1866. 357 pp. D. HA—B642

——— Récits du seizième siècle. Seconde série. Paris, 1885. 342 pp. D. HA—B643
Gift of Dr. Abram Du Bois.

——— La réforme au Chateau de Saint-Privat, étude historique. Paris, 1873. 48 pp. O. HA—B645
Gift of Dr. Abram Du Bois.

——— Souvenirs de l'église réformée de la Calmette. Pages d'histoire locale. Paris, 1884. 91 pp. map. O. HA—B645
Gift of Dr. Abram Du Bois.
Bound with his "La réform au Chateau de Saint-Privat . . . in l'Eglise Reformée," volume.

BONZON, Jacques. La direction des pauvres réfugiés français de Nyon. 1688-1860. 22 pp. O. [Paris, 1901?] HA—D74
Reprint: Bulletin Soc. hist. prot. français (Mars. 1901).
Autograph gift of the Author.

[BORDIER, Henri Léonard.] Editor. Le chansonnier Huguenot du XVIe siècle. Paris, 1870. 2 vols. S. HA—B646

——— La Saint-Barthélemy et la critique moderne. Genève, 1879. 116 pp. illustrated, folio. HA—B647

BOURCHENIN, DANIEL. Etude sur les académies protestantes en France au XVIᵉ et au XVIIᵉ siècle. Paris, 1882. 480 pp. O.   HA—B66
Gift of Dr. Abram Du Bois.

BOURGEON, G. La réforme à Nérac, les origines (1530-60). Toulouse, 1880. 118 pp. O.   HA—B645
Gift of Dr. Abram Du Bois.

BOWER, HERBERT M. The fourteen of Meaux: An account of the earliest "Reformed Church" within France proper, organized by Estienne Mangin, and Pierre LeClerc; who with twelve other persons, suffered death by fire in 1546. 124 pp. 1 chart, 1 fac-sim., 2 pl., 1 plan, 1 port. O. London, 1894.   HA—B67
Reprint: Vol. V, Proceedings Huguenot Soc. of London.

BRIET, ELISÉE. Le protestantisme en Brie et basse Champagne du XVIᵉ siècle à nos jours. Vallées de la Marne et du Grand-Morin, d'après des documents inédits. Paris, 1885. 254 pp. fac-similes. O.   HA—B76
Publié à l'occassion du second centenaire de la révocation de l'Edit de Nantes.
Gift of the Author.

BROWNING, WILLIAM S. History of the Huguenots. New edition continued to the present time. XII, 13-452 pp. O. Philadelphia, 1845.   HA—B82

BUJEAUD, VICTOR. Chronique protestante de l'Angoumois, XVIᵉ, XVIIᵉ, XVIIIᵉ siècles. Paris, 1860. 394 pp. O.   HA—B86
Gift of Dr. Abram Du Bois.

[CASEIRAC, JEAN HOVI DE.] Apologie de Louis XIV. et de Conseil, sur la Révocation de l'Edit de Nantes, pour Servir de Résponse à la Lettre d'un Patriote sur la tolérance civile des Protestans de France. Avec une dissertation sur la Journée de la S. Barthelemi. 566 pp., I-LXIII, n.p. 1758. D.   HA—C337
Gift of Herbert Dupuy.

CASTEL, ELIE. Les Huguenots et la constitution de l'église réformée de France en 1559. Paris, 1859. 240 pp. D.   HA—C27
Publié à l'occasion du jubilé de 1859.

CASTELNAU, MICHEL DE. Memoirs of the reigns of Francis II. & Charles IX. of France . . . with an account of the three first civil wars, carried on by the Huguenots, done into English by the Rev. Kelly. 426 pp. Folio. London, 1724.   HA—C272

CATLIN, GEORGE L., Translator. See: DELMAS, LOUIS. Huguenots of La Rochelle.

CHEVRIER, EDMOND. Notice historique sur le protestantisme dans le département de l'Ain (Bresse, Bugey, pays de Gex) et lieux circonvoisins (Savoie, Lyon, Mâcon). Paris, 1883. 304 pp. portrait. O.   HA—C42

CLAPAREDE, R., Editor. See: NAEF, F. La réforme en Bourgogne: notice sur les Eglises réformées de la Bourgogne avant la Révocation de l'Edit de Nantes. 258 pp., 5 pl., 1 port., 1 map. D. Paris, 1901.   HA—N12

CLAPAREDE, THÉODORE. Histoire des églises réformées du pays de Gex. Genève, 1856. 351 pp. O.   HA—C53
Gift of Dr. Abram Du Bois.

——— Histoire de la Réformation en Savoie. 680 pp., 1 map fld. D. Geneve, 1893.   HA—C53S

CLASSIQUES (Les) du protestantism Français XVIe, XVIIe, XVIIIe siècles. (CLAUDE, JEAN. Les plaintes des protestants. 1885.)   HA—C571

[CLAUDE, JEAN.] Account of the persecutions and oppressions of the protestants in France. 1886. 48 pp. Square O.   HA—C57

——— Les plaintes des protestans cruellement opprimez dans le royaume de France. Edition nouvelle avec commentaires par Frank Puaux. Paris, 1885. 148 pp. Square O. (Les classiques du protestantisme Français XVIe, XVIIe, XVIIIe siècles).   HA—C571
Gift of Dr. Abram Du Bois.

——— Short account of the complaints and cruel persecutions of the Protestants in the kingdom of France. With a biographical sketch of the author by N. Cyr. XIV, 212 pp., 1 port. T. London, 1707.   HA—C572
First American reprint of English translation. Boston, 1893.

CLOUZOT, H., Editor. See MIGAULT, JEAN. Journal . . . maitre d'école (1681-1688). Publié pour la première fois d'après le texte original avec une introduction et des notes. . . . D. Paris, 1910.   HA—M634

COMBA, EMILIO. History of the Waldenses of Italy, from origin to the Reformation; translated from the . . . revised edition by T. E. Comba. 357 pp. O. London, 1889.   HA—C73
Contains an account of their religious life, literature and dispersion in France, Switzerland and Italy.

COMBA, TEOFILO E., Translator. See COMBA, EMILIO. History of the Waldenses of Italy. . . .

COMBES, M. F. Entrevue de Bayonne de 1565, et la Question de la Saint-Barthélemy d'après les archives de Simancas. Paris, 1882. 49 pp. O.   HA—D74
Gift of the French Société.

CONSEIL D'ESTAT DU ROY. Arrest du Conseil d'Estat du Roy portant deffenses aux Ministres de la R. P. R. de faire leur demeure aux lieu où l'exercice de leur Religion aura esté interdit. . . . Toulouse, 1683. 4 pp. Sq. O.   HA—L888

CONSEIL D'ESTAT DU ROY. Arrest du Conseil . . . pour le paye-
ment des Pensions ou gratifications accordées par sa Majesté sur les
Economars & Biens des Religionnaires fugitifs, ensemble des arrerages
qui en sont dûs du pas fé. [Paris, 1720.] 4 pp. Sq. Q.

———— Arrest de Conseil . . . qui ordonne qu'il sera informé par les
Intendans & Commissaires départis dans ses Provinces & Generalitez,
contre les Ministres de la R. P. R. qui ont mal interpreté l'Arrest
du 19 May denier. Paris, 1681. 4 pp. Sq. O.

———— Arrest du Conseil . . . qui ordonne que les Commis à la regie
des biens des Consistoires Ministres, & autres de la R. P. R. . . .
dans les Generalitez de Roüen, Caën, Limoges, Moutauban, Bordeaux, Tours, Portiers, Amiens, Dijon; & dans les Provinces de
Dauphiné & Flanders, remettront és mains de Sieur Clement la
Somme de 121855 liv. pour employer au payedes Pensions de Nouveaux Convertis. . . . Paris, 1689. 6 pp. Sq. Q.

———— Arrest . . . par lequel Sa Majesté interdit l'exercice de la
Religion . . . & à une lieue à laronde, Ordonne à cette fin que les
Temples qui y sont construits seront incessamment démolis. Tou-
louse, 1685. 4 pp. Sq. O.

———— Arrest . . . portant defenses à ceux de la R. P. R. d'avoir des
Cimetieres dans les Villes; Bourgs & lieux de Royaume où il n'y a
plus d'exercice de ladite Religion Pretenduë Reformée. Toulouse,
1685. 4 pp. Sq. O.

———— Arrest du Conseil . . . Portant reglement par rapport aux pen-
sions assignées sur les Oeconomats & sur la Regie des Biens des
Religionnaires fugitifs ou refractaires aux ordres de sa Majesté.
[Paris, 1727.] 4 pp. Sq. Q.

———— Instruction pour l'Execution des Arrests du conseil d'Estat des
26. Aoust & 4e Dec. 1727, qui regle les Formalités qui doivent estre
observées dans l'Adjudication qui sera faite à l'avenir des Baux
des Biens des Réligionnaires. en Régie. . . . 13 pp. [Paris, 1727.]
Sq. Q.
A collection of very rare pamphlets bound in one volume, square
  octavo, half calf.   HA—L888
Gift of Herbert DuPuy, Esq.

COQUEREL, fils, ATHANASE JOSUÉ. Précis de l'histoire de l'église
réformée de Paris, d'après des documents en grande partie inédits,
premièr époque 1512-1594. De l'origine de l'église à l'Edit de
Nantes. Paris, 1862. 184 pp. O.   HA—C79
Gift of Dr. Abram Du Bois.

———— See: SMILES, SAMUEL. Huguenots (Les) . . . Traduction
autorisée par l'auteur avec une preface par A. C., fils XVI, 464 pp.
Paris, 1870. O.   HA—Sm4F
Gift:

CORBIERE, PHILIPPE. Histoire de l'église réformée de Montpellier depuis son origine jusqu'à nos jours avec de nombreuses pièces inédites sur le Languedoc, les Cévennes et le Vivarais. Montpellier, 1861. 610 pp. O.
Gift of Dr. Abram Du Bois.
HA—C81

CORTEIZ, PIERRE. Mémoires de Pierre Carrière, dit Corteis [pasteur du désert. Histoire des misères d'autrefois, 1685-1730. Publiés pour la première fois d'après un manuscrit de la bibliothèque de Zurich, par J. G. Baum. Genève, 1871]. *No title page.* 88 pp. O.
HA—C812

CREISSEIL, E. 18 octobre, 1685; la révocation de l'Edit de Nantes dans la Saintonge & l'Angoumois. Saintes, 1885. 20 pp. O.
HA—C84
Reprint from the *Bulletin évangélique de l'Ouest,* 3 Oct. 1885.
Gift of Louis Marie Meschinet de Richemond.

CREVAIN, PHILIPPE LE NOIR, SIEUR DE. Histoire ecclesiastique de Bretagne depuis la réformation jusqu'à l'Edit de Nantes ouvrage publié par B. Vaurigaud. Paris, 1851. 370 pp. O.   HA—C86

CUNITZ, EDOUARD, Editor. Histoire ecclésiastique des églises réformées au royaume de France . . . par T. Béze. 3 vols. 1883-'89.
HA—B46

DARRAGON, B. See: BARRAU, J. J., and DARRAGON, B. Montfort and les Albigeois. 1840.   HA—B27

DAVAL, GUILLAUME and JEAN. Histoire de la réformation à Dieppe, 1557-1657. Publiée pour la première fois, avec une introduction et des notes, par Emile Lesens. Rouen, 1878-79. 2 vols. O. (Publié par la Soc. rouennaise de bibliophiles.)   HA—D27
Gift of Dr. Abram Du Bois.

DE LA FERRIERE, HECTOR. La Saint-Barthélemy: la veille le jour, le lendemain. 288 pp. Paris, 1892. O.   HA—D37
Autograph gift of the Author.

DELMAS, LOUIS. L'église réformée de La Rochelle étude historique. 10 to 453 pp. D. Toulouse, 1870. (Pub. Soc. de livres religieux de Toulouse.)   HA—D381
Gift of The Hon. John Jay.

——— Huguenots of La Rochelle. A translation of "The Reformed Church of La Rochelle," from the French, by G. L. Catlin. N. Y. [1880]. 295 pp. D.   HA—D38

DE TRIQUETI, H. Les premiers jours de Protestantisme en France. Depuis son origine jusqu'au Premier Synode national de 1559. Ouvrage publié à l'occasion de 3e Jubilé séculaire de ce Synode. 302 pp. D. Paris, 1859.   HA—D48

DE VAYNES, JULIA H. L., Editor. A Huguenot garland. Hertfore, England, 1890. XVI, 304 pp. O.   HA—D49
Collection of French national songs with descriptive notes in English.
No. 26 of 50 copies privately printed.
Gift of the Editor.

DISOWAY, GABRIEL POILLON. Huguenots in America. In: SMILES, SAMUEL. The Huguenots . . . in England & Ireland. pp. 427-448. 1868. O.   HA—Sm4

DOUEN, EMMANUEL ORENTIN. Essai historique sur les églises réformées du département de l'Aisne, d'après des documents pour la plupart inédits. Paris, 1860. 186 pp. O.   HA—D74
Extrait du "Bulletin de la Société de l'histoire du protestantisme francais."
Gift of Dr. Abram Du Bois.

———— Editor. Révocation de l'Edit de Nantes, d'après des documents inédits. Vols. I-III. Paris, 1894. Q.   HA—R32
Gift of Dr. N. Weiss, through Mrs. J. M. Lawton.

———— Editor. Relation des tourments . . . par J. Bion.   HA—B52

DU BOIS-MELLY, CHARLES. Le récit de Nicolas Muss, serviteur de Mr. l'Admiral; épisode de la Saint-Barthélemy, avec notes historiques et gloses. Genève, 1878. 258 pp. D.   HA—D85
Gift of Dr. Abram Du Bois.

DU MOULIN, PIERRE. Bouclier de la foi; ou, Défense de la confession de foi des églises réformées du royaume de France contre les objections du sieur Arnoux, jésuite. Paris, 1846. 650 pp. D.   HA—D89

DUPIN DE SAINT-ANDRE, ARMAND. Histoire du protestantisme en Touraine. Paris, 1885. 306 pp. D.   HA—D92

EGLISE ÉVANGÉLIQUE VAUDOISE. Rapport annuel sur l'oeuvre d'évangélisation en Italie et à l'étranger. . . . 47 pp. Torre Pellice, 1887. O.   HA—Pamphlet
Gift of Rev. Alfred V. Wittmeyer.

EGLISE REFORMEE DE LA ROCHELLE. Etude Historique par L. Delmas, Pasteur, Président du Consistoire. Toulouse: Société des Livres Religieux, 1870. 453 pp. D.   HA—D381
Gift of The Hon. John Jay.

FELICE, G. DE. Histoire des protestants de France, depuis l'origine de la réformation jusqu'au temps présent, Deuxième édition. Paris, 1851. 655 pp. O.   HA—F33P

———— Histoire des Synodes nationaux des Eglises réformées de France. 2 leaves, 324 pp. Paris, 1864. D.   HA—F33S
Gift of Col. Henry A. DuPont.

FELICE, Paul de. Mer (Loir et Cher) son église réformée; établissement, vie intérieure, décadence, restauration. Paris, 1885. 301 pp. map. O. HA—F332
Gift of the author through Henry M. Baird.

———— La Réforme en Blaisors: documents inédits. Registre du consistoire. (1665-1677.) lxi, 1 leaf, 111 pp., 2 leaves. D. Orleans, 1885. HA—F332R

[FETIZON, Paul.] Apologie pour les réforméz; où, On voit la juste idée des guerres civiles de France, et les vrais fondements de l'Edit de Nantes entretiens curieux, entre un protestant et un catholique. La Haye, 1683. 250 pp. D. HA—F43
Gift of the Rev. Alfred V. Wittmeyer.

FLOURNOIS, Jacques. Extraits contenans tout ce qu'ily à d'important dans les registres publics de Geneve. Dés l'an 1532 à 1536. i-ccix pp., 3 leaves. HA—F922
Bound with: FROMMENT, Anthoine. Les actes et gestes merveilleux de la cité de Geneve. . . .
Gift of The French Société.

FOOTE, William Henry. Huguenots; or, Reformed French Church; their principles delineated; their character illustrated; their sufferings and successes recorded. Richmond [Va. 1870]. 627 pp. O. HA—F73

FRANKLIN, Alfred Louis Auguste. Les grandes scènes historiques du XVIe siècle, reproduction fac-similé du recueil de J. Tortorel et J. Perrisson. Paris, 1886. Illustrated, portrait, folio, half morocco. HA—F85

FRENCH Refugees. Letter to the French refugees, concerning their behavior to the Government. . . . 24 pp. S. London, 1711. HA—B88
No. 5 of Pamphet Volume.

FROMMENT, Anthoine. Actes (Les) gestes merveilleux de la cité de Gene. Nouuellement conuertie à l'Euangille faictz de temps de leur Reformation et comment ils l'ont receue redigez par escript en fourme de Chroniques Annales ou Hystoyres commençant l'an MDXXXII. Mis en lumiere par Gustave Revilliod. Geneve, 1854. xxxi, 250 pp., 63 pl., 4 port. O. HA—F922
Bound with: FLOURNOIS, Jacques. Extraits . . . registres publics de Geneve. Des l'an 1532 à 1536.
Gift of The French Société.
Bound in vellum, and beautifully illustrated.

FROSSARD, Charles Louis. L'église sous la Croix pendant la domination Espagnole, chronique de l'église réformée de Lille. Paris, 1857. 336 pp. illustrated. O. HA—F921
Gift of Dr. Abram Du Bois.

———— Numismatique protestante. Description de quarante et un méreaux de la communion réformée. Paris, 1872. 19 pp. O. HA—B645
Gift of Dr. Abram Du Bois.

FROSSARD, Charles Louis. La réforme dans le Cambrésis au XVIe siècle (1566). Paris, 1855. 47 pp. Q. (Bulletin de la Société de l'histoire du protestantisme français.) HA—B645
Gift of Dr. Abram Du Bois.

GALLAND, J. A. Essai sur l'histoire du Protestantisme à Caen et en Basse-Normandie de l'Edit de Nantes à la Révolution (1598-1791). Thèse pour le doctorat présentée à la Faculté des Lettres de l'Université de Paris. xxxviii, 550 pp., 1 map. Paris, 1889. Q. HA—G13
Gift of The French Société.

GAULLIEUR, Ernest. Histoire de la réformation à Bordeaux, et dans le ressort du parlement de Guyenne. Bordeaux, 1884. Vol. I.
O. HA—G23
Gift of Dr. Abram Du Bois.

GENEVE. See: FROMMENT, Anthoine. Les actes et gestes merceilleux de la cité of Geneve. . . . Together with: FLOURNOIS, J. Extraits . . . registres publics de Geneve. Des l'an 1532 à 1536. Geneve, 1854. O. HA—F922

GILLETT, William Kendall. See: JACKSON, S. M. Edict of Nantes: . . . with a translation of the Edict together with that of the Revocation of the Edict . . . revised by W. K. G. New York, 1898. O. HA—N19

GOLDSMITH, Oliver, translator. See: MARTEILHE, Jean. Huguenot galley-slave; being the autobiography of a French protestant condemned for his religion. Trans. from the French. 15 to 24 pp. D. New York, 1867. HA—M36

GUNITZ, E., Editor. Histoire ecclesiastique des églises réformées au royaume de France . . . par T. de Bèze. 1883-1889. HA—B46

GUYOT, Henri Daniel. Episode de la Révocation de l'Edit de Nantes. 23 pp. Groningue, 1907. O. HA—N19

HANNA, William. Wars of the Huguenots. N. Y., 1882. 344 pp. plates. HA—H19
Gift of Peter Carter.

HERBERT, Henry William, Translator. See: WEISS, Charles. History of the French Protestant refugees. 1854. HA—W43

HISTOIRE DE L'EDIT DE NANTES. Contenant Les choses les plus remarquables qui se sontpassées en France avant & après sa publication, à l'occasion de la diversité des Religions: Et principalement les Contraventions, In executions, Chicanes, Artifices, Violences & autres Injustices, que les Reforme se plaignent d'y avoir souffertes, jusques à L'Edit de Revocation, en Octobre, 1685. A Delft, Chez Adrien Beman, 1693-1695. 3470 pp. Tomes i-v. Q. The covers of this set of volumes bear the Ducal Arms. 5 vols.
Gift of The Hon. John Jay.

——— Same: plain binding, except tooling on back. BENOIT, Elie, Editor. Delft, 1693-1695. 5 vols. Q. 1 pl. (Frontispiece in Vol. i.) HA—B44

HISTORY of the Protestant reformation in France. By Mrs. Anne Marsh. London, 1849. 2 vols. New edition. O. HA—M35

HUGUENOTS in France and America. By Mrs. Anna F. Sawyer Lee. Cambridge, Mass., 1843. Vol. II. D. HA—L51 (Vol. I wanting.)

HUGUES, EDMOND. Histoire de la restauration du protestantisme en France au XVIIIᵉ siècle. Antoine Court d'après des documents inédits. Quatrième édition. Paris, 1875. 2 vols. O. HA—H87 Gift of Dr. Abram Du Bois.

——— Inauguration du Musée du Désert . . . 24 Sept. 1911. Allocution de . . . E. Hugues. Cevennes, 1912. pp. 27-43. O. HA—M986

——— Les synodes du désert, actes et réglements des synodes nationaux et provinciaux tenus au désert de France de l'an 1715-1793. Paris, 1885-86. 3 vols. portraits, plates, fac-similes. Q. HA—H871

——— Supplement aux synodes du desert . . . par A. Arnaud. Sq. Q. Paris, 1892. HA—H871A

HUISSEAU, J. D'. Discipline (La) des églises réformées de France; ou, l'Ordre lequel elles sont conduites & gouvernées. . . . New ed. Genéve, 1666. 245 pp. O. HA—H875

JACCARD, E. l'Eglise Française de Zurich. Une page de l'histoire du grand refuge. 425 pp. Zurich, 1889. D. HA—J11 Gift of the French Société.

JACKSON, SAMUEL MACAULEY. The Edict of Nantes; its scope and its place in the development of religious toleration. With a complete translation of the Edict . . . together with that of the Revocation of the Edict . . . revised by W. E. Gillette. New York, 1898. pp. 51-104, 6 pp. O. HA—N19 With the exception of the translation of the Revocation, this is a Reprint from the Tercentenary Volume of The Huguenot Society of America.

KELLY, ——— REV., Translator. See: CASTELNAU, MICHEL DE. Memoirs of the reigns of Francis II. and Charles IX. of France. 1724. HA—C27.2

KERLING, J. B. J., and DOZY, R. B., compilers. Catalogue de pamphlets et d'estampes concernant les Traites de paix, conclus avec les Pay-Bas depuis 1576-1815. 40 pp., 6 pl. Sq. Q. HA—Pamphlet Gift:

LAFON, MARY. Histoire d'une ville Protestante [Montaubon]. xv, 316 pp. O. Paris, 1862. HA—L132 Gift of The French Société.

LAGARD, ALPHONSE. Chronique des églises réformées de l'Agenais. Toulouse, 1870. 340 pp. D. (Société des livres religieux de Toulouse.) HA—L13 Gift of Dr. Abram Du Bois.

LA ROCHELLE ET SES ENVIRONS. Avec un Précis Historique, de M. A. De Quatrefages, Membre De l'Institut, et un Nouveau Plan De La Ville. La Rochelle: C. Chartier, 1866. D. 368 pp.   HA—Qu2
Gift of The Hon. John Jay.

LEE, Mrs. HANNAH F. (SAWYER). Huguenots in France and America. Cambridge [Mass.], 1843. Vol. ii. D.   HA—L51

LEGENDRE, PHILIPPE. Histoire de la persécution faite à l'église de Rouen sur la fin du dernier siècle, précédée d'une notice historique et bibliographique par Emile Lesens. Rouen, 1874. 185 pp. plates. Sq. O.   HA—L52
Gift of Dr. Abram Du Bois.

LE HARDY, GASTON. Histoire du protestantisme en Normandie depuis son origine jusqu'à la publication de l'Edit de Nantes. Caen, 1869. 456 pp. O.   HA—L522
Gift of Dr. Abram Du Bois.

LEROUX, ALFRED. Histoire de la Réforme dans la Marche et le Limousin (Creuse, Haute-Vienne, Correze). xlvii, 391 pp. O. Limoges, 1888.   HA—L56
Gift of The French Société.

LESENS, EMILE, Editor. See: BIANQUIS, J. La Revocation de l'édit de Nantes. 1885.   HA—B47

———— Editor. See: DAVAL, GUILLAUME and JEAN. Histoire de la reformation à Dieppe 1557-1657 . . . 1878-'79.   HA—D27

———— Editor. See: LEGENDRE, PHILLIPE. Histoire de la persecution faite a l'église de Rouen. 1874.   HA—L52

LIEVRE, AUGUSTE FRANÇOIS. Histoire des Protestants et des églises réformées du Poitou. 3 vols., map. Paris, 1856-'60. O.   HA—L62
Gift of Dr. Abram Du Bois.

LOMBARD, ALEXANDRE. Paulicens Bulgares et bons-hommes en Orient et en Occident, etude sur quelaues sectes du Moyen age. xxiv, 319 pp. Fac-simile. D. Geneve, 1879.   HA—L62
Gift of the Author, through Prof. Henry M. Baird.

LOUIS, ROY DE FRANCE. Arrest de reglement de la cour de Parlement de Toulouse: sur les choses qui doivent estre observées par ceux de la Religion Pretenduë Réformée. . . . Toulouse, 1682. 6 pp., 1 leaf. Square O.   HA—L888

———— Declaration de Roy concernant les pensions sur les Benefices, cures et prebandes. Verifiee & Enregistrée au Parlement de Bourdeaux le treisiéme Aoust, 1671. Saintes, 1671. 8 pp. Square S.

———— Declaration . . . Contreceux qui s'étant convertis, fortiront de Rayaume sans permission du Roy. . . . Paris, 1686. 4 pp. Square O.

LOUIS, ROY DE FRANCE. Declaration du Roy, portant deffences aux Ministres, et aux consitoires de recevoir les relaps, et apostats, sur paine de desobeissence de suppression des Consistoires, & d'interdiction des Ministres. . . . To[u]louse, 1679. 7 pp. Square O.

—— Declaration du Roy, portant interdiction de l'Exercise de la Religion P. R. & démolition des Temples où il aura esté fait des mariages entre personnes [Roman] Catholiques & de ladite R. P. R. Toulouse, 1685. 6 pp. Square O.

—— Declaration du Roy, portant, que ceux de la R. P. R. ne pourront tenir leurs Consistoires qu'uene fois en quinze jours, & en presence d'un Iuge Royal. . . . Toulouse, 1685. 7 pp. Square O.

—— Declaration du Roy, qui défend aux Sujets de la Religion prétenduë Reformée, de vendre aucuns biens sans permission de sa Majesté, pendant le temps detroisans. [Paris], 1723. 3 pp. Square Q.

—— Declaration du Roy, portant que l'exercice de la R. P. R. ne pourra estre fait dans les lieux où il y aura moins dix familles de ladite R. P. R. sans comprendre celle du Ministre. . . . Toulouse, 1685. 6 pp. Square O.

—— Declaration du Roy, portant que les Ministres de la R. P. R. ne pourront exercer leur Ministere plus de trois ans en un même lieu d'Exercice, soit réel ou personnel. Toulouse, 1685. 4 pp. Square O.

—— Declaration . . . portant que les Ministres de la R. P. R. ne pourront demeurer plus prés que de six lieues des endroits où l'Exercice de ladite Religion ne se fait plus. . . . Toulouse, 1685. 4 pp. Square O.

—— Declaration du Roy, portant qu'il sera marquéun lieu dans les Temples de ceux de la R. P. R. pour les [Roman] Catholiques qui y voudront aller. . . . Toulouse, 1683. 4 pp. Square O.

—— Declaration . . . pour changes la peine des Galeres en celle de mort, contre ceux qui favoriseront l'évasion des nouveaux Catholiques hors du Royaume. Paris, 1687. 4 pp. Square O.

—— Edit . . . portant défenses de faire aucun Exercice public de la R. P. R. dans son Royaume. . . . [Toulouse?], 1685. 4 pp. Square O.

—— Edict du Roy d'abolition en faveur de ses subjets de la Religion prétendue réformée qui s'estoient sousleues en armes contre son service. Castres, 1630. 16 pp. Square O.

—— Lettres patentes du Roi, portant défenses aux personnes qui ont fait profession de la Religion Prétendue Réformee, de vendre leurs biens, & l'universalité de leurs meubles, sans la permission du Roi. [Paris], 1757. 3 pp. Square Q.

LOUIS, ROY DE FRANCE. Ordonnance du Roy pour empescher les Assemblées des Nouveaux Convertis dans les Provinces de son Royaume. . . . Toulouse, 1689. 4 pp. Square O.

——— Ordonnance . . . portant exemption delogement de Gens de Guierre & Contributions à iceux pendant deux ans, en faveur de ceux qui estans de la R. P. R. . . . se sont convertis & faits Catholiques, depuis le premier Janvier dernier, & qui se convertiront cy-aprés. . . . Paris, 1681. 7 pp. Square O.
A collection of very rare pamphlets bound in one volume, square
    octavo, half calf.   HA—L888
Gift of Herbert DuPuy, Esq.

LUTTEROTH, HENRI. La réformation en France pendant sa première période. Paris, 1859. 233 pp. O.   HA—L97

MARSH, MRS. ANNE. History of the Protestant reformation in France. 2 vols. O. New ed. London, 1849.   HA—M35

MARTEILHE, JEAN. Huguenot galley-slave: being the autobiography of a French protestant condemned to the galleys for the sake of his religion. Translated from the French [by Oliver Goldsmith]. N. Y., 1867. 241 pp. D.   HA—M36
Gift of J. C. Pumpelly.

MARTIN. ALPHONSE. Notice historique sur Sanvic et le Protestantisme. Dans cette 'Paroisse au Havre et dans les Environs. (XVIe et XVIIe siècles.) . . . x, 407 pp., 5 leaves, 2 pl. D. Fécamp, 1877.   HA—M362
Gift:

MARTIN, HENRI. Les cinq étudiants de l'académie de Lausanne brulés vifs à Lyon sur la Place des Terreaux, le 16 Mai, 1553, étude historique. Lausanne, 1863. 62 pp. S.   HA—R67
No. 2 in volume "French Church History."

MARTYN, REV. WILLIAM CARLOS. History of the Huguenots. 528 pp. D. N. Y., 1866.   HA—M364

MASSON, GUSTAVE. The Huguenots: a sketch of their history from the beginning of the Reformation to the death of Louis XIV. . . . 192 pp. S. London, 1881.   HA—M38

MEGE, SALVADORE, artist. The great painting, "The massacre of the Huguenots," in Paris, on Saint Bartholomew's Day, August 24th, 1572. O. 15 pp. N. Y., 1888.   HA—Pamphlet
MS. description by J. O'Donoghoe inserted.

MEILLE, W. Le réveil de 1825 dans les Vallées Vaudoises Piémont raconté à la génération actuelle. 105 pp., 1 port. O. Turin, 1893.   HA—R67
No. 4 in volume "French Church History."
Gift of Société d'histoire Vaudoises, Torre Pellice.

[MESCHINET DE RICHEMOND, Louis Marie.] Origine et progrès de la réformation à La Rochelle, précédé d'une notice sur Philippe Vincent. Deuxième édition. Paris, 1872. 128 pp. D.　　　　　　　　　　　　　　　　　　　　　　HA—R67
No. 1 in volume "French Church History."
Gift of Dr. Abram Du Bois.

MICHEL, Adolphe. Louvois et les protestants. Paris [no date]. 350 pp. D.　　　　　　　　　　　　　　　　　　　　HA—M58

MIGAULT, Jean. Journal de Jean Migault, maitre d'école (1681-1688). Publié pour la première fois d'après le texte original avec une introduction et des notes par N. Weiss & H. Clouzot. 302 pp., 3 fac-sim., 1 map folded, 19 pl., 3 port. Paris, 1910. D.　　HA—M634
Gift of the French Société.

MONASTIER, Antoine. Histoire de l'église Vaudois depuis son origine et des Vaudois du Piémont jusqu'a nos jours. Paris, 1847. 2 vols. in 1, portrait, map. O.　　　　　　　　　　HA—M74

MONTAUBON. See: LAFON, Mary. Histoire d'une ville Protestante. xv, 316 pp. O. Paris, 1862.　　　　　　　HA—L132

MOUTARDE, E. La Réforme en Saintonge: les églises reformées de Saujon et de la presqu'ile d'Arvert. 215 pp., fac-sim. O. Paris, 1892.　　　　　　　　　　　　　　　　　　　　HA—M86
Gift of the Author, with his autograph.

MUHLENBECK, Eugene. See: ROUGET, Claude. Une Eglise Calviniste au XVI me siècle 1550-1581. Histoire de la comminauté réformée de Sainte-Marie-aux-Mines (Alsace). Publiée . . . avec notes et commentaries par E. M. xiv, 515 pl. Q. Paris, 1881.　　　　　　　　　　　　　　　　　　　HA—R75
Gift of the French Société.

MUSEE de Désert. Inauguration de Musée de Désert le Dimanche 24 Septembre 1911. Allocutions de F. Praux, . . . E. Hugues, et C. Babut. en Cévennes, 1912. 60 pp., 4 pl. O.　　HA—M986
Gift of the French Société.

MUSS, Nicolas. De récit de Nicolas Muss, serviteur de Mr. l'Admiral, épisode de la Saint-Barthélemy . . . par C. Dubois-Melly. 1878.　　　　　　　　　　　　　　　　　　　　HA—D85
Gift of Dr. Abram Du Bois.

NAEF, F. La réforme en Bourgogne: notice sur les Eglise réformées de la Bourgogne avant la Révocation de l'Edict de Nantes. Editée . . . par R. Claparède. 258 pp., 5 pl., 1 port., 1 map. D. Paris, 1901.　　　　　　　　　　　　　　　　　　　　HA—N12
Gift of The French Société.

NICOLAS, Michel. Histoire de l'ancienne académie protestante de Montauban (1598-1659), et de Puylaurens (1660-1685). Montauban, 1885. 440 pp. O.　　　　　　　　　　　　HA—N54
Gift of Dr. Abram Du Bois.

15

ŒUVRES (Les) du protestantisme français au XIXᵉ siècle. Edited by F. Puaux. Paris, 1893. Folio. HA—P96

ORIGINE & progrès de la réformation à La Rochelle . . . [par Meschinet de Richemond, Louis Marie] 1872. HA—R67

PANNIER, Jacques. Etudes historiques sur la réforme, dans l'Arrandissement de Corbeil. 1. Le prieuré et la seigneurie de Longjumeau au milieu de XVIᵉ siècle. Théodore de Beze et Michel Gaillard. Paris, 1898. 20 pp., illus. Q. HA—D74
Gift of the Author.

PASCAL, César. La révocation de l'Edit de Nantes et Mme. de Maintenon, sa vie, son caractère, son influence. Deuxième édition. Paris, 1885. 108 pp. HA—P26

PERRENOUD, Henri. Etude historique sur les progrès de protestantisme en France ay point de vue statistique, 1802-1888. Paris, 1889. 253 pp. Q. HA—P42

PERRISSON, J. See: FRANKLIN, Alfred Louis Auguste. Les grandes scènes histoire du XVIᵉ siècle. 1886. Folio volume, fully illustrated. HA—F85

[PILATTE, Leon.] Edits, déclarations, et arrests concernans la réligion p. réformée, 1662-1751, précédés de l'Edit de Nantes, réimprimés pour le deuxième centenaire de la révocation de l'Edit de Nantes. Paris, 1885. 660 pp. D. HA—P64

PITHOU, Nicolas. Le protestantisme en Champagne; ou, Récits extraits d'un manuscrit concernant l'histoire de la fondation et du développement de l'église réformée de Troyes dès 1539-95. Par C. L. B. Recordon. Paris, 1863. 259 pp. O. HA—P68
Gift of Dr. Abram Du Bois.

POOLE, Reginald Lane. History of the Huguenots; of the dispersion at the recall of the Edict of Nantes. London, 1880. 208 pp. D. HA—P78
Lothian essay. 1879.

PUAUX, Frank. Défence de la Réformation. Conférence faite à Saint-Jean-du-Gard. Le 25 Septembre 1910. 31 pp. Paris, 1892. HA—R67

———— Histoire de l'establissement des protestants français Suede. 212 pp. Paris, 1892. O. HA—P961

———— Inauguration de Musée de Désert . . . 24 Sept. 1911. Allocutions de F. Puaux, E. Hugues et C. Babut. Cévennes, 1912. 19-26 pp. O. HA—M986

———— Editor. Œuvres du protestantisme française au XIXᵉ siècle. Paris, 1893. 480 pp., 18 port. Folio. HA—P96

———— Editor. Les plaintes des protestants cruellement opprimez dans le royaume de France. Par Jean Claude. 1885. (Classiques du protestantisme français, XVIᵉ, XVIIᵉ, XVIIIᵉ siècles.) HA—C571
Gift of Dr. Abram Du Bois.

QUATREFAGES DE BREAU [JEAN LOUIS] A[RMAND] DE. La Rochelle et ses environs avec un précis historique. . . . 385 pp., 1 pl., 1 map. D. La Rochelle, 1866. HA—Qu2
Gift of the Hon. John Jay.

QUICK, JOHN, compiler. Synodicon in Gallia reformata; or, The acts, decisions, decrees, and canons of those famous national councils of the reformed churches in France collected and composed out of those renowned synods. A work never before extant in any language. London, 1692. 2 vols. folio, *half calf.* HA—Qu4

RABAUD, CAMILLE. Histoire du protestantisme dans l'Albigeois et le Lauragais, depuis son origine jusqu'à la révocation de l'Edit de Nantes (1685). Paris, 1873. 514 pp. O. HA—R11
Gift of Dr. Abram Du Bois.

REVILLIOD, GUSTAVE, Illustrator. Les actes et gestes merceilleux de la cite de Geneve. . . . par A. Fromment. Geneve, 1854. O. HA—F922
Gift of The French Société.

REVOCATION de l'Edit de Nantes; discours prononcés à l'occasion du deuxième anniversaire det événement. Montreal, 1885. 157 pp. O. HA—R32
Gift of Dr. Abram Du Bois.

ROBERT-LABARTHE, U. DE. Pasteur. Histoire du protestantisme dans le Haut-Languedoc, le Bas-Quercy et le comté de Foix de 1685-1789. D'après des documents pour la plupart inédits par . . . pasteur. 2 vols. O. Paris, 1896. HA—R54
Vol. I, 1685-1715.
Vol. II, 1715-1789.
Gift of The French Société.

ROSSIER, L. Histoire des protestants de Picardie particulièrement de ceux du département de la Somme d'après des documents pour la plupart inédits. Paris, 1861. 328 pp. D. HA—R73
Gift of Dr. Abram Du Bois.

ROUGET, CLAUDE. Une Eglise Calviniste au XVIme siècle, 1550-1581. Histoire de la communauté réformée de Sainte-Marie-du-Mines (Alsace). Publier pour la premiète fois avec notes et commentaires par E. Muhlenbeck. XIV, 515 pp. Paris, 1881. Q. HA—R75

SCHAEFFER, ADOLPHE. Les Huguenots du seizième siècle. Paris, 1870. 331 pp. HA—Sch1

[SCHMIDT, CHARLES GUILLAUME ADOLPHE], editor. Poésies huguenotes du 16e siècle. Strasbourg, 1882. 44 pp. Q. HA—Sch5

SMEDLEY, Rev. Edward. History of the reformed religion of France. N. Y., 1834. 3 vols. portraits. S. HA—Sm3
Gift of Mrs. Maria C. Dusenbury.

—— History of the reformed religion of France. London, 1832-34. 3 vols. portraits. S. HA—Sm31
Index in Vol. III of London edition.

SMILES, Samuel. Les Huguenots: leurs colonies, leurs industries, leurs Eglises, en Angleterre et en Irlande. Traduction autorisee par l'auteur, avec une preface par A. Coquerel, fils. xvi, 464 pp. O. Paris, 1870. HA—Sm4.F

—— The Huguenots: their settlements, churches and industries in England & Ireland, with an appendix relating to the Huguenots in America by G. P. Disosway. 448 pp. O. New York, 1868. HA—Sm4
List of Huguenot refugees & their descendants, pp. 397-426.

SOCIETE des livres religieux de Toulouse. See: LAGARDE, Alphonse. Chronique des églises réformées de l'Agenais. Toulouse, 1870. D.

SOULICE, Louis. L'intendant Foucault et la révocation en Béarn. Pau, 1885. 151 pp. O. (In Documents pour l'histoire du protestantisme en Béarn, Vol. III.) HA—D74
Gift of Dr. Abram Du Bois.

TORTOREL, J. See: FRANKLIN, Alfred Louis Auguste. Les grandes scènes historiques du XVIe siècle. HA—F85

TRAICTE d'Association faice par Monseigneur le Prince de Condé avec les Princes, Chevaliers de l'Ordre, Seigneurs, Capitaines, Gentilshommes, & aultres de tous estats, qui sont entrez ou entreront cy apres en la dicte association pour mantenir, l'honneur de Dieu, le repos de ce Royaume, & l'estat & libetté de Roy sous le legouvernemet de la Roine sa mere, auctorisee & establie par les Estats. [Orleans?] 1562. 7 leaves. T. HA—L888
Herbert DuPuy; Collection French Pamphlets.

TRAITES de paix: Catalogue de pamphlets et d'estampes concernant . . . conclus avec les Pays-Bas, depuis 1576-1815. La Haye, [1913]. 40 pp., 6 pl. Square O. par J. B. Kerling and R. B. Dozy.
HA—Pamphlet

Gift of Authors.

TRIQUETI, Henri, Baron de. Les premiers jours du protestantisme en France, depuis son origine jusqu'au premier synode national de 1559. Paris, 1859. 300 pp. D. HA—T73
Ouvrage publié à l'occasion du 3e jubilé, séculaire de ce synode.

ÜBERSICHT der wanderungen und niederlassungen französischer, savoyischer und niederländischer religionsflüchtlinge besonders nach und in Deutschland. Karlsruhe, 1854. 130 pp. O. HA—Ub3

VAUDOIS du Dauphine. ARNAUD, Eugene. Memoirs historiques. A volume of 6 of his pamphlets (in French). HA—Ar6

VAUDOIS (Les). Leur histoire sur les deux versants des Alpes de IVe siècle au XVIIIe. par Alexandre BERNARD. Lyon, 1892. O.   HA—B461

VAURIGAUD, Benjamin. Essai sur l'histoire des églises réformées de Bretagne, 1535-1808. Paris, 1870. 3 vols. O .   HA—V461

———— Histoire de l'église réformée de Nantes, depuis l'origine jusqu'au temps présent. Paris, 1880. 377 pp. O.   HA—V46
Gift of Dr. Abram Du Bois.

———— Editor. See: CREVAIN, Phillipe le Noir. Sieur de Histoire ecclesiastique de Bretagne. 1851.   HA—C86

VINET, A. Histoire de la predication parmi les réformés de France au dix-septieme siècle. viii, 718 pp. Paris, 1860. O.   HA—V783
Gift of The French Société.

WADDINGTON, Francis. Le Protestantisme en Normandie depuis la Révocation de l'Edit de Nantes jusqu'a la fin du dix-huitieme siècle. (1685-1797.) vii, 140 pp. Q. Paris, 1862.   HA—W11
Gift of The French Société.

WEISS, Charles. History of the French protestant refugees, from the revocation of the Edict of Nantes to our own days. Translated from the French by Henry William Herbert. N. Y., 1854. 2 vols. portrait. D.   HA—W43

WEISS, Nathanël. La chambre ardente; étude sur la liberté de conscience en France sous François Ier et Henri II; suivie d'environ 500 arrêts inédits, rendus par le Parlement de Paris, 1547-1550. Publié pour le premier centenaire de la liberté de conscience sous les auspices de la Société de l'histoire du protestantisme français. Paris, 1889. 432 pp. plates. D.   HA—W432
Gift of Charles M. du Puy.

———— Editor. Journal de Jean Migault, maitre d'ecole (1681-1688). Publie pour la première fois d'après le texte original avec une introduction et des notes. . . . D. Paris, 1910.   HA—M634

AGNEW, Rev. David C. A. Protestant exiles from France reign of
Louis XIV.; or, The Huguenot refugees and their descendants in
Great Britain and Ireland. 1 p.l., viii, 403 pp., 2 fac-sim., 3 pl.,
4 port. Square Q. no place, 1866.   HB—A273D
Gift of H. R. Duval, with his Bookplate. Privately Printed.

———— Protestant exiles from France in the reign of Louis XIV; or,
Huguenot refugees and their descendants in Great Britain and Ire-
land. Second edition, enlarged. London, 1871. 2 vols. Square
O.   HB—A273

ALGERIE: Colonie de Vaudois. See: REVEILLAUD, Eugene.
Etablissement d'une Colonie de Vaudois français en Algérie. . . .
Paris, 1893. S. Plate & 1 map.   HB—R32

ALLEN, Charles E. Huguenot settlers in Dresden, Maine. 31 pp.
Read before the Maine Hist. Society, March 17, 1892.   HB—AL5

AUGUR, C. H. New Rochelle through seven generations. 65 pp.
Square D. [New Rochelle, N. Y.], cop. 1908.   HB—Au4
Gift of H. M. Lester.
Printed for private distribution only. Fully illustrated. (Invi-
tation and programme inserted.)

BEARD, Augustus F. Churches of the Huguenots and the religious
condition of France. 1884. O.   HB—H12
From the *Andover Review.* 1884. Vol. i.
Presented by the publisher.

BEARD, Rev. Augustus F., editor. See: WESTPHAL—Castelnau.
Yesterday and to-day. 1885.   HB—A2H

BAIRD, Rev. Charles Washington. History of the Huguenot emigration to America. N. Y. [1885]. 2 vols. illustrated, maps, fac-
simile. O.   HB—B16

BEAUFORT DISTRICT,—past, present, and future. In: CONTI-
NENTAL Monthly. Vol. i, No. iv, pp. 381-388. O. [Boston],
1862. By Frederic Kidder.   HB—H897

BODE, prediger. GESCHICHTE der wallonisch-reformirten Kirchengemeinde zu Magdeburg 17 pp. Magdeburg, 1892. (Deutsche
Hugenotten Verein. Geschichtsblätter. 1892 V. 5. O.)   HB—T57

BROWNING, Arthur Giraud. The influence exerted by Huguenot refugees of the seventeenth and early eighteenth centuries upon the social and professional life of England. 20 pp. O. Aberdeen, 1904. (Privately reprinted from Pro. Huguenot Society of London, Vol. VII.)   HB—B88
Gift of Mrs. J. M. Lawton; Author's presentation copy.

—— A lecture on the peaceful invasion of England by French Protestants in 1685. 37 pp. O. [London], 1906. (St. Mark's Literary Soc'y.)   HB—B88

BUSSIERRE, Marie Théodore Renouard, Vicomte de. Histoire de l'établissement du protestantisme à Strasbourg et en Alsace, d'après des documents inédits. Paris, 1856. 509 pp. O. *Half roan.*   HB—B961
Gift of Dr. Abram Du Bois.

—— Histoire du développement du protestantisme à Strasbourg et en Alsace, depuis l'abolition du culte catholique jusqu'à la Paix de Haguenau (1529-1604). Strasbourg, 1859. 2 vols. in 1. O. *Half roan.*   HB—B96
Gift of Dr. Abram Du Bois.

[CAAN, H. J.] Eglise (l') Française de Voorburg, Recueil de documents relatifs . . . l'origine et l'état actuel de la dite institution religieuse. [La Haye], 1859. 42 pp., 1 pl. 1 port., 2 fac-sim. O.   HB—C11
Gift of M. G. Wildeman.

CHAMPION de CRESPIGNY, Mrs. Philip. See: de CRESPIGNY, Mrs. Philip Champion.

CHAPTER (A) in Huguenot history, pp. 414-418. No place [March, 1896]. No. 2, of Volume "Huguenot Essays."   HB—H89

CHARLESTON, South Carolina, French Protestant Church. See: FRENCH Protestant Church, Charleston, South Carolina.

CHAVANNES, Jules. Les réfugiés français dans le pay de Vaud, et particulièrement à Vevey. Lausanne, 1874. 331 pp. D.   HB—C39
Gift of Dr. Abram Du Bois.

CLUTE, Robert F., compiler. Annals and parish register of St. Thomas and St. Denis parish in South Carolina, 1680-84. Charleston, 1884. 111 pp. O.   HB—C62

COLLES, Julia K. Josiah Collins Pumpelly. Extract from "Authors and writers associated with Morristown, New Jersey." 1893. Typewritten Ms., Bd. with: PUMPELLY, J. C. Mahlon Dickerson. . . . Paterson, N. J., 1892. O.   HB—P87

COLONIAL DAMES: New York. Catalogue, Van Cortlandt House Museum Huguenot Memorials of the refugees who came to America. . . . 15 pp., 2 leaves. New York, 1910. O.   HB—B88

CONTINENTAL (THE) MONTHLY. Vol. I, Nos. II-IV, pp. 113-492. Boston, 1862. O.   HB—B897

CUNO, FRIEDERICH WILHELM. Geschichte der wallonisch-reformirten gemeinde zu Annweiler. 14 pp. Magdeburg, 1893. (In Der Deutsche Hugenotten verein. Geschichtsblätter. 1893. No. 10, part 1.) HB—T57

———— Geschichte der Wallonisch-reformirten gemeinde zu Heidelberg. 13 pp. Magdeburg, 1893. (Der Deutsche Hugenotten verein. Geschichtsblätter. 1893. No. 10, part 4.) HB—T57

DANIELS, GEORGE F. Huguenots in the Nipmuck country; or, Oxford prior to 1713. With an introduction by Oliver Wendell Holmes. Boston, 1880. 168 pp. map. O. HB—D22
Gift of Mrs. Poor.

DE CRESPIGNY, MRS. PHILIP CHAMPION, compiler. Key to the Roll of the Huguenots: containing brief historical notices of the Huguenot refugees to England, and explaining the object of the Roll of the Huguenots. Second edition. London, 1886. D. 18 pp. HB—B88

DEMAREST, DAVID D. Huguenots on the Hackensack. New Brunswick, N. J., 1886. Q. 24 pp. HB—D39
Gift of the author.

DEMAREST, REV. W. H. S., D.D., LL.D. Commemorative address, 225th anniversary of the founding of the French Protestant Church in the City of Charleston, "The Huguenot Church." Pages 23-38. In:—French Prot. Church, Charleston, S. C., 1912. HB—F875

DUBOSE, SAMUEL. Contribution to the history of the Huguenots of South Carolina: consisting of pamphlets by Samuel Dubose and Frederick A. Porcher. Republished for private circulation by T. Gaillard Thomas. N. Y., 1887. 175 pp. O. HB—D85
Contents: Address delivered at the 17th anniversary of the Black Oak agricultural society, April 27, 1858, with Reminiscences of St. Stephen's parish and notices of her old homesteads, by Samuel Dubose. Historical and social sketch of Craven County, South Carolina, by Frederick A. Porcher.
Gift: Dr. Theodore Gaillard Thomas.

———— A second copy in volume, "French Protestant Church, Charleston, S. C." HB—F875

EGLISE (l') Française de Voorburg. Recueil de documents relatifs à l'Eglise . . . conçernant l'origine et l'état actuel de la dite institution religieuse: par H. J. Caan. [La Haye], 1859. O. HB—C11
Gift: M. G. Wildeman.

EGLISES WALLONNES de la BARRIERE: Tournai, Armentières, Menin, Ypres et Namur. Registres des baptêmes, mariages and inhumations. Liste des membres . . . hors de Tournai. Abjurations à Tournai et à Menin. XVIIIᵉ siècle. 528 pp. O. LeCateau, 1894. HB—Wa16
Gift of the Rev. Alfred V. Wittmeyer.

———— Same.

EGLISES en PRUSSE. See: PARISET (Georges). L'état et les Eglises en Prusse sous Fréderic-Guillaume I.er. (1713-1740) . . . xx, 990 pp. Paris, 1896. O. HB—P21

ENGLISH (The) CHURCH in the HAGUES. The eldest Church-book of the English Congregation in the Hague . . . a transcript by M. G. Wildeman. 84, IV pp. The Hague, 1906. O. HB—W67E

FISHER, E. T., translator. Report of a French Protestant refugee, in Boston, 1687 . . . 1868. HB—R29

FLORIDA. See: SIMMS, W. G. The lily and the totem, or, the Huguenots in Florida. HB—Si4

FORDHAM, New York. See: WALDRON, WILLIAM WATSON. Huguenots of Westchester and parish of Fordham. N. Y., 1864. S. HB—W14

FOSDICK, LUCIAN J. The French blood in America. 448 pp., 8 groups, 20 pl., 4 port. New York, cop. 1906. O. HB—F74
Autograph gift through Mrs. J. M. Lawton.

FRENCH Protestant Hospital. Charter and By-laws of the Corpora-tion of the Hospital for poor French Protestants . . . residing in Great Britain. XXVI, 65 pp., 2 plans, 3 plates. London, 1892. O. HB—F875I
Gift of the Directors.

FRENCH Protestant (Huguenot) Church, Charleston, South Caro-lina. Liturgy; or, Forms of divine service. Translated from the liturgy of the church of Neufchatel and Vallagin, the whole adapted to public worship in the United States of America. Third edition. N. Y. [1853]. 228 pp. D. HB—H875L
Presented by the French Protestant Church of Charleston, S. C.

FRENCH Protestant (Huguenot) Church in the City of Charleston, S. C. Historical notes: a Biographical list of Mural tablets in the . . . Church [and] Rules of the French Protestant Church adopted after revision, March 7, 1869. Square O. Charleston, 1898. 23 pp., 2 pl. No. 2, of P. V. HB—F875
Gift: Rev. C. S. Vedder, through Mrs. Jas. M. Lawton.

——— "The Huguenot Church." A brief history of the Church, and two addresses delivered on the 225th Anniversary . . . April 14th, 1812. 1 pl., 38 pp. Charleston, S. C., 1912. Square O. HB—F875

GILMAN, THEODORE. Huguenots as founders and patriots. An Ad-dress . . . before the N. Y. Society, Order of Founders and Patriots of America . . . March 27, 1913. 16 pp. New York, 1913. O. No. 4, in P. V. HB—B88

GODET, FRÉDÉRIC. Histoire de la réformation et du refuge dans le pays de Neuchatel, conférences tenues à Neuchatel. Neuchatel, 1859. 302 pp. D. HB—G54
Gift of Dr. Abram Du Bois.

GRAVES, Horace. HUGUENOT (The) in New England. n.p., n.d. HB—H89
No. 3 of Vol. of "Huguenot essays."
Gift of the Author.

GUMBEL, Th. Die wallonisch-französische fremdengemeinde in St. Lambrecht-Grevenhausen. 21 pp. Magdeburg, 1893. (In Der Deutsche Hugenotten verein. Geschichtsblätter, 1893. No. 10, pt. 2.) HB—T57

GUYOT, Henri Daniel. Deux (Les) compagnie de français refugiés à Groningue . . . 15 pp. [Groninque, 189?.] No title page. Bound with: VERMILYE, A. G. Huguenot element among the Dutch. HB—A2H

HAGUE, William. Old Pelham and New Rochelle. 1882. Portrait. O. HB—H12
From the *Magazine of American History,* 1882, vol. 8.

HAGUE (The) Holland. See: ENGLISH (The) Church in the Hague. The eldest Church-book . . . a transcript by M. G. Wildeman. The Hague, 1906. O. HB—W67E

HIGGINSON, Thomas Wentworth. French voyageurs. 1883. Illustrated. O. HB—H12
From *Harper's Magazine,* 1883, vol. 66.
Gift of Rev. Alfred V. Wittmeyer.

HUGUENOT (The) element in Charleston's pronunciation. Pages 214-244. O. Charleston, S. C., 1889. By PRIMER (Sylvanus) Ph.D. In: "Huguenot essays." HB—H89

"HUGUENOT ESSAYS," a collection bound together in one volume. HB—H89

HUGUENOT (The) in New England. Pages 497-503. By GRAVES (Horace). In: "Huguenot Essays." HB—H89

HUGUENOT Memorials of the Refugees who came to America before and after the Revocation of the Edict of Nantes, 1685. HB—B88

HUGUENOT College at Wellington, Cape Colony, South Africa. Boston, 1881. 20 pp. D. HB—H87SA

—— Catalogue. Cape Town, 1882. O. HB—H87SA
Gift: Miss E. F. Brewer.

—— [An appeal] 1907. HB—H87SA

HUGUENOTS in South Africa. See: TEALL, G. McC., and others. HB—H87SA

KERSHAW, S. W. Protestants from France in their English home. XII, 170 pp., 1 fac-sim., 1 pl., 1 port. London, 1885. D. HB—K47

KIDDER, Frederic. Beaufort District,—past, present, and future. Pages 381-388. Boston, 1862. O. (In: Continental (The) Monthly, Vol. i, Nos. ii-iv.) HB—H897

KNECHT, J. Die Wallonische gemeinde zu Otterberg. 21 pp. O. Magdeburg, 1892. (Der Deutsche Hugunotten-verein. Geschichtsblätter, 1892. Vol. 7.) HB—T57

LECLERCQ, J. B. Une église réformé au 17ᵉ siècle; ou, Histoire de l'église wallonne de Hanau, depuis sa fondation jusqu'à l'arrivée dans son sein des réfugiés français. Hanau, 1868. 293 pp. O. HB—L49
Gift of Dr. Abram Du Bois.

LETTER to the French refugees concerning their behavior to the government. London, 1711. 24 pp. S. HB—B88

LILY (The) and the totem, by SIMMS, WILLIAM GILLMORE. 1850. HB—S14

MAGDEBURG. See: TOLLIN, HENRI. Geschichte der französischen Colonie zu Magdeburg . . . Halle and Magdeburg, 1886-'94. 3 Vols. in 5. O.
Contents given under main entry.

MOERIKOFER, J. C. Histoire des réfugiés de la réforme en Suisse. Traduit de l'allemand et illustré par G. Roux. Paris, 1878. 432 pp. illustrated. O. HB—M72
Gift of Dr. Abram Du Bois.

MORRIS, REV. WILLIAM, translator. See: VERREN, REV. ANTOINE. The Huguenots in this Country. 1862.

MURRAY, REV. ANDREW. De Hugenoten-school; verslag over de jaren van Januari, 1874, tot December, 1878. [No date.] 7 pp. O. HB—H87SA
Gift of Miss E. F. Brewer.

NATURALIZATIONS and names. See: AGNEW, REV. DAVID C. A. Protestant exiles from France in the reign of Louis XIV or, Huguenot refugees . . . in Great Britain and Ireland. 2 Vols. London, 1871. Square O. HB—A273

NEDERDUITSCHE GEREFORMEERDE KERK IN ZUID-AFRIKA. Almanak. Kaapstad, 1886. Vol. 37. HB—H87SA

NEW ROCHELLE, New York. Photographs of houses built by Huguenot settlers at New Rochelle, N. Y. 23 photographs with names of original and present owners. Square folio, half morocco. HB—P56
Gift of Henry M. Lester.

NEW ROCHELLE, New York. See: AUGUR, C. H. New Rochelle through seven generations. 65 pp., illus. New Rochelle, N. Y. [cop. 1908]. Square D. HB—Au4

——— See: HAGUE, W. Old Pelham and New Rochelle. HB—H12

NEW ROCHELLE on the Sound. Illustrated by Joseph Rösch. A brochure of 48 pp. White Plains, N. Y. [cop. New York, 1903.] Square Q. (Two copies.) HB
Gift of Henry M. Lester.

NOBLE, John. De geschiedenis der Hugenoten in Zuid Afrika. 1860. 41 pp. S. HB—H87SA

OLD PELHAM AND NEW ROCHELLE. Hague, W. No title page, 1882. Pages 521-537. Magazine of Amer. Hist., 1882. Vol. 8. HB—H12
No. 1 of a Vol. of 7 pamphlets.

OLLIER, Daniel. Guy de Brès, étude historique sur la réforme au pays Wallon (1522-1567). Paris, 1883. 200 pp. O. HB—Ol4

OXFORD, Massachusetts. See: DANIELS, D. F. Huguenots in the Nipmuck Country, or, Oxford prior to 1713. . . . Boston, Mass. O. HB—D22

PARISET, Georges. Etat (l') et les Eglises en Prusse sous Frédéric-Guillaume Ier. (1713-1740.) Thèse pour le doctorat présentée à la faculté des lettres de Paris. xx, 990 pp. O. Paris, 1896. HB—P21

PENNSYLVANIA Huguenots. See: STAPLETON, Rev. Ammon. "Huguenots Pennsylvanianica." A collection of items and articles from newspapers and elsewhere mounted in book: interesting information, etc. Lewisburg, Pa., 1898-1901. Square O. HB—S794.1
Gift of the Compiler.

PIERREFLEUR, Pierre de. Mémoires de Pierrefleur grand banderet d'Orbe où sont contenus les commencements de la réforme dans la ville d'Orbe et au pays de Vaud (1530-61), publiés [avec] de notes historiques par A. Verdeil. Lausanne, 1856. 412 pp. O. HB—P61
Gift of Dr. Abram Du Bois.

PORCHER, Frederick A. Historical and social sketch of Craven County, South Carolina. In: DUBOSE, Samuel. Contributions to the history of the Huguenots of South Carolina. . . . 1887. Pages 87-168. HB—D85

———— Same in pamphlet volume. HB—F875

PRIMER, Sylvester, Ph.D. The Huguenot element in Charleston's pronunciation. Pages 214-244. Charleston, S. C., 1889. O. In: Volume entitled: "Huguenot Essays." HB—H69
This Essay is the gift of William D. Gaillard.

PUMPELLY, Josiah Collins. Volume entitled: Addresses and Papers. HB—P87
Contents: Huguenot builders of New Jersey. Pages 49-60, 1 port. Incidents in the early history of Berkshire County, Mass., and the Pumpelly, Pixley, Paterson, and Avery families. Pages 65-72, 1 pl. (N. Y. Gen. and Biographical Record, April, 1893, and April, 1896.)
Mahlon Dickerson, industrial pioneer and old time patriot. 26 pp. (A paper read before the New Jersey Historical Society, January 27th, 1891.) Paterson, N. J., 1892. O.
Gift of the Author.

RAVENEL, Daniel, compiler. "Liste des François et Suisses." From an old manuscript list of French and Swiss protestants settled in Charleston, on the Santee, and at the Orange Quarter in Carolina, who desired naturalization. Prepared about 1695-6. N. Y., 1888. 77 pp. map. O.   HB—R19

REPORT of a French protestant refugee in Boston, 1687. Translated from the French by E. T. Fisher. Brooklyn, N. Y., 1868. 42 pp. square O.   HB—R29

REVEILLAUD, Eugene. Etablissement d'une Colonie de Vaudois français en Algérie; publié sous les auspices de le Société Coligny, XXXII, 118 pp., 4 pl., 1 map folded. Paris, 1893. S.   HB—R32
Gift of Rev. Dr. Atterbury.

ROSENGARTEN, Joseph George. French colonists and exiles in the United States. 234 pp. O. Philadelphia, 1907.   HB—R71

ROUX, G., translator. Moerikofer, J. C. Histoire des réfugiés de la réforme en Suisse. 1878.   HB—M72

ST. JACOBSKERK: Grafboeken der Groote of St. Jacobskerk, te s'Gravenhage, 1620-1830. Bewerkt door M. G. WILDEMAN. 2 p.l., 209 pp., 8 leaves. Square folio. s'Hertogenbosch, 1898.   HB—W67

SCHICKLER, Fernand baron de. Les églises du refuge en Angle-terre. Paris, 1892. Vols. 1-3, fac-similes. Q. 3 vols.   HB—Sch3
Tome 1: Edouard VI.—Jacques I. 1547-1625.
Tome 2: Charles I.—Jacques II. 1625-1685.
         Les églises réformées des Iles de la manche.
Tome 3: Pièces justificatives et complémentaires du tome 1 et du tome 2.
         Table générale alphabétique.

SILLEM, Carl Hieronymus Wilhelm. Die Wallonisch gemeinde in Stade. 32 pp. Magdeburg, 1893. O. (Der Deutsche Huge-notten Verein. Geschichtsblätter. 1893. No. 10, pt. 6.)   HB—T57

[SIMMS, William Gilmore.] Lily and the totem; or, Huguenots in Florida. 1562-1570. Second edition. N. Y., 1850. 470 pp. O.   HB—Si4

SOUTH CAROLINA. 1680-'84. See: CLUTE, R. F. Annals and parish register of St. Thomas' and St. Denis' parish. . . . O. Charleston, 1884.   HB—C62

SOUTH CAROLINA. 1695-1696. See: RAVENEL (D.) compiler, "Liste des François et Suisses." . . . O. N. Y., 1888.   HB—R19

STAPLETON, Rev. Ammon. Memorial of the Huguenots in Amer-ica, with special reference to their emigration to Pennsylvania. IX, 164 pp., 1 fac-sim., 7 pl., 6 port. O. Carlisle, Pa., 1901. HB—S794

——— "Huguenota Pennsylvanianica." Series of Articles; clippings from newspapers, etc., in which they were published; mounted in blank book. 75 leaves, 1 port. Square O. Lewisburg, Pa., 1898-1901.   HB—S794.1
Gift of the Author.

STURSBURG, Johannes. Die französische-reformirte gemeinde in Erlanger. 27 pp. O. Magdeburg, 1892. (Der Deutsche Hugenotten-
Verein. Geschichtsblätter. 1892. Vol. 6.)   HB—T57

THEAL, George McCall. Boers and Bantu: a history of the emi-
grant farmers, from their leaving the Cape Colony to the overflow of
Dingau. Cape Town, 1886. 128 pp. S.   HB—H87SA
Reprint from the *South African Illustrated News.*
          No. 1, of P. V. "Huguenots in South Africa."

——— Republic of Natal: the origin of the present Pondo tribe, imperial treaties with Panda, and establishment of the colony of Natal.
Cape Town, 1886. 69 pp. S. (Reprint from the "Cape Mercantile Advertiser. No. 2, of P. V.)   HB—H87SA
Gift of Chr. C. de Villiers.

THOMAS, Theodore Gaillard, Editor. See: DUBOSE, Samuel.
Contributions to the history of the Huguenots of South Carolina
. . . 1887.

——— Same, in Volume entitled "FRENCH Protestant Church in
Charleston, S. C.   HB—F875

TOLLIN, Henri. Geschichte der französischen colonie zu Magde-
burg, jubilausschrift. Vols. I-III in 5 Vols. Halle (Vol. III Magde-
burg), 1886-1894. Port. pl. 3 v. in 5.   HB—T57
Vol. I.   Buch 1. Die Hugenotten in Frankreich.
           Buch 2. Das Refuge.
Vol. II.   Buch 3. Die Französischen Colonieen in der Provinz
                    Sachsen.
Vol. III. Abthelung 1, A. Der kampf der hugenottischen glau-
                    bensfluchtlinge inbesondere in Magde-
                    burg.
Vol. III. Abthelung 2, B. Vom nutzen des refuge inbesondere in
                    Magdeburg.
Vol. III. Abthelung 3, C. Kirche des Refuge insondere in Mag-
                    deburg.
Gift of the Author.

——— Ueber den Namen "Hugenotten." Erlangen, 1899. Pages 387-
415. Q. (Reformirte Kirchen-Beitung. Nos. 49-52.)   HB—T571
Gift of Author.

——— Concerning the name "Huguenot." A translation. HUGUE-
NOT Society of London. Proceedings. Vol. VI. Pages 327-355.)
                                                     HK—H876

TRAITS and stories of the Huguenots. Pages 185-190. n.p., n.d.
No. 1 of Volume "Huguenot Essays."   HB—H89

VEDDER, Rev. CHARLES S., D.D., LL.D. Historical address, 225th anniversary, April 14th, 1912. The Huguenot Church. Pages 12-22. (In: FRENCH Protestant Church, Charleston, S. C., 1912.)   HB—F875

—————— Huguenot church of Charleston, S. C.: an apostolic and true church. Two discourses preached May, 1879, and 1880. Charleston, S. C., 1880. 32 pp. O.   HB—F875V
Gift of the author.

—————— "This day shall be unto you for a memorial." A communion sermon preached in the Huguenot church, Charleston, S. C., May 11, 1873, the 28th anniversary of the dedication of the present edifice. Charleston, S. C., 1873. 15 pp. O.   HB—F875V
Gift of the author.
These three sermons bound in one volume: "French Protestant Church."

VERDEIL, A., Editor. See: PIERREFLEUR, PIERRE. Memoires . . . 1856.

VERMILYE, ASHBEL GREEN. Huguenot element among the Dutch. Schenectady [no date]. 23 pp. O.   HB—A2H
Gift of the Author.

VERREN, Rev. ANTOINE. The Huguenots in this country, in Pine, Franklin and West 22d Sts.; or, A discourse delivered June 26, 1862, on the occasion of laying the corner-stone of their new temple. Translated from the French by Rev. William Morris. N. Y., 1862. 24 pp. O.   HB—A2H
Gift of the Rev. Alfred V. Wittmeyer.

VILLIERS, CHR. C. DE. Aankondiging: iets belangrijks voor onze oude Afrikaansche familien. Kaapstad, 1885. 8 pp. O.   HB—H87SA
Reprint from Ned. Geref. kerk-almanak.
Gift of the Author.

WALDRON, WILLIAM WATSON. Huguenots of Westchester and Parish of Fordham . . . with introduction by Rev. S. H. Tyng, Jr. 126 pp., 1 pl. New York, 1864. S.   HB—W14
Gift of Dr. R. B. Coutant.

WEISS, CHARLES. The Huguenot families in America. (In: The Continental Monthly, Vol. I, Nos. II-IV, pp. 231-232, 151-155, 298-302, 461-465.) Boston, 1862. O.   HB—H897

WESTCHESTER, New York. See: WALDRON, WM. WATSON. Huguenots of Westchester and Parish of Fordham. New York, 1864. S.   HB—W14

WESTPHAL-CASTELNAU. Yesterday and to-day: or, The activities of French protestants since the commencement of this century, with an introduction and notes by Rev. A. F. Beard. Translated by permission. Paris, 1885. 48 pp. O.   HB—A2H
Gift of Edward F. De Lancey.

WILDEMAN, Marinus Godefridus. The Eldest Church-book of the English congregation in the Hague. . . . A transcript. 84, i-iv pp. The Hague, 1906. O. HB—W67E
Gift of the Compiler.

—— Compiler. Grafboeken (De) der Groote of St. Jacobskerk te s'Gravenhage, 1620-1830. 2 p.l., 209 pp., 8 leaves. s'Hertogen-gosch, 1898. Square folio. HB—W67
Gift of the Compiler.

WILLIAMS, Rev. J. N. Our debt to the Huguenots; or, What we owe to French protestantism. 1882. O. HB—H12
From the *Baptist Quarterly Review,* 1882, vol. 4.
Gift of Charles Marseilles.

WITTMEYER, Rev. Alfred V. Historical sketch of the "Eglise François à la Nouvelle York," from 1688-1804. N. Y., 1886. 82 pp. plate. Q. HB—Wit77
Reprint from the Huguenot Society of America *Collections,* vol. i.

CHURCH HISTORY

BAILEY, J. C.   Erasmus and the Reformation.   Pages 207-219. n.p.,
n.d.   HC—Pamphlet

BAIRD, ROBERT.   Religion in America; or, Account of the origin, progress, relation to the state and present condition of the Evangelical
Church. N. Y., 1844. 343 pp. O.   HC—B16

BEESLEY, CHARLES NORBURY.   Illustrated guide to St. Michael's
Church, Charleston, South Carolina. 76 pp. Tt. oblong. Charles-
ton, S. C., 1898.   HC—Pamphlet
A brochure containing 33 plates and an historic description of the
Church.
Gift of B. K. Neu.

BERINGUIER, RICHARD.   Ausführliche beschreibung der feier zum
200 jähringen gedächtnisse des ediktes von Potsdam, 29 Oct., 1685.
Berlin, 1885. 103 pp. O.   HC—Sy6

BERRIAN, REV. WILLIAM.   Historical sketch of Trinity Church, New
York, N. Y., 1847. 386 pp. plates. O.   HC—B45
Gift of Edward F. De Lancey.

BONNET, JULES.   Aonio Paleario, études sur la réforme en Italie.
Paris, 1863. 348 pp. D.   HC—B64

BOURLIER, E.   Souvenir de troisième centenaire de l'eglise Wallonne de la Haye. . . . Et sermon par E. Lacheret. . . . 105 pp.,
2 pl., 3 port. La Haye, 1891. O.   HC—B66
Gift of M. G. Wildeman.

BREEN, GILLIS VAN, translator.   See: GILLIS, PETRUM.   Kercke-
lijcke historie.   1657.

BRIEGER, THEODORE, Editor.   ZEITSCHRIFT für kirchengeschichte.   1877-'82.   Vols. 1, 2, and 5.   O.   HC—Ze3

CHARLESTON, S. C.   See: French Protestant Church.

CHARLESTON, S. C.   See: St. Phillip's Church.   Special services
held on the 12th and 13th of May, 1875.

CORWIN, REV. EDWARD TANJORE, D.D., Compiler.   Ecclesiastical
records, State of New York.   Vol. VII.   Index.   682 pp., 1 port.
Albany, 1916.   O.   (Univ. State of N. Y., Div. Archives and
Hist.)   HC—C832
Gift of Univ. State of N. Y.

——— Manual of the Reformed Church in America (formerly Reformed protestant Dutch Church).   Third edition, enlarged.   N. Y.,
1879.   675 pp. illustrated, portraits.   O.   HC—C81

31

DEMAREST, David D. Reformed Church in America; its origin, development, and characteristics. 215 pp., port., pl. N. Y., 1889. 4 ed., enlarged. O.   HC—D39
History of the coat-of-arms of the Reformed Church in America by John S. Bussing, pp. 9-13.
Gift of Mrs. Martha J. Lamb.

DE MEAUX, le vicomte. Les luttes religieuses en France au seizième siècle. LXVII, 41 pp. Paris, 1879. O.   HC
Gift of the French Société.

De WITT, Thomas. Discourse delivered in the North Reformed Dutch (Collegiate) Church in the city of New York. August, 1856. N. Y., 1857. 100 pp. plates. O.   HC—D51

DIMAN, Jeremiah Lewis. Religion in America. 1776-1876. O. Pages 1-47.   HB—H12
From the *North American Review,* 1876, vol. 122.
Gift of Rev. Alfred V. Wittmeyer.

DISOSWAY, Gabriel Poillon. Earliest churches of New York and its vicinity. N. Y., 1865. 416 pp. plates. O.   HC—D63

DIX, The Rev. Morgan, S.T.D., Editor. A History of the Parish of Trinity Church in the City of New York. . . . part 1, pl., port., N. Y., 1898.   HC—D64
Part 1: To the close of the Rectorship of Rev. Dr. Inglis, A.D., 1783.
One of 750 copies.
(This Library wants Part 2.)

EGLE, William H., M.D., Editor. See: PENNSYLVANIA Archives.

EGLISE Evangelique Vaudoise. Resume historique des fetes du bicentenaire de la glorieuse rentree des Vaudois et compterendu du synode de 1889 tenu a La Tour, 2-7 Sept. 62,138 pp. plates. La Tour, 1889. O.   HC—Sy6
No. 3 of Pamphlet Volume.
Gift of the Société d'Hist. Vaudoise.

EGLISE réformée de France. Actes et décisions du synode général officieux. Toulouse, 1881. O.   HC—Sy6
No. 2 of Pamphlet Volume.

ERASMUS and the Reformation. By J. C. Bailey. N.p., n.d. O.   HC—Pamphlet

FISHER, George Parke. History of the Christian Church. N. Y., 1887. 701 pp. maps. O.   HC—F53
Gift of Mrs. Martha J. Lamb.

FRIEDRICHSDORF: Colonie Réformée Française. Chronique de la Colonie . . . suivie de documents et pièces explicatives. Hambourg-és-Monts, 1887. VIII, 190 pp., 5 pl., 1 coloured plate, 2 port. O.   HC—F81
Gift of Rev. Mr. Kleinhaus.

GAILLARD, THOMAS. History of the Reformation in the Church of Christ, continued from close of the 15th century. N. Y., 1847. 557 pp. O.   HC—G12
Gift of Gen. W. G. De Saussure.

GILLIS, PETRUM. Kerckelijck Historie van de Gereformeerde Kercken . . . uyt het Frans in 'tNederduyts vertaalt door Gillis van Breen. [26], 496 [44] pp. Amsterdam, 1657. Square D.
Gift of Mrs. Pierre Van Cortlandt.
Bound in ancient vellum.

HACKENSACK, New Jersey. See: ROMEYN, REV. T. B. Historical discourse. . . . First Reformed (Dutch) Church. N. J., 1870. O.   HC—R66

HARLEM, New York. See: TILTON, REV. EDGAR, JR., D.D. Reformed Low Dutch Church of Harlem, organized 1660. Historical sketch. [New York], 1910. O.   HC—T58

HILL, HAMILTON ANDREWS. History of the Old South Church (Third Church), Boston, 1669-1884. 2 Vols., port., pl., fac-sim. O.   HC—H55
Gift of Mrs. Martha J. Lamb.

HOES, REV. ROSWELL RANDALL. Baptismal and marriage registers of the Old Dutch Church of Kingston, Ulster County, N. Y. (formerly named Wiltwyck, and often familiarly called Esopus or 'Sopus), for 150 years from their commencement in 1660. 795 pp. New York, 1891. Folio.   HC—Hoes67

HOWE, RT. REV. WILLIAM BELL WHITE, Bishop of the Diocese of S. C. Sermon preached in St. Philip's Church, Charleston, S. C., May 12, 1875. (Charleston, S. C., St. Philip's Church, Special services, . . . 1876 . . . pp. 51-76.)   HC—C38

INDEX to . . . Bishop Meade's Old Churches, ministers and families of Virginia. Compiled by J. M. Toner. Washington, 1898. O.   HC—M461

KETCHAM, REV. WILLIAM E. Memoir of J. B. Wakeley. In: WAKELEY, J. B. Lost chapters of American Methodism. [Cop. 1889.] Pages 597-635.   HC—W13

KINGSTON [New York], Records, 1660-1809. See: HOES, REV. R. R. Baptismal and marriage registers of the Old Dutch Church.

KURTZ, JOHN HENRY. Text-book of church history. 2 vols. in 1. Philadelphia, 1876. O.   HC—K96

LACHERET, E. Sermon . . . prononcé le 27 Septembre, 1891. (In: BOURLIER, E. Souvenir du troisième centenaire de l'èglise Wallonne de La Haye. . . . La Haye, 1891.) O.   HC—B66

LAWRENCE, EUGENE. Historical studies. N. Y., 1876. 508 pp. O.   HC—L43

LINN, JAMES B., and EGLE, W. H., M.D., Editors. See: PENN-
SYLVANIA Archives. Vols. 8 and 9. Harrisburg, Pa., 1895-
'96.   HC—Pa.11

MacSPARRAN, The REV. JAMES, D.D. America dissected . . . in
sundry letters from a Clergyman there. (In: UPDIKE, WILKINS.
History of the Episcopal Church in Narragansett, R. I. . . . With
an appendix . . . reprint of a work now extremely rare. . . .
"America dissected.") New York, 1847. Pages 483-533. O.
                                                           HC—Up1

MEADE, The RT. REV. WILLIAM, D.D., Bishop of Vermont. Old
Churches, ministers, and families of Virginia. Philadelphia, 1900.
2 vols. Q.   HC—M46
Index by J. M. Toner, bound separately and published by the Southern Historical Assoc., as, Extra Vol. I.   HC—M461

MERLE D'AUBIGNE, JEAN HENRI. Histoire de la réformation en
Europe au temps de Calvin. Paris, 1863-66. 4 vols. O.   HC—M54

———— History of the reformation in the 16th century, translated by
David Dundas Scott and H. White. Lancaster, Pa. [no date]. 2
vols. illustrated, portraits. O.   HC—M541

MORRISON, HUGH A., Reviser. See: TONER, J. M., M.D. Index
to Meade's Old Churches of Virginia.

NEW YORK STATE: Ecclesiastical records. Vol. VIII. Index, compiled by Rev. E. T. CORWIN, D.D. Albany, 1816. O.   HC—C832

OLD FIRST Presbyterian Church, New York City. Dedication of the
Huguenot Window, given by Dr. Benjamin G. Demarest as a
Memorial to his Mother, in the Church, on Sunday, December 19th,
1915. N. Y., Huguenot Society of America, 1916. 25 pp., 2 plates.
Square Q.   HC—Pamphlet

PENNSYLVANIA Archives. Vols. 8 and 9. Edited by J. B. Linn
and W. H. Egle, M.D. [Harrisburg, Pa.], 1895-'96. O. 2nd
series.   HC—Pa.11

PENNSYLVANIA marriages, prior to 1810. See: PENNSYL-
VANIA Archives. [Harrisburg, Pa.], 1895-'96. Vols. 8 and 9.
2nd series. O.

PERRY, The RIGHT REV. WILLIAM STEVENS, D.D., LL.D., Second
Bishop of Iowa. History of the American Episcopal Church. 1587-
1883. Boston, 1885. 2 vols. Square Q.   HC—P43
Vol. I. The planting and growth of the American Colonial
Church. 1587-1783.
Vol. II. The organization and progress of the American Church,
1783-1883.
Gift of the Rev. Alfred V. Wittmeyer.

REFORMED Dutch Church: North America. List of Ministers prior
to 1800. (In: DEWITT, T. Discourse delivered. . . . August,
1856. . . . N. Y., 1857. , Pages 71-79. O.)   HC—D51

REFORMED (First) Dutch Church: Hackensack, N. J. Register of the members. 1686-1870. (In: ROMEYN, Rev. T. B. Historical discourse. . . . New Jersey, 1870. O. Pages I-XXIII. Appendix.) HC—R66

REFORMED Low Dutch Church of Harlem. Organized 1660. Historical Sketch by Rev. Edgar Tilton, Jr., D.D. New York, 1910. 181 pp., 1 coloured plate, other plates paged in. O. HC—T58

REFORMED Protestant Dutch Church, Albany, New York. Register of members of the . . . Church, 1683-1700[?]. In: ROGERS, Rev. E. P. Historical discourse. . . . Nov. 26, 1857. . . . Pages 67-80. N. Y., 1858. O. HC—R63

REFORMED Protestant Dutch Church: New York City. Celebration of the quarter-millennial anniversary, Nov. 21, 1878. 104 pp., N. Y., [1878]. O. HC—N48
Gift of the Rev. Alfred V. Wittmeyer.

REFORMED Protestant Dutch Church: New York City: Year book of Collegiate Reformed Protestant Dutch Church. N. Y., 1882. D. HC—Pamphlet
Gift of the Rev. Alfred V. Wittmeyer.

ROGERS, REV. E. P. Historical discourse on the Reformed protestant Dutch church of Albany, Nov. 26, 1857, delivered in the North Dutch Church. N. Y., 1858. 120 pp. illustrated, plates. O. HC—R63

ROMEYN, REV. THEODORE BAYARD. Historical discourse delivered on the occasion of the re-opening and dedication of the First Reformed (Dutch) church at Hackensack, N. J., May 2, 1869. N. Y., 1870. 131 pp. plate, fac-simile. O. HC—R66

SAINT MARK'S Church-in-the-Bowery. Services in commemoration of the 100th Anniversary of the Consecration of the Church, on May 9th, 1899. New York, 1899. 4 leaves. Square Q. HC—Pamphlet

SAINT MICHAEL'S Church, Charleston, S. C. See: BEESLEY, C. N. Illustrated guide to St. Michaels. . . .

ST. PHILLIP'S Church, Charleston, S. C. Special services held at St. Phillip's Church on the 12th and 13th of May, 1875, in commemoration of the planting of the Church of England in the province of Carolina; with the sermon preached by Rev. W. B. W. Howe and the historical address by J. J. Pringle Smith. [Charleston, 1876.] 172 pp. portrait, plates. HC—C38
Gift of Rev. Alfred V. Wittmeyer.

SCOTT, DAVID DUNDAS. Translator. See: MERLE d'AUBIGNE, JEAN HENRI. History of the Reformation in the XVI century.

SMITH, J. J. PRINGLE. Address . . . in St. Phillip's Church, Charleston, May 13th, 1875. (In: Charleston, S. C., St. Phillip's Church. Special services . . . 1876. Pages 77-127.) HC—C38

STOUDT, John Baer. Rev. Michael Schlatter in the Lehigh Valley, June 24-July 2, 1747. N.p., n.d. 15 pp. O. HC—Pamphlet Reprint: The Reformed Church Review, Vol. xx. No. 1, Jan., 1916.
Gift of Miss Minnie F. Mickley.

TILTON, Rev. Edgar, Jr., D.D. REFORMED Low Dutch Church of Harlem, organized 1660. Historical sketch. New York, 1910. 181 pp., 1 coloured plate, 19 pl., 6 port., 1 plan, paged in. O. HC—T58
Gift of the Consistory.

TONER, James Meredith. Index to names of persons and Churches in Bishop Meade's "Old Churches, Ministers and Families of Virginia." Washington, D. C., 1898. 63 pp. O. (Southern Hist. Assoc., Pub. Supplement to Vol. 2, No. 4. No. 1.) HC—M461

UPDIKE, Wilkins. History of the Episcopal Church in Narragansett, Rhode Island; including . . . other Episcopal Churches in the State; with an Appendix containing a reprint . . . entitled, "America dissected," by the Rev. J. MacSPARRAN, D.D. With . . . genealogical and biographical accounts. . . . xxxiii, 34-533 pp., 1 port. New York, 1847. O. HC—Up.1
Gift of Mrs. Levi P. Holbrook.

VENNEMA, Rev. Ame. History of the Reformed Church of New Paltz, Ulster Co., N. Y., 1683-1883. Rondout, N. Y., 1884. 40 pp. HC—V56
Gift of the Author.

WAKELEY, Joseph B. Lost chapters recovered from the early history of American Methodism, with a memoir of the author by Rev. W. E. Ketcham. . . . 635 pp., port., pl., fac-sim. New York [cop., 1889]. O. HC—W13

WHITE, H., Translator. See: MERLE d'AUBIGNE, Jean Henri. History of the Reformation in the xivth century.

ZEITSCHRIFT für kirchengeschichte in verbindung mit W. Gass, H. Reuter, u. A. Ritschl. hrsg., T. BRIEGER. Gotha, 1877-1882. Vols. 1, 2, and 5. O. HC—Ze3

FRENCH HISTORY

ACADEMIE royale des médailles & des inscriptions. See: PARIS-ACADEMIE royale des médailles & des inscriptions.

ANQUEZ, LÉONCE. Histoire des assemblées politiques des Réformés de France. (1573-1622.) xv, 520 pp., 1 map, folded. O. HD—An6
Gift of the French Société.

———— Same. HA—An7

ARC, JEANNE D'. See: JEANNE LA PUCELLE D'ORLEANS.

AYLESBURY, WILLIAM, Translator. See: DAVILA, A. C. Historie of the civill warres of France. 1647. HD—D281

BEAUVAU, HENRI, MARQUIS DE. Mémoires du Marquis de Beauvau, pour servir à l'histoire de Charles IV, duc de Lorraine et de Bar. Cologne, 1690. 456 pp. S. HD—B38

BLACK, ROBERT, Translator. See: GUIZOT, FRANÇOIS PIERRE GUILLAUME. History of France. 1887. HD—G94

BONGARS, JACQUES. 1546-1612. Lettres latines, de . . . Bongars . . . ambassadeur sous . . . Henry IV en diverses négociations importantes; traduites en François. . . . 391 pp. Paris, 1681. S. HD—B64
Gift of Edward F. Delancey.

BORDIER, L., Illustrator. See: Henry IV. Job le bon Roy Henry. 48 pp., Coloured plates. Tours, 1894? Oblong. O. HD—H55

CHARLES IX. Roi de France. Correspondance du Roi . . . et du Sieur de Mandelot, gouverneur de Lyon, pendant l'année 1572, époque du massacre de la Saint-Barthélemy. Edited by P. Paris. D. Paris, 1830. (Monumens inedits de l'histoire de France. Part 1, pp. 1-103.) HD—M815

COLLECTION Universelle des Mémoires particuliers, relatifs à l'histoire de France. Tome VII. . . . Mémoires de la Pucelle d'Orléans, ceux du Connétable de Richemont, & ceux de Florent Sire d'Illiers. XIVe & XVe siècles. 467 pp. Paris, 1785. D. HD—C696
Gift of Herbert Du Puy.

COTTEREL, SIR CHARLES, Translator. See: DAVILA, A. C. Histoire of the civill warres of France. 1647.

37

DAVILA, Arrigo Caterino. Dell'istoria delle guerre civili di Francia. Firenze, 1823. 6 vols. O. *Vellum.*   HD—D28
Gift of William S. Pelletreau.

—— Historie of the civill warres of France, translated out of the original [by William Aylesbury and Sir Charles Cotterel]. London, 1647. 1478 pp., folio.   HD—D281
Gift of William S. Pelletreau.

[DUBOIS DE RIACOURT, Nicolas.] Histoire de l'emprisonnement de Charles IV duc de Lorraine. 132 pp. Cologne, 1688. S.   HD—B38
Bound with Beauvau, H. marquis de. Mémoires.

[GODEFROY, Denys.] Mémoires concernant la Pucelle d'Orléans, XVᵉ siècle. 222 pp. D. (Collection Universelle des Mémoires . . . relatifs à l'hist. de France. Tome VII.)   HD—C696

GUIZOT, François Pierre Guillaume. History of France from the earliest times to 1848; by Guizot and Madame Guizot de Witt. Translated by Robert Black. N. Y., 1887. 8 vols. portraits, plates. D.   HD—G94
Gift of Mrs. Martha J. Lamb.

HANOTAUX, Gabriel. Etudes historiques sur le 16ᵉ et le 17ᵉ siècle en France. Paris, 1886. 350 pp. D.   HD—H19
Gift of Rev. Alfred V. Wittmeyer.

HENRY IV. Job le bon Roy Henry. 48 pp. coloured plates. Tours, 1894? Oblong O. Hermant, A.   HD—H55
Gift of Mrs. J. M. Lawton, with autograph of E. Belleroche.

HERMANT, A. Job le bon Roy Henry. 48 pp. Coloured plates. Tours [1894?] oblong O. [Bordier, L., Illustrator.]   HD—H55

HOUGHTON, Louise Seymour. Idealism of the French people. 3 leaves, 7-80 pp. Boston [cop. 1918]. O.   HD—H81
Author's presentation copy, through Mrs. James M. Lawton.

INVENTAIRE-sommaire des archives départementales antérieures à 1790 Charente-inférieure . . . [par, L. M. Meschinet de Richemond].   HD—M56

[LENNOX, Mrs. C. R.], Translator. See: SULLY, Maximilian de Bethune duc de Mémoires . . . 1763.

MANDELOT, Sieur de, Gouverneur de Lyon. Correspondance du Roi Charles IX, et du . . . gouverneur de Lyon, pendant l'année 1572, epoque du massacre de la Saint-Barthélemy. [Edited by P. Paris.] D. Paris, 1830. (Monumens inedits de l'histoire de France. Part 1, pp. 1-103.)   HD—M815

MEMOIRES concernant la Pucelle d'Orléans. XVᵉ siècle par Denys Godefroy. Pages 1-222. (Coll. Univ. Mém. . . . relatifs à l'hist. France. Tome VII.) Paris, 1785. D.   HD—C696

MENESTRIER, Claude François. Histoire du roy Louis le Grand, par les médailles, emblêms, armoiries et autres monumens publics. Paris, 1691. 64 pp. illustrated, folio, *calf.*   HD—L888
Gift of William S. Pelletreau.

MESCHINET de RICHEMOND, Louis Marie. Inventaire-sommaire des archives départementales antérieures à 1790. Charente-inférieure, archives civiles et ecclésiastiques. Séries C. D. G. et H. Paris, 1877. Vol. 2, folio, *morocco.*   HD—M56
Gift of Henry M. Lester.

———— List of books, dated at La Rochelle, 29 Mars, 1909. MS. bibliography of his books and writings, in letter form to the Secretary of the Huguenot Society of America. 6 letter sheets, closely written on both sides, closing with the Author's signature. O.   HD—M56.1
(Inserted in a volume of his pamphlets, gifts of the Author, through Mrs. James M. Lawton.)

———— Rapport de l'archiviste du département. [Charente-Inférieure] 1885. 19 pp. O.   HD—M56.1
Gift of the Author.

———— Relations inédites et autographes des voyages, dans l'Europe centrale de Jean Godeffroy, d'Orléans (de 1568-1571), et de Jacques Esprinchard, sieur du Plomp, Rochelois (de 1593-1598). Paris, 1882. 9 pp. O.   HD—M56.1
Reprint from Association française pour l'avancement des sciences. Congrès de la Rochelle. 1882.
Gift of the Author.

———— Une famille d'ingénieurs, geographes, Claude Masse (1650-1737) sa vie et ses œuvres. Rochefort, 1882. 20 pp. O.   HD—M56.1
Reprint from Société de Géographie de Rochefort. *Bulletin,* 1882, vol. 3.
Gift of the Author.

———— Voyage à le cité souterraine; le dernier explorateur des catacombes de Rome. Rochefort, 1882.   HD—M56.1
Reprint from Société de Géographie de Rochefort. *Bulletin,* 1882, vol. 3.
Gift of the Author.

MONUMENS inédits de l'histoire de France.
   I.   Correspondence du roi Charles XI, et du Sieur de Mandelot, gouverneur de Lyon, pendant l'année 1572, époque de massacre de la Saint-Barthélemy.
   II. Lettre des seize au roi d'Espagne Philippe II année 1591.
[Edited by P. Paris.] 2 en 1 tome. Paris, 1830. vii-xvi, 128 pp. D.   HD—M815
Gift of Herbert DuPuy.

PARIS-Académie royale des médailles et des inscriptions. Médailles sur les principaux evenements du regne de Louis le Grand; avec des explications historiques. Paris, 1702. 286 leaves, illustrated, folio.   HD—L888.1
Gift of William S. Pelletreau.

PHILIPPE II., Roi d'Espagne. Lettre envoyée au Roi d'Espagne . . . par le Conseil des Seize, en 1591, pendant le siége de Paris. [Edited by P. Paris.] D. Paris, 1830. (Monumens inédits de l'histoire de France. Part 2.)   HD—M815

RAMBAUD, Alfred. Histoire de la civilisation contemporaine en France. Paris, 1888. 750 pp. D.   HD—R14
Gift of Mrs. Martha J. Lamb.

RIBARD, Clement. Notes d'histoire Cévenole d'après des documens la plupart inédits. 344 pp. O. SeVend [190?].   HD—R35
Gift of the Author.

RICHEMONT, Comte de. See: ARTUS III duc de Bretagne.

SULLY, Maximilien de Béthune, duc de. Memoirs containing history of the life and reign of [Henry the Great] translated from the French [by Mrs. C. R. Lennox] with tryal of Ravaillac. Fourth edition. London, 1763. 6 vols. map. D.   HD—Su5

WASHBURNE, Elihu Benjamin. Recollections of a minister to France, 1869-77. N. Y., 1887. 2 vols. illustrated, portraits, facsimiles. O.   HD—W27
Gift of Mrs. Martha J. Lamb.

WITT, Mme. Pauline Guizot de. See GUIZOT, François Pierre Guillaume. History of France . . . 1887.   HD—G94

AMERICAN HISTORY

ADAMS, CHARLES FRANCIS. Struggle for neutrality in America. Address before N. Y. Historical Soc'y, Dec. 13, 1870. 52 pp.   HE—Z3

ADAMS, HERBERT BAXTER. Maryland's influence in founding a National Commonwealth. Paper read before the Maryland Historical Society, April 9, 1877. 123 pp., 1 pl. Baltimore, 1877. O.   HE—Z4

ALBANY, New York. Early records of the City and County of Albany and Colony of Rensselaerswyck. Translated from the original Dutch by J. Pearson. Revised and edited by A. J. F. vanLaer. Vols. 2-4. Albany, N. Y., 1916-1919. 3 vols. Q. (University State N. Y., State Library Historical Bulletin, 9-11.)   HE—A326
Gift of the University, State of New York.

AMERICAN Almanacs, 1639-1800. See: MORRISON, H. A.

AMERICAN Revolution Naval Records, 1775-1778. See: LINCOLN, CHARLES H., Compiler.

BACON, WILLIAM JOHNSON. The Continental Congress, some of its actors and their doings, with the results thereof. Address before the Oneida Historical Society . . . 31st of Dec., 1880. 26 pp. Utica, 1881.   HE—Z1

BACON, REV. WILLIAM THOMPSON. Sires and Sons; Historical poem pronounced at the Woodbury Centennial Celebration, July 4th, 1859. In: COTHREN, WILLIAM. Second Centennial Celebration. . . . Ancient Woodbury, pp. 78-99.   HE—W885
Volume—"Ancient Woodbury."

BAGG, M. M., M.D. Historical sketch of the Utica Orphan Asylum; an Address read at its 50th Anniversary, Oct. 13th, 1880. 24 pp. Utica, 1880.   HE—Z4

BAIRD, CHARLES WASHINGTON. History of Rye, Westchester County, New York, 1660-1870, including Harrison and the White Plains till 1788. xvi, 2 maps, 1 fac-sim. New York, 1871. O.   HE—B16

BALCH, EDWIN SWIFT, and BALCH, ELISE WILLING, Translators. See: BALCH, THOMAS. The French in America during the War of Independence. . . . Translation of his "Francais en Amerique pendant la guerre de l'independance des Etats-Unis. Philadelphia, 1895. O.   HE—B18E

BALCH, Thomas. Les Français en Amérique pendant la guerre de l'indépendance des Etats-Unis, 1777-83. Paris, 1872. 237 pp. illustrated, portraits, maps. O.   HE—B18F
Gift of Thomas Willing Balch.

—— The French in America during the War of Independence . . . 1777-1783. A translation by E. S. Balch and E. W. Balch, of [his] "Français en Amerique pendant la guerre de l'independance des Etats-Unis." IV, 252 pp. Philadelphia, 1895. O.   HE—B18E
Gift of Thomas Willing Balch.
English edition is Volume II.
French edition is Volume I.

—— Letters and papers relating chiefly to the provincial history of Pennsylvania, with some notices of the writers. Philadelphia, 1855. 312 pp. D.   HE—B18I
These are known as the Shippen papers.
Gift of Thomas Willing Balch.

BANCROFT, George. The necessity, the reality, and the promise of the progress of the human race. Oration delivered before the N. Y. Historical Soc., Nov. 20, 1854. (N. Y. Historical Soc. Semi-centennial celebration, 1854, pp. 5-37.)   HE—Z3

BARRY, John Stetson. The history of Massachusetts. Boston, 1855. 3 Vols. O.   HE—B27
Vol. 1. Colonial period.
Vol. 2. Provincial period.
Vol. 3. Commonwealth period.

BARTLETT, Homer L., M.D. History of initiation, as practiced by the ancient rites and perpetuated by Freemasonry; read before the Long Island Historical Society, Jan. 23d, 1877. 21 pp. Flatbush, L. I., 1877.   HE—Z7

BAXTER, James Phinney. Campaigns of Carleton and Burgoyne from Canada, 1776-77. (See: DIGBY, W. British invasion from the north. 1887, pp. 1-75.)   HE—D56

—— Editor. See: DIGBY, W. British invasion of the North. 1887.   HE—D56

BEARD, George Miller, M.D. Scientific basis of delusions. . . . 47 pp. N. Y., 1877.   HE—Z2

BEEKMAN, James William. Centenary address delivered before the Society of the New York Hospital. . . . July 24, 1871. 44 pp. N. Y., 1871.   HE—Z1

—— The Founders of New York; an Address delivered before the Saint Nicholas Society of . . . New York . . . Dec. 4, 1869. 36 pp. N. Y., 1870.   HE—Z9

BELLAMONT, Richard Coote, first Earl of. 1636-1701. See: DePEYSTER, Frederic. Life and administration of Bellomont, Governor of the Provinces of New York, Massachusetts, and New Hampshire, from 1697-1701. An address delivered before the N. Y. Historical Society, November 18th, 1879. 5 p.l., 60, xvii pp., 3 port. New York, 1879. Q.   HE—D44
Another copy, portrait of Earl lacking, in pamphlet Vol.   HE—Z9

BELLOWS, Rev. Henry Whitney. Oration at the funeral of William Cullen Bryant, June 14, 1878. 11 pp. No title-page.
                                                           HE—Z7

BENEDICT, Erastus Cornelius. . . . Address on . . . taking the Chair of the University Convocation at the Capitol in . . . Albany, July 9, 1878. 19 pp. Albany, 1878.   HE—Z7

——— Battle of Harlem Heights, Sept. 16, 1776; read before the New York Historical Society, Feb. 5, 1878. . . . 11-62 pp. N. Y. [pref. 1880].   HE—Z5

——— 1800-80. The beginning of America; a Discourse delivered before the New York Historical Society on its 59th anniversary . . . Nov. 17, 1863. . . . 64 pp. N. Y., 1864.   HE—Z2

BERTOLET, Benjamin. Camp Pottsgrove, September 18th to 26th, 1777. General Washington with his Continental Army at Fagleysville, New Hanover Township, Montgomery County, Pennsylvania. 1 leaf, 19 pp., 1 leaf. Illustrated. Philadelphia, 1903. O. Privately printed.   HE—Pamphlet
Gift of the Author.

BIOGRAPHICAL memoir of William J. Duane. 28 pp. Philadelphia, 1868.   HE—Z7

BLACKET, W. S. Researches into the lost histories of America. . . . 336 pp., ill., pl. London, 1884.   HE—B56

BLAKE, Mrs. Euphenia Vale. Modern American literature. Pages 35-53. (From the Oriental Church Magazine.)   HE—Z5

BOGGILD, F. The anti-Columbian discovery of the American Continent by the Northmen. Pages 171-178. 1869. From the Historical Magazine, 1869. Vol. 5.   HE—Z6

BOLTON, Rev. C. W., Editor. See: BOLTON, Rev. Robert. History of . . . Westchester County, 1881.

BOLTON, Reginald Pelham. *Washington's* Headquarters, New York. A sketch of the history of the Morris mansion (or Jumel mansion), in the city of New York, used by Washington as his Headquarters in 1776. 1 port., 40 pp., 1 pl. S. New York, 1903.   HE—A512
Gift of Mrs. James M. Lawton.

43

BOLTON, Rev. Robert. History of the several towns, manors and patents of the county of Westchester from its first settlement to the present time. Edited by Rev. C. W. Bolton. N. Y., 1881. 2 vols. illustrated, tables, maps. O.   HE—B63

BROOKLYN'S Garden: views of picturesque Flatbush. With an historical introduction by C. A. Ditmas. 24 coloured plates, mounted. Oblong. O. [Brooklyn, N. Y., 1908.]   HE—D615
Gift of the Compiler.

BRAINERD, Rev. D. S. Sermon preached in Old Lyme, on the 25th anniversary of his pastorate, July 1st, 1866. 20 pp. O. New Haven, 1867.   HE—Z1

BREWSTER, Charles W. Rambles about Portsmouth. Sketches of persons, localities, and incidents of two centuries. . . . 376 pp. O. Portsmouth, N. H., 1859.   HE—P83B

BRODHEAD, John Romeyn. N. Y. (state)-Legislature. Documents relative to the Colonial History. 1856-61.   HE—N482

BROKAW Brothers' New Home. Reminiscence of the old neighborhood: i.e.: Astor Place, Fourth Avenue and Lafayette Place. Facts worthy of preservation. 4 pp.; in cover, ill. Oblong. O. New York City, 1916.   HE—A512
Gift of Messrs. Brokaw.

BROWN, Alexander, Editor. Genesis of the United States . . . 1605-1616 . . . through a series of historical manuscripts now first printed . . . with a re-issue of rare contemporaneous tracts . . . bibliographical memoranda, notes, and brief biographies. 2 vols. illus., 100 port., pl. maps, fac-sim. Q. Boston, 1890-91.
Biography of persons connected with the founding of Virginia, Vol. 2, pp. 807-1068.   HE—B81

BULLARD, Gen. Edward F. History of Saratoga; an Address delivered at Schuylerville, N. Y., July 4, 1876. 22 pp. Ballston Spa, 1876.   HE—Z1

BURDGE, Franklin. A notice of John Haring, a patriotic statesman of the Revolution. 11 pp. N. Y., 1878.   HE—Z4

—— Memorial of Henry Wisner, the only New Yorker who voted for the Declaration of Independence. 14 pp. N. Y., 1878.   HE—Z4

—— Simon Boerum, of Brooklyn, N. Y., written . . . for the committee on the restoration of Independence Hall, Philadelphia. 28 pp. 1876.   HE—Z4

BURNS celebration, held at Delmonico's, Jan., 1880; report of speeches by H. E. Partridge and A. W. Granville. 48 pp. N. Y., 1880. HE—Z1

BURRELL, A. B. Reminiscences of George La Bar, the centenarian of Monroe county, Pa., and incidents in the early settlement of the Pennsylvania side of the river valley from Easton to Bushkill. Philadelphia, 1870. 111 pp. portrait. O.   HE—B94

CAPRON, HORACE. Japan; some remarks in connection with [his] visit . . . to Japan in 1871-1875 . . . read before the Philosophical society of Washington, May 6, 1876. 19 pp. Philadelphia, n.d.   HE—Z2

——— Letters addressed during the year 1875 to Kuroda Kiyotaka. 2 pamph. Tokei, 1875.   HE—Z7

CARY, WILLIAM B. Memorial discourse of the First Congregational Church, 1693-1876, of Old Lyme, Conn. July 9, 1876. 19 pp. Hartford, 1876. O.   HE—Z4

CHAILLE-LONG, COL. CHARLES. Association of the Freeman of Maryland, N. Y., 1890. Q. (Republic Magazine, Vol. 1, No. 1, pp. 42-48.) (Chaillé family genealogical notes herein.)   HE—Cha35 Gift of the Author.

CHAMBERS, THEODORE FRELINGHUYSEN. Early Germans of New Jersey, their history, Churches, and genealogies. [Dover, N. J., cop. 1895.] XIII, 667 pp., 18 pl., 38 gr. port., 3 maps. Q. 3 parts in 1 vol.   HE—C445
Part 1. Their arrival, settlement, and Churches. . . .
Part 2. Genealogies.
Part 3. Appendices.

CHARLESTON (SOUTH CAROLINA)—CITY COUNCIL. Centennial of incorporation, 1670, 1783, 1883. [Charleston, 1883.] 259 pp. plate, maps, fac-similes. O.   HE—C38
Gift of William A. Courtney.

CLINTON, GEORGE. 1st Governor of New York. Public papers of George Clinton . . . 1777-1795-1801-1804. Military, Vols. 1-8, and 10. With an introduction by H. Hastings, State Historian. Published by the State of New York, as appendix "N"—3d annual report of the State Historian. 9 Vols. N. Y. and Albany, 1899-1914. O.   HE—C61
Gift of the State University, N. Y.

COLLEVILLE, VICOMTE DE. Les missions secrètes du Général Major Baron de Kalb et son rôle dans la guerre de l'indépendance Américaine. Paris, 1885. 161 pp. D.   HE—C68

CONNECTICUT marriages. Church records prior to 1800. Vols. I-III. New Haven [cop. 1896-'98.] Edited by Fred'k W. Bailey. 3 Vols. in 1. O.   HE—B15

CONE, M. The first settlement in Ohio. Pages 241-259, il. 1 map. 1881. (From Magazine of Amer. History. April, 1881.)   HE—Z6

COOLIDGE, SUSAN. pseudonym. See: WOOLSEY, SARAH CHAUNCEY.

COOPER, PETER. 1791-1883. Political and financial opinions, with an autobiography of his early life, edited by J. C. Zachos. 101 pp. 1 port. N. Y., 1877.   HE—Z2

COTHREN, WILLIAM, Editor. Second centennial celebration . . . of ancient Woodbury . . . held at *Woodbury, Conn.,* July 4 and 5, 1859. 223 pp. O. Woodbury, Conn, 1859. In: Volume "Ancient Woodbury." HE—W885

COUTANT, REV. L. J. John LeFevre. A biographical sketch. (In: New Rochelle Press Almanac, 1879-84. D. Pages 37-43.) HE—NR87S

COWDIN, ELLIOT CHRISTOPHER. Tribute of the Chamber of Commerce of the State of New York, to the memory of Moses H. Grinnell, Dec. 6, 1877, Address. 9 pp. N. Y., 1877. HE—Z4

DALY, [CHARLES PATRICK]. The geographical work of the world in 1872; annual Address before the American Geographical Society, delivered Feb. 17th, 1873. 60 pp. N. Y., 1873. HE—Z2

DANIELS, GEORGE FISHER. History of the town of Oxford, Massachusetts, with genealogies and notes on persons and estates. 856 pp., ill., pl., 1 fac-sim. Oxford, Mass., 1892. O. HE—D22

DAWSON, HENRY BARTON. Sons of Liberty in New York; a Paper read before the N. Y. Historical Society, May 3, 1859. 118 pp. Poughkeepsie, 1859. HE—Z3

DEDHAM, Massachusetts. Record of . . . the town of Dedham, 1635-1706. Edited by Don Gleason Hill. Dedham, Mass., 1886-1894. In 5 Vols. O. Illustrations, fac-similes, etc. HE—D299H

Vol. I. Records of births, marriages and deaths, and intentions of marriage in the town of Dedham. . . . With an appendix containing records of marriages before 1800, returned from other Towns, under the Statute of 1857. (1635-1845.)

Vol. II. Record of baptisms, marriages and deaths, and admissions to the Church and dismissals therefrom, transcribed from the Church Records in the town of Dedham. 1638-1845. Also all the Epitaphs in the ancient burial place in Dedham . . . with the other inscriptions in the three Parish Cemeteries.

Vol. III. Early records of . . . Dedham, 1636-1659. Complete transcript of Book I. . . . General Records of the Town . . . with the Selectmen's Day Book, covering a portion of the same period. . . .

Vol. IV. Early records of . . . Dedham, 1659-1673. Complete transcript of the Town Meeting and Selectmen's records contained in . . . general records of the Town. . . . Appendix containing transcripts from the Mass., Archives, and from the . . . Court Records, 1635-'73. . . .

Vol. V. Early Records of the town of Dedham, 1672-1706. Complete transcript of the Town Meeting and Selectmen's Records contained in Book V., of the General Records of the Town. . . .

DELAFIELD, MATURIN L. William Smith, Judge of the Supreme Court of the province of New York. Pages 260-282. 1881. (From Magazine of Amer. History, April, 1881.) HE—Z6

DE LANCEY, EDWARD FLOYD. Memoir of James William Beekman, prepared at the request of the Saint Nicholas Society of . . . New York. 17 pp. N. Y., 1877. HE—Z9

———— William Allen, chief justice of Pennsylvania, a Biographical sketch prepared for the Centennial Celebration of the adoption of the "Resolutions respecting Independency," held at . . . Philadelphia, July 1, 1876. 12 pp. Phil., 1877. (Reprinted from the "Pennsylvania Magazine of History.") HE—Z9

———— Editor. See: JONES, THOMAS. History of New York, 1879. HE—J72

[DENHAM, EDWARD.] *Why* is history read so little? an Address to parents, teachers, and members of . . . society. . . . 27 pp. New Bedford, 1876. HE—Z7

DE PEYSTER, FREDERIC. 1796-1882. Early political history of New York; an Address delivered before the New York Historical Society on its 60th anniversary . . . Nov. 22, 1864. 76 pp. N. Y., 1865. HE—Z3

———— Life and administration of Richard, Earl of Bellomont, Governor of the Provinces of New York, Massachusetts and New Hampshire, from 1697-1701. An Address delivered before the New York Historical Society, at the celebration of its 75th Anniversary, Nov. 18, 1879. 5 p.l., 60, XVII pp., 3 portraits, 1 fac-sim. New York, 1879. Q. HE—D44

———— Another copy in Pamphlet Volume: (The portrait of the Earl is lacking in this copy). HE—Z9

———— Moral and intellectual influence of Libraries upon social progress. . . . Address delivered before the N. Y. Historical Society . . . Nov. 21, 1865. 96 pp. N. Y., 1866. HE—Z3

———— [William the Third as a reformer.] Address delivered before the N. Y. Historical Society . . . Jan. 6, 1874. 36 pp., 1 port. N. Y., 1874. HE—Z3

DE PEYSTER, JOHN WATTS. Burgoyne's Campaign . . . 1777; justice to Schuyler. 4 pp. n.t.p. HE—Z3

———— Major-General George H. Thomas. Address before the New York Historical Society. 24 pp., n.t.p., n.d. HE—Z9

———— Major-General George H. Thomas; A Biographical sketch. Pages 545-576, with a steel-engraved portrait. N.t.p., n.d. HE—Z9

———— Major-General Philip Schuyler and the Burgoyne campaign in the Summer of 1777. 26 pp. N.t.p. Address before the N. Y. Hist. Soc. HE—Z3

DE PEYSTER, JOHN WATTS. Nashville, the decisive Battle of the Rebellion; Address delivered before the N. Y. Historical Society, Jan. 4, 1876. 14 pp. n.t.p. HE—Z3

────── Sir John Johnson, the first American-born baronet; Address delivered before the N. Y. Historical Society . . . Jan. 6th, 1880. HE—Z3

DE ST. BRIS, THOMAS. Discovery of the origin of the name of America. 140 pp., 1 map, New York, 1888. O. HE—D476

DIGBY, WILLIAM. British invasion from the north. The campaigns of Carleton and Burgoyne, 1776-1777, with the journal of William Digby and historical notes by J. P. Baxter. Albany, 1887. 412 pp. portraits, plate, square O. HE—D56
The original title of Digby's book reads: "Some account of the American war between Great Britain and her colonies." 1776.
Gift of Mrs. Martha J. Lamb.

DITMAS, CHARLES ANDREW, Compiler and Publisher. Brooklyn's Garden. Views of picturesque Flatbush, with an introduction. 24 coloured plates, mounted. Brooklyn, N. Y., 1908. Oblong O. HE—D615F
Gift of the Compiler.

────── Historic homesteads of Kings County. 120 pp., 20 hand-coloured photogravures. (Paged.) Brooklyn, [1909?]. HE—D615K
No. 311 of First edition, limited to 500 copies, signed and numbered.
Gift of the Compiler.

DUXBURY, Massachusetts. Copy of the old records of the town of Duxbury, Mass. From 1642-1770. Made in the year 1770. 348 pp. O. Plymouth, Mass., 1893. HE—D95

────── See: WINSOR, JUSTIN. History of Duxbury, with Genealogical registers. Boston, 1849. O. HE—W721

EARLY Connecticut marriages. See: CONNECTICUT.

EARLY RECORDS of the City and County of Albany and Colony of Rensselaerswyck. Translated from the original Dutch by J. PEARSON. Revised and edited by A. J. Van LAER. Vols. II-IV. Albany, 1916-19. 3 vols. Q. (University State N. Y., N. Y. State Lib'y History Bull. 9-11.) HE—A326

EAST-Hampton, Long Island, Suffolk County, New York. Records of the town, with other ancient documents of historic value. . . . From 1639-1849. Vols. 1-4. Sag-Harbor, 1887-89. 4 Vols. Q. HE—E7

ECCLESIASTICAL Records, State of N. Y. See: CORWIN, REV. EDWARD TANJORE, D.D., Compiler. Index. Vol. VII. Albany, 1916. HC—C832

ELLIS, George Edward. History of the battle of Bunker's (Breed's) Hill . . . June 17, 1775; from authentic sources. 69 pp., 1 map. Boston, 1875. HE—ZL

FAIRBANKS, George Rainsford. History and antiquities of the city of St. Augustine, Florida, founded A. D. 1565. N. Y., 1858. 200 pp. plates, portrait, maps. O. HE—F15

FAIRFIELD, Conn. 1779-1879. Centennial commemoration of the burning of Fairfield, Conn., by the British troops under Gov. Tryon, July 8, 1779. 104 pp. N. Y., 1879. HE—Z3

FERNOW, Berthold. Albany and its place in the history of the U. S. A memorial sketch written for the 200th anniversary of its birthday as a city. Albany, 1886. 98 pp. O. HE—F39
Gift of the Author.

———— Editor. See: NEW AMSTERDAM. The Records of New Amsterdam . . . 1653-1674. 7 Vols. New York, 1897. Folio. HE—N42

FERREE, Barr. Sentiment as a National asset. Oration delivered at the Fourth of July Celebration in Tenafly, N. J. . . . 13 pp. New York, 1908. HE—A512
Gift of the Author.

FISKE, John. Beginnings of New England, or, the Puritan theocracy of its relations to civil and religious liberty. 296 pp., map. Boston, 1889. O. HE—F54

FITCH, William Edward. The First founders in America, with facts to prove that Sir Walter Raleigh's lost Colony was not lost. Paper read at a Meeting of the N. Y. Society of the Order of the Founders and Patriots of America. . . . 40 pp., 1 map, folded. New York, 1913. O. HE—A512

FORD, William F. Industrial interests of Newark, N. J., containing an historical sketch of the City. . . . 271 pp., illustrated. 1 map. N. Y., 1874. HE—Z8

FORD, Worthington Chauncey, Compiler. List of the Benjamin Franklin Papers in the Library of Congress. 322 pp. Washington, D. C., 1905. Square Q. HE—F711

———— Papers of James Monroe listed in chronological order from the original MSS., in the Library of Congress. 6 fac-sim.; 114 pp. Washington, D. C., 1904. Q. (The fac-simile is the Purchase of Louisiana.) HE—F711m
(Monroe's Journals of Negotiations, 1803.)
Gift of the Library of Congress.

FREELAND, Mary de Witt. The records of Oxford, Mass. Including chapters of Nipmuck, Huguenot and English history from . . . 1630. . . . Square O. 429 pp. Albany, N. Y., 1894. (Munsell's Hist. Ser. No. 22.) HE—F87

FRENCH settlement of the Mississippi Valley. Pages 136-147. (Extract Amer. Hist. Mag. Vol. VII, No. 2.) O.   HE—N533
By Peter J. Hamilton.

GAFFAREL, PAUL. Histoire de la Floride française. Paris, 1875.
522 pp. map. O.   HE—G12

GARRETT, W. R. History of the South Carolina cession and the northern boundary of Tennessee. Nashville, 1884. 32 pp. O.
(Tennessee Historical Society. Papers.)   HE
Gift of the Tennessee Historical Society.

GERARD, JAMES WATSON. The old stadt Huys of New Amsterdam; a Paper read before the New York Historical Society, June 15, 1875.
59 pp. N. Y., 1875.   HE—Z3

———— The old Streets of New York under the Dutch; a Paper read before the New York Historical Society, June 2, 1874. 65 pp.
N. Y., 1874.   HE—Z3

GREEN, FRANK BERTANGUE. History of Rockland county [N. Y.].
N. Y., 1886. 444 pp. map. Q.   HE—G82
Gift of Mrs. Martha J. Lamb.

GRIFFITH, THOMAS W. Sketches of the early history of Maryland.
76 pp.; 1 pl. Baltimore, 1821. O.   HE—G854

HALE, JOHN P. Trans-Allegheny pioneers: historical sketches of the first white settlements west of the Alleghenies. 1748 and after.
Cincinnati [1886]. 330 pp. illustrated, portraits, fac-simile.
D.   HE—H13
Gift of Mrs. Martha J. Lamb.

HALL, REV. EDWIN, Compiler. Ancient historical records of Norwalk, Conn.; with a plan of the ancient settlement, and of the town in 1847, (and the Genealogical register of marriages, births and deaths.) 320 pp., 1 map. Norwalk, Conn., 1847. D.   HE—N831H
Contains Autograph of the compiler.

HAMILTON, FRANK HASTINGS, M.D. Eulogy on the life and character of Theodric Romeyn Beck, M.D., delivered before the Medical Society of the State of New York. 90 pp., 1 port. Albany,
1856.   HE—Z1

HAMILTON, PETER J. The French settlement of the Mississippi Valley. (Pages 136-147, Amer. Hist. Mag., Vol. VII, No. 2.)
O.   HE—N533

HARTLEY, REV. ISAAC S. Historical discourse delivered on the occasion of the semi-centennial year of the Reformed Church, Utica,
N. Y., Jan., 1880. 68 pp., 2 pl. Utica, 1880.   HE—Z1

HARVEY, CORNELIUS BURNHAM, Editor. Genealogical history of Hudson and Bergen counties, New Jersey. 617 pp., 1 map. New
York, 1900. Q.   HE—H26

HASTINGS, Hugh, Compiler and Editor. Military minutes of the Council of Appointment of the state of New York, 1783-1821. 4 Vols. Albany, N. Y., 1901-02. O. HE—H27

HAZARD, Willis P. See: WATSON, J. F. Annals of Philadelphia and Pennsylvania, in the olden time. . . . Illustrated. 3 Vols. Phila., 1891. O. HE—WATS33

HENRY, William Wirt. Oration on the 100th anniversary of the introduction of the "Resolutions respecting Independency," delivered on June 7, 1876 at Philadelphia. 31 pp. Philadelphia, 1876.
HE—Z9

HISTORICAL SOCIETY, Newburgh Bay and the Highlands. Historical Papers. Newburgh, N. Y., 1894-1901. 2 Nos. O.
Fevre. HE—N533
No. viii for 1901: M. E. Church, Newburgh, N. Y., Record of Births and Marriages, 1789-1835.

———— Same, in another Pamphlet Volume. HE—H62V

HOFFMAN, Charles Fenne. The Pioneers of New York. Anniversary discourse before St. Nicholas Society of Manhattan, Dec. 6, 1847. 55 pp. O. N. Y., 1848. HE—A512
(Reprint, January, 1915.)
No. 1, of Volume "Americana."

HOLDEN, James Austin, State Historian. The Centenary of the Battle of Plattsburg, 1814,—September 11, 1914, at Plattsburg, N. Y., Sept. 6-11, 1914. 98 pp., 1 fac-sim. Albany, N. Y., 1914. O. (University State, N. Y.) HE—H726
Fully illustrated; plates paged.
Gift of the Author.

HORSFORD, Eben Norton. Defences of Norumbega and a review of the reconnaissances of T. W. Higginson, Henry W. Haynes . . . and others. . . . 84 pp., ill., pl., maps. Square folio. Boston, 1891. HE—H782

———— Discovery of America by Northmen; Address at the unveiling of the statue of Leif Eriksen . . . Oct. 29, 1887. 113 pp., ill., pl., maps. Square folio. Boston, 1888. HE—H78

———— Discovery of the ancient city of Norumbega; a communication to the . . . American geographical society . . . Nov. 21, 1889. 55 pp., pl., maps. Square folio. Boston, 1890. HE—H781

HOWARD, George E[lliotte]. Introduction to the local Constitutional History of the United States. Balt., 1889. (In Johns Hopkins University Studies in Historical and Political Science. Extra volumes, No. 4.) HE—H83
Vol. i. Development of the township, hundred, and shire.

HOWE, Henry. The sad, heart-touching, but ennobling history of Captain Nathan Hale, the hero-martyr of the American Revolution. 21 pp., ill. New Haven, Conn., 1881. HE—Z2

HUIDEKOPER, FREDERIC LOUIS. Sieges of Louisbourg in 1745 and 1758. Address . . . before Soc. Colonial Wars, D. C., February 12th, 1914. 18 pp.; plans and maps, folded, 1 view, folded. Washington, D. C., 1914. (Hist. Papers Soc. Col. Wars, D. C., No. 8. "Some important military operations.")   HE—A512

—— Struggle (The) between the French and English for the Valley of the Ohio, 1749-1758. Address delivered before the Soc. Col. Wars, D. C. . . . March 5th, 1914. 21; 3-18; 21-43 pp.; 4 plans, 2 maps, 1 view, folded. Washington, D. C., 1914. O. (Hist. papers Soc. Col. Wars, D. C., No. 8. "Some important military operations.")   HE—A512
Volume "Americana."

HUNTINGTON, REV. WILLIAM REED, D.D. The Puritan strain. . . . A sermon preached in Grace Church before the New England Society, in the City of New York, on Sunday, March 10, 1901. 19 pp. N. Y., 1901.   HE—W885
In: "Ancient Woodbury."
Gift of the New England Society.

HURD, D. HAMILTON, Compiler. History of Fairfield county, Conn., with illustrations and biographical sketches of its prominent men and pioneers. Philadelphia, 1881. 878 pp. illustrated, portraits. Q.   HE—H93

IPSWICH, Mass. The ancient records of the town of Ipswich, Massachusetts. Edited by G. A. Schofield. Vol. 1, 1899. O.   HE—I6
Vol. 1. From 1634-1650.

JAY, The HON JOHN. 1817-94. The American foreign service. Pages 419-433. 1877. (From the International Review, May, 1877.)   HE—Z6

—— Battle of Harlem Plains; Oration before the New York Historical Society, Sept. 16, 1876. (In New York Historical Society. Commemoration of the battle of Harlem Plains. 1876. Pages 5-38.)   HE—Z5

—— Same.

—— Columbia College; her honourable record in the past, with a glance at her opportunities in the future, a Centennial discourse delivered before the Association of the Alumni, Dec. 21st, 1876. 48 pp. N. Y., 1876.   HE—Z1

JOHNS HOPKINS University Studies in History and Political Science; Extra volumes. Baltimore, 1889.—Edited by H. B. Adams. No. 4: HOWARD, G. E. Introduction to the local Constitutional History of the United States.   HE—H83

JOHNSON, ELLEN TERRY. The House of Hope of the first Connecticut settlers. Paper read before the Connecticut Society of Holland Dames . . . November 19, 1895. . . . 46 pp. Hartford, Conn., 1896.   HE—A512
Gift of Mrs. James M. Lawton.

JONES, Henry R. Sketches of the people and places of New Hartford, Connecticut, in the past and present. 33 pp. Hartford, Conn., 1883. HE—A512

JONES, Thomas. History of New York during the Revolutionary War, and of the leading Events in the other Colonies at that period. Edited by Edward Floyd de Lancey, with notes, contemporary documents, maps, and portraits. In 2 Vols. New York, 1879. Q. (N. Y. Hist. Soc'y, John D. Jones Fund Series of Histories and Memoirs.) HE—J72

KINGSBURY, J. D. Memorial History of Bradford, Massachusetts, from the earliest period to the close of 1882. Including Addresses . . . at the 200th Anniversary of the First Church of Bradford, Dec. 27, 1882. xii, 192 pp. Haverhill, Mass., 1883. O. HE—B73K

LAMB, Mrs. Martha Joan Reade Nash. History of the City of New York; its origin, rise and progress. 2 Vols. port., pl., maps. New York, 1877-80. Q. HE—L16
Vol. I. Period prior to the Revolution, closing in 1774.
Vol. II. Embracing the Century of National Independence, closing in 1876.

———— Souvenir of the centennial anniversary of Washington's inauguration, April 30, 1789, with the program of ceremonies. N. Y., 1889. 86 pp. illustrated, portraits. O. HE—L161
From the *Magazine of American History,* Dec., 1888, Feb. and March, 1889.
Gift of the Author.

LATROBE, John Hazlehurst, Boneval. . . . A lost chapter in the history of the steamboat. 44 pp. O. Baltimore, 1871. HE—Z2

LeFEVRE, Ralph. History of New Paltz, New York, and its old families. (From 1678-1820.) Including the Huguenot pioneers and others who settled in New Paltz previous to the Revolution. xiv, 593 pp., 1 port., ill. Q. Albany, N. Y., 1903. HE—L52

———— [History of New Paltz, New York, and its old families.] Appendix giving additional information concerning the Revolutionary Period: likewise Wills of a number of the Patentees and their sons. . . . Notice of those who moved from New Paltz in the early days and . . . other matter. vi, 208 pp. Illustrations paged. New Paltz, N. Y., [1918?]. Q. HE—L52A
Gift of the Author.

LESCARBOT, Marc. Histoire de la Nouvelle,France, contenant les navigations, découvertes et habitations faites par les Français ès Indes occidentales et Nouvelle-France; suivi des muses de la Nouvelle-France. Nouvelle édition, publiée par Edwin Tross. Paris, 1866. 3 vols. maps. O. HE—L56

LESTER, Henry M. New Rochelle's 221st Anniversary. (In: Westchester Co.; Magazine, Vol. iii, No. 4, pp. 13-15.) O. HE—N533

LETTERS and papers relating . . . to the history of Pennsylvania, 1855. By Thomas Balch.   HE—B18P

LINCOLN, CHARLES HENRY, Compiler. Naval records of the American Revolution, 1775-1788. Prepared from the originals in the Library of Congress. 54 pp. Washington, 1906. Q.   HE—L737
Gift of the Library of Congress.

LOUISIANA: Purchase of Louisiana. Monroe's Journals of Negotiations, 1803. [Fac-simile on 6 pp. of List of] "Papers of James Monroe . . . in Chronological order from . . . original MSS., in the Lib'y of Congress." Washington, D. C., 1904. Q.   HE—F711M
Compiled by W. C. Ford.

LOWER WALL STREET Business Men's Association. New York's Commercial Tercentenary. . . . A few Historical events as given by historians compared with their actual occurrence. By A. Wakeman, Secretary. 40 pp. Square Q. New York, 1914. (2 mounted illustrations paged in.)   HE—N483
Gift of the Association.

———— Unveiling of the Commemorative Tablet on the site of the Merchants Coffee House (The Birthplace of our Union), Southeast corner of Wall and Water Streets, New York City. 4 leaves, illustrated. Square Q. New York, 1914.   HE—N485

LUCAS, FREDERICK W. Appendiculæ historicæ: or, Shreds of history hung on a horn. . . . 216 pp., 1 pl., maps. London, 1891. Q. Contains an account of the discovery, settlement and Anglo-French Wars of America.   HE—L96

McCRADY, EDWARD. The history of South Carolina under the proprietary government, 1670-1719. IX, 762 pp., 1 map. New York, 1897. O.   HE—M13

MARSH, LUTHER RAWSON. Oration before the Society of the army of the Potomac, at Burlington, Vermont, June 16, 1880. 29 pp. n.t.p.   HE—Z1

MARSHALL, REV. JAMES. The Lebanon Club; an Address before the Lebanon Club for workingmen. . . . Dec. 13, 1878. 31 pp., N. Y., 1879.   HE—Z7

MARYLAND: Association of the Freemen of Maryland, by Col. C. Chaille-Long. (In: Republic Magazine. Vol. 1, No. 1. New York, 1890. Q. Pages 42-48.)   HE—Cha35

MARYLAND Historical Society. Proceedings in connection with the celebration of the 150th anniversary of the settlement of Baltimore. 123 pp., ill. Baltimore, 1880.   HE—Z4

MASSACHUSETTS—JUDICIARY COMMITTEE. Report on the state seal. [Boston, 1885.] 18 pp. O. (House documents, 1885. No. 345.)   HE—Q4
Presented by the secretary of the Commonwealth.

MASSACHUSETTS of to-day. A memorial of the state, historical, issued for the World's Columbian Exposition at Chicago. Edited by T. C. Quinn. Illustrated, 619 pp., folio. Boston, 1892.   HE—Q4
Gift of Mr. Hosea Starr Ballou.

MATHER, FREDERIC GREGORY. The Refugees of 1776 from Long Island to Connecticut. Albany, N. Y., 1913. 1204 pp., 1 port., fully illustrated throughout. Square O.   HE—M427
Part I.   Historical: I. Division; Short story of the Revolutionary War. II. Division; Military and Civil service. III. Division; Effects of the Battle of Long Island—The Refugees. IV. Division; Local conduct of the War.
Part II.   Biographical. I. Division; Captains and Masters of Ships. II. Division; Refugees from Long Island to Connecticut. III. Division; Refugees from Canada and Nova Scotia. IV. Division; Refugees from New York City.
Part III. Documentary.
Gift of Miss Cornelia Horsford, with an etched plate of Sylvester Manor, inserted to face page 450.

MEADS, ORLANDO. Annual address before the Albany Institute. May 25th, 1871. . . . 36 pp. Albany, 1871.   HE—Z1

MELLICK, ANDREW D., JR. Story of an old farm [Bedminster, Somerset Co., N. J.] or, Life in New Jersey in the 18th century; with a genealogical appendix. 743 pp. pl. Q. Somerville, N. J., 1889. (Bibliography, pp. 714-720.)   HE—M48

MEMORIAL of Fitz-Greene Halleck; a description of the dedication of the monument erected to his memory at Guilford, Conn., and of the proceedings connected with the unveiling of the poet's statue in the Central Park, N. Y. 72 pp., 2 pl. N. Y., 1877.   HE—Z9

MERCHANTS (The) Coffee House, N. Y. City. See: LOWER WALL STREET Business Men's Association.

METHODIST Episcopal Church. Record of Baptisms and Marriages, copied from and compared with the original entries in Stewards' Book, Newburgh, N. Y., circuit . . . 1789-1835, by A. Leslie and Mrs. W. Vanamee. (Hist. Soc., Newburgh Bay and The Highlands, Hist. Papers No. 8, 1901.) O. Pages 7-35.   HE—N533

MONROE, JAMES, 4th President, U. S. A. Papers . . . listed in chronological order from the original MSS.; in the Library of Congress. (Also Purchase of Louisiana, Fac-simile from his Journals of Negotiation, 1803.) 6 fac-sim., 114 pp. Washington, D. C., 1904. Q. Compiled by W. C. Ford.   HE—F711M
Gift of the Library of Congress.

MORGAN, CHRISTOPHER. New York (state) State Dept. Documentary history of the State. . . . 1849-51.   HE—N48

MORRISON, HUGH ALEXANDER. American almanacs, 1639-1800: A preliminary check list. 160 pp. Washington, D. C., 1907. Square Q.   HE—M879
Gift of the Library of Congress.

MULFORD, WILLIAM REMSEN. Genealogy of the family of Mulford. 12 pp. O. Boston, 1880. (Reprint New England Historical and Genealogical Register.)   HE—Z2

MURPHY, HENRY CRUDE. Voyage of Verrazzano; a chapter in the early history of maritime discovery in America. 198 pp., ill., 4 maps. N. Y., 1875. O.   HE—Z5

NAVAL records of the American Revolution, 1775-1788. Prepared from the originals in the Library of Congress, by C. H. Lincoln. 549 pp. Washington, 1906. Q.   HE—L737
Gift of the Library of Congress.

NEILL, EDWARD DUFFIELD. History of the Virginia company of London, with letters to and from the first colony, never before printed. Albany, 1869. 432 pp. portrait, square Q.   HE—N31

NEW AMSTERDAM. Records of New Amsterdam from 1653-1674, Domini. Edited by B. Fernow. Vols. 1-7. New York, 1897. 7 vols. folio. Index in Vol. 7.   HE—N42

NEW HAVEN, Conn. Proceedings in commemoration of the settlement of the town of New Haven. 68 pp. O. New Haven, 1888.

NEW ROCHELLE Press Almanac. Vols. 1-6. New Rochelle, 1879-'84. D.   HE—NR87S

NEW YORK (CITY)—COMMON COUNCIL. Manual of corporation. 1853-70. 17 vols., illustrated, portraits, maps, fac-similes. D., cloth.   HE—N481
Note: These Volumes are best known as "Valentine's Manuals of the City of New York."
Volumes prior to 1853 would be acceptable for our Collection and any other volumes, as they are no longer obtainable.

NEW YORK: Colony and State. Civil list and Constitutional History of the Colony and State of New York, by E. A. Werner. 663 pp., 16 pl. Albany, 1886. O.   HE—W5
Gift of Mrs. James M. Lawton.

NEW YORK: Executive Council of the Province. Minutes. Administration of Francis Lovelace. 1668-1673. Edited by Victor H. Paltsits, State Historian. Vols. I-II. Albany, 1910. 2 vols. Q.   HE—N46
Vol. I. Minutes. Collateral & Illustrative Documents, I.-XIX.
Vol. II. Collateral & Illustrative Documents, XX.-XCVIII.
   Fac-similes, plan, port., 2 maps, folded in pockets.
   Gift of the State Historian.

NEW YORK Genealogical & Biographical Society. By-laws. 16 pp. N. Y., 1882.   HE—Z7

NEW YORK Historical Society. Charter & By-laws, revised Jan., 1858, with the amendments and a list of resident members. 39 pp. N. Y., 1870.   HE—Z1

———— Commemoration of the Battle of Harlem Plains on its 100th Anniversary. 98 pp. N. Y., 1876.   HE—Z5

———— Same. 52 pp. N. Y., 1876.   HE—Z3

———— John D. Jones Fund Series of Histories & Memoirs. See: JONES, THOMAS. History of New York, 1879.

———— Semi-centennial celebration; 50th Anniversary of the Founding of the New York Historical Society. . . . Nov. 20th, 1854. 96 pp. N. Y., 1854.   HE—Z3

NEW YORK: Need of a History of New York. 55 pp., 1 port. N. Y., 1915. O. (United Historical & Patriotic Soc'y & Assoc., of N. Y.)   HE—H726
Bound with: HOLDEN, J. A. Centenary. . . . Battle of Platts-burg. . . .
Gift of the Author.

NEW YORK (State) Commissioners of the correct Arms of the State of New York. Report transmitted to the Senate, April 13, 1881. 31 pp., 4 pl. Albany, 1881.   HE—Z7

———— (State). Military Minutes of the Council of Appointment. 1783-1821. 4 vols. O. Edited by Hugh Hastings.   HE—N482.2

———— (State)—State Dept. Documentary history of the state, ar-ranged under the direction of Christopher Morgan by E. B. O'Cal-laghan. Albany, 1849-51. 3 vols. illustrated, portraits, maps. O. *cloth.*   HE—N48

———— (State)—Legislature. Documents relative to the colonial his-tory of the state, procured in Holland, England and France by John Romeyn Brodhead. Edited by E. B. O'Callaghan. Albany, 1856-61. 11 vols. maps. Square Q. *Cloth.*   HE—N482

NEW YORK (State)—Regiment. (VIIth.) The Veteran's room, Seventh Regiment, National Guard, State of New York, Armory, N. Y., 1881. 24 pp.   HE—Z7

NEWBERRY, JOHN STRONG. Geological history of New York Island and Harbor. 20 pp., illustrated. n.t.p.   HE—Z2

NORWOOD, ANDREW SICKLES, deponent. Deposition relating to various historical facts "in New York City during the period of our Revolutionary history." Sworn to before F. E. Westbrook, Comm'r of Deeds, 20th of May, 1854. 4 leaves. Typewritten MS. New York, 1854.   HE—Pamphlet

NOTICE sur la vie et les œuvres de William Beach Lawrence. 74 pp. Gand, 1876.   HE—Z1

O'CALLAGHAN, Edmund Burke. Register of New Netherlands, 1626-1674. Albany, 1865. 198 pp. Q.   HE—Oc1
Gift of Edward F. De Lancey.

—— Editor. New York (State) State Department. Documentary history of the State of New York. 1849-1851.   HE—N48

—— Editor. New York Legislature. Documents relative to the Colonial history of New York. 1856-1861.   HE—N482

OHIO SOCIETY of New York. Eighteenth annual banquet given for the Hon. William Howard Taft, Secretary of War, at the Waldorf-Astoria. . . . March 5th, 1904. . . . Full page illustrations of the American Battles with portraits of their Commanding Officers. A brochure designed and executed by Thomas A. Sindelar. 4 leaves, 16 plates, 4 portraits, 2 groups of portraits. Square Q.   HE—Pamphlet
Gift of the Society.

OSGOOD, Rev. Samuel. Thomas Crawford and Art in America; Address before the New York Historical Society. . . . April 6, 1875. 40 pp. N. Y., 1875.   HE—Z2

PALTSITS, Victor Hugo, State Historian. The Function of State Historian of New York. Read before The N. Y. State Hist. Assoc. . . . at its Annual Meeting. . . . 1908. 14 pp. O. Albany, N. Y., 1909. In Vol. "Americana."   HE—A512
Gift of the Author.

—— Editor. See: New York: Executive Council of the Province. . . . Minutes. Administration of Francis Lovelace, 1668-1673. Albany, 1910. 2 vols. Q.   HE—N48
Vol. i. Minutes. Collateral & Illustrative Documents, I-XIX.
Vol. ii. Minutes. Collateral & Illustrative Documents, XX-XCVIII.
Gift of the Author.

PAMPHLET Volumes, containing a collection of many rare and interesting American pamphlets.   HE—Z1—HE—Z9
Gift of Mrs. Martha J. Lamb.

PARIS (P.), Editor. See: Monumens inedits de l'histoire de France. Paris, 1830. D.

PARIS (The) Memorial. Re-interment of Col. Isaac Paris. 32 pp. n.p., 1880.   HE—Z7

PARKHURST, Rev. Charles Henry. Madison Square Presbyterian Church to its first pastor the Rev. William Adams, a tribute. A sermon by the pastor, Nov. 7th, 1880. 23 pp. N. Y., 1880.   HE—Z1

—— Sermon preached on Sabbath morning following the death of President James A. Garfield (Sept. 25, 1881), at the Madison Square Presbyterian Church. . . . 16 pp. N. Y., 1881.   HE—Z7

PARKMAN, Francis. Conspiracy of Pontiac and the Indian war after the conquest of Canada. Tenth edition, enlarged. Boston, 1882. 2 vols. maps. D.   HE—P23

——— Count Frontenac and New France under Louis XIV. Tenth edition. Boston, 1882. 463 pp. maps. D. (France and England in North America, Vol. v.)   HE—P231

——— Jesuits in North America in the 17th century. Sixteenth edition. Boston, 1882. 463 pp. maps. D. (France and England in North America, Vol. II.)   HE—P232

——— La Salle and the discovery of the great west. Twelfth edition, enlarged. Boston, 1882. 483 pp. maps. D. (France and England in North America, Vol. III.)   HE—P233

——— Old régime in Canada. Eleventh edition. Boston, 1882. 448 pp. map. D. (France and England in North America, Vol. IV.)   HE—P234

——— Oregon trail, sketches of prairie and Rocky Mountain life. Eighth edition. Boston, 1882. 381 pp. D.   HE—P235

——— Pioneers of France in the new world. Nineteenth edition. Boston, 1882. 427 pp. portrait, maps. D. (France and England in North America, Vol. I.)   HE—P236

PARMENTER, C. O. History of Pelham, Massachusetts, from 1738-1898, including the early history of Prescott. . . . 531 pp., 8 port., 35 pl., 1 fac-sim. Amherst, Mass., 1898. O.   HE—P21

PEARSON, Jonathan, Translator. See: ALBANY, New York. Early records of the City and county of Albany and colony of Rensselaerswyck. Translated from the original Dutch. Revised and edited by A. J. F. Van Laer. Vols. II-IV. Albany, 1916-1919. 3 vols. Q. (Univ. State N. Y. N. Y. State Lib'y Hist. Bull. Nos. 9-11.)   HE—A326

PENNSYLVANIA; Historical items. Letters and papers relating . . . to the . . . history of Pennsylvania, 1855. By Thomas Balch.   HE—B18P

PEPPERELLBOUROUGH, Massachusetts. First Book of Records of the Pepperellbourough, now the City of Saco. Printed by vote of the City Council, March 18, 1895. 299 pp. Portland, Me., 1896. O.   HE—Sa1

PERKINS, Mary E. Old houses of the antient town of Norwich, Connecticut, 1660-1800. Norwich, Conn., 1895. XVIII, 62 pp., 23 port., 8 group port., 3 pl., 3 maps, 2 plans. Square O.   HE—P41
Gift of the Author.

PHILADELPHIA: Short history of the City from its foundation to the present time. [By Sarah Chauncey Woolsey.] Boston, 1887. D.   HE—W88

PLYMOUTH, MASSACHUSETTS. Records of the town of Plymouth. Plymouth, 1889. Vol. I. 1636-1705. O. HE—P74

PORTER, REV. NOAH. 1781-1866. Half century discourse, on occasion of the 50th anniversary of his ordination as pastor of the First Church in Farmington, Conn., delivered Nov. 12th, 1856. 54 pp. Farmington, 1857.

POTTER, ELISHA REYNOLDS, JR. Early history of Narragansett; with an appendix of original documents, many of which are now for the first time published. XIX, 423 pp. Providence, 1835. 2nd edition. O. (R. I. Hist. Soc'y. Collections. Vol. III.) HE—P85N

——— A second copy. HK—P85N
Memorial Gifts of William H. Potter.

——— Memoir concerning the French settlements and French settlers in the colony of Rhode Island. Providence, 1879. 138 pp. 2 maps. O. (Rhode Island Historical Tracts. No. 5.) HE—P85F
Gift of William H. Potter.

PUMPELLY, JOSIAH COLLINS. Historical sketches of the Hampton Settlements on Long Island. pp. 217-236, 1 port., 5 pl. n.p., 1911. O. (In: "Americana," March, 1911.) HE—A512
Gift of the Author.

——— Our French Allies in the Revolution and other addresses. Morristown, [pref. 1889]. 64 pp. D. HE—Pu986
Gift of the Author.

QUINN, THOMAS C., Editor. See: MASSACHUSETTS of to-day, A memorial of the State, historical and biographical. Boston, 1892. Folio. HE—Qu4

REFORMED Protestant Dutch church of the city of N. Y. Celebration of the quarter-millennial anniversary, Nov. 21, 1878. [N. Y., 1878?] 104 pp. HE—Z8
In a volume of pamphlets.

——— Same. A separate volume in Class C. (Church History.)

RENSSELAERSWYCK, New York. See: ALBANY, New York.

REPUBLIC Magazine. Vol. I, No. 1. N. Y., 1890. Q. See: CHAILLE-LONG, COL. CHARLES. The Association of the Freemen of Maryland. pp. 42-48. Cha335

RHODE ISLAND Historical Tracts. No. 5. Memoir concerning the French . . . settlers in . . . Rhode Island. By Elisha Reynolds Potter. Providence, 1879. Square O. HE—P85
Gift of William H. Potter.

RICE, FRANKLIN P., Editor. Worcester town records, from 1753-1783. 472 pp. Worcester, Mass., 1882. O. (Worcester Society of Antiquity. Collections, Vol. IV.) HE—W89

RIKER, JAMES. Annals of Newtown, in Queens County, New York: containing its history from its first settlement . . . also, a particular account of numerous Long Island families now spread over this and various other States. New York, 1852. 437 pp., 2 maps. O.   HE—R44N

———— "Evacuation Day," 1783 . . . with recollections of Captain John Van Arsdale . . . by whose efforts on that day . . . the American Flag successfully raised on the Battery (New York City). 56 pp. N. Y., 1883. O.   HE—A512 Gift.

———— Harlem (city of N. Y.): its origin and early annals, prefaced by home scenes in the fatherlands; or, Notices of its founders before emigration; also sketches of numerous families, and the recovered history of the land-titles. N. Y., 1881. 636 pp. illustrated, maps. O.   HE—R44

ROGERS, REV. EBENEZER PLATT. 1817-81. The glory of New York; a discourse delivered in the South Reformed Church on Thanksgiving Day, Nov. 26th, 1874. 18 pp. N. Y., 1874.   HE—Z1

ROSENGARTEN, JOSEPH GEORGE. The German soldier in the Wars of United States. 2nd edition, enlarged. 298 pp. Philadelphia, 1890 (cop. 1886).   HE—R72 Gift of Mrs. Martha J. Lamb.

———— Reynolds Memorial address. March 8th, 1880. 34 pp. O. Philadelphia, 1880.   HE—A512

RYAN, DANIEL J. History of Ohio, with biographical sketches of her governors, and the ordinance of 1787. Columbus, 1888. 210 pp. portrait. O.   HE—R95 Gift of Mrs. Martha J. Lamb.

SALEM (THE) BOOK: Records of the past and glimpses of the present. Prepared for publication by a group of Salem's sons and daughters. 250, VIII pp., 1 port., 5 pl. Salem, N. Y., 1896. O.   HE—Sa3 Gift of Mrs. Byron H. Painter.

SALTER, EDWIN. A history of Monmouth and Ocean counties, . . . a genealogical record of earliest settlers . . . and their descendants. XIII, 442, LXXX pp., 2 port. Bayonne, N. J., 1890. O.   HE—S277

SCHENCK, MRS. ELIZABETH HUBBELL. History of Fairfield, Fairfield Co., Conn., from 1639-1818. N. Y., 1889. Vol. I, map. O. Genealogies of Fairfield, pp. 347-423.   HE—Sch2

SCHOFIELD, GEORGE A., Editor. See: IPSWICH, Mass. The Ancient Records. . . . Vol. I. 1899. O.   HE—I6

SENTER, ORAMEL S. Civic and scenic New England. Newport in 1877. pp. 1-15. IL. 1877. (From Potter's American monthly. 1877. Vol. IX.)   HE—Z6

SEYMOUR, HORATIO. Address at Wells Female College, Aurora, N. Y., June 16, 1880. 15 pp. Utica, N. Y., 1880. HE—Z4

———— Address before the New York State Agricultural Society, at the annual meeting . . . Jan. 21, 1880. . . . 37 pp., 1 map. Albany, 1880. HE—Z4

———— History and topography of New York; a lecture at Cornell University, June 30th, 1870. 32 pp. Utica, 1870. HE—Z2

———— Influence of New York on American jurisprudence. pp. 217-230. 1879. (From Magazine of American History. 1879. Vol. III, No. 4.) HE—Z6

SHERMAN, REV. HENRY BEERS. These three. A sermon preached at Woodbury, Conn., on occasion of its Bi-centennial celebration, July 5, 1859. 18 pp. O. (In: Second centennial . . . Woodbury . . . pp. 107-125.) HE—W885
Volume "Ancient Woodbury."

SMITH, SAMUEL. The history of the Colony of Nova-Caesaria, or New Jersey: an account of its first settlement, . . . and other events of the year 1721. With . . . a view of its present state. XIV, 613 pp., 4 maps folded. O. Burlington, N. J., 1765. HE—S759
Reprint, Trenton, N. J., 1890.

SMITH, WILSON CARY. The Roger Morris house, Washington's headquarters on Harlem Heights. pp. 89-104, illus., 1 pl. 1881. (From Magazine of American History, Feb., 1881.) HE—Z6

STEVENS, JOHN AUSTIN. The Burgoyne campaign, an Address delivered on the Battle-field, on the 100th celebration of the battle of Bemis Heights, Sept. 19, 1877. 43 pp. N. Y., 1877. HE—Z2

———— New York in the Continental Congress. pp. 151-159. (From the Galaxy, 1876, Vol. II.) HE—Z2

———— Progress of New York in a Century, 1776-1876, an Address delivered before the New York Historical Society, Dec. 7, 1875. 66 pp. N. Y., 1876. HE—Z2

STEVENS, THE REV. WILLIAM BACON, M.D., D.D. History of Georgia from its first discovery by Europeans to the adoption of the present Constitution in MDCCXCVIII. In 2 vols. New York, 1847, Vol. I; Philadelphia, 1859, Vol. II. O. HE—S843

STONE, WILLIAM LEETE. 1792-1844. George Clinton. pp. 329-354. 1879. (From Magazine of American History, 1879.) Vol. III, No. 6. HE—Z6

———— Memoir of the Centennial Celebration of Burgoyne's Surrender, held at Schuylerville, N. Y., under the auspices of the Saratoga Monument Association, on the 17th of Oct. 1877. 189 pp., 1 pl. Albany, 1878. HE—Z2

THOMPSON, Gilbert. Historical military powder-horns. 21; 16 pp., 3 plans, 6 pl., 2 maps. O. [Washington], 1901.   HE—A512

TICONDEROGA Historical Society. Memorial tablet at Ticonderoga. A corporation's gift to history. 30 pp., 1 pl. Cambridge, 1911. O. Reprinted by the Ticonderoga Pulp & Paper Co.   HE—H726
Gift of the Society.

TOWNSHEND, Charles Hervey. The British invasion of New Haven, Conn. . . . with some account of their landing and burning the towns of Fairfield and Norwalk, July, 1779. 112 pp., 5 pl. New Haven, 1879.   HE—Z1

TREDWELL, Daniel M. Personal reminiscences of men and things on Long Island. One Volume in two parts, paged consecutively. Brooklyn, N. Y., 1912, Part 1; 1917, Part 2. Q.   HE—T78
Part 1: 3 p.l., 182 pp., 1 map, 1 port.
Part 2: 4 p.l., 197-250 pp., 1 fac-sim., 1 map, 4 pl., 1 port.
Gift of Charles Andrew Ditmas, with autograph letter.
No. 176 of 500 copies.

UNITED Historical & Patriotic Societies of New York. The need of a history of New York. 55 pp., 1 port. New York, 1915. O. Bound with: HOLDEN, J. A. Centenary . . . Battle of Plattsburg. . . .   HE—H726
Gift of Author.

UNITED STATES—Congress. Congressional directory . . . 2nd ed. corrected to Jan. 21, 1881. 167 pp., 4 pl. Washington, 1881. HE—Z5

UNITED STATES—State Dept. Letter from the Secretary transmitting a report of Theodore F. Dwight on the papers of Benjamin Franklin offered for sale by Henry Stevens, & recommending their purchase by Congress. 99 pp. Washington, 1882. No title-page.   HE—Z7

UNIVERSITY State of New York. New York State Library History Bulletin. Nos. 9-11. Albany, N. Y., 1916-1919. 3 vols. Q. Vols. ii, iv: Early Records of Albany & Rensselaerswyck. Revised & edited by A. J. F. van Laer. Translated from the original Dutch by J. Pearson.   HE—A326

UTICA (N. Y.). Manufacturing and Mercantile Association. Constitution and a commercial history of Utica. 44 pp. 1880. n.t.p.   HE—Z4

VALENTINE, David Thomas. History of the city of New York. N. Y. 1853. 404 pp. plates, maps. O.   HE—V23

——— Editor. See: NEW YORK City Common Council. Manual of Corporation. 1853-1870. 17 vols.

VAN LAER, A. J. F., Editor. Early records of the city and county of Albany and colony of Rensselaerswyck. Translated from the original Dutch by J. Pearson. Vols. ii-iv. Albany, 1916-1919. 3 vols. Q. (University State of N. Y., N. Y. State Library Hist. Bull. Nos. 9-11.)   HE—A362
Vol. ii: Deeds 3 & 4, 1678-1704. 438 pp. Albany, 1916. Q.
Vol. iii: Notarial Papers, 1 & 2. 1660-1696. 644 pp. Albany, 1918. Q.
Vol. iv: Mortgages 1, 1658-1660, & Wills 1-2, 1681-1765. 220 pp. Albany, 1919. Q.
Gift of the University.

VERMILYE, Rev. Ashbel Green, D.D. Patriot clergy and the New York City Chaplains in the War of the Revolution. An address before the N. Y. Historical Society. 28 pp. O. New York, 1895.   HE—A512

VIRGINIA: Colonial History. See: Colonial Virginia Register.

VOSSION, Louis. Constitution (La) Américaine et ses amendements texte, notice historique et commentaire. Avec une préface par J. Chailley. . . . v-xxiv, 74 pp., 3 port. Paris, 1889. O. (Facsim. paged in.)   HE—V97

WAGER, Charles, admiral. List of the Vernon-Wager MSS.; in the Library of Congress. With fac-similes. Compiled by W. C. Ford. 148 pp. Washington, D. C., 1904. Q.   HE—F711
Gift of the Library of Congress.

WAKEMAN, Abram. New York's Commercial Tercentenary. . . . A few Historical events as given by historians compared with their actual occurrence. 40 pp. Square Q. New York, 1914.   HE—N485
Gift of Lower Wall Street Business Men's Assoc.

WALLACE, John William. Discourse pronounced on the inauguration of the new Hall, March 11, 1872, of the Historical society of Pennsylvania. . . . 66 pp. O. Philadelphia, 1872.   HE—Z4

WASHINGTON, George. 1732-1777. Journal from the original MS. in the Library of the Department of State at Washington, May to August, 1781. pp. 108-125. From Magazine of American History, February, 1881.   HE—Z6

—— Letters, 1754-1777. pp. 125-240. From Magazine of American History, February, 1881.   HE—Z6

WASHINGTON'S Headquarters, New York. Sketch of the history of the Morris Mansion (or Jumel Mansion) used by Washington as his Headquarters in 1776. By R. P. Bolton. 2 leaves, 1 pl., 1 port., 3-40 pp. New York, 1903. S.   HE—A512
Gift of Mrs. J. M. Lawton.

WATERMAN, Elijah. A century sermon, preached before the First Church in Windham, December 10, A.D. 1800, in commemoration of its institution, December 10, A.D. 1700. Containing historical facts. . . . 43 pp. O. Windham, 1801.   HE—W885
Volume "Ancient Woodbury."

WATSON, John Fanning. Annals of Philadelphia, & Pennsylvania, in the olden time; being a collection of memoirs, anecdotes, and incidents of the city and its inhabitants, and of the earliest settlements of the inland part of Pennsylvania. . . . Enl. & rev. by W. P. Hazard. 3 vols., illustrated. O. Philadelphia, 1891.   HE—WATS33

———— 1780-1860. Olden time researches & reminiscences of New York city . . . [1828]. 78 pp. O. No place, no date.   HE—Z7

WERNER, Edgar A. Civil list and Constitutional history of the Colony and State of New York. III-VII, 3-663 pp., 16 pl. Albany, 1886. O.   HE—W5
Gift of Mrs. James M. Lawton.

WESTCHESTER County Magazine. Vol. III, No. 4, & Vol. IV, No. 2. White Plains, New York, July & November, 1909. O.   HE—N533
Gift of W. H. Falconer.

WHITMORE, William Henry. The Massachusetts civil list for the Colonial and Provincial periods, 1630-1774. Being a list of the names . . . of all the civil officers. . . . 172 pp. O. Albany, 1870.   HE—W61

WHY is history read so little? [By Edward Denham.]   HE—Z7

WILLIAMS, Rev. Solomon. Historical sketch of Northampton, from its first settlement: in a sermon, delivered on the National Thanksgiving, April 13, 1815. 24 pp. O. Northampton, 1815. Volume "Ancient Woodbury."   HE—W885

WILSON, Gen. James Grant. Memorial of Col. John Bayard; read before the New Jersey Historical Society . . . May 16th, 1878. O. pp. 141-160.   HE—Z7

WILSON, Thomas Woodrow, Pres. U. S. A. President Wilson's War Address to Congress and Proclamation, together with joint Resolution of House and Senate, giving names of those voting for and against the measure. Illus. cover. 6 leaves, 1 pl., 1 port. Q. New York, 1917.   HE—Pamphlet
Gift of J. P. M. M.

WINFIELD, Charles Hardenbergh. History of the county of Hudson, New Jersey. . . . 568 pp., il., port., pl. O. N. Y., 1874.   HE—W72

WINSOR, Justin. A history of the town of Duxbury, Mass.; with genealogical registers. VIII, 9-36 pp., 1 port. O. Boston, 1849.   HE—W721
Contains autograph of Author.

WOOD, Jervis A. My Flag. 10 leaves with color illustrations. O. Philadelphia, 1917.   HE—Pamphlet
Gift of John Wanamaker.

[WOOLSEY, Sarah Chauncey.] Short history of Philadelphia from its Foundation to the present time, by Susan Coolidge. 288 pp. Boston, 1887. D.   HE—W88
Gift of Mrs. Martha J. Lamb.

WORCESTER Society of Antiquity. Collections. Vol. iv. O. Worcester, Mass., 1882.   HE—W89

WORTHINGTON, Erastus. The history of Dedham, Mass., from the beginning of its settlement in September, 1635, to May, 1827. 146 pp. Boston, 1827. O.   HE—Ded36

ZACHOS, John Celivergos, Editor. See: COOPER, Peter. 1791-1883. Political and financial opinions. 1877.   HE—Z2

ALBANY, New York. Early records of the City and County of Albany and Colony of Rensselaerswyck. Translated from the original Dutch by J. Pearson. Revised and edited by A. J. F. van LAER. Vols. II-IV. Albany, N. Y., 1916?-19. 438 pp. Q. (University State N. Y., State Library Historical Bulletin, 9-11.)

HE—A326—Vols. II,III,IV

PEARSON, JONATHAN, Translator. See: Albany, N. Y. Early records of the city and county of Albany and Colony of Rensselaerswyck. Revised and edited by A. J. F. vanLaer. Albany, 1916-1919. Vols. II-IV. Q. 3 vols. Univ. State N. Y. N. Y. State Lib'y Hist. Bull. No. 11.

HE—A326

UNIVERSITY State of New York. New York State Library History Bulletin. Nos. 9-11. Albany, N. Y., 1916-1919. 3 vols. Q. Early Records of Albany and Rensselaerswyck. Vols. II-IV. Revised and edited by A. J. F. van Laer. Translated from the original Dutch by J. Pearson.

HE—A362

VAN LAER, A. J. F., Editor. Early records of the city and county of Albany and colony of Rensselaerswyck. Translated from the original Dutch by J. Pearson. Vols. II-IV. Albany, 1916-1919. 3 vols. Q. (University State of N. Y. N. Y. State Library Hist. Bull., Nos. 9-11.)

HE—A362

Vol. II.   Deeds 3 & 4, 1678-1704. 438 pp. Albany, 1916. Q.

"   III.   Notarial Papers, 1 & 2.   1660-1696.   644 pp.   Albany, 1918. Q.

"   IV.   Mortgages 1, 1658-1660, & Wills 1-2, 1681-1765. 220 pp. Albany, 1919. Q.

OTHER HISTORY

ACADIA. See: CANADIAN ARCHIVES; Appendix H. Letter of Father Ignace re Acadia. According to a photographic copy of the original in the Archives of the Propaganda, Rome. pp. 331-341. (Vol. I.)   HF—C213

ACADIAN genealogy and notes. By P. Gauder. xxxiv, 372 pp. O. (Appendix A, part III, Canadian Archives.) Vol. II.   HF—C213

"ANCHOR," pseudonym. See: DE PEYSTER, JOHN WATTS, Brev. Major General, U. S. A.

ANDREWS, E. BENJAMIN. Brief institutes of general history. Boston, 1887. 440 pp. D.   HF—An2
Gift of Mrs. Martha J. Lamb.

AUBIGNE, THÉODORE AGRIPPA D'. Histoire universelle. Edition publiée pour la Société de l'histoire de France, par Baron Alphonse de Ruble. Paris, 1886. Vol. I. O.   HF—Au1
Gift of Baron Alphonse de Ruble.

BOTHWELL, JAMES HEPBURN, fourth Earl of Bothwell, third husband of Mary, Queen of Scots. An historical drama by J. Watts de Peyster. New York, 1884. O.   HF—D419
No. 3 of de Peyster volume.

BOURINOT, JOHN GEORGE. Manual of the constitutional history of Canada from the earliest period to 1888. Montreal, 1888. 238 pp. D.   HE—B66
Gift of Mrs. Martha J. Lamb.

CANADIAN ARCHIVES. Report . . . for the year 1905. Vols. I-II. Ottawa, 1905-1906. 2 vols. Q.   HF—C213
Vol. III wanting to complete Report.
Gift of Howland Pell.

DE PEYSTER, JOHN WATTS, Brev. Major General, U. S. A. Authorities cited and referred to in his three pamphlets. . . . "Waterloo," . . . and other Works on Napoleon. . . . With a biographical sketch of the author, by W. L. Stone. New York, 1894. 1-16, 1-16 pp. Square Q.   HF—D419W
Gift of the Author.

———— Bothwell: (James Hepburn, fourth Earl of Bothwell, third husband of Mary, Queen of Scots). An historical drama. New York, 1884. 48 pp., 2 port. (Also 2 port., on covers, & pages illustrated.) O.   HF—D419
No. 3 of de Peyster Volume.
Gift of Mrs. J. M. Lawton.

DE PEYSTER, JOHN WATTS, Brev. Major General, U. S. A., Editor. Genuine (The) letters of Mary, Queen of Scots, to James, Earl of Bothwell: . . . Trans. from the French originals, by Edw. Simmonds. . . . Added Remarks on each letter, with an abstract of her life . . . from an unknown hand. 2nd ed., Westminster, n.d. New York, 1891-'92. II-III pp. O.   HF—D419
No. 5 of de Peyster Volume.
Gift of Mrs. James M. Lawton.

———— Inquiry (An) into the career and character of Mary Stuart . . . and a justification of Bothwell. . . . New York, 1883. 260 pp., 2 port. O. Illustrated.   HF—D419
No. 2 of de Peyster Volume.
Gift of Mrs. James M. Lawton.

———— Mary, Queen of Scots. A study. By "Anchor." 144 pp. New York, 1882. O.   HF—D419
No. 1 of de Peyster Volume.
Gift of Mrs. James M. Lawton.

———— Mary Stuart, Bothwell, & the casket letters, something new. . . . 40 pp., illus. N. Y., 1890. O.   HF—D419
No. 4 of de Peyster Volume.
Gift of the Author.

———— Prussians (The) in the Campaign of Waterloo. n.p., n.d. 21 pp., 1 plan. Square Q. Reprint, "The College Student," Lancaster, Pa.   HF—D419W
Gift of the Author.

DUCOUDRAY, GUSTAVE. History of modern civilization translated & adapted from the French by J. V. 587 pp., illustrated. New York, 1891. O.   HF—D85
Gift of Mrs. Martha J. Lamb.

FLETCHER, CHARLES ROBERT LESLIE. Gustavus Adolphus and the struggle of Protestantism for existence. XVIII, 316 pp., 12 pl., 13 port., 3 maps, 1 table. O. New York, 1890. (Heroes of the nations.)   HF—F62
No. 139 of 250 copies printed.

FORD, WORTHINGTON CHAUNCEY, Compiler. List of the Vernon-Wager MSS., in the Library of Congress. With fac-simile of Letter of Admiral Charles Wager. 4 fac-sim.; 148 pp. Washington, D. C., 1904. Q.   HF—F711V-W
Gift of the Library of Congress.

FORGUES, The Abbé Michel. Genealogy of the families of the Island of Orleans. 360 pp. O. (Appendix A; part II, Canadian Archives.) Vol. II.   HF—C213

FRANKLIN, BENJAMIN. List of the Benjamin Franklin Papers in the Library of Congress, edited by W. C. Ford. Washington, D. C., 1905. 322 pp. Square Q.   HF—F711F

FROUDE, James Anthony. Divorce of Catherine of Aragon . . . a supplementary volume to . . . Froude's "History of England." 476 pp. N. Y., 1891. O. HF—F93

GAFFAREL, Paul. Histoire du Brésil français au 16e siècle. Paris, 1878. 512 pp. map. O. HF—G12
Gift of Dr. Abram Du Bois.

GAUDET, Placide. Acadian genealogy and notes. xxxiv, 372 pp. O. (Appendix A, part iii, Canadian Archives. Vol. ii.) HF—C214

GIGLIOTTI, Nicola. Cor Mundi. The Heart of the World. A contribution to the Mission of the United States of America in the Modern War. 2 leaves, 6-84 pp., 1 leaf. [Erie, Pa.], 1918. O. HF—Pamphlet
Gift of Mrs. James M. Lawton, with autograph letter of Author.

GROVE, Lilly M., Translator. See: MADELIN, Louis. Victory (The) of the Marne. Paris, 1917. O. HF—Pamphlet

GUSTAVUS Adolphus and the struggle of Protestantism for existence, by C. R. L. Fletcher. N. Y., 1890. O. HF—F62

HART, Gerald E. Fall of New France, 1755-1760. Montreal, 1888. 175 pp. portraits, plates, fac-simile. O. HF—H25
Gift of Mrs. Martha J. Lamb.

ISLAND of Orleans. See: Genealogy of the families of the Island of Orleans, by the Abbé Michel Forgues. O. (Appendix A, part ii, Canadian Archives. Vol. ii.) HF—C213

KAHN, Otto. When the tide turned. The American attack at Chateau-Thierry and Belleau Wood in the first week of June, 1918. Address at the Meeting of the Boston Athletic Assoc., Nov. 12, 1918. 18 pp. Boston, 1918. O. HF—Pamphlet
Gift of the Author.

LESCARBOT, Marc. Histoire de la Nouvelle-France, contenant les navigations, découvertes et habitations faites par les Français ès Indes occidentales et Nouvelle-France; suivi des muses de la Nouvelle-France. Nouvelle édition, publiée par Edwin Tross. Paris, 1866. 3 vols. maps. O. HF—L56

[MACAULAY], Thomas Babington. Macaulay, 1st baron, 1800-1859. History of England. 5 vols. in 1, 1 port. Philadelphia. (Vol. v, edited by Lady Treveylan.) HF—M11
Gift of Mrs. Martha J. Lamb.

MADELIN, Louis. Victory of the Marne. The enemy's onslaught—Order to stand firm—The Battle—Immediate results—Historic consequences. Translated by Lilly M. Grove. 1 leaf, 3-64 pp., 2 maps folded. Paris, 1917. O. (Studies & Documents on the War.) HF—Pamphlet
Gift of the Author.

[MALLET, EDMOND, ABBÉ.] Négociations de le comte d'Avaux en
  Hollande depuis 1679 jusqu'en 1684. Paris, 1754. 6 vols. in 2.
  S.   HF—M29

MARTIN, E. K. The Mennonites. 17 pp. Philadelphia, 1883.
  O.   HF—M36

MARY, QUEEN OF SCOTS. A study. By "Anchor." 144 pp. New
  York, 1882. O.   HF—D419
  No. 1 of de Peyster volume.

MEILLEUR, J. B. Mémorial de l'éducation du Bas-Canada. . . .
  1615-1855. . . . 389 pp. Montreal, 1860. S.   HF—M47

NEGOCIATIONS de M. le comte d'Avaux en Hollande. . . . par
  l'abbé Edme. Mallet. 1754.   HF—M29

RUBLE, ALPHONSE, LE BARON DE, Editor. See: AUBIGNE, THÉ-
  ODORE AGRIPPA D'. Histoire universelle. . . . 1886.   HF—Au.1

SAGARD-THEODAT, GABRIEL. Histoire du Canada et voyages
  que les frères mineurs recollects y ont faicts pour la conversion des
  infidèles depuis l'an 1615, avec un dictionnaire de la langue huronne.
  Nouvelle édition publiée par Edwin Tross. Paris, 1866. 4 vols.
  O.   HF—Sa.1

SELLAR, ROBERT. History of the county of Huntingdon and of the
  seigniories of Chateaugay and Beauharnais from their first settlement to 1838. Huntingdon, Quebec, 1888. 584 pp. O.   HF—Se4
  Gift of Mrs. Martha J. Lamb.

SOCIETE de l'histoire de France. See: DAUBIGNE, THÉODORE
  AGRIPPA D'. Histoire universelle. 1886.   HF—Au1

STONE, WILLIAM L. . . . Biographical sketch of Brev. Maj. Gen.
  J. W. de Peyster. New York, 1894. 16 pp. Square Q.   HF—D419W
  Bound with: de Peyster, J. W., Authorities cited. . . . Waterloo.
  N. Y., 1894.
  Gift of Author.

THEAL, GEORGE McCALL, compiler. Chronicles of Cape commanders; or, An abstract of original manuscripts in the archives of
  the Cape Colony, 1651-91. Compiled with printed accounts of the
  settlement. Cape Town, 1882. 428 pp. maps, O.   HF—T34
  Gift of C. de Villiers.

TREVEYLAN, LADY HANNAH MORE MACAULAY, Editor. See:
  MACAULAY, T. B. M. 1st baron. 1800-59. History of England. Vol. v.   HF—M11

TROSS, EDWIN, Editor. See: LESCARBOT, MARC. Histoire de la
  Nouvelle-France. . . . 1866.   HF—L56

——— Editor. See: SAGARD-THEODAT, GABRIEL. Histoire du
  Canada. . . . 1866.   HF—Sa.1

VERNON, EDWARD, Vice-Admiral. List of the Vernon-Wager MSS.,
  in the Library of Congress. With fac-similes. 148 pp. Washington, D. C., 1904. Q.   HF—F711V-W
  Gift of Library of Congress.

BIOGRAPHY

ACADEMIE DE GENÈVE. Le livre du recteur catalogue des étudiants de l'Académie de Genève de 1559-1859. Genève, 1860. 391 pp. Q.   HG—Ac1

[ALBOUIS] D' AZINCOURT, [JOSEPH JEAN BAPTISTE]. 1747-1809. Mémoires. (In: Barrière, J. F., editor. Bibliothèque des mémoires relatifs à l'histoire de France. 1857. Vol. VI. pp. 193-236.)   HG—B27

ALLABEN, FRANK. General John Watts de Peyster, Author, Soldier, Historian, Military biographer, and Critic. 36 pp., 1 port., 2 pl. O. New York, 1894.   HG—D419
Reprint Natl. Mag., Oct., 1894.
Gift of Mrs. James M. Lawton.

ANCESTRAL sketches, [by Mrs. Sarah Van Rensselaer]. New York, 1882. Square Q.   HG—V351

ARGENSON, [RENÉ LOUIS DE VOYER], MARQUIS D'. 1694-1757. Mémoires. (In: Barrière, J. F., editor. Bibliothèque des mémoires relatifs à l'hist. de France. 1853. Vol. I, pp. 243-327.)   HG—B27

ARNAUD, EUGENE. Guillaume Rabot de Salène, humaniste ignoré de XVIe siècle; étude historique. 46 pp. O. Paris, 1890.   HG—S33
Gift of the Author.
Volume of Biographical & Historical Essays.

AUSTIN, MARY S. Philip Freneau, the Poet of the Revolution. A history of his life and times. Edited by H. K. Vreeland. 285 pp., 1 fac-sim., 2 pl., 3 port. O. New York, 1901.   HG—F88A
Gift of Mrs. H. K. Vreeland.

BACHAUMONT, [LOUIS]. -1771. Mémoires historiques et littéraires de . . . 1762-1782. (In: Barrière, J. F., editor. Bibliothèque des mémoires relatifs l'histoire de France. 1846. Vol. III, pp. 209-524.)   HG—B27

[BACON, NATHANIEL.] Relation of the fearful estate of Francis Spira, . . . apostate from the Protestant Church . . . also lives and deaths of John Child . . . and Geo. Edwards. 138 pp. T. London, 1718.   HG—Sp4

[BAIRD, MRS. MARGARET E. STRANG,] Editor. Memorials of Rev. C. W. Baird . . . with a few . . . sermons and . . . poems. 235 pp., port., pl. O. New York, 1888.   HG—B16
Gift of Mrs. Baird.

BAKER, William Spohn, Compiler. Bibliotheca Washingtonia; descriptive list of the biographies . . . of George Washington. 179 pp., 1 port. Square Q. Philadelphia, 1889.　　　　HG—W277
Gift of Mrs. Martha J. Lamb.

────── Medallic portraits of Washington with historical and critical notes and . . . catalogue of the coins, medals, tokens and cards. 252 pp., 1 pl. Square Q. Philadelphia, 1885.　　　　HG—W276
Gift of Mrs. Martha J. Lamb.

BARBAULD, Mrs. Anna Laetitia Atkin. Life and works, memoir, letters and a selection from (her) poems and prose works. 2 vols. D. Boston, 1874.　　　　HG—B23

BARRIERE, Jean François. Bibliothèque des mémoires relatifs à l'histoire de France pendant le 18me siècle. Paris, 1846-53. 12 vols. D.　　　　HG—B27

BATES, James L. Alfred Kelley; his life and work. 210 pp., 1 port. Columbus, O., 1888. O.　　　　HG—K29
250 copies, privately printed.
Gift of Mrs. Martha J. Lamb.

BEAUCHET-FILLEAU, Henri, et Beauchet-Filleau, P.　Dictionnaire historique et généalogique des familles du Poitou. Tome I-IV. A-Gue. 2nd ed. Q. 4 vols. Poitiers, 1891-1909.　　　　HG—B38
Pub. en fasc. Tome IV contains fasc. 1-3.
Tomes I-III. Gift of The French Society.

BEAUCHET-FILLEAU, Paul. See above.　　　　HG—B38

BENJAMIN, Marcus. Charles Frederick Tiffany Beale. 13 pp., 1 port. O. Washington, D. C., 1902. (Soc. Col. Wars, D. C., Mem. Papers, No. 2.)　　　　HG—Mem.512

────── Francis Asbury Roe. 35 pp., 8 pl., 1 port. O. Washington, D. C., 1903. (Soc. Col. Wars, D. C., Mem. Papers, No. 4.)　　　　HG—Mem512

BENNEVILLE, George de. See: DE BENNEVILLE, George.

BENOIT, Daniel. Frères (Les) Gibert. Deux pasteurs du désert et du refuge. (1722-1817.) 429 pp., 1 port., 1 fac-sim. D. Toulouse, 1899.　　　　HG—G35
Gift of The French Society.

────── Marie Durand, prisonnière a la Tour de Constance (1730-1736): sa famille et ses compagnes de captivité, d'aprés des documents inédits. 320 pp., 1 pl., 1 fac-sim., folded. D. Toulouse, 1884.　　　　HG—D93
Gift of The French Society.

────── See: CRESPIN, Jean. Histoire des martyrs. . . . Introduction par D. B. 3 vols. Toulouse, 1885-'89. Q.　　　　HG—C.86.2

BERSIER, Eugène. Coligny: the earlier life of the great Huguenot. Trans. by Annie Harwood Holmden. 36-351 pp. O. London, 1886. HG—C68—Bersier

BESANT, Walter. Gaspard de Coligny, (Marquis de Chatillon), Admiral of France. . . . 228 pp., 1 port. Tt. New York, 1879. (Harper's Half-hour Ser.) HG—C68—Copy 1
Gift of Mrs. James M. Lawton.
Autograph letter of Gen. F. A. Roe inserted.

——— Gaspard de Coligny. . . . 232 pp., 1 port. D. New York. (The New Plutarch Ser.) HG—C68—Copy 2
Gift of Josiah Collins Pumpelly.

BESENVAL, Pierre Victor, Baron de. 1722-'91. Mémoires. (In: Barrière, J. F., editor. Bibliothèque des mémoires relatifs à Histoire de France. 1846. Vol. IV, pp. 1-383.) HG—B27—Vol. 4

BIBLIOTHEQUE des Mémoires relatifs à l'histoire de France pendant le 18e siècle. See: BARRIERE, J. F. 1786-1868.

BIDDLE, Charles. 1745-1821. Autobiography. 423 pp. O. Philadelphia, 1883. HG—B47
Privately printed.

BIDDLE, Henry D., Editor. See: DRINKER, Mrs. E. S. Extracts from (her) journal, from 1759-1807. 1889. HG—D83

BLANCHON, Pierre. Jean Guiton et le Siège de la Rochelle. 65 pp., 1 port., inserted. Square D. La Rochelle, 1911. HG—G968
Gift: le Comité.

BLISS, Eugene F., editor. See: ZEISBERGER, David. Diary, 1885. HG—Ze5

BONNET, Jules. Vie d'Olympia Morata épisode de la Renaissance & de la réforme en Italie. Ed. 2, enl. 255 (1) pp. O. Paris, 1851. HG—M34

——— Editor. See: Marolles de. fils. Histoire des souffrances du bienheureux martyr Louis de Marolles. . . . 1883. HG—M34

BORDIER, Henri Leonard, editor. See: HAAG, Eugene & Emile. La France Protestante. 1877-'88. HG—H11

BORREL, Abraham. Biographie de Paul Rabaut, pasteur du désert & de ses trois fils. 168 pp. D. Nimes, 1854. HG—R111
Bd. with: CUVIER, O. Trois martyrs de la Réforme. . . .
Gift of The French Société.

BOWEN, Rev. L. P. Days of Makemie, or, The vine planted. . . .
1680-1708. With an appendix. 558 pp., 1 map. D. Philadelphia,
1885. HG—M29
Gift of Mrs. Martha J. Lamb.

BROWNING, ARTHUR G[IRAUD]. Odet de Coligny, Cardinal de
Châtillon. A paper read at Canterbury, on the occasion of . . .
visit of the French Hospital (Victoria Park), London, July 26,
1884. Canterbury, 1884. 20 pp. D. HG—C681—Vol. III
Author's Presentation Copy: through Mrs. J. M. Lawton.
(Inserted in Volume III of Delaborde, L. J., comte de. Gaspard de
Coligny, amiral de France. . . .)

CAMPAN, MME. [JEANNE LOUISE HENRIETTE (GENET)]. 1752-
1822. Mémoires sur le vie de Marie Antoinette . . . suivis de
souvenirs et anecdotes historiques sur les règnes de Louis XIV., de
Louis XV. et Louis XVI. . . . 488 pp. D. Paris, 1849. (In:
BARRIERE, J. F., Editor. Bibliothèque des mémoires relatifs à
l'hist. de France. . . . Vol. x.) HG—B27

CHARLESTON, S. C. See: French Protestant Church.

CLERY, [JEAN BAPTISTE CANT HANET]. Mémoires. [Journal de
ce qui s'est passé à la tour du Temple.] (In: Barrière, J. F., Editor.
Bibliothèque des mémoires relatifs à l'hist. de France. 1847. Vol.
IX, pp. 15-171.) HG—B27

COLLE, [CHARLES]. 1709-'83. La vérité dans le vin; ou, Les desa-
grements de la galanterie, comédie. (In: Barrière, J. F., Editor.
Bibliothèque des mémoires relatifs à l'hist. de France. 1846. Vol.
IV, pp. 385-437.) HG—B27

COLONEL, DE HEER, ABRAHAM DE PEYSTER, Mayor of New York
City, Commander of City Troops, Chief-Justice . . . Supreme
Court, 2 p.l., 5 pp., 1 port., 2 colored pl. O. New York,
1895. HG—D419
Reprint, "Mem. Hist. of N. Y."
In "de Peyster" Volume.

COUVRAY, JEAN BAPTISTE LOUVET DE. 1760-'97. See: LOUVET
DE COUVRAY, JEAN BAPTISTE. 1760-'97.

CRESPIN, JEAN. Histoire des martyrs: persécutez et mis à mort
pour la vérité de l'Evâgile, depuis le temps des Apostres insques à
present (1619). Ed. nouvelle. . . . Introduction par D. Benoit,
et . . . notes par M. Lelièvre. Tome 1-3. Toulouse, 1885-1889.
3 vols. Q. HG—C86.2
Gift of the French Société.

———— et GOULART, S. Histoire des martyrs persécutez et mis
à mort pour la vérité de L'Evâgile depuis le temps des Apostres
insques à l'an 1597. . . . 8 p.l., 1526 pp. Folio. No place, 1597.
Vélin blanc ancien aux armes frappees en or sur les plats et au dos
de la ville d'Amsterdam. HG—C86
Gift of Herbert Dupuy.

CUVIER, OTHON. Trois martyrs de la Réforme brules en 1525 a Vic, Metz et Nancy. 1 leaf, VIII, 1 leaf, 116 pp. D. Paris, 1889.   HG—R111
Chastelain, Jean.
Leclerc, Jean.
Schuch, Wolfgang.
Bound with: BORREL, A. Biographie de Paul Rabaut. . . .
Gift of The French Société.

CYR, NARCISSE. Heroism of Huguenot women imprisoned for life in the Tower of Constance. 19 pp. T. Springfield, Mass., 1894. (Cyr's Huguenot Sketches, No. 1.)   HG—Qu3
Inserted in Volume.

DARDIER, CHARLES. See: BABAUT, PAUL. Letters à Antoine Court (1739-1755). [No date.]   HG—R11

DAUNOU, [PIERRE CLAUDE FRANÇOIS]. 1761-1840. Mémoires pour servir à l'histoire de la Convention nationale. (In: Barrière, J. F. Bibliothèque des mémoires relatifs à l'hist. de France pendant le 18me siècle. 1848. Vol. XII, pp. 405-464.)   HG—B27

DAVIS, REUBEN. 1813-1873. Recollections of Mississippi and Mississippians. 446 pp., 1 port. O. Boston, 1889.   HG—D29
Gift of Mrs. Martha J. Lamb.

DAZINCOURT, JOSEPH JEAN BAPTISTE ALBOUIS. See: ALBOUIS D'AZINCOURT, JOSEPH JEAN BAPTISTE. 1747-1809.

DE BENNEVILLE, GEORGE. 1703-'93. Some remarkable passages in the life of Dr. George de Benneville . . . with . . . account of his . . . persecution in France. Trans. from the French of his own MS. . . . by Rev. E. Winchester. 55 pp. D. Germantown, 1890.   HG—D351
Reprint from American edition of 1800, revised & enlarged.
Gift of Converse Cleaves, publisher.

DE BUDE, EUGÈNE. Vie de Bénédict Pictet, théologien Génevois. 1655-1724. 304 pp. D. Lausanne, 1874.   HG—P58
Gift of The French Société.

——— Vie de Guillaume Budé, fondateur de Collège de France. 300 pp., 1 port. D. Paris, 1884.   HG—B86
Gift of The French Société.

——— Vie de Jacob Vernet, théologien Génevois, 1698-1789. 304 pp. D. Lausanne, 1893.   HG—V59
Gift of The French Société.

——— Vie de Jean Diodati, théologien Génevois, 1576-1649. 302 pp., 1 leaf. D. Lausanne, 1869.   HG—D62
Gift of The French Société.

——— Vie de Jean-Alphonse Turrettini, théologien Génevois. 1671-1737. 324 pp. D. Lausanne, 1880.   HG—T86
Gift of The French Société.

DE CHERGE, CHARLES. See: BEAUCHET-FILLEAU, HENRI et
PAUL. Dictionnaire . . . genealogique des familles du Poitou. . . .
HG—B38

DE COSTA, THE REV. BENJAMIN FRANKLIN, D.D. Memorial
brochures of the De Costa family.   HG—D35—also D351
Gifts of the Author.
In Memoriam: Elizabeth De Costa. 8 pp. New York, 1880. S.
Privately printed.
In Memoriam: Harriet Cooper Spencer De Costa. New York,
1901. 18 pp., 1 pl., 1 port. Square D. One of 75 copies printed
privately.
In Memoriam: Mary Rebecca De Costa. New York, 1896. 12
pp. S. Privately printed.
In Memoriam: Mary Rebecca Theresa De Costa. Sister Sainte
Claire, Order of St. Ursula. Charlestown, 1876. 25 pp. O.
One of 100 copies, no copy sold.
In Memoriam: William Hickling De Costa. Charlestown, 1878.
8 pp., 1 port. S. Privately printed.
Souvenir: St. Michael and All Angels. September 29th, 1858-
1894. New York, 1894. 1 port., 2 illustrations, and a poem in
booklet. S.

DE FOREST, DAVID C. Copy of the Acts and doings respecting the
De Forest Fund at Yale College, in New Haven . . . established
September, 1823. New Haven, 1823. 8 pp. O.   HG—Mis68
No. 1 of Pamphlet Volume.

DELABORDE, [LOUIS] JULES, COMTE DE. Gaspard de Coligny,
Amiral de France. . . . 3 vols. Paris, 1879-1882. O.   HG—C681

DE LANCEY, EDWARD FLOYD. Memoir of James William Beekman;
prepared at the request of the St. Nicholas Society of New York.
New York, 1877. 17 pp. Q.   HG—Mem51

DE PEYSTER, COL. ARENT SCHUYLER. Miscellanies by an Officer
. . . edited by J. Watts de Peyster. . . . 80 pp., 1 port.: 202, 6 pp.,
1 map, 1 map fld., 1 port. In 2 parts. O. (Dumfries, 1813.)
New York, 1888.   HG—D419
Gift of the Editor.

DE PONTBRIANT, A. Guerres de religion. Le Capitaine Merle,
Baron de Lagorce, gentilhomme de Roy de Navarre et ses descendants, avec lettres et documents inédits. . . . 2 p.l., 306 pp.,
1 map folded. Paris, 1886. O.   HG—D44

DE RICHEMOND, LOUIS MARIE MESCHINET. See: MESCHINET
DE RICHEMOND.

DE SCHICKLER, FERNAND, BARON. Discours prononce a l'assemblée
générale de la Société de l'Histoire de France, le 5 mai 1903. 22
pp. O. Nogent-le-Rotrou, 1903.   HG—S33
Author's autograph: Gift of Mrs. J. M. Lawton.
P. V., "Biographical & Historical Essays."

DICTIONNAIRE historique et généalogique des familles du Poitou. See: BEAUCHET-FILLEAU, H[ENRI] & PAUL.   HG—B38

DOUEN, [EMMANUEL ORENTIN]. Clément Marot & le psautier Huguenot, étude historique littéraire, musicale & bibliographique, contenant les mélodies primitives des psaumes & des specimins d'harmonie de Clement, Jannequin. . . . 2 vols. Q. Paris, 1878-'79. HG—M341 Gift of Dr. Abram Du Bois.

——— Les premiers pasteurs du désert (1685-1700) d'après des documents pour la plupat inédits. Paris, 1879. 2 vols. O.   HG—D74

DRINKER, MRS. ELIZABETH [SANDWITH]. 1734-1807. Extracts from her journal, from 1759-1807 . . . edited by H. D. Biddle. 423 pp. O. Philadelphia, 1889.   HG—D83 Gift of Mrs. Martha J. Lamb.

DUBUS-PREVILLE, P[IERRE] L[OUIS]. 1721-'99. Mémoires. (In: Barrière, J. F., Editor. Bibliothèque des mémoires relatifs à l'histoire de France. 1857. Vol. VI. pp. 143-192.)   HG—B27

DUCHESNE, ANDRÉ. History of the Bethune family, translated from the French, with additions . . . & a Sketch of the Faneuil family . . . by Mrs. J. A. Weisse. 54 & 3 pp., 1 pl. Q. New York, 1884.   HG—B67

DUCLOS, [CHARLES PINEAU]. 1704-1772. Mémoires secrets le règne de Louis XIV, la régence et le règne de Louis XV. (In: Barrière, J. F., Editor. Bibliothèque des mémoires relatifs à l'histoire de France. 1854. Vol. II.)   HG—B27

DU HAUSSET, MME. N. Mémoires de Madame du Hausset, femme de chambre de Madame de Pompadour. (In: Barrière, J. F., Editor. Bibliothèque des mémoires relatifs à l'histoire de France. 1846. Vol. III, pp. 49-154.)   HG—B27

DUMOURIEZ, [CHARLES FRANÇOIS DUPÉRIER]. 1739-1823. Mémoires. (In: Barrière, J. F., Editor. Bibliothèque des mémoires relatifs à l'histoire de France. 1848. Vols. XI & XII. pp. 1-207.)   HG—B27

[DUNCAN, MRS. M. G. LUNDY], anon. Memoirs of the life and character of the Rev. Matthias Bruen, late pastor of the Presbyterian Church in Bleecker Street, New York. 358 pp., 1 port. O. N. Y., 1831.   HG—B83.1

[DU PUY, PIERRE.] Histoire des plus illustres favoris anciens et modernes, recueillie par . . . P. D. P. Avec un journal de ce qui s'est passé à la mort de Mareschal d'Ancre. 10 p.l., 340 pp. Square O. Leide, 1659.   HG—D92

DURYEE, REV. JOSEPH R., D.D., and others. Funeral address: memorial tributes, resolutions, etc., for the Hon. Henry W. Bookstaver, LL.D. 1834-1907. 30 pp., 1 portrait inserted. O. New York, 1907.   HG—Mem512

DUYCKINCK, Evert T., Editor. See: FRENEAU, Philip Morin. Poems. . . . 1865.

DWIGHT, Timothy. Noah Porter; address delivered at the funeral service of President Porter, March 7, 1892. 14 pp. D. New Haven, 1892.   HG—Mis68
No. 2 of a P. V.

[ELIZABETH CHARLOTTE, Duchesse d'Orléans, 1652-1722]. Mémoires de Madame, mère du régent. (In: Barrière, J. F., Editor. Bibliothèque de mémoires relatifs à l'histoire de France. 1853. Vol. i, pp. 329-355.)   HG—B27

ELLERY, Harrison, Editor. Memoirs of Gen. J. G. Swift . . . with a genealogy of the family of Thomas Swift. Worcester, Mass., 1890. Q.   HG—Sw.5
Privately printed.

ELLIS, Grace Atkinson. Memoir of Mrs. Anna Laetitia Barbauld. In: BARBAULD, Mrs. Anna Laetitia. Life & Works. 2 vols.   HG—B23

FAIRCHILD, Helen Lincklaen, Editor. See: van der KEMP, Francis Adrian, 1752-1829. An autobiography . . . edited, with an historical sketch by H. L. F. N. Y., 1903.   HG—V28

FELICE, Paul de. See: FRANCE, H. de. Les Montalbanais & le refuge . . . 1887.   HG—F84

FERET, P., Abbé. Un curé de Charenton au XVIIe siècle, [François Veron]. Paris, 1881. iv, 5-160 pp. S.   HG—F37
Author's autograph letter inserted.
Gift of E. Belleroche.

FERGUSON, Henry. Sir Edmund Andros. 32 pp. O. no place, no date. Address delivered before the Westchester Co. Historical Society, Oct. 28, 1892.   HG—Mis68
No. 4 of P. V.

FILLEAU. See: BEAUCHET-FILLEAU.

FISKE, John, abridger. See: IRVING, Washington. Washington and his Country. 1887.

FISKE, Willard. Lost (The) MS. of the Rev. Lewis Rou's "Critical remarks upon the letter to the craftsman on the game of chess" written in 1734 and dedicated to his Excellency William Cosby, Gov. of N. Y. (Signed W. F., i. e., Willard Fiske). 18 pp. O. Florence, (Italy), 1902.   HG—Pamphlet
Reprint: Notes and Queries, July 19, 1902, with additions.
Gift of Huguenot Society of London.

FONTAINE, Rev. James. Born 1658. Memoirs of a Huguenot family, translated and compiled from the original autobiography and other family manuscripts, comprising an original journal of travels in Virginia, New York, etc., in 1715 and 1716, by Ann Maury, with an appendix containing a translation of the Edict of Nantes. N. Y., 1853. 512 pp. portraits. D. HG—F73
Gift of C. M. Maury.

FRANCE, H. de. Les Montalbanais et le refuge, augmenté des notes recueillies dans les archives de Berlin par Paul de Félice. Montauban, 1887. 553 pp. O. HG—F84

FRENCH PROTESTANT CHURCH, Charleston, S. C. In Memoriam William Ravenel and Peter Charles Gaillard. 16 pp. Charleston, 1889. O. HG—Mem51
Gift of the author.

FRENEAU, Philip [Morin]. Poems relating to the American Revolution, with an introductory memoir and notes by E. A. Duyckinck. N. Y., 1865. 288 pp. portrait, fac-simile. Q. HG—F88

GARRICK, David. 1717-1779. Mémoires. (In: Barrière, J. F., Editor. Bibliothèque des mémoires relatifs à l'histoire de France. 1857. Vol. vi, pp. 279-320.) HG—B27

GOLDONI, [Carlo]. 1707-1793. Mémoires pour servir à l'hist. de sa vie et à celle de son théatre. (In: Barrière, J. F., Editor. Bibliothèque des mémoires relatifs à l'histoire de France. 1857. Vol. vi, pp. 321-465.) HG—B27—Vol. vi

GOSS, Elbridge Henry. Life of Col. Paul Revere. 2 vols., illus., port., pl., fac-sim. Boston, 1891. O. HG—R32

[GOULART, Simon.] See: [CRESPIN, Jean, et GOULART, S.] Histoire des martyrs. . . . Avec deux indices. . . . 8 p.l., 1526 pp. Folio. no place, 1597. HG—C86
Gift of Herbert Dupuy.

———— Ed. nouvelle. en 3 tomes. Q. Toulouse, 1885-'89. HG—C86.2
Gift of The French Société.

GOUTTEPAGNON, Maurice de. See: BEAUCHET-FILLEAU, Henri & Paul. Dictionnaire . . . des familles du Poitou. . . . 2nd ed. Poitiers, 1891. HG—B38

GRAYSON, William J. James Louis Petigru, a biographical sketch. 178 pp., 1 port. New York, 1866. D. HG—P44

GUYOT, Henri Daniel. Marquis de Venours, protecteur des victimes de l'intolérance de Louis XIV. 31 pp. O. Groninque, 1906. HG—S33
Volume: Biographical & Historical Essays.

HAAG, Emile. See: HAAG, Eugene & Emile. La France Protestante. . . .

HAAG, Eugène & Emile. La France protestante. Deuxième édition publiée sous les auspices de la Société de l'histoire du protestantisme français et sous la direction de Henri Bordier. Paris, 1877-88. Vols. i-vi. O.   HG—H11 A—Gas.

HARTLEY, Robert Milham. 1796-1881. Memorial of R. M. H., edited by his son, I. S. Hartley, D.D. 549 pp., portrait and plate. (Extracts from his diary, and other writings included.) Utica, 1882. O.   HG—H25

HARTLEY, Rev. Isaac Smithson, D.D., Editor. See: HARTLEY, Robert Milham. Memorial. . . . Utica, 1882. O.   HG—H25

HENRY CLAY PAYNE. A life. [By William W. Wight.] 196 pp., 1 port. Milwaukee, 1907. Q.   HG—P346

HESTER, Rev. St. Clair, D.D. Lafayette, the Apostle of Liberty. Sermon preached in the Church of the Messiah . . . Brooklyn, N. Y., May 13, 1917. . . . Brooklyn, 1917. 6 leaves, 1 pl. O.   HG—Pamphlet
Illustrated cover.
Gift of the Author.

HISTOIRE des martyrs persécutez et mis à mort pour la vérité de l' Evâgile depuis le temps des Apostres insques à l'an 1597. . . . Avec deux indices . . . par Jean CRESPIN et Simon GOULART. 8 leaves, 1526 pp. Folio. no place, 1597. Vélin blanc ancien aux armes frappées en or sur les plats et au dos de la ville d'Amsterdam.   HG—C86
Gift of Herbert Dupuy.

——— Edition nouvelle. En 3 tomes. Q. Toulouse, 1885.   HG—C86.2
Gift of The French Société.

HISTOIRE des plus favoris anciens et modernes, recueillie par feu . . . P. d[u] P[uy]. Avec un journal de ce qui s'est passé à la mort du mareschal d'Ancre. Square O. Leide, 1659.   HG—D92
Gift of Herbert Dupuy.

HISTOIRE des souffrances du bienheureux martyr Louis de Marolles. 1883. par MAROLLES, de. fils.   HG—M34

HITCHCOCK, Roswell Dwight. Life and writings of Edward Robinson. . . . 100 pp. New York, 1863. D.   HG—R56
Gift of the Rev. Alfred V. Wittmeyer.

HOLMDEN, Annie Harwood, translator. See: BERSIER, Eugene. Coligny: the earlier life of the great Huguenot . . . 1886.

HUNTINGTON, Rev. William Reed, D.D. Address commemorative of Eugene Augustus Hoffman. 28 pp., 1 port. New York, 1903. Read before the N. Y. Historical Society, Dec. 2, 1902.   HG—Mem512
Gift of the Author.

IRVING, WASHINGTON. 1783-1859. Washington & his Country; being Irving's "Life of Washington" abridged by John Fiske. 618 pp., 15 maps. Boston, 1887. D. HG—W272
Gift of Mrs. Martha J. Lamb.

JACCARD, E. Trois homes de grand refuge: Reboulet, Corteiz, Sagnol. . . . 152 pp. O. Lausanne, 1900. HG—B83
Gift of The French Society.
No. 3 of volume "Etude Biographique."

JACKSON, REV. SAMUEL MACAULAY, & SCHAFF, REV. PHILIP. Editors. Encyclopedia of living divines. 1887. HG—Sch.1
Gift of Mrs. Martha J. Lamb.

JAL, A. Abraham Du Quesne et la marine de son temps. Tome 1-2. 2 tomes. Paris, 1873. Q. HG—J21
Gift of The French Society.

JAUCOURT, ARNAIL FRANÇOIS, MARQUIS DE. Discours . . . 17 juillet 1889 pour l'inauguration du monument de l'amiral Coligny, par . . . J. et par E. Bersier. 22 pp., 1 pl. D. Paris, 1889.
HG—C683
Gift of E. Bersier.

JENKS, WILLIAM. Eulogy . . . of Hon. James Bowdoin, with notices of his family; pronounced in Brunswick, Maine, at the request of the Trustees . . . of Bowdoin College. Sept. 2, 1812. 40 pp. Boston, 1812. HG—B67
Gift of Rev. A. G. Vermilye.

JOHNSTON, ELIZABETH BRYANT. Original portraits of Washington including statues, monuments and medals. . . . 22-257 pp., illus., 32 pl. Square folio. Boston, 1882. HG—W271
Gift of Mrs. Martha J. Lamb.

JUBILE DE M. AIMÉ-LOUIS HERMINJARD, docteur ès lettres et en théologie, profeseur honoraire de l'universite de Lausanne, editeur de la Correspondance des réformateurs dans les pays de langue française. 7 Novembre, 1896. 119 pp., 1 port. Square Q. [Lausanne, 1896?] HG—H55

LALLY-TOLLENDAL, TROPHIME GÉRARD, MARQUIS DE. 1751-1830. Mémoires concernant Marie Antoinette. See: WEBER, JOSEPH. 1755-. Mémoires de Weber, frère de lait Marie Antoinette, reine de France. HG—B27
Ascribed to Marquis Lally-Tollendal.

LALOT, J. A. Devant la statue de l'amiral Coligny. Ed. 3. 69 pp., 1 pl. D. Paris, [pref. 1890]. HG—C683
Gift of Charles M. DuPuy.

LANIER, J. F. D. Born 1800. Sketch of the life of J. F. D. Lanier. N. Y., 1871. 62 pp. portrait. O. *Cloth.* HG—L27
Gift of J. C. Pumpelly.
Printed for the use of his family only.

LAUNAY, Marguerite Jeanne Cordierde. 1684?-1750. See: STAAL, Marguerite Jeanne Cordier (de Launay).

LEKAIN, [Henri Louis Cain]. 1728-1778. Mémoires. (In: Barrière, J. F., Editor. Bibliothèque des mémoires relatifs à l'histoire de France. 1857. Vol. vi, pp. 105-142.)   HG—B27

Le LABOUREUR, J. Mémoires de Messire Michel de Castelnau, seigneur de Mauvissière . . . avec . . . l'histoire genealogique de la maison de Castelnau, et les genealogies de plusieurs maisons illustres alliées à celle de Castelnau. Nouvelle ed. Tome i-iii. Bruxelles, 1731. 3 vols. Folio.   HG—L53
Gift of Herbert Dupuy.

LELIEVRE, Matthieu. See CRESPIN, Jean. Histoire des martyrs . . . introduction par D. Benoit . . . [et notes par M. L.]. Édition nouvelle. Toulouse, 1885-1889. 3 tomes. Q.   HG—C86.2

LORRAINE, Charles IV, Duc de. 1604-75. Histoire de l'emprisonnement de Charles IV, Duc de Lorraine. By Nicolas Du Bois de Riacourt. Cologne, 1688. 132 pp. S. *Calf.*   HD—B38
Bound with *Beauvau, Henri, Marquis de, Memoires.*

LOST MS. of the Rev. Lewis Rou's "Critical remarks upon the letter to the craftsman on the game of chess" written in 1734 and dedicated to . . . William Cosby, Gov. of N. Y. Signed W. F., i.e., Willard Fiske. 18 pp. Florence, 1902.   HG—Pamphlet
Reprint: Notes & Queries, July 19, 1902. With additions.
Gift of Huguenot Society of London.

LOUVET [de COUVRAY, Jean Baptiste]. 1760-1797. Mémoires. (In: Barrière, J. F., Editor. Bibliothèque des mémoires relatifs à l'histoire de France. 1848. Vol. xii, pp. 209-404.) HG—B27
Sub-title: "QUELQUES NOTICES pour l'histoire et le recit de mes perils depuis le 31 mai."

McPIKE, Eugene F., Editor. Tales of our forefathers and Biographical annals of families allied to those of McPike, Guest and Dumont. . . . Square Q. 181 pp. Albany, N. Y., 1898.   HG—M17

MARMONTEL, [Jean François]. 1723-1799. Mémoires. (In: Barrière, J. F., Editor. Bibliothèque des mémoires relatifs à l'histoire de France. 1846. Vol. v.)   HG—B27

[MAROLLES, Louis de]. 1629-92. Histoire des souffrances du bienheureux martyr Louis de Marolles, réimprimée sur la seconde édition avec une préface et des notes par Jules Bonnet. Paris, 1883. 132 pp. D.   HG—M34

MAURY, Ann, Editor. See: FONTAINE, Rev. James. Memoirs of a Huguenot family. . . . 1853.   HG—F73

MESCHINET de RICHEMOND, [Louis Marie]. Don fait par
Louis XIII, pendant le siège de la Rochelle. 30 Octobre 1627.
Paris, 1901. 8 pp. O.   HG—S33
Reprint: Bull. Hist. et Philologique, 1900.
Gift of the Author.
In: Biographical & Historical Essays.

MOLE, François René. 1734-1802. Mémoires. (In: Barrière,
J. F., Editor. Bibliothèque des mémoires relatifs à l'histoire de
France. 1857. Vol. VI, pp. 237-277.)   HG—B27

MONTPENSIER, [Antoine Philippe d'Orleans,] duc de. 1775-
1807. Mémoires sur son arrestation et sa captivité. (In: Barrière,
J. F., Editor. Bibliothèque des mémoires relatifs à l'histoire de
France. 1847. Vol. IX, pp. 241-370.)   HG—B27

MORRIS, Anne Cary, Editor. See: MORRIS, Gouverneur.
Diary and Letters. 2 vols. New York, 1888. O.

MORRIS, Gouverneur. 1752-1816. Diary and letters, edited by
Anne Cary Morris. 2 vols., 2 port. New York, 1888. O.   HG—M83
Gift of Mrs. Martha J. Lamb.

NEGRE, Léopold. Vie et ministère de Claude Brousson, 1647-1698.
. . . 230 pp. Paris, 1878. O.   HG—B83
Gift of The French Société.

NOTES & QUERIES: a Medium of intercommunication for literary
men. . . . No. 238 (9th Ser.), Sat., July 19, 1902, containing arti-
cle: "The 'craftsman' on chess: L. Rou." Signed W. F., i.e.,
Willard FISKE.   HG—Pamphlet
See entry under Author for reprint with additions and comments.
See also: Reverend Louis Rou.

ORLEANS, Elizabeth Charlotte, Duchesse d'Orleans, 1652-
1722. See: ELIZABETH Charlotte, Duchesse d'Orleans,
1652-1722.

PALISSY, the Huguenot potter. A true tale. 204 pp., 18 pl. Philadelphia, cop. 1864. S.   HG—P16
Gift of Josiah Collins Pumpelly.

PERRY, Amos. Memorial of Zachariah Allen, 1795-1882. 108 pp.,
port. Cambridge, 1883. O.   HG—Al 5
Gift of the Rhode Island Historical Society.

PEYRAT, Napol. Histoire des pasteurs du désert: depuis la Révocation de l'Edit de Nantes: jusqua la Revolution française. 1685-
1789. 2 vols. Paris, 1842. O.   HG—P45
Gift of The French Société.

PICHEREL-DARDIER, Mme. A. See: RABAUT, Paul. Lettres
a Antoine Court, 1739-1755.

POITOU: familles du. See: BEAUCHET-FILLEAU, Henri & Paul. Dictionnaire historique et genealogique. . . . 2nd ed. T. I-IV. Poitiers, 1891-1901.   HG—B38
Pub. en fasc.

POPE, Joseph. Jacques Cartier; his life and voyages. 168 pp., 1 pl. Ottawa, 1889. D.   HG—C24
Gift of Mrs. Martha J. Lamb.

PRETENDUE (La) trahison de Coligny. [By N. Weiss.] 11 pp. 1900.   HG—S33
Reprint: Bull. Soc. Hist. Prot. François.
In: Biographical & Historical Essays.
Gift of the Author.

PREVILLE, Pierre Louis Dubus-. See: DUBUS-PREVILLE, Pierre Louis.

PUAUX, Frank. Le Baron Fernand de Schickler. Discours prononce à la Assemblée Générale de la Société de l'Histoire de protestantisme français, le 28 avril, 1910. 18 pp. Paris, 1910. O.   HG—S33
Gift of the Author with autograph.
No. 1 of volume Biographical & Historical Essays.

PUTNAM, Ruth. William the silent, prince of Orange, the moderate man of the XVIth century. The story of his life. 2 vols. 2nd ed. pl., tables. New York, 1898. O.   HG—P98

QUELQUES femmes de la réforme, recueil biographique. Seconde édition. Lausanne, 1865. 12mo.   HG—Qu3

RABAUT, Paul. Lettres à Antoine Court (1739-1755). Dix-sept ans de la vie d'un apôtre du désert, avec notes, portrait et autographe par A. Picheral-Dardier, et une préface par Ch. Dardier. Paris [1884]. 2 vols. portrait, fac-simile. O.   HG—R11
Gift of Dr. Abram Du Bois.

RAHLENBECK, Charles. Expositions (Les) Belges a la cour d' Elizabeth. 1558-1603. (Extrait de la Revue de Belgique.) 16 pp. Bruxelles, 1880. O.   HG—S33
Gift of E. Belleroche.
Biographical & Historical Essays.

RAMSEY, David. Memoirs of the life of Martha Laurens Ramsay, with an appendix containing extracts from her diary, letters and other private papers. Fourth edition. Boston, 1814. 219 pp.
Gift of the Rev. Alfred V. Wittmeyer.   HG—R14

READ, Charles, & WADDINGTON, Francis. Mémoires inédits de Dumont de Bostaquet, gentilhomme Normand. Sur les temps qui ont précédé et suivi la Révocation de l'Edit de Nantes, sur le refuge et les expéditions de Guillaume III. en Angleterre et en Irlande. Et précédés d'une introduction historique. XLVI, 376 pp. Paris, 1864. O.   HG—R22

REUSS, RODOLPHE. Pierre Brully: ancient Dominicain de Metz, ministre de l'Eglise française de Strasbourg, 1539-1545.   HG—B83
No. 1 in P. V. "Etude Biographique."
Gift of The French Société.

REVEREND LOUIS ROU, Pastor, French Protestant Church, N. Y.
City, and the Missing MS., of his tract . . . (1734) entitled: Critical remarks on the game of chess, occasioned by his paper of . . .
15th Sept., 1733, and dated from Slaughter's Coffee-house, Sept.
21. Florence, (Italy), 1902. 14 pp. D.   HG—Pamphlet
Gift of The Huguenot Society of London.

RIOUFFE, HONORÉ, BARON 1764-1813. Mémoires d'un détenu, pour servir à l'histoire de la tyrannie de Robespierre. (In: Barrière, J. F.,
Editor. Bibliothèque des mémoires relatifs à l'histoire de France.
1847. Vol. IX, pp. 371-464.)   HG—B27—Vol. IX

RODOCANACHI, E. Une protectrice de la Réforme en Italie et en
France. Rénee de France, duchesse de Ferrare. 573 pp., 1 port.
Paris, 1896. O.   HG—R29
Gift of The French Société.

ROE, FRANCIS ASBURY, U. S. N. An American sea Captain of Colonial times. A paper read before Soc. Colonial Wars, D. C., March
12, 1900. 11 pp. O. (No. 2, Hist. Papers, Soc. Col. Wars,
D. C., 1900.)   HG—Mem512
Gift of the Author.

ROLAND [DE LA PLATIERE, MME. MANON JEANNE (PHILIPON)]. 1754-1793. Mémoires particuliers suivis des notices historiques sur la revolution. . . . (In: Barrière, J. F., Editor. Bibliothèque des mémoires relatifs à l'histoire de France. 1847. Vol.
VIII.)   HG—B27

ROSER, FRANCIS, M. Memorial of Adrian Oliver Iselin. New
York, 1885. 34 pp. O.   HG—Mem51

ROU, JEAN. 1638-1711. Mémoires inédits et opuscules . . . pub.
pour la Société de l'hist. du Protestantisme Français . . . par F.
Waddington. 2 vols., tables. Paris, 1857. O.   HG—R75

SAINT-SIMON, [LOUIS DE ROUVROI,] DUC DE. 1695-1755. Extraits des mémoire de Saint-Simon en ce qui touche le régence. (In:
Barrière, J. F., editor. Bibliothèque des mémoires relatifs à l'histoire de France. 1853. Vol. I, pp. 357-453.)   HG—B27

SCHAFF, D.D., LL.D., REV. PHILIP, and REV. SAMUEL MACAULAY
JACKSON, M.A., editors. Encyclopedia of living divines and Christian workers of all denominations in Europe and America. N. Y.,
1887. 271 pp. O.   HG—Sch1
Gift of Mrs. Martha J. Lamb.

SIMMS, WILLIAM GILMORE. Life of Francis Marion.   HG—M33

SMITH, HENRY B. Remarks on the announcement of the death of
Dr. Robinson. (In Hitchcock, R. D. Life of Edward Robinson.)
1863. pp. 3-16.   HG—R56

SMITH, Rev. Samuel Francis. Discourse in Memory of William Hague. Boston, 1889. 67 pp., 1 port. O. HG—H12

SOCIETY of Colonial Wars, D. C. Memorial papers, Nos. 2-4. 1902-'03. (In: P. V. "Memorial Addresses and Sketches. Nos. 9 & 10.) HG—Mem512

SPARKS, Jared. Life of George Washington. 562 pp., pl. O. Title page wanting. HG—W273
Gift of Mrs. Martha J. Lamb.

STAAL, [Marguerite Jeanne Cordier] (de Launay), baronne de. 1684?-1750. Mémoires. (In: Barrière, J. F., Editor. Bibliothèque des mémoires relatifs à l'histoire de France. 1853. pp. 6-24.) HG—B27

SWIFT, Joseph Gardner. Memoirs of Gen. Joseph Gardner Swift, first graduate of the U. S. Military Academy, West Point . . . with a genealogy of the family of Thomas Swift . . . 1634, by H. Ellery. 292, 58, 21 pp., illus., port., 1 pl. Worcester, Mass., 1890. Q. Privately printed. HG—Sw5
Gift of Mrs. Martha J. Lamb.

TALES of our forefathers, and Biographical annals of families allied to those of McPike, Guest & Dumont. . . . Edited by Eugene F. McPike. 181 pp. Albany, N. Y., 1898. Square Q. HG—M17

TOLLENDAL, Trophime Gérard, marquis de Lally. See: LALLY-TOLLENDAL, Trophime Gérard, marquis de.

TOLLIN, Henri. Johann Duraeus. Magdeburg, 1898. 2 vols. in 1. pp. 227-285, 26-81. No title page. HG—D947
Gift of the Author.

TREE PLANTING ASSOC., & The Washington Square Assoc., N. Y. City. In memoriam Cornelius Berrien Mitchell. Minute and Resolution. . . . 5 leaves. S. New York, 1902. HG—Mem512
No. 1 of volume "Memorial."
Gift of Mrs. James M. Lawton.

VAN DER KEMP, Francis Adrian. 1752-1829. An autobiography, together with extracts from his correspondence. Edited, with an historical sketch by H. L. Fairchild. xii, 230 pp., 3 fac-sim., 8 port. New York, 1903. O. HG—V28
Gift of Mrs. James M. Lawton.

VAN NEST, Rev. Abraham Rynier. Memoir of Rev. George W. Bethune. vi, 446 pp., 3 port., 1 pl. D. HG—B46

VAN RENSSELAER, Rev. Maunsell. Annals of the Van Rensselaers in the United States, especially as they relate to the family of Killian K. Van Rensselaer. 241 pp., port., fac-sim. Albany, N. Y., 1888. O. HG—V35
Gift of Mrs. Martha J. Lamb.

[VAN RENSSELAER, Mrs. Sarah.] Ancestral sketches and records of olden times. . . . 375 pp. Square Q. New York, 1882. HG—V351

VERMILYE, Ashbel Green, D.D. Memorial sketch of the Hon. John Jay, first President of The Huguenot Society of America. Delivered before the Society . . . January 29, 1895. 15 pp., 1 port. New York, 1895. HG—Mem512

VIE de Jean Frédéric Oberlin. Pasteur au Ban de la Roche. Toulouse, 1854. 223 pp. S. HG—Ob2

VIE de Pierre Du Bosc. Enrichie de lettres, harangues, dissertations et autres pieces importantes. Rotterdam, 1694. 610 pp. O. HG—D85
Bound in vellum.

VINCENT, Rev. John Hey, D.D. Centennial souvenir of John Himrod Vincent, born in Milton, Pa., April 20, 1798. no place, 1898. D. HG—Mem512
One of very few copies printed.

VOYER, Rene Louis de. See: ARGENSON, Rene Louis de Voyer, marquis d'.

VREELAND, Helen Kearny, Editor. See: AUSTIN, M. S. Philip Freneau, the poet of the Revolution: A history of his life and times. 1901. HG—F88A

WACE, The Very Rev. Henry, D.D. John Calvin. 10 pp. O. London, 1909. HG—Mem512
Reprinted, after revision by the Author, from The Churchman, for July, 1909.

WADDINGTON, Francis. See: READ, Charles, & WADDINGTON, F. Memoires inedits de Dumont de Bostaquet, gentilhomme Normand. . . . xlvi, 376 pp. O. Paris, 1864. HG—R22

——— See: ROU, Jean. Mémoires inédits et opuscules. 1857. HG—R75

WAGER, Daniel E. Col. Marinus Willett, the hero of Mohawk Valley; an Address before The Oneida Historical Society. Utica, N. Y., 1891. 50 pp. O. HG—Mis68

WALTER, James. Memorials of Washington and of Mary, his mother, and Martha, his wife, from letters and papers of Robert Cary and James Sharples. . . . 362 pp., illus., port. New York, 1887. Q. HG—W27
Gift of Mrs. Martha J. Lamb.

WEAVER, Ethan Allen. William Herman Wilhelm. 9 pp., 1 port. Washington, D. C., 1902. O. (Soc. Col. Wars, D. C., Mem. Papers. No. 3.) HG—Mem512

WEBER, Joseph. Mémoires de Weber, frère de lait de Marie Antoinette, reine de France. (In: Barrière, J. F., Editor. Bibliothèque des mémoires relatifs à l'histoire de France. 1847. Vol. VII.) HG—B27
Ascribed also to Marquis Lally-Tollendal.

[WEISS, Nathaniel]. Prétendue trahison de Coligny. Paris(?), 1900. 11 pp. O. HG—S33
Reprint: Bull. Soc. Hist. Prot. Fr.
Autograph gift of the Author.
Biographical & Historical Essays.

WEISSE, Mrs. John A., Translator. See: DUCHESNE, André. History of the Bethune family. 1884. HG—B67

[WIGHT, William W.]. Henry Clay Payne. A life. 196 pp., 1 port. Milwaukee, 1907. Q. HG—P346
Gift of Mrs. Henry C. Paine.

WILLIAM the Silent, Prince of Orange. The story of his life. By Ruth Putnam. New York, 1898. 2 vols. 2nd ed. O. HG—P98

WILSON, Rev. William T. The death of President Lincoln. A sermon preached in St. Peter's Church, Albany, 1865. 25 pp. Albany, 1865. O. HG—Mem.512

WINCHESTER, Rev. Elhanan, Translator. See: DeBENNEVILLE, George. Some remarkable passages in the life of Dr. George de Benneville. 1890. HG—D35

WINTHROP, Robert Charles. Life and services of James Bowdoin. Second edition, enlarged. Boston, 1876. 50 pp. O. HG—B67
Privately printed.
Presented by the author.

BIOGRAPHY—INDIVIDUAL

ADAMS, Rev. William. 1807-1880. See: PARKHURST, Rev. C. H. Madison Square Presbyterian Church to its first Pastor . . . a tribute . . . Nov. 7, 1880. 23 pp. New York, 1880.   HE—Z1

ALLEN, WILLIAM. 1710?-'80. See: DeLANCEY, Edward F. William Allen, Chief Justice of Pennsylvania, a Biographical sketch prepared for the Centennial Celebration of the "Resolutions respecting Independency," held at . . . Philadelphia, July 1, 1876. 12 pp. Philadelphia, 1877.   HE—Z9

ALLEN, Zachariah. 1795-1882. Memorial of Zachariah Allen. By Amos Perry. Cambridge [Mass.], 1883. 108 pp. portrait, fac-simile. O.   HG—Al5

AMYRAUT, Moise. 1596-1664.. VINET, A. Histoire de la prédication parmi les réformés de France. . . . Paris, 1860. O.   HA—V783

ANDERSON, Robert, Gen. U. S. A. 1805-1871. See: PELLE-TREAU, William S. Historic homes . . . genealogical and family history of New York. 4 vols. N. Y., 1907. Q.   HH—P36

ANDROS, Sir Edmund. See: FERGUSON, Henry. Sir Edmund Andros. Address before the Westchester County Historical Society, October 28, 1892.   HG—Mis68

ARTUS III. duc de Bretagne. See: GRUEL, G. Mémoires . . . comte de Richemont, et Connetable de France. Paris, 1785. D. (Coll. Univ. Memories Hist. France.) pp. 223-442.   HD—C696

BACOT, Thomas Sinclair. 1860-1917. Obituary from the Utica Daily, 1917. Inserted on first leaf.   HG—Mem.512

BAIRD, Rev. Charles Washington. 1828-87. [Baird, Mrs. Margaret E. Strang], editor. Memorials of Rev. Charles Washington Baird, with a few sermons and poems. N. Y., 1888. 235 pp. portrait, plate. O.   HG—B16

BARBAULD, Mrs. Anna Laetitia (Aikin). 1743-1825. Memoir of Mrs. Anna Laetitia Barbauld, with many of her letters. By Grace Atkinson Ellis. Boston, 1874. 2 vols.   HG—B23

BARNES, Mrs. Cornelia Chevalier. 1830-1901. A biographical sketch of a beautiful life. 2 pp. Utica Daily Press, 1901.   HG—Mem.512

BAYARD, John. 1738-1807. See: WILSON, Gen. James Grant. Memorial of Col. John Bayard. Read before the New Jersey Historical Society . . . May 16, 1878. pp. 141-160.   HE—Z7

BEALE, CHARLES FREDERICK TIFFANY. 1857-1901. See: BENJA-
MIN, MARCUS. Charles Frederick Tiffany Beale. 13 pp., 1 portrait. (Soc. Col. Wars, D. C., Mem. Papers, No. 2.)   HG—Mem.512

BEAUVAU, HENRI, MARQUIS DE. d. 1684. Mémoires pour servir
a l'histoire de Charles IV. 456 pp. S. Cologne, 1690.   HD—B38

BECK, THEODORE ROMEYN, M.D. 1791-1855. See: HAMILTON,
F. H., M.D. Eulogy on life and character of Theodric Romeyn
Beck, delivered before the Medical Society of the State of New
York. 90 pp., 1 port. Albany, 1856.   HE—Z1

BEEKMAN, JAMES WILLIAM. 1815-1877. See: DeLANCEY,
EDWARD FLOYD. Memoir . . . prepared at the request of the St.
Nicholas Society, New York, 1877.   HG—Mem.51

——— Same. No. 5 of a Volume of Pamphlets.   HE—Z9

BOERUM, SIMON. 1724-1775. See: BURDGE, FRANKLIN. Simon
Boerum, of Brooklyn, New York. Written for the Committee on
the Restoration of Independence Hall, Philadelphia. 28 pp. 1876.
No title page.   HE—Z4

BOOKSTAVER, THE HON. HENRY W., LL.D. 1834-1907. See:
DURYEE, REV. J. R., and others. Memoirs, Funeral address,
memorial tributes, Resolutions. 30 pp., portrait inserted. New
York, 1907. O.   HG—Mem.512

BOTHWELL, JAMES HEPBURN, IV. EARL OF. 1536?-1577? See:
DE PEYSTER, JOHN WATTS. In his Works on Mary Stuart and
Bothwell.   HF—D419

BOWDOIN, JAMES. 1752-1811. See: JENKS, WILLIAM. Eulogy
of Hon. James Bowdoin, with notices of his family, pronounced in
Brunswick [Me.] at the request of the trustees of Bowdoin College, Sept. 2, 1812. Boston, 1812. 40 pp. Q.   HG—B67

BOWDOIN, JAMES. 1726-90. See: WINTHROP, ROBERT
CHARLES. Life and services of James Bowdoin. Second edition,
enlarged. Boston, 1876. 50 pp.   HG—B67

BRES, GUY DE. d. 1567. See: OLLIER, DANIEL. Guy de Bres,
étude histoire sur la réforme au pays Wallon (1522-1567). 200
pp. O. Paris, 1883.   HB—O14

BROUSSON, CLAUDE. See NEGRE, Léopold. Vie et ministère de
Claude Brousson. . . . D'après des documents. . . . XII, 13-230 pp. O.
Paris, 1878.   HG—B83

BRUEN, REV. MATTHIAS. 1793-1829. Memoirs of the life and character of the Rev. Matthias Bruen, late pastor of the presbyterian
church in Bleecker St., N. Y. By Mrs. Mary G. Lundy Duncan.
N. Y., 1831. 358 pp. portrait. Q.   HG—B83

BRULLY, Pierre. See: REUSS, Rodolphe. Pierre Brully: ancien dominicain de Metz, ministre de l'Eglise française de Strasbourg, 1539-1545. Etude biographique. 152 pp., 2 leaves. O. Strasbourg, 1878. HG—B83

BRYANT, William Cullen. 1794-1878. See: BELLOWS, Rev. H. W. Oration at the Funeral of William Cullen Bryant, June 14, 1878. 11 pp. No title-page. HE—Z7

BUDE, Guillaume. See: DE BUDE, Eugène. Vie de Guillaume Budé, fondateur du College de France. (1467-1540.) 300 pp., 1 port. D. Paris, 1884. HG—B86

CALVIN, John. 1509-1515. See: WACE, Very Rev. Henry, D.D. John Calvin. 10 pp. O. London, 1909. Reprint (after revision by the Author) of "The Churchman," July, 1909. HG—Mem.512

CARTIER, Jacques. 1494-1554. See: POPE, Joseph. Jacques Cartier; his life and voyages. 168 pp., 1 pl. D. Ottawa, 1889. HG—C24

CATHARINE of Aragon. 1486-1536. See: FROUDE, J. A. Divorce of Catherine of Aragon. A supplementary volume to [Froude's] "History of England." 476 pp. O. N. Y., 1891. HF—F93

CAZENOVE, Theophilus. 1740-1811. See: LINCKLAEN, John. Travels . . . 1791 and 1792 in Pennsylvania; New York; and Vermont. Journals of J. L. . . . With a biographical sketch . . . by H. L. Fairchild. New York, 1897. O. HI—L63

CHAILLE, Pierre. See: MESCHINET de RICHEMOND, Louis Marie. Medecin le Pierre Chaillé de la Tremblade et sa famille. Paris, 1895. O. HH—C434
MS. genealogies of the Chaillé & Chevalier families inserted. Bound with: WEISS, N. Independance des Etats d'Amerique et Pierre Chaillé.

CHASTELAIN, Jean. See: CUVIER, Othon. Trois martyrs de la Reforme brutes en 1525 a Vic, Metz et Nancy. VIII, 116 pp. Paris, 1889. O. HG—R11.1
Bound with BORREL, A. Biographique P. Rabaut.

CHERIGNY, Claude. See: PORCHER, Mrs. Claude Cherigny.

CLAIRON, Claire Joseph Hippolyte Legris de Latude. 1723-1803. Mémoires. (In: Barrière, J. F., Editor. Bibliothèque des memoires relatifs à l'histoire de France. 1857. Vol. vi, pp. 17-104.) HG—B27

CLINTON, George. 1739-1812. See: STONE, William L. George Clinton. pp. 329-1844. HE—Z6
From Magazine of American History, Vol. iii, No. 6, 1879.

CLAUDE, JEAN. 1619-1667. CYR, NARCISSE. Biographical sketch: Claude and his masterpiece. In: CLAUDE, JEAN. Cruel persecutions of the Protestants. . . . Boston, 1893. pp. V-XIV. T.　　　　　　　　　　　　　　　　　　　　　　　　HA—C572

―――― See: VINET, A. Histoire de la predication parmi les reformes de France. . . . Paris, 1860. O.　　　　　　HA—V783

COLIGNY, GASPARD DE. Admiral of France. 1517-1572. See: BERSIER, EUGENE. Coligny; the earlier life of the great Huguenot. Translated by A. H. Holmden. XXXVI, 351 pp. London, 1884. O.　　　　　　　　　　　　　　　HG—C68—Bersier

―――― See: BESANT, WALTER. Gaspard de Coligny, Marquis de Chattillon, Admiral of France. . . . 228 pp., 1 port. New York, 1879. Tt. (Harper's Half-Moon Series.)　　HG—C68—Besant

―――― See: BESANT, WALTER. Gaspard de Coligny. . . . "232 pp.," 1 port. New York, 1884. D. (New Plutarch Series.) Paging in this volume imperfect.　　HG—C68—Besant—Copy 2

―――― See: DELABORDE, [LOUIS] J., COMTE DE. Gaspard de Coligny. 3 vols. Paris, 1879-1882. O.　　HG—C68—Delaborde

―――― See: JAUCOURT, ARNAIL-FRANÇOIS. Marquis de. Discours . . . 17 juillet 1889 pour l'inauguration du monument de l'amiral Coligny, par . . . J. et E. Bersier. 22 pp., 1 pl. Paris, 1869. D.　　　　　　　　　　　　　　　　　HG—C68—Lalot Bound with: LALOT, J. A. Devant la statue . . . Coligny.

―――― See: LALOT, J. A. Devant la statue de l'Amiral Coligny. 4 p.l., 69 pp., 1 leaf, 1 plate. Paris, pref. 1890. D.　HG—C68—Lalot

COLIGNY, ODET DE. Cardinal de Chatillon. 1517-1568. See: BROWNING, ARTHUR GIRAUD. Odet de Coligny, Cardinal de Chattillon. A Paper read at Canterbury, on the . . . visit of the Directors of the French Hospital, Victoria Park, London, July 26, 1884. Canterbury, 1884. 20 pp. D.
　　　　　　　　　　　　　HG—C68—Delaborde—Vol. III

CORTEIZ, PIERRE. 1684-1767. See: JACCARD, E. Trois hommes du grand refuge; Reboulet, Corteiz, Sagnol. 152 pp. Lausanne, 1900.　　　　　　　　　　　　　　　　　　HG—B83

―――― See also, his Mémoires . . . Edited by BAUM, JEAN GUILLAUME. Geneve, 1871.　　　　　　　　　　　HA—C812

CRAEY, METJE. 1650?-17?. See: WOODRUFF, FRANCIS E. The Coursen's of Sussex County, New Jersey. . . . New York, 1909. O.　　　　　　　　　　　　　　　　　　　　H—C86

CRAWFORD, THOMAS. 1814-1857. See: OSGOOD, REV. SAMUEL. Thomas Crawford and Art in America; Address before the New York Historical Society . . . April 6, 1875. 40 pp. N. Y., 1875.　　　　　　　　　　　　　　　　　　　HG—Z2

DAILLE, Jean. 1594-1670. See: VINET, A. Histoire de la predication parmi les reformes de France. . . . Paris, 1860. O. HA—V783

DE BENNEVILLE, George. 1703-1793. Some remarkable passages in the life of Dr. de Benneville . . . with an account of his persecution in France. Translated from the French of his own MS., by Rev. E. Winchester. Germantown, 1890. 55 pp. D. HG—D351

DE BOSTAQUET, Dumont. See: READ, Charles, et WADDINGTON, F. Mémoires inedits de Dumont de Bostaquet, gentilhomme Normand. . . . xlvi, 376 pp. Paris, 1864. O. HG—R22

DE COSTA, The Rev. Benjamin Franklin, D.D. See: Memorial brochures of members of his family. HG—D35 & D351 & D35.1.1 Collected and bound together according to the numbers given.

———— In Memoriam: Elisabeth De Costa. 8 pp. New York, 1880. S. Privately printed.

———— Harriett Cooper Spencer De Costa. 18 pp., portrait and 1 plate. Square D. D35.1.1 One of 100 copies, printed privately.

———— Mary Rebecca De Costa. New York, 1896. 12 pp. S. Privately printed.

———— Mary Rebecca Theresa De Costa. Sister Sainte Claire, Order of St. Ursula. Charlestown, 1876. 25 pp. O. One of 100 copies, no copy sold.

———— William Hickling De Costa. Charlestown, 1878. 8 pp., and a portrait. S. Privately printed.

———— Souvenir: St. Michael and All Angels. September 29th, 1858-1894. New York, 1894. Containing—a poem, 2 illustrations, and a portrait. S. D35.1.1

DE FOREST, Jesse. 1576?-1624. See: DE FOREST, Emily Johnston. A Walloon family in America. . . . Together with . . . the Journal of Jesse de Forest and his colonists, 1623-'25. 2 vols. Boston, 1914. O. H—D315

DE FOREST, Lockwood. 1775-1848. See: DE FOREST, Emily Johnston. A Walloon family in America; L. de Forest and his forebears, 1500-1848. . . . Boston, 1914. 2 vols. O. HG—D315

DE PEYSTER, Abraham. July 8, 1657-August 7, 1728. See: Colonel, de Heer Abraham de Peyster, Mayor of New York City, Commander of City Troops, Chief-Justice . . . Supreme Court. . . . 5 pp., 1 port., 2 colored plates. New York, 1895. O. HG—D419 Reprint: Memorial History of New York. (de Peyster Volume.)

DE PEYSTER, JOHN WATTS. 1821-19. See: ALLABEN, FRANK.
General John Watts de Peyster; author, soldier, historian, military
biographer, and critic. 36 pp., 1 port., 2 pl. New York, 1894.
O.   HG—D419
Reprint, National Magazine, October, 1894.

———— See: STONE, WILLIAM L. Biographical sketch. . . . New
York, 1894. 16 pp. Square Q.   HG—D419W

DE SAUSSURE, ANTOINE. See: FRENCH Protestant Church,
Charleston, S. C. Mural Tablets. . . . Charleston, 1898. Page
10.   HB—F875

———— HENRI. Obit. 1761. See: FRENCH Protestant Church,
Charleston, S. C. Mural Tablets. Charleston, 1898. Page
10.   HB—F875

DE SCHICKLER, FERNAND. See: PUAUX, FRANK. Le Baron
Fernand de Schickler. Discours prononcé a l'Assemblée Générale de
la Soc. de l'Hist. Prot. Fran. . . . Paris, 1910. O.   HG—S33

DE VENOURS, MARQUIS. See: GUYOT, HENRI DANIEL. Marquis
de Venours, protecteur des victimes de l'intolérance de Louis XIV.
Gronique, 1906. O.   HG—S33

DICKERSON, MAHLON. 1770-1858. See: PUMPELLY, JOSIAH
COLLINS. Mahlon Dickerson, industrial pioneer and old time patriot. Paterson, N. J., 1892. O.   HB—P87

DIODATI, JEAN. See: DE BUDE, EUGÈNE. Vie de Jean Diodati,
theologien, Génevois, 1576-1649. 302 pp. D. Lausanne,
1869.   HG—D6

DRELINCOURT, REV. CHARLES. 1595-1669. The Christian's con-
solation . . . with prayers and meditations . . . To which is prefixed the life of the author, [Rev. C. D.]. Philadelphia, 1834. D.
                                                       HM—D81

DUANE, WILLIAM JOHN. 1780-1865. See: Biographical memoir of
W. J. D. 28 pp. Philadelphia, 1868.   HE—Z7

DU BOSC, PIERRE. 1623-92. La vie de Pierre Du Bosc, enrichie de
lettres, harangues, dissertations et autres pieces importantes. Rotterdam, 1694. 610 pp. Vellum.   HG—D85

———— See: VINET, A. Histoire de la prédiction parmi les reformes
de France. Paris, 1860. O.   HA—V783

DU MOULIN, PIERRE. 1568-1658. See: VINET, A. A Histoire
de la predication parmi les reformes de France. Paris, 1860.
O.   HA—V783

DU PUY, BARTHOLOMEW. See: HARPER, LILLIAN DUPUY VANC.
Colonial men and times. The Huguenots. Genealogy, with sketches
of allied families. Philadelphia, 1916. Q.   HH—H294

Du QUESNE, Abraham. See: JAL, A. Abraham Du Quesne et la marine de son temps. Tomes 1-2. Paris, 1873. 2 vols. Q.   HG—J21

DURAEUS, Johann. 1595?-1616. See: TOLLIN, Henri. Johann Duraeus. Magdeburg, 1898? O.   HG—D947

DURAND, Marie. 17?-17?. See: BENOIT, Daniel. Marie Durand, prisonniere a la Tour de Constance (1730-1736): Sa famille et ses compagnes de captivite. 320 pp., pl., fac-sim., fld. Toulouse, 1884. D.   HG—D93

DURRELL, Edward Henry. 1810-87. Hon. Edward Henry Durrell. 1888. Portrait. O.   HB—H12
From the *Granite Monthly*, 1888, vol. II.

ESPRINCHARD, Jacques. See: MESCHINET de RICHEMOND, L. M. Relations inedites et autographes des voyages, dans l'Europe centrale de Jean Godeffroy, d'Orleans (de 1568 à 1571) & de J. E. (de 1593 a 1598). Paris, 1882.   HO—R39
Reprint: Assoc. Fr. Adv. Sci., 1882.

FAUCONEER, John. 17?-178?. See: John Falconer, Patriot, Supervisor & Public Servant. In: Westchester Co., Magazine, Vol. III, No. 4, page 15.   HE—N533

FAUCONNIER, Pierre. 1560-16?. See: HELFENSTEIN, Abraham E. Pierre Fauconnier and his descendants . . . with some account of the allied Valleaux. Philadelphia, 1911.   HH—F25

FIELD, David Dudley. 1805-1894. See: PIERCE, Frederick C. Field genealogy of all the Field family in America, . . . prior to 1700. . . . All . . . of England, whose ancestor, Hurbutus De la Field, was from Alsace-Lorraine. 2 vols. Chicago, 1901.   HH—F45

FIELD, Cyrus West. 1819-1891. See: PIERCE, Frederick C. Field genealogy. . . . 2 vols. Chicago, 1891.   HH—F45

FLORENT, Sire de'Illiers. See: GODFROY, Denys. Mémoires de Florent . . . capitaine au service de Charles VII, XVe siècle. In: Coll. Univ. Memoires Hist. France, Paris, 1785. pp. 443-467.   HD—C696

FONTAINE, Rev. James. Born 1658. Memoirs of a Huguenot family, translated and compiled . . . by Ann MAURY. N. Y., 1853. 512 pp. portraits. D.   HG—F73

FORMAN, Samuel S., Major. 1765-1862. See: DRAPER, L. C. Memoir. . . . In: FORMAN, Samuel S. Narrative of a journey down the Ohio & Mississippi. 1888. pp. 5-18.   HI—F76

FREEMAN, Joel Francis. See: Obituary notices reprinted from local Newspapers in New Jersey. 1910.   HG—Mem512

FRENEAU, Philip [Morin]. 1752-1832. . See: AUSTIN, Mary
A. Philip Freneau the Poet of the Revolution. . . . Edited by H. K.
Vreeland. New York, 1901.   HG—F88A

—— See: NEW YORK GEN. & BIOG. RECORD. Biographical
Sketch: In Volume XVI.   HK—N49

—— In: FRENEAU, Philip [Morin]. Poems relating to the
American Revolution, with . . . memoir and notes by E. A.
DUYCKINCK. New York, 1865.   HG—F88

FRONTENAC, Louis de Buade, Comte de. 1620-1698. See:
PARKMAN, Francis. Count Frontenac & New France under
Louis XIV. Ed. 10. Boston, 1882. (In his: France & England in
North America. 1882. Vol. v.)   HE—P231

GACHES, Raymond. 1615-1668. See: VINET, A. Histoire de la
predication parmi les reformes de France. . . . Paris, 1860.   HA—V783

GAILLARD, Peter Charles. 1812-1866. See: French Protestant
Church, Charleston. . . . Mural tablets. Charleston, S. C., 1898.
page 10.   HB—F875

—— In memoriam William Ravenel & Peter Charles Gaillard. 16
pp. Charleston, 1889.   HG—Mem51

GODEFFROY, Jean, d'Orleans. See: MESCHINET de RICHE-
MOND, L. M. Relations inedits et autographes des voyages, dans
l'Europe centrale. . . . Paris, 1882.   HO—R39
Reprint: Assoc. Fr. Adv. Sci., 1882.

GOURDIN, Louis. Obit., 1716. See: FRENCH Protestant Church,
Charleston, S. C. Mural Tablets. Charleston, 1898.   HB—F875

GRINNELL, Moses H. 1803-1877. See: COWDIN, E. C. Tribute
the Chamber of Commerce of the State of New York, to his memory
December 6, 1877. An address.   HE—Z4

GRIGSBY, Hugh Blair. 1806-1881. See: BROCK, R. A. Biographical sketch of H. B. Grigsby. In: VIRGINIA Hist. Soc. Collections. New Series. Vol. IX. pref. pp. 5-27.   HG—V81

GRUNER, Louis. 1809-1883. See: EGLESTON, Thomas. Biographical notice of Louis Gruner, Inspector-general of Mines of
France. A paper read before American Institute of Mining Engineers
at Roanoke Meeting, June, 1883. 5 pp. 1884. O.   HH—Var4
Author's edition.

GUITON, Jean. 1585-. See: BLANCHON, Pierre. Jean Guiton
et le Siège la Rochelle. 65 pp., 1 port. inserted. La Rochelle, 1911.
Square D.   HG—G968

GYSBERT, "the Huguenot." 1535-16—?. See: Royal descent and
Colonial ancestry of Mrs. Harley Calvin Gage. 32 pp. O. N. P.,
cop. 1910.   HH—A54

HAGUE, William. 1808-1887. See: SMITH, Rev. Samuel Francis. Discourse in memory of William Hague. Boston, 1889. 66 pp., portrait. O.   HG—H12

HALE, Nathan. 1755-1776. See: HOWE, Henry. The sad . . . but ennobling history of Captain Nathan Hale, the hero-martyr of the American Revolution. . . . New Haven, Conn., 1881.   HE—Z2

HALLECK, Fitz-Greene. 1790-1867. See: Memorial . . . dedication of the monument erected to his memory at Guilford, Conn., and . . . the proceedings connected with the unvailing of the poet's statue in the Central Park, New York. N. Y., 1877.   HE—Z9

HAMELIN, Philibert. 15?-15?. See: PALISSY, the Huguenot potter. A true tale. Philadelphia, 1864.   HG—PL6

HARING, John. 1748?-1810?. See: BURDGE, Franklin. A notice of J. H., a patriotic Statesman of the Revolution. N. Y., 1878.
                                                        HE—Z4

HORRY, Elias. 1664-1736. See: French Protestant Church. . . . Mural tablets. Charleston, S. C., 1898. page 11.   HB—F875

HERMAN, Augustine. 1621?-1686. See: MALLERY, Rev. Charles P. Ancient families of Bohemia Manor; their homes & their graves. 1888. pp. 7-24.   HH—M253

HERMINJARD, Aime-Louis. See: JUBILE de M. Aime-Louis Herminjard. . . . 7 Novembre, 1896. Lausanne, 1896?.   HG—H55

HOFFMAN, Rev. Charles Frederick, D.D. 1830-1897. See: HOFFMAN, Very Rev. Eugene Augustus, D.D., LL.D. Genealogy of the Hoffman family, descendants of Martin Hoffman. . . . N. Y., 1899.   HH—H65

HOFFMAN, Very Rev. Eugene Augustus, D.D., LL.D. 1829-1902. In: GENEALOGY of the Hoffman Family. . . . N. Y., 1899.   HH—H65

——— See: HUNTINGTON, The Rev. William Reed, D.D. Address commemorative of Dr. Hoffman. Read before the N. Y. Historical Society, Dec. 2nd, 1902.   HG—Mem512

HOFFMAN, The Hon. John Thompson. 1828-1888. See: HOFFMAN, Very Rev. E. A., D.D. Genealogy of the Hoffman family. . . . New York, 1899.   HH—H65

HOFFMAN, Martin Hermanzen. 1625-1689. See: HOFFMAN, Very Rev. E. A., D.D., LL.D. Genealogy of the Hoffman Family. N. Y., 1899.   HH—H6

ISELIN, Adrian Oliver. 1873-1885. See: ROSER, F. M. Memorial. . . . New York, 1885.   HG—Mem51

JAY, The Hon. John. See: VERMILYE, Rev. Ashbel Green, D.D. Memorial sketch of the Hon. John Jay, First President of the Huguenot Society of America. Delivered before the Society . . . January 29th, 1895. 15 pp., 1 port. N. Y., 1895. HG—Mem512

JOAN of Arc, Maid of Orleans See: Jeanne d'Arc, la Pucelle d'Orléans.

JEANNE d'ARC, la Pucelle d'Orleans. See: GODEFROY, Denys. Memoires concernant la Purcelle d'Orleans XVᵉ siècle. (Coll. Univ. Mem. Hist. France. tome VIII.) HD—C.696

JOHNSON, Ellen Terry. Obit. Dec. 25, 1896. See: Her "House of Hope of the first Connecticut settlers." . . . Hartford, Conn., 1896. HE—A512

JOHNSON, Sir John. 1742-1830. See: de PEYSTER, John Watts. Sir John Johnson, the first American-born Baronet. Address before the New York Historical Society, January 6th, 1880. HE—Z3

KELLY, Alfred. 1789-1859. See: BATES, J. L. Alfred Kelly, his life and work. Columbus, Ohio, 1888. HG—K29

LaBAR, George. Born 1763. See: BURRELL, A. B. Reminiscences of . . . the centenarian of Monroe County, Pennsylvania and incidents in the early settlement of the Pennsylvania side of the River Valley. Philadelphia, 1870. HE—B94

LABAREE. See: LABORIE.

LABORIE, Dr. James. Biographical sketch by Mrs. Marie Graham Snitzler. (HUGUENOT Society of America. Publications. Vol. IV. pp. 8-11. 1915.) HK—H87

LAFAYETTE, de Marquis. See: HESTER, The Rev. St. Clair, D.D. Lafayette the Apostle of Liberty. . . . Brooklyn, N. Y., 1917. HG—Pamphlet

LANIER, J. F. D. Born 1800. Sketch of the life of J. F. D. Lanier. N. Y., 1871. 62 pp. portrait. O. HG—L27
Printed for the use of his family only.

LaSALLE, Robert Cavelier, sieur de. 1643?-1687. See: PARKMAN, Francis. LaSalle and the discovery of the great West. In his France and England in North America. 1882. Vol. III. HE—P233

LAWRENCE, William Beach. 1800-1881. Notice sur la vie et les œuvres. . . . Gand, 1876. HE—Z1

LeCLERC, Jean. See: CUVIER, Othon. Trois martyrs de la Reforme brules en 1525 a Vic, Metz et Nancy. Paris, 1889. HG—R11.1

LeCLERC, Pierre. 14?-1546. See: Bower, Herbert M. The fourteen of Meaux: An account of the earliest "Reformed Church" within France proper, organized by E. Mangin and Pierre LeClerc. . . . London, 1894. HA—B67

LeFAUCHER, Michel. 1585-1657. See: VINET, A. Histoire de la predication parmi les reformes de France. . . . Paris, 1860.
HA—V783

LeFEVRE, John. 1762-1837. See: COUTANT, Rev. L. J. John LeFevre. A biographical sketch. In: The New Rochelle Press Almanac. 1879-'84. pp. 37-43. HE—NR87S

LINCOLN, Abraham. See: WILSON, Rev. William T. The Death of President Lincoln. A Sermon preached in St. Peter's Church, Albany, N. Y., April 19, 1865. 25 pp. O. Albany, 1865. HG—Mem512

LORRAINE, Charles IV, Duc de. 1604-75. Histoire de l'emprisonnement de Charles IV, Duc de Lorraine. By Nicolas Du Bois de Riacourt. Cologne, 1688. 132 pp. S. HD—B38
Bound with *Beauvau, Henri, Marquis de, Memoires.*

LOUIS XIV, King of France, 1638-1715. See: MENESTRIER, C. F., Compiler. Histoire du roy Louis le Grand par les medailles, emblems . . . armoires and autres monumens publics. . . . Paris, 1691. HD—L888

MAKEMIE, Francis. Died 1708. Days of Makemie; or, The vine planted. 1680-1708. By Rev. L. P. Bowen. Philadelphia [1885]. 558 pp. map. D. HG—M29

MALTBIE, Jonathan. Brief sketch of J. M., who was in the Service of the United States during the Revolution; compiled from the Archives in the State Department. Washington, 1883. HJ—MSS.

MANGIN, Estienne. 14?-1546. See: BOWER, Herbert M. The fourteen of Meaux: An account of the earliest "Reformed Church" within France proper, organized by E. M., and Pierre LeClerc. . . . London, 1894. HA—B67

MARIE ANTOINETTE, Queen of France. 1755-1793. See: CAMPAN, Mme. J. L. Memoires sur la vie de Marie Antoinette. 488 pp., Paris, 1849.

——— See: WEBER, Joseph. Memoires de Weber, frere de lait de Marie Antoinette. Ascribed also to Marquis LALLY-TOLLENDAL. Both Memoires in: BARRIERE, J. F., Editor. Bibliotheque des Memoires relatifs a l'histoire de France. 1849. Vol. x.
HG—B27

MARION, Francis. 1732-95. Life of Francis Marion. By William Gilmore Simms. N. Y., 1856. 347 pp., illustrated. D. HG—M33

MAROLLES, Louis de. 1629-92. Histoire des souffrances du bienbeureux martyr Louis de Marolles, réimprimée sur la seconde édition avec une préface et des notes par Jules Bonnet. Paris, 1883. 132 pp. D. HG—M34

99

MAROT, Clément. 1495-1544. Clément Marot et le psautier huguenot; étude historique, littéraire, musicale et bibliographique, contenant les mélodies primitives des psaumes et des spécimens d'harmonie de Jannequin, Bourgeois, Louis, Jambe-de-fer, Sureau, Servin, Stobée, etc. By Emmanuel Orentin Douen. Paris, 1878-79. 2 vols., *half roan.* Q.   HG—M341
Gift of Dr. Abram Du Bois.

MARY, Queen of Scots. 1542-1587. See: DE PEYSTER, John Watts, Maj. Gen., U. S. A. In his Works on Mary Stuart, bound in de Peyster volume.   HF—D419

MASSE, Claude. 1650-1737. See: MESCHINET de RICHEMOND, L. M. Une famille d'ingenieurs geographes, Claude Masse, (1650-1737) sa vie et œuvres. Rochefort, 1882.   HO—R39
Reprint: Soc. de Geographie de Rochefort, Bulletin. Vol. III. 1882.

MAZYCK, Isaac. 1661-1735. See: FRENCH Protestant Church, Charleston, S. C., 1898. page 9. Mural Tablets. . . .   HB—F875

MAZYCK, Isaac, fils. 1700-1770. See: FRENCH Protestant Church, Charleston, S. C. Mural Tablets. . . . Page 9.   HB—F875

MAZYCK, Paul. 1744-1835. See: FRENCH Protestant Church, Charleston, S. C. Mural Tablets. . . . Page 9.   HB—F875

MERLE, Mathieu de, Capitaine. 1548-16?. See: DePONT-BRIANT, A. Guerres de religion Le Capitaine Merle, Baron de Lagorce, gentilhomme du Roy de Navarre et ses descendants, avec lettres et documents inedits. . . . Paris, 1886.   HG—D44

MESTREZAT, Jean. 1592-1627. See: Vinet, A. Histoire de la predication parmi les reformes de France. . . . Paris, 1860.   HA—V783

MITCHELL, Cornelius Berrien. 1852-1910. In Memoriam. . . . Minute and Resolution of the Tree Planting Association of New York City & the Washington Square Association. New York, 1910.   HG—Mem512

MONNET, Isaac, & MONNET, Pierre. See: MONNETTE, Orra Eugene, Compiler. Monnet genealogy . . . a noble Huguenot heritage. Somewhat of the first immigrants, Isaac and Pierre Monnet: . . . Los Angeles, Cal., 1911.   HH—M748

MORATA, Olympia Fulvia. 1526-55. Vie d'Olympia Morata, épisode de la renaissance et de la réforme en Italie. By Jules Bonnet. Seconde édition. Paris, 1851. 255 pp. O.   HG—M79

NEELY, The Right Rev. Henry Adams, D.D. Bishop of the Diocese of Maine. 1830-1899. Biographical sketch from "The Living Church," Chicago, Ill. 1899. Inserted in this Memorial Volume.   HG—Mem512

NORTH, Rev. Simeon. 1802-84. Memorial of Rev. Simeon North, fifth president of Hamilton college. Utica, N. Y., 1884. 111 pp. portrait. O.   HG—N81
Gift of Prof. North.

OBERLIN, JEAN FRÉDÉRIC. 1740-1826. Vie d'Oberlin, pasteur au Ban de la Roche. Toulouse, 1854. 223 pp. S. HG—Ob2

OPDYCK, GYSBERT. See: JOHNSON, ELLEN TERRY. The House of Hope of the first Connecticut settlers. . . . HE—A512
In: Volume "Americana."

PALEARIO, AONIO. 1500?-1570. See: BONNET, JULES. Aonio Paleario, etude sur la reforme en Italie. Paris, 1863. HC—B64

PALISSY, BERNARD. 1507?-1588?. See: PALISSY, the Huguenot potter. A true tale. Philadelphia, 1864. HG—P16

―――― See: FOSDICK, LUCIEN J. The French blood in America. pp. 58-60. HG—P16

PARIS, COLONEL ISAAC. 1761-1790. The Paris memorial. Reinterment of Col. Isaac Paris. 1880. HE—Z7

PAYNE, HENRY CLAY. 1843-1904. See: WIGHT, WILLIAM W. Henry Clay Payne: a life. Milwaukee, Wis., 1907. HG—P346

PERRIN, DANIEL. 16?-1719?. See: PERRINE, HOWLAND DE-LANO. Daniel Perrin, "The Huguenot," and his descendants in America of the surnames Perrine, Perine, and Prine, 1665-1910. South Orange, N. J., 1910. HH—P458.1

PETIGRU, JAMES LOUIS. 1789-1863. James Louis Petigru: a biographical sketch. By William J. Grayson. N. Y., 1866. 178 pp. portrait. D. HG—P44

PICTET, BÉNÉDICT. 16?-17?. See: DE BUDE, EUGÈNE. Vie ede B. P., théologien Gènevois. . . . Lausanne, 1874. HG—P58

PIERREFLEUR, [PIERRE DE] fl. 16th century. See: PIERRE-FLEUR, PIERRE DE. Mémoires . . . published with notes historique par A. Verdeil. Lausanne, 1856. HB—P61

POCAHONTAS. 1595?-1617. See: ROBERTSON, WYNDHAM. Pocahontas, alias Matoaka, and her descendants through her marriage with John Rolfe . . . with notes by R. A. Brock. Richmond, Va., 1887. HH—P75

PORCHER, MRS. CLAUDE CHERIGNY: -1726. PORCHER, ISAAC, M.D.: 1726-. See: FRENCH Protestant Church, Charleston, S. C. Mural tablets . . . page 10. HB—F875

PORTER, NOAH. 1811-1892. See: DWIGHT, TIMOTHY. Address delivered at the Funeral Service of President Porter, March 7th, 1892. HG—Mis68

PRIOLEAU, REV. ELIAS. 16?-1699. See: FRENCH Protestant Church, Charleston, S. C. . . . Mural Tablets. . . . 1898. Page 9. HB—F875

QUANTAIN, MOYSE. 16?-17?. See: JULIEN, MATTHEW CANTINE. Preliminary statement of the Cantine genealogy. Boston, 1903. HH—A54

QUINTARD, The Right Rev. Charles Todd, M.D., S.T.D., LL.D. Bishop of the Diocese of Tennessee. 1824-1898. HG—Mem512 Biographical sketch from the New York "Churchman," inserted in this Memorial Volume. **New York, 1898.**

RABAUT, Paul. 1718-94. Lettres à Antoine Court (1739-1755). Dix-sept ans de la vie d'un apôtre du désert, avec notes, portrait et autographe par A. Picheral-Dardier, et une préface par Ch. Dardier. Paris [1884]. 2 vols. portrait, fac-simile. O.   HG—R11

—— Biographie de Paul Rabaut, pasteur du désert et de ses trois fils. By Abraham Borrel. Nîmes, 1854. 168 pp. O.   HG—R111

RABOT de SALENE, Guillaume. See: ARNAUD, Eugene, pasteur. Guillaume Rabot de Salene, humaniste, ignore de XVIe siècle, etude historique. Paris, 1890.   HG—S33

RAMSAY, Mrs. Martha (Laurens). 1759-1811. See: RAMSAY, David. Memoirs of the life of Martha Laurens Ramsay, with an appendix containing extracts from her diary, letters and other private papers. Fourth edition. Boston, 1814. 219 pp. T. HG—R14

RAVENEL, Daniel. Memorial sketch by Hon. W. A. COURTNAY. (HUGUENOT Society of America. Proceedings. Vol. iii, part 1, pp. 117-120. 1896.)   HK—H87.1

—— 1789-1873. See: FRENCH Protestant Church, Charleston, S. C. . . . Mural Tablets. . . . 1898. Page 11.   HB—F875

—— St. Julien, M.D. See: FRENCH Protestant Church, Charleston, S. C. . . . Mural Tablets. . . . 1898. Page 12.   HB—F875

—— William. 1805-1888. See: FRENCH Protestant Church, Charleston, S. C. In Memoriam: William Ravenel & Peter Charles Gaillard. Charleston, 1889.   HG—Mem51

REBOULET, Paul. 1655-1710. See: JACCARD, E. Trois hommes du grand refuge. . . . Lausanne, 1900.   HG—B83

RENEE de France, duchesse de FERRAR. See: RODOCA-NACHI, E. Une protectrice de la Reforme en Italie et en France. . . . Paris, 1896.   HG—R29

REVERE, Paul. 1735-1818. See: GOSS, E. H. Life of Colonel Paul Revere. Boston, 1891.   HG—R32

REYNOLDS, John Fulton, Colonel, U. S. Army. 1820-1863. See: ROSENGARTEN, Joseph G.   HE—A512

REYNOLDS, William, Rear-Admiral, U. S. Navy. See: ROSEN-GARTEN, Joseph G. Reynolds Memorial address, March 8th, 1880. Philadelphia, 1880.   HE—A512

ROBINSON, Edward. See: HITCHCOCK, Roswell Dwight. Life and writings of Edward Robinson. Read before the New York Historical Society. N. Y., 1863. 100 pp.   HG—R56 Remarks on the announcement of the death of Dr. Robinson, by Henry B. Smith, pp. 3-16.

ROE, Francis Asbury. 1823-1901. See: BENJAMIN, Marcus. Francis Asbury Roe. (Society Colonial Wars, Washington, D. C., Memorial Papers, No. 4.) Washington, 1903. HG—Mem512

ROMBOUT, Francis. 1625?-1691. See: SUTCLIFFE, Alice Cary. The Homestead of a Colonial Dame. A monograph. Poughkeepsie, New York, 1909. HH—A54

ROUS, John. 1730?-1758. See: ROE, Francis Asbury, U. S. Navy. An American sea Captain of Colonial times. (Society Colonial Wars, Washington, D. C., Historical Papers, No. 2.) Washington, D. C., 1899. HG—Mem512

SAGNOL [DE LACROIX], Isaac. See JACCARD, E. Trois hommes du grand refuge. . . . Lausanne, 1900. HG—B83

SANXAY, Rev. Jacques. 16?-1693. See: SANXAY, Theodore F. The Sanxay family and descendants of Rev. Jacques Sanxay, Huguenot refugee to England in 1685. New York, 1907. HH—Sa5 Privately printed.

SAURIN, Jacques. 1677-1730. See: VINET, A. Histoire de la predication parmi les reformes de France. . . . Paris, 1860. HA—V783

SCHLATTER, Rev. Michael. 17?-?. See: STOUDT, John Baer. Rev. Michael Schlatter in the Lehigh Valley, June 24th-July 2nd, 1847. (Reprint: Reformed Church Review, Vol. xx, No. 1. January, 1916.) HC—Pamphlet

SCHUCH, Wolfgang. See: CUVIER, Othon. Trois martyrs de la Réforme Brulés en 1525 a Vic, Metz et Nancy. viii, 116 pp. Paris, 1889. D. HG—R111 Bound with: BORREL, A. Biographique . . . P. Rabout.

SCHUYLER, Philip John, Major-General, U. S. Army. 1733-1804. See: DE PEYSTER, John Watts, Brev. Major Gen. U. S. A. Major-General Philip Schuyler and the Burgoyne Campaign in the Summer of 1777. An Address before the New York Historical Society. HE—Z3

SMITH, William. 1697-1769. See: DELAFIELD, M. L. William Smith, Judge of the Supreme Court of the Province of New York. 1881. (From the Magazine of American History, April, 1881.) HE—Z6

SUPERVILLE, Daniel de. 1657-1728. See: VINET, A. Histoire de la prédication parmi les réformés de France. Paris, 1860. HA—V783

SWIFT, Joseph Gardner, General U. S. Army. 1738-1865. See: SWIFT, J. G. Memoirs of General Swift, first graduate of the United States Military Academy, West Point. . . . Worcester, Mass., 1890. HG—SW5

THOMAS, George Henry, Major-General U. S. Army. 1816-1870. See: DE PEYSTER, John Watts, Brev. Major-Gen., U. S. A. Maj.-Gen. George H. Thomas; an Address before the New York Historical Society. HE—Z9

TOLLIN, Henri Wilhelm Nathanael. See: DEUTSCH Hugenotten-Vereins. Geschichtsblätter. Zehnt XI, Heft 8-9. Magdeburg, 1902. 46 pp., and portrait. HK—D49

TURRETTINI, Jean Alphonse. See: DE BUDE, Eugene. Vie de J. A. Turrettini, théologien Genevois. 1671-1737. Lausanne, 1880. HG—T86

Van ARSDALE, John. 1756-1836. See: RIKER, James. "Evacuation Day," 1783. . . . Recollections of Capt. John Van Arsdale . . . by whose efforts on that day . . . the American flag successfully raised on the Battery. New York, 1883. HE—A512

van CAPELLEN TOT den POL, Jan Derck, Baron. 1741-1784. See: HOLLAND Society of New York. Report on a Tablet commemorative of the services rendered . . . on behalf of the North American Colonies in . . . the Revolution. . . . New York, 1909. HK—H71.1.van

van der KEMP, Francis Adrian. 1752-1829. See: LINCKLAEN, John. Travels in 1791—& 1792 in Pennsylvania & New York & Vermont. Journals of J. L. . . . With a biographical sketch . . . by H. L. Fairchild. New York, 1897. HI—L63

———— See: Van der Kemp, Francis Adrian. . . . An autobiography . . . with extracts from his correspondence. Edited with an historical sketch by H. L. Fairchild. New York, 1903. HG—V28

Van RENSSELAER, Killian Killiansen. 1763-1845. See: Van Rensselaer, Rev. Maunsell. Annals of the Van Rensselaers in the United States, especially as they relate to the family of K. K. Van R. . . . Albany, 1888. HG—V35

VERNET, Jacob. See: DE BUDE, Eugène. Vie de Jacob Vernet, théologien Genevois. 1698-1789. Lausanne, 1893. HG—V59

VERON, François. 1575?—?. See: FERET, P., abbé. Un curé de Charenton au XVIIᵉ siècle. Paris, 1881. HG—F37

VINCENT, John Himrod. 1798-1873. See: VINCENT, Rev. John Heyl, D.D. A Centennial souvenir of John Himrod Vincent, born in Milton, Pa., April 20, 1798. (One of very few copies printed.) HG—Mem512

VINCENT, Philippe. 1595-1651. See: MESCHINET de RICHEMOND, L. M. Origine & progrès de la réformation à La Rochelle précédé d'une notice sur Ph. Vincent. ed. 2. Paris, 1872. HA—R67 Volume lettered "French Church History."

WAKELEY, Joseph B. 1809?-1876. See: KETCHAM, Rev. William E. Memoir of . . . Wakeley. In: "Lost Chapters . . . of American Methodism." 1889. By J. B. Wakeley. pp. 597-635. HC—W13

WASHINGTON, GEORGE. 1732-1799. See the following:
BAKER, WILLIAM SPOHN, Compiler. Bibliotheca Washingtoniana;
a descriptive list of the biographies and biographical sketches of
George Washington. Square Q. Philadelphia, 1889.   HG—W277

———— Character portraits . . . arranged in chronological order
with . . . notes. Philadelphia, 1887. Square Q.   HG—W275

———— Medallic portraits . . . with historical . . . notes and . . .
catalogue of the coins, medals, tokens and cards. Philadelphia,
1885. Square Q.   HG—W276

IRVING, WASHINGTON. Washington and his Country; being
Irving's "Life of Washington," abridged by John Fiske. D. Boston, 1887.   HG—W272

JOHNSTON, ELIZABETH BRYANT. Original portraits of Washington, including statues, monuments and medals. Square folio.
Boston, 1882.   HG—W271

SPARKS, JARED. Life of George Washington. O. Title page
wanting.   HG—W273

WALTER, JAMES. Memorials of Washington and of Mary, his
mother, and Martha, his wife, from letters and papers of Robert
Cary and James Sharples. Q. New York, 1887.   HG—W27

WASSENAER, -STARRENBURG, COMTES VAN. See: WILDE-
MAN, M. G. Les Worbert, comtes van Wassenaer-Starrenburg.
Amersfoort, 1899.   HH—W673N

WILBOUR, MRS. BELINDA OLNEY HATHAWAY. See: Mrs.
Joshua Wilbour: sketch of her work as a member of various
historical and patriotic Societies.   HH—A54

WILHELM, WILLIAM HERMAN. 1867-1901. See: WEAVER,
ETHAN ALLEN. William Herman Wilhelm. (Society Colonial
Wars, D. C., Memorial Papers, No. 3.) Washington, D. C.,
1902.   HG—Mem512

WILLETT, MARINUS. 1740-1830. See: WAGER, DANIEL E.
Col. Marinus Willett, the hero of Mohawk Valley; an Address
before the Oneida Historical Society. Utica, N. Y., 1891. HG—Mis68

WILLIAM III, King of England. 1650-1702. See: DE PEYSTER,
Frederic. William the Third as a Reformer. Address before the
New York Historical Society . . . January 6, 1874.   HE—Z3

WILLIAMS, ROGER. 1615?-1660?. See: AUSTIN, J. O. Sketch
of his career. In his: The Roger Williams Calendar. Rhode Island,
1897. pp. V-VI.   HO—C13

WINTHROP, ROBERT CHARLES. See: CURRY, J. L. M. Robert Charles Winthrop. Necrology Virginia Historical Society, 1894. In: The Virginia Magazine, Vol. II, pp. 328-330. HK—V81

WISNER, HENRY. 1720?-1790. See: BURDGE, FRANKLIN. Memorial of Henry Wisner, the only New Yorker who voted for the Declaration of Independence. New York, 1873. HE—Z4

ZEISBERGER, DAVID. 1721-1808. Diary of David Zeisberger, a Moravian missionary among the Indians of Ohio. Translated from the original German manuscript and edited by E. F. Bliss. Cincinnati, 1885. Vol. I. O. HG—Ze5

GENEALOGY

ABBOTT, William Henry. Heraldry illustrated: being a short account of the origin of heraldry . . . with . . . directions for drawing and painting coats of arms, to which is added a Glossary of terms used in heraldry. 127 pp., 31 plates. O. N. Y., 1897.
Gift of Mrs. Chas. Doremus.   HH—A.134

ADAMS' Magazine of Revolutionary Records. New York, 1892. Vol. I, 4; II, 5-8. O. Title of Vol. I, "Adams' Magazine of general literature."   HH—Unbound

AMERICAN (The) Historical Register, Philadelphia, 1894, Vol. I, No. 1 & No. 3.   HH—Unbound

AMERICAN RECORD Series A. 2 vols. plates, fac-similes. Square O. New York, 1906. Vols. I-II, Ulster County, New York, Wills.   HH—An5

AMORY, Thomas Coffin. Life of Admiral Sir Isaac Coffin, baronet; his English and American ancestors. Boston, 1886. 141 pp. portrait. O.   HG—C65
Gift of Mrs. Martha J. Lamb.

ANDERSON, Thomas McArthur, LL.D., Brig. Gen. U. S. A. Monograph of the Anderson, Clark, Marshall and McArthur connection. 36 pp., 1 chart folded. Portland, Oregon, 1915. O.
In volume—"A Genealogical Collection."   HH—A54
Gift of Mrs. James M. Lawton.

ANJOU, Gustave, Ulster County, N. Y. Probate records in the office of the Surrogate, and in the County Clerk's office at Kingston, N. Y. A careful abstract and translation of the Dutch and English wills, letters of administration after interstates, and inventories from 1665, with genealogical . . . notes, and list of Dutch and Frisian Baptismal names with their English equivalents. With introduction by Judge A. T. Clearwater. 2 vols. pls., fac-sims. Square O. N. Y., 1906. (American Record Series A.:—Wills. Vols. I-II.)   HH—An5

ANSPACH, Jacob. Van Bodegem (Bodegom). 14 pp. D. n.p. 1894. Reprint: Maandblad van hat Geneal.-herald. genootschap "de Nederlandsche Leeuw," 1894.   HH—W66
In Volume "Genealogical & Historical pamphlets in Dutch."
Gift of M. G. Wildeman.

AUSTIN, John Osborne. Genealogical dictionary of Rhode Island: comprising three generations of settlers who came before 1690. Albany, 1887. 440 pp. Square folio. HH—Au7
Contains: "Additions & Corrections—continued and concluded."

AYMAR, Benjamin. Aymar of New York. New York, 1903. 65 pp. (A reprint of Huguenot Soc'y of America. Proceedings. Vol. III, Part 2, pp. 167-229.) O. HH—A54
Gift of the Author.
No. 140 of 150 copies printed.

BAILEY, Frederic W., Editor. Early Connecticut marriages as found on ancient Church records prior to 1800. Vols. I-III, New Haven, cop. 1896-'98. 3 vols. in 1. O. HH—B15

BANTA, Theodore Melvin. A Frisian family. The Banta genealogy. Descendants of Epke Jacobse, who came from Friesland, Netherlands, to New Amsterdam, February, 1659. New York, 1893. XIII, 412 pp., 4 port., 3 pl., 1 table. O. HH—B22
Gift of the Author.

——— Genealogical table of the Banta family. New York, no date. (Inserted in Volume.) HH—S425
Gift of the Author.

——— Sayre family: lineage of Thomas Sayre, a founder of Southampton. New York, 1901. 759 pp., fac-sim., 14 pl., 19 port., 2 tables. Q. HH—Sa94
Gift of the Author.

BERGEN, Teunis G. Register in alphabetical order, of the early settlers of Kings County, Long Island, N. Y., from its first settlement by Europeans to 1700; with biographies and genealogies. New York, 1881. 452 pp. O. HH—B35

BEURDEN, A. F. van. De familie van Lom. 15 pp. O. n.p., 1894. HH—W66
Repr.: Maandblad van het Geneal.-herald. genootschap "De Nederlandsche Leeuw," 1894.
"Genealogical & Historical pamphlets in Dutch."
Gift of M. G. Wildeman.

BLAINE, Laura Cowan. Maxwell history & genealogy, including the allied families. . . . Also Baptismal record of Rev. J. Craig, D.D., of Augusta Co., Va., 1740-1749. . . . By F. A. W. Houston & others. Indianapolis, Ind., [cop. 1916]. O. HH—M465

BLODGETTE, George B. Inscriptions from the old cemetery in Rowley, Mass. 78 pp. O. Salem, Mass., 1893. HH—R77B

BOHEMIA Manor, Delaware. Ancient families . . . their homes & their graves. By Rev. C. P. Mallery. O. Wilmington, 1888. HH—M253

BOLTON, CHARLES KNOWLES. Marriage notices, 1785-1794, for the whole United States. Copied from the Massachusetts Centinel and the Columbian Centinel. 1 p.l., 4, 1-139 pp. Salem, Mass., 1900. O.   HH—B69
Gift of Mrs. J. M. Lawton.

BOOTH, CHARLES EDWIN. One branch of the Booth family showing the lines of connection with one hundred Massachusetts Bay colonists. 2 p.l., v-vi, 259 pp., 1 fac-sim., 1 pl., 1 port. New York, 1910. O.   HH—B72
Gift of the Author.

BOSCH, R. P. VAN DER. De Kaap de Goede Hoop, tijdens het Nederlandsch bewind, (1652-1806, met Engelsch tusschenbestunr). 17 pp. O. n.p., 1894.   HH—W66
Repr. Maandblad van het Geneal.-herald. genootschap "De Nederl. Leeuw," 1894.
Gift of M. G. Wildeman.

BOSTON, Mass. See: BRIDGEMAN, T. Memorials of the dead. . . . Inscriptions, epitaphs & records on the monuments . . . in Copp's Hill Burying Ground. . . . Boston, 1852. D.   HH—B76

BRIDGMAN, THOMAS. Memorials of the dead in Boston; . . . Inscriptions, epitaphs and records on the monuments and tombstones in Copp's Hill Burying Ground . . . Boston . . . Historical and biographical notices of the early settlers of the metropolis of New England. 1 plate, xxiv, 252 pp. D. Boston, 1852.   HH—B76

BROCK, R. A., Editor. See: ROBERTSON, WYNDHAM. Pocahontas.   HH—P75

BULLOCH, JOSEPH GASTON BAILLIE, M.D. History and genealogy of the Habersham family . . . and . . . many other names . . . related or connected to some family in this work. vi, 222 pp. O. Columbia, S. C., 1901.   HH—H14
Gift of Mrs. James M. Lawton.

BUTLER, JAMES DAVIE, Butleriana, genealogica, et biographica; or, Genealogical notes concerning Mary Butler & her descendants. . . . 162 pp., port., pl., fac-sim. O. Albany, 1888.   HH—B97

CAEN, NORMANDY. Registers of the Protestant Church. Vannes, 1907. Edited by C. E. LART.   HH—L33—Vol. I
Vol. I. Baptemes et Mariages, 1560-1572.

CALAND, FRED. Une branche de la famille van Soest en Belgique—van Soust de Borckenfeldt. 13 pp. D. n.p., 1895.   HH—W66
Reprint: Maandblad. Genealogisch-heraldik genootschap, "De Nederlandsche Leeuw," 1895.
Gift of M. G. Wildeman.

CANTON, Mass. Record (The) of births, marriages and deaths. . . . 1797-1845. . . . Edited by F. Endicott. O. Canton, Mass., 1896.   HH—St.6

CHATEAU (Au) de Loches: le médecin Pierre Chaillé, de La Tremblade, et sa famille, 1693-1775. Paris, 1895. O. HH—C434
Bound with: WEISSE (N.). Indépendance des Etats d'Amerique
et Pierre Chaillée.
MS. Genealogy of the Chaille famille by M. de Richmond, inserted
in volume.
Gift of Louis Marie Meschinet de Richemond.

CLEARWATER, ALPHONSO TRUMPBOUR, LL.D. See: ANJOU. Gus-
tave, Ulster County, N. Y. Probate records . . . Kingston, N. Y.
. . . With introduction by A. T. C. 2 vols. pls., fac-sims. Square O.
N. Y., 1906. (Amer. Rec. Ser. A.:—Wills. Vols. I-II.) HH—An5

COLE, REV. DAVID, D.D., Editor. FIRST (The) Reformed Church
of Tarrytown, N. Y. First record book of the "Old Dutch Church
of Sleepy Hollow." Q. Yonkers, N. Y. HH—F44
No. 122 of 500 copies printed.

COLONIAL men and times: containing, The Journal of Col. Daniel
Trabue: . . . The Huguenots: Genealogy, . . . of allied families.
Edited by Lillie DuP. VanC. Harper. Q. Philadelphia, 1916.
Gift of the Editor. HH—H294

COLONIAL (The) Virginia Register. A list of governors . . .
other higher officials . . . members of the house of burgesses, and
the Revolutionary conventions of the Colony of Virginia. Compiled by Wm. G. & M. N. Stanard. 249 pp. Q. Albany, N. Y.,
1902. HH—V817

COLVER, HENRY CLAY, Compiler. Hasbrouck. Historical facts and
chronological table of Hasbrouck family. 12 pp. Seattle, Wash.,
1904. O. HH—A54
Gift of the compiler.
In: "A genealogical collection."

CONCORD, Mass. See: Potter, C. E., Editor. Genealogies of some
old families . . . Vol. I. Boston, 1887. Square Q. HH—P85

CONNECTICUT marriages: . . . as found on ancient Church records prior to 1800. New Haven, [cop. 1896-1898]. 3 vols. in 1.
O. Edited by F. W. Bailey. HH—B15

CORSON, HIRAM, M.D. Corson family—A history of the descendants of Benjamin Corson. son of Cornelius Corssen of Staten Island,
New York. Philadelphia, [Pa., 1919]. 5 leaves, 9-192 pp., 2
leaves, 20 port., 11 pl. Q. HH—C86
Gift of Percival G. Ullman.

COSTER, MORRIS, Editor. New Amsterdam Gazette. Historical
sketches . . . of the Dutch régime of New Amsterdam & the New
Netherlands. Vols. I-VII. Square Q. New York, 1883-1893.
7 vols. in 4. HH—N421

CRAB, A. J. E. VAN DER. Het geslacht van der Eeckhout. 6 pp. n.p.,
1895. O. Reprint. HH—W66
Gift of M. G. Wildeman.

CRAIG, Rev. John, D.D. Baptismal record of Augusta County, Virginia, 1740-1749, containing 1,474 names. First publication of the original Record. (In: Houston, F. A. W., & others. Maxwell history & genealogy.) Indianapolis, Ind., [cop. 1916]. O. pp. 573-597.   HH—M465

CRANDALL, A. P. Genealogy of a branch of the Crandall family. Chattanooga, 1888. 62 pp. D.   HH—C85
Gift of the Author.

CREGAR, William Francis, Compiler. Ancestry of the children of James William White, M.D., with accounts of the families of White, Newby, Rose [& others]. 194 pp., pl., 1 fac-sim. Q. Philadelphia, 1888.   HH—W58
Gift of Mrs. Martha J. Lamb.

DE BOER, Louis P. Van der Veer family in the Netherlands, 1150-1660, and 1280 to 1780. 62 pp., 1 chart, 8 pl., 1 map, 1 port. O. Brooklyn, N. Y., cop. 1913.   HH—V28
No. 59 of 125 copies.
Gift of Charles A. Ditmas.

DE COSTA, Rev. Benjamin Franklin, D.D. Genealogical chart of the De Costa family.   HH—S425
Gift of the Compiler.

DE FOREST, Emily Johnston. A Walloon family in America; Lockwood de Forest and his forebears, 1500-1848. Together with A voyage to Guiana; being the Journal of Jesse de Forest and his colonists, 1623-1625. Vols. I-II. Portraits, plates, maps, fac-similes. Boston, 1914. 2 vols. O.   HH—D315
Gift of the Author, with her autograph letter.

DE FOREST, Mrs. Robert Weeks. See: DE FOREST, Emily Weeks.

DELANO, Major Joel Andrew. The genealogy, history, and alliances of the American house of Delano, 1621-1899. With the history and heraldry of the Maison de Franchimont and DeLannoy to Delano, 1096 to 1621 . . . and . . . Lannoy from Guelph, . . . to Philippe de Lannoy, 476 A. D., to 1621. . . . Arranged by M. D. de Lannoy. 561 pp., 22 pl. (colored pl.). Q. New York, 1899.
                                                              HH—D37

DELAVAN, Edward C., Jr. The Guyon house. A history based upon personal researches and family data supplied by Miss S. G. Clark. pp. 113-138, 1 fac-sim., 2 plans, 1 pl. New York, 1916. (Reprint: Staten Island Assoc. Arts & Sciences, Proceedings, Vol. VI, Part 2. February, 1916.)   HH—Pamphlet
Gift of the Author.

DE RESSEGUIE. See: RESSEQUIE.

DE VILLIERS, Christoffel Goetzee, Compiler. See: GESLACHT-REGISTER der oude Kaapsche familien.   HH—G33

DE VOE, THOMAS F.   Genealogy of the DeVoe family . . . the numerous forms of spelling the name by various branches and generations in the past eleven hundred years.   302 pp., illus.   New York, 1885.   O.   HH—D49
Autograph gift of the Author.

DODGE, RICHARD DESPARD.   Condensed table of the Block Island branch of the Dodge family in America.   A chart folded.   Brooklyn, New York, 1898.   HH—D66
Gift of the Author.

———— Dodge (The) lands at Cow Neck, Long Island; an Appendix to Robert Dodge's History of Tristram Dodge and his descendants in America.   32 pp.   O.   Brooklyn, New York, 1898.   HH—D66
Gift of the Author.
Note: The Chart and this pamphlet are bound with: DODGE, ROBERT TRISTRAM DODGE, and his descendants in America. . . .

DODGE, ROBERT.   Tristram Dodge and his descendants in America, with historical and descriptive accounts of Block Island, Rhode Island, and Cow Neck, Long Island; their original settlements. New York, 1886.   233 pp., and Chart of the Block Island branch of the Dodge family, by R. D. Dodge, inserted.   O.   HH—D66
Gift of Mrs. Martha J. Lamb.

DORCHESTER, Massachusetts.   In: RECORD of Births, marriages and deaths . . . in . . . Stoughton . . . and . . . Canton . . . preceded by Records of Dorchester . . . 1715-1717.   Edited by F. ENDICOTT.   Canton, Mass., 1896.   O.   HH—St6

DOUCHETT, ANDREW THOMPSON.   Douchett and Ward families; genealogical notes.   36 pp., 1 portrait.   Pittsburgh, Pa., 1889. S.   HH—D74
Gift of the Author.

DUBOIS, ANSON, and JAMES G.   Documents and genealogical chart of the family of Benjamin Du Bois of Catskill, New York.   Being an addition to the History of the descendants of Louis and Jacques Du Bois, as given at the Bi-centenary reunion held at New Paltz, New York, 1875.   IV, 104 pp., 1 plan.   New York, 1878.   Square Q.   HH—D85.2
Gift of Anson Du Bois.

———— Same: Bound with: DU BOIS, W. E., and P.   Bi-centenary reunion. . . . Philadelphia, 1876.   Square Q.   HH—D85

DU BOIS, GEORGE W.   Descendants of Jacques Du Bois.   A genealogical chart, 58 x 64, inserted in volume.   no place, no date.   HH—D85

DU BOIS, JAMES G.   See: DU BOIS, ANSON, and Du Bois, J. G. Documents and genealogical chart of the family of Benjamin Du Bois of Catskill, New York. . . . New York, 1878.   Square Q.
                                                                    HH—D85.2

[Du BOIS, WILLIAM E., and PATTERSON.] Bi-centenary reunion of the descendants of Louis and Jacques Du Bois, (Emigrants to America, 1660 and 1665), at New Paltz, New York, 1875. Compiled for the family connection. Philadelphia, 1876. 158 pp., 9 port., 7 pl., 1 fac-sim. Square Q. HH—D85
The coat-of-arms plate is in color.
Gift of Dr. Abram Du Bois.

DuBOIS, PATTERSON, & DuBOIS, W. E. Bi-centenary reunion of the descendants of Louis and Jacques DuBois. . . . 1876. HH—D85

DuPUY, CHARLES MEREDITH. Genealogical history of the DuPuy family. With additions by his son, Herbert DuPuy. x, 165 pp., 8 fac-sim., 11 plates, 16 groups, 9 port., 1 survey, 6 charts. Square Q. Privately printed, Philadelphia, 1910. HH—D94
Gift of Herbert DuPuy.

DuPUY, HERBERT. See: DuPUY, CHARLES MEREDITH. Genealogical history of the DuPuy family. With additions by his son. Philadelphia, 1910. Square Q. HH—D94

DUTCH CHURCH, New York. Baptisms: 1697-1720. In: VALENTINE, D. T. Manual of the city of New York, N. Y., 1864. pp. 777-837. HE—N481

DUTCH CHURCH, New York, Burials. Record of burials in the Dutch Church, New York. 309-311 pp. Q. N. Y., 1899. HH—D95
Reprint: Holland Soc. of N. Y. Year-book.
Gift of Thomas M. Banta.

EGLESTON, THOMAS. Biographical notice of Louis Gruner, Inspector-General of mines of France. 5 pp. O. N. Y., 1884. HH—Var4
A paper read before Amer. Inst., Mining Engineers, June, 1883.
   Author's edition, and gift.
In volume—"Ancestry."

ELLERY, HARRISON, Editor. See: SWIFT, J. G. Memoirs . . . with a genealogy of the family of Thomas Swift. 1890. HG—Sw5

ENDICOTT, FREDERIC, ed. Record (The) of births, marriages and deaths . . . in . . . Stoughton . . . and . . . Canton. . . . Canton, Mass., 1896. O. HH—St6

FABER, REGINALD STANLEY. The buried book; or, The Bible of Henri de Dibon. London, 1885. 24 pp. portrait. MS. Genealogical notes inserted. HH—Fa.11
1 of 35 copies privately printed.
Gift of the Author.

FAMILY (A) History. 44 pp. O. Taneytown, Md., 1909. HH—A54
Gift of the Author.

FEEN, B. VAN DER. Genealogie de Dieu. 8 pp. O. n.p., 1895. HH—W66
Reprint: Maanblad van het Geneal.-herald. genootschap "De Nederlandsche Leeuw," 1895.
Gift of M. G. Wildeman.

FIRST (The) Reformed Church of Tarrytown, N. Y. First record book of the "Old Dutch Church of Sleepy Hollow," organized in 1697, and now the First Reformed Church of Tarrytown, N. Y. An original translation of its brief historical matter, and a copy . . . of its four registers . . . from its organization to 1791, by Rev. D. COLE, D.D., Yonkers, N. Y., 1901. HH—F44
No. 122 of 500 copies printed.
Gift of Yonkers Historical & Library Association.

FLUDD, MRS. ELIZA C. K. Biographical sketches of the Huguenot Solomon Legare and of his family . . . also Reminiscences of the Revolutionary struggle with Great Britain. . . . 142 pp. O. Charleston, S. C., 1886. HH—L53
Gift of the Author.

FREDERIKS, J. G. De familie Vorsterman te Amsterdam. 8 pp. O. n.p., 1895. HH—W66
Reprint: Maanblad . . . Geneal.-herald. genootschap "De Nederlandsche Leeuw," 1895.
Gift of M. G. Wildeman.

GENEALOGICAL (The) Advertiser. A quarterly magazine of family history. Vols. I-IV. Cambridge, Mass., 1898. 4 vols. in 3. Edited by L. H. Greenlaw. HH—G32
Title page & index wanting for Vol. IV.

GENEALOGICAL Queries and memoranda. A quarterly magazine devoted to genealogy, family history, heraldry and topography. Edited by G. F. T. Sherwood. Vol. I, Nos. 1-3, 8-10. O. London, 1896-'98. HH—Pamphlets
Unbound.

GENEALOGIES: Reprints of N. Y. Gen. & Biog. Record. Collected and bound together, representing 18 families. No title page. N. Y., 1863-97. O. HH—V42G

GENEALOGY of the Hoffman family, descendants of Martin Hoffman, with biographical notes. O. New York, 1899. See: [HOFFMAN, VERY REV. EUGENE AUGUSTUS, D.D.]. HH—H65

GEROULD, [SAMUEL L.], Compiler. Genealogy of the family of Gamaliel Gerould, son of Dr. Jacques (or James) Jerould of the Province of Languedoc, France. 84 pp. Bristol, N. H., 1885. 84 pp. O. HH—G31
Gift of the Author.

GESLACHT-Register der oude Kaapsche familien. Gecompileerd door Christoffel Coetzee de Villiers. In 3 vols. Vols. I-III. Square O. kaapstad, 1894. HH—G33
Deel 1. A. tot J.
 "   2. K. " O.
 "   3. P. " Z.
Gift of Prof. Samuel Macauley Jackson.

GESLACHTLIJST der familie de Comte later genaamd Voûte. 11 pp., 1 pl. Square folio. 's-Gravenhage, 1893. HH—V97 Behoort bij No. 2, van het algemeen Nederlandsch Familieblad, 10e jaargang.
Gift of M. G. Wildeman.
Bound with: "De Nederlandsche Leeuw"—Maandblad. . . .

GOODE, George Brown. Virginia cousins; a study of the ancestry & posterity of John Goode of Whitby . . . with notes upon related families, a key to Southern genealogy and a history of the English surname Gode, Goad, Goode or Good from 1148-1887 with a preface by R. A. Brock. xxxvi, 526 pp., illus., port., pl. Q. Richmond, Va., 1887. HH—G54
Copy No. 139.
Gift of Mrs. Martha J. Lamb.

GREEN, Thomas Marshall. Historic families of Kentucky, with special reference to stocks derived from the valley of Virginia. First series. Cincinnati, 1889. 304 pp. portrait. O. HH—G82
Gift of Mrs. Martha J. Lamb.

GREENLAW, Lucy Hall, Editor. Genealogical (The) Advertiser. A quarterly magazine of family history. Vols. i-iv. Cambridge, Mass. 1898-1901. 4 vols. in 3. O. HH—G32
Title page and index for Vol. iv wanting.

GUYOT, Henri Daniel. Généalogie de la famille Guyot avec pièces justificatives. 38 pp. [1st ed.] O. Groninque, 1892. HH—Var4

——— Généalogie de la famille Guyot avec pièces justificatives. 40 pp. [2nd ed.] O. Groninque, 1900. HH—Var4
Gift of the Author.

HANOVER, Mass. A copy of the records of births, marriages and deaths . . . of the town of Hanover, Mass., 1727-1857. Prepared under . . . direction of . . . a Committee appointed by said town. . . . 319 pp. O. Rockland, 1898. HH—H19

HARPER, Lillie DuPuy VanCulin, Editor. Colonial men and times. Containing the Journal of Col. Daniel Trabue, some account of his ancestry, life and travels in Virginia and . . . Kentucky during the Revolutionary period: The Huguenots: Genealogy, with brief sketches of the allied families. 6 p.l., 3-624 pp., 2 groups, 36 pl., 15 port. Philadelphia, 1916. Q. HH—H294
Gift of the Author.

HASBROUCK. Historical facts and Chronological table of Hasbrouck family. [Compiled by H. C. Colver.] 12 pp. Seattle, Washington, 1904?. O. HH—A54
Gift of H. C. Colver.

HAYDEN, Rev. Horace Edwin. Oliver genealogy: a record of the descendants of Joseph, Reuben and Levi Oliver, and of Pierre Elisée Gallaudet. N. Y., 1888. 23 pp. portrait. O. HH—Var4
Gift of Paul A. Oliver.

HELFFENSTEIN, Abraham Ernest. Pierre Fauconnier, and his descendants; with some account of the allied Valleaus. 4 p.l., vii-ix, 226 pp., 2 colored pl., 6 pl., 20 port. Philadelphia, 1911. Q. HH—F25
Author's Autograph presentation copy.

HERALDRY illustrated . . . with directions for drawing & painting coats of arms. . . . By W. H. ABBOTT. New York, c. 1897. O. HH—A2

HERALDRY: See: LANNOY, Mortimer Delano. Bibliography of American Heraldry. 12 pp. D. New York, 1896. HH—D37

HERALDRY: See: Volume iii of LeLABOUREUR, J. Mémoires de Messire Michel de Castelnau . . . avec . . . genealogies de plusieurs maisons illustres alliees à celle de Castelnau. Nouvelle ed. Tome i-iii. Bruxelles, 1731. F. HG—L53

HERRICK, Lucius C., Editor. See: HERRICK, Jedediah. Herrick genealogy. . . . 1885. HH—H43

HERRICK, Jedediah. Herrick genealogy, genealogical register of the name & family of Herrick . . . 1629-1846 . . . revised, augmented and brought down to A. D. 1885, by Lucius G. Herrick. 516 pp., port., pl., fac-sim. O. Columbus, 1885. HH—H43

HILL, William G., compiler. Family record of . . . James W. Converse and Elisha S. Converse, including some of the descendants of Roger de Coigneries . . . Edward Convers . . . Robert Wheaton . . . William Edmonds . . . John Coolidge. . . . iv, 241 pp., 19 port., 8 pl. O. Boston, 1887. HH—Con74
Privately printed.
Gift of the Author.

[HOFFMAN, Very Rev. Eugene Augustus, D.D.] Genealogy of the Hoffman family, descendants of Martin Hoffman, with biographical notes. 545 pp., 1 fac-sim., 3 pl., 14 port. O. New York, 1899. HH—H65
No. 7 of 25 copies.
Gift of the Author.

HOLGATE, Jerome B. American genealogy . . . some of the early settlers of North America and their descendants . . . their intermarriages and collateral branches, . . . with . . . genealogical tables. 3 pl., 244 pp. Albany, N. Y., 1848. Square folio. HH—H731

[HOOGSTRATEN, Johan van.] Afscheidsgroete, aan den heeren . . . diaconen der Walsche gereformeerde kerke in 's Graavenhaage. 3 pp. no place, 1780. O. HH—W66
Gift of M. G. Wildeman.

HOTTEN, John Camden, Editor. The original lists of persons of quality; emigrants; religious exiles; political rebels; . . . and others who went from Great Britain to the American plantations, 1600-1700. With . . . other interesting particulars. From MSS. preserved in the State paper dept., of Her Majesty's public record office, England. 2nd ed. xxxii, 33-580 pp. Q. New York, 1880.

HH—H79

HOUSTON, Florence [Amelia] Wilson. Blaine, L. C., & Mellette, E. D. Maxwell history and genealogy, including the allied families. . . . Also Baptismal record of the Rev. John Craig, D.D., of Augusta County, Virginia, 1740-1749. . . . 8 p.l., 642 pp., 7 pl., 4 groups, 34 port. Indianapolis, Ind., [cop. 1916]. O.   HH—M465

HUGHES, Thomas P. American ancestry: giving the name and descent in the male line of Americans whose ancestors settled in the United States previous to the Declaration of Independence, A. D. 1776. Albany, 1887. Vols. i, ii and iii, Part 1, illustrated.
Q.   HH—H87
Vol. i.   City of Albany, N. Y.
Vol. ii.   Columbia Co., N. Y.
Vol. iii.   Embracing lineages from the whole of the U. S.

HURLBUT, Henry Higgins. Hurlbut genealogy; or, Record of the descendants of Thomas Hurlbut, of Saybrook & Wethersfield, Conn. . . . 545 pp., il. port. Albany, 1888. O.   HH—H93
Gift of Mrs. Martha J. Lamb.

INDEX to American Genealogies and to genealogical material contained in all works. . . . 282 pp. 4th ed. O. Albany, N. Y., J. Munsell & Sons, 1895.   HH—M96

——— Supplement, 1900-1908. Q. Albany, N. Y.   HH—M96

JAMES, Edmund J. The Stites and James Genealogy. 6 pp. O.
New York, 1898.   HH—Pamphlet
Reprint: N. Y. Genealogical & Biographical Record.
Gift of the Author.

JAMES, Edward W., Editor. See: Lower Norfolk County Virginia Antiquary.

JULIEN, Rev. Matthew Cantine. Preliminary statement of the Cantine genealogy, or, The descendants in America of the Huguenot refugee Moses Cantine. 14 pp. O. [Boston?], 1903.   HH—A54
Gift of the Author.

KEIM, DeBenneville Randolph, Editor. See: KEIM (The) and allied families. . . . Harrisburg, Pa., 1898-1900.

KEIM (The) and allied families in America and Europe. A monthly serial of history, biography, genealogy and folklore, . . . of the German, French and Swiss emigrations to America from the 17th century. . . . Edited by DeB. R. Keim. Harrisburg, Pa., 1898-1900.
O. Vols. i-ii, Nos. 1-23.   HH—K27
Volume ii unbound.

LANCASTER, Massachusetts. Birth, Marriage and Death register, Church records and epitaphs, 1643-1850. Edited by H. S. Nourse. 508 pp. O. Lancaster, 1890. HH—L22

LANNOY, Mortimer Delano de. Bibliography of American heraldry. New York, 1896. 12 pp., il. D. HH—D37
Inserted in his Hist. & Gen. of Delano and Lannoy.
Gift of the Author.

LANNOY, Mortimer Delano de. See: DELANO, Major J. A. Genealogy . . . of the American house of Delano, 1621-1899. With the history and heraldry of the Maison de Franchimont and de Lannoy to Delano, 1096-1621. . . . New York, 1899. Q.
One of 400 copies published. HH—D37

[LARPENT, Frederic DeH.] Note concerning the family of Larpent settled between 1695-1705 in Denmark and Norway. 7 pp. Square O. [London, S. E., 1916.] HH—A54
Gift of the Author.

[LART, Charles Edmund], Editor. Registers of the Protestant Church at Caen, Normandy. Vol. i. Vannes, 1907. Q. xxiv, 712 pp. HH—L33—Vol. i
Vol. i. Baptèmes et Mariages, 1560-1572.
Gift of Col. Henry A. Du Pont.

——— Editor. Registers of the Protestant Church at Loudun, 1566 to 1582. Vol. i. Lymington, 1905. O. x, 69 pp. HH—L33L
Vol. i. Baptèmes, 1566-1577.
Gift of Mrs. James M. Lawton.

LEACH, Josiah Granville, Editor. See: ROEBLING, Emily Warren. Journal of the Rev. Silas Constant . . . Presbyterian Church at Yorktown, N. Y. . . . Records of the Church. . . . Notes on families mentioned. . . . Philadelphia, 1903. O. HH—C758

LEE, William, Compiler. John Leigh of Agawam, (Ipswich) Mass., 1634-1671, and his descendants of the name of Lee. . . . 999 pp., 1 map, il. Albany, N. Y., 1888. O. HH—L51
Gift of Mrs. Martha J. Lamb.

LISTS of persons . . . who went from Great Britain to . . . America . . . 1600-1700. (In: HOTTEN, J. C., Editor. Original lists. . . . New York, 1880. 2nd ed. Q.) HH—H79

LOUDON; Registers of the Protestant Church. 1566-1582. [Vol. i.] Edited by C. E. LART. HH—L33L—Vol. i

LOWER NORFOLK COUNTY Virginia Antiquary. Edited by E. W. JAMES. Vols. i-ii, iii, Nos. 1, 2, & iv, v, Nos. 1, 2, & 3. Richmond, Va., cop. 1895-1905. O. HH—J28
Note: Unbound because numbers wanting.

118

LYLE, Maria Catherine Nourse, Compiler. James Nourse and his descendants. 138 pp., 4 pl., 6 port., 4 group port., 1 fac-sim., 1 table. Lexington, Ky., 1897. Q. (Printed by request.)   HH—N85
Gift of the Author.

MAANDBLAD van het Genealogisch-heraldiek genootschap "De Nedersche Leeuw." XIIIᵉ Jaargang, 1895. Nos. 1-12, & Index. s'Gravenhage, 1895. Square Q.   HH—V97
Illustrated with coats-of-arms, & 2 heraldry plates paged.
Bound with: VOUTE family genealogy.
Gift of M. G. Wildeman.

McALLISTER, James Gray. Family records: compiled for the descendants of Abraham Addams McAllister and his wife Julia Ellen (Stratton) McAllister, of Covington, Virginia. Containing a sketch of A. A. McAllister. 88 pp., 1 port. O. Easton, Pa., 1912.
Illustrated throughout.   HH—A54

MAGAZINE of the Daughters of the Revolution. New York, 1893. Vol. i, No. 1. O.   HH—Unbound

MAINE (The) Historical & Genealogical Recorder. Edited by S. M. Watson. Vols. i-vi. Portland, Me. 1884-1889. 6 vols. Square O.   HH—M28
Gift of the Society.

MALLERY, Rev. Charles Payson. Ancient families of Bohemia Manor; their homes and their graves. 74 pp. Wilmington, Del., 1888. O. (Papers of the Historical Society of Del., No. 7.)
HH—M253

MARRIAGE notices, 1785-1794, for the whole United States. See: BOLTON, Charles Knowles.

MARSH, Lucius B. Genealogy of John Marsh, of Salem, and his descendants 1633-1888, revised & edited by Rev. D. W. Marsh. 283 pp. Amherst, Mass., 1888. O.   HH—M35
Gift of Mrs. Martha J. Lamb.

MARSHALL, Edward Chauncey. Ancestry of General Grant, and their contemporaries. 186 pp. N. Y., 1869. O.   HH—G76
Gift of the Author.

[MEE, Isaac du.] Oprechte uitboezeming aan den . . . diaconen der Walsche gereformeerde kerke in s'Graavenhaage. . . . 3 pp. O. n.p., 1780.   HH—W66
Gift of M. G. Wildeman.

MEEKER, Mary Falconer Perrin. See: Perrin, Anna Fauconnier, & M. F. P. Meeker. Allied families of Purdy, Fauconnier, Archer, Perrin. New York, cop. 1911. O.   HH—P458
No. 36 of 79 copies.
Autograph Gift: William H. Falconer.

MELLETTE, Ella Dunn, Houston, Florence A. Wilson, & others.
Maxwell history & genealogy, including the allied families. . . .
Also Baptismal record of Rev. J. Craig, D.D., of Augusta Co., Va.,
1740-1749. O. Indianapolis, Ind., cop. 1916.   HH—M465

MESCHINET de Richemond, [Louis Marie]. Medécin (Le)
Pierre Chaillé de la Tremblade et sa famille, 1693-1775. pp. 39-42.
O. [Paris, 1895.] Contains insert; MS. Genealogy of Chaillé
family, also of Chevallier family.   HH—C434
Bd. with: Weiss, N. Indépendance des Etats d'Amerique et Pierre
   Chaillé. . . .
Gift of the Author.

MICKLEY, Minnie Fogel. Genealogy of the Mickley family of
America . . . with a . . . record of the Michelet family of Metz,
and some . . . biographical . . . and historical memorabilia. 182
pp., 3 leaves, 2 port. O. Mickleys, Pa., 1893.   HH—M62
Additional items inserted in volume, Oct., 1917, regarding the Un-
   vailing of the Huguenot and Revolutionary Memorial of the
   Mickley family by the Michelet Chapter, N. S. D. A. R.
Gift of the Author.

MINET, William, Compiler. Some account of the Huguenot family of Minet from their coming out of France at the revocation of
the Edict of Nantes 1686; founded on Isaac Minet's "Relation of
our family." 240 pp., il., fac-sim. tables. Square folio. London,
1892.   HH—M63
250 large paper copies privately printed.

MINNICH, Michael Reed. Some data of the Hillegas family.
(The American Historical Register, Philadelphia, 1894. No. 1.)
                                         HH—Unbound

MOENS, William John Charles, Editor. Marriage, baptismal and
burial registers, 1571-1874, and monumental inscriptions in the
Dutch reformed church, Austin Friars, London, and a short account
of the strangers and their churches. Lymington, 1884. 227 pp.
illustrated. Square Q.   HH—M72
Gift of the editor.

MONNETTE, Orra Eugene, Compiler. Monnet family genealogy:
an emphasis of a noble Huguenot heritage. Somewhat of the first
immigrants, Isaac and Pierre Monnet: being a presentation of those
in America bearing the name as variously spelled . . . and . . . .
short account of . . . families connecting with the ancestral lines.
. . . Los Angeles, Cal., 1911. 1150, 16, lxxviii pp. Q. HH—M748
Illustrations paged in.
Compiler's autograph presentation copy.
No. 100 of 350 copies.

MONOGRAPH of the Anderson, Clark, Marshall & McArthur con-
nection. 36 pp., 1 chart folded. Portland, Ore. By Brig. Gen.
Thomas McArthur Anderson.   HH—A54
Gift of the Author.

MORRIS, JOHN EMERY, Compiler. Ancestry of Daniel Bontecou, of
Springfield, Massachusetts. 29 pp. Hartford, Conn., 1887. O.
Gift of the Author. HH—Var4

———— Bontecou genealogy; a record of the descendants of Pierre
Bontecou, a Huguenot refugee from France, in the lines of his sons.
271 pp. O. Hartford, 1885. HH—B64
Gift of the Author.

———— The Felt genealogy. A record of the descendants of George
Felt of Casco Bay. 568 pp. O. Hartford, Conn., 1893. HH—F36
Gift of the Author.

———— Resseguie family, a historical and genealogical record of Alex.
Resseguie of Norwalk, Conn., and four generations of his descend-
ants. 99 pp. O. Hartford, 1888. HH—R31
Gift of the Author.

MUELEN, J. C. VAN DER. Kwartierstaten betreffende het geslacht
Martini. 14 pp. O. no place, 1895. HH—W66
Reprint: Maandblad van het Geneal.-herald. genootschap "De
Nederlandsche Leeuw" 1895. HH—W66
Gift of M. G. Wildeman.

MUNSELL'S, JOEL, Sons. Supplement, 1900-1908. Being supplement to the Index to Genealogies published in 1900. 207 pp.
Albany, N. Y., 1908. Q. HH—M96

———— Same. 4th edition. 1885.

NEDERLANDSCHE (De) Leeuw. See: MAANDBLAD van het
Genealogisch-heraldiek genootschap.

NEW YORK MARRIAGES. Names of persons for whom Mar-
riage licenses were issued by the Secretary of the Province of N. Y.,
previous to 1784. 480 pp. Albany, 1860. O. HH—N42
Gift of Mrs. J. M. Lawton.

———— Supplementary list of Marriage licenses; years 1752-1753, 1755-
1756, & 1758. Albany, 1898. O. (University of N. Y., State
Library Bulletin History, No. 1.) HH—N42—Supplement
Gift of State Librarian.

NOTES upon the ancestry of Ebenezer Greenough . . . and . . . wife
Abigail Israel . . . also a list of their descendants. Compiled by
F. Platt. Philadelphia, 1895. O. HH—P69

NOURSE, HENRY STEDMAN, Editor. Lancaster, Massachusetts.
Births, marriage, and death register, Church records and epitaphs,
1643-1850. 508 pp. Lancaster, 1890. O. HH—L22

"OLD DUTCH CHURCH of Sleepy Hollow." The First Reformed
Church of Tarrytown, New York. First Record Book, a copy . . .
by Rev. D. COLE. Yonkers, N. Y., 1901. Q. HH—F44
No. 122 of 500 copies printed.

"OLD NORTHWEST" Genealogical Quarterly. Columbus, Ohio. 1898-1900. Vol. I, complete; Vol. II, No. 5, and Index; Vol. III, Nos. 1 & 2.   HH—Unbound
(All this Library has.)

PAXTON, WILLIAM McCLUNG. Marshall family; genealogical chart of the descendants of John Marshall and his wife . . . and notices of families connected with them. 415 pp., 1 port., 1 pl. Cincinnati, 1885. O.   HH—M351

PELLETREAU, WILLIAM S. Historic homes and institutions, and genealogical and family history of New York. Vols. I-IV. New York, 1907. 4 vols. Illus., pl., port., fac-sim. Q.   HH—P36
Gift of Mrs. James M. Lawton.
Note:—In Volume III is inserted a "Photograph of Register in the old Family Bible which belonged to Benjamin L'Hommedieu, Jr., of Southold, son of Benjamin L'Hommedieu the Emigrant from La Rochelle, France, after the Revocation of the Edict of Nantes. This Bible belongs to Katherine Ward Lane of Boston, who also owns the portrait by Earle of her great-great-grandfather, Ezra L'Hommedieu, of Southold, who was for over 40 years in the service of his Country." Photograph faces page 194, in Vol. III.
Photograph is Gift of Miss Cornelia Horsford.

PERRIN, ANNA FALCONER, & Meeker, M. F. P. Allied families of Purdy, Fauconnier, Archer, Perrin. 114 pp., 2 charts, folded, 9 pl., 8 port., 2 maps. New York, [cop. 1911]. O.   HH—P458
No. 36 of 79 copies.
Autograph Gift of William H. Falconer.

PERRINE, HOWLAND DELANO. Daniel Perrin, "The Huguenot," and his descendants in America, of the surnames Perrine, Perine, and Prine, 1665-1910. 547 pp., 1 fac-sim., 11 groups, 25 port., 5 pl., 3 maps. South Orange, N. J., 1910. O.   HH—P458.1
Author's autograph presentation copy.
No. 150 of 250 copies printed.

PHŒNIX, STEPHEN WHITNEY. Whitney family of Connecticut and its affiliations; being an attempt to trace the descendants . . . of Henry Whitney from 1649-1878 . . . with some account of the Whitneys of England. 3 vols., pl. tables. Q. New York, 1878.   HH—W61
Gift of the Phœnix Estate.

PIERCE, FREDERICK CLIFTON. Field genealogy, being the record of all the Field family in America, whose ancestors were in this country prior to 1700. . . . All descendants of the Fields of England, whose ancestor, Hurbutus De la Field, was from Alsace-Lorraine. 2 vols., pl. port. Q. Chicago, Ill. 1901.   HH—F45
Gift of Marshall Field.

[PLATT, FRANKLIN, Compiler.] Notes upon the ancestry of Abenzer Greenough . . . and of his wife . . . Abigail Israel . . . also a list of their descendants. 38 pp. O. Philadelphia, 1895.   HH—P69

POTTER, CHARLES EDWARD, Editor. Genealogies of some old families of Concord, Mass., and their descendants in part to the present generation. . . . 14 port., 1 pl., 143 pp. Vol. I. Boston, 1887. Square Q.   HH—P85

PRIME, TEMPLE. Some account of the Bowdoin family, with notes on the families of Pordage, Lynde, Newgate, Erving. 52 pp. 2nd ed. O. New York, 1894.   HH—A54
Gift of the Author.

PROTESTANT Church at Loudin: See: Loudin: Registers of the Protestant Church. . . .

PUTNAM, EBEN., Editor. Salem Press Historical & Genealogical Record. Vol. I, No. 1; Vol. II, No. 3. Salem, Mass., 1890-92.
                                     HH—Sa.1

RAVENEL, HENRY EDMUND. Ravenel records. A history of genealogy of the Huguenot family of Ravenel, of South Carolina; with some . . . account of the parish of St. John's, Berkeley, which was their principal location. 279 pp., 9 pl., 2 port. Atlanta, Ga., 1898. O.   HH—R11

RECORD (The) of births, marriages, and deaths . . . in the town of Stoughton, . . . 1727 to 1800, and . . . Canton, . . . 1797 to 1845, preceded by . . . records of the south precinct of Dorchester, . . . 1715 to 1727. Edited by F. Endicott. 317 pp. O. Canton, Mass., 1896.   HH—St6

REGISTERS (The) of the Protestant Church at Loudun. 1566-1582. Vol. I. O. Lymington, 1905. Edited by C. E. LART.
                                     HH—L33L

REQUA, REV. AMOS CONKLIN. The family of Requa. 1678-1898. XXXVIII, 1-63 pp., 18 port., 1 pl. O. Peekskill, New York, 1898.
Gift of the Author.   HH—Rq31

RHODE ISLAND. See: AUSTIN, JOHN OSBORNE. Genealogical dictionary . . . 3 generations . . . before 1690. Albany, N. Y., 1887. Square folio.   HH—A93

ROBERTSON, WYNDHAM, Pocahontas, alias Matoaka, and her descendants through her marriage . . . with John Rolfe . . . notes by R. A. Brock. 84 pp., 1 port. Richmond, Va., 1887. O.   HH—P75
Gift of Mrs. Martha J. Lamb.

R[OBINSON,] [MRS. I[DA] M[AY]. Items of ancestry, by a descendant. 93 pp. O. Boston, 1894.   HH—Rob56
Privately printed.
Gift of the Author.

ROEBLING, EMILY WARREN. Journal of the Rev. Silas Constant
. . . Presbyterian Church at Yorktown, N. Y. . . . Records of the
Church . . . list of marriages, 1784-1825 . . . notes on families
mentioned. Edited by J. G. Leach. 561 pp., 1 chart, 3 fac-sim., 5
groups, 15 plates, 11 port. Philadelphia, 1903. O.   HH—C788
names of German, Swiss, Dutch, French, and other immigrants in
No. 18 of 300 copies, privately printed.
Gift of the Author.

ROXBURY CHURCH. Records relating to Brookline. (Brook-
line Hist. Pub. Society Publications, No. 5, pp. 55-57.)   HH—Pamphlet
A reprint, Vol. VI, Reports of Record Commissioners of Boston, 2nd
edition, 1884.

ROYAL (The) descent and Colonial ancestry of Mrs. Harley Calvin
Gage. 32 pp. O. no place, [cop. 1910].   HH—A54

RUPP, I. DANIEL, Professor. A collection of . . . thirty thousand
Pennsylvania, from 1727 to 1776 . . . With . . . historical and
other notes, also, an appendix containing lists of more than one thousand German and French names in New York prior to 1712. 495
pp. Philadelphia, 1880. 2nd ed., revised . . . with German translations. D.   HH—R82

ST. DUNSTAN'S, Stepney, England. Marriage registers. Edited by
Thomas Colyer-Fergusson (I). 3 vols. Canterbury, 1898 to 1902.
Q.   HH—F38
Vol. I. 1568-1639.
Vol. II. 1640-1696.
Vol. III. 1697-1719.

SALEM PRESS Historical & Genealogical Record. No. 1, Vol. I;
No. 3, Vol. II. Salem, Mass., 1890-1892.   HH—Sal

SALISBURY, EDWARD ELBRIDGE. Family memorials. A series of
genealogical and biographical monographs. . . . With 15 pedigrees
and an appendix. 2 vols. Square folio. New Haven, 1885.
Gift of Mrs. James M. Lawton.   HH—Sa3M

SALISBURY, EDWARD ELBRIDGE, & Salisbury, E. McC. Family
Histories & genealogies; a series of genealogical and biographical
monographs. . . . With 29 pedigree-charts & 2 charts of combined
descents (in a supplement separately bound). 3 vols in 5 vols.,
pl., charts. New Haven, 1892. Square folio. 5 vols.   HH—Sa3H
Gift of Mrs. James M. Lawton.

SANXAY, THEODORE FREDERIC. The Sanxay family, and descendants
of Rev. Jacques Sanxay, Huguenot refugee to England in sixteen
hundred and eighty-five. . . . 217 pp. Square O. New York,
printed privately. 1907.   HH—Sa5
Gift of the Author.

SAVAGE, JAMES. Genealogical dictionary of the first settlers of New
England, showing three generations of those who came before May
1692, on the basis of Farmer's Register. Vols. I-IV. Boston, 1860-
1862. 4 vols. O.   HH—Sa9

SCHENCK, Alexander Du Bois, Compiler. Rev. William Schenck, his ancestry and descendants. Washington, 1883. 163 pp., plate, table. O.   HH—Sch2
Gift of the Compiler.

SCHOUTEN, H. J. De Hollandsche tak van het Schotschegeslacht Craffort of Crawfurd. 13 pp. O. n.p., 1895.   HH—W66
Reprint: Maadblad van het Geneal.-herald genootschap "De Neder-landsche Leeuw," 1894.
Gift of M. G. Wildeman.

SCOTT, Mrs. Fannie J. Platt. French Protestant exiles in Eng-land and Sweden. Reproduced from recognized authorities, from privately printed family histories, and . . . MS., pedigrees. Roches-ter, N. Y., 1909. 11 leaves. Square Q.   HH—S425
Typewritten MS., in Swedish with English translation.
Gift of the Compiler.

——— Miscellaneous genealogies of the Huguenot refugees in England, Ireland, Holland, and America, 1514-1900. 47 leaves, oblong folio. Rochester, N. Y., 1905. MS. typewritten, presentation page en-grossed.   HH—S425
Gift of the Author.

SCOTT, Mrs. Jacob de la Barre. See: SCOTT, Fannie J. Platt.

SHERWOOD, George F. Tudor, Editor. Genealogical Queries and Memoranda. . . . London, 1896.   HH—Pamphlet

STANARD, Mary Newton, & William G., Compilers. See: COLONIAL (The) Virginia Register.

STANARD, William G., & M. N., Compilers. See: COLONIAL (The) VIRGINIA Register. Albany, 1902.   HH—V817

STILES, Henry R., M.D. The history and genealogies of ancient Windsor, Connecticut; including East Windsor, South Windsor, Bloomfield, Windsor Locks, and Ellington. 1635-1891. 2 vols., fac-sim., maps, pl., port. Quarto. Hartford, Conn., 1891-'92. (Revised and enlarged edition.)   HH—Sti5
Vol. I. History.
Vol. II. Genealogy & Biography.

SUTCLIFFE, Alice Crary. Homestead (The) of a Colonial dame. A monograph. 3 p.l., 5-57 pp., 1 map, 8 pl., 5 port. Poughkeepsie, New York, 1909. O.   HH—A54
Author's autograph gift.
No. 4 of P. V.

SWOPE, Gilbert Ernest, Compiler. History of the Swope family and their connections. 1678-1896. 398 pp., 3 fac-sim., 18 group port., 42 port., 7 pl., 1 table. Lancaster, Pa., 1896. Q.   HH—Sw7
Gift of the Author.

TARRYTOWN, New York. First (The) Reformed Church. . . .
First record book of the "Old Dutch Church of Sleepy Hollow" . . .
a copy . . . by Rev. D. COLE. . . . Yonkers, N. Y., 1901. Q.
HH—F44

TUCKER, GIDEON J., Compiler. See: UNIVERSITY State of New
York. Supplementary list of Marriage licenses. (State Lib'y Bulletin, History, No. 1.) HH—N46—Supplement

ULLMAN, PERCIVAL' GLENROY, Compiler. The Coursens from
1612-1917: compiled from ancient and modern records, with the
Staten Island branch. 88 pp., 2 pl., 1 port. New York, 1888.
O. HH—C86.1
Gift of the Compiler.

ULSTER COUNTY, New York. See: ANJOU, GUSTAVE.

UNIVERSITY State of New York. Supplementary list of Marriage
licenses, years 1752-'53, 1755-'56, & 1758. Albany, 1898. O.
(State Library Bulletin. History, No. 1.) G. J. TUCKER,
Compiler. HH—N42—Supplement
Gift of the University.

VAIL, CHARLES MONTGOMERY. Vail and Armstrong. A short rec-
ord of my ancestors beginning with John Vail, Southold, Long
a reference to the L'Hommedieu family. 57 pp., 1 pl., 1 fac-sim.
Island, 1670-1760. Francis Armstrong (from Ireland) 1727. With
Goshen, N. Y., 1894. O. HH—V19
Gift of the Author.

VAN VOORHIS, E. W., Compiler. Tombstone inscriptions from the
church-yard of the First reformed Dutch church of Fishkill Village, Dutchess co., N. Y. N. Y. [1882]. 229 pp. plate. O. HH—V37
Gift of the Compiler.

VIVIEN, LOUIS. Familles du refuge en pays Neuchatelois. . . . 204
pp. O. Paris, 1899. HH—V861
Note: pages illus., with port., & crests.
Autograph Gift: Mrs. J. M. Lawton.

VOS, P. D. DE. De Grafschriften der voormalige St. Lievens-
Monsterkerk te Zierikzee. 46 pp. O. 1895. HH—W66
Reprint: Maandblad Geneal.-herald. genootschap "De Nederl.
Leeuw." 1895.
Gift of M. G. Wildeman.

WALLOON (A) family in America: Lockwood de Forest and his
forebears . . . Together with a Voyage to Guiana . . . the Journal
of Jesse de Forest and his colonists . . . by Emily Johnston de
Forest. Boston, 1914. 2 vols. O. HH—D315

WATERS, HENRY F. Genealogical gleanings in England. O. Boston, 1901. HH—W31
Index of persons and places in Vol. II.

WATSON, Stephen Marion, Editor. See: MAINE Historical & Genealogical Recorder. Vols. I-VI. Portland, Me., 1884-1889. 6 vols. Square O. HH—M28

WEISS, Nathaniel. Indépendance des Etats d'Amerique et Pierre Chaillé fils du Médecin de la Tremblade, prisonnier pour la foi, 1693-1775. Paris, 1895. O. 22 pp. HH—C434
Ext.: Bull. Soc. Prot. Fr., Juin, 1895.
Bound with: Meschinet de Richemond, L. M. . . . Le Médecin Pierre Chaillé.
Gift of the Author, through Rev. Dr. Atterbury.

WELLES, Theodore W., D.D. Hardenbergh. Leaves out of ancestral tablets; from Colonial days to the present era. 1 pl., 79-176 pp. n.p., n.d. O. HH—H25
Autograph gifts of Mrs. Q. Gillmore.

WETMORE, James Carnahan. Wetmore family of America and its collateral branches. 670 pp. Q. Albany, N. Y., 1861. HH—W53
Gift of Mrs. Martha J. Lamb.

WHITMORE, William Henry, Compiler. Graveyards of Boston. Albany, 1878. Vol. I, illustrated. O. HH—W59
Vol. I, *Copp's Hill epitaphs.*

WHITTEMORE, Henry, Compiler. History of the Sage and Slocum families of England and America, including the allied families of . . . Jermain or Germain . . . Hon. Russell Sage and Margaret Olivia (Slocum) Sage. . . . 27, xix, 44, 1-50 pp., 4 plates, 5 port. New York, 1908. Square folio. HH—S12
Gift of Mrs. Russell Sage.

WILDEMAN, Marinus Godefridus. Aanteekeningen van Benckendorff en Crommelin. 11 pp. n.p., 1899. O. HH—W673N
Overgedrukt . . . Maandb. . . . Geneal.-her. genoots. de Nederl. Leeuw, 1899.
Gift of the Author.

———— Delfsche poorters. 10 pp. n.p., 1896. O. HH—W673N
Reprint: Maandblad . . . Geneal.-herald. genootschap "De Nederl. Leeuw," 1896.
Gift of the Author.

———— Doodsberichten 1597-1743, rakende de geslach ten: v.Arnhem, v.Balveren, v.Boelzelaar, v.d.Bongert, v.Brederode, Cloeck, Cock, v.Delen, v.Essen, v.Harften, v.Langen, de Lannoy, v.Lynden, v.Matenesse, Pieck, v.Randwyck, v.Rechteren, v.Reede, v.Spuelde, v.Tellicht Vygh, v.Welderen, v.Wyhe. No place, no date, no title page. HH—W66
Gift of the Author.

WILDEMAN, Marinus Godefridus. Eenige kwartierborden der Wassenaer's zovals zij indertijd aanwezig waven in de kerken van Giessen, Warmond, Leiden en Leiderdorp. n.p., 1895. 13 pp.
O.   HH—W66
Gift of the Author.
Reprint: Maandblad . . . Geneal.-herald. genootschap "Neder-landsche Leeuw." 1894.

———— Familie-aanteekeningen Gerlings. 12 pp. O. n.p., 1897.
                                                                          HH—W673N
Rept. Maandblad . . . Geneal.-herald. . . . 1897.
Gift of the Author.

———— Genealische kwartierstaten van Nederlandsche Geslachten samengesesteld en byeengebrachtdoor . . . 's Gravenhage, 1894.
Square folio.   HH—W673W
This is the Author's family chart, cut and bound in 7 leaves. Also his portrait and autograph, and a card showing his connections and standing in many historical and genealogical societies, the latter having been collected and added to his chart, by F. M. C. L.
Gift of the Author.

———— Geslacht Brandwijk van Blokland. 20 pp. n.p., 1896. O.
                                                                          HH—W66
Reprint: Maandblad van het Geneal.-herald. . . .

———— Het geslacht Goekoop. 3 p.l., 57 leaves, 1 pl. 's Gravenhage, 1914. Q.   HH—G59
Gift of the Author.

———— Namen der . . . burgemeesteren, Schepenen, Vroddschappen en tresoriers van 's Gravenhage die sedert . . . 1738 tot 1794. . . .
Een vervolg op de lijst can J. DeRiemer. . . . n.p., 1896. 32 pp.
O.   HH—W66
Reprint: Maandblad . . . Gen.-Herald. . . . 1896.
Gift of the Author.

———— Nassau en Oranje-Nassau te Haarlem. (1515-1897.) Archi-valia. 124 pp. Haarlem, 1898. O.   HH—W673N
Autograph gift of the Author.

———— Ontwerp van een Wapen voor H. M. de Koningen. 14 pp., 1 pl. no place, 1897. O.   HH—W673N
Rep't, het Maandblad . . . Genealogisch-heraldiek . . . "Neder-landsche." 1897.
Gift of the Author.

———— Prins Willem I. 1533-1558. 29 pp., 1 port. no place, 1898.   HH—W673N
Gift of the Author.

———— Worbert (Les) comtes van Wassenaer-Starrenburg devant le tribunal de l'histoire. 49 pp. Amersfoort, 1899. O.   HH—W673N
Gift of the Author.

WOODRUFF, Francis E. The Coursens of Sussex County, New Jersey. A reprint from "The Woodruffs of New Jersey." 123 pp. New York, 1909. O.   HH—C86
Gift of the Author.

YORKTOWN, New York, Presbyterian Church Records. See: ROEBLING, Emily Warren. Journal of the Rev. Silas Constant . . . with . . . Records . . . List of marriages, 1784-1825. O. Philadelphia, 1903.   HH—C758

ZIEBER, Eugene. Rules for the proper usage of Heraldry in the United States, and other extracts from the popular authority, "Heraldry in America." 34 pp. S. Philadelphia, Pa., 1900.
                                    HH—Pamphlet

GENEALOGY

FAMILY NAMES

GENEALOGY

FAMILY NAMES

ADAMS FAMILY. Magazine of the Daughters of the Revolution. Vol. I, No. 1, pp. 8-12. N. Y., 1893. HH—Unbound

AGACE FAMILY. See: HUGUENOT Society of London. Proceedings. Vol. XI. HK—H876—Vol. XI

ALDWORTH-ELBRIDGE FAMILY. SALISBURY, EDWARD ELBRIDGE. Family memorials. . . . 2 vols. Folio. New Haven, 1885. (In Vol. I.) HH—Sa3M

ALLAIRE FAMILY. BOLTON, REV. ROBERT. History . . . of . . . Westchester. Family chart of Pierre Allaire the Huguenot and his New Rochelle (New York) descendants. In: Vol. I, facing page 677. HE—B63

AMONNET. See: MONNET.

AMYAND FAMILY. SCOTT, FANNIE J. PLATT. Miscellaneous genealogies. . . . oblong folio. Rochester, N. Y., 1905. HH—S425

AMYOT FAMILY. SCOTT, FANNIE J. PLATT. Miscellaneous genealogies . . . Huguenot refugees. . . . Oblong folio. Rochester, N. Y., 1905. HH—S425

ANDRE FAMILY. See: HUGUENOT Society of London. Proceedings. Vol. X. HK—H876—Vol. X

ANDROVETTE FAMILY. PELLETREAU, WILLIAM S. Historic homes. . . . Genealogical and family history of New York. Vol. II, page 300. Q. N. Y., 1907. (Index in Vol. IV.) HH—P36

ANDERSON FAMILY. [ANDERSON, THOMAS McA., Brig.-Gen.] Monograph of the Anderson . . . connection. Portland, Ore., 19?. O. HH—A54

ARCHER FAMILY. PERRIN, ANNA F., & Meeker, M. F. P. Allied families of . . . Perrin. N. Y., cop. 1911. O. HH—P458

ARMSTRONG FAMILY. VAIL, C. M. Vail and Armstrong. A short record of . . . ancestors. Goshen, N. Y., 1894. O. HH—V19

AUFRERE FAMILY. See: HUGUENOT Society of London. Proceedings. Vol. XI. HK—H876—Vol. XI

AURIOL FAMILY. See: HUGUENOT Society of London. Proceedings. Vol. XI. HK—H876—Vol. XI

AYMAR FAMILY. AYMAR, BENJAMIN. Aymar of New York. N. Y., 1903. O. (Reprint: Proc. H. S. of A.)   HH—A54

BANTA FAMILY. BANTA, THOMAS M. A Frisian family. The Banta genealogy. N. Y., 1893. O.   HH—B22

BARTO FAMILY. PELLETREAU, WILLIAM S. Historic homes. . . . Genealogical and family history of New York. Vol. III, page 280. N. Y., 1907. Q. (Index in Vol. IV.)   HH—P36

BARTOW FAMILY. See: BARTOW, MOREY HALE. Brief account of the Bartow family. In: HUGUENOT Society of America. Proceedings. New York, 1889. Vol. I, pp. V-VI. 1889. 2nd Edition.   HK—H871—Vol. I
An addition to the Reprint of the Proceedings of 1883, which is Part 1 of Vol. I.

BAYARD FAMILY. MALLERY, CHARLES P. Ancient families of Bohemia Manor; . . . Wilmington, 1888. O. (Papers, Hist. Soc. of Del., No. 7.)   HH—M253

——— PELLETREAU, WILLIAM S. Historic homes . . . genealogical and family history of New York. Vol. I, p. 95, and Vol. III, p. 179. N. N., 1907. Q. (Index, Vol. IV.)   HH—P36

——— WILSON, JAMES GRANT, Gen., U. S. A. Bayard family of America & Judge Bayard's London diary of 1795 to 1796. (HUGUENOT Soc'y of Amer., Proceedings, 1891. Vol. II, pp. 135-154.)   HH—H872

BEAUFORT FAMILY. HARPER, LILLIE DUP. VAN C., Editor. Colonial men and times . . . The Huguenots . . . Genealogy . . . allied families. Philadelphia, 1916. pp. 513-550.   HH—H294

BEAUREGARD FAMILY. See: HUGUENOT Society of London. Proceedings. Vol. XI.   HK—H876—Vol. XI

BELLIVEAU FAMILY. GOUDET, PLACIDE. Acadian genealogy and notes. See: Appendix A, Part 3. Canadian Archives. pp. 22-55.   HF—C213

BENEDICT FAMILY. BENEDICT, H. M. Genealogy of the Benedicts in America. Albany, 1870. O.   HH—B43

BERANGER FAMILY. In: FRANZOSISCHE Colonie. Biography, etc., Jean Abraham Béranger, and a table. page 104. No. 7/8. 1895.   HK—D491

BERNON FAMILY. PERRY, AMOS. Memorial of Zachariah Allen. 1795-1882. page 51. Cambridge, 1883. O.   HG—A15

BERTHELOT FAMILY. In: The KEIM and allied families in America and Europe. . . . Edited by DeB. R. Keim. Harrisburg, Pa., 1898-. Vol. I, pp. 49-50, 78-79, 107-110.   HH—K27

BETHUNE FAMILY. History of the Bethune family. By André DUCHESNE. Translated from the French with additions, and a sketch of the Faneuil family, by Mrs. J. A. Weisse. N. Y., 1884. 54 pp. plate. Q.   HG—B67
Gift of Dr. F. D. Weisse.

BERTOLET. See: BERTHELOT.

BLANCHAN. See: CANTINE family.

BLANCHARD FAMILY. See: SALEM (The) Book: records of the past. . . . Salem, N. Y., 1896. pp. 35-37.   HE—Sa3

BOARDMAN FAMILY. SALISBURY, EDWARD ELBRIDGE, & Salisbury, E. McC. Family histories and genealogies. . . 3 vols. in 5. Folio. New Haven, 1892. 5 vols.   HH—Sa3H

BOCHETELS FAMILY. LeLABOUREUR, J. Mémoires de Messire Michel de Castelnau. . . . T. 1-3. Folio. Bruxelles, 1731. HG—L53
In: Vol. III, pp. 140-161, 200 and following.

BODEGEM (VAN) FAMILY. ANSPACH, JAC. Van Bodegem (Bodegom) 1894.   HH—W66

BOISRAGON FAMILY. See: HUGUENOT Society of London. Proceedings. Vol. VI.   HK—H876—Vol. VI

BOND FAMILY. SALISBURY, EDWARD ELBRIDGE, & Salisbury, E. McC. Family histories and genealogies. . . . 3 vols. in 5. Folio. New Haven, 1892.   HH—Sa3H

BONTECOU FAMILY. MORRIS, JOHN E. Ancestry of Daniel Bontecou. . . . Hartford, 1887.   HH—Var4
Pamphlet Volume, "Ancestry."

BONTECOU FAMILY. Bontecou genealogy: a record of the descendants of Pierre Bontecou, a Huguenot refugee from France, in the lines of his sons. Compiled by John E. MORRIS. Hartford, 1885. 271 pp. O.   HH—B64

BOOTH FAMILY. BOOTH, CHARLES E. One branch of the Booth family . . . lines of connection with 100 Mass. Bay Colonists. N. Y., 1910.   HH—B72

BOSANQUET FAMILY. See: HUGUENOT Society of London. Proceedings. Vol. II.   HK—H876—Vol. II

BOUCHE FAMILY. In: FRANZOSISCHE (Die) Colonie. . . . No. 1, 1900. pp. 15-17.   HH—D491

BOUDINOT FAMILY. See: ATTERBURY, REV. WILLIAM WALLACE, D.D. Elias Boudinot: Reminiscences of the American Revolution. See: HUGUENOT Society of America. Proceedings, 1891. pp. 296-298.   HK—H871—Vol. II

BOUHEREAU FAMILY. See: HUGUENOT Society of London. Proceedings. Vol. VII.   HK—H876—Vol. VII

BOULIER (DE) FAMILY. See: HUGUENOT Society of London.
Proceedings. Vol. XI.   HK—H876—Vol. XI

BOURDINS FAMILY. LeLABOUREUR, J. Mémoires de Messire
Michel de Castelnau. . . . Vol. III, pp. 199-200. Bruxelles, 1731.
Folio.   HG—L53

BOURGEOIS FAMILY. GOUDET, PLACIDE. Acadian genealogy and
notes. (Appendix A, Part 3. Canadian Archives.) pp. 1-14.
                                                        HF—C-213

BOUTON FAMILY. HALL, REV. E. Ancient records, Norwalk,
Conn., and Genealogical registers. Norwalk, Conn., 1847. D.
pp. 182-183, and Appendix A, pp. 305-307.   HE—N83H

BOWDOIN FAMILY. PRIME, TEMPLE. Some account of the Bowdoin family. . . . New York, 1894. 2nd edition. O.   HH—A54

BOWTEN. See: BOUTON.

BRANDWIJK VAN BLOKLAND FAMILY. WILDEMAN, M. G.
Geslacht. . . . 20 pp. no place, 1896.   HH—W66

BREESE FAMILY. SALISBURY, EDWARD E. Family memorials.
2 vols.   HH—Sa3M

BREVARD FAMILY. HARPER, L. DuP., VanC. Editor. Colonial
men and times . . . The Huguenots . . . Genealogy . . . allied
families. Philadelphia, 1916. Q. pp. 573-575.   HH—H294

BROUSSON FAMILY. NEGRE, LÉOPOLD. Vie et ministère de Claude
Brousson, 1647-1698. . . . Paris, 1878. O.   HG—B83
(Descent of Barthèlmy, fils au Claude.)

BRUERE FAMILY. In: FRANZOSISCHE Colonie. No. 4. Page
47. 1896.   HK—D491

BUCHANAN FAMILY. SALISBURY, EDW. E., & Salisbury, E.
McC. Family Histories and genealogies. . . . 3 vols. in 5. Folio.
New Haven, 1892.   HH—Sa3H

BURNETT FAMILY. In: ADAMS' Magazine of Revolutionary Records. Vol. II, No. 5. pp. 6-7. N. Y., 1892. O.   HH—Unbound

BUTLER FAMILY. Butleriana, genealogica et biographica; or, Genealogical notes concerning Mary Butler and her descendants. By
James Davie BUTLER. Albany, 1888. 162 pp. portraits, plates,
fac-similes. O.   B97—HH

CANTINE FAMILY. JULIEN, MATTHEW CANTINE. Preliminary
statement of the Cantine genealogy. . . . Boston?, 1903. O.
                                                        HH—A54

CASTELNAU FAMILY. LeLABOUREUR, J. Mémoires de Messire
de Castelnau. . . . Tome 3, pp. 61-137. Bruxelles, 1731. Folio.
                                                        HG—L53

CASTRES FAMILY. SCOTT, FANNIE J. P. Miscellaneous genealogies . . . Huguenot refugees. Oblong F. Rochester, N. Y. 1905. HH—S425

CERJAT FAMILY. SCOTT, FANNIE J. P. . . . Genealogies . . . Huguenot refugees. . . . Rochester, N. Y., 1905. Oblong F.
HH—S425

CHAILLE FAMILY. MESCHINET DE RICHEMOND, LOUIS M. MS., genealogical chart, Arms in colour, inserted in his: "Médecin Pierre Chaillé, de la Tremblade, et sa famille, 1693-1775." Paris, 1895. O. HH—C434
Bound with: WEISS, N. Indépendance des Etats d'Amerique et Pierre Chaillé.

———— CHAILLE-LONG, COL. CHARLES. Association of Maryland. In: The Republic Magazine, Vol. I, No. 1. New York, 1890. Square Q. pp. 42-48. HE—Cha35

CHASSEREAU FAMILY. SCOTT, FANNIE J. P. Genealogies . . . Huguenot refugees. Rochester, N. Y., 1905. Oblong folio. HH—S425

CHENEVIX FAMILY. See: HUGUENOT Society of London. Proceedings. Vol. VI. HK—H876—Vol. VI

CHEVALIER-ANDERSON FAMILY. SALISBURY, EDW. E. Family memorials. . . . 2 vols. New Haven, 1885. Folio. HH—Sa3M

CHEVALLIER FAMILY. MESCHINET DE RICHEMOND, LOUIS M. MS. genealogical chart, Arms in color, inserted in his: Médecin Pierre Chaillé, de La Tremblade, et sa famille, 1693-1775. Paris, 1895. O. HH—C434

CLARKE FAMILY. SALISBURY, EDW. E., & Salisbury, E. McC. Family histories and genealogies. . . . Folio. 3 vols in 5. New Haven, 1892. HH—Sa3H

COLE FAMILY. SALISBURY, EDW. E., & Salisbury, E. McC. Family histories and genealogies. . . . Folio. New Haven, 1892.
HH—Sa3H

COMARQUE FAMILY. SCOTT, FANNIE J. P. French Protestant exiles in England & Sweden. . . . Rochester, N. Y., 1909. Square Q. HH—S425
Typewritten MS., Swedish & English.

CONVERSE FAMILY. HILL, W. G., Compiler. Family record . . . James W. Converse and Elisha S. Converse. . . . Boston, 1887, pp. 95-177. O. HH—Con74

COOLIDGE FAMILY. HILL, W. G., Compiler. Family record . . . James W. and Elisha Converse. Boston, 1887. pp. 2-7. Q.
HH—Con74

CORSON FAMILY. CORSON, HIRAM, M.D. History of the Descendants of Benjamin Corson, son of Cornelius Corssen of Staten Island, New York. Philadelphia, [1919?]. O. HH—C86

137

CORSON: See also COURSEN.

COURSEN FAMILY. ULLMAN, PERCIVAL GLENROY, Compiler. The Coursens from 1612-1917 . . . with the Staten Island branch. N. Y., 1918. O. HH—C861

——— WOODRUFF, FRANCIS E. The Coursens of Sussex County, New Jersey. A reprint from the "Woodruffs of N. J." 123 pp. N. N., 1909. O. HH—C86

COURTAULD FAMILY. See: HUGUENOT Society of London. Proceedings. Vol. XI. HK—H876—Vol. XI

CRAFFORT FAMILY. SCHOUTEN, H. J. Hollandsch tak van het Schotsche geslacht Craffort of Crawfurd. 1895. O. HH—W66 No. 4 of Dutch P. V.

CRANDALL FAMILY. Genealogy of a branch of the Crandall family. By A. P. Crandall. Chattanooga, 1888. 62 pp. D. *Half roan.* HH—C85 Gift of W. J. and A. P. Crandall.

CRUGER FAMILY. See: BOLTON, REV. ROBERT. History of the County of Westchester, edited by Rev. C. W. Bolton. 2 vols. New York, 1881. O. pp. 98-112. HE—B63

D'ESPARD. See: DESPARD.

D'HERVART FAMILY. SCOTT, FANNIE J. P. . . . Genealogies . . . Huguenot refugees. . . . Rochester, N. Y., 1905. Oblong folio. HH—S425

DEBENNEVILLE FAMILY. STAPLETON, REV. AMMON. Memorials of the Huguenots. . . . Harrisburg, Pa., Square O. HH

DEBONNAIRE FAMILY. SCOTT, FANNIE J. P. . . . Genealogies . . . Huguenot refugees. . . . Rochester, N. Y., 1905. Oblong folio. HH—S425

DEBOW. See: DUBOIS.

DE CERJAT. See: CERJAT.

DECOIGNERIES FAMILY. HILL, W. G., Compiler. Family record of. . . . Boston, 1887. pp. 77-93. O. HH—Con74

DECOMTE FAMILY. See: GESLACHTLIJST der familie de Comte, later genaamd Voute. Square folio. 'sGravenhage, 1893. HH—V97

DE COSNE FAMILY. See: HUGUENOT Society of London. Proceedings. Vol. VII. HK—H876—Vol. VII

DE COSTA FAMILY. DE COSTA, REV. BENJAMIN FRANKLIN, D.D. Genealogical chart of the De Costa family. HH—S425

DE CROY FAMILY. See: WOODRUFF, FRANCIS E. The Coursens of Sussex Co., N. J. HH—C86

DE DIBON FAMILY. [FABER, REGINALD S.] The buried book, or, the Bible of Henri de Dibon. (Genealogical notes in MS., inserted.) London, 1885. Q. HH—Fa.11

DeDIEU FAMILY. FEEN, B. van der. Genealogie de Dieu. No place, 1895. O. HH—W66 No. 7 of Dutch P. V.

DE FOREST FAMILY. DE FOREST, EMILY JOHNSTON. A Walloon family in America: Lockwood de Forest and his forebears. . . . Together with . . . the Journal of Jesse de Forest. . . . 2 vols. Boston, 1914. O. HH—D315

DE GIGNILLIAT FAMILY. BULLOCH, JOSEPH G. B., M.D. History and genealogy of the Habersham family . . . and . . . other names. . . . Columbia, S. C., 1901. O. pp. 102-103, & 84.
HH—H14

DE GRAEFF FAMILY. WILDEMAN, M. G. Genealogische kwartierstaten van Nederlandsche Geslachten samengesteld en byeengebrachtdoor. . . . 'sGravenhage, 1894. Square folio. HH—W673 Gift of the Author.

DeGROOT FAMILY. R[OBINSON], [Mrs.] I. M. Items of ancestry. . . . Boston, 1894. O. pp. 56-58. HH—Rob56

DE HABRINCHSHAM. See: HABERSHAM.

DE LA BALLE FAMILY. See: HUGUENOT Society ^f London. Proceedings. Vol. x. HK—H876—Vol. x

DE LA CHASTRE FAMILY. LeLABOUREUR, J. Mémoires de Messire Michel de Castelnau. . . . Bruxelles, 1731. Folio. Tome 3, pp. 181-189. HG—L53

DE LA CHEVALLERIE FAMILY. See: HUGUENOT Society of London. Proceedings. Vol. II. HK—H876—Vol. x

DE LA GRANGE FAMILY. SCOTT, FANNIE J. P. French Protestant exiles in England and Sweden. . . . Rochester, N. Y., 1909. Square Q. Typewritten MS., Swedish and English. HH—S425

DE LANNOY FAMILY. The Royal descent and Colonial ancestry of Mrs. Harley Calvin Gage. cop. 1910. O. HH—A54

DE LANNOY. See: LANNOY.

DELANO FAMILY. DELANO, MAJOR J. A. Genealogy . . . American house of Delano, 1621-1899. With the history and heraldry of the Maison de Franchimont and DeLannoy to Delano, 1096-1621. . . . N. Y., 1899. Q. HH—D37

DELAPLAINE FAMILY. A family history. Taneytown, Maryland. 44 pp. O. HH—A54

DE LIMOGES FAMILY. LeLABOUREUR, J. Mémoires de Messire Michel de Castelnau. . . . Bruxelles, 1731. Folio. Tome 3, pp. 213, & following. HG—L53

DELPRAT FAMILY. SCOTT, Fannie J. P. . . . Genealogies . . . Huguenot refugees. . . . Rochester, N. Y., 1905. Oblong folio.
HH—S425

DE MOROGUES FAMILY. LeLABOUREUR, J. Mémoires . . . de Castelnau. . . . Bruxelles, 1731. Folio. Tome 3, pp. 197-198, & following. HG—L53

DE MORTAIGNE FAMILY. SCOTT, FANNIE J. P. French Protestant exiles in England and Sweden. . . . Rochester, N. Y., 1909. Square Q. Typewritten MS., Swedish & English. HH—S425

DE MORVILLIER FAMILY. LeLABOUREUR, J. Mémoires . . . de Castelnau. . . . Bruxelles, 1731. Folio. pp. 161-171, table page 202, in Tome 3. HG—L53

DE PEYSTER FAMILY. DePEYSTER, COL. ARENT S. Miscellanies . . . edited by J. Watts de Peyster. (Dumfries, 1813), New York, 1888. O. HG—D419

DeRAPALLE FAMILY. WELLES, THEODORE W., D.D. Hardenbergh. Leaves out of ancestral tablets from Colonial days to the present era. No place, no date. O. pp. 96-98. HH—H25

DeREIMER FAMILY. WELLES, THEODORE W., D.D. Hardenbergh. Leaves out of ancestral tablets from Colonial days to the present era. No place, no date. O. pp. 162-163. HH—H25

DE ROCHECHOUART FAMILY. LeLABOUREUR, J. Mémoires . . . de Castelnau. . . . Bruxelles, 1731. Folio. pp. 214-following, Tome 3. HG—L53

DESCARRIERES FAMILY. SCOTT, FANNIE J. P. . . . Genealogies . . . Huguenot refugees. . . . Rochester, N. Y., 1905. Oblong folio. HH—S425

DES MAREST FAMILY. See: HUGUENOT Society of America. Proceedings. Vol. I, Part 2. pp. 30-36. 1889. HK—H87.1—Vol. I

DE SOUCHE FAMILY. See: HUGUENOT Society of London. Proceedings. Vol. II. HK—H876—Vol. II

DESPARD FAMILY. See: DODGE, RICHARD DESPARD. The Despard family. In: HUGUENOT Society of America. Proceedings. Vol. III, Part 2. pp. 230-244. New York, 1903.
HK—H871—Vol. III

DES TOMBE FAMILY. WILDEMAN, M. G. Genealogische kwartierstaten van Nederlandsche Geslachten samengesteld en byeengebrachtdoor. . . . 'sGravenhage, 1894. Square F. HH—W673

DE VANTIER FAMILY. See: HUGUENOT Society of London. Proceedings. Vol. II. HK—H876—Vol. II

——— SCOTT, FANNIE J. P. . . . Genealogies . . . Huguenot refugees. . . . 1514-1900. Rochester, N. Y., 1905. Oblong folio. p. 42. HH—S425

DE VEAUX FAMILY. Genealogy of the De Veaux family: introducing the numerous forms of spelling the name by various branches and generations in the past eleven hundred years. By Thomas F. DE VOE. N. Y., 1885. 302 pp. illustrated. O.   HH—D49

DE VENOURS FAMILY. GUYOT, HENRI DANIEL, Marquis de Venours protecteur des victimes de l'intolérance de Louis XIV. 31 pp. Groninque, 1906. O.   HG—S33
Biographical & Historical Essays.

DE VICOSE FAMILY. See: HUGUENOT Society of London. Proceedings. Vol. x.   HK—H876—Vol. x

DE VICOUSE. See: DE VICOSE.

DE VILLETTES FAMILY. See: HUGUENOT Society of London. Proceedings. Vol. x.   HK—H876—Vol. x

DEVOE. See: DEVEAUX.

DEVOTION FAMILY. DEVOTION, SARA, Compiler. Genealogy of the DeVotion family; a brief account copied from records. MS. Square Q. New York, 1894.   HJ—D49

DE WOLF FAMILY. SALISBURY, EDW. E., & Salisbury, E. McC. Family histories and genealogies. . . . 3 vols. in 5. Folio. New Haven, 1892.   HH—Sa3H

DE ZOUCHE. See: DE SOUCHE.

DIGBY FAMILY. SALISBURY, EDW. E., & Salisbury, E. McC. Family histories and genealogies. . . . 3 vols in 5. Folio. New Haven, 1892.   HH—Sa3H

DIGUES (DE) FAMILY. See: HUGUENOT Society of London. Proceedings. Vol. xi.   HK—H876—Vol. xi

DIODATI FAMILY. SALISBURY, EDW. E., & Salisbury, E. McC. Family histories and genealogies. . . . 3 vols in 5. Folio. New Haven, 1892.   HH—Sa3H

DODGE FAMILY. Tristam Dodge and his descendants in America: with historical and descriptive accounts of Block Island and Cow Neck, L. I., their original settlements. By Robert DODGE. N. Y., 1886. 233 pp. O.   HH—D66

DOUCHETT FAMILY. DOUCHETT, A. T., Compiler. Douchett and Ward families, genealogical notes. . . . Pittsburgh, Pa., 1889.   HH—D74

DRAKE FAMILY. SALISBURY, EDW. E., & Salisbury, E. McC. Family histories and genealogies. . . . 3 vols. in 5. Folio. New Haven, 1892.   HH—Sa3H

DU BOIS FAMILY. Bi-centenary reunion of the descendants of Louis and Jacques Du Bois (emigrants to America, 1660 and 1675), at New Paltz, N. Y., 1875. [Compiled by William E. and Patterson Du Bois.] Philadelphia, 1876. 158 pp. portraits, plates, fac-simile. Q. HH—D85

—— Documents and genealogical chart of the family of Benjamin Du Bois, of Catskill, N. Y., being an addition to the history of the descendants of Louis and Jacques Du Bois, as given at the Bi-centenary reunion held at New Paltz, Ulster Co., N. Y., 1875. Compiled by Anson and James G. Dubois. N. Y., 1878. 104 pp. Bound with the "Bi-centenary." HH—D85

—— Documents and genealogical chart of the family of Benjamin DuBois, of Catskill, N. Y. . . . N. Y., 1875. Compiled by Anson and James G. DuBois. 104 pp. Square Q. HH—D852
This copy bound as separate volume.
Gift of Anson DuBois.

—— Descendants of Jacques Du Bois [genealogical chart]. By George W. Du Bois. In HH—D85

—— PELLETREAU, WILLIAM S. Historic homes . . . genealogical and family history of New York. N. Y., 1907. Vol. I, page 175; Vol. III, page 275. Q. HH—P36

—— WELLES, THEODORE W., D.D. Hardenbergh. Leaves out of ancestral tablets, from Colonial days to the present era. pp. 106-113. O. HH—H25

DU HOUX FAMILY. GUYOT, HENRI DANIEL. Deux compagnies de français réfugies à Groningue. No title page. HB—A2H

DUMONT FAMILY. McPIKE, Eugene F., Editor. Tales of our forefathers and Biographical annals of families allied to those of McPike, Guest, and Dumont. . . . Square Q. Albany, N. Y., 1898. HG—M17

DUNBAR FAMILY. SALISBURY, EDW. E., & Salisbury, E. McC. Family histories and genealogies. . . . 3 vols. in 5. Folio. New Haven, 1892. HH—Sa3H

DuPUY FAMILY. DuPUY, CHARLES MEREDITH. Genealogical history of the DuPuy family. With additions by his son, H. DuPuy. Square Q. Privately printed, Philadelphia, 1910. HH—D94

—— DuPUY, CHARLES MEREDITH. MS., historical sketch of the DuPuy family. 1883. HH—MSS.

—— In: HARPER, LILLIE DuP. VANC., Editor. Colonial men and times. . . . The Huguenots. Genealogy, with . . . sketches of the allied families. Philadelphia, 1916. Q. pp. 164-194, 369-417. HH—H294

—— PETTETREAU, WILLIAM S. Historic homes and institutions and genealogical and family history of New York. N. Y., 1907. Q. Vol. III, p. 274. HH—P36

DURAEUS FAMILY. TOLLIN, HENRI. Johann Duraeus. 2 vols. in
1. Magdeburg, 1898. O. HG—947

DUROURE FAMILY. See: HUGUENOT Society of London. Proceedings. Vol. x. HK—H876—Vol.x

DURYEA FAMILY. PELLETREAU, WILLIAM S. Historic homes
. . . genealogical and family history of New York. N. Y., 1907.
Q. Vol. IV, page 325. HH—P36

DUS FAMILY. In: FRANZOSISCHE Colonie. Vol. für 1896, heft.
3, page 41. HH—D491

DUTILH. See: RIGAUD.

DUVAL FAMILY. See: HUGUENOT Society of London. Proceedings. Vol. VIII. HK—H876—Vol. VIII

DUVALL FAMILY. DUVAL, MARY REBECCA. Duvalls (The) of
Maryland. (HUGUENOT Society of America. Proceedings.
Vol. III, Part 2, pp. 137-148. 1903.) HK—H871—Vol. III

DU VERGER DE MONROY FAMILY. In: FRANZOSISCHE Colonie. Genealogische notizen. . . . No. 7/8, 1895, pp. 98-104.
HK—D491

DU VERGIER DE MONROY. See: DU VERGER DE MONROY.

EDMONDS FAMILY. HILL, W. G. Family record of James W. &
Elisha S. Converse. . . . Boston, 1887. O. pp. 9-40. HH—Con74

EECKHOUT (VAN DEN) FAMILY. CRAB, A. J. E. VAN DER. Geslacht van den Eeckhout. No place, 1895. HH—W66
No. 6 of Dutch P. V.

EROUARD FAMILY. WATERS, EDWARD STANLEY. Notes on some
Huguenot families. (HUGUENOT Society of America. Proceedings. Vol. III, Part 2. pp. 245-271. 1903.) HK—H87.1—Vol. III

ERVING FAMILY. PRIME, TEMPLE. Some account of the Bowdoin
family, with notes on the families of . . . Erving. N. Y., 1894.
2nd ed. O. HH—A54

FALCONER. See: FAUCONIER, and FAUCONNIER.

FANEUIL FAMILY. DUCHESNE, ANDRE. History of the Bethune
family . . . together with a sketch of the Faneuil family. N. Y.,
1884. Q. pp. 45-49. HG—B67

—————— Genealogical records of the Faneuil family. MS. HH—MS.

FAUCONIER FAMILY. The famous Falconeer House . . . John
Fauconiere or Falconeer's ancestry . . . old families . . . White
Plains, N. Y., 1909. In: Westchester County Magazine, Vol. IV,
No. 2, pp. 13-15; Vol. III, No. 4, p. 15. HE—N533

FAUCONNIER FAMILY. HELFFENSTEIN, ABRAHAM ERNEST.
Pierre Fauconnier and his descendants; With some account of the
allied Valleaux. Philadelphia, 1911. Q.   HH—F25

———— PERRIN, ANNA F., & Meeker, M. F. P. Allied families of
Purdy, Fauconnier, Archer, Perrin. N. Y., cop. 1911. O.   HH—P458

FELT FAMILY. MORRIS, John E. Record of the descendants of
George Felt of Casco Bay. Hartford, Conn., 1893. O.   HH—F36

FERRIS FAMILY. In: ADAMS' Magazine of general literature. Vol.
I. No. 4, pp. 26-29. New York, 1891. O.   HH—Unbound

FIELD FAMILY. PIERCE, F. C. Field genealogy . . . record of all
the Field family in America . . . prior to 1700. . . . All descendants of the Fields of England, whose ancestor, Hurbutus de la Field,
was from Alsace-Lorraine. Chicago, 1901. Q.   HH—F45

FLOURNOY FAMILY. HARPER, LILLIE DUP. VANC., Editor.
Colonial men and times. . . . The Huguenots. Genealogy . . .
allied families. Philadelphia, 1916. Q. pp. 289-300.   HH—H294

———— RIVERS, FLOURNOY, Compiler. Genealogy: the Flournoy
family. In: VIRGINIA Magazine of History & Biography.
Vol. II, pp. 81-90, 190-213, 318-327, 437-447.   HK—V81

FOURDRINIER FAMILY. See: HUGUENOT Society of London.
Proceedings.   HK—H87.6—Vol. VI

FRENEAU FAMILY. AUSTIN, MARY A. Philip Freneau, the Poet
of the Revolution. A history of his life and times. . . . Edited by
Mrs. H. V. Vreeland. N. Y., 1901. O.   HG—F88A

———— FRENEAU, PHILIP MORIN. Poems . . . American Revolution, with . . . memoir and notes by E. A. Duyckinck. N. Y.,
1865. Q.   HG—F88

GAILLARD FAMILY. Table (Chart) of the descendants of the Huguenot Peter Gaillard. Complete to the present time. (A large
broadside; heavy cardboard.)   HG—Gaillard Chart

———— LELABOUREUR, J. Mémoires . . . de Castelnau . . .
Bruxelles, 1731. Folio. Tome 3, pp. 171-180, 190-196; table, pp.
203-204.   HG—L53

GALLAUDET FAMILY. HAYDEN, REV. H. E. Oliver genealogy,
a record of the descendants of Joseph, Reuben, and Levi Oliver . . .
and of Pierre Elisée Gallaudet. . . . N. Y., 188?. O.   HH—Var4
No. 5 of P. V., "Ancestry."

GARNAULT FAMILY. See: HUGUENOT Society of London. Proceedings. Vol. XI.   HK—H876—Vol. XI

GERARD FAMILY. PELLETREAU, WILLIAM S. Historic homes
. . . Genealogical and family history of New York. N. Y., 1907.
Q. Vol. I, page 388.   HH—P36

GERLINGS FAMILY. WILDEMAN, M. G. Familie-aanteekeningen
Gerlings. n.p., 1897. HH—W673N

GERMAIN. See: JERMAIN.

GEROULD FAMILY. Genealogy of the family of Gamaliel Gerould,
son of Dr. Jacques (or James) Jerould of the province of Languedoc,
France. Compiled by Samuel L. Gerould. Bristol, N. H., 1885.
84 pp. O. HH—G31

GERVAISE FAMILY. SCOTT, FANNIE J. P. . . . Genealogies . . .
Huguenot refugees. . . . Rochester, N. Y., 1905. Oblong folio.
HH—S425

GIBERT FAMILY. BENOIT, DANIEL. Les Frères Gibert. Deux
pasteurs du désert et du refuge, 1722-1817. Torlouse, 1889. D.
HG—G35

GILBERT FAMILY. See: HUGUENOT Society of London. Proceedings. Vol. XI. HK—H876—Vol. XI

GODDE FAMILY. SCOTT, FANNIE J. P. . . . Genealogies . . .
Huguenot refugees. . . . Rochester, N. Y., 1905. Oblong folio.
HH—S425

GODIN FAMILY. BULLOCH, JOSEPH G. B., M.D. History & genealogy of the Habersham family . . . and other names. . . . Columbia, S. C., 1901. O. Page 165. HH—H14

GOEKOOP FAMILY. WILDEMAN, GESLACHT GOEKOOP. 'sGravenhage, 1814. 57 leaves, 1 pl. Q. HH—G59

GOELET FAMILY. PELLETREAU, WILLIAM S. Historic homes
. . . genealogical and family history of New York. New York,
1907. Q. Vol. I, page 186. HH—P36

GOODE FAMILY. GOODE, G. B. Virginia cousins; a study of the
ancestry and posterity of John Goode of Whitby . . . with notes
upon related families. . . . Preface by R. A. Brock. 526 pp., port.,
pl. Richmond, Va., 1887. Q. HH—G54

GOOKIN FAMILY. SALISBURY, EDW. E. Family memorials. . . .
2 vols. New Haven, 1885. Square folio. HH—Sa3M

GOUVERNEUR FAMILY. PELLETREAU, WILLIAM S. Historic
homes . . . genealogical and family history of New York. N. Y.,
1907. Vol. I, page 143. HH—P36

GRANT FAMILY. Ancestry of General Grant, and their contemporaries. By Edward Chauncey MARSHALL. N. Y., 1869. 186 pp.
D. HH—G76

GREENOUGH FAMILY. PLATT, F., Compiler. Notes upon the
ancestry of Ebenezer Greenough . . . and of his wife . . . Abigail
Israel. . . . Philadelphia, 1895. O. HH—P69

GRISWOLD FAMILY. SALISBURY, EDW. E., & Salisbury, E. McC.
Family histories and genealogies. . . . 3 vols. in 5. New Haven,
1892. Folio. HH—Sa3H

GUICHARD FAMILY. GUYOT, HENRI DANIEL. Deux compagnies de français réfugiés à Groningue. 15 pp. Groningue, 189?. n.t.p. HH—A2H

GUSTINE FAMILY. In: FRANZOSISCHE Colonie. No. 1, 1900. pp. 15-17. HK—D491

GUYON FAMILY. DELAVAN, E. C., JR. The Guyon house. A history based upon personal researches and family data supplied by Miss S. G. Clark. pp. 113-138, 1 fac-sim., 2 plans, 1 pl. New York, 1916. O. (Reprint, Proceedings S. I., Assoc. Arts & Sciences, Vol. VI, Part 2.) HH—G

GUYOT FAMILY. GUYOT, HENRI DANIEL. Généalogie de la famille Guyot, avec pièces justificatives. 40 pp. 2nd ed. Groningue, 1900. O. HH—Var4

———— Same: first edition. 38 pp. Both editions in this volume.

HABERSHAM FAMILY. BULLOCH, JOSEPH G. B., M.D. History and genealogy of the Habersham family . . . and other names . . . related . . . to some family in this work. Columbia, S. C., 1901. O. pp. 4, 58 & 59. HH—H14

HARDENBERGH FAMILY. WELLES, THEODORE W., D.D. Hardenbergh. Leaves out of ancestral tablets from Colonial days to the present era. O. n.p., n.d. HH—H25

HARWAY. See: EROUARD.

HASBROUCK FAMILY. [COLVER, HENRY CLAY, Compiler.] Hasbrouck. Historical facts and chronological table of Hasbrouck family. 12 pp. Seattle, Wash., 1904?. O. HH—A54

———— WELLES, THEODORE W., D.D. Hardenbergh. Leaves out of ancestral tablets, from Colonial days to the present era. n.p., n.d. O. page 114. HH—H25

HAVERSHAM. See: HABERSHAM.

HERICOURT, (DE) FAMILY. KEIM (The) and allied families. . . . Edited by DeB. R. Keim. Harrisburg, Pa., 1898-. O. In: Vol. I, p. 50. HH—K27

HERRICK FAMILY. Herrick genealogy: genealogical register of the names and family of Herrick from the settlement of Henerie Hericke, in Salem, Mass., 1629-1846, with a concise notice of their English ancestry. By Jedediah Herrick. Revised, augmented and brought down to 1885, by Lucius C. Herrick. Columbus, Ohio, 1885. 516 pp. illustrated, portraits. O. HH—H43

HILLEGAS FAMILY. The American historical register. No. 1, pp. 23-28. Philadelphia, 1894. O. HH

HOFFMAN FAMILY. HOFFMAN, Very Rev. E. A., D.D. Genealogy of the Hoffman family, descendants of Martin Hoffman, with biographical notes. N. Y., 1899. O. HH—H65 No. 7 of 250 cop.

HOO FAMILY. SALISBURY, Edward Elbridge, and Salisbury, E. McC. Family histories and genealogies. . . . 3 vols. in 5. F. New Haven, 1892. 5 vols. HH—Sa3H

HUGER FAMILY. HUGUENOT Society of South Carolina. Transactions. Vols. I, II, & subsequent. HH—H87-8

HUGUENOT (The) families in America. [By Charles Weiss.] pp. 231-232, 151-155, 298-302, 461-465. Boston, 1862. O. (In: Continental Monthly. Vol. I, Nos. 2-4.) HB—H897

HURLBUT FAMILY. Hurlbut genealogy; or, Record of the descendants of Thomas Hurlbut of Saybrook and Wethersfield, Conn., who came to America as early as 1637, with notices of others not identified as his descendants. By Henry Higgins Hurlbut. Albany, 1888. 545 pp. illustrated, portraits. O. HH—H93

JAMES FAMILY. See: JAMES, EDMUND J. Stites and James genealogy. 6 pp. O. New York, 1898. HH—Pamphlet Reprint, N. Y. Gen. & Biog. Record, October 1897, April 1898.

JERMAIN FAMILY. WHITTEMORE, HENRY, Compiler. History of the Sage and Slocum families . . . including the allied families of Jermain or Germain. . . . Hon. Russell Sage. . . . pl., port. N. Y., 1908. Square folio. HH—S12

JOHNSON FAMILY. SALISBURY, Edward Elbridge, and Salisbury, E. McC. Family histories and genealogies. . . . 3 vols. in 5. Folio. New Haven, 1892. HH—Sa3H

KEIM FAMILY. KEIM (The) and allied families in America and Europe. . . . Harrisburg, Pa., 1898-1900. O. HH—K27

KNIGHT FAMILY. ROBINSON, [Mrs.] I. M. Items of ancestry. . . . pp. 45-46. O. Boston, 1894. HH—Rob56

L'HOMMEDIEU FAMILY. Holgate, Jerome B. American genealogy . . . early settlers . . . their descendants . . . intermarriages and collateral branches, . . . with . . . genealogical tables. 244 pp. Albany, 1848. Square folio. pp. 64-65. HH—H731

———— MATHER, FREDERIC GREGORY. Refugees of 1776 from Long Island to Connecticut. Albany, N. Y., 1913. O. pp. 446-452. HE

———— PELLETREAU, WILLIAM S. Historic homes. Genealogical and family history of New York. Vol. III. HH—P36
In this volume is inserted a "Photograph of Register in the old Family Bible which belonged to Benjamin L'Hommedieu, Jr., of Southold, son of Benjamin L'Hommedieu, the Emigrant from La Rochelle, France, after the Revocation of the Edict of Nantes. This Bible belongs to Katherine Ward Lane of Boston, who also owns the portrait by Earle of her great-great-grandfather, Ezra L'Hommedieu, of Southold, who was for over 40 years in the service of his Country."
This Photograph faces page 194 in Vol. III.

———— VAIL, C. M. Vail and Armstrong. A short record of my ancestors. . . . Goshen, New York, 1894. O. pp. 13-17. HH—V19

LABOUCHERE FAMILY. See: HUGUENOT Society of London. Proceedings. Vol. x   HK—H876—Vol. x

LA CHEVALLERIE FAMILY. See: HUGUENOT Society of London. Proceedings. Vol. VI.   HK—H876—Vol. VI

LA CHEVALLERIE. See also DE LA CHEVALLERIE.

LAFARGUE FAMILY. See: HUGUENOT Society of London. Proceedings. Vol. VII.   HK—H876—Vol. VII

LA MELONIERE FAMILY. SCOTT, F. J. P. Miscellaneous genealogies of the Huguenot Refugees. . . . Rochester, N. Y., 1905. Oblong folio.   HH—S42

LANGLOIS FAMILY. SCOTT, F. J. P. Miscellaneous genealogies of the Huguenot refugees. . . . Rochester, N. Y., 1905. Oblong folio.   HH—S42

LANIER FAMILY. LANIER, J. F. D. Sketch of life. 62 pp., port. N. Y., 1871. O.   HH—L27

LANNOY FAMILY. DELANO, MAJOR JOEL ANDREW. Genealogy, . . . of the American house of Delano, 1621-1899. With the history and heraldry of the Maison de Franchimont and DeLannoy to Delano, 1096 to 1621. . . . Arranged by M. D. deLannoy. N. Y., 1899. Q.   HH—D37
One of 400 copies.

LANOUE FAMILY. GOUDET, PLACIDE. Acadian genealogy & notes. (Appendix A, Part 3. Canadian Archives.) pp. 15-21.
                                                          HF—C213

LARPENT FAMILY. LARPENT, F. DEH. Note concerning the family of Larpent settled between 1695-1705 in Denmark and Norway. 7 pp. Square O. [London, S. E., 1916.]   HH—A54

LA TOUCHE FAMILY. See: HUGUENOT Society of London. Proceedings. Vol. XI.   HK—H876—Vol. XI

LAULHE FAMILY. SCOTT, F. J. P. Miscellaneous genealogies . . . Huguenot. . . . Rochester, N. Y., 1905. Oblong folio.
                                                          HH—S42

LaVILLAIN FAMILY. HARPER, L. DUP. VANC. Colonial men and times. . . . The Huguenots. Genealogy . . . allied families. Philadelphia, 1916. Q. (Also spelled LaVilain.)   HH—H294

LAY FAMILY. SALISBURY, EDWARD ELBRIDGE, and Salisbury, E. McC. Family histories and genealogies. . . . 3 vols. in 5. Folio. New Haven, 1892. 5 vols.   HH—Sa3H

LAYARD FAMILY. See: HUGUENOT Society of London. Proceedings. Vol. VIII.   HK—H876—Vol. VIII

LeBRUN, or LEBRUN. See: RIOU FAMILY.

LEE FAMILY. Lee, William, Compiler. John Leigh of Agawam
(Ipswich) Massachusetts, 1634-1671, and his descendants of the
name of Lee. Albany, 1888. O. HH—L51

———— SALISBURY, EDWARD ELBRIDGE, and Salisbury, E. McC.
Family histories and genealogies. . . . 3 vols. in 5. Folio. New
Haven, 1892. HH—Sa3H

LEGARE FAMILY. FLUDD, MRS. ELIZA C. K. Biographical sketches
of the Huguenot Solomon Legaré and of his family, extending down
to the fourth generation of his descendants. . . . Charleston, S. C.,
1886. 142 pp. O. HH—L53

LeKEUX FAMILY. SCOTT, FANNIE J. P. Miscellaneous Genealogies . . . Huguenot refugees. . . . Rochester, N. Y., 1905. Oblong
folio. HH—S42

LE MONTRESOR. See: MONTRESOR.

LeROY FAMILY. PELLETREAU, WILLIAM S. Historic homes and
institutions and genealogical and family history of New York. 4
vols. illustrated, port., fac-sim. Q. N. Y., 1907. HH—P36

LESESNE FAMILY. BULLOCH, JOSEPH G. B., M.D. History &
genealogy of the Habersham family . . . and . . . other names.
. . . Columbia, S. C., 1901. O. Page 7. HH—H14

LINCOLN FAMILY. MORRIS, JOHN E., Compiler. Stephen Lincoln of Oakham. . . . O. Hartford, Conn., 1895. HH—M831

LOCKE FAMILY. SALISBURY, Edward Elbridge, and Salisbury, E.
McC. Family histories and genealogies. . . . 3 vols. in 5. Folio.
New Haven, 1892. HH—Sa3H

LOGONIER FAMILY. See: HUGUENOT Society of London. Proceedings. Vol. VI. HK—H876—Vol. VI

LORD FAMILY. SALISBURY, Edward Elbridge, and Salisbury, E.
McC. Family histories and genealogies. . . . 3 vols. in 5. Folio.
New Haven, 1892. HH—Sa3H

LYNDE FAMILY. PRIME, TEMPLE. Some account of the Bowdoin
family. With notes on the families of . . . Lynde. . . . 52 pp. 2nd
ed. O. New York, 1894. HH—A54

———— SALISBURY, Edward Elbridge, and Salisbury, E. McC. Family histories and genealogies. . . . 3 vols. in 5. Folio. New Haven,
1892. HH—Sa3H

MacCURDY FAMILY. SALISBURY, Edward Elbridge, and Salisbury, E. McC. Family histories and genealogies. . . . 3 vols. in 5.
New Haven, 1892. HH—Sa3H

McALLISTER FAMILY. McALLISTER, JAMES GRAY. Family
records. . . . 88 pp., illus. O. [Easton, Pa.], 1912. HH—A54

MAGNY FAMILY. WATERS, EDWARD STANLEY. Notes on some Huguenot faimlies. . . . (HUGUENOT Society of America. Proceedings. Vol. III, Part 2. pp. 245-271. 1903.)

HK—H87.1—Vol.III

MAJENDIE FAMILY. See: HUGUENOT Society of London. Proceedings. Vol. VIII.　　　　　　　　　　　HK—H876—Vol. VIII

MANGIN FAMILY. BOWER, HERBERT M. The Fourteen of Meaux. Account of the earliest "Reformed Church" within France proper, organized by Estienne Mangin and Pierre Le Clere. London, 1894. O.　　　　　　　　　　　　　　HA—B67
(A reprint from Vol. V, HUGUENOT Soc'y of London. Proceedings.)

—— See: HUGUENOT Society of London. Proceedings. Vol. V.

HK—H876—Vol. V

MANY. See: MAGNY.

MARSH FAMILY. MARSH, LUCIUS B. Genealogy of John Marsh of Salem and his descendants, 1633-1888. Revised and edited by Rev. D. W. Marsh. Amherst, Mass., 1888. 283 pp. O.　HH—M35

MARSHALL FAMILY. PAXTON, W. M. Marshall family; genealogical chart of the descendants of John Marshall and . . . his wife, sketches of individuals & notices of families connected with them. 415 pp., 1 port., 1 pl. O. Cincinnati, 1885.　　HH—M351

MARTINI FAMILY. MUELEN, J. C. VAN DER. Kwartierstaten betreffende het geslacht Martini. 14 pp. O. n.p., 1895. Reprint: Maandblad van het Geneal.-herald. genootschap "De Nederlandsche Leeuw," 1895.　　　　　　　　　　　HH—W66
No. 9 of Dutch P. V.

MARVIN FAMILY. SALISBURY, Edward Elbridge, and Salisbury, E. McC. Family histories and genealogies. . . . 3 vols. in 5. Folio. New Haven, 1892.　　　　　　　　　　　　　　HH—Sa3H

MAUVE FAMILY. BULLOCH, JOSEPH G. B., M.D. History and genealogy of the Habersham family . . . and many other names . . . related or connected. . . . 222 pp. Columbia, S. C., 1901. O. Page 74.　　　　　　　　　　　　　　　　　HH—H14

MAXWELL FAMILY. HOUSTON, FLORENCE A. WILSON, & others, Maxwell history and genealogy, including the allied families. . . . Indianapolis, Ind., cop. 1916.　　　　　　　　HH—M465

MELLICK FAMILY. MELLICK, A. D., JR. Story of an old farm, or, Life in New Jersey in the 18th century; with a Genealogical appendix. Somerville, N. J., 1889. Q.　　　　　HE—M48

MENANTAUX FAMILY. In: FRANZOSISCHE (Die) Colonie. . . . Volume für 1896, heft 3, page 41.　　　　　HK—D491

MERSEREAU FAMILY. In: ADAMS' Magazine of Revolutionary records. Vol. II, No. 6, pp. 6-10. New York, 1892.　HH—Pamphlet

—— PELLETREAU, WILLIAM S. Historic homes and institutions and genealogical and family history of New York. 4 vols. Illustrated. New York, 1907. Q. Vol. II, page 377, & Vol. IV, page 28.

HH—P96

MICHELET FAMILY. MICKLEY, MINNIE F. Genealogy of the Mickley family of America . . . with a . . . record of the Michelet family of Metz. . . . Mickleys, Pa., 1893. O.   HH—M62

MICKLEY FAMILY. See: MICHELET family.

MIGAULT FAMILY. MIGAULT, JEAN. Journal de Jean Migault, maitre d'ecole, 1681-1688. . . . Paris, 1910. D.   HA—M634

MINET FAMILY. MINET, WILLIAM, Compiler. Some account of the Huguenot family of Minet from their coming out of France at the Revocation of the Edict of Nantes, 1686. . . . 7 to 240 pp., illus., port., fac-sim., tab. Square folio. London, 1892.   HH—M63

MITCHELL FAMILY. SALISBURY, Edward Elbridge, and Salisbury, E. McC. Family histories and genealogies. . . . 3 vols. in 5. Folio. New Haven, 1892.   HH—Sa3H

MOLINIER FAMILY. See: HUGUENOT Society of London. Proceedings. Vol. x.   HK—H876—Vol. x

MONNET FAMILY. MONNETTE, ORRA EUGENE, Compiler. Monnet family genealogy . . . Somewhat of the first immigrants, Isaac & Pierre Monnet. . . . [Los Angeles, Cal., 1911.] Q.   HH—M748

MORTRESOR FAMILY. See: HUGUENOT Society of London. Proceedings. Vol. II.   HK—H876—Vol. II

——— SCULL, G. D., Editor. The Montresor journals. XII, 578 pp., 2 port. New York, 1881. O. In: NEW YORK Historical Soc'y. Collections. Vol. XIV.   HK—N532

MOTT FAMILY. ROYAL descent and Colonial ancestry of Mrs. Harley Calvin Gage, (Mary Eldora Mott). 32 pp. O. cop. 1910.   HH—A54

MULFORD FAMILY. MULFORD, W. R. Genealogy of the family of Mulford. 12 pp. O. Boston, 1880.   HE—Z2

NASSAU FAMILY. PUTNAM, RUTH. William the Silent, Prince of Orange. . . . 2 vols. O. N. Y., 1898. (In: Vol. I, pp. 6-22.)   HG—P98

NEWDIGATE FAMILY. SALISBURY, EDWARD ELBRIDGE, and Salisbury, E. McC. Family histories and genealogies. . . . 3 vols. in 5. Folio. New Haven, 1892.   HH—Sa3H

NEWGATE FAMILY. PRIME, TEMPLE. Some account of the Bowdoin family, with notes on the families of . . . Newgate. . . . 52 pp., 2nd ed. O. New York, 1894.   HH—A54

NOURSE FAMILY. LYLE, M. C. N., Compiler. James Nourse and his descendants. Lexington, Ky., 1897. Q.   HH—N85

OGDEN FAMILY. SALISBURY, EDWARD ELBRIDGE, & Salisbury, E. McC. Family histories and genealogies. . . . 3 vols. in 5. Folio. New Haven, 1892.   HH—Sa3H

OLIVER FAMILY. HAYDEN, REV. H. E. Oliver genealogy, a record of the descendants of Joseph, Reuben, and Levi Oliver, and of Pierre Elisée Gallaudet. . . . 23 & 4 pp., portrait. New York, 1888. O.   HH—Var4

OLIVIER FAMILY. OLIVIER, DANIEL JOSIAS. Memoirs of the ancient and worthy families D'OLIVIER and their alliances: 1520-1808. (HUGUENOT Society of America. Publications. Vol. IV. pp. 88-161. 1915.)   HK—H87—Vol. IV

ORANGE FAMILY. BOURLIER, E. Souvenir du troisième centenaire de leglise wallonne de la Haye. . . . LaHaye, 1891. O.
HC—B66

ORANGE-NASSAU FAMILY. PUTNAM, RUTH. William the Silent, Prince of Orange. . . . 2 vols. New York, 1898. O. In: Volume II, page 433.   HG—P98

OURRY FAMILY. SCOTT, FANNIE J. P. Miscellaneous genealogies . . . Huguenot refugees. . . . Rochester, N. Y., 1905. Oblong folio.   HH—S425

PAPIN FAMILY. FRANZOSISCHE (Die) Colonie . . . für 1896. No. 3, page 41.   HK—D491

PARMELEE FAMILY. SALISBURY, EDWARD ELBRIDGE, & Salisbury, E. McC. Family histories and genealogies. . . . 3 vols. in 5. New Haven, 1892. Folio.   HH—Sa3H

PEIRET FAMILY. MS. genealogy of the Peiret family.

PERINE. See: PERRIN, also PERRINE.

PERREAUX FAMILY. LELABOURER, J. Mémoires de Messire Michel de Castelnau. . . . Tomes I-III. Folio. Bruxelles, 1731. pp. 200-203, table, on page 205.   HG—L53

PERRIN FAMILY. PERRIN, ANNA F., & Meeker, M. F. P. Allied families of Purdy, Fauconnier, Archer, & Perrin. New York, [cop. 1911]. O.   HH—P458

———— PERRINE, HOWLAND DELANO. Daniel Perrin "The Huguenot," and his descendants in America, of the surnames Perrine, Perine, and Prine, 1665-1910. 547 pp., 1 fac-sim., 3 maps, 9 group port., 28 port. South Orange, N. J., 1910. Q.   HH—P45

PERROTT FAMILY. HARPER, LILLIE DUP. VANC., Editor. Colonial men and times. . . . The Huguenots. Genealogy . . . allied families. Philadelphia, 1916. Q. pp. 435-444.   HH—H294

PETIT DES ETANS FAMILY. SCOTT, FANNIE J. P. Miscellaneous genealogies . . . Huguenot refugees. . . . Rochester, N. Y., 1905. Oblong folio.   HH—S425

PETITOT FAMILY. See: HUGUENOT Society of London. Proceedings. Vol. VI.   HK—H876—Vol. VI

PHILLIPS FAMILY. SALISBURY, EDWARD ELBRIDGE. Family memorials. . . . 2 vols. Square folio. New Haven, 1885.   HH—Sa3M

PHILIPSE FAMILY. PELLETREAU, WILLIAM S. Historic homes . . . genealogical and family history of New York. 4 vols., illus. N. Y., 1907. Q. Vol. I, page 143.   HH—P36

PIERRE FAMILY. See: HUGUENOT Society of London. Proceedings. Vol. IV.   HK—H876—Vol. IV

PITKIN FAMILY. SALISBURY, EDWARD ELBRIDGE, and Salisbury, E. McC. Family histories and genealogies. . . . 3 vols. in 5. Folio. New Haven, 1892.   HH—Sa3H

POINGDESTRE FAMILY. VIRGINIA Magazine of history and biography. Beginning in Vol. XIX, No. 2, p. 217, and continuing. (Virginia Historical Society.)   HK—V81

PORDAGE FAMILY. PRIME, TEMPLE. Some account of the Bowdoin family, with notes on the families of Pordage. . . . 52 pp. 2nd edition. O. New York, 1894.   HH—A54

PRINE. See: PERRIN.

PRIOLEAU FAMILY. GALLAUDET, EDWARD M., LL.D. The family of Priuli, also called Prioli, Priolo, Prioleau. In: Huguenot Soc. of America, Proceedings. 1891. Vol. II, pp. 299-321.
HK—H871

PURDY FAMILY. PERRIN, ANNA F., & Meeker, M. F. P. Allied families of Purdy, Fauconnier, Archer, Perrin. New York, [cop. 1911]. O.   HH—P458

PYLDREN-DUMMER FAMILY. SALISBURY, EDWARD ELBRIDGE. Family memorials. . . . 2 vols. Folio. New Haven, 1885.
HH—Sa3M

QUINCY FAMILY. SALISBURY, EDWARD ELBRIDGE. Family memorials. . . . 2 vols. Folio. New Haven, 1885.   HH—Sa3M

RAPALJE FAMILY. HOLGATE, JEROME B. American genealogy . . . early settlers . . . their descendants . . . intermarriages and collateral branches . . . with . . . genealogical tables. 244 pp. Albany, 1848. Square folio. pp. 15-21.   HH—H731

RAPELYE FAMILY. PELLETREAU, WILLIAM S. Historic homes and institutions & genealogical & family history of New York. 4 vols. Q. N. Y., 1907. Vol. III, page 132.   HH—P36

RAVAUD FAMILY. SCOTT, FANNIE J. P. . . . Genealogies . . . Huguenot refugees. . . . Rochester, N. Y., 1905. Oblong folio.
HH—S42

RAVENEL FAMILY. RAVENEL, HENRY E. Ravenel records. A history of the Huguenot family . . . of South Carolina; with some account of the parish of St. Johns', Berkeley. . . . O. Atlanta, Ga., 1898.   HH—R11

REBOULET FAMILY. JACCARD, E. Trois hommes du grand
refuge; Reboulet, Cortéiz, Sagnol. pp. 44-51. O. Lausanne,
1900.   HG—B83

RECLAM FAMILY. FRANZOSISCHE (Die) Colonie. . . . In:
Volume "1896," pp. 88-89, 111, etc., etc.   HK—D491

RECLAN. See: RECLAM.

REGIS FAMILY. See: HUGUENOT Society of London. Proceedings. Vol. VIII.   HK—H876—Vol. VII

RENEU FAMILY. SCOTT, FANNIE J. P. French Protestant exiles
in England and Sweden . . . from . . . family histories and MSS.
pedigrees. Rochester, N. Y., 1909. Square Q.   HH—S425
Typewritten MS., Swedish, with English translation.

RENOUARD FAMILY. See: HUGUENOT Society of London.
Proceedings. Vol. VIII.   HK—H876—Vol. VIII

REQUA FAMILY. REQUA, REV. AMOS CONKLIN. The family of
Requa. 1678-1898. Peekskill, N. Y., 1898. O.   HH—Rq31

RESSEGUIE FAMILY. Resseguié family: a historical and genealogical
record of Alexander Resseguié of Norwalk, Conn., and four generations of his descendants. Compiled by John E. MORRIS. Hartford, 1888. 99 pp. O.   HH—R31

RHINELANDER FAMILY. Table (Chart) of the descendants of the
Huguenot to the present time. Large broadside. Framed. HH—Chart
Gift of T. J. Oakley Rhinelander.

RIVAL FAMILY. SCOTT, FANNIE J. P. Miscellaneous genealogies
. . . Huguenot refugees. . . . Rochester, N. Y., 1905. Oblong
folio.   HH—S425

ROLFE FAMILY. ROBERTSON, WYNDHAM. Pocahontas, alias
Matoaka, and her descendants through her marriage . . . with John
Rolfe. With . . . notes by R. A. Brock. 84 pp., 1 port. Rich-
mond, Va., 1887. O.   HH—P75

ROMILLY FAMILY. See: HUGUENOT Society of London. Proceedings. Vol. VI.   HK—H876—Vol. VI

ROUFFIGNAC FAMILY. See: HUGUENOT Society of London.
Proceedings. Vol. V.   HK—H876—Vol. V

ROUXEL MEDAVY (DE) FAMILY. LALEBOUREUR, J. Me-
moires de Messire Michel de Castelnau. . . . Tomes I-III. Folio.
Bruxelles, 1731. pp. 206-212. Vol. III.   HG—L53

ROWE FAMILY. ADAMS' Magazine of Revolutionary Records.
Vol. II, No. 5, pp. 7-9. New York, 1892.   HH—Pamphlet

SAGE FAMILY. WHITTEMORE, HENRY, Compiler. History of
the Sage and Slocum families of England and America, including the allied families of . . . Jermain, or, Germain . . . Hon.
Russell Sage and Margaret Olivia (Slocum) Sage. . . . New York,
1908. Square folio.   HH—S12

SALISBURY FAMILY. SALISBURY, EDWARD ELBRIDGE. Family Memorials. . . . 2 vols. Folio. New Haven, 1885. HH—Sa3M

SANXAY FAMILY. SANXAY, THEODORE FREDERIC. The Sanxay family, and descendants of Rev. Jacques Sanxay, Huguenot refugee to England in 1685. . . . 217 pp. Square O. New York, 1907. Privately printed. HH—Sa5

———— PELLETREAU, WILLIAM S. Historic homes . . . genealogical and family history of New York. 4 vols. New York, 1907. Q. Vol. I, page 328. HH—P36

SAYRE FAMILY. BANTA, THEODORE MELVIN. Sayre family. Lineage of Thomas Sayre, a founder of Southampton. XIV, 759 pp., 1 fac-sim., 14 plates, 19 port., 2 tables. New York, 1901. HH—Sa9.4

SCHENCK FAMILY. Rev William Schenck, his ancestry and descendants. Compiled by Alexander Du Bois SCHENCK. Washington, 1883. 163 pp., plate, table. HH—Sch2

SEIGNORET FAMILY. SCOTT, FANNIE J. P. Miscellaneous genealogies . . . Huguenot refugees . . . 1514-1900. Rochester, New York, 1905. Oblong folio. Page 20. HH—S425

SELLEW FAMILY. SELLEW, PHILIP, Compiler. Genealogical sketch of the Sellew family. A manuscript. HH

SEWALL FAMILY. SALISBURY, EDWARD ELBRIDGE. Family memorials. 2 vols. Folio. New Haven, 1885. HH—Sa3M

SHIPPEN FAMILY. BALCH, THOMAS. Letters and papers relating . . . to the . . . history of Pennsylvania . . . with . . . notices of the writers. Philadelphia, 1855. HE—B18P

SLOCUM FAMILY. WHITTEMORE, HENRY, Compiler. History of the Sage and Slocum families . . . including the allied families of Jermain or Germain . . . Hon. Russell Sage and Margaret Olivia Sage. Square Folio. New York, 1908. HH—S12

STITES FAMILY. See: JAMES, EDMUND J. Stites and James genealogy. 6 pp. O. New York, 1898. HH—Pamphlet
Reprint, N. Y. Gen. & Biog. Record, October, 1897, April, 1898.

SWAYNE FAMILY. SALISBURY, EDWARD E., & Salisbury, E. McC. Family histories and genealogies. . . . 3 vols. in 5. New Haven, 1892. Folio. HH—Sa.3.H

SWIFT FAMILY. ELLERY, HARRISON. Genealogy of the family of Thomas Swift of Dorchester, Mass., 1634. Worcester, Mass., 1890. Q. (In: SWIFT, J. G. Memoirs . . . 1890.) HG—Sw5

SWOPE FAMILY. SWOPE, GILBERT ERNEST, Compiler. History of the Swope family and their connections. 1678-1896. 390 pp., 3 fac-sim., 18 group port., 42 port., 7 pl., 1 table. Lancaster, Pa., 1896. Q. HH—Sw7

TEISSONIERE FAMILY. SCOTT, FANNIE J. P. Miscellaneous genealogies . . . Huguenot refugees . . . 1514-1900. Rochester, N. Y., 1905. Oblong folio. HH—S425

THIERRY FAMILY. In: FRANZOSISCHE Colonie . . . für 1896. No. 10, page 154. HK—D491

TOURTELLOT FAMILY. TOURTELLOT, J. S. Genealogy of the Tourtellot family, 1854. MS. HH—MSS.

TRABUE FAMILY. HARPER, L. DuP. VanC. Colonial men and times. Containing . . . Journal of Col. Daniel Trabue. . . . The Huguenots. Genealogy . . . allied families. Philadelphia, 1916. Q. pp. 207-275. HH—H294

TRENCH FAMILY. See: HUGUENOT Society of London. Proceedings. Vol. VI. HK—H876—Vol. VI

VAIL FAMILY. VAIL, C. M. Vail and Armstrong. A short record of my ancestors. . . . Goshen, N. Y., 1894. O. HH—V19

VALLEAUX FAMILY. HELFFENSTEIN, ABRAHAM ERNEST. Pierre Fauconnier, and his descendants; with some account of the allied Valleaux. Philadelphia, 1911. Q. HH—F25

VAN BORSSELEN FAMILY. DeBOER, LOUIS P. Van der VEER family in the Netherlands, 1150-1660, and 1280-1780. Brooklyn, N. Y., cop. 1913. O. HH—V28

VAN CORTLANDT FAMILY. BOLTON, REV. ROBERT. History of the . . . County of Westchester . . . edited by Rev. C. W. Bolton. 2 vols. New York, 1881. O. pp. 98-112. HE—B63

——— ROEBLING, EMILY WARREN. Journal of the Rev. Silas Constant . . . Presbyterian Church at Yorktown, N. Y. . . . Records of the Church. . . . Notes on families mentioned. . . . Edited by J. G. Leach. Philadelphia, 1903. O. HH—C758 No. 18 of 300 copies privately printed.

VAN DER VEER FAMILY. DeBOER, LOUIS P. Van der Veer family in the Netherlands, 1150-1660, and 1280-1780. Brooklyn, N. Y., cop. 1913. HH—V28

VAN LOM FAMILY. BEURDEN, A. F. VAN. Familie (De) van Lom. No place. 1894. O. (A reprint.) HH—W66 No. 5 of Dutch P. V.

VAN SCAGHEN FAMILY. DeBOER, LOUIS P. Van der Veer family in the Netherlands, 1150-1660, and 1280-1780. Brooklyn, N. Y., cop. 1913. HH—V28

VANSOEST DE BORCKENFELDT FAMILY. CALAND, F. Une branche de la famille van Soesten en Beligique—van Soust de Borckenfeldt. No place, 1895. D. HH—W66

VINCENT FAMILY. VINCENT, REV. JOHN H., D.D. A centennial souvenir of John Nimrod Vincent, born in Milton, Pa., April 20, 1798. No place, 1898. HG—Mem.512

—— WATERS, EDWARD STANLEY. Notes on some Huguenot families. (HUGUENOT Society of America. Proceedings. Vol. III, Part 2. pp. 245-271. 1903.) HK—H87.1—Vol. III

VORSTERMAN FAMILY. FREDERIKS, J. G. De familie Vorsterman te Amsterdam. No place, 1898. O. HH—W66 No. 3 of Dutch P. V.

VOUTE FAMILY. GESLACHTLIJST de familie de Comte later genaamd Voute. Square folio. s'Gravenhage, 1893. HH—V97 Behoort bij No. 2, van het Algemeen Nederlandsch Familieblad, 10e jaargang.

WALLEY FAMILY. SALISBURY, EDWARD ELBRIDGE. Family memorials. . . . 2 vols. Folio. New Haven, 1885. HH—Sa3M

WANTY. WANTIE. WANTIER. For either or all of these names see DE VANTIER.

WARD FAMILY. DOUTHETT, A. T., Compiler. Douthett and Ward families; genealogical notes. Pittsburgh, Pa., 1889. HH—D74

WARREN FAMILY. ROEBLING, EMILY WARREN. Journal of the Rev. Silas Constant . . . notes on families mentioned. . . . Edited by J. G. Leach. Philadelphia, 1903. HH—C758

WASSENAER (VAN) FAMILY. WILDEMAN, M. G. Eenige kwartierborden der Wassenaer's, zooals zj indertijd aanwezig waren in de kerken van Giessen, Warmond, Leiden en Leiderdorp. No place, 1895. O. HH—W66 In Dutch P. V.

WATTS FAMILY. DE PEYSTER, COL. A. S. Miscellanies . . . edited by John Watts de Peyster. 2 parts in 1 vol. (Dumfries, 1813.) New York, 1888. O. HG—D419

WENDELL FAMILY. SALISBURY, EDWARD ELBRIDGE. Family memorials. 2 vols. Folio. New Haven, 1885. HH—Sa3M

WETMORE FAMILY. Wetmore family of America, and its collateral branches, with genealogical, biographical and historical notices. By James Garnaham WETMORE. Albany, 1861. 670 pp. O.
HH—W53

WHEATON FAMILY. HILL, W. G., Compiler. Family record of . . . James W. . . . and Elisha S. Converse. . . . Boston, 1887. pp. 41-76. O. HH—Con74

WHITE FAMILY. CREGAR, WILLIAM F., Compiler. Ancestry of the children of James William White, M.D., with accounts of the families of White, Newby, Rose . . . and others. Philadelphia, 1888. Q. HH—W58

WHITNEY FAMILY. Whitney family of Connecticut and its affiliations; being an attempt to trace the descendants of Henry Whitney from 1649-1878, [with] some account of the Whitneys of England. By Stephen Whitney PHŒNIX. N. Y., 1878. 3 vols. plates, tables. Q.   HH—W61

WILDEMAN FAMILY. WILDEMAN, MARINUS GODEFRIDUS. Genealogische kwartierstaten van Nederlandsche Geslachten samengesteld en byeengebrachtdoor. . . . s'Gravenhage, 1894. Square folio.
HH—W673

Portrait and autograph inserted: this volume consists of family charts and coat-of-arms of Wildeman, Des Tombe, and De Graeff families.

WILLOUGHBY FAMILY. SALISBURY, EDWARD ELBRIDGE, & Salisbury, E. McC. Family histories and genealogies. . . . 3 vols. in 5. New Haven, 1892.   HH—Sa3H

WINN FAMILY. SCOTT, FANNIE J. P. Miscellaneous genealogies. . . . Huguenot refugees. . . . Rochester, 1905. Oblong folio.
HH—S425

WOLCOTT FAMILY. See: SALISBURY, EDW. ELBRIDGE, & Salisbury, E. McC. Family histories and genealogies. 3 vols in 5. Folio. New Haven, 1892. 5 vols.   HH—Sa3H

DESCRIPTION AND TRAVEL

BATES, ARLO, Editor. See: BATES, MRS. HARRIET L. (Vose). Old Salem.

[BATES, MRS. HARRIET L. VOSE.] Old Salem by Eleanor Putnam; edited by Arlo Bates. 120 pp. Boston, 1886. S.   HI—B31

BARRINGTON, GEORGE. Voyage (A) to New South Wales; with a description of the country; manners, customs, religion, etc., of the natives, in the vicinity of Botany Bay. Philadelphia, 1796. VII, 150 pp. Narrow S.   HI—B276

DE COSTA, REV. BENJAMIN FRANKLIN, D.D. Cabo de Arenas; or, The place of Sandy Hook in the old cartology. N. Y., 1885. 16 pp. map. Q.   HI—D.35
Reprinted from the *New England Historical and Genealogical Register.*
Gift of the Author.

——— Cabo de Baros; or, The place of Cape Cod in the old cartology, with notes on the neighboring coasts. N. Y., 1881. 13 pp., 1 map. Q.   HI—D35
Reprinted from the *New England Historical and Genealogical Register,* Jan., 1881.
Gift of the Author.

——— Myvyrian archæology: the pre-Columbian voyages of the Welsh to America. 12 pp. O. Albany, 1891.   HI—D35
Gift of the Author.

——— Editor. Relation of a voyage to Sagadahoc: now first printed from the original manuscript in the Lambeth Palace library, with preface, notes and appendix. Cambridge, 1880. 43 pp., illustrated, fac-simile. Q.   HI—D35
Gift of the editor.

DRAPER, LYMAN COPELAND, Editor. FORMAN, SAMUEL S. 1765-1862. Narrative of a journey down the Ohio & Mississippi in 1789-90. 1888.   HI—F76

FAIRCHILD, HELEN LINCKLAEN, Editor. See: LINCKLAEN, JOHN. Travels in the years 1791 and 1792 in Pennsylvania, New York and Vermont. Journals of J. L., agent of the Holland Land Company. With a biographical sketch and notes.   HI—L63

FORMAN, SAMUEL S. 1765-1862. Narrative of a journey down the Ohio & Mississippi in 1789-'90; with a memoir & . . . notes by Lyman C. Draper. 67 pp. Cincinnati, 1888. D.   HI—F76

HOLMES, Oliver Wendell. Our hundred days in Europe. Boston, 1887. 329 pp. D. HI—H73
Gift of Mrs. Martha J. Lamb.

HUNNEWELL, James F. Historical monuments of France. Boston, 1884. 336 pp. plates. O. HI—H89
Gift of Mrs. Martha J. Lamb.

LINCKLAEN, John. Travels in the years 1791 and 1792 in Pennsylvania, New York, and Vermont. Journals of J. L., agent of the Holland Land Company. With a biographical sketch and notes by H. L. Fairchild. iv, 1-4, v-xi, 1-162 pp., 1 fac-sim., 1 pl., 1 port., 2 maps, & 1 map folded in pocket. O. New York, 1897. HI—L63

NEW South Wales. See: BARRINGTON, George. Voyage to New South Wales, with a description of the Country, the manners, customs, religion, etc., in the vicinity of Botany Bay. Philadelphia, 1796. Narrow S. HI—B276

PUTNAM, Eleanor, pseudonym. See: BATES, Mrs. Harriet L. (Vose).

SALEM: Old Salem, by Mrs. Harriet L. (Vose) BATES. Edited by Arlo Bates. 120 pp. Boston, 1886. S. HI—B276

TRAVELS in . . . 1791 and 1792 in Pennsylvania, New York, and Vermont. Journals of John LINCKLAEN. With a biographical sketch, by Helen L. Fairchild. New York, 1897. O. HI—L63

WILDEMAN, Marinus Godefridus. Archæography of Delft curiosities. Delft, 1903. 74 pp., 16 pl., 1 map. D. HI—W673
Bound with his: Itineraire archeologique de Delft.
Gift of Mrs. James M. Lawton.

——— Itinéraire archéologique de Delft. 2nd ed., revue, corrigée et augmentée. 96 pp., 19 pl. Delft, 1906. D. HI—W673
Bound with his English edition.
Gift of Mrs. James M. Lawton.

MANUSCRIPTS

BALCH, Thomas Willing, Compiler. Genealogy of the de Trouville family. 1886.

CAPE Colony, South Africa. See: VILLIERS (de). MS. Brief notices of the Huguenot families who sought refuge in Cape Colony.
HJ—V792—MS.

DEVOTION, Sara, Compiler. Genealogy of the De Votion family: A brief account copied from records. MSS., 2 portraits. New York, 1894. Square Q.   HJ—D49
Gift of the Compiler.
Contains also a small Journal of Ebenezer DeVotion. MS.

Du BOIS, William Ewing. Translator. See: FRENCH CHURCH, New Paltz, New York. Copy and translation of the First Record Book, 1683-1704. MS. 19 pp. Folio. Philadelphia, 1846.
Gift of the Translator.   HJ—MS.

Du PUY, Charles M. Historical sketch of the Du Puy family. 1883.

EGLISE de Narragansett. Papier du Consistoire de l'Eglise de Narragansett, 1687. The original MS. 34 pp. Bound in parchment. Small square O.   HJ—N23
Gift of the Rev. Alfred V. Wittmeyer.
Artistically enclosed in a double case of red buckram.

———— A true copy in French, from the original MS., page 1-175 written upon: paging numbered 1-253. New York, 1893. O.
Gift of the Rev. Alfred V. Wittmeyer.   HJ—N23.1—W

———— A type-written MS., copy in French, with an English translation made and verified by Mrs. E. M. C. A. Lawton. 2 leaves, 47, 49, xi leaves. New York, 1896. Square O.   HJ—N23.1—L
Gift of the Translator.

ENGLAND: Huguenot Refugees. Order of Council relating to the Royal action in favor of the Huguenot refugees to England. 4 pp. Q. 1681.   HJ—MS—Case

FISHKILL, New York. Original deed of partition of land in the vicinity of Fish Kill, New York, between James Bontineau, Gillam Phillips and John Jones. 1751. MS.   HJ—MS.

FRENCH Church; The Hague, Holland. Trouwboek waalsche Gemeente 15 April 1691—27 December 1699. MS. Folio.
HJ—H12W

A true copy of the entrances of Marriage made and presented to the Society by M. G. Wildeman.

—————— New Paltz, New York. Copy and translation of the First Record Book, 1683-1704. MS. 19 pp. Folio. Philadelphia, 1846. Translated by William E. DuBOIS, and Indexed by Mrs. E. M. C. A. Lawton.
HJ—N558

HAGUE (The), Holland. French Church; Trouwboek waalsche Gemeente 14 April 1691—27 December 1699. Folio.
HJ—H12W
MS. copy of the entrances of Marriage, made by M. G. Wildeman, in A.D. 1895. Original Registers . . . at the Town House, (Record Office).
Gift of M. G. Wildeman.

LAWTON, Mrs. Eliza Mackintosh Clinch Anderson, Translator. See: EGLISE de Narragansett. Papier du Consistoire de l'Eglise de Narragansett, A.D. 1687. A type-written MS., copy in French from the original MS., with an English translation. 2 leaves, 47, 49, xi leaves. New York, 1896. Square O.
Gift of the Translator.
HJ—N23.1—L

LeMERCIER, Rev. André. MS. Sermons (French) Preached at the French Church in Boston, Mass. Dated, 1714-1719. Square O.
Gift of Abbott Brown.
HJ—L54

LORD, Rev. Charles E., Compiler. List of Huguenots who settled in various parts of the United States.
HJ—MS.
Gift of the Compiler.

LOUIS XIV, king of france. Original decree of Louis XIV in relation to the Temple (Protestant Church) of Bergerac, with an English translation by Rev. Alfred V. Wittmeyer. Fontainebleau, 1679.
HJ—MS. Case

MALTBIE, Jonathan, of the United States Revolutionary Army. A brief sketch of Jonathan Maltbie, who was in the Service of the U. S., during the Revolution, compiled from the Archives in the State Department. Washington, D. C., 1883. MS.
HJ—Case

MARTIN, Rev. J. H. Dominic De Gourgues, a poem. 1883.
HJ—MS. Case

NARRAGANSETT, Rhode Island. See: EGLISE de Narragansett. Papier du Consistoire, 1687. MS., et Translation.

NEW PALTZ (N. Y.) French church. Copy of the first record book of the French church at New Paltz, Ulster Co., N. Y., 1683-1702, with an English translation by William Ewing Du Bois. 1846.
HJ—MS.—Bound

OGILVY, GABRIEL, Compiler. French families in England. List of marriages at the foreign churches in London, from 1688-1740, with the names, dates, professions, places in France whence they came; consisting of thousands of names taken from the original registers now in Somerset House. 4 vols. in 2 vols. [No place, no date.] 2 vols.   HJ—Og4

ROGERS, S. H. Tradition of the "Betrothal Medal," supposed to have been brought to South Carolina from Holland, by the Ioor family, Huguenot refugees from France, with a copy of the "Medal" taken from the original.   HJ—& the Medal in Case

SELLEW, PHILIP. Genealogical sketch of the Sellew family.   HJ—Case

SOUTH Africa. See: VILLIERS (DE). Brief notices of the Huguenot families who sought refuge in Cape Colony. MS.   HJ—V752

STOUPPE, REV. PIERRE. MS. Sermons (in French) preached in the Huguenot Church in New Rochelle, New York, A. D., 1724-1740. Also one dated, Charleston, S. C., 1720. Square O. Gift of Abbott Brown.   HJ—S88

TRABUE, ANTOINE. Letter of commendation given to Antoine Trabue. Dated 1687. MS.   HJ—Case

VILLIERS, DE. Manuscript containing brief notices of the Huguenot families who sought refuge in Cape Colony, South Africa. Folio, half roan.   HJ—V71

VIRGINIA: Huguenot emigration, 1700. RECORDS relating to the Huguenot emigration to Virginia in A. D. 1700. Copied by G. D. SCULL, Oxford, England. Unpaged. MS. Folio.   HJ—V817

WITTMEYER, REV. ALFRED V., Compiler. Genealogy of the Fresneau family, copied from an old family Bible.   HJ—Case

——— Translator. See: LOUIS XIV., King of France. Original decree of Louis XIV. in relation to the Temple (Protestant Church) of Bergerac. A. D. 1679. MS.   HJ—Case

SULLY, Maximilien de Béthune, Duc de. Autograph letter signed.
1 page folio.

DU PLESSIS MORNAY, Philippe.
1. Autograph letter signed. 2 pages, folio. Dated 1610.
2. Autograph letter signed. 1 page, folio. Dated 1610.

HENRY IV, King of France.
1. Autograph letter signed. 1 page, 4to. Dated at Fontainebleau.
2. Autograph letter signed. 1 page, folio. Dated 1601.
3. Signature on a document. 1 page, folio. Dated 1578.
4. Signature countersigned by Du Plessis. 1 page, folio. 1588.
5. Letter. 2 pages, folio. Dated 1583.

PHILIP II, King of Spain.
1. Letter signed in French. Dated 15 March, 1578.
2. Letter. 1 page, folio. Dated February 9, 1579.
3. Letter signed in French. 6 pages, folio. Dated 1577.
4. Letter. 1 page, folio. Dated 1579.
5. An official copy of the King's Orders. Dated 1578.

CHARLES IX.
1. Document on vellum signed. Dated 1570.
2. Document on vellum signed. Dated 1566.
3. Letter signed. 1 page, folio. Dated Paris, 1568.

FRANCIS II (Duc de Lorraine).
1. Letter signed. 2 pages, folio. Dated 1632.

MORNAY, Philippe de.
1. Letter signed. 1½ pages, folio. Dated 1606.

COLIGNY, Gaspard de.
Letter signed. 1 page, folio. Dated 1554.

SOCIETIES

AMERICAN ANTIQUARIAN SOCIETY. Proceedings April 30, 1862, April 7, 1864. Boston, 1862-64. 8vo.   HK—H62V

AMERICAN HISTORICAL ASSOCIATION. Annual Report for 1889-'90, 1892-1915. 26 vols. in 40 vols. Washington, D. C., 1890-1918. 40 volumes. O.   HK—Am3

Note:—"The Publications of this Association cover its activities from . . . its organization in . . . 1884 to the present time. The first five volumes bear the title 'Papers of the American Historical Association.' "

"The ANNUAL REPORTS are of the period 1889 to date."

The interesting and valuable material in these volumes will be found accessible by reference to Vol. II of Report for 1914, and published in 1918. This volume is the—

GENERAL INDEX to Papers and Annual Reports of the American Hist. Assoc., 1884-1914. Compiled by David Maydole Matteson.
Gift of the Association.

—— Officers, Act of Incorporation, Constitution, List of Members, Historical Societies in the United States. 1896. Baltimore, Md., 1896. S.   HK—Am3.1
Gift of the Association.

AMERICAN Orders and Societies and their decorations. The Objects of the Military and Naval Orders, commemorative and patriotic Societies of the United States and the requirements for Membership therein. 107 pp., 18 coloured plates. O. Philadelphia, 1917.   HK—A5
Compiled by Jennings Hood & C. J. Young.
Gift of Bailey, Banks & Biddle.

AMES, HERMAN V. The proposed Amendments to the Constitution of the United States during the first Century of its History. (AMERICAN Hist. Assoc. Annual Report, 1896. 1 vol. in 2. See Vol. II.)   HK—Am3

ASSOCIATIONS (Les) Protestantes, religieuses et charitables de France. Résumé . . . rapports et budgets, statisques, etc. Compiled by Edouard Borel. Paris, 1884. 150 pp. 2nd ed. O.   HK—B731

ATTERBURY, REV. WILLIAM WALLACE, D.D. Elias Boudinot. Reminiscences of the American Revolution. (HUGUENOT Society of America. Proceedings. 1891. Vol. II. pp. 261-298.)   HK—H871

AYMAR, BENJAMIN. Aymar of New York. (In: HUGUENOT
Society of America. Vol. III. pp. 167-178, & 178-229. Genealogy
and Index, Part 2, New York, 1903. O.)   HK—H87
Read before the Society, November 25th, 1899.

BACOT, THOMAS WRIGHT. Huguenots in South Carolina.
(HUGUENOT Society of America. Publications. Vol. III.
1900.)   HK—H87

—— Orange Quarter, (St. Denis). (HUGUENOT Society of
South Carolina. Transactions, No. 23. Charleston, 1917. pp.
37-50. O.)   HK—H87.8

BAIRD, REV. HENRY MARTYN, D.D., LL.D. Edict (The) of Nantes
and its Recall. (HUGUENOT Society of America. Commemoration of the Bi-Centenary of the Revocation of the Edict of Nantes
pp. 14-41. Q. New York, 1886.)   HK—H87

—— Huguenots of the "Desert." (HUGUENOT Society of
America. Proceedings. New York, 1891. Vol. II, pp. 8-26. Q.)
Read before the Society, November 15th, 1888.   HK—H87.1

—— Recovery (The) of Religious liberty of the Huguenots.
(HUGUENOT Society of America. Proceedings. New York,
1894. Vol. III. pp. 36-51.)   HK—H871
Read before the Society, December 14, 1894.

—— Some traits of Huguenot character. (HUGUENOT Society of
America. Proceedings. Vol. I, Part 1. New York, 1884. pp.
9-16. Q.)   HK—H871
Read at the First Public Meeting of the Society, November 15th,
1883.

—— Strength (The) and weakness of the Edict of Nantes.
(HUGUENOT Society of America. Publications. Vol. III.
1900.)   HK—H87—Vol. III

BALDWIN, ELIZABETH G., Compiler. See: HUGUENOT Society
of America. Catalogue of the books, pamphlets and MSS. belonging
to the Society. New York, 1890. 1st Edition.   HK—H87

BARBARO, MARCO ANTONIO MAURICIO. Dispacci di Marc' Antonio
Barbaro estratti dal cod. CDV. classe VII. dei MSS. Italiani
della r. biblioteca Marciana di Venezia. (HUGUENOT Soc. of
London. Pub. 1891. Vol. VI, appendix, pp. 59-149. Preceded by
an English translation.)   HK—H875

BARNABAS, REV. J. R., D.D. Address on the Huguenot Crypt at
Canterbury, at Canterbury, England. (HUGUENOT Society of
America, Proceedings. Vol. V. New York, 1906. pp. 38-50.)
Delivered before the Society, February 18, 1905.   HK—H871

BARTLETT, HENRIETTA C., Editor. See: ROBISON, JEANNIE
F. J., & Bartlett, H. C., ed. Genealogical records. Manuscript
entries of births, deaths, and marriages, taken from family Bibles,
1581-1917. New York, 1917. Square O. (Colonial Dames, State
of New York.)   HK—C711

BARTOW, MOREY HALE. Brief account of the Bartow family. (HUGUENOT Society of America. Proceedings. Vol. I, Part 1. New York, 1883; Reprint, 1889. pp. v-vi.)   HK—H871—Vol. I
Added to the Reprint of first edition of Vol. I, Part 1.

BERGMAN, J. T., Compiler. EGLISES Wallonnes. Catalogue de la Bibliothèque Wallonne.   HK—Unbound

BERINGUIER, RICHARD, & Tollin, Henri. Die Französische colonie in Berlin. (In: Der Deutsche Hugenotten Verein. Geschichtsblätter. 1891. Vol. IV.)   HK—D49

BIBLIOTHEQUE de la Providence, London, England. See: FRENCH Protestant Hospital Library.

BISSELL, MRS. SANFORD. Huguenot's (A) ride. From the History of New York, by Todd, copied by Mrs. Bissell & read before the Society, April 13th, 1913. (HUGUENOT Society of America. Publications, pp. 165-66. Vol. IV.)   HK—H87

BLAIR, EMMA HELEN, Editor. STATE HISTORICAL SOCIETY of Wisconsin. Annotated catalogue of newspaper files in the Library. . . . O. Madison, Wis., 1898.   HK—W75

BOREL, EDOUARD. . . . Associations Protestantes, religieuses et charitables de France. Résumé . . . rapports et budgets, statistiques, etc. 150 pp. O. 2nd ed. Paris, 1884.   HK—B731

BRIGGS, REV. CHARLES A., D.D. Elias Neau, the confessor and catechist of Negro and Indian slaves. (HUGUENOT Society of America. Vol. III. New York, 1903. Part 2. pp. 103-116.) Read before the Society, April 18, 1889.   HK—H871

BROCK, ROBERT ALONZO, Editor. Documents relating to the Huguenot emigration to Virginia and to the settlement of Manakintown, with genealogies, etc. (VIRGINIA Historical Society. Collections. New Series. 1886. Vol. V.)   HK—V81—Vol. V

———— Miscellaneous Papers, 1672-1865, printed from the MSS. in the Collections of the Society. (Same, Vol. VI.)   HK—V81—Vol. VI

———— See: GRIGSBY, H. B. History of the Virginia Federal Convention of 1788. (Same. Vols. IX-X.)   HK—V81—Vols. IX-X

———— See: ROBINSON, CONWAY, Compiler. Abstract of the Proceedings of the Virginia Company of London. 1619-'24. (Same. Vols. VI-VIII.)   HK—V81—Vols. VI-VIII

BROOKLINE HISTORICAL PUBLICATION SOCIETY. Publications. Nos. 1-5. Paged continuously. Brookline, Mass., 1895-'06. O.   HK—Pamphlet

BROWNING, ARTHUR GIRAUD. History of the French Hospital in London and the lives of the Huguenots who founded it. (HUGUENOT Society of America. Publications. Vol. III. 1900.)   HK—H87—Vol. III.

———— See: FRENCH Protestant Hospital-Library. Bibliotheque de la Providence. Catalogue . . . with an introduction by A. G. B. London, 1887, & 1890. Q. & O.   HK—L84 & L84.1

BUFFALO (N. Y.) HISTORICAL SOCIETY. Annual report. Buffalo, 1886-89. 4 vols. O.   HK—B86

———— Obsequies of Red Jacket at Buffalo, Oct. 9, 1884. Buffalo, 1885. 117 pp. plates. O. (Transactions, Vol. III.)
Gift of the Society.

CALIFORNIA HISTORICAL SOCIETY. Papers. San Francisco, 1887. Vol. I. Q.   HK—C12
Gift of the Society.

CHAMIER, ADRIAN CHARLES, Editor. Les actes des colloques des Eglises Françaises et des synodes des églises étrangères refugiées en Angleterre 1581-1654. 118 pp. Q. Lymington, 1890. (Huguenot Soc. of London. Publications. 1887-90. Vol. II.)
Bound with Volume III.   HK—H875—Vols. II & III

CHAVANNES, REV. C. G., Compiler. EGLISES Wallonnes. Catalogue de la bibliotheque Wallonne. sup. 4e-5e. 1890-1901.
                                                           HK—Unbound

CLARK, A[LONZO] HOWARD, & Ford, P. L., Compilers. Bibliography of the writings of the members of the American Historical Association for . . . 1890. (AMERICAN Hist. Association. Annual Rept., 1891. pp. 117-160.)   HK—Am3—1891

CLEARWATER, ALPHONSE TROMPBOUR, LL.D. Description of the Set of Huguenot Medals presented to the Society, February 28th, 1899; with historic notes thereon.   (HUGUENOT Society of America. Proceedings. Vol. III, Part 2, pp. 132-136. New York, 1903.)   HK—H87.1—Vol. III
These Medals are the Gift of the Author.

———— Huguenot influence in the Colonial Capital of New York. (HUGUENOT Society of America. Publications. Vol. III. 1900.)   HK—H87—Vol. III

———— See: ANJOU, GUSTAVE. Ulster County, New York, Probate Records, at Kingston, New York. With introduction by A. T. C.   HH—An5

COLONIAL Dames: State of New York. Annual register. 1893-1901, 1913. New York, 1893-1913. 3 vols. O.   HK—C71

———— Calendar of Wills on file and recorded in the offices of the clerk of the Court of Appeals, . . . County Clerk at Albany, and . . . Secretary of State. 1626-1836. Compiled & edited by S. Fernow. III-XV, 657 pp. New York, 1896. Q.   HK—C71.1

———— Catalogue of the Genealogical and Historical Library. 518 pp. Square O. New York, 1912.   HK—C71.1
No. 5 of 250 copies.

———— Colonial Book-plates. Catalogue of the Loan Exhibition at the Van Cortlandt House, New York. April-June, 1908. IV, 40 pp., 6 plates. S.   HK—Pamphlet
Gift of Mrs. James M. Lawton.

COLONIAL Dames: State of New York. Publications of the Committee on History and Tradition. 2 vols. New York, 1902-1917. Vol. Nos. I-II. Square O.   HK—C71.1

No. 1. FERNOW, BERTHOLD. Minutes of the Orphanmasters of New Amsterdam. 1655-1663.

No. 2. ROBISON, JEANNIE FLOYD-JONES, and Bartlett, H. C., Editors. Genealogical records. MS. entries . . . taken from Family Bibles. 1581-1917.

COLYER-FERGUSSON, THOMAS, Editor. Marriage registers of St. Dunstan's, Stepney, in the County of Middlesex, England. Vols. I-III. Canterbury, 1898-1902. Q.   HH—F38

Vol. I, 1568-1639.
" II, 1640-1696.
" III, 1697-1719.
Only 100 copies privately printed.

———— Registers of the French Church, Threadneedle Street, London. Vols. III & IV. Q. Aberdeen, 1906, & London, 1916. (HUGUENOT Society of London. Publications. Vols. XVI & XXIII.) 450 copies printed. Nos. 411 & 357.   HK—H875—Vols. XVI & XXIII

CONGRESS of Archæological Societies. Report on the transcription and publication of Parish Registers, etc. 16 pp. O. London, 1892; Reprint, 1896.   HK—Pamphlets

———— Second report of the Committee for promoting the transcription and publication of Parish Registers, with Calendar of registers printed and transcribed since the first report of 1892. 18 pp. O. London, 1896.   HK—Pamphlet

CONNECTICUT HISTORICAL SOCIETY. Papers and reports presented at the Annual Meeting. O. Hartford, 1893, '94. 2 vols. Nos. 3 & 4 of P. V.   HK—H62V

COURTENAY, HON. W. ASHMEAD. Extracts from a Memorial of Daniel Ravenal of South Carolina, a Vice-president of the Huguenot Soc. of America. (HUGUENOT Soc. of America, Proceedings, 1894. Vol. III, pp. 117-120.)   HK—H871 Read before the Society, February 27, 1896.

CROSS, FRANCIS W. History of the Walloon & Huguenot Church, Canterbury. VIII, 272 pp., 1 pl. Q. Lymington, 1898. HUGUENOT Society of London. Publications. 1898. Vol. XV.)   HK—H875—Vol. XV

CUMMINGS, ANNA M. Huguenots in South Africa. (HUGUENOT Society of America. Proceedings. New York, 1903. Vol. III, Part 2, pp. 117-131. Q.)   HK—H871

DANKERS, JASPER, & Sluyter, P. Journal of a voyage to New York & a tour in several of the American colonies in 1679-'80. Translated from the Dutch . . . & edited by H. C. Murphy. (In: LONG ISLAND Hist. Soc. Memoires, 1867. Vol. I.)   HK—L86—Vol. I

DARLING, CHARLES. W. New Amsterdam, New Orange, New York, with chronological data. [Utica, N. Y.], 1889. 43 pp. plate. O.
Gift of the Author.

DAUGHTERS of the American Revolution of Arkansas. Proceedings. Sixth and Seventh Annual State Conference, 1914-'15. 2 vols. n.p., 1914-'15. O. pl., port.   HK—Pamphlet
Gift of Mrs. Louis Flickinger.

DAUGHTERS of the Cincinnati. Year Book, for 1910-1911. New York, cop. 1911. Edited by Miss Ruth Lawrence. Contains 42 portraits, reproduced through the courtesy of members who have the originals in their possession.   HK—C57
Gift of Mrs. James M. Lawton.

DAUGHTERS of the Revolution. Ancestral register of the general Society, 1896. 417 pp. Square Q. Philadelphia, 1897.
HK—SO.DR78

DAVIS, GEORGE T. Huguenots and New Rochelle. (HUGUENOT Society of America. Publications. Vol. III. 1900.)
HK—H87—Vol. III

DE LANCEY, EDWARD FLOYD. Philip Freneau, the Huguenot patriot poet of the Revolution and his poetry. (HUGUENOT Society of America. Proceedings. New York, 1891. Vol. II, pp. 66-84.)
Read before the Society, February 21st, 1889.   HK—H871

—————— & DeCosta, Rev. B. F., D.D. Memorial notice of Charles Martyn Baird, D.D. February 10th, 1887. (HUGUENOT Society of America. Proceedings. New York, 1889. Vol. I, Part 2, pp. 74-75.)   HK—H871

DELAWARE Historical Society Papers. No. 7. See: MALLERY, REV. C. P. Ancient families of Bohemia Manor. 1888.   HH—D37

DEPEW, HON. CHAUNCEY M. Characteristics and influence of the Huguenots. An address before the Society, April 20th, 1888. (HUGUENOT Society of America. Proceedings. Vol. I, Part 2, pp. 96-101. 1889.)   HK—H87.1—Vol. I

DE SAUSSURE, W. C., Gen. U. S. A. Two hundredth anniversary of the Revocation of the Edict of Nantes. Address before the Society in the Eglise du Sainte Esprit, Oct. 2nd, 1885. (HUGUENOT Society of America. Publications. Vol. I, pp. 44-56. 1886.)
HK—H87—Vol. I

DEUTSCHE Hugenotten Verein. Geschichtsblätter. Vols. I-XIII, Nos. 1-8. O. Magdeburg, 1890-1908. 13 vols.   HK—D49
Gift of the Society.

DEVARANNE, pfarrer. Die Französisch-reformirten gemeinden zu Gross und Klein-Ziethen in der mark Brandenburg. 15 pp. O. Magdeburg, 1893. (In: Der Deutsche Hugenotten Verein. Geschichtsblätter. 1893. No. 10, Part 5.)   HK—D49

DITTMAR, W., and Robert, pfarrer. Die Waldenser und ihre colonie
Walldorf. (In: Der Deutsche Hugenotten Verein. Geschichtsblätter. 1891. Vol. III.)   HK—D49

DODGE, RICHARD DESPARD. The Despard family. (HUGUE-
NOT Society of America. Proceedings, Vol. III, Part 2, pp. 230-244.
New York, 1903.)   HK—H871—Vol. III

DU FAIS, F. F., Translator. See: FELICE, PAUL DE. "Comment
l'Edit de Nantes fut observé." (HUGUENOT Society of America. Publications. Vol. III. 1900.)   HK—H87—Vol. III

DUPUY, CHARLES M. Saint Bartholomew's Day; its causes and re-
sults. (HUGUENOT Society of America. Proceedings. New
York. Vol. III, Part 2, pp. 83-102. Q.)   HK—H871
Read before the Society at the Summer Meeting held at New
Rochelle, N. Y., August 24th, 1885.

DuRIEU, W. N., Compiler. EGLISES Wallonnes. Catalogue de la
Bibliotheque Wallonne. Sups. 1e-3e. 1875-'90.   HK—Unbound

DUTCH Records: City Clerk's Office, N. Y. Extracts from Dutch
documents, . . . labelled "Original records of burgomasters and
Orphanmasters." "Surrogates." (HOLLAND Soc., N. Y., Year
Book, 1900.)   HK—H711

DUTCH Reformed Church of Brooklyn, N. Y. First Book of Records.
(Holland Society, N. Y., Year Book, 1897, pp. 133-194.)   HK—H711

DUTCH settlers in Esopus. Names compiled from the old Court Records of Wildwyck (Kingston). . . . Marriages recorded . . . 1667-
1672. (HOLLAND Society, New York, Year-book, 1897, pp.
117-132.)   HK—H711

DUVAL, MARY REBECCA. Duvall's (The) of Maryland. (HUGUE-
NOT Society of America. Proceedings. Vol. III, Part 2, pp. 137-
148. 1903.)   HK—H871—Vol. III

EDWARDS, REV. JOHN H., D.D. The First home of the Huguenots
in North America. (HUGUENOT Society of America. Proceedings. Vol. III, pp. 125-143.)   HK—H871—Vol. III
Read before the Society, March 27th, 1896.

EGLISES Wallonnes. Bulletin de la Commission pour l'Histoire. . . .
T. I-VIII, port., pl., tables. O. LaHaye, 1885-1902.   NK—Eg5

——— Catalogue de la Bibliotheque Wallonne . . . redige par J. T.
Bergman, 12, 202 pp. O. Leide, 1875. Supplement 1875-1908.
Redige par W. N. duRieu & C. G. Chavannes. Vols. I-V. O.
Leide, 1880-1908. 6 vols.   HK—Unbound

EVANS, THOMAS GRIER, Editor. Records of the Reformed Dutch
Church in New Amsterdam and New York. Baptisms from 25 De-
cember, 1639, to 27 December, 1730. 664 pp., 1 port. Vol. I.
N. Y., 1901. Q. (N. Y. Gen. & Biog. Soc. Coll., Vol. II.)
No. 54 of 100 copies.   HK—N491

FABER, REGINALD STANLEY, Compiler. See: FRENCH Protestant Hospital-Library. Bibliotheque de la Providence. Catalogue: with an Introduction by A. G. Browning. London, 1887, & 1890. Q. & O. HK—L84—L84.1—L84.111

FAVRE, REV. ROBERT. Present condition of the French-American Committee of Evangelization, Paris. (HUGUENOT Society of America. Proceedings, 1894. Vol. III, pp. 92-95.) HK—H871 Read before the Society, January 23, 1896.

FELICE, PAUL DE. "Comment l'Edit de Nantes fut observé." (HUGUENOT Society of America. Publications. Vol. III. 1900.) Translated by F. F. Du Fais. HK—H87—Vol. III

FERGUSSON, THOMAS COLYER. See: COLYER-FERGUSSON, THOMAS.

FERNOW, BERTHOLD, Editor & Compiler. Calendar of Wills . . . 1626-1836. Q. New York, 1896. (COLONIAL Dames, State of New York.) HK—C71

—— Editor & Translator. Minutes of the Orphanmasters of New Amsterdam, 1655-1663. VIII, 259 pp. Square O. New York, 1902. (COLONIAL Dames, State of N. Y. Vol. I.) One of 300 copies. HK—C71.1—Vol. I

FLATBUSH Dutch Church, Flatbush, Long Island, N. Y. Records: Marriages, 1677, October 14,—1757, November 5th. Baptisms, 1677, September 16th,—1754, December 29th. (HOLLAND Society, New York, Year-book, 1898. pp. 87-152.) HK—H711

FORD, PAUL LEICESTER, Compiler. Partial bibliography of the published works of members of the American Historical Association. (AMERICAN Hist. Association. Annual Report, 1890. pp. 163-386.) HK—Am3—1890

—— & Clark, A. H., Compiler. Bibliography of the writings of the members of the American Historical Association for . . . 1890. (AMERICAN Hist. Association. Annual Report, 1891. pp. 117-160.) HK—Am3—1891

FRANCKE, RUDOLF. Die Französische colonie in Karlshafen. 16 pp. O. Magdeburg, 1892. (In: Der DEUTSCHE Hugenotten-Verein, Geschichtsblätter. 1892. Vol. IX.) HK—D49

FRANZOSISCHE Colonie. Zeitschrift für Vergangenheit und Gegenwart der Französische-reformirten Gemeinden Deutschlands. Organ des Deutsche Hugenotten Vereins. Hrsg. VON R. BERINGUIER. Vols. IX-X, XI, Nos. 9-12; XII, Nos. 2-12; XIII-XIV, XV, Nos. 1-11; XVI, Nos. 2-5, 8-11. Berlin, 1895-1902. Q. HK—D491 All of these bound into 3 volumes: Vols. IX-X, XIII-XIV are complete. Largely composed of Huguenot history and genealogy, and 12 or more of the French Huguenot families whose genealogies in part or in whole are to be found therein are to be found under Family Genealogies in this Bibliography. Gift of Henri Tollin.

FRENCH Protestant Hospital, London, England. Bibliotheque de la Providence. Catalogue of the Library, compiled by R. G. FABER, with an introduction by A. G. BROWNING. London, 1887, & 1890. (1st & later editions.) Q. & O.   HK—L84—L84.1—L84.1.1
Gifts of the Compiler and A. G. Browning.

FURNAS, Robert W., Editor. See: NEBRASKA State Historical Society. Transactions & Reports.

GAILLARD, Thomas. Names of French Refugees who emigrated to South Carolina. (HUGUENOT Society of America. Proceedings. New York, 1884. Vol. I, Part 1. pp. 53-54. Q.)
HK—H87.1—Vol. I

GALLAUDET, Edward M., LL.D. The family of Priuli, also called Prioli, Priolo, Prioleau. (HUGUENOT Soc. of America. Proceedings, 1891. Vol. II, pp. 299-321.)   HK—H871
Read before the Society, April 13, 1894.

GERARD, James Watson. Retribution of Louis XIV. (HUGUENOT Society of America. Proceedings. 1891. Vol. II, pp. 155-175.)   HK—H871—Vol. II
Read before the Society, March 20th, 1890.

GODFRAY, Humphrey Marett, Editor. Registre des baptesmes, mariages & morts, et jeusnes de l'église Wallonne et des Isles de Jersey, Guernesey . . . etc. établie à Southampton par patente du roy Edouard six et la reine Elizabeth. 172 pp. Q. Lymington, 1890. (HUGUENOT Soc. of London. Pub. 1890. Vol. IV.)
HK—H875—Vol. IV

GOODE, George Brown. Origin of the national scientific & educational institutions of the United States. (In: AMERICAN Historical Association. Annual Report, 1890. pp. 53-161.)
HK—Am3—1889

GRIFFIN, Appleton Prentiss Clark, Compiler. Bibliography of the Historical Societies of the United States. (AMERICAN Hist. Association. Annual Report, 1891. pp. 161-267.) Part 1.
HK—Am3—1891

GRIFFIN, George Butler, Editor & Translator. Documents from the Sutro collection. 213 pp., 1 fac-sim. O. Los Angeles, 1891. (SOUTHERN Cal. Hist. Soc. Publications. 1891. Vol. II, Part 1.) Spanish text with English translation.   HK—C13

GRIGSBY, Hugh Blair. History of the Virginia Federal Convention of 1788 . . . with a . . . sketch of the author & . . . notes by R. A. Brock. Vols. I-II. O. Richmond, Va., 1890-91. (VIRGINIA Hist. Soc. Coll. New ser. Vols. IX-X.)   HK—V81—Vol. IX
Vol. II contains accounts of the Virginians who were members of the convention.

GROSE, G. Address on Huguenot influence upon our early Colonial life. (HUGUENOT Society of America. Proceedings. New York, 1906. Vol. V. pp. 51-56. Q.)   HK—H871—Vol. V
Delivered before the Society, April 17th, 1906.

173

GUILLE-ALLES Library & Museum. Encyclopædic catalogue of the lending department, compiled under the direction of A. Cotgreave, assisted by H. Boland. xviii, 1220 pp. S. Guernsey, 1891.　　HK—C94

Bound with: Bibliothèque Guille-Alles . . . section française . . . par Henri Boland. 273 pp. S. Londres, 1889.

HAWKS, John, Major. Orderly book and journal, on the Ticonderoga-Crown Point campaign, under General Jeffrey. Amherst, 1759-1760. Introduction by Hon. Hugh Hastings. New York, 1911. xii, 92 pp. O. (Pub. Soc. Colonial Wars.)　　HK—CW712N
Gift of the Society.

HOLLAND Society of New York. Annual dinner, 1886. port., pl. New York, 1886. Q.　　HK—H711
(Subsequent Annual Dinners bound with the Year Book.)
Volume lettered: "First Annual Dinner."

———— Collections. Vols. i & iii. 2 vols. in 3. New York, 1891, 1896.　　HK—H71
Vol. i, Part 1. Records. Reformed Dutch Church of Hacken-
　　　　　sack, N. J. 1891.
" i, " 2. Records. Reformed Dutch Church of Schraelen-
　　　　　burgh, N. J. 1891.
" iii, 　　Records. Reformed Dutch Church of New Paltz,
　　　　　New York. 1896.

———— Constitution, by-laws, officers and members. New York, 1891-'94. 3 vols.　　HK—H71
Gift of the Society.

———— Report on a Tablet commemorative of the services rendered by Baron Joan Derck van Calellen Tot den Pol, of Overyssel, Holland, on behalf of the North American Colonies in . . . the Revolution. . . . June 6, 1908. New York, 1909. 33 pp., 6 pl. O.
Gift of J. R. Van Wormer.　　HK—H711—Van

———— Year Book, 1886-'89, 1894-1900, 1902-1907, 1913-1914, 1917, 1918. New York, 1886-1918. 20 vols. Q.　　HK—H71.1
Illustrated with portraits and plates.
Earlier Volumes are the Gift of the late Theodore M. Banta. Later Volumes are the Gift of the Society.
These Volumes are catalogued separately by Title or Author entry, in this Class, and by various Cross-reference entries in the Dictionary Section of this Bibliography.

HOOD, Jennings, & Young, C. J., Compilers. American Orders and their decorations. The objects of the military and naval orders, Commemorative and patriotic societies of the United States and the requirements for membership therein. 107 pp., 18 coloured plates. O. Philadelphia, cop. 1917.　　HK—A5
Gift of Bailey, Banks & Biddle.

HOVENDEN, ROBERT, Editor. Registers of the Wallon or Strangers'
Church in Canterbury. Lymington, 1891. (HUGUENOT Society of London. Publications. 1891. Vol. V, Parts 1-3. 1 vol.
in 3 vols.   HK—H87.5

HUGUENOT SOCIETY OF AMERICA. Collections. Vol. I. Rev. Alfred V. Wittmeyer, Editor. Registers of the births, marriages and
deaths of the "Eglise François à la Nouvelle York," from 1688-1804;
and historical documents relating to the French protestants in N. Y.
during the same period. N. Y., 1886. 431 pp. plates, fac-simile.
O. Half-morocco.   HK—H87.3

———— Proceedings. May 29th, 1883—June 15th, 1914. Vols. I-VIII.
New York, 1884-1915. 8 vols. in 5. O.   HK—H871
Vol. I, Part 1, reprinted, December, 1889.
Vol. VI, reprinted June, 1914.
A complete set of the Proceedings, including the two reprints and
   the separate volume of "Huguenot Ancestry," Vol. VII (that was
   also issued bound with reprint of Vol. VI), together with copies
   of the several editions of the Constitution, By-laws, and list of
   Members, are beautifully bound in half-morocco, and actually
   comprise eleven volumes bound in five.

———— Publications. New York, 1885-1915. 4 vols. Q.   HK—H87
Vol. I.   Commemoration of the Bi-Centenary of the Revocation
           of the Edict of Nantes, October 22nd, 1885, at New
           York. 86 pp. New York, 1886. Q. Half-morocco.
Vol. II.   Catalogue of the books, pamphlets, and MSS. belonging
           to the Huguenot Society of America. Compiled by
           Elizabeth G. Baldwin. x, 107 pp. New York, 1890.
           Q.
Vol. III. Ter-Centenary Celebration of the Promulgation of the
           Edict of Nantes, April 13th, 1598. 2 p.l., LXIII, 464
           pp., 1 fac-sim. (1st & last pages of the Edict), 7 pl.,
           28 port. New York, 1900. Q. Blue morocco.
Vol. IV.   Addresses read before the Society. IV, 175 pp. New
           York, 1915. Q. Half morocco.
Author analytical entry will be found for every paper or article
   contained in our Publication Series, and Genealogical analytical
   entry for every family, will be found under Class H, family
   division.

HUGUENOT SOCIETY OF LONDON. Proceedings. Vols. I-VI, VII, Nos.
2 & 3; VIII-XI. London, 1885-1918. 11 vols. Illustrations and
portraits. O. Half-morocco.   HK—H87.6
Part 1 of Vol. VII wanting.
Genealogical analytical entry for every family pedigree or chart contained in these Proceedings will be found under Class H, family
   division.

———— Publications. Vols. I-XXIII. Lymington, 1887-1916. 23 vols.
in 22. Q.   HK—H875

CONTENTS

Vol. i.   MOENS, W., Editor. Walloons and their Church at Norwich. 1887-1888.

Vol. ii.   CHAMIER, ADRIAN CHARLES, Editor. Les Actes des colloques des eglises Francaises et des synodes des eglises etrangeres refugiees en Angleterre. 1581-1654.

Vol. iii.   MINET, WILLIAM, & Waller, W. C., Editors. Transcript of the Registers of the Protestant Church at Guisnes from 1668-1685.
Bound with Volume ii.

Vol. iv.   GODFRAY, HUMPHREY MARETT, Editor. Registre des baptesmes, mariages and morts, et jeusnes de l'eglise Walloon et des Isles de Jersey . . . etablie a Southampton par patente du Roy Edouard Sixe.

Vol. v.   HOVENDEN, ROBERT, Editor. Registers of the
1 vol. in 3   Wallon or Strangers' Church in Canterbury.
One Volume in three parts, bound separately.

Vol. vi.   LAYARD, SIR HENRY, Editor. Despatches of Michele Suriano and Marc' Antonio Barbaro. 1560-1563.

Vol. vii.   LA TOUCHE, J. J. D., Editor. Registers of the French Conformed Churches of Saint Patrick and Saint Mary, Dublin.

Vol. viii.   PAGE, WILLIAM, Editor. Letters of Denization and Acts of Naturalization for aliens in England.

Vol. ix.   MOENS, WILLIAM JOHN CHARLES, Editor. Registers of the French Church, Threadneedle Street, London, Vols. i-iv. 4 vols.
Vol. i is Vol. ix of Publications.
" ii " " XIII " "
" iii " " XVI " "
" iv " " XXIII " "

Vol. x.   KIRK, R. E. G., & Kirk, E. F., Editors. Returns of
1 vol. in 4   aliens dwelling in the City and Suburbs of London from . . . Henry VIII-James I.
1 vol. in 4.   Part 1, 1523-1571.
Part 2, 1571-1597.
Part 3, 1598-1625.
Part 4, The Index.

Vol. xi.   MINET, WILLIAM, & Waller, W. C., Editors. Reg-
Bd. with   isters of the Church . . . La Patente, . . . Spittle-
Vol. xiii.   fields, . . . 1689-1785.

MOENS, WILLIAM JOHN CHARLES, Editor. Register of Baptisms in the Dutch Church at Colchester . . . 1645-1728.

Vol. xiii.   ——— Registers of the French Church, Threadneedle Street, London. Vol. ii.

176

Vol. xiv.   Le FANU, THOMAS PHILIP, Editor. Registers of
Bd. with   the non-conformist Churches of Lucy Lane and Peter
Vol. xv.   Street, Dublin.

CROSS, FRANCIS W., Editor. History of the Walloon
and Huguenot Church at Canterbury.

Vol. xvi.   COLYER-FERGUSSON, THOMAS COLYER, Editor.
Registers of the French Church, Threadneedle Street,
London. Vol. iii.

Vol. xvii.   PEET, HENRY, Editor. Register of the French
Bd. with   Church at Thorney, Cambridgeshire. 1654-1727.
Vol. xviii.   SHAW, WILLIAM A., Editor. Letters of denization
and Acts of naturalization for aliens in England
and Ireland. 1603-1700.

Vol. xix.   Le FANU, THOMAS PHILIP, Editor. Registers of the
Bd. with   French Church of Portarlington, Ireland.

Vol. xx.   LART, CHARLES EDMUND, & Waller, William C.,
Editors. Registers of the French Churches of Bristol, Stonehouse, . . . Plymouth, and Thorpe-le-Soken.

Vol. xxi.   MINET, WILLIAM, & Minet, Susan, Editors. Livre
Bd. with   des tesmoignages de l'Eglise de Threadneedle Street.
Vol. xxii.   1669-1789.

———— Livre des Conversions et des Reconnoissances
faites a l'Eglise Françoise de la Savoye. 1684-1702.
Vols. xxi and xxii bound together in one volume.

Vol. xxiii.   COLYER-FERGUSSON, THOMAS COLYER, Editor,
Registers of the French Church, Threadneedle Street,
London. Vol. iv.

———— Royal Institute of Painters in water colours, Piccadilly. Conversazione, on Wednesday, May 22nd, 1895. Programme of Music,
etc. (Words and music.) 16 pp. London, 1895. Square O.
Privately printed.
Gift of the Society.

HUGUENOT SOCIETY OF SOUTH CAROLINA. Transactions. Nos.
1-23. Charleston, S. C., 1889-1917. Nos. 1-22, bound in 4 volumes. Illustrated. O.   HK—H87.8
Binder's title—"Proceedings."
Gift of the Society.

"HUGUENOT'S (A) Ride." Copied from Todd's "History of New
York," and read before the Society by Mrs. Sanford Bissell, April
14th, 1913. (HUGUENOT Society of America. Publications.
Vol. iv, pp. 165-166. 1915.)   HK—H87

IKEN, J. FR. Wallonisch-franzosische fremdengemeinde in Bremen.
Magdeburg, 1892. 24 pp. O. (In: Deutsche Hugenotten-Verein.
Geschichtsblatter. 1892. Vol. viii.)   HK—D49

JAY, Hon. John. Demand for education in American history. (AMERICAN Hist. Assoc. Annual Report. 1891.)
HK—Am3—1890

——— Huguenot Society of America and Columbia College. (HUGUENOT Society of America. Proceedings. New York, 1891. Vol. ii, Part 1, pp. 1-7.)   HK—H871—Vol. ii
Read before the Society, November 15th, 1888.

——— Introductory remarks at the First Public Meeting of the Society in the French Church du Saint Esprit, New York, November 15th, 1883. (pp. 5-7. Proceedings, Vol. i, No. 1. Abstract of Proceedings, HUGUENOT Society of America.)   HK—H871—Vol. i

——— The President's Annual Address to the Society on April 13th, 1893. (HUGUENOT Society of America. Proceedings. New York, 1894. Vol. ii, Part 2, pp. 246-251.)   HK—H871—Vol. ii

JULIEN, Rev. Matthew Cantine. Huguenots of old Boston. (HUGUENOT Society of America. Proceedings, 1894. Vol. iii, Part 1, pp. 52-72.)   HK—H871—Vol. iii
Read before the Society, April 30th, 1895.

KANSAS State Historical Society. Biennial report (8th) for 1890-1892. Topeka, 1892. O.   HK—H62V
No. 5 of Pamphlet Volume.

KINGS County Historical Society Magazine. Special Year-book and program of the Festival given by the Society in Commemoration of the Long Island Tercentenary. Vol. ii, November, 1914. 24 pp. O.   HK—Pamphlet
Gift of the Society.

KIRK, Ernest F. See: KIRK, R. E. G., & Kirk, E. F. Returns of aliens dwelling in . . . London. . . . (HUGUENOT Society of London, Publications. 1900-1908. Vol. x.)   HK—H875—Vol. x

KIRK, R. E. G., & Kirk, E. F., Editors. Returns of aliens dwelling in the city and suburbs of London from . . . Henry VIII to . . . James I. 1 vol. in 4 parts. Q. Aberdeen, 1900-1908. (HUGUENOT Society of London, Publications. Vol. x.)   HK—H875—Vol. x
450 copies printed: Nos. 392, 422, 420, & 427.

LAKE Champlain Association & The Ter-Centenary Commissions of New York & Vermont. Banquet given by the Delegation from the People of France presenting a bronze bust of La France to the People of the United States of America. New York, 1914. A brochure of 4 leaves and 4 plates, mounted. Square Q.   HK—Pamphlet
Gift of Mrs. James M. Lawton.

LAMB, Mrs. Martha Joan Reade Nash. Career and times of Nicholas Bayard, son of an exiled Huguenot. (HUGUENOT Society of America, Proceedings. 1891. Vol. ii, pp. 27-57.)
Read before The Society, Dec. 20th, 1888.   HK—H871—Vol. ii

LART, CHARLES EDMUND, Editor. Registers of the French Churches of Bristol, Stonehouse and Plymouth. XXVIII, 156 pp. Q. London, 1912.   HK—H875—Vol.xx
Bound with: WALLER, W. C., Editor. Register . . . French Church at Thorpe-le-Soken in Essex. . . . (HUGUENOT Society of London. Publications. 1912. Vol. xx.)
450 copies printed: No. 414.

LA TOUCHE, JOHN JAMES DIGGES, Editor. Registers of the French conformed Churches of St. Patrick and St. Mary, Dublin. 312 pp. Q. Dublin, 1893. (HUGUENOT Society of London, Publications. Vol. VII.)   HK—H875—Vol. VII
500 copies printed. No. 38.

LAUX, JAMES B. Huguenot element in Pennsylvania. (HUGUENOT Society of America. Proceedings, 1894. Vol. III, pp. 96-116.)   HK—H871—Vol. III
Read before the Society, February 27th, 1896.

LAWTON, ELIZA MACKINTOSH CLINCH ANDERSON. Abstract of report of . . . visit abroad as the representative of the Society. (HUGUENOT Society of America, Proceedings. Vol. III. pp. 73-79.)   HK—H871—Vol. III
Read before the Society, Nov. 26th, 1895.

——— The Emblematic flower and distinguishing colour of the Huguenots. (HUGUENOT Society of America. Proceedings. 1891. Vol. II. pp. 237-260.)   HK—H871—Vol. II
Read before the Society, April 13th, 1893.

——— Compiler. Index to Flatbush Dutch Church Marriage Records. Typewritten MS.   HK—H71.1—L—1898
Gift of the Compiler.
(The Records are in: HOLLAND Society Year Book, for 1898.)

——— Societe de l'Histoire de Protestantisme Français Extracts . . . account of Meeting . . . at La Rochelle and Sainte Martin-en-Ré, . . . A translation. (HUGUENOT Society of America. Proceedings. 1894. Vol. III. pp. 121-124.)   HK—H871—Vol. III

LAYARD, SIR HENRY. Despatches of Michele Suriano and Marc' Antonio Barbaro, Venetian ambassadors at the Court of France. 1560-1563. XII, 107, CLVI pp. Q. Lymington, 1891. (HUGUENOT Society of London, Publications. Vol. VI.) HK—H875—Vol. VI
500 copies printed. No. 366.

LAYARD, IDA L. H. Huguenot (A) miniaturist at home. Paper read before the Society at the Annual Meeting of April 14th, 1913. (HUGUENOT Society of America. Publications. Vol. IV. pp. 67-87. New York, 1915.)   HK—H87—Vol. IV
Note: Hand-sketches illustrating Miss Layard's paper are preserved in separate cover.   HK—H87—Appendix to Vol. IV

——— Martyrs (The) of Salies. Paper read before the Annual Meeting, April 13th, 1903. (HUGUENOT Society of America. Proceedings. pp. 55-67.) Also an Appendix-Pièces justificatives. pp. 68-77. Vol. IV. New York, 1904.   HK—H—Vol. IV

LE FANU, THOMAS PHILIP, Editor. Registers of the French Church of Portarlington, Ireland. XIX, 176 pp. Q. London, 1908. (HUGUENOT Society of London, Publications, Vol. XIX. 1908.) 450 copies printed. No. 411.　　　　　　　HK—H875—Vol. XIX

———— Registers of the Nonconformist Churches of Lucy Lane and Peter Street, Dublin. XIV. 167 pp. Q. Aberdeen, 1901. (Huguenot Society of London. Publications. Vol. XIV. 1901.
　　　　　　　　　　　　　　　　　　HK—H875—Vol. XIV

LE FEVRE, REV. JAMES, D.D. Huguenot patentees of New Paltz, New York. (HUGUENOT Society of America. Proceedings, New York, 1894. Vol. III, Part 1, pp. 80-95.)　　HK—H871—Vol. III
Read before the Society, January 23rd, 1896.

LE FEVRE, RALPH. Huguenots of Ulster County, New York. In: Historical Society Newburgh Bay & The Highlands. pp. 41-55. Newburgh, N. Y., 1894. O.　　　　　　　　　　HK—H62V
Read before the Newburgh Hist. Society, December 13th, 1889.

LISTS of passengers, 1657-1664, and of owners of houses and lots in New Amsterdam about 1674. . . . (HOLLAND Society Year-Book, 1896.)　　　　　　　　　　　　　　　HK—H711

LONG ISLAND HISTORICAL SOCIETY. Catalogue of the Library . . . 1863-1893. 801 pp. Brooklyn, N. Y., 1893. Q.　　　HK—L861

———— Memoirs. Volume I, plates, map. Brooklyn, New York, 1867. O.　　　　　　　　　　　　　　　　　　　HK—L86

LUTHERAN Church, New York City. See: ST. MATTHEW'S Lutheran Church, New York City.

MARQUAND, PROF. ALLAN. Huguenot Industries in America. Read before the Society, April 20th, 1888. (HUGUENOT Society of America. Proceedings. pp. 87-96. Vol. I, No. 2.) New York, 1884.　　　　　　　　　　　　　　　HK—H871—Vol. I

MAURY, COL. RICHARD L. Huguenot (The) Martyrs of Meaux, commonly called the Fourteen of Meaux. (HUGUENOT Society of America. Proceedings. Vol. III, Part 2, pp. 149-166.) New York, 1903.　　　　　　　　　　　HK—H871—Vol. III
Read before the Society, March 21, 1899.

———— Huguenots in Virginia. (HUGUENOT Soc'y of America. Publications. Vol. III. 1900.)　　　　　　　　HK—H87

MINET, WILLIAM, and Minet, Susan, Editors. Livre des Conversions et des Reconnoissances faites à l'Eglise Francois de la Savoye. 1684-1702. . . . XXXVI, 42 pp. Q. London, 1914. (HUGUENOT Society of London, Publications. Vol. XXII.) HK—H875—Vol. XXII 450 copies printed. No. 379.

———— and Waller, W. C., Editors. Registers of the Church known as La Patente, in Spittlefields, from 1689-1785. XXVI, 254 pp. Q. Lymington, 1898. (HUGUENOT Society of London, Publications. Vol. II.) HK—H875—Vol. II 450 copies printed. No. 427.

———— Transcript of the Registers of the Protestant Church at Guisnes from 1668-1685. . . . VII, 329 pp., [1 p.], 1 map. Q. Lymington, 1891. (HUGUENOT Society of London. Publications. Vol. III.) HK—H875—Vol. III 500 copies printed. No. 359.
Vols. II & III bound in one volume.

———— Susan. See: MINET, WILLIAM, & Minet, S. Livre des Conversions et des Reconnoissances faites a l'Eglises Francois de la Savoye. . . .

———— See: MINET, WILLIAM, & Minet, S. Livre des tesmoignages de l'Eglise de Threadneedle Street. . . .

MOENS, WILLIAM JOHN CHARLES, Editor. Register of Baptisms in the Dutch Church at Colchester, from 1645-1728. . . . XLIII, 177 pp. Q. Lymington, 1905. (HUGUENOT Society of London. Publications. 1905. Vol. XII.) HK—H875—Vol. XII 450 copies printed. No. 363.

———— Registers of The French Church, Threadneedle Street, London. Vol. I. VI, 364 pp. Q. Lymington, 1896. (HUGUENOT Society of London. Publications. 1896. Vol. IX.) HK—H875—Vol. IX 450 copies printed. No. 402.

———— Walloons and their Church at Norwich: their history and registers. 1565-1832. 2 parts in 1 vol. Q. Lymington, 1887-1888. (HUGUENOT Society of London. Publications. 1887-'88. Vol. I.) HK—H875—Vol. I
Only 309 copies printed.

MORAVIAN Church: Staten Island, New York. See: NEW YORK Genealogical & Biographical Society. Collections. WRIGHT, TOBIAS ALEXANDER, Editor. Records. . . . Vol. IV. HK—N49.1

MURPHY, HENRY C., Editor. See: DANKERS, JASPER, & Sluyter, P. Journal of a voyage to New York. . . . HK—L86

NAMES of about 8000 persons a small portion of the number confined on board the British prison ships during the War of the Revolution. 61 pp. Brooklyn, N. Y., 1888. (Society of Old Brooklynites.) HK—Br79

NARRAGANSETT, Rhode Island: See: POTTER, Elisha Reynolds, Jr. Early history of Narragansett. Providence, 1835. 2nd ed. O. (Collections. R. I. Historical Soc'y. Vol. iii.)   HK—P85N

NATIONAL Historical Society. Journal of American History. Produced in Quarterly editions. Vol. xi, Nos. 2-4. Greenfield, Ind., Cop. 1917. Q.   HK—N277
Gift of Mrs. James M. Lawton.

NEBRASKA State Historical Society. Transactions and reports, edited by R. W. Furnas. Lincoln, 1885. Vol. i, 3-5. 4 vols. O.
Gift of the Society.   HK—N27

——— Proceedings and Collections. Second Series. Vol. ii. Lincoln, Neb., 1898. O.   HK—N27
Gift of the Society.

NEW AMSTERDAM. See: COLONIAL Dames, State of New York. Minutes of the Orphanmasters. . . .

NEW AMSTERDAM, New Orange, New York, with chronological data. By C. W. DARLING. Utica, 1889.   HK—H62V
No. 7 of Pamphlet Volume.

NEW ENGLAND Historic Genealogical Society. Memorial biographies. Volume iv. Boston, 1885. O.   HK—NR44
Gift of Mrs. Martha J. Lamb.

——— Proceedings, 1887, 1894, & 1901 (unbound), and 1908-1916, bound in two volumes.   HK—NR44

——— Historical and Genealogical Register. Vols. i-v, 66-71; portraits and plates. Boston, 1847-1917. 12 vols. O.   HK—NR44
The Volumes of more recent years, and current numbers are the gift of Mr. & Mrs. Levi P. Holbrook.

——— Index to genealogies and pedigrees in the . . . Register for 50 years. . . . From January, 1847, Vol. i—October, 1896, Vol. l. Compiled by W. W. Wright. xi, pp. —. O. Boston, 1896. Reprint: N. E. Hist. & Gen. Register, Oct., 1896.   HK—NR44—Index

NEW ENGLAND Society. Ninety-seventh Anniversary Celebration of the . . . Society, in the City of New York, . . . December 22, 1902. 136 pp. New York, 1902. O.   HK—Pamphlet

NEW HAVEN (Connecticut) Historical Society. Papers. New Haven, 1865-1894. 5 vols. O.   HK—N45

NEW NETHERLAND. Early immigrants to New Netherland. A bibliographical sketch "concerning . . . names, etc., of early settlers." . . . (HOLLAND Society Year-Book, 1896. pp. 124-129.)   HK—H711

NEW NETHERLAND. Passengers to New Netherland. List of passengers, 1654-1664. From New York Colonial MSS., Vol. xiv, pp. 83-123. (HOLLAND Society Year-Book, 1902. pp. 1-37.)
HK—H711

NEW PALTZ, New York. See: Reformed Dutch Church Records. In: HOLLAND Society of New York. Collections. Vol. iii. See also: VENNEMA, Rev. Ame. Reformed Church . . . History . . . 1683-1883. See also: LE FEVRE, Ralph. History of New Paltz, N. Y., & its old families (1678-1820). . . .

NEW YORK Genealogical & Biographical Society. Collections. Vols. i-iv. Q. New York, 1890-1909.　　　　　　　　HK—N491
> Volume i. PURPLE, S. S., Editor. Records . . . Ref. Dutch Ch. in New Amsterdam New York. Marriages . . . 1639-1801. 1890.
> Volume ii. EVANS, T. G., Editor. Records . . . Ref. Dutch Ch., New Amsterdam & New York. Baptisms . . . 1639-1730. Vol. i.
> Volume iii. WRIGHT, T. A., Editor. Records . . . Ref. Dutch Ch., New Amsterdam & New York. Baptisms . . . 1731-1800. Vol. ii.
> Volume iv. ——— Staten Island Church Records. Dutch Ref. Ch., Port Richmond, S. I., Baptisms, 1696-1772. Moravian Ch., S. I., Births & Baptisms, 1749-1853; Marriages, 1764-1863; Deaths & Burials, 1758-1828. St. Andrew's Ch., Richmond, S. I., Births & Baptisms, 1752-1795; Marriages, 1754-1808. 1909.

——— See: NEW YORK Genealogical & Biographical Record. Published Quarterly by the Society.

——— Officers, Committees, By-laws, Members. New York, 1900, '02, '06, '08, '10, '15. 5 vols. 1900-1915. D.　　　　　HK—N481

NEW YORK Genealogical & Biographical Record. Devoted to the Interests of American Genealogy and Biography. Vols. i-xlix. New York, 1870-1919. 49 vols. Illustrations, portraits, fac-similes, coats-of-arms. Q.　　　　　　　　　　　　　　　　HK—N49
Gift of Mrs. Levi P. Holbrook. Various numbers of earlier volumes were gifts of Mrs. James M. Lawton and others.

NEW YORK Historical Society. Collections, for the years 1868-1918. Vols. i-li. New York, 1868-1918. 51 vols. O. Perpetual Gift of Mrs. James M. Lawton.　　　　　　　　　HK—H53.2

NEW YORK STATE Historical Association. Proceedings. Vols. ii & iii. Annual Meeting, with Constitution & By-laws and List of Members. pl., port. New York, 1901-'02. 2 vols. Q.　HK—N42
Note: Proceedings of First Annual Meeting not published.

NEWPORT (R. I.) HISTORICAL SOCIETY. Annual report. Newport, 1886. Vol. I, 8vo.   HK—H62V
No. 9 of P. V.

NORTH American Colonies. See: HOLLAND Society of New York.
Report . . . on a Tablet commemorative of . . . services rendered
. . . on behalf of the No. American Colonies in . . . the Revolution. . . . New York, 1909. 33 pp., 6 plates. O.   HK—H711—Van
Gift of J. R. Van Wormer.

NORTH CAROLINA Huguenots. See: RAND, JAMES HALL. Indians of N. C., and their relations with the settlers.   HK—Pamphlet

O'GILVY, GABRIEL. Nobiliaire de Normandie. Proces-verbaux . . .
1463 . . . 1727. . . . Origines et genealogies des familles eteinnes
et existantes jusqu'a 1789. (HUGUENOT Society of America,
Publications. Vol. IV. pp. 45-66. New York, 1915.)
                                                  HK—H87—Vol. IV

OHIO STATE ARCHÆOLOGICAL & HISTORICAL SOCIETY. 8th Annual
Report. Columbus, 1892. O.   HK—H62V
No. 10 of Pamphlet Volume.

OLIVIER, DANIEL JOSIAS. Memoirs of the ancient and worthy family,
D'Olivier and their alliances, 1520-1803. Also a family table.
(HUGUENOT Society of America. Publications. Vol. IV. pp.
88-161.) New York, 1915.   HK—H87—Vol. IV

OLNEY, HON. PETER B. Huguenot Settlement at Oxford, Massachusetts, its Park, Monuments, etc. A Paper read at the Meeting
held at New Rochelle, August 24, 1885. (HUGUENOT Society
of America. Proceedings. Vol. I, Part 2, pp. 56-64.)
                                                  HK—H871—Vol. I

ORDERLY Book and Journal of Major John Hawks on the Ticonderoga-Crown Point Campaign, under General Jeffrey Amherst,
1759-1760. N. Y., 1911. 92 pp. (Society Colonial Wars: N. Y.,
Publication No. 15.)   HK—CW712N

OSWEGO HISTORICAL SOCIETY. Publication No. 1. 1899. Oswego,
N. Y., 1899. 1 vol. O.   HK—Os8

OXFORD, Massachusetts. See: OLNEY, HON. PETER B. The Huguenot Settlement at Oxford, Mass., its Park, Monuments, etc.
(HUGUENOT Society of America. Proceedings. Vol. I, Part 2,
pp. 56-67.)   HK—H871

PAGE, WILLIAM, Editor. Letters of denization and Acts of Naturalization for aliens in England. 1509-1603. LIII, 1, 258 pp. Q.
Lymington, 1893. (HUGUENOT Society of London. Publications. 1893. Vol. VIII.)   HK—H875—Vol. VIII
500 copies printed. No. 385.

PEET, Henry, Editor. Register of Baptisms of the French Protestant refugees settled at Thorney, Cambridgeshire. 1654-1727. xvi, 138 pp., 1 fac-sim., 1 leaf. Q. Aberdeen, 1903. (HUGUENOT Society of London. Publications. Vol. xvii.)   HK—H875—Vol. xvi 450 copies printed. No. 390.

PELLETREAU, William S. Huguenot (The) Church Lot and its neighbors. Read at the Unveiling of the Commemorative Tablet, marking the Site of the First French Church in New York, at the N. Y. Produce Exchange, May 10, 1902. (HUGUENOT Society of America. Proceedings. Vol. iv. pp. 53-54. See also page 8. New York, 1904.)   HK—H871—HK

PENNSYLVANIA Society of New York. First Annual Dinner, 1899. 54 pp. New York, 1899. O.   HK—P37 Subsequent Annual Dinners bound with Year Book. Gift of the Society.

———— Year Book, 1901-'03. 3 vols. port., pl., maps. New York, 1901-'03. O.   HK—P371 Gift of the Society.

PLEINE, J. N. Französische reformirte kirche in Emden. 20 pp. O. Magdeburg, 1890. (DEUTSCHE Hugenotten Vereins. Geschichtsblätter. 1890. Vol. ii.)   HK—D49

POTTER, Elisha Reynolds, Jr. Early (The) History of Narragansett; with an appendix of original documents, many of which are now for the first time published. xix, 423 pp. 2nd ed. Providence, 1835. O. (RHODE ISLAND Historical Society. Collections. Vol. iii.)   HK—P85

———— Same.   HE—P85N Gifts of Wm. H. Potter, in memory of his brother, the Author.

PUMPELLY, Josiah Collins. Huguenot Settlement in New Jersey. (HUGUENOT Society of America. Publications. Vol. iii. 1900.)   HK—H87—Vol. iii

PURPLE, Samuel Smith, M.D., Editor. Records of the Reformed Dutch Church in New Amsterdam and New York. Marriages from 11 December, 1639, to 26 August, 1801. xii, 9-351 pp., 1 fac-sim., 1 pl. New York, 1890. Q. (NEW YORK Genealogical & Biographical Collections. Vol. i.)   HK—N491

RAND, James Hall. Indians (The) of North Carolina and their relations with the settlers. 41 pp. O. (Univ. of No. Carolina. The James Sprunt Hist. Pub. Vol. xii, No. 2.) Chapel Hill, N. C., 1913.   HK—Pamphlet Gift of the University. Contains references to N. C., Huguenots, pp. 22, 23, & 35.

REFORMED DUTCH CHURCH, Albany, New York. Records.
1683-1764. Vols. I-IV. Q. (HOLLAND Society, New York.
Year Book, 1904-1907.) 4 vols. Albany Book, Nos. 1, 2, 3 & 4.
HK—H71.1

——— Hackensack and Schraalenburg, New Jersey. Records of the
Churches . . . with the Registers . . . and the Consistories to the
beginning of the 19th century. (HOLLAND Society, New York.
Collections. Vol. I. 2 vols. in 1. 1891.) HK—H71

——— New Amsterdam and New York. Records. Q. 3 vols. New
York, 1890, 1901-'02. HK—N491
  Marriages, Dec. 11, 1639—August 26, 1801. PURPLE,
  S. S., Editor.
  Baptisms, Dec. 25, 1636—Dec. 27, 1730. Vol. I. EVANS,
  T. G., Editor.
  Baptisms, Jan. 1, 1731—Dec. 29, 1800. Vol. II. WRIGHT,
  T. A., Editor.
(N. Y. Gen. & Biog. Soc'y. Collections, Vols. I, II, III, & IV.)

——— New Paltz, New York. Records: containing an account of the
Church, and Registers of Consistories, Members, and Baptisms.
(HOLLAND Society of New York. Collections. Vol. III. 1891.
O.) HK—H71H

——— Port Richmond, Staten Island, New York. Records of the
Baptisms from 1692 to 1772. Edited by T. A. WRIGHT. (N. Y.
Gen. & Biog. Soc'y. Collections. Vol. IV. 1909. Q.) HK—N491

——— PROTESTANT DUTCH CHURCH, Bergen, New Jersey.
Bergen Church Records. Vols. I-II. 2 vols. Q. HK—H711
  Vol. I. Baptisms, 1666-1788.
  Vol. II. Marriages, 1665-1788, & Register of Members.
(HOLLAND Society of New York, Year Book. 1913 & 1914.)

RENSSELAERSWYCK: Settlers from 1630-1646, compiled from the
books of monthly wages and other MSS. From O'Callaghan's "History of New Netherland," pp. 430-441. (HOLLAND Society
Year Book, 1896. pp. 130-140.) HK—H711
  NOTE:—Also Passenger Lists, 1657-1664. (From "Doc. Hist.
  of New York." Vol. II. pp. 52-63.) See pp. 141-166 in this
  Volume.

RHODE ISLAND HISTORICAL SOCIETY. Collections. Vol. III.
Providence, R. I., 1835. HK—P85
  Vol. III. POTTER, E. R. Early History of Narragansett.

——— Same. Another copy. HK—P85N

ROBERT, pfarrer, & Dittmar, W. Waldenser (Die) und ihre Colonie
Walldorf. 23 pp. O. Magdeburg, 1891. (In: DEUTSCHE
Hugenotten Verein. Geschichtsblätter. 1891. Vol. III.) HK—D49

ROBERTSON, Charles Franklin. Historical Societies in their relation to local historical interest. An address . . . before the Missouri Historical Society, September 19, 1883. 16 pp. St. Louis, 1883. O. HK—H62V
No. 6 of pamphlet volume.

ROBINSON, Conway, Compiler. Abstract of the Proceedings of the Virginia Company of London, 1619-1624. . . . Edited by R. A. BROCK. 2 vols. O. Richmond, 1888-'89. (VIRGINIA Historical Society Collections. New Series. 1888-'89. Vols. VII-VIII.)
HK—V81—Vols. VII-VIII

ROBISON, Jeannie Floyd-Jones, & Bartlett, H. C., Editors. Genealogical records. Manuscript entries of births, deaths, and marriages, taken from family Bibles, 1581-1917. xv, 331 pp., 3 fac-sim., 7 pl., 6 port. New York, 1917. Square O. (COLONIAL Dames, State of New York.) HK—C711
200 copies. No. 85.

ROE, Francis Asbury, Rear Admiral, U. S. N. Huguenots (The). Some account of their persecution, sufferings, wanderings, and achievements, together with an estimate of their character and influence in America. HK—H87
Read before the Society in 1899. (HUGUENOT Society of America, Publications. Vol. IV, pp. 1-7.) New York, 1915.

ST. ANDREW'S (Episcopal) Church, Richmond, Staten Island, New York. Births and Baptisms from 1752-1795. HK—N491
Marriages from 1754-1808.
Edited by T. A. WRIGHT (N. Y. Gen. & Biog. Soc'y. Collections. Vol. IV. 1909. Q.)

ST. GEORGE'S Society of New York. History of St. George's Society of New York from 1770-1913. 389 pp., 1 coloured plate. New York, 1913. O. (Also port., etc., paged in.) HK—G23
No. 176 of 1000 copies printed.
Gift of Charles W. Bowring, Pres. of the Society.

ST. MATTHEW'S Evangelical Lutheran Church, New York City. Some early records of the Lutheran Church (Broome Street), New York. Marriages prior to the Revolution, and the earlier Baptisms. September 14, 1704-1723. (HOLLAND Society, N. Y., Year Book. 1903. pp. 1-118.) HK—H711

ST. NICHOLAS Society of New York. Genealogical record, containing the lines of descent of members of the Society . . . to July 1, 1916. Vols. I-II. New York, 1905, 1916. 2 vols. HK—N48
Gift of the Society.

—— Record of the Semi-centennial Anniversary, February 28, 1885. 42 pp., 1 leaf. New York, 1885. O. HK—N481A

SCHAFF, Rev. Philip. History of the Edict of Nantes. (HUGUENOT Society of America. Proceedings. 1891. Vol. II, pp. 85-114.) HK—H87
Read before the Society, March 21st, 1889.

SCULL, G. D., Editor. Montrésor (The) Journals. XII, 578 pp., 2 port. O. New York, 1881. (NEW YORK Hist. Soc'y. Collections. Vol. XIV.)　　　　　　　　　　　　　　　HK—N532

SHARP (The) Papers in the Brookline Public Library. (BROOKLINE Historical Society. Publications. No. 2, pp. 7-14.)
　　　　　　　　　　　　　　　　　　　　　　　HK—Pamphlet

SHAW, WILLIAM A., Editor. Letters of denization and acts of naturalization for aliens in England and Ireland. 1603-1700. XXXVI, 413 pp. Q. Lymington, 1911. (HUGUENOT Society of London. Publications. 1911. Vol. XVIII.)　　HK—H875—Vol. XVIII
450 copies printed. No. 405.

SHEPHERD, WILLIAM R. Story (The) of New Amsterdam. (HOLLAND Society of New York. Year Book, 1917. pp. 1-111. Q.)　　　　　　　　　　　　　　　　　　HK—H711

SLUYTER, PETER, and Dankers, Jaspar. Journal of a voyage to N. Y., 1679-80. (Long Island Historical Society. *Memoirs,* Vol. I.)
　　　　　　　　　　　　　　　　　　　　　　　HK—L86—Vol. I

SNITZLER, MARIE GRAHAM. Biographical sketch of Dr. Jacques Laborie. (Dr. James Labaree.) (HUGUENOT Society of America. Publications. Vol. IV. pp. 8-11.)　　　　　　HK—H87

SOCIETÉ DE L'HISTOIRE DU PROTESTANTISME FRANÇAIS. Bulletin historique et litteraire. Vols. 1-69. Series 1-5. Illustrated. Paris, 1853-1919.　　　　　　　　　　　　　　　　　　HK—So.1
Vols. I-XIV, title, "Doc. His. inedits & originaux."

———— Tab. générale des matières de la 1ᵉ ser. Vols. I-XIV.　HK—So.1

———— Commémoration de l'Enregistrement de l'Edit de Nantes par le Parlement de Paris (25 février 1599). Paris, 1899. 87 pp., 1 plan.　　　　　　　　　　　　　　　　　　HK—So.1.N
Bound with: Troisiéme centenaire de l'Edit de Nantes.
Gift of Mrs. James M. Lawton.

———— Jubilé cinquantenaire de la Société . . . (25 mai au 4 juin 1902). IV, 240 pp. O. Paris, 1902.　　　　　HK—So.1—1902
Extr. Bull. Soc. Hist. Prot. Fran., Sept. 1902.
Gift of N. Weiss.

———— Notice sur la Société . . . 1852-1872. 195 pp. Paris, 1874. S.　　　　　　　　　　　　　　　　　　　HK—So.1.N
Gift of Mrs. James M. Lawton.

———— Quarante-deuxiéme assemblée générale tenue a la Rochelle et à Saint-Martin-en-Ré les 18, 19 en 20 juin 1895. 172 pp. [Paris, 1895.] O.　　　　　　　　　　　　　　　　HK—So.1.R
Gift of N. Weiss.

————Troisiéme centenaire de l'Edit de Nantes en Amérique et en France. 224 pp., 1 fac-sim. Paris, 1898. O. (Il., pl., port., paged in.)　　　　　　　　　　　　　　　　　　HK—So.1.N
Gift of N. Weiss.
Bound with: Commemoration l'Enregistrement de l'Edit de Nantes.

SOCIETE D'HISTOIRE VAUDOISE. Bulletin. Nos. 1-26, bound in 8 volumes. Pignerol, & Alpina, 1884-1912. port., illus. O.   HK—V46

Title of No. 6, "Bulletin du bi-centenaire de la glorieuse rentrée, 1689-1889." 158, 1, pp., illus. O. Turin, 1889.

Title of No. 15, "Bollettino del cinquatenario della emancipazione," 1848-1898. VIII, 176 pp., illus., pl. O. Torino, 1898.

SOCIETY OF AMERICAN WARS: Commandery of the State of New York. Book of the Society. Vol. I-II. New York, 1911-1917. 2 vols.   HK—A51
Gift of Rufus G. Shirley.

SOCIETY OF COLONIAL WARS: Commonwealth of Massachusetts. Publication. No. 8. 1 vol. Boston, 1906. O.   HK—CW712M
Gift of the Society.

———— District of Columbia. Register for 1904. port., pl. O. Washington City, 1904. 1 vol.   HK—CW712D.C
Gift of the Society.

———— State of New York. Publications. No. 16-28. 4 vols. O. New York, 1911-1916. (Addresses and Year Book.)   HK—CW712
Gift of the Society.

SOCIETY OF DAUGHTERS OF HOLLAND DAMES. Descendants of the Ancient and Honourable families of New Netherland. Second Record Book. New York, 1913. O.   HK—H7

SOCIETY OF OLD BROOKLYNITES. Names of about 8000 persons, a small portion of the number confined on board the British prison ships during the War of the Revolution. 61 pp. Brooklyn, New York, 1888. O.   HK—Br79
Gift of H. M. Fisher.

SOCIETY FOR PROPAGATING THE GOSPEL AMONG THE INDIANS. Historical sketches of the Society by James F. Hunnewell & Rev. Peter Thacher; list of officers & members; by-laws adopted May 26, 1887. 52 pp., 1 pl. Square O. Boston?, 1887.   HK—P.956.I
225 copies, privately printed.
Gift of Mrs. Martha J. Lamb.

SOCIETY FOR THE PROPAGATION OF THE GOSPEL IN FOREIGN PARTS. Classified digest of the Records, . . . 1701-1892. (With much supplementary information.) XVI, 980 pp. London, 1893. O. Port. & group port., paged in.   HK—P.956.F
Gift of the Rev. Alfred V. Wittmeyer.

SOCIETY OF SONS OF THE REVOLUTION. Constitution, by-laws, membership. 87 pp. O. New York, 1890.   HK—So.32

———— 282 pp., illus., port., pl. New York, 1892. Q.   HK—So.32

————Year Book, 1899, and Supplement to Year Book of 1899. 2 vols. New York, 1899, & 1903. Q. fac-sim., port., pl.   HK—So.321
Gift of the Society.

SOUTH Carolina Society. Transactions, upon the occasion of the Centennial Celebration, July 25, 1904, of the Occupancy of the Society's Hall on . . . Meeting Street . . . in the City of Charleston, S. C. Charleston, 1905. 22 pp., 5 pl., 7 group port. D.
Gift of the Society.   HK—Pamphlet

SOUTHERN California Historical Society. Annual publication, 1888-'91. 3 vols. in 2. San Francisco, 1889-'91. O.   HK—C131
Gifts of B. A. Stephens & George Butler Griffen.
Vol. for 1888-'89 bound separately.

—— Publications. Vol. II, Part 1. 1 fac-sim. O. Los Angeles, 1891.   HK—C131
Vol. II, Part 1: GRIFFIN, G. B., Editor & Translator. Documents from the Sutro collection.
Gift of the Editor.
Bound with: Annual publications, 1890-'91.

STATE Historical Society of Wisconsin. Annotated catalogue of Newspaper files in the Library of the Society. Prepared by E. H. Blair. XII, 375 pp. O. Madison, Wis., 1898.   HK—W.75
Gift of the Society.

—— Proceedings. Nos. 37-41, and 45. Also Annual Report of 1886. Madison, 1886, 1890-'98. O.   HK—W75
Also unbound Nos.
Gift of the Society.

STATEN Island Church Records. See: WRIGHT, Tobias A. Records. . . . (N. Y. Gen. & Biog. Society.) Collections. Vol. IV. 1909. Q.

SURIANO, Michele. fl. 1560. Dispacci di Michele Suriano estratti dal cod. MXLV. classe VII dei MSS. Italiani della r. biblioteca Marciana di Venezia. (HUGUENOT Society of London. Publications. 1891. Vol. VI, Appendix, pp. 1-57.)   HK—H875—Vol. VI
Preceded by an English translation.

TENNESSEE Historical Society. Papers. GARRETT, History of the South Carolina cession, 1889.   HK—Pamphlet

THOMAS, Theodore Gaillard, M.D. Short sketch of two South Carolina Huguenots of the fourth generation. Read before the Society's Annual Meeting, April 13, 1904.   HK—H877
(HUGUENOT Society of America. Proceedings. Vol. IV. New York, 1904. pp. 78-82.)

THREADNEEDLE Street French Church. Registers. London, 1599-1840. 4 vols.   HK—H875
See: HUGUENOT Society of London. Publications.
Vol. I is Vol. IX   of Publications.
  " II   "   " XIII   "   "
  " III   "   " XVI   "   "
  " IV   "   " XXIII   "   "

TILLEY, R[ISBROUGH] H[AMMETT]. Huguenots (The) of Rhode Island. (HUGUENOT Society of America. Proceedings. Vol. III, Part 1, pp. 144-149.)   HK—H871—Vol. III
Read before the Society, April 13th, 1896.

TOLLIN, HENRI WILHELM NATHANAEL. 1833-1902. Deutschen Hugenotten-Vereins Würdigung durch das Hugenottische Ausland. 15 pp. O. Berlin, 1895.   HK—D491
Reprint of, & Bound with: Französische Colonie, Vol. 1895-'96. Gift of the Author.

——— Geschichte der französischen colonie von Halberstadt. (In: Deutsche Huguenotten Verein. Geschichtsblätter. 1893. No. 10, Part 3.)   HK—D49

——— Huguenotten (Die) in Magdeburg. (In: Deutsche Huguenotten Verein. Geschichtsblätter. 1890. Vol. I, pp. 9-40.)   HK—D49

——— & Béringuier, Richard. Französische colonie in Berlin. 42 pp. O. Magdeburg, 1891. (In: Deutsche Huguenotten Verein. Geschichtsblätter. 1891. Vol. IV.)   HK—D49

VAN DYKE, REV. PAUL, Prof. Huguenots (The) and the Beggars. (HUGUENOT Society of America. Proceedings. New York, 1894. Vol. II. pp. 210-223.)   HK—H871—Vol. II
Read before the Society, January 21st, 1892.

VAN SLYKE, REV. J. G., D.D. Huguenots (The) of Ulster County. (HUGENOT Society of America. Proceedings. New York, 1894. Vol. II. pp. 224-236.)   HK—H871—Vol. II
Read before the Society, March 16th, 1893.

VEDDER, REV. CHARLES S., D.D. Huguenots (The) of South Carolina and their Churches. (HUGUENOT Society of America. Proceedings. Vol. I, Part 1. New York, 1884. pp. 31-48. O.)   HK—H87.1—Vol. I
Read before the Society at the first public Meeting, held at the Eglise du Saint Esprit, New York, November 15th, 1883.

VERMILYE, REV. ASHBEL GREEN, D.D. Huguenot element among the Dutch. Schenectady, N. Y., 18?. 23 pp. O.   HK—A2H
No. 1 of volume of four pamphlets.

——— Mingling of the Huguenots and Dutch in Early New York. (HUGUENOT Society of America. Proceedings. New York, 1884. pp. 24-31.)   HK—H871
Read at the second Meeting of the Society, April 24th, 1884.

——— Memorial sketch of the Honorable John Jay, First President of the Huguenot Society of America, 1883-1894. (Huguenot Society of America. Proceedings. New York, 1896, pp. 22-36.)   HK—H871
Read before the Society, January 29th, 1895.

VERSTEEG, DINGMAN, Editor. See: REFORMED Dutch Church Records. 2 vols. 1666-1788. Q. (HOLLAND Society, New York. Year Book. 1913 & 1914.)

VIRGINIA HISTORICAL SOCIETY. Catalogue of the MSS. in the Collection of the Society, and also of some printed papers. Richmond, 1901. 120 pp. O.
Supplement to the VIRGINIA Magazine of History & Biography. Gift of the Society.

———— Collections. New Series. Richmond, 1886-1891. Vols. v-x. O.   HK—V81

    Vol. v.   BROCK, R. A., Editor. Huguenot emigration to Virginia.

    " vi.   ———— Miscellaneous Papers, 1672-1865.

    " vii-viii. ROBINSON, C., Compiler. Virginia Company, 1619-1624.

    " ix-x.   GRIGSBY, H. B. History of the Virginia Federal Convention of 1788.

Volumes v, vi, & vii, Gift of the Society. Volumes vii (a second copy), viii, ix, & x, Gift of Mrs. Martha J. Lamb.

———— Proceedings of the Society at its Annual Meeting. Richmond, 1894, 1898, 1903-'04, 1914-'17. O.   HK—V81
Bound with the Virginia Magazine of History & Biography.

———— VIRGINIA Magazine of History & Biography. Vols. ii, vi, xi-xii, xxii-xxvii, No. 1. Richmond, Va., 1894-1919. O.   HK—V81
Also Vols. iv, No. 2; xix, No. 2; xx, No. 2.
Gift of Mrs. James M. Lawton, and continued currently as her gift.
Note: Numbers to complete the early volumes of our file would be acceptable.
(Vols. ii, vi, xi-xii, xxii-xxvii bound.)

VIRGINIA Magazine of History and Biography. See: VIRGINIA Historical Society.

WAKEFIELD, EDWARD. Waifs and strays of American History. (HUGUENOT Society of America. Proceedings. 1891. Vol. ii. pp. 115-134.)   HK—H87—Vol. ii
Read before the Society, December 19th, 1889.

WALLER, WILLIAM CHAPMAN, Editor. Register of the French Church at Thorpe-le-Soken in Essex. 1684-1726. x, 27 pp. Q. London, 1912.   HK—H875—Vol. xx
Bound with: LART, C. E. Registers . . . French Churches . . . Bristol, Stonehouse, & Plymouth. (HUGUENOT Society of London. Publications. 1912. Vol. xx.)
450 copies printed. No. 414.

———— & Minet, William, Editors. Registers of the Church known as La Patente in Spittlefields, from 1689-1785. (HUGUENOT Society of London. Publications. Vol. xi. 1898.)   HK—H875—Vol. xi
450 copies printed. No. 427.

———— Transcript of the Registers of the Protestant Church at Guisnes from 1668-1685. (HUGUENOT Society of London. Publications. Vol. iii. 1891.)   HK—HK
500 copies printed. No. 359.

WATERS, EDWARD STANLEY. Notes on some Huguenot families: Vincent, Magny (Many), Aymar, Erouard (Harway), and others. (HUGUENOT Society of America. Proceedings. New York, 1903. Vol. III, Part 2, pp. 245-271.)   HK—H871—Vol. III

WEISS, NATHANIEL. Ennemis (Les) de l'Edit de Nantes. (HUGUENOT Society of America. Publications. Vol. III. 1900.)   HK—H87—Vol. III

WIGHT, WILLIAM W., Compiler. See: NEW ENGLAND Historical & Genealogical Register. Index to genealogies and pedigrees in the Register. . . . Vol. I-Vol. X. Boston, 1896. 11 pp. O. Reprint: N. E. Hist. & Gen. Register, October, 1896.   HK—NR44

WILSON, GEN. JAMES GRANT, U. S. A. Bayard family of America and Judge Bayard's London diary of 1795-'96. (HUGUENOT Society of America. Proceedings. New York, 1891. Vol. II. pp. 135-154.)   HK—H8.71—Vol. II
Read before the Society, April 17th, 1890.

PERIODICALS

FRENCH CHURCH du Saint Esprit, New York City. Historical sketches of the first and second edifices, with wood-cut illustrations. In: NEW YORK MIRROR, Vol. VIII, No. 2, page 9; Vol. XII, No. 22, page 168; No. 23, page 176; No. 24, page 148. New York, 1830-1835. Square folio. HL—N48

JOURNAL of American History. See: NATIONAL Historical Society. HK—N277

LONG ISLAND Historical Bulletin. Vol. I, Nos. 1-4. Brooklyn, N. Y., 1913. Published and copyrighted by Chas. A. Ditmas. HL—N421.1

This volume contains articles in reference to the Works of Daniel M. Tredwell, and is largely composed of his historical sketches about Long Island.
Gift of the Publisher.

MAGAZINE of American History, with notes and queries, edited by Mrs. Martha J. Lamb. N. Y., 1885-89. Vols. XIII-XXII, illustrated, square roan. O. HL—M27

MARSEILLAIS Hymn: words and music. In: NEW YORK MIRROR, Vol. VIII, No. 13, pp. 103-104. New York, 1830. Square folio. HL—N48—Vol. VIII

With notes on the author and composer, its origin, etc.

NEW AMSTERDAM Gazette. Historical sketches and reminiscences of the Dutch régime of New Amsterdam and the New Netherlands: History of the early Churches: Dutch progress in later years in Holland and America: Views of Holland and other illustrations. Edited by Morris Coster. Vols. I-VII. New York, 1883-1893. 7 vols. in 4. Square quarto. HL—L421

Gift of the Editor through Wm. Gayer Dominick.

—————— Year Book. Vol. I, Nos. 1-3, 1897-1899. Edited by Morris Coster. New York, 1897-'99. O. HL—N421.1
Publication discontinued.
Gift of the Editor.

NEW YORK Mirror and Ladies' Literary Gazette. N. Y., 1831-34. Vols. VIII & XII, illustrated, folio. HL—N48

THEOLOGY

BALLOU, Hosea. Treatise on atonement. Boston, 1858. Sixth edition. 228 pp. D. HM—B21

BEZE, Thedore de, Translator. See: NOVUM testamentum. 1574. Dedication by P. de Loyseleur. Title-page wanting. HM—N851 Latin and Greek in parallel columns.

—— Les PSEAUMES de David, 1652. HM—P95

BROWN, Rev. William Adams, Ph.D., D.D. Calvin's influence upon Theology. (UNION Theo. Seminary. Three Addresses delivered by Professors in the Seminary, at a Service in commemoration of the 400th Anniversary of the birth of John Calvin.) New York, 1909. 47 pp. O.. pp. 20-35. HM—Pamphlet

CAILLOT, Antoine. Morceaux d'éloquence, extraits des sermons des orateurs protestans français, les plus célèbres du dix-septième siècle, précédés d'une courte notice sur la vie de chacun d'eux. Paris, 1810. 375 pp. O. Half calf. HM—C12 Gift of Edward F. De Lancey.

CALVIN, John. Le catéchisme français de Calvin, publié en 1537, réimprimé pour la première fois d'après un exemplaire nouvellement retrouvé et suivi de la plus ancienne Confession de foi de l'église de Genève avec deux notices par Albert Rilliet et Théophile Dufour. Genève, 1878. 146 pp. D. Half morocco. HM—C13

CHARLESTON, S. C., French Protestant Church. See: LITURGY. . . .

CHRISTIAN (The) hero: . . . proving no principles but . . . religion . . . sufficient to make a great man. London, 1727. [By R. Steele.] HM—S814

CORWIN, Rev. Edward Tanjore, D.D. Amsterdam (The) correspondence. 1 leaf, pp. 81-107. New York, 1897. (Reprinted from Vol. VIII American Soc'y of Church History.) HM—Pamphlet Gift of the Author.

CUSHMAN, Robert. Self-love. 1621. "The first sermon preached in New England; and the oldest extant of any delivered in America." N. Y., 1847. 47 pp. fac-simile. D. Boards. HM—C95 Gift of the Rev. Alfred V. Wittmeyer.

de BUDE, Eugene, Editor. See: TURRETTINI, Jean-Alphonse. Lettres inedites adressees de 1686 a 1737. . . . Vols. I-III. Paris, 1887. 3 vols. D. HM—T86

DODDRIDGE, Philip. Les Commencemens et les progrès de la vraie
piété . . . traduit de l'Anglois, par J. S. Vernede . . . 24,472, 31
pp. La Haye, 1751. O.   HM—D66
Gift of Mrs. Maria Dusenbury.

DRELINCOURT, Rev. Charles. The Christian's consolations
against the fears of death. With . . . prayers and meditations. . . .
To which are prefixed the Life of the author. . . . 24,444 pp., 1 pl.
Philadelphia, 1884. D.   HM—D81
Contains bookplate of John Pintard, LL.D.
Gift of Mrs. Maria Dusenbury.

DUFOUR, Théophile. Notice bibliographique fur le catéchisme et
la confession de foi de Calvin (1537) et fur les autres livres im-
primés à Genève et à Neuchatel dans les premiers temps de la Réforme (1533-'40).   HM—C13
(See: CALVIN, Jean. Catéchisme Français de Calvin. . . . 1878.
pref. pp. 99-237.)

DU MOULIN, Pierre. Huictieme decade de sermons. Genève, 1653-
54. 3 vols. in 1. S. Vellum.   HM—D89
Vol. ii, Neufvieme decade de sermons.
Vol. iii, Dixieme decade de sermons.
Gift of Charles M. Du Puy.

EGLISE FRANCAISE de Cantorbéry. Le Livre du Sanctuaire. . . .
Crypte de Cathédrale, fondée en 1550. xxiv, 176 pp. 2nd ed. Tt.
Cantorbéry, [1877?]. Compiled par Rev. J. A. Martin.   HM—L78
Gift of Mrs. James M. Lawton.

———— Service du Culte Divin pour les Solennites de l'Eglise Française et autres occasions speciales. . . . Dans ces Solennites, comme
signe d'Union Chretienne, le LIVRE du Sanctuaire est remplace par
la LITURGIE de l'Eglise d'Angleterre. Canterbury, no date.
Cover & 16 pp. S. This is the Office of Morning Prayer in French
and English, parallel columns, with "Collectes Speciales," appended,
in both languages.   HM—L78.1
Gift of Mrs. James M. Lawton.

EGLISE PROTESTANT EPISCOPAL: Livre des prières publiques
de l'administration des sacremens et des autres rites et cérémonies
de l'église, selon l'usage de l'église protestante épiscopale dans les
Etats-Unis d'Amérique avec le psautier. Nouvelle édition. N. Y.,
1831. 464 pp. Q. Sheep.   HM—L78.2F
Gift of the Rev. Alfred V. Wittmeyer.

Note:—This Prayer Book used in the Chancel, l'Eglise du Saint
Esprit, A.D., 1832. Original binding preserved, the cover bearing name and date.

EGLISES Evangeliques Françaises des Etats-Unis. Confession de foi
et liturgie. [Edited et trans., par Rev. J. Provost. Springfield,
Mass., 1897.] vii, 72 pp. O.   HM—L73P
Gift of the Translator.

ESPRIT (l') de Jesus-Christ sur la Tolérance; pour servir de résponse à plusieurs Ecrits de ce tems sur la même matiere, & particulierement à l'Apologie de Louis XIV sur la Revocation de l'Edic de Nantes, & a la Dissertation sur le Massacre de la Saint Barthelemi. 360 pp. n.p., 1759. D.   HM—E77
Gift of Herbert Dupuy.

FRENCH PROTESTANT Church, Charleston, S. C.   See: LITURGY.

HALL, Rev. Thomas Cuming. D.D.   The inner spirit of the Calvinistic Puritan State.   (In: UNION Theo. Seminary.   Three addresses delivered at a Service in commemoration of the 400th Anniversary of the birth of John Calvin.)   New York, 1909.   47 pp. O.   pp. 36-47.   HM—Pamphlet

HOPITAL (L') pour les Pauvres Français Protestants.   Ordre à Suivre au Culte Divin a l'occasion de l'Anniversaire.   Londres, no date.   8 pp.   Small square O.   HM—L78.1
Gift of Mrs. James M. Lawton.

Bound with: Eglise Protestant Française de Canterbury.   Service du Culte Divin pour les Solennités de l'Eglise Française et autres occasions spéciales.

HYMNAL Companion to the Book of Common Prayer of the Church of England.   Edited by the Rev. E. C. Bickersteth.   [189?.]   Title page missing.   III-VII pp., remainder unpaged; Hymns numbered 1-550, 11 leaves ff. S.   HM—HB99
Gift of Mrs. James M. Lawton.

JAQUELOT, Isaac. 1647-1708.   Sermons sur divers textes prononcéz dans la Chapelle royale en présence de sa Majesté [le roi de Prusse].   Amsterdam, 1710. Tome 2. S.   HM—J27
Gift of Edward F. de Lancey.

JULIEN, Rev. Matthew Cantine.   Harvest (The) of Life.   A thought for the New Yorr.   12 pp.   D.   New Bedford, Mass., January 7, 1906.   HM—Pamphlet
Gift of the Author.

———— Reason in Religion.   12 pp.   New Bedford, Mass., 1907.   D.
Gift of the Author.   HM—Pamphlet

La PLACETTE, Jean de.   La Communion dévote; ou, la Maniére de participer saintement & utilement à l'Eucaristie.   Ed. 4.   2 parts in 1 vol. Amsterdam, 1699. S.   No title page.   HM—L31

Note:—Edition 4 is enlarged by Part 2.   First edition printed in 1695.   The title page for this copy of the fourth edition has been supplied evidently from that of the *first* edition: the date of the *fourth* edition is as given—1699.
Gift of the Hon. John Jay.

Le MERCIER, Rev. André.   Treatise on detraction.   303 pp.   Boston, 1733. D.   HM—L54
Gift of the French Huguenot Church of Charleston, S. C.

LIBERTINS (Les) spirituels traités mystiques écrits dans les années 1547-1549. Publiés d'après le manuscrit original. Bale, 1876. 251 pp. D. Edited par C. SCHMIDT.　　　　　　　　　　　HM—Sch5

LITURGIE pour les protestans de France ou prieres pour les familles des fidelés privés de l'exercice public de leur religion. Avec un discourse Préliminaire *sur quelques Matieres intéressantes.* A Amsterdam, Chez Marc-Michel Rey, 1758. 8vo, pp. 294.　　　　HM—L73

LITURGY; or, Forms of divine service of the French Protestant Church of Charleston, S. C. Translated from the liturgy of the Churches of Neufchatel and Vallagin, editions of 1737 and 1772, with some additional prayers carefully selected. The whole adapted to public worship in the United States of America. Third edition. New York, [1853]. xxiv, 228 pp. D. Morocco.　　　　　　HM—L53
Presented by the French protestant church of Charleston, S. C.

———— Same. Fourth edition. Charleston, S. C., 1886. xxiv, 230 pp. (Contains as Additional Canticles, the Nunc Dimittis and the Magnificat.) Inside of front cover is printed: "This Edition of the Liturgy of the French Protestant Church of Charleston, South Carolina, is presented to the Church by William Ravenel, Esq. 1886." Gift of H. A. De Saussure.　　　　　　　　　　　　　HM—L53P

MAIMBOURG, Louis. Histoire de Calvinisme. New edition. 21, 1-514, 26 pp. T. Paris, 1682.　　　　　　　　　　　　　HM—M2₹
Gift of the Hon. John Jay.

MAROT, Clement, Translator. Les Pseaumes de David. 1652.
　　　　　　　　　　　　　　　　　　　　　　　　　　　HM—P9₴

MARTIN, Rev. J. A., Compiler. See: EGLISE l' Française de Cantorbéry. Livre du Sanctuaire.

NICHOLE, P. De l'unité de l'église; ou, Refutation du nouveau systême de M. Jurieu. Paris, 1687. 484 pp. S.　　　　　HM—N₹1
Gift of Edward F. De Lancey.

NOUVEAU TESTAMENT, c'est-a-dire, la nouvelle alliance de notre Seigneur Jesus Christ. Amsterdam, 1770. S. Russia leather.
Gift of Charles E. Lord.　　　　　　　　　　　　　　HM—N 5

———— Revu sur les originaux par David Martin. New York, 1846. S.　　　　　　　　　　　　　　　　　　　HM—N85.1₊1
Gift of Mrs. James M. Lawton.

———— texte grec, Vulgate et traduction latine avec notes, de Theodore de Bèze. Cinquiéme Edition. Dédidace de Ch. de Bèze à Louis de Bourbon, 1565. Dédidace de Loselerius Villerius á henri d'Hastings, 1573. L'Imprimeur au Lecteur. Exhortation à la lecture de Nouveay Testament (h'Etienne). (Deux parties en un volume.) Londres: Loselerius Villerius, 1574. 8vo, pp. 514.　　　HM—N₹₊1

PROTESTANTISME (Le) réfuté par luimême; Résponse aux ministres du canton de Sainte-Foy. 2 leaves, 5-224 pp. Bordeaux, 1838. O.　　　　　　　　　　　　　　　　　　　　　　HM— 96
Gift of Herbert DuPuy.

PROVOST, Rev. J. See: EGLISES Evangeliques Françaises des Etats-Unis. Confession de foi et liturgie.

PSEAUMES DE DAVID. Mis en rime Francoise. Par Clement Marot et Theodore de Beze. Paris: Pierre Des-Hayes, 1652. O.   HM—P95
Contains also les Dix commandemens, Le Catechisme, Confession de foi faite d'un commun accord par les églises réformées du royaume de France, La forme des prieres ecclesiastiques.
Gift of the Hon. John Jay.

———— mis en vers François, revus & approuvez par le synode Walon des Provinces-Unies. 269 pp. S. Amsterdam, 1770. (In: le NOU-VEAU Testament, 1770.)   HM—N85
Gift of Charles E. Lord.

PSEAUMES DE DAVID. Mis en Vers François; *Revus & approuvés par les Pasteurs & Professeurs de l'Eglise & de l'Académie de Genève.* Nouvelle Edition. A Genève, Chez Pierre-Isaac Faber, 1790. 12mo, pp. 652. CANTIQUES SACRES POUR LES PRINCIPALES SOLENNITES DES CHRETIENS, et sur autres sujets. Nouvelle Edition, *augmentée de plusieurs Cantiques & Prières.* A Niort, Chez Jean-Baptiste Lefranc-Elies, Imprimeur-Libraire, 1790. 12mo, pp. 313. (Both works bound in one volume.)   HM—P952
Contains also Les Prieres ecclésiastiques; La Liturgie du baptême, mariage; Confession de foi.
Gift of the Hon John Jay.

RILLIET, Albert. Notice fur la premier sejour de Calvin a Geneve. (See: CALVIN, Jean. Catechisme François de Calvin publie en 1878, pref. pp. 5-98.)   HM—C13

ROCKWELL, William Walker, S.T.B., Lic. Th. Calvin and the Reformation. (UNION Theo. Seminary. Three addresses delivered by Professors in the Seminary, at a Service in commemoration of the 400th Anniversary of the birth of John Calvin.) New York, 1909. 47 pp. O. pp. 5-19.   HM—Pamphlet

ROISSELET de Sauelieres, fils. Histoire de Protestantisme en France, precedee de la Refutation d'un libelle de E. B. D. Fressard . . . intitule: Evenemens de Nismes. . . . Vol. i. v-xlviii, 415 pp. O. Nismes, 1836. (Imprint on cover: Montpellier, 1837.) HM—P96
Bound with: Protestantisme (Le) refute. . . .
Gift of Herbert DuPuy.

ROMAN forgeries, or a True account of false records discovering the impostures and counterfeit antiquities of the Church of Rome. By a Faithful Son of the Church of England. i.e., T. TRAHERNE. London, 1673.   HM—E9

ROY, Joseph E. Manual of the principles, doctrines and usages of congregational churches. Revised edition. Boston, no date. 48 pp. D.   HM—Pamphlet
Gift of the author.

SCHMIDT, CHARLES, Editor. Les libertins spirituels, traités mystiques écrits dans les années 1547-1549. Publiés d'après le manuscrit original. Bale, 1876. 251 pp. D. Half roan.　　　HM—Sch5

SCHUYLER, THE REV. MONTGOMERY, D.D. Sermon on the 25th anniversary of his rectorship, Christ church, Oct. 5, 1879. St. Louis, 1879. 26 pp. O.　　　HM—Pamphlet
Gift of Charles F. Robertson.

SOULIER, ———. Explication (L') de l'Edit de Nantes, de M. Bernard. Avec de nouvelles observations, and les Nouveaux Edits, Declarations & Arrests donnez jusqu'a present, touchant la Religion pretendue reformee. Paris, 1683. 13 leaves, 566 pp. D.　　HM—S723
Gift of Herbert M. DuPuy.

STEELE, RICHARD. Christian (The) hero: an Argument proving principles of religion sufficient to make a great man. London, 1727. 8th ed. S.　　　HM—S814
Gift of Miss Sara Devotion.

TURRETTINI, JEAN-ALPHONSE. Lettres inédites adressées de 1686 a 1737 à J-A. T., théologien Genevois. Publiées et annotées par E. de Budé. Vols. I-III. Paris, 1887. 3 vols. D.　　　HM—T86
Gift of the French Société.

TRAHERNE, THOMAS, B. D. Roman forgeries, or a true account of false records discovering the impostures and counterfeit antiquities of the Church of Rome. By a Faithful Son of the Church of England. 17 leaves, 316 pp. London, 1673. S.　　　HM—E9
Gift of Miss Sara Devotion.

UNION Theological Seminary. Three addresses delivered by Professors . . . at a Service in commemoration of the 400th Anniversary of the birth of John Calvin, in the Adams Chapel, third of May, 1909. New York, 1909. 47 pp. O.　　　HM—Pamphlet
　I. Calvin and the Reformation. Prof. Wm. W. Rockwell, S.T.B., Lic.
　II. Calvin's Influence upon Theology. Prof. Wm. A. Brown, Ph.D.
　III. Inner (The) spirit of the Calvinistic Puritan State. Prof. Thos. C. Hall, D.D.
Gift of the Seminary.

UNITE (De l') de l'Eglise. 1678. By P. NICHOLE.　　HM—N51

VERNEDE, JEAN SCIPION, Translator. See: DODDRIDGE, PHILIP. Commencemens (Les) de la vraie piété. 1751.　HM—D66

LITERATURE

BUNGENER, LAURENCE LOUIS FÉLIX. Priest and the Huguenot; or, Persecution in the age of Louis XV, [translated] from the French. Boston, 1854. 2 vols. D. HN—B88

BURGOYNE, [SIR] J[OHN]. Heiress (The). A Comedy in five acts, with Prologue by the Right Hon. Richard Fitzpatrick. Also gives dramatis personae. III-XII, 80 pp. Hertford street, Feb. 1st, 1786, title page wanting. D. HN—B957
Gift of Mrs. James M. Lawton.

BURGWYN, COLLINSON PIERREPONT EDWARDS. Huguenot (The) lovers. A tale of the Old Dominion. 4 pl., 219 pages. S. Richmond, Va., 1889. HN—B95
Autograph Gift of Evert Jansen Wendell.

CANNON, LEGRAND BOUTON. Personal reminiscences of the Rebellion. 1861-1866. 228 pp. New York, 1895. D. HN—C16
Gift of the Author.

CASPIPINA'S letters, [by Jacob Duché], 1777. HN—D85

[COOKE, JOHN ESTEN.] Story (The) of a Huguenot's sword. Derived from authentic papers and traditions. (In: Harper's New Monthly Magazine, No. LXXXIII, April, 1857, Vol. XIV, pp. 618-631.) O. N. Y., 1857. HN—C77
Gift of H. M. Ames.

COUNT, HANNIBAL. Romance (A) of the Court of France, by STANLEY J. WEYMAN. D. N. Y., 1901. W54—W54

[DeCOSTA, REV. BENJAMIN FRANKLIN, D.D.] Pilgrim (The) of old France, or, The Huguenots on the Hudson. 1613-'14. To which are added . . . other pieces of verse. 2nd ed. 48 pp., 3 pl., 1 port. New York, 1893. T. HN—D35
Autograph Gift of the Author.

[DUCHE, JACOB.] Caspipina's letters, containing observations on subjects literary, moral and religious, [with] the life and character of Wm. Penn. Bath, 1777. 2 vols. in 1. S. HN—D85
Gift of Charles Marseilles.

DOYLE, A[RTHUR] CONAN. Refugees (The): a Tale of two Continents. 366 pp., 20 pl. D. New York, 1893. HN—D77

[DuPUY, ELIZA A.] Huguenot (The) exiles, or, The times of Louis XIV. An historical novel. 2 pl., 6-453 pp. New York, 1856. D. HN—D94
Gift of Prof. Samuel Macauley Jackson.

[————] Miser's (The) curse. A veritable ghost story. (Harper's New Monthly Magazine. April, 1857. pp. 641-646.) O. N. Y., 1857.   HN—C77

FONTAINE, Francis. The exile: a tale of St. Augustine. N. Y., 1878. 114 pp. square D.   HN—F73
Gift of the Author.

GILLE Tilleman et les siens; ou, La Bible aux Pays-Bas sous la domination espagnole: drame historique en cinq actes, par un Huguenot. 88 pp. D. Bruxelles, 1896.   HN—AH8
Gift of E. Belleroche.

HARPER'S New Monthly Magazine. No. lxxxiii, April, 1857. Vol. xiv. New York, 1857. O.   HN—C77
Gift of H. M. Ames.

HEIRESS (The). [A Comedy in five acts, by Sir John BURGOYNE.] With Prologue by the Right Hon. Richard Fitzpatrick. [Also gives] Dramatis personae. Hertford-street, Feb. 1st, 1786. D.   HN—B957

HENTY, G. A. St. Bartholomew's eve. A tale of the Huguenot wars. 384 pp., 12 pl., 1 map. D. New York, 1893.   HN—H38

HOUSE (The) of the wolf. By S. J. WEYMAN. Philadelphia, 1898?. S.   HN—W54

HUGUENOT (A), pseudonym. Gille Tilleman et les siens; ou LaBible aux Pays-Bas sous la domination espagnole: drame historique en cinq actes. 88 pp. D. Bruxelles, 1896.   HN—AH8
Gift of E. Belleroche.

HUGUENOT (The) exiles, or, The times of Louis XIV. A historical novel. New York, 1856. [By Eliza A. DuPUY.]   HN—D94

HUGUENOT Lovers (The). A Tale of the Old Dominion. By C. P. E. Burgwyn. Richmond, Va., 1889.   HN—B95

HUGUENOTS (The). A tale of the French Protestants. [By George P. R. JAMES.] D. New York, 1839.   HN—Hug87

[JAMES, George Payne Rainsford.] The Huguenot. A Tale of the French Protestants. 2 vols. D. New York, 1839.   HN—Hug87
Gift of Charles Volney Wheeler.

KING'S (The) Signet: or, the Story of a Huguenot family. By Eliza Pollard. London, 1900. O.   HN—P91

"LITTLE (The) Huguenot." A Romance of Fontainebleau. By Max Pemberton. New York, 1895.   HN—P37

LUCANUS, Marcus Annæus. Pharsalia; sive, De bello civili, libri decem, ad fidem editionis Oudendorpianæ, re-editi, cum supplemento Thomæ Maii. London, 1815. 296 pp. O.   HN—L96

MANN, Florian A. Story of the Huguenots. A sixteenth century narrative wherein the French, Spaniards, and Indians were the actors. St. Augustine, Fla. 197 pp. 1898. HN—M13
Gift of Prof. Samuel Macauley Jackson.

MAY, Thomas. Supplementum Lucani. (In Lucanus, M. A. Pharsalia.) HN—L96

MISER'S (The) curse. A veritable ghost story. By Eliza A. DuPuy. (In Harper's New Monthly Magazine. April, 1857. pp. 641-646.) O. N. Y., 1857. HN—C77

MONNIER, Marc. Histoire de la littérature moderne; la réforme, de Luther à Shakespeare. 495 pp. D. Paris, 1885. HN—M75

MUSICK, John R. Saint Augustine. A story of the Huguenots in America. vi, 309 pp., 8 pl. D. New York, 1892. M97—M97

PEMBERTON, Max. "The little Huguenot." A Romance of Fontainebleau. 177 pp., 1 port. S. New York, 1895. HN—P37

PIERRE and his family; or, a Story of the Waldenses. vi, 7-214 pp., 4 pl. Revised edition. Philadelphia, 1842. S. HN—P81
Gift of J. P. M. M., through Mrs. James M. Lawton.

PILGRIM (The) of old France or, the Huguenots on the Hudson, 1613-'14 . . . and other pieces of verse. By Rev. B. F. DeCOSTA, D.D. 2nd ed. T. New York, 1893. HN—D35

POLLARD, Eliza. King's (The) Signet; or, the Story of a Huguenot family. 1 leaf, v-vi, 1 leaf, 9-288 pp., plates. London, 1900. O. HN—P91
Gift of J. P. M. M., through Mrs. J. M. Lawton.

PRIEST and Huguenot; or, Persecution in the Age of Louis XV. By Laurence Louis Felix BUNGENER. Translated from the French. Boston, 1854. 2 vols. D. HN—B88

READ, Charles, Editor. See: SATYRE Ménipée. . . . 1876. HNn—Sa8

REFUGEES (The): a Tale of two Continents. By Arthur Conan Doyle. N. Y., 1893. D. HN—D77

SAINT Augustine: a story of the Huguenots in America. By J. R. Musick. N. Y., 1892. D. HN—M97

SAINT Bartholomew's eve. A tale of the Huguenot wars. By G. A. HENTY. D. New York, 1893. HN—H38

SATYRE Ménippée; ou, La vertu du catholicon selon l'édition princeps de 1594, avec introduction et éclaircissements par Charles Read. Edition nouvelle. Paris, 1876. 322 pp. T. HN—Sa8

STORY (The) of a Huguenot's sword. [By John Esten Cooke.] [New York, 1857?.] O. (In: Harper's New Monthly Magazine, April, 1857.) HN—C77

STORY of the Huguenots. A Sixteenth Century narrative wherein the French, Spaniards and Indians were the actors. By Florian A. Mann. St. Augustine, Fla., 1898. Tt.   HN—M13

WEYMAN, STANLEY JOHN. Count Hannibal: a Romance of the Court of France. VI, 403 pp., 1 pl. New York, 1901. D.   HN—W54 Gift of Mrs. James M. Lawton.

—————— House (The) of the wolf. 234 pp., 1 port. Philadelphia, 1898. S.   HN—W541

MISCELLANEOUS

AUSTIN, John Osborne, Compiler. The Roger Williams calendar.
VI, 370 pp. D. Central Falls, R. I., 1897. HO—C13
Gift of the Compiler.

BIBLIOPHILE Huguenot, bulletin trimestriel de livres rares . . .
sur le protestantisme pendant les 16e-18e siècles. 48 pp. O. Paris,
1889. HO—Pamphlet

BYLES, Dr.—The Huguenot refugee. Song (with chorus). Music
by W. Ryves. Q. 6 pp. n.p., n.d. HO—Pamphlet

CHARENTE-Inferieure-Archiviste. MESCHINET de Richemond,
L. M. Rapport de l'archiviste. 1885. HO—R39

DE PEYSTER, John Watts, Brev. Maj. Gen., U. S. A. Wolverene
(The). (Carcajou or Glutton.) With information from trust-
worthy authorities, and illustrations. 4 pl., 4 leaves, XLIV, 30 pp.
Tivoli, N. Y., 1901. O. HO—Pamphlet
Gift of the Author.

DICTIONNAIRE historique de l'ancien langage François. . . . Tomes
1-10. Niort, [187?]-1882. Square Q. 10 Tomes. LaCURNE
DE SAINTE-PALAYE. HO—Pal.18

DOZY, Charles M. The Pilgrim fathers. Exhibition of documents
from public and private collections at Leiden, relating to the Dutch
settlements in North America. Aug., 1888. [Leiden, 1888.]
HO—Pamphlet

ESPRINCHARD, Jacques. See: MESCHINET de RICHE-
MOND, L. M. Relations inédites et autographes des voyages, dans
l'Europe centrale de Jean Godeffroy, d'Orleans (de 1568 à 1571)
& de J. E. (de 1593 à 1598). Paris, 1882. HO—R39
Reprint: Assoc. Fr. Adv. Sci., 1882.

FEW (A) plain facts by "Justice" concerning the plagiarisms . . . of
the Merchant Prince of Cornville: an original drama by Capt.
Samuel Eberly Gross. . . . N. Y., 1910. HO—Pamphlet
Gift of S. E. Gross, Capt. U. S. A.

GALERIES histoire de Versailles. n.d. GAVARD, J. D. C. HO—G24

[GAVARD, Jacques Dominique Charles.] Galeries historiques de
Versailles [text]. 2 vols. in 1, folio, half morocco. HO—G24

HOLLANDSCH-AMERIKAANSCH almanak en jaarboekje. N. Y.,
1883. D. HO—Pamphlet
Gift of the Rev. Alfred V. Wittmeyer.

HUGUENOT (The) refugee. Song (with chorus). Words by Dr. Byles, music by W. Ryves. Q. 6 pp. n.p., n.d.   HO—Pamphlet

LaCURNE DE SAINTE-PALAYE. Dictionnaire historique de l'ancien langage François; ou, Glossaire de la langue Françoise depuis son origine jusqu-au siècle de Louis XIV. . . . A-Z. Vols. 1-10. Square Q. 10 vols. Niort, [187?]-1882.   HO—Pal 18z Gift of Mrs. J. M. Lawton.

OUDIN, Antonin. Curiositez françoises. . . . In: LaCURNE DE SAINTE-PALAYE. Dictionnaire historique de l'ancien langage François. . . . Square Q. Niort, [187?]-1882. A-Z. Tomes 1-10.
HO—Pal 18z

ROGER Williams (The) Calendar. Compiled by J. O. Austin. Central Falls, R. I., 1897. D.   HO—C13

RYVES, Windham. The Huguenot refugee. Song (with chorus). Words by Dr. Byles. Q. 6 pp. n.p., n.d.   HO

SWORDS'S pocket almanack, Christian's calendar and ecclesiastical register. N. Y., 1829-59. 12 vols. in 3. S. & Tt.   HO Gift of Rev. Alfred V. Wittmeyer.

VEDDER, Rev. Charles S., D.D., LL.D. Holland. A poem written for the anniversary of the Holland Society of New York, 1892. Square O. New York, 1898. (1 of 300 copies.)   HO—Pamphlet Gift of the Author.

———— Poem: read at the celebration by the Huguenot Society of Charleston, S. C., April 14, 1890, of the Promulgation of the Edict of Nantes, 1598. Charleston, 1890. S. Oblong, 21 leaves. Privately printed.   HO—Pamphlet Gift of the Author.

VOLTAIRE, François Marie Arouet de. Lettres de Voltaire à Louis Necker de Germany. 13 pp. O. [Genève, 1882.] (Ext. Bulletin de la Soc. d'hist. et d'archeologie de Genève. Tome i, livre 2.)   HO—Nec 28

PART II

A DICTIONARY

OR

STRICTLY ALPHABETICAL CATALOGUE

with numerous cross-references, names of places, "catch-words," etc.

Individual Indexes of Biography, Class G, and Genealogy, Class H, immediately follow their respective Classes in PART I.

DICTIONARY

ABBOTT, William Henry. Heraldry illustrated: being a short account of the origin of heraldry . . . with . . . directions for drawing and painting coats-of-arms, to which is added a Glossary of terms used in heraldry. 2 leaves, 127 pp., 31 pl. N. Y., [C. 1897].
O.   HH—A134

ACADEMIE de Genève. Le livre du recteur catalogue des étudiants de l'Académie de Genève de 1559-1859. Genève, 1860. 391 pp.
D.   HG—Ac1

ACADEMIE Royale des médailles & des inscriptions. See: PARIS Académie Royale des médailles & des inscriptions.

ACADIA. See: CANADIAN Archives: Appendix H. Letter of Father Ignace re Acadia. (According to a photographic copy of the original in the Archives of the Propaganda, Rome.) pp. 331-341.   HF—C213—Vol. I

ACADIAN genealogy and notes. By P. Gaudet. I-XXXIV, 372 pp. (Appendix A, Part III, Canadian Archives.)   HF—C213—Vol. II

ACCOUNT of the persecutions & oppressions of the Protestants in France. . . . 1686. By Jean CLAUDE.   HA—C57

ADAMS, Charles Francis. Struggle for neutrality in America. Address before N. Y. Historical Soc'y, Dec. 13, 1870. 52 pp.   HE—Z3

ADAMS, Herbert Baxter. Maryland's influence in founding a National Commonwealth. Paper read before the Maryland Historical Society, April 9, 1877. 123 pp., 1 pl. Baltimore, 1877. O.   HE—Z4

ADAMS' Magazine of Revolutionary records. New York, 1892. Vol. I, No. 4; Vol. II, Nos. 5-8. Title of Vol. I, "Adams' Magazine of general literature."   HH—Pamphlet

AGNEW, Rev. David C. A. Protestant exiles from France in Reign of Louis XIV; or, The Huguenot refugees and their descendants in Great Britain and Ireland. 1 pl., VIII, 403 pp., 2 fac-sim., 3 pl., 4 port. Square Q. n.p., 1866.   HB—A273D
Contains Bookplate of H. R. Duval.

——— Protestant exiles from France in the reign of Louis XIV; or, Huguenot refugees and their descendants in Great Britain and Ireland. Second edition, enlarged. London, 1871. 2 vols. Square
O.   HB—A273

AGUESSE, Laurent. Histoire de l'établissement du protestantisme en France, contenant l'histoire politique et religieuse de la nation depuis François Ier jusqu'à l'Edit de Nantes. Paris, 1882-86. 4 vols. O.   HA—Ag9

AIGUES-MORTES, South of France. See: CYR, N. Heroism of Huguenot women imprisoned for life in the Tower of Constance. (Cyr's Huguenot Sketches, No. 1.) A Pamphlet inserted in this volume.   HG—Qu3

ALBANY, New York. Early records of the City and County of Albany and Colony of Rensselaerswyck. Translated from the original Dutch by J. Pearson. Revised and edited by A. J. F. van LAER. Vols. ii-iv. Albany, N. Y., 1916?-19. 438 pp. Q. (University State N. Y., State Library Historical Bulletin, 9-11.)
                                          HE—A326—Vols. ii,iii,iv

——— See: COLONIAL Dames, State of New York. Calendar of Wills . . . 1626-1836. New York, 1896. Q. Edited by B. FERNOW.   HK—C71

ALBANY; its place in the United States. See: FERNOW, Berthold. Albany, N. Y., 1886. O.   HE—F39

[ALBOUIS] d' AZINCOURT, Joseph Jean Baptiste. 1747-1809. Mémoires. (In: Barrière, J. F., Editor. Bibliothèque des mémoires relatifs à l'histoire de France. 1857. Vol. vi. pp. 193-236.) HG—B27

ALBY, Ernest. Les Camisards (1702-11). Paris, [1857]. 241 pp. D.   HA—All

ALGERIE: Colonie de Vaudois. REVEILLAUD, Eugene. Etablissement d'une Colonie de Vaudois français en Algérie. . . . Paris, 1893. S. pl. & 1 map.   HB—R32

ALLABEN, Frank. General John Watts dePeyster, Author, Soldier, Historian, Military biographer, and Critic. 36 pp., 1 port., 2 pl. O. New York, 1894.   HG—D419
Reprint, Natl. Magazine, Oct., 1894.

ALLEN, Charles E. Huguenot settlers in Dresden, Me. 31 pp. No place, no date. O. Read before the Maine Hist. Society, March 17, 1892.   HB—AL5

ALLEN, William. 1710-80. See: DELANCEY, E. F. William Allen, Chief Justice of Pennsylvania, a biographical sketch prepared for the Centennial Celebration of the "Resolutions respecting Independency," held at . . . Philadelphia, July 1, 1876. 12 pp. Phila., 1877.   HE—Z9

ALLEN, Zachariah. 1795-1882. Memorial of Zachariah Allen. By Amos Perry. Cambridge, [Mass.], 1883. 108 pp., portrait, facsimile. O.   HG—Al5

ANCESTRAL sketches, by Mrs. Sarah VAN RENSSELAER. New York, 1882. Square Q.   HG—V351

"ANCHOR," pseud. See: dePEYSTER, JOHN WATTS.

ANDERSON, ROBERT, General U. S. Army. 1805-1871. See: Pelletreau, William S. Historic homes . . . genealogical and family history of New York. 4 vols. Q. N. Y., 1907.   HH—P36

ANDERSON, THOMAS MCARTHUR, LL.D., Brig. Gen. U. S. A. Monograph of the Anderson, Clark, Marshall and McArthur connection. 36 pp., 1 chart folded. Portland, Oregon. 1915. O. (Volume: "A Genealogical Collection.")   HH—A54

ANDREWS, E. BENJAMIN. Brief institutes of general history. Boston, 1887. 440 pp. D.   HF—An2

ANDROS, SIR EDMUND. 1637-1617. See: FERGUSON, HENRY. Sir Edmund Andros. Address before the Westchester County Historical Society, October 28, 1892.   HG—Mis68

ANJOU, GUSTAVE. Ulster County, N. Y.: Probate records in the office of the Surrogate, and in the County Clerk's office at Kingston, N. Y. A careful abstract and translation of the Dutch and English Wills, letters of administration after interstates, and inventories from 1665, with genealogical . . . notes, and list of Dutch and Frisian Baptismal names with their English equivalents. With introduction by Judge A. T. Clearwater. 2 vols., pls., fac-sims. Square O. N. Y., 1906. Amer. record ser. A.:—Wills. Vols. I-II.   HH—An5

ANQUEZ, LÉONCE. Histoire des assemblées politiques des réformées de France (1573-1622). Paris, 1859. 519 pp., map. O.   HA—An7

ANSPACH, JAC. Van Bodegem (Bodegom). 14 pp. D. n.p., 1894. Reprint: Maandblad van hat Geneal.-herald. genootschap "de Nederlandsche Leeuw," 1894.   HH—W66

APOLOGIE de Louis XIV et de son conseil, sur la Revocation de l'Edit de Nantes pour Servir de Reponse a la Lettre d'un Patriote sur la tolerance civile des Protestans de France. Avec une dissertation sur la Journee de la S. Barthelemi. 2 leaves, VI, 2 leaves, 566 pp. I-LXIII, 1 leaf. No place, 1758. D. Edited by CASEIRAC, JEAN HOVI DE.   HA—C337

APOLOGIE pour les reformez. 1683. See: FETIZON, PAUL.
                                                                HA—F43

AMERICAN Almanacs, 1639-1800. See: MORRISON, H. A.

AMERICAN ANTIQUARIAN SOCIETY. Proceedings April 30, 1862, April 7, 1864. Boston, 1862-64.   HK—H62V

AMERICAN Battles. See: OHIO Society of New York. Eighteenth annual banquet. . . . Full page illustrations.   HE—Pamphlet

AMERICAN Historical Association. Annual Report for 1889-'90, 1892-1915. 26 vols. in 40 vols. Washington, D. C., 1890-1918. 40 volumes. O. HK—Am3

Note:—"The Publications of this Association cover its activities from . . . its organization in . . . 1884 to the present time. The first five volumes bear the title 'Papers of the American Historical Association.'"

"The ANNUAL REPORTS are of the period 1889 to date."

The interesting and valuable material in these volumes will be found accessible by reference to Vol. II, of Report for 1914, and published in 1918. This volume is the—

GENERAL INDEX to Papers and Annual Reports of the American Hist. Assoc., 1884-1914. Compiled by David Maydole Matteson.

———— Officers, Act of Incorporation, Constitution, List of Members, Historical Societies in the United States. 1896. Baltimore, Md., 1896. S. HK—Am 3.1

AMERICAN (The) Historical Register, Philadelphia, 1894, Vol. I, No. 1; No. 3. HH—Pamphlet

AMERICAN Orders and Societies and their decorations. The Objects of the Military and Naval Orders, commemorative and patriotic Societies of the United States and the requirements for Membership therein. 107 pp., 18 colored plates. O. Philadelphia, 1917. Compiled by Jennings Hood & C. J. Young. HK—A5

AMERICAN RECORD, Series A. 2 vols., plates, fac-similes. Square O. New York, 1906. Vols. I-II, Ulster County, New York, Wills. HH—An5

AMERICAN Revolution Naval Records, 1775-1778. See: LINCOLN, Charles H., Compiler.

AMES, Herman V. The proposed Amendments to the Constitution of the United States during the first Century of its History. (AMERICAN Historical Assoc., Annual Report, 1896. 1 vol. in 2. See Vol. II.) HK—Am3

AMYRAUT, Moise. 1596-1664. See: VINET, A. Histoire de la predication parmi les reformes de France. . . . Paris, 1860. O. HA—V.783

ARC, Jeanne d'. See: Jeanne la Pucelle d'Orléans.

ARNAUD, Eugène. Guillaume Rabot de Salène, humaniste ignoré de XVIᵉ siècle; étude historique. 46 pp. O. Paris, 1890. HG—S33

———— Histoire de l'académie protestante de Die en Dauphiné au XVIIᵉ siècle. Paris, 1872. 116 pp. O. HA—Ar62

———— Histoire des églises réformées de la vallée de Bourdeaux en Dauphiné. Paris, 1876. 50 pp. O. HA—Ar6

ARNAUD, Eugène. Histoire des protestants de Crest en Dauphine pendant les trois derniers siècle. 102 pp., 1 leaf. Q. Paris, 1893.

HA—Ar6

Bound with his "Memoires historiques."

―――― Histoire des protestants de Provence du Comtat Venaissin et de la principauté d'Orange. Paris, 1884. 2 vols., map, 8vo.   HA—Ar61

―――― Histoire des protestants de Vivarais et du Veelay pays de Langue-doc de la Reforme a la Recolution. 2 vols. Q. Paris, 1888.   HA—Ar66
Vol I: 1st, 2d, & 3d periode.
Vol II: 4th periode.

―――― Memoirs historiques sur l'origine les moeurs, les souffrances et la conversion au protestantisme des Vaudois de Dauphine. 3 leaves, 90-126, 17-40, 1-70 pp. O. 1896.   HA—Ar6

―――― Notice historique et bibliographique sur les controverses reli-gieuses en Dauphine pendant la periode de l'Edit de Nantes. 64 pp. O. Grenoble, 1872.   HA—Ar6
Bound with his "Memoirs historiques."

―――― Notice historique sue les deux Cathechismes officiels de l'Eglise reformee de France, Calvin & Ostervald. . . . 2 leaves, 5-38 pp. O. Paris, 1885.   HA—Ar6
Bound with his "Memoirs historiques."

―――― Supplement aux Synodes du desert, de Edmond Hugues. Renfer-mant vingt-un synodes ou colloques inedits du Desert de Dauphine. 2 pl., 5-60 pp. Square Q. Paris, 1892.   HA—H871A

ASSOCIATIONS (Les) Protestantes, religieuses et charitables de France. Résumé . . . rapports et budgets, statisques, etc. Compiled by Edouard Borel. Paris, 1884. 150 pp. 2nd ed. O.   HK—B731

ATTERBURY, Rev. William Wallace, D.D. Elias Boudinot. Reminiscences of the American Revolution. (HUGUENOT So-ciety of America. Proceedings. 1891. Vol. II. pp. 261-298.)

HK—H871

AUBIGNE, Théodore Agrippa d'. Histoire universelle. Edition publiée pour la Société de l'histoire de France, par Baron Alphonse de Ruble. Paris, 1886. Vol. I. O.   HF—Au1

AUGUR, C. H. New Rochelle through seven generations. 65 pp. Square D. (New Rochelle, N. Y., cop. 1908.)   HB—Au4
Printed for private distribution only. Fully illustrated. Invitation and programme inserted.

AUSTIN, John Osborne. Genealogical dictionary of Rhode Island: comprising three generations of settlers who came before 1690. Albany, 1887. 440 pp. square folio.   HH—Au7

―――― Compiler. The Roger Williams Calendar. VI, 370 pp. D. Central Falls, R. I., 1897.   HO—C13

AUSTIN, Mary S. Philip Freneau, the Poet of the Revolution. A history of his life and times. Edited by H. K. Vreeland. 285 pp., 1 fac-sim., 2 pl., 3 port. O. New York, 1901. HG—F88A

AYLESBURY, William, Translator. DAVILA, A. C. Historie of the civill warres of France. 1647. HD—D28.1

AYMAR, Benjamin. Aymar of New York. New York, 1903. 65 pp. (A reprint of HUGUENOT Soc'y of America. Proceedings. Vol. iii, Part 2, pp. 167-229.) O. HH—A54

——— Aymar of New York. (In: HUGUENOT Society of America Proceedings. Vol. iii, Part 2, pp. 167-178, & 178-229. Genealogy and Index.) HK—H87
Read before the Society, November 25th, 1899.

BABUT, Charles, Pasteur. Inauguration du Musee du Desert . . . 24 Sept. 1911. Allocutions de F. Praux, E. Hugues, et C. Babut. Cevennes, 1912. O. (pp. 44-55.) HA—M986

BACHAUMONT, [Louis]. -1771. Mémoires historiques et litté-raires de . . . 1762-1782. (In: BARRIERE, J. F., Editor. Biblio-thèque des mémoires relatifs l'histoire de France. 1846. Vol. iii, pp. 209-524.) HG—B27

[BACON, Nathaniel.] Relation of the fearful estate of Francis Spira, . . . apostate from the Protestant Church . . . also lives and . . . deaths of John Child . . . and Geo. Edwards. 138 pp. T. London, 1718. HG—Sp4

BACON, William Johnson. The continental congress, some of its actors and their doings, with the results thereof; an address before the Oneida historical society . . . 31st . . . of Dec. 1880. 26 pp. O. Utica, 1881. HE—Z1

BACON, Rev. William Thompson. Sires and Sons; Historical poem pronounced at the Woodbury Centennial Celebration, July 4th, 1859. In: COTHREN, William. Second Centennial celebration . . . Ancient Woodbury, pp. 78-99. HE—W885
Volume "Ancient Woodbury."

BACOT, Thomas Wright. Huguenots in South Carolina. (HUGUENOT Society of America. Publications. Vol. iii. 1900.) HK—H87.1

——— Orange Quarter (St. Denis). (HUGUENOT Society of South Carolina. Transactions, No. 23. Charleston, 1917. pp. 37-50. O.) HK—H87.8

BAGG, M. M., M.D. Historical sketch of the Utica Orphan Asylum; an Address read at its 50th Anniversary, Oct. 13th, 1880. 24 pp. Utica, 1880. O. HE—Z4

BAILEY, J. C. Erasmus and the Reformation. pp. 207-219. No place, no date. HC—Pamphlet

BAILEY, FREDERIC W., Editor. Early Connecticut marriages as found on ancient Church records prior to 1800. Vols. I-III. New Haven, cop. 1896-'98. 3 vols. in 1. O. HH—B15

BAIRD, REV. CHARLES WASHINGTON. 1828-87. [Baird, Mrs. Margaret E. Strang], Editor. Memorials of Rev. Charles Washington Baird, with a few sermons and poems. N. Y., 1888. 235 pp., portrait, plate. O. HG—B16

———— History of the Huguenot emigration to America. N. Y., [1885]. 2 vols. illustrated, maps, fac-simile. O. HB—B16

———— History of Rye, Westchester County, New York, 1660-1870, including Harrison and the White Plains till 1788. XVI, 1 leaf, 2 maps, 1 fac-sim. New York, 1871. O. HE—B16

BAIRD, REV. HENRY MARTYN, D.D., LLD. Edict (The) of Nantes and its Recall. (HUGUENOT Society of America. Commemoration of the Bi-Centenary of the Revocation of the Edict of Nantes. pp. 14-41. Q. New York, 1886.) HK—H87

———— Huguenots of the "Desert." (HUGUENOT Society of America. Proceedings. New York, 1891. Vol. II, pp. 8-26. Q.) HK—H87

———— History of the rise of the Huguenots. London, 1880. 2 vols., map. O. HA—B16

———— Recovery (The) of Religious liberty of the Huguenots. (HUGUENOT Society of America. Proceedings. New York, 1894. Vol. III, pp. 36-51.) HK—H871

———— Some traits of Huguenot character. (HUGUENOT Society of America. Proceedings. Vol. I, Part 1. New York, 1884. pp. 9-16. Q.) Read at the First Public Meeting of the Society, November 15th, 1883. HK—H871

———— Strength (The) and weakness of the Edict of Nantes. (HUGUENOT Society of America. Publications. Vol. III. 1900.) HK—H87

[BAIRD, MRS. MARGARET E. STRANG], Editor. Memorials of Rev. C. W. Baird . . . with a few . . . sermons & . . . poems. 235 pp., port., pl. O. New York, 1888. HG—B16

BAIRD, ROBERT. Religion in America; or, Account of the origin, progress, relation to the state and present condition of the evangelical church. N. Y., 1844. 343 pp. O. HC—B16

BAKER, WILLIAM SPOHN, Compiler. Bibliotheca Washingtonia; descriptive list of the biographies . . . of George Washington. 179 pp., 1 port. Square Q. Philadelphia, 1889. HG—W277

———— Medallic portraits of Washington with historical and critical notes and . . . catalogue of the coins, medals, tokens and cards. 252 pp., 1 pl. Square Q. Philadelphia, 1885. HG—W276

BALCH, THOMAS. Calvinism and American independence. [No title page.] 13 pp. O. HE—Pamphlet

——— Les Français en Amérique pendant la guerre de l'indépendance des Etats-Unis, 1777-83. Paris, 1872. 237 pp., illustrated, portraits, maps. O. HE—B18

——— French (The) in America during the War of Independence . . . 1777-1783. A trans. by E. S. Balch & Elise W. Balch, of "François en Amerique pendant la guerre de l'Independance des Etats-Unis. Phila., 1895. IV, 252 pp. O. HE—B18E
The English edition is Vol. I, the French edition is Vol. II.

——— Letters and papers relating chiefly to the provincial history of Pennsylvania, with some notices of the writers. Philadelphia, 1855. 312 pp. D. HE—B181
These are known as the Shippen papers.

BALCH, THOMAS WILLING, Compiler. Genealogy of the de Trouville family. 1886.

BALCH, EDWIN SWIFT, & BALCH, ELISE WILLING, Translators. See: BALCH, THOMAS. The French in America during the War of Independence. . . . Translation of his "Francais en Amerique pendant la guerre de l'independance des Etats-Unis." Philadelphia, 1895. HE—B18E

BALCH, ELISE WILLING, Translator. See: BALCH, THOMAS. The French in America during the War of Independence. . . . A translation of his "Francais en Amerique pendant la guerre de l'independance des Etats-Unis." Philadelphia, 1895. O. HE—B18E

BALDWIN, ELIZABETH G., Compiler. See: HUGUENOT Society of America. Catalogue of the books, pamphlets and MSS. belonging to the Society. New York, 1890. HK—H87.2

BANCROFT, GEORGE. The necessity, the reality, & the promise of the progress of the human race. Oration delivered before the N. Y. Historical Soc. Nov. 20, 1854. (In: N. Y. Historical Soc. Semi-Centennial Celebration, 1854, pp. 5-37.) HE—Z3

BANTA, THEODORE MELVIN. A Frisian family. The Banta genealogy. Descendants of Epke Jacobse, who came from Friesland, Netherlands, to New Amsterdam, February, 1659. New York, 1893. XIII, 412 pp., 4 port., 3 pl., 1 table. HH—B22

——— Genealogical table of the Banta family. New York, no date. (Inserted in Volume.) HH—S425

——— Sayre family: lineage of Thomas Sayre, a founder of Southampton. New York, 1901. 759 pp., fac-sim., 14 pl., 19 port., 2 tables. Q. HH—Sa94

BARDARO, Marco Antonio Mauricio. Dispacci di Marc' Antonio Barbaro estratti dal cod. CDV. classe VII. dei mss. italiani della r. biblioteca Marciana di Venezia. (Huguenot Soc. of London. Pub. 1891. Vol. vi, appendix, pp. 59-149.) Preceded by an English translation.　　　　　　　　　　　　　　　　　　　HK—H875

BARBAULD, Mrs. Anna Laetitia Aikin. Life and works, memoir, letters and a selection from (her) poems and prose works. 2 vols. D. Boston, 1874.　　　　　　　　　　　　　　　　　　　HG—B23

BARNABAS, Rev. Dr. Address on the Huguenot Crypt at Canterbury, at Canterbury, England. (HUGUENOT Society of America. Proceedings. Vol. v. New York, 1906. pp. 38-50.)　　HK—H871

BARRAU, J. J., and DARRAGON, B. Montford et les Albig ois. Bruxelles, 1840. 2 vols. S.　　　　　　　　　　　　　　　HA—B27

BARRIERE, Jean François. Bibliothèque des mémoires relatifs à l'histoire de France pendant le 18me siècle. Paris, 1846-53. 12 vols. D.　　　　　　　　　　　　　　　　　　　　　　　　HG—B27

BARRINGTON, George. Voyage (A) to New South Wales; with a description of the country; manners, customs, religion, etc., of the natives, in the vicinity of Botany Bay. Philadelphia, 1796. vii, 150 pp. Narrow S.　　　　　　　　　　　　　　　　　　HI—B276

BARRY, John Stetson. History of *Massachusetts*. Boston, 1855. 3 vols. O.　　　　　　　　　　　　　　　　　　　　　HE—B27
　　Vol. i.　Colonial period.
　　"　　ii.　Provincial period.
　　"　　iii.　Commonwealth period.

BARTLETT, Henrietta C., Editor. See: ROBISON, Jeannie, F-J, & Bartlett, H. C., Editors. Genealogical records. Manuscript entries of births, deaths, and marriages, taken from family Bibles, 1581-1917. New York, 1917. Square O. (COL. DAMES, State of N. Y.) No. 85 of 200 cop.　　　　　　　　HK—C711

BARTLETT, Homer L., M.D. History of initiation, as practiced by the ancient rites and perpetuated by Freemasonry. Read before the Long Island Historical Society, Jan. 23d, 1877. 21 pp. D. Flatbush, L. I., 1877.　　　　　　　　　　　　　　　　　HE—Z7

BARTOW, Morey Hale. Brief account of the Bartow family. (HUGUENOT Society of America. Proceedings. Vol. i, Part 1. New York, 1883.)　　　　　　　　　　　　　　　　　　HK—H871
　　Added to the Reprint of first edition of Vol. i, Part 1. New York, 1889. pp. v-vi.

BATES, Arlo, Editor. See: BATES, Mrs. Harriet L. (Vose). Old Salem.

BATES, Mrs. Harriet L. Vose. Old Salem by Eleanor Putnam; edited by Arlo Bates. 120 pp. S. Boston, 1886.　　　HI—B31

BATES, James L. Alfred Kelley; his life and work. 210 pp., 1 port.
Columbus, O., 1888. HG—K29
250 copies, privately printed.

BATTLES, famous in History of Army and Navy. Illustrations. See:
OHIO SOC., of N. Y. 18th Annual banquet given for the Hon.
Wm. H. Taft, Sec'y of War . . . Mch. 5, 1904. HE—Pamphlet

BAUM, G. U., Editor. BEZE, Theodore de. Histoire ecclesiastique
des églises reformées au royaume de France. . . . 1883-'89. HA—B46

BAUM, J. G., Editor. Corteis, P. Memoirs de Pierre Carriere dit.
Corteis. . . . 1871. HA—C812

BAXTER, James Phinney. Campaigns of Carleton & Burgoyne
from Canada. 1776-77. (See: DIGBY, W. British invasion from
the North. 1887. pp. 1-75.) HE—D56

———— Edited by DIGBY, William. British invasion of the North.
1887. HE—D56

BEARD, Augustus F. Churches of the Huguenots and the religious
condition of France. 1884. O. HB—H12
From the *Andover Review*. 1884. Vol. I.

———— Editor. See: WESTPHAL—Castelnau. Yesterday and to-day.
1885. HB—A2H

BEARD, George Miller, M.D. Scientific basis of delusions. New
York, 1877. 47 pp. HE—Z2

BEAUCHET-FILLEAU, Henri, et Beauchet-Filleau, P. Dictionnaire
historique et généalogique des familles du Poitou. Tomes I-IV. A-
Gue. 2nd ed. Q. 4 vols. Poitiers, 1891-1909. HG—B38
Pub. en fasc. Tome IV contains fasc. 1-3.

BEAUCHET-FILLEAU, Paul. See above. HG—B38

BEAUFORT DISTRICT,—past, present, and future. By Frederic
KIDDER. In: CONTINENTAL Monthly. Vol. I, No. IV, pp.
381-388. O. Boston, 1862. HB—H897

BEAUJOUR, Sophronyme. Essai sur l'histoire de l'église réformée
de Caen. Caen, 1877. 597 pp. O. HA—B38

BEAUVAU, Henri, Marquis de. Mémoires du Marquis de Beauvau, pour servir à l'histoire de Charles IV, duc de Lorraine et de Bar.
Cologne, 1690. 456 pp. S. HD—B38

BEEKMAN, James William. 1815-77. Centenary address delivered
before the Society of the New York Hospital . . . July 24, 1871.
44 pp. O. N. Y., 1871. HE—Z1

———— The Founders of New York. Address delivered before the
Saint Nicholas Society of New York . . . Dec. 4th, 1869. 36 pp.
Q. N. Y., 1870. HE—Z9

BEESLEY, CHARLES NORBURY. Illustrated guide to St. Michael's Church, Charleston, South Carolina. 76 pp. Tt. oblong. Charleston, S. C., 1898. HC—Pamphlet
A brochure containing 33 plates and an historic description of the Church.

BELLEROCHE, EDWARD. Edit (l') de Nantes et les evenements successifs qui en ont amene la promulgation. Conference du 13 Avril 1898, à New York. (The HUGUENOT Soc. of America.) 50 pp. D. Liege, 1898. HA—N19

BELLOMONT, RICHARD COOTE, first Earl of. 1636-1701. See: DePEYSTER, FREDERIC. Life and administration of Bellomont, Governor of the Provinces of New York, Massachusetts, and New Hampshire, from 1697-1701. An address delivered before the N. Y. Historical Society, November 18th, 1879. 5 p.l., 60, XVII pp., 3 port. New York, 1879. Q. HE—D44

———— Another copy: (portrait of Earl lacking), in pamphlet Volume. HE—Z9

BELLOWS, REV. HENRY WHITNEY, 1814-82. Oration at the funeral of William Cullen Bryant, delivered . . . June 14, 1878. 11 pp. O. No title-page. HE—Z7

BENEDICT, ERASTUS CORNELIUS. 1800-81. . . . Address on . . . taking the chair of the university convocation at the capitol in . . . Albany, July 9, 1878. 19 pp. O. Albany, 1878. HE—Z7

———— Battle of Harlem Heights, Sept. 16, 1776; read before the New York historical society, Feb. 5, 1878. . . . 11+62 pp. Q. N. Y., pref. 1880. HE—Z5

———— 1800-80. The beginning of America; a discourse delivered before the New York historical society on its 59th anniversary . . . Nov. 17, 1863. . . . 64 pp. O. N. Y., 1864. HE—Z2

BENEDICT, HENRY MARVIN. Genealogy of the Benedicts in America. 19-474 pp., 1 port. Albany, New York, 1870. O. HH—B43

BENJAMIN, MARCUS. Charles Frederick Tiffany Beale. 13 pp., 1 port. O. Washington, D. C., 1902. (Soc. Col. Wars, D. C., Mem. Papers, No. 2.) HG—Mem. 512

———— Francis Asbury Roe. 35 pp., 8 pl., 1 port. O. Washington, D. C., 1903. (Soc. Col. Wars, D. C., Mem. Papers, No. 4.) HG—Mem. 512

BENNEVILLE, GEORGE DE. See: DE BENNEVILLE, GEORGE.

BENOIT, Daniel. Frères (Les) Gibert. Deux pasteurs du désert et du refuge. (1722-1817.) 429 pp., 1 port., 1 fac-sim. D. Toulouse, 1889.   HG—G35

———— Marie Durand, prisonnière a la Tour de Constance (1730-1736): sa famille et ses compagnes de captivité, d'aprés des documents inédits. 320 pp., 1 pl., 1 fac-sim., folded. D. Toulouse, 1884.   HG—D93

———— See: CRESPIN, Jean. Histoire des martyrs. . . . Introduction par D. B. Q. 3 vols. Toulouse, 1885-'89.   HG—C.86.2

[BENOIT, Elie.] Histoire de l'Edit de Nantes. Delft, 1693-95. 5 vols., plates. Q.   HA—B44

BERARD, Alexandre. Les Vaudois: leur histoire sur les deux versants des Alpes du IVe siècle au XVIIIe. 3 p.l., v, 328 pp., 1 pl., fld. O. Lyon, 1892.   HA—B461

BERGEN, Teunis G. Register in alphabetical order, of the early settlers of Kings County, Long Island, N. Y., from its first settlement by Europeans to 1700; with . . . biographies and genealogies. . . . 2 p.l., 5-452 pp. New York, 1881. O.   HH—B35

BERGEN County, New Jersey. See: HARVEY, C. B. Genealogical history of Hudson & Bergen Counties, New Jersey. N. Y., 1900. Q.   HE—H26

BERGMAN, J. T., Compiler. EGLISES Wallonnes. Catalogue de la bibliotheque Wallonne. 1875.   HK—Unbound

BERINGUIER, Richard. Ausführliche beschreibung der feier zum 200 jähringen gedächtnisse des ediktes von Potsdam, 29 Oct. 1685. Berlin, 1885. 103 pp. O.

———— & Tollin, Henri. Französische colonie in Berlin. (In: Deutsche Hugenotten Verein Geschichtsblätter. 1891. Vol. IV.)   HK—D49

BERRIAN, Rev. William. Historical sketch of Trinity Church, New York. N. Y., 1847. 386 pp., plates. O.   HC—B45

BERSIER, Eugène. Coligny: the Earlier life of the great Huguenot. Trans. by Annie Harwood Holmden. 36-351 pp. O. London, 1886.   HG—C68—Bersier

BERTOLET, Benjamin. Camp Pottsgrove, September 18th to 26th, 1777. General Washington with his Continental Army at Fagleysville, New Hanover Township, Montgomery County, Pennsylvania. 1 leaf, 19 pp., 1 leaf. Illustrated. Philadelphia, 1903. O. Privately printed.   HE—Pamphlet

BESANT, Walter. Gaspard de Coligny, (Marquis de Chatillon), Admiral of France. . . . 228 pp., 1 port. Tt. New York, 1879. (Harper's Half-hour Ser.)   HG—C68—Copy 1

———— Gaspard de Coligny. . . . 232 pp., 1 port. D. New York. (The New Plutarch Ser.)   HG—C68—Copy 2

BETHUNE, Rev. George Washington. 1805-62. Memoir of Rev. George W. Bethune. By Rev. Abraham Rynier Van Nest. N. Y., 1867. 446 pp., portrait, plate. D. HG—B46

BEURDEN, A. F. van. De Familie van Lom. 15 pp. O. n.p., 1894. Repr.: Maandblad van het Geneal.-herald. genootschap "De Nederlandsche Leeuw," 1894. HH—W66

[BEZE, Théodore de.] Histoire ecclésiastique des églises réformées au royaume de France. Edition nouvelle avec commentaire, notice bibliographique. Par G. Baum et par Ed. Cunitz. Paris, 1883-89. 3 vols. O. Half morocco. HA—B46
Vol. iii, contenant la préface, l'introduction et la table alphabétique par R. Reuss.

——— Translator. See: NOVUM testamentum. 1574. Dedication by P. de Loyseleur. Title-page wanting. HM—N851
Latin and Greek in parallel columns.

——— Les PSEAUMES de David, 1652. O. HM—P95

BIANQUIS, Jean. La révocation de l'Edit de Nantes à Rouen; essai historique suivi de notes sur les protestants de Rouen, par Emile Lesens. Rouen, 1885. 103 pp. O. HA—B47

BIBLIOPHILE Huguenot, bulletin trimestriel de livres rares . . . sur le protestantisme pendant les 16e-18e siècles. 48 pp. O. Paris, 1889. HO

BIBLIOTHEQUE des Mémoires relatifs à l'histoire de France pendant le 18e siècle. See: BARRIERE, J. F. 1786-1868.

BIBLIOTHEQUE de la Providence, London, England. See: FRENCH Protestant-Hospital-Library.

BIDDLE, Charles. 1745-1821. Autobiography. 423 pp. O. Philadelphia, 1883. HG—B47
Privately printed.

BIDDLE, Henry D., Editor. See: DRINKER, Mrs. E. S. Extracts from (her) journal, from 1759-1807. 1889. HG—D83

BIOGRAPHICAL memoir of William J. Duane. 28 pp. Philadelphia, 1868. O. HE—Z7

BION, Jean. Relation des tourments qu'on fait souffrir aux protestants qui sont sur les galères de France; réimprimée sur la seconde édition avec une préface par O. Douen. Paris, 1881. 53 pp. O. HA—B52

BLACK, Robert, Translator. See: GUIZOT, François Pierre Guillaume. History of France. 1867. HD—G94

BLACKET, W. S. Researches into the lost histories of America. . . . 8-336 pp., il., pl. Q. 1884. HE—B56

BLAINE, Laura Cowan. Maxwell history & genealogy, including the allied families. . . . Also Baptismal record of Rev. J. Craig, D.D., of Augusta Co., Va., 1740-1749. . . . O. Indianapolis, Ind., [Cop. 1916]. HH—M465

BLAIR, Emma Helen, Editor. See: STATE HISTORICAL SOCIETY of Wisconsin. Annotated catalogue of newspaper files in the Library. . . . O. Madison, Wis., 1898. HK—W75

BLAKE, Mrs. Euphenia Vale. Modern American literature. pp. 35-53. O. (From: The Oriental Church Magazine.) HE—Z5

BLANCHON, Pierre. Jean Guiton et le Siège de la Rochelle. 65 pp., 1 port., inserted. Square D. La Rochelle, 1911. HG—G968 Gift of le Comité.

BLISS, Eugene F., Editor. See: ZEISBERGER, David. Diary, 1885. O. HG—Ze5

BLODGETTE, George B. Inscriptions from the old Cemetery in Rowley, Mass. 2 p.l., 78 pp. O. Salem, Mass., 1893. HH—R77B

BODE, prediger. GESCHICHTE der wallonisch-reformirten Kirchengemeinde zu Magdeburg. 17 pp. Magdeburg, 1892. (In: Der Deutsche Hugenotte Verein. Geschichtsblätter. 1892. Vol. v.) HB—T57

BOGGILD, F. The anti-Columbian discovery of the American Continent by the Northmen. pp. 171-178. O. 1869. (From: The Historical Magazine. 1869. Vol. v.) HE—Z6

BOHEMIA Manor, Delaware. See: Mallery, Rev. Chas. P. Ancient families of Bohemia Manor, their homes and their graves. Wilmington, 1888. O. HH—M253

BOLTON, Rev. C. W., Editor. See: BOLTON, Rev. Robert. History of Westchester County, 1881. HE—B63

BOLTON, Charles Knowles. Marriage notices, 1785-1794, for the whole United States. Copied from the Massachusetts Centinel and the Columbian Centinel. 139 pp. Salem, Mass., 1900. O. HH—B69

BOLTON, Reginald Pelham. Washington's Headquarters, New York. A sketch of the history of the Morris Mansion, (or Jumel Mansion,) in the City of New York, used by Washington as his Headquarters in 1776. 1 port., 3-40 pp., 1 pl. New York, 1903. S. HE—AA12

BOLTON, Rev. Robert. History of the several towns, manors and patents of the county of Westchester from its first settlement to the present time. Edited by Rev. C. W. Bolton. N. Y., 1881. 2 vols., illustrated, tables, maps. O. HE—B63

BONGARS, Jacques. 1546-1612. Lettres latines de . . . Bongars . . . ambassadeur sous . . . Henry IV en diverses négociations importantes; traduites en François. . . 391 pp. Paris, 1681. S. HD—B64

BONNET, Jules. Aonio Paleario, étude sur la réforme en Italie.
Paris, 1863. 348 pp. D.   HC—B64

———— Derniers récits du seizième siècle. Paris, 1876. 350 pp. D.
                                                       HA—B64

———— Nouveaux récits du seizième siècle. Paris, 1870. 361 pp.
D.   HA—B641

———— Récits du seizième siècle. Paris, 1866. 357 pp. D.   HA—B642

———— Récits du seizième siècle. Seconde Série. Paris, 1885. 342
pp. D.   HA—B643

———— La réforme au Chateau de Saint-Privat, étude historique. Paris,
1873. 48 pp. O.   HA—B644

———— Souvenirs de l'église réformée de la Calmette. Pages d'histoire
locale. Paris, 1884. 91 pp., map. O.   HA—B645

———— Vie d'Olympia Morata épisode de la renaissance & de la réforme en Italie. Ed. 2. Enlarged. 255 (1) pp. O. Paris,
1851.   HG—M34

———— Editor. See: MAROLLES de, fils. Histoire des souffrances du
bienheureux martyr Louis de Marolles. . . .1883.   HG—M34

BONZON, Jacques. La direction des pauvres refugies français de
Nyon. 1688-1860. 22 pp. O. Paris, 1901.   HA—D74
Reprint: Bulletin Soc. Hist. Prot. Français (Mars. 1901).

BOOTH, Charles Edwin. One branch of the Booth family showing
the lines of connection with one hundred Massachusetts Bay colonists.
2 p.l., v-vi, 259 pp., 1 fac-sim., 1 pl., 1 port. New York, 1910.
O.   HH—B72

[BORDIER, Henri Léonard], Editor. Le chansonnier Huguenot du
XVIe siècle. Paris, 1870. 2 vols. S. Half morocco.   HA—B646

———— La Saint-Barthélemy et la critique moderne. Genève, 1879. 116
pp., illustrated, folio.   HA—B647

———— See: HAAG, Eugene & Emile. La France Protestante.
1877-'88.   HG—H11

[BORDIER, L., Illustrator.] See: Henry IV. Job le bon Roy
Henry. 48 pp., colored plates. Tours, [1894?]. Oblong O.
                                              H5D—H55

BOREL, Edouard. . . . Associations Protestantes, religieuses et Charitables de France. Résumé . . . rapports et budgets, statistiques, etc.
150 pp. O. 2nd ed. Paris, 1884.   HK—B731

BORREL, Abraham. Biographie de Paul Rabaut, pasteur du désert
et de ses trois fils. 168 pp. D. Nimes, 1854.   HG—R111
Bound with: CUVIER, O. Trois martyrs de la Réforme. . . .

BOSCH, R. P. VAN DER. De Kaap de Goede Hoop, tijdens het Nederlandsch bewind, (1652-1806, met Engelsch tusschenbestunr). 17
pp. O. n.p., 1894. Repr. Maandblad van het Geneal.-herald.
genootschap "De Nederl. Leeuw," 1894.   HH—W66
No. 12 of Volume of Dutch Pamphlets.

BOSTON, Mass. See: Bridgeman, T. Memorials of the dead. . . .
Inscriptions, epitaphs & records on the monuments . . . in Copp's
Hill Burying Ground . . . Boston. . . . Boston, 1852.   HH—B76

BOURCHENIN, DANIEL. Etude sur les académies protestantes en
France au XVIᵉ et au XVIIᵉ siècle. Paris, 1882. 480 pp. O.
                                                         HA—B66

BOURGEON, G. La réforme à Nérac, les origines (1530-60). Toulouse, 1880. 118 pp. O.   HA—B661

BOURINOT, JOHN GEORGE. Manual of the constitutional history
of Canada from the earliest period to 1888. Montreal, 1888. 238
pp. D.   HF—B66

BOURLIER, E. Souvenir de troisième centenaire de l'église Walloonne
de la Haye. . . . Et sermon par E. Lacheret. . . . 105 pp., 2 pl., 3
port. La Haye, 1891. O.   HC—B66

BOWEN, REV. L. P. Days of Makemie, or, The Vine planted. . . .
1680-1708. With an appendix. 558 pp., 1 map. D. Philadelphia, 1885.   HG—M29

BOWER, HERBERT M. The fourteen of Meaux: An account of the
earliest "Reformed Church" within France proper, organized by
Estienne Mangin, and Pierre LeClerc; who with twelve other persons, suffered death by fire in 1546. 3 p.l., 124 pp., 1 leaf, 1 chart,
1 fac-sim., 2 pl., 1 plan, 1 port. O. London, 1894.   HA—B67
Reprint: Vol. v, Proceedings Huguenot Society of London.

BRADFORD, Massachusetts. See: KINGSBURY, J. D. Memorial
history of Bradford. . . . O. Haverhill, Mass. 1883.   HE—B73K

BRAINERD, REV. D. S. Sermon preached in Old Lyme, on the 25th
Anniversary of his pastorate, July 1st, 1866. 20 pp. New Haven,
1867.   HE—Z1

BREEN, GILLIS VAN, Translator. See: GILLIS, PETRUM. Kercke-
lijcke historie. 1657.

BREWSTER, CHARLES W. Rambles about Portsmouth. Sketches
of persons, localities, and incidents of two centuries. . . . 376 pp.
O. Portsmouth, N. H., 1859.   HE—P83B

BRIDGMAN, THOMAS. Memorials of the dead in Boston; . . . Inscriptions, epitaphs and records on the monuments and tombstones
in Copp's Hill Burying Ground . . . Boston. . . . Historical and
biographical notices of the early settlers of the metropolis of New
England. 1 pl., xxIV, 252 pp. D. Boston, 1852.   HH—B76

BRIEGER, THEDORE, Editor. ZEITSCHRIFT für kirchengeschichte. 1877-'82. Vols. I, II, & v. O. HC—Ze3

BRIET, ELISÉE. Le protestantisme en Brie et basse Champagne du
XVIᵉ siècle à nos jours. Vallées de la Marne et du Grand-Morin,
d'après des documents inédits. Paris, 1885. 254 pp., fac-similes.
O. HA—B76
Publié à l'occassion du second centenaire de la révocation de l'Edit de
Nantes.

BRIGGS, REV. CHARLES A., D.D. Elias Neau, the confessor and
catechist of Negro and Indian slaves. (HUGUENOT Society of
America. Vol. III. New York, 1903. Part 2. pp. 103-116.)
HK—H87.1

BROCK, ROBERT ALONZO, Editor. Documents relating to the Huguenot emigration to Virginia and to the settlement of Manakintown,
with genealogies, etc. (Virginia Historical Society. Collections.
New Series. 1886. Vol. v.) HK—V81

———— Miscellaneous Papers, 1672-1865, printed from the MSS. in the
Collections of the Society. (Same, Vol. VI.) HK—V81

———— See: GRIGSBY, H. B. History of the Virginia Federal Convention of 1788. (Same. Vols. IX-X.) HK—V81

———— See: ROBERTSON, WYNDHAM. Pocahontas. HH—P75

———— See: ROBINSON, CONWAY, Compiler. Abstract of the Proceedings of the Virginia Company of London. 1619-'21. (Same.
Vols. VII-VIII.) HK—V81

BRODHEAD, JOHN ROMEYN. N. Y. (state)—Legislature. Documents relative to the colonial hist. 1856-61. HE—N482

"BROKAW Brothers' New Home." Reminiscence of the old neighborhood: i.e., Astor Place, Fourth Avenue, & Lafayette Place. Facts
worthy of preservation. 4 pp., in cover, illustrated. Oblong O.
New York City, 1916. HE—A512

BROOKLINE Historical Publication Society. Publications. Nos. 1-5.
Paged continuously. Brookline, Mass., 1895-'06. O. HK—Pamphlets

BROOKLYN'S Garden: views of picturesque Flatbush. With an historical introduction. 1 leaf, 24 colored plates, mounted. Oblong O.
Brooklyn, N. Y., 1908. C. A. DITMAS, Compiler. HE—D615

BROWN, ALEXANDER, Editor. Genesis of the United States . . .
1605-1616 . . . through a series of historical manuscripts now first
printed . . . with a re-issue of rare contemporaneous tracts . . .
bibliographical memoranda, notes, & brief biographies. 2 vols. 38,
1157 pp., illus., 100 port., pl., maps, fac-sim. Q. Boston, 1890-91.
Paged continuously. (Biography of persons connected with the
founding of Virginia, Vol. II, pp. 807-1068.) HE—B81

BROWN, Rev. William Adams, Ph.D., D.D. Calvin's influence upon Theology. (In: UNION Theo. Seminary. Three Addresses delivered by Professors in the Seminary, at a Service in commemoration of the 400th Anniversary of the birth of John Calvin. New York, 1909. 47 pp. O. pp. 20-35. HM—Pamphlet

BROWNING, Arthur Giraud. History of the French Hospital in London, and the lives of the Huguenots who founded it. (HUGUENOT Society of America. Publications. Vol. iii. 1900.) HK—H87

——— Huguenot influence in the Colonial Capital of New York. (HUGUENOT Society of America. Publications. Vol. iii. 1900.) HK—H87

——— Influence exerted by Huguenot refugees of the seventeenth, and early eighteenth centuries, upon the social and professional life of England. 20 pp. O. Aberdeen, 1904. (Privately Reprinted from Proceedings Huguenot Society of London. Vol. vii.) HB—B88

——— Lecture on the Peaceful Invasion of England by French Protestants in 1685. 37 pp. O. London, 1906. (St. Mark's Literary Soc'y.) HB—B88

——— Odet de Coligny, Cardinal de Chatillon. A paper read at Canterbury, on the occasion of . . . visit of the French Hospital (Victoria Park), London, July 26, 1884. Canterbury, 1884. 20 pp. D. HG—C681

——— See: FRENCH Protestant Hospital Library. Bibliotheque de la Providence. Catalogue . . . with an introduction by A. G. B. London, 1887, & 1890. Q. & O. HK—L84 & L84.1

BROWNING, William S. A history of the Huguenots. New edition, continued to the present time. xii, 13-452 pp. O. Philadelphia, 1845. HA—B82

BUFFALO (N. Y.) Historical Society. Annual report. Buffalo, 1886-89. 4 vols. 8vo. HK—B86

——— Obsequies of Red Jacket at Buffalo, Oct. 9, 1884. Buffalo, 1885. 117 pp., plates. O. (In its Transactions, Vol. iii.) HK—B86

BULLARD, Gen. Edward F. History of Saratoga; an Address delivered at Schuylerville, N. Y. July 4, 1876. 22 pp. O. Ballston Spa, 1876. HE—Z1

BULLOCH, Joseph Gaston Baillie, M.D. History and genealogy of the Habersham family . . . and . . . many other names . . . related or connected to some family in this work. vi, 222 pp. O. Columbia, S. C., 1901. HH—H14

BUNGENER, Laurence Louis Félix. Priest and the Huguenot; or, Persecution in the age of Louis XV, [translated] from the French. Boston, 1854. 2 vols. D. HN—B88

BURDGE, Franklin. A notice of John Haring, a patriotic Statesman of the Revolution. 11 pp., 1 leaf. O. N. Y., 1878. No title-
page.   HE—Z4

—— Memorial of Henry Wisner, the only New Yorker who voted
for the Declaration of Independence. 14 pp. O. N. Y., 1878. No
title-page.   HE—Z4

—— Simon Boerum, of Brooklyn, N. Y. Written . . . for the
Committee on the Restoration of Independence Hall, Philadelphia.
28 pp. O. 1876. No title-page.   HE—Z4

BURGOYNE, J[ohn]. Heiress (The). A Comedy in five acts,
with Prologue by the Right Hon. Richard Fitzpatrick. Also gives
Dramatis personae. iii-xii, 80 pp. Hertford street, Feb. 1st, 1786.
Title page wanting. D.   HN—B957

BURGWYN, Collinson Pierrepont Edwards. Huguenot (The)
lovers. A tale of the Old Dominion. 4 pp., 1, 219 pp. Richmond,
Va., 1889. S.   HN—B95

BURIED (The) book, or, the Bible of Henri de Dibon. By R. S.
Faber. 24 pp., 1 port. Q. London, 1885.   HH—Fa.11
MS. genealogical notes inserted.
35 copies privately printed.

BURNS celebration, held at Delmonico's, Jan. 1880; report of speeches,
by H. E. Partridge & A. W. Granville. 48 pp. N. Y., 1880.
O.   HE—Z1

BURRELL, A. B. Reminiscences of George La Bar, the centenarian of
Monroe county, Pa., and incidents in the early settlement of the
Pennsylvania side of the river valley from Easton to Bushkill.
Philadelphia, 1870. 111 pp., portrait. O.   HE—B94

BUSSIERRE, Marie Théodore Renouard, Vicomte de. Histoire
de l'établissement du protestantisme à Strasbourg et en Alsace, d'après
des documents inédits. Paris, 1856. 509 pp. O.   HB—B961

—— Histoire du développement du protestantisme à Strasbourg et en
Alsace, depuis l'abolition du culte catholique jusqu'à la Paix de
Haguenau (1529-1604). Strasbourg, 1859. 2 vols. in 1. O.   HB—B96

BUTLER, James Davie. Butleriana, genealogica, et biographica; or,
Genealogical notes concerning Mary Butler & her descendants. . . .
162 pp., port., pl., fac-sim. O. Albany, 1888.   HH—B97

BYLES. Dr. The Huguenot refugee. Song (with chorus). Music
by W. Ryves. Q. 6 pp. No place, no date.   HO—Pamphlet

CAAN, H. J. Eglise Française de Voorburg, Recueil de documents
relatifs . . . l'origine et l'état actuel de la dite institution relegieuse
La Hayes, 1859. 9, 1-42 pp., 1 pl., 1 port., 2 fac-sim. O   HB—C11

CAEN, Normandy. Registers of the Protestant Church. Vannes,
1907. Edited by C. E. Lart.   HH—L33
Vol. I. Baptemes et Mariages, 1560-1572.

CAILLOT, Antoine. Morceaux d'éloquence, extraits des sermons des orateurs protestans français, les plus célèbres du dix-septième siècle, précédés d'une courte notice sur la vie de chacun d'eux. Paris, 1810. 375 pp. O. Half calf. HM—C12

CALAND, Fred. Une branche de la famille van Soest en Belgique— van Soust de Borckenfeldt. 13 pp. D. n. p. 1895. Repr. Maand-blad., Genealogisch-heraldiek genootschap "De Nederlandsche Leeuw," 1895. HH—W66
No. 2 of Dutch pamph. Volume.

CALIFORNIA Historical Society. Papers. San Francisco, 1887. Vol. i. Q. HK—C12

CALVIN, John. Le catéchisme français de Calvin, publié en 1537, réimprimé pour la première fois d'après un exemplaire nouvellement retrouvé et suivi de la plus ancienne Confession de foi de l'église de Genève avec deux notices par Albert Rilliet et Théophile Dufour. Genève, 1878. 146 pp. D. Half morocco. HM—C13

CAMPAN, Mme. [Jeanne Louise Henriette (Genet)]. 1752-1822. Mémoires sur le vie de Marie Antoinette . . . suivis de souvenirs et anecdotes historiques sur les règnes de Louis XIV., de Louis XV., et Louis XVI. . . . 488 pp. D. Paris, 1849. (In: BARRIERE, J. F., Editor. Bibliotheque des memoires relatifs à l'hist. de France. . . . Vol. x.) HG—B27—V10

CANADIAN ARCHIVES. Report . . . for the year 1905. Vols. i-ii. Ottawa, 1905-1906. 2 Vols. Q. HF—C213

CANNON, LeGrand Bouton. Personal reminiscences of the Rebellion. 1861-1866. 228 pp. New York, 1895. D. HN—C16

CANTON, Mass. See: Record (The) of births, marriages and deaths . . . 1797-1845 . . . Edited by F. Endicott. O. Canton, Mass. 1896. HH—St.6

CAPE COLONY, South Africa. See: VILLIERS (de). MS. Brief notices of the Huguenot families who sought refuge in Cape Colony. HJ—D494

CAPRON, Horace Japan. Some remarks in connection with the visit of Horace Capron to Japan in 1871-1875 . . . read before the Philosophical Society of Washington, May 6, 1876. 19 pp. O. Philadelphia. HE—Z2

———— Letters addressed during the year 1875 to Kuroda Kiyotaka. O. 2 pam. Tokei 1875. HE—Z7

CARY, William B. Memorial discourse of the First Congregational Church, 1693-1876, of Old Lyme, Conn., July 9, 1876. 19 pp. O. Hartford 1876. HE—Z4

CASEIRAC, JEAN HOVI DE. Apologie de Louis XIV. et de Conseil, sur la Revocation de l'Edit de Nantes, pour Servir de Response a la Lettre d'un Patriote sur la tolerance civile des Protestans de France. Avec une dissertation sur la Journee de la S. Barthelemi. VI. 566 pp. I-LXIII, no place, 1758. D.　　　　　　　　　HA—C337

CASPIPINA'S letters, by Jac. Duche. 1777.　　　　　　　　HN—D85

CASTEL, ELIE. Les Huguenots et la constitution de l'église réformée de France en 1559. Paris, 1859. 240 pp. D.　　　　　　HA—C27
Publié à l'occasion du jubilé de 1859.

CASTELNAU, MICHEL DE. Memoirs of the reigns of Francis II. & Charles IX. of France . . . with an account of the 3 first civil wars . . . carried on by the Huguenots . . . done into English by the Rev. Kelly. 426 pp. London, 1724. Folio.　　　　HA—C272

CATLIN, G. L. Translator. Delmas, L. Huguenots of La Rochelle. 1880.　　　　　　　　　　　　　　　　　　　　　HA—D38

CHAILLE-LONG, COL. CHARLES. Association of the Freeman of Maryland. N. Y., 1890. Q. (Republic Magazine, Vol I, No. 1., pp. 42-48.) (Chaille family genealogical notes herein.)　HE—Cha35
Gift of the Author.

CHAMBERS, THEODORE FRELINGHUYSEN. Early Germans of New Jersey, their history, churches and genealogies. Dover, N. J., 1895. 1 p.l. v-XIII, 11, 667 pp., 18 pl., 38 group port., 3 maps. Q. 3 parts in 1 vol.　　　　　　　　　　　　　　　HE—C445
Pt. 1. Their arrival, settlement, and churches.
Pt. 2. Genealogies.
Pt. 3. Appendices.

CHAMIER ADRIAN CHARLES. Editor. Actes des colloques des Eglises Françaises et de synodes des églises étrangères refugiees en Angleterre, 1581-1654. 118 pp. Q. Lymington, 1890. (HUGUENOT Soc. of London. Publications. 1887-90. Vol II.)　HK—H875
Bound with Volume III.

CHAMPION de CRESPIGNY, MRS. PHILIP. See: De CRESPIGNY, Mrs. Philip Champion.

CHANSONNIER (LE) Huguenot du XVIe siècle. By Henri Leonard Bordier, 1870.　　　　　　　　　　　　　　HA—B646

CHAPTER (A) in Huguenot history, pp. 414-418., n. p., March, 1896. No. 2, (Vol. "Huguenot Essays.")　　　　　HB—H89

CHARENTE-INFERIEURE-ARCHIVISTE. Par L. M. Meschinet de Richemond, Rapport de l'archiviste. 1885.　　　　HO—R39

CHARLES IX. Roi de France. Correspondance du Roi . . . et du Sieur de Mandelot, gouverneur de Lyon, pendant l'année 1572, époque du massacre de la Saint-Barthélemy. [Edited by P. Paris.]. D. Paris, 1830. (en: Monumens inedits de l'histoire de France. Part 1., pp. 1-103.)　　　　　　　　　　　HD—M815

CHARLESTON (South Carolina)—City Council. Centennial of incorporation, 1670, 1783, 1883. [Charleston, 1883.] 259 pp. plates, maps, fac-similes. O.   HE—C38

CHARLESTON, South Carolina, French Protestant Church. See: FRENCH Protestant Church, Charleston, South Carolina.

CHARLESTON, S. C. St. Phillip's Church. Special services held on the 12th and 13th of May, 1875.   HC—C38

CHATEAU (Au) de Loches: le médecin Pierre Chaillé, de La Tremblade, et sa famille, 1693-1775. Paris, 1895. O.   HH—C434
Bound with: WEISSE (N.) Indépendance des Etats d'Amerique et Pierre Chaillée.
MS. Genealogy of the Chaillé famille by M. de Richmond, inserted in volume.

CHAVANNES, Rev. C. G. compiler. See: EGLISES Wallonnes. Catalogue de la bibliotheque Wallonne. Sup. 4e-5e. 1890-1901.

CHAVANNES, Jules. Les réfugiés francais dans le pay de Vaud, et particulièrement à Vevey. Lausanne, 1874. 331 pp. D.   HB—C39

CHEVRIER, Edmond. Notice historique sur le protestantisme dans le département de l'Ain (Bresse, Bugey, pays de Gex) et lieux circonvoisins (Savoie, Lyon, Mâcon). Paris, 1883. 304 pp. portrait, O.   HA—C42

CHRISTIAN (The) hero: . . . proving no principles but . . .religion . . . sufficient to make a great man. London, 1727. By R. Steele. S.   HM—S814

CHRONIQUE de la colonie réformée française. See: Friedrichsdorf.

CHURCH ALMANAC. 1880-83. No. 50-53. Edited by W. G. Farrington. N. Y. 1880-83. D.   HC—C47

CLAPAREDE, R., Editor. See NAEF, F. La reforme en Bourgogne: notice sur les Eglises réformées de la Bougogne avant la Revocation de l'Edit de Nantes. Edited . . . par R. C. 258 pp., 5 pl., 1 port., 1 map. D. Paris, 1901.   HA—N12

CLAPAREDE, Théodore. Histoire des églises réformées du pays de Gex. Genève, 1856. 351 pp.   HA—C53

——— Histoire de la Reformation en Savoie. 680 pp., 1 map., folded. D. Geneve, 1893.   HA—C53S

CLARK, Alonzo Howard, and Ford, P. L., Compilers. Bibliography of the writings of the members of the American Historical Association for . . . 1890. (In: American hist. association. Annual report. 1891. pp. 117-160.)   HK—Am3—1891

CLASSIQUES (Les) du protestantism Français XVI, XVII, XVIII, siècles.   HA—C571
Claude, J. Les plaintes des protestants. 1885.

[CLAUDE, Jean.] Account of the persecutions and oppressions of the protestants in France. 1886. 48 pp. Square O. HA—C57

—————— Les plaintes des protestans cruellement opprimez dans le royaume de France. Edition nouvelle avec commentaires par Frank Puaux. Paris, 1885. 148 pp. square. O. (Les classiques du protestantisme Français, XVIᵉ, XVIIᵉ, XVIIIᵉ siècles). HA—C571

—————— A short account of the complaints and cruel persecutions of the Protestants in the kingdom of France. With a biographical sketch of the author by N. Cyr. XIV, 212 pp., 1 port., T. London, 1707. First American reprint of English translation. Boston, 1893.
HA—C572

——————VINET, A. Histoire de la predication parmi les réformées de France. . . . Paris, 1860. O. HA—V783

CLEARWATER, Alphonse Trompbour. LL.D. Description of the Set of Huguenot Medals presented to the Society, February 28th, 1899; with historic notes thereon. (HUGUENOT Society of America. Proceedings. Vol. iii., Part 2. pp. 132-136. New York, 1903.) HK—H87.1

—————— Huguenot influence in the Colonial Capital of New York. (HUGUENOT Society of America. Publications. Vol. iii. 1900.)
HK—H87

—————— See: ANJOU, Gustave. Ulster County, N. Y., Probate Records . . . at Kingston, N. Y. With introduction by A. T. C.
HH—An5

CLINTON, George. 1st Gov. of N. Y. Public papers of George Clinton . . . 1777-1795-1801-1804. Military—v. 1-8 & 10. With an introduction by H. Hastings, state historian. Published by the state of New York, as appendix "N"—3 ann. report of the state historian. O. 9 Vols. N. Y. & Albany, 1899-1914. HE—C61

CLOUZOT, H., Editor. MIGAULT, Jean. Journal . . . maitre d'école (1681-1688). Publie pour la premiere fois d'apres le texte original avec une introduction et des notes. . . . D. Paris, 1910.
HA—M634

CLUTE, Robert F., Compiler. Annals and parish register of St. Thomas and St. Denis parish in South Carolina, 1680-84. Charleston, 1884. 111 pp. O. HB—C62

COLE, Rev. David, D.D., Editor. See: FIRST (The) Reformed Church of Tarrytown. N. Y. First record book of the "Old Dutch Church of Sleepy Hollow." . . . Q. Yonkers, N. Y. HH—F44 No. 122 of 500 copies printed.

COLLECTION Universelle des Mémoires particuliers, relatifs, à l'histoire de France. Tome VII. . . . Mémoires de la Pucelle d'Orléans, ceux du Connétable de Richemont, & ceux de Florent Sire d'Illiers. XIVᵉ & XVᵉ siècles. 467 pp. Paris, 1785. D. HD—C696

COLLES, Julia K. Josiah Collins Pumpelly. Extract from "Authors & writers associated with Morristown, New Jersey." 1893. Typewritten Ms., Bound with: PUMPELLY, J. C. Mahlon Dickerson. . . . O. Paterson, N. J., 1892. HB—P87

COLLEVILLE, Vicomte de. Les missions secrètes du Général Major Baron de Kalb et son rôle dans la guerre de l'indépendance Américaine. Paris, 1885. 161 pp. D. HE—C68

COLONEL, de herr, Abraham de Peyster, Mayor of New York City, Commander of City Troops, Chief-Justice . . . Supreme Court, 2 p.l., 5 pp., 1 port., 2 colored pl. O. New York, 1895. Re-print, "Memorial History of New York." HG—D419

COLONIAL Dames: State of New York. Annual register. 1893-1901, 1913. New York, 1893-1913. 3 Vols. O. HK—C71

——— Calendar of Wills on file and recorded in the offices of the clerk of the Court of Appeals . . . County Clerk at Albany, and . . . Secretary of State. 1626-1836. Comp. & ed., by S. Fernow. XV, 657 pp. New York, 1896. Q. HK—C71.1

——— Catalogue of the Genealogical and Historical Library. 9-518 pp., square. O. New York, 1912. HK—C71.1 No. 5 of 250 copies.

——— Catalogue, Van Cortlandt House Museum Huguenot Memorials of the refugees who came to America. . . . 15 p., 21-. New York, 1910. O. HB—B88

——— Colonial Book-plates. Catalogue of the Loan Exhibition at the Van Cortlandt House, New York. April-June, 1908. IV, 40 pp., 6 plates. S. HK—Pamphlet

——— Publications of the Committee on History and Tradition. 2 Vols. New York, 1902-1917. V. Nos. 1-2. Square O. HK—C71.1 No. 1: Fernow, Berthold. Minutes of the Orphanmasters of New Amsterdam. 1655-1663. No. 2: Robison, Jeannie Floyd-Jones and Bartlett, H. C. ed. Genealogical records. MS. entries . . . taken from family Bibles. 1581-1917.

COLONIAL men and times: containing the Journal of Col. Daniel Trabue: . . . The Huguenots: Genealogy . . . of allied families. Ed. by Lillie DuP. Van C. Harper. Q. Philadelphia, 1916. HH—H294

COLONIAL (The) Virginia Register. A list of governors . . . other higher officials . . . members of the house of burgesses, and the Revolutionary conventions of the Colony of Virginia. Compiled by Wm. G., & M. N. Stanard. 249 pp. Q. Albany, N. Y., 1902. HH—V817

COLVER, Henry Clay, Compiler. Hasbrouck. Historical facts and chronological table of Hasbrouck family. 12 pp. Seattle, Wash., 1904. O. HH—A54 (A Genealogical collection.)

COLYER, Fergusson Thomas. The marriage registers of St. Dunstan's, Stepney, in the county of Middlesex, England. Vols. I-III. Canterbury, 1898-1902. Q.   HH—F38
Vol. I, 1568-1639.
Vol. II, 1640-1696.
Vol. III, 1697-1719.
No. 1 of only 100 copies privately printed.

—— Registers of the French Church, Threadneedle Street, London, Vols. III & IV. Q. Aberdeen, 1906, & London, 1916. (Huguenot Society of London. Publications. Vols. 16 & 23.)
450 copies printed. Nos. 411 & 357.   HK—H875—Vols. 16 & 23

COMBA, Emilio. History of the Waldenses of Italy, from origin to the Reformation; trans. from the . . . revised edition by T. E. Comba. 5-357 p. O. L. 1889.   HA—C73
Contains an account of their religious life, literature & dispersion in France, Switzerland & Italy.

COMBA, Teofila E., Translator. COMBA, Emilio. History of The Waldenses in Italy. 1889.   HA—C73

COMBES, M. F. Entrevue de Bayonne de 1565, et la Question de la Saint-Barthelemy d'apres les archives de Simancas. 8 pl., 7-49 pp. O. Paris, 1882.   HA—D74
No. 5 of pamphlet Volume.

CONCORD, Massachusetts. See: POTTER, Chas. Edw. ed. Genealogies of some old families . . . and their descendants . . . Vol. I. Boston, 1887.   HH—P85

CONE, M. The first settlement in Ohio. pp. 241-259, il., 1 map. O. 1881. (From Magazine of Amer. History. April, 1881.)   HE—Z6

CONGRESS of Archæological Societies. Report on the transcription and publication of Parish Registers, etc. 16 pp. O. London, 1892, Reprint, 1896.   HK—Pamphlet

—— Second report of the committee for promoting the transcription and publication of parish registers, with calender of registers printed and transcribed since the first report of 1892. 18 pp. O. London, 1896.   HK—Pamphlet

CONNECTICUT Historical Society. Papers and reports presented at the Annual Meeting. O. Hartford, 1893-'94.   HK—H62V

CONNECTICUT marriages. Church records prior to 1800. Vols. I-III. New Haven [cop. 1896-'98.] Edited by Fred'k W. Bailey. 3 Vols. in 1. O.   HH—B15

CONTINENTAL (The) Monthly. Vol. I, Nos. II-IV, pp. 113-492. O. Boston, 1862.   HB—H897

COOKE, John Esten. Story (The) of a Huguenot's sword. Derived from authentic papers and traditions. (In: Harper's New Monthly Magazine, No. LXXXIII, April, 1857, Vol. XIV. pp. 618-631.) O. N. Y. 1857.   HN—C77

COOLIDGE, Susan. Pseudonym. See: WOOLSEY, Sarah Chauncey.

COQUEREL, fils, Athanase Josué. Précis de l'histoire de l'église réformée de Paris, d'après des documents en grande partie inédits, premièr époque 1512-1594. De l'origine de l'église à l'Edit de Nantes. Paris, 1862. 184 pp. 8vo. HA—C79

———— Translator. SMILES, Samuel. Les Huguenots: leurs colonies, leurs industries, leurs Eglises, en Angleterre et en Irlande. Traduction autorisee par l'auteur avec une preface par A. C., fils. 2 pl., XVI, 464 pp. O. Paris, 1870. HA—Sm4F

CORBIERE, Philippe. Histoire de l'église réformée de Montpellier depuis son origine jusqu'à nos jours avec de nombreuses pièces inédites sur le Languedoc, les Cévennes et le Vivarais. Montpellier, 1861. 610 pp. O. HA—C81

CORTEIZ, Pierre. Mémoires de Pierre Carrière, dit Corteis [pasteur du désert. Histoiire des misères d'autrefois, 1685-1730. Publiés pour la première fois d'après un manuscrit de la bibliothèque de Zurich, par J. G. Baum. Genève, 1871]. No title page. 88 pp. O. HA—C812

CORWIN, Edward Tanjore. Amsterdam (The) correspondence. 1 leaf, pp. 81-107. New York, 1897. (Reprinted from Vol. viii. American Soc'y of Church History. HM—Pamphlet

———— Compiler. Ecclesiastical records, State of New York. Vol. vii. Index. 682 pp., 1 port. Albany, 1916. O. (Univ. State of N. Y., Div. Archives & Hist.) HC—C832

———— Manual of the Reformed Church in America (formerly Reformed protestant Dutch Church). Third edition, enlarged. N. Y. 1879. 675 pp. illustrated, portraits. O. HC—C81

COSTER, Morris, Editor. See: NEW AMSTERDAM Gazette. Historical sketches . . . of the Dutch regime of New Amsterdam & the New Netherlands. . . . Vols. i-vii. Square Q. New York, 1883-1893. 7 v. in 4. HH—N421

COTHREN, William, Editor. Second Centennial celebration . . . of ancient Woodbury . . . held at Woodbury, Conn., July 4 and 5, 1859. 223 pp. O. Woodbury, Conn., 1859. HE—W885 Volume "Ancient Woodbury."

COTTEREL, Sir Charles, Translator. See: DAVILA, A. C. Historie of the civill warres of France. 1647.

COUNT Hannibal. A romance of the Court of France, by S. J. WEYMAN. D. New York, 1901. HN—W54

COURTENAY, Hon. W. Ashmead. Extracts from a Memorial of Daniel Ravenal of South Carolina, a vice-president of the Huguenot Soc. of America. (In: Huguenot Soc. of America, Proceedings, 1894. Vol. iii, pp. 117-120.) HK—H871 Read before the Society, Feb'y 27, 1896.

COUTANT, Rev. L. J. John LeFevre. A biographical sketch. (In: New Rochelle (The) Press Almanac. 1879-84. D. pp. 37-43.) HE—NR87S

COWDIN, Elliot Christopher. Tribute of the Chamber of commerce of the state of New York, to the memory of Moses H. Grinnell, Dec. 6, 1877; Address. 9 pp. O. N. Y., 1877. HE—Z4

CRAB, A. J. E. van der. Het geslacht van der Eeckhout. 6 pp. n.p., 1895. O. Reprint. HH—W66
No. 6 of P. V.

CRAIG, Rev. John, D.D. Baptismal record of Augusta County, Virginia, 1740-1749, containing 1,474 names. First publication of the original Record. (In: Houston (F. A. W.), Blaine (L. C.) & Mellette (E. D.). Maxwell history & genealogy. . . . Indianapolis, Ind., [Cop. 1916]. O. pp. 573-597. HH—M465

CRANDALL, A. P. Genealogy of a branch of the Crandall family. 62 pp. D. Chattanooga, 1888. HH—C85

CREGAR, William Francis, Compiler. Ancestry of the children of James William White, M.D., with accounts of the families of White, Newby, Rose . . . & others. VIII, 194 pp., pl., 1 fac-sim. Q. Philadelphia, 1888. HH—W58

CREISSEIL, E. 18 octobre, 1685; la révocation de l'Edit de Nantes dans la Saintonge & l'Angoumois. Saintes, 1885. 20 pp. 8vo. HA—C84
Reprint from the Bulletin évangélique de l'Ouest, 3 Oct., 1885.

CRESPIN, Jean. Histoire des martyrs: persécutez et mis à mort pour la vérité de l'Evâgile, depuis le temps des Apostres insques à present (1619). Ed. nouvelle. . . . Introduction par D. Benoit, et . . . notes par M. Lelièvre. Tomes 1-3. Toulouse, 1885-1889. 3 vols. Q. HG—C86.2

[———— et GOULART, S.] Histoire des martyrs persécutez et mis à mort pour la vérité de l'Evâgile depuis le temps des Apostres insques à l'an 1597. . . . 8 p.l., 1526 pp. Folio. n.p., 1597. HG—C86
Vélin blanc ancien aux armes frappées en or sur les plats et au dos de la ville d'Amsterdam.

CREVAIN, Philippe le Noir, sieur de. Histoire ecclesiastique de Bretagne depuis la réformation jusqu'à l'Edit de Nantes ouvrage publié par B. Vaurigaud. Paris, 1851. 370 pp. O. HA—C86

CROSS, Francis W. History of the Walloon & Huguenot Church, Canterbury. VIII, 272 pp., 1 pl. Q. Lymington, 1898. (Huguenot Society of London. Publications. 1898. Vol. xv.)
HK—H875—Vol.xv.

CUMMINGS, Anna M. Huguenots in South Africa. (HUGUENOT Society of America. Proceedings. New York, 1903. Vol. III, Part 2, pp. 117-131. Q.) HK—H871

CUNITZ, Edouard, Editor. Histoire ecclésiastique des églises réformées au royaume de France. Par T. Béze. 3 vols. 1883-'89.   HA—B46

CUNO, Friedrich Wilhelm. Geschichte der wallonisch-reformirten gemeinde zu Annweiler. 14 pp. O. Magdeburg, 1893. (In: Der deutsche hugenotte verein. Geschichtsblätter. 1893. No. 10, Part 1.)   HB—T57

———— Geschichte der Wallonisch-reformirten gemeinde zu Heidelberg. 13 pp. O. Magdeburg, 1893. (Der Deutsche Hugenotte Verein. Geschichtsblätter. 1893. No. 10, Part 4.)   HB—T57

CUSHMAN, Robert. Self-love. 1621. "The first sermon preached in New England; and the oldest extant of any delivered in America." N. Y., 1847. 47 pp., fac-simile. D. Boards.   HM—C95

CUVIER, Othon. * Trois martyrs de la Réforme brulés en 1525 à Vic, Metz et Nancy. 1 leaf, viii, 1 leaf, 116 pp. D. Paris, 1889.   HG—R111
    * Chastelain, Jean.
    Leclerc, Jean.
    Schuch, Wolfgang.
    Bound with: BORREL, A. Biographie de Paul Rabaut. . . .

CYR, Narcisse. Heroism of Huguenot women imprisoned for life in the Tower of Constance. 19 pp. T. Springfield, Mass., 1894. (Cyr's Huguenot Sketches, No. 1.)   HG—Qu3

———— Claude and his masterpiece. (See: CLAUDE, Jean. Cruel persecutions of the Protestants. . . . Boston, 1893. T. pp. v-xiv.)   HA—C572

DALY, Charles Patrick. The geographical work of the world in 1872; annual address before the American Geographical Society, delivered Feb. 17th, 1873. 60 pp. O. N. Y., 1873.   HE—Z2

DANIELS, George F. Huguenots in the Nipmuck country; or, Oxford prior to 1713. With an introduction by Oliver Wendell Holmes. Boston, 1880. 168 pp., map. O.   HB—D22

———— History of the town of Oxford, Massachusetts, with genealogies and notes on persons and estates. 4-2-856 pp., illus., pl., 1 facsim. O. Oxford, Mass., 1892.   HE—D22

DANKERS, Jasper & Sluyter, P. Journal of a voyage to New York & a tour in several of the American colonies in 1679-'80. Translated from the . . . Dutch . . . & edited by H. C. Murphy. (Long Island Hist. Soc. Memoires, 1867. Vol. i.)   HK—L86

DARLING, Charles W. New Amsterdam, New Orange, New York, with chronological data. [Utica, N. Y.], 1889. 43 pp., plate. O.   HK—H62V

DARRAGON, B. See: BARRAU, J. J., & Darragon, B. Montfort et les Albigeois. 1840.   HK—B27

DAUGHTERS of the American Revolution of Arkansas. Proceedings. Sixth and Seventh Annual State Conference, 1914-'15. 2 vols. n.p., 1914-'15. O. pl., port. HK—Pamphlet

DAUGHTERS of the Cincinnati. Year Book, for 1910-1911. New York, cop. 1911. Edited by Miss Ruth Lawrence. Contains 42 portraits, reproduced through the courtesy of members who have the originals in their possession. HK—C57

DAUGHTERS of the Revolution. Ancestral register of the general Society, 1896. 417 pp. Square Q. Philadelphia, 1897. HK—SO.DR78

DAVAL, GUILLAUME and JEAN. Histoire de la réformation à Dieppe, 1557-1657. Publiée pour la première fois, avec une introduction et des notes, par Emile Lesens. Rouen, 1878-79. 2 vols. 8vo. HA—D27 (Publié par la Soc. rouennaise de bibliophiles.)

DAVILA, ARRIGO CATERINO. Dell' istoria delle guerre civili di Francia. Firenze, 1823. 6 vols. 8vo. Vellum. HD—D28

———— Historie of the civil warres of France, translated out of the original [by William Aylesbury and Sir Charles Cotterel]. London, 1647. 1478 pp. Folio. HD—D281

DAVIS, GEORGE T. Huguenots and New Rochelle. (HUGUENOT Society of America. Publications. Vol. III. 1900.)
HK—H87—Vol.III

DAVIS, REUBEN. 1813-1873. Recollections of Mississippi and Mississippians. 446 pp., 1 port. O. Boston, 1889. HG—D29

DAWSON, HENRY BARTON. 1821- Sons of Liberty in New York; A paper read before the N. Y. Historical Society, May 3, 1859. 118 pp. O. Poughkeepsie, 1859. HE—Z3

DAZINCOURT, JOSEPH JEAN BAPTISTE ALBOUIS. See: ALBOUIS D'AZINCOURT, JOSEPH JEAN BAPTISTE. 1747-1809.

DE BENNEVILLE, GEORGE. 1703-'93. Some remarkable passages in the life of Dr. George de Benneville . . . with . . . account of his . . . persecution in France. Trans. from the French of his own MS. . . . by Rev. E. Winchester. 55 pp. D. Germantown, [Pa.]. 1890. HG—D351
Reprint from American edition of 1800, revised & enlarged.

DE BOER, LOUIS P. Van der Veer family in the Netherlands, 1150-1660, and 1280 to 1780. 62 pp., 1 chart, 8 pl., 1 map, 1 port. Brooklyn, N. Y., cop. 1913. O. HH—V28
No. 59 of 125 copies.

DE BUDE, EUGÈNE. Vie de Bénédict Pictet, théologien Génevois. 1655-1724. 304 pp. D. Lausanne, 1874. HG—P58

—— Vie de Guillaume Budé, fondateur de Collège de France. 300 pp., 1 port. D. Paris, 1884. HG—B86

—— Vie de Jacob Vernet, théologien Génevois, 1698-1789. 304 pp. D. Lausanne, 1893. HG—V59

—— Vie de Jean Diodati, théologien Génevois, 1576-1649. 302 pp., 1 leaf. D. Lausanne, 1869. HG—D62

—— Vie de Jean-Alphonse Turrettini, théologien Génevois. 1671-1737. 324 pp. D. Lausanne, 1880. HG—T86

—— Editor. See: TURRETTINI, Jean-Alphonse. Lettres inedites adressees de 1686 a 1737. . . . Vols. I-III. Paris, 1887. 3 Vols. D. HM—T86

DE CHERGE, CHARLES. See: BEAUCHET-FILLEAU, Henri et Paul. Dictionnaire . . . genealogique des familles du Poitou . . .

DE COSTA, BENJAMIN FRANKLIN. Cabo de Arenas; or, The place of Sandy Hook in the old cartology. N. Y. 1885. 16 pp. map. Q. HI—D35
Reprinted from the *New England Historical and Genealogical Register.*

——Cabo de Baros; or, The place of Cape Cod in the old cartology, with notes on the neighboring coasts. N. Y. 1881. 13 pp. 1 map. Q. HI—D35
Reprinted from the *New England Historical and Genealogical Register,* Jan. 1881.

—— Genealogical chart of the De Costa family. HH—S425

—— Memorial brochures of the De Costa family. 3 Vols. D. HG—D35—Also D35.1 & D35.1.1

—— Myvyrian archaeology: the pre-Columbian voyages of the Welsh to America. 12 pp. Albany, 1891. O. HI—D35

—— Pilgrim (The) of old France, or, The Huguenots on the Hudson, 1613-'14. To which added . . . other pieces of verse. 2 ed. 48 pp., 3 pl., 1 port. New York, 1893. T. HN—D35

—— Editor. Relation of a voyage to Sagadahoc: now first printed from the original manuscript in the Lambeth Palace library, with preface, notes and appendix. Cambridge, 1880. 43 pp. illus., facsim. Q. HI—D35

DE CRESPIGNY, MRS. PHILIP CHAMPION, Compiler. Key to the Roll of the Huguenots: containing brief historical notices of the Huguenot refugees to England, and explaining the object of the Roll of the Huguenots. Second edition. London, 1886. 18 pp. D. HH—

DEDHAM, Massachusetts. Record of . . . the town of Dedham, 1635-1706. Edited by Don Gleason Hill. Dedham, Mass., 1886-1894. In 5 Vols. O. Illus., fac-sim., etc. HE—D299H

Vol I. Record of births, marriages & deaths, & intentions of marriage in the town of Dedham. . . . With an appendix containing records of marriages before 1800, returned from other Towns, under the Statute of 1857. (1635-1845.)

Vol. II. Record of baptisms, marriages and deaths, and admissions to the Church and dismissals therefrom, transcribed from the Church Records in the town of Dedham. 1638-1845. Also all the Epitaphs in the ancient burial place in Dedham . . . with the other inscriptions in the three Parish Cemeteries.

Vol. III. Early records of . . . Dedham, 1636-1659. Complete transcript of Book I. . . . General Records of the Town . . . with the Selectmen's Day Book, covering a portion of the same period. . . .

Vol. IV. Early records of . . . Dedham, 1659-1673. Complete transcript of the Town Meeting and Selectmen's records contained in . . . general records of the Town. . . . Appendix containing transcripts from the Mass. Archives and from the . . . Court Records, 1635-'73. . . .

Vol. V. Early Records of the town of Dedham, 1672-1706. Complete transcript of the Town Meeting and Selectmen's Records contained in Book V., of the General Records of the Town. . . .

——— See: WORTHINGTON, E. The history of Dedham. . . .
O. Boston, 1827. HE—Ded36

DE FOREST, EMILY JOHNSTON. A Walloon family in America; Lockwood de Forest and his forbears, 1500-1848. Together with A voyage to Guiana; being the Journal of Jesse de Forest and his colonists, 1623-1625. Vols. I-II. Portraits, plates, maps, fac-sims. Boston, 1914. 2 Vols. O. HH—D315

DE FOREST, MRS. ROBERT WEEKS. See: de FOREST, Emily Weeks.

DELABORDE, LOUIS JULES, COMTE DE. Gaspard de Coligny, Amiral de France. 3 vols. HG—C681

DE LA FERRIERE, HECTOR. La Saint-Barthelemy: la veille, le jour, le landemain. IX, 288 pp. O. Paris, 1892. HA—D37

DELAFIELD, MATURIN L. William Smith, Judge of the Supreme Court of the Province of New York. pp. 260-282. O. 1881. From Magazine of Amer. History, April, 1881. HE—Z6

DE LANCEY, Edward Floyd. Memoir of James William Beekman; prepared at the request of the St. Nicholas Society of N. Y. N. Y. 1877. 17 pp. Q.   HG—Mem.51

——— A Second copy in Pamphlet Volume.   HE—Z9

——— Philip Freneau, the Huguenot patriot poet of the Revolution and his poetry. (HUGUENOT Society of America. Proceedings. New York, 1891. Vol. II. pp. 66-84.)   HK—H87.1

——— William Allen, chief justice of Pennsylvania, a biographical sketch prepared for the centennial celebration of the adoption of the "Resolutions respecting independency," held at . . . Philadelphia, July 1, 1876. 12 pp. Q. Philadelphia, 1877. Reprint, "Pennsylvania Magazine of History."   HE—Z9

——— Editor. See: JONES, Thomas. History of New York, during the Revolutionary War. New York, 1879. Q. 2 Vols.   HE—J72

——— & De Costa, Rev. B. F., D.D. Memorial notice of Charles Martyn Baird, D.D. February 10th, 1887. (HUGUENOT Society of America. Proceedings. New York, 1889. Vol. I, part 2, pp. 74-75.)   HK—H871

DELANO, Joel Andrew, Major U. S. Army. The genealogy, history, and alliances of the American house of Delano, 1621-1899. With the history and heraldry of the Maison de Franchimont and DeLannoy to Delano, 1096 to 1621 . . . and . . . Lannoy from Guelph . . . to Philippe de Lannoy, 476 A. D. to 1621 . . . arranged by M. D. de Lannoy. New York, 1899. 561 pp., 22 pl. (1 colored plate). Q.   HH—D37

DELAVAN, Edward C., Jr. The Guyon house. A history based upon personal researches and family data supplied by Miss S. G. Clark. pp. 113-138, 1 fac-sim., 2 plans, 1 pl. New York, 1916. (Reprint: Staten Island Assoc. Arts & Sciences. Proceedings, Vol. VI, part 2. February, 1916.)   HH—Pamphlet

DELAWARE Historical Society Papers. No. 7. See: MALLERY, Rev. C. P. Ancient families of Bohemia Manor. 1888.
                                                     HH—D37

DELMAS, Louis. Eglise reformée de La Rochelle etude historique. 10 & 453 pp. D. Toulouse, 1870. (Pub. Soc. de livres religieux de Toulouse.)   HA—D381

——— Huguenots of La Rochelle. A translation of "The Reformed Church of La Rochelle," from the French, by G. L. Catlin. N. Y. [1880]. 295 pp. D.   HA—D38

DEMAREST, David D.   Huguenots on the Hackensack.   New
Brunswick, N. J., 1886.   HB

—— Same.   HK—H87.1

—— Reformed Church in America; its origin, development, and
characteristics.   215 pp., port., pl.   N. Y., 1889.   4 ed., enlarged.
O.   HC—D39
History of the coat-of-arms of the Reformed Church in America by
John S. Bussing, pref. pp. 9-13.

—— Rev. W. H. S., D.D., LL.D.   Commemorative address, 225th
anniversary of the founding of the French Protestant Church in the
City of Charleston, "The Huguenot Church."   pp. 23-38.   In:
French Prot. Church.   Charleston, S. C., 1912.   HB—F875

DE MEAUX, le vicomte.   Les luttes religieuses en France au seizième
siècle.   LXVII.   41 pp.   Paris, 1879.   O.   HC—D394

DENHAM, Edward.   Why is history read so little?   An address to
parents, teachers, and members of . . . society . . . 27 pp.   O.
New Bedford, 1876.   HE—Z7

DEPEW, Hon. Chauncey M.   Characteristics and influence of the
Huguenots.   An address before the Society, April 20th, 1888.
(HUGUENOT Society of America.   Proceedings.   Vol. I., part 2.
pp. 96-101.   1889.)   HK—H87.1—Vol. I

DE PEYSTER, Col. Arent Schuyler.   Miscellanies by an Officer
. . . edited by J. Watts de Peyster. . . . 80 pp., 1 port.: 202, 6 pp.,
1 map, 1 map folded, 1 port.   In 2 parts.   Q.   (Dumfries, 1813.)
New York, 1888.   HG—D419
Nos. 3 & 4 of de Peyster Volume.

DE PEYSTER, Frederic.   Early political history of New York; an address delivered before the New York historical society on its 60th
anniversary. . . . Nov. 22, 1864.   3-76 pp.   O.   N. Y., 1865.   HE—Z3

—— Life and administration of Richard, Earl of Bellomont, Governor of the Provinces of New York, Massachusetts and New Hampshire, from 1697-1701.   An address delivered before the New York
Historical Society, at the celebration of its 75th Anniversary, Nov.
18, 1879.   5 pl., 60, XVII pp., 3 port., 1 fac-sim.   New York,
1879.   Q.   HE—D44

—— Same.   2 portraits—(Port. of the Earl, missing.)   HE—Z9

—— 1796-1882.   Moral and intellectual influence of libraries upon
social progress . . . address delivered before the N. Y. historical
society . . . Nov. 21, 1865.   96 p.   O.   N. Y. 1866.   HE—Z3

—— 1796-1882.   William the Third as a reformer, an address delivered before the N. Y. historical society . . . Jan. 6, 1874.   36 pp.
1 port.   O.   N. Y., 1874.   HE—Z3

DE PEYSTER, JOHN WATTS, BREV. MAJ. GEN. U. S. A. Authorities cited or referred to in [his] three pamphlets . . . "Waterloo," . . . and other Works on Napoleon. . . . With a biographical sketch of the author, by W. L. Stone. New York, 1894. 1-16, 1-16 pp. Square Q. HF—D419W

—— Bothwell: (James Hepburn, fourth Earl of Bothwell, third husband of Mary, Queen of Scots.) An historical drama. New York, 1884. 48 pp., 2 port. (also 2 port. on covers, & pp. illus.) O. HF—D419

—— Burgoyne's Campaign . . . 1777; justice to Schuyler. 4 pp. n. t. p. HE—Z3

—— Editor. Genuine (The) letters of Mary, Queen of Scots, to James, Earl of Bothwell: . . . Trans. from the French originals, by Edw. Simmonds. . . . Added Remarks on each letter, with an abstract of her life . . . from an unknown hand. 2 ed. Westminster, n. d. New York, 1891-'92. 124, ii-iii pp. O. HF—D419

—— Ho! For the North Pole. 8 pp., illus. O. HG—D419

—— Inquiry into the career and character of Mary Stuart . . . and a justification of Bothwell. . . . New York, 1883. 260 pp., 2 port. O. Illust. HF—D419

—— Major-General George H. Thomas. Address before the New York Historical Society. 24 pp. n. t. p., n. d. HE—Z9

—— Major-General George H. Thomas. A Biographical sketch. pp. 545-576, with a steel-engraved portrait. n. t. p., n. d.

—— Major-General Philip Schuyler and the Burgoyne campaign in the summer of 1777. 26 pp. O. No title-page. HE—Z3 Address before the N. Y. Hist. Society.

—— Mary, Queen of Scots. A study. By "Anchor." 144 pp. New York, 1882. O. HF—D419

—— Mary Stuart, Bothwell, and the casket letters, something new. . . . 40 pp., illus. N. Y. 1890. O. HF—D419

—— Nashville, the decisive battle of the rebellion; address delivered before N. Y. Historical Society, Jan. 4, 1876. 14 pp. O. No title-page. HF—Z3

—— Prussians (The) in the Campaign of Waterloo. n. p., n. d. 21 pp., 1 plan. Square Q. Reprint "The College Student," Lancaster, Pa. HF—D419w

—— Sir John Johnson, the first American-born baronet; an address delivered before the N. Y. historical society . . . Jan. 6th, 1880. 12-36 pp. O. No place, no date. HE—Z3

—— Wolverene (The) (Carcajou or Glutton.) With information from trustworthy authorities, and illustrations. 4 pl., 4 leaves, XLIV, 30 pp. Tivoli, N. Y., 1901. O. HO—Pamphlet

DE PONTBRIANT, A. Guerres de religion. Le Capitaine Merle, Baron de Lagorce, gentilhomme de Roy de Navarre et ses descendants, avec lettres et documents inedits. . . . 2 pl., 306 pp., 1 map folded. Paris, 1886. O.   HG—D44

DE RICHEMOND, Louis MARIE MESCHINET: See: MESCHINET de RICHEMOND.

DE ST. BRIS, THOMAS. Discovery of the origin of the name of America. 140 pp., 1 map. New York, 1888. O.   HE—D476

DESAUSSURE, GEN W. G., U. S. A. Address on the Occasion of the 200th Anniversary of the Revocation of the Edict of Nantes. Read at the Meeting in the Eglise du St. Esprit, October 22nd, 1885. (HUGUENOT Society of America. Commemoration of the Bi-Centennial of the Revocation of the Edict of Nantes. N. Y., 1886. pp. 44-56. Q.)   HK—H87.1

DE SCHICKLER, FERNAND, BARON. Discours prononce a l'assemblée generale de la Societe de l'Histoire de France, le 5 mai 1903. 22 pp. O. Nogent-le-Rotrou, 1903.   HG—S33

DE TRIQUETI, H. Les premiers jours de Protestantisme en France. Depuis son origine jusqu'au Premier Synode national de 1559. Ouvrage publie a l'occasion de 3 Jublie seculaire de ce Synode. 302 pp. D. Paris, 1859.   HA—D48

DEUTSCHE HUGENOTTEN VEREIN. Geschichtsblätter. Vols. I-XIII, I-VIII. O. Magdeburg, 1890-1908.   HK-D49

DEVARANNE, pfarrer. Die französisch-reformirten gemeinden zu Gross und Klein-Ziethen in der mark Brandenburg. 15 pp. O. Magdeburg, 1893. (Der DEUTSCHE Hugenotten Verein. Geschichtsblätter. 1893. No. 10, pt. 5.)   HK—D49

DE VAYNES, JULIA H. L., Editor. A Huguenot garland. Hertford, England, 1890. XVI, 304 pp. O.   HA—D49
Collection of French national songs with descriptive notes in English. No. 26 of 50 copies privately printed.

DE VILLIERS, CHRISTOFFEL COETZEE, Compiler. See: GESLACHT-REGISTER der oude Kaapsche familien.   HH—G33

DE VOE, THOMAS F. Genealogy of the DeVoe family . . . the numerous forms of spelling the name by various branches and generations in the past eleven hundred years. 302 pp., illus. New York, 1885. O.   HH—D49

DE VOTION, SARA, Compiler. Genealogy of the De Votion family: A brief account copied from records. MSS., 2 port. New York, 1894. Square Q.   HJ—D49
Contains also a Journal of Ebenezer De Votion. MS.

DE WITT, THOMAS. Discourse delivered in the North Reformed Dutch (Collegiate) Church in the city of New York. August, 1856. N. Y. 1857. 100 pp., plates. O.   HC—D51

DICTIONNAIRE historique de l'ancien langage François. . . .
Tomes 1-10. Niort, 187?-1882. 10 Vols. Square Q. LaCURNE
de SAINTE PALAYE, Editor. HO—Pal. 182

DICTIONNAIRE historique et généalogique des familles du Poitou.
See: BEAUCHET-FILLEAU, Henri & Paul. HG—B38

DITTMAR, W., & ROBERT, pfarrer. Die Waldenser und ihre colonie
Walldoef. (In: DEUTSCHE Hugenotten Verein. Geschichtsblätter. 1891. Vol. III.) HK—D49

DIGBY, WILLIAM. British invasion from the north. The campaigns of
Carleton and Burgoyne, 1776-1777, with the journal of William
Digby and historical notes by J. P. Baxter. Albany, 1887. 412
pp., portraits, plate. Square O. Cloth. HE—D56
The original title of Digby's book reads: "Some account of the
American war between Great Britain and her colonies." 1776.

DIMAN, JEREMIAH LEWIS. Religion in America. 1776-1876. O.
From the *North American Review*, 1876, vol. 122. HB—H12

DISOSWAY, GABRIEL POILLON. Earliest churches of New York and
its vicinity. N. Y. 1865. 416 pp., plates. O. HC—D63

———— Huguenots in America. See: SMILES, Samuel. Huguenots
(The). pp. 427-448. 1868. HA—Sm4

DITMAS, CHARLES ANDREW, Compiler & Publisher. Brooklyn's Garden. Views of picturesque Flatbush, with an introduction. 24 colored plates, mounted. Brooklyn, N. Y., 1908. Oblong O.
HE—D615F

———— Historic homesteads of Kings County. 120 pp., 20 hand-col-
ored photogravures. (Paged.) Brooklyn, 1909? HE—D615K
No. 311 of First edition, 500 copies, signed and numbered.

DIX, THE REV. MORGAN, S.T.D., Editor. A History of the Parish of
Trinity Church in the City of New York . . . part 1, pl., port.
N. Y., 1898. HC—D64
Part 1: To the close of the Rectorship of Rev. Dr. Inglis, A.D.
1783.
One of 750 copies.

DODDRIDGE, PHILIP. Les Commencemens et les progres de la
vraie piete . . . traduit de l'Angleis, par J. S. Vernede. 24, 472,
31 pp. La Haye, 1751. O. HM—D66

DODGE, RICHARD DESPARD. Condensed table of the Block Island branch of the Dodge family in America. A chart folded. Brooklyn, New York, 1898.   HH—D66

———— Despard (D'Espard) family. (HUGUENOT Society of America. Proceedings. Vol. III, part 2. pp. 230-244. New York, 1903. Q.)   HK—H87.1

———— Dodge (The) lands at Cow Neck, Long Island; an Appendix to Robert Dodge's History of Tristram Dodge and his descendants in America. 32 pp. O. Brooklyn, New York, 1898.   HH—D66
Gift of the Author.
Note: The Chart and this pamphlet are bound with: DODGE, Robert. Tristram Dodge and his descendants in America. . . .

DODGE, ROBERT. Tristram Dodge and his descendants in America, with historical and descriptive accounts of Block Island, Rhode Island; and Cow Neck, Long Island; their original settlements. New York, 1886. 233 pp., and chart of the Block Island branch of the Dodge family, by R. D. Dodge, inserted. O.   HH—D66

DORCHESTER, Mass. In: RECORD of births, marriages and deaths . . . in . . . Stoughton . . . and . . . Canton . . . preceded by records of . . . Dorchester . . . 1715-1727. . . . Edited by F. Endicott. Canton, Mass., 1896. O.   HH—St6

DOUEN, EMMANUEL ORENTIN. Clément Marot & le psautier Huguenot, étude historique littéraire, musicale & bibliographique, contenant les mélodies primitives des psaumes et des specimins d'harmonie de Clement, Jannequin. . . . 2 vols. Q. Paris, 1878-'79.
                                                        HG—M341

———— Essai historique sur les églises réformées du département de l'Aisne, d'après des documents pour la plupart inédits. Paris, 1860. 186 pp. O. Boards.   HA—D74
Extrait du "Bulletin de la Société de l'histoire du protestantisme français."

———— Les premiers pasteurs du désert (1685-1700) d'après des documents pour la plupat inédits. Paris, 1879. 2 vols. O.   HG—D74

———— Editor. Revocation (La) de l'Edit de Nantes, d'apres de documents inedits. Vols. I-III. Q. 3 Vols. Paris, 1894.   HA-R32

———— Editor. BION, Jean. Relation des tourments. . . . 1881.
                                                          HA—B52

DOUTHETT, ANDREW THOMPSON, Compiler. Douthett and Ward families; genealogical notes. 36 pp., portrait. Pittsburgh, Pa., 1889. S.   HH—D74

DOYLE, ARTHUR CONAN. The Refugees: a Tale of two Continents. 366 pp., 20 pl. D. New York, 1893.   HN—D77

DOZY, CHARLES M. The Pilgrim fathers. Exhibition of documents from public and private collections at Leiden, relating to the Dutch settlements in North America. Aug., 1888. [Leiden, 1888.]
HE—Pamphlet

DOZY, R. B., Compiler. Kerling, J. B. J. & Dozy, R. B., Compiler. Catalogue de pamphlets et d'estampes concernant les Traites de paix, conclus . . . Pay-Bas depuis, 1576-1815. 40 pp., 6 pl. Square O.
HA—Pamphlet

DRELINCOURT, REV. CHARLES. The Christian's consolations against the fears of death. With . . . prayers and meditations. . . . To which are prefixed the Life of the author. . . . 24, 444 pp., 1 pl. Philadelphia, 1884. D.
HM—D81

DRINKER, MRS. ELIZABETH [SANDWITH]. 1734-1807. Extracts from her journal, from 1759-1807 . . . edited by H. D. Biddle. 423 pp. O. Philadelphia, 1889.
HG—D83

DRAPER, LYMAN COPELAND, Ed. FORMAN S.: S. 1765-1862. Narrative of a journey down the Ohio & Mississippi in 1789-90. 1888.
HI—F76

DuBOIS, ANSON, and JAMES G. Documents and genealogical chart of the family of Benjamin DuBois of Catskill, New York. Being an addition to the History of the descendants of Louis and Jacques DuBois, as given at the Bi-centenary reunion held at New Paltz, New York, 1875. IV, 104 pp., 1 plan. New York, 1878. Square Q.
HH—D85.2

———— Same: Bound with: DU BOIS, W. E. and P. Bi-centenary reunion. . . . Philadelphia, 1876. Square Q.
HH—D85

DU BOIS, GEORGE W. Descendants of Jacques Du Bois. A genealogical chart, 58 x 64, inserted in volume. No place, no date.
HH—D85

DU BOIS, JAMES G[OELET]. See DU BOIS, Anson, and Du Bois, J. G. Documents and genealogical chart of the family of Benjamin Du Bois of Catskill, New York. . . . New York, 1878. Square Q.
HH—D85.2

DU BOIS, PATTERSON, & DUBOIS, W. E. Bi-centenary reunion of the descendants of Louis and Jacques DuBois. . . .
HH—D85

DU BOIS, WILLIAM E. and PATTERSON. Bi-centenary reunion of the descendants of Louis and Jacques Du Bois, (Emigrants to America, 1660 and 1665), at New Paltz, New York, 1875. Compiled for the family connection. Philadelphia, 1876. 158 pp., 9 port., 7 pl., 1 fac-sim. Square Q.
HH—D85
The coat-of-arms plate is in color.

DU BOIS, WILLIAM EWING. Translator. See: FRENCH CHURCH, New Paltz, New York. Copy and translation of the First Record Book, 1683-1704. MS. 19 pp., folio. Philadelphia, 1846.
HJ—N558

[DUBOIS DE RIACOURT, NICHOLAS.] anon. Histoire de l'emprisonnement de Charles IV. duc de Lorraine. 133 pp. S. Cologne 1688. Bound with: BEAUVAU, H. (marquis de.) Mémoires. HD—B38

DU BOIS-MELLY, CHARLES. Le récit de Nicolas Muss, serviteur de Mr. l'Amiral; épisode de la Saint-Barthélemy, avec notes historiques et gloses. Genève, 1878. 258 pp. D. HA—D85

DU BOSC, PIERRE. 1623-92. La vie de Pierre Du Bosc, enrichie de lettres, harangues, dissertations et autres pieces importantes. Rotterdam, 1694. 610 pp. O. Vellum. HG—D85

DUBOSE, SAMUEL. Contribution to the history of the Huguenots of South Carolina: consisting of pamphlets by Samuel Dubose and Frederick A. Porcher. Republished for private circulation by T. Gaillard Thomas. N. Y. 1887. 175 pp. O. HB—D85

Contents: Address delivered at the 17th anniversary of the Black Oak agricultural society, April 27, 1858, with Reminiscences of St. Stephen's parish and notices of her old homesteads, by Samuel Dubose. Historical and social sketch of Craven County, South Carolina, by Frederick A. Porcher.

———— Second copy in: HB—F875

DUBUS-PREVILLE, P[IERRE] L[OUIS]. Mémoires. (In: Barrière, J. F., Editor. Bibliothèque des mémoires relatifs à l'histoire de France. 1857. V. 6. pp. 143-192. HG—B27—V. 6

[DUCHE, JACOB.].Caspipina's letters, containing observations on subjects literary, moral and religious, [with] the life and character of Wm. Penn. Bath, 1777. 2 vols. in 1, calf. D. HN—D85

DUCHESNE, ANDRÈ. History of the Bethune family, translated from the French, with additions . . . and a Sketch of the Faneuil family . . . by Mrs. J. A. Weisse. 54 & 3 pp., 1 pl. Q. New York, 1884. HG—B67

DUCLOS, CHARLES PINEAU. Mémoires secrets le règne de Louis XIV, la règence et le règne de Louis XV. (In: Barrière, J. F., Editor. Bibliothèque des mémoires relatifs à l'histoire de France. 1854. Vol. II.) HG—B27

DUCOUDRAY, GUSTAVE. History of modern civilization translated & adapted from the French by J. V. 587 pp., illust. New York, 1891. O. HF—D85

DU FAIS, F. F., Translator. See: FELICE, Paul de. "Comment l'Edit de Nantes fut observé." (HUGUENOT Society of America. Publications. Vol III. 1900.) HK—H87

DUFOUR, THEOPHILE. Notice bibliographique fur le catechisme and la confession de foi de Calvin (1537) and fur les autres livres imprimes a Geneve and a Neuchatel dans les premiers temps de la Reforme (1533-'40). HM—C13
See: CALVIN, Jean. Catechisme Français de Calvin . . . 1878. Pref. pp. 99-237.

Du HAUSSET, Mme. N. Mémoires de Madam du Hausset, femme de chambre de Madam de Pompadour. (In: Barrière, J. F., Editor. Bibliothèque des mémoires relatifs à l'histoire de France. 1846. Vol. 3, pp. 49-154.) HG—B27—V. 3

DU MOULIN, Pierre. Bouclier de la foi; ou, Défense de la confession de foi des églises réformées du royaume de France contre les objections du sieur Arnoux, jésuite. Paris, 1846. 650 pp. D.
HA—D89

——— Huictieme decade de sermons. Genève, 1653-54. 3 vols. in 1. S. Vellum. HM—D89
Vol. ii, Neufvieme decade de sermons.
Vol. iii, Dixieme decade de sermons.

DUMOURIEZ, Charles Francois Dupérier. Mémoires. (In: Barrière, J. F., Editor. Bibliothèque des mémoires relatifs à l'histoire de France. 1848. Vols. xi & xii. pp. 1-207.)
HG—B27—V.11 & 12

[DUNCAN, Mrs. M. G. Lundy.] anon. Memoirs of the life and character of the Rev. Matthias Bruen, late pastor of the Presbyterian Church in Bleecker Street, New York. 358 pp., 1 portrait. O. N. Y., 1831. HG—B83.1

DUPIN DE SAINT-ANDRE, Armand. Histoire du protestantisme en Touraine. Paris, 1885. 306 pp. D. HA—D92

DuPUY, Charles Meredith. Genealogical history of the DuPuy family. With additions by his son, Herbert DuPuy. x, 165 pp., 8 fac-sim., 11 plates, 16 groups, 9 port., 1 survey, 6 charts. Square Q. Privately printed, Philadelphia, 1910. HH—D94

——— Historical sketch of the DuPuy family. 1883. HJ

——— Plea for better distribution; read [before] the Philadelphia Social Science Association, June 17, 1884. Philadelphia [1884]. 19 pp. 8vo. HO—Pamphlet

——— Saint Bartholomew's Day: its causes and results. (HUGUENOT Society of America. Proceedings. New York. Vol. iii., part 2, pp. 83-102. Q.) Read before the Society at the Summer Meeting held at New Rochelle, N. Y., August 24th, 1885. HK—H87.1

DuPUY, Eliza A. Huguenot (The) exiles, or The times of Louis XIV. A historical novel. 2 p.l., 6-453 pp. New York, 1856. D.
HN—94

——— Miser's (The) curse. A veritable ghost story. (Harper's New Monthly Magazine. April, 1857. pp. 641-646.) O. N. Y. 1857. HN—C77

DuPUY, Herbert. See: DuPUY, Charles Meredith, Genealogical history of the DuPuy family. With additions by his son. Philadelphia, 1910. Square Q. HH—D94

[DU PUY, PIERRE.] Histoire des plus illustres favoris anciens et modernes, recueillie par . . . P. D. P. Avec un journal de ce qui s'est passé à la mort de Mareschal d'Ancre. 10 p.l., 340 pp. Square O. Leide, 1659.　　　　　　　　　　　　　　　　　　　HG—D92

DuRIEU, W. N. Compiler. EGLISES Wallonnes. Catalogue de la bibliotheque Wallonne. Sups. 1e-3e. 1875-'90.　　　HK—Unbound

DURYEE, REV. JOSEPH R., D.D., and others. Funeral address: memorial tributes, resolutions, etc., for the Hon. Henry W. Bookstaver, LL.D. 1834-1907. 30 pp., 1 port., inserted. O. New York, 1907.　　　　　　　　　　　　　　　　　　　HG—Mem.512

DUTCH CHURCH, N. Y., Baptisms: 1697-1720. See: VALENTINE, D. T. Manual of the city of New York. N. Y., 1864. pp. 777-837.　　　　　　　　　　　　　　　　　　　HE—N481

——— Burials. Record of burials in the Dutch Church, New York. 1 p. l. 309-211 pp. Q. N. Y., 1899.　　　　　　HH—D95 Reprint: Holland Soc. of N. Y. Year-book.

DUTCH Records: City Clerk's Office, N. Y. Extracts from Dutch documents . . . labeled "Original records of burgomasters and orphanmasters." "Surrogates." (Holland Society. N. Y. Year book, 1900.)　　　　　　　　　　　　　　　　　　HK—H711

DUTCH Reformed Church of Brooklyn, N. Y. First Book of Records. (Holland Society, N. Y. Year book, 1897. pp. 133-194.)　HK—H711

DUTCH settlers in Esopus. Names compiled from the old Court Records of Wildwyck (Kingston) . . . Marriages recorded . . . 1667-1672. (HOLLAND Society, New York, Year book, 1897. pp. 117-132.)　　　　　　　　　　　　　　　　　HK—H711

DUVAL, MARY REBECCA. Duvalls (The) of Maryland. (HUGUENOT Society of America. Proceedings. Vol. III, part 2. pp. 137-148. 1903.　　　　　　　　　　　　　　　　　HK—H871

DUXBURY, Massachusetts. Copy of the old records of the town of Duxbury, Mass. From 1642 to 1770. Made in the year 1770. 348 pp. O. Plymouth, Mass., 1893.　　　　　　　HE—D95

——— See: WINDSOR, Justin. A history of Duxbury . . . with genealogical registers. O. Boston, 1849.　　　　　HE—W721

DUYCKINCK, EVERT T., Editor. See: FRENEAU, Philip Morin. Poems. . . . 1865.

DWIGHT, TIMOTHY. Noah Porter; address delivered at the funeral service of President Porter, March 7, 1892. 14 pp. D. New Haven, 1892.　　　　　　　　　　　　　　　　　HG—Mis68

EARLY Connecticut marriages. See: CONNECTICUT.

EARLY RECORDS of the City and County of Albany and Colony of Rensselaerswyck. Translated from the original Dutch by J. PEARson. Revised and edited by A. J. Van LAER. Vol II. Albany, 1916-19. 3 Vols. Q. IV. (University State N. Y., N. Y. State Lib'y. History Bull. 9-11.)　　　　　　　　　　HE—A326—Q

EAST Hampton, Long Island, Suffolk Co., New York. Records, of the town, with other ancient documents of historic value. . . . From 1639-1849. Vol. I-IV. Sag-Harbor, 1887-89. 4 Vols. Q.   HE—E7

EDWARDS, REV. JOHN H., D.D. The First home of the Huguenots in North America. (HUGUENOT Society of America. Proceedings. Vol. III. pp. 125-143.)   HK—H87.1

EGLE, WILLIAM H., M.D., Editor. See: PENNSYLVANIA Archives.

EGLESTON, THOMAS. Biographical notice of Louis Gruner, inspector-general of mines of France. N. Y. 1884. 5 pp. 8 vo.   HH—Var4
Extract from the *American Institute of Mining Engineers. Transactions.*
In: Pamphlet Volume "Ancestry."

EGLISE ÉVANGÉLIQUE VAUDOIS. Rapport annuel sur l'œuvre d'évangélisation en Italie et à l'étranger Torre Pellice, 1887. 47 pp. O.
HA—Pamphlet

———— Résumé historique des fêtes du Bi-centenaire de la glorieuse rentrée des Vaudois et compterendu du synode de 1889 tenu à La Tour, 2-7 Sept. 62, 138 pp., plates. La Tour, 1889. O.   HC—Sy6

EGLISE FRANCAISE de Cantorbéry. Le Livre du Sanctuaire. . . . Crypte de Cathédrale, fondée en 1550. XXIV, 176 pp. 2nd ed. T.t. Cantorbéry, [1877?]. Compiled par Rev. J. A. Martin.   HM—E31

———— Service du Culte Divin pour les Solennites de l'Eglise Francaise et autres occasions speciales. . . . Dans ces Solennites, comme signe d'Union Chretienne, le LIVRE du Sanctuaire est remplace par la LITURGIE de l'Eglise d'Angleterre. Canterbury, no date. Cover and 16 pp. S.   HM—L78.1
This is the Office of Morning Prayer in French and English, parallel columns, with "Collectes Speciales," appended, in both languages.

EGLISE (L') Française de Voorburg. Recueil de documents relatifs à l'Eglise . . . concernant l'origine et l'état actuel de la dite institution religieuse, [par H. J. CAAN]. [La Haye]. 1859. O.
HB—C11

EGLISE de Narragansett. Papier du Consistoire de l'Eglise de Narragansett, 1687. The original MS. 34 pp. Bound in parchment. (Small.) Square O.   HJ—N23

———— A true copy in French, from the original MS. One side of pages 1-175 written upon (paging numbered 1-253). New York, 1893. O.   HJ—N23.1—W

———— A typewritten MS. copy in French, with an English translation made and verified by Mrs. E. M. C. A. Lawton. 2 leaves, 47; 49, XI leaves. New York, 1896. Square O.   HJ—N23.1—L

EGLISE PROTESTANT EPISCOPAL: Livre des prières publiques de l'administration des sacremens et des autres rites et cérémonies de l'église, selon l'usage de l'église protestante épiscopale dans les Etats-Unis d'Amérique avec le psautier. Nouvelle édition. N. Y., 1831. 464 pp. Sheep. Q. HM—L78.2F

EGLISE RÉFORMÉE DE FRANCE. Actes et décisions du synode général Officieux. Toulouse, 1881. O.

EGLISE REFORMEE DE LA ROCHELLE. Etude Historique par L. Delmas, Pasteur, Président du Consistoire. Toulouse: Société des Livres Religieux, 1870. pp. 453. D. HA—D38.1

EGLISES Evangeliques Françaises des Etats-Unis. Confession de foi et liturgie. [Edited et trans., par Rev. J. Provost. Springfield, Mass., 1897.] VII, 72 pp. O. HM—L73P

EGLISES en PRUSSE. See: PARISET, Georges. L'état et les Eglises en Prusse sous Frédéric-Guillaume Ier. (1713-1740) . . . xx, 990 pp. Paris, 1896. O. HB—P21

EGLISES Wallonnes. Bulletin de la commission pour l'histoire . . . Tome 1-8., port., pl., tables. O. La Haye, 1885-1902. HK—Eg5

—— Catalogue de la bibliotheque Wallonne . . . redige par J. T. Bergman. 12-202-[1] pp. O. Leide, 1875. Supplement 1875-1908. Rédigé par W. N. duRieu & C. G. Chavannes. Vols. I-V. O. Leide, 1880-1908. 6 Vols. in all. HK—Unbound

EGLISES WALLONNES de la BARRIERE: Tournai, Armentières, Menin, Ypres et Namur. Registres des baptêmes, mariages & inhumations. Liste des membres . . . hors de Tournai. Abjurations à Tournai et à Menin. XVIIIe siècle. 528 pp. 1 leaf. Le Cateau, 1894. O. HB—Wa.16

—— A second copy. HH—B16

ELLERY, Harrison, Editor. See: SWIFT, J. G. Memoirs . . . with a genealogy of the family of Thomas Swift. 1890. HG—Sw5

ELLIS, George Edward. History of the Battle of Bunker's (Breed's) Hill . . . June 17, 1775; from authentic sources . . . 69 pp., 1 map. Boston, 1875. HE—Z1

ELLIS, Grace Atkinson. Memoir of Mrs. Anna Laetitia Barbauld. (In: BARBAULD, Mrs. Anna Laetitia. Life & Works.) 2 vols. HG—B23

ENDICOTT, Frederic, Editor. Record (The) of births, marriages and deaths in Stoughton and . . . Canton . . . O. Canton, Mass. 1896. HH—St6

ENGLAND: Order of Council relating to the Royal action in favor of the Huguenot refugees to England. 4 pp. Q. 1681. HJ—MS

ENGLISH (The) CHURCH in the HAGUE. The eldest Church-book of the English Congregation in the Hague . . . a transcript by M. G. Wildeman. 84, i-iv pp. The Hague, 1906. O.

HB—W67E

ESPRIT (l') de Jesus-Christ sur la Tolerance; pour servir de response a plusieurs Ecrits de ce tems sur la meme matiere, & particuliere-ment a l'Apologie de Louis XIV sur la Revocation de l'Edic de Nantes, & a la Dissertation sur le Massacre de la Saint Barthelemi. 360 pp., n. p., 1759. D.

HM—E77

ETHERIDGE, George. See: DUXBURY, Mass. Copy of the old records . . . 1642-1770. O. Plymouth, Mass., 1893.

HE—D95

EVANS, Thomas Grier, Editor. Records of the Reformed Dutch Church in New Amsterdam and New York. Baptisms from 25 De-cember, 1639, to 27 December, 1730. 664 pp., 2 leaves, 1 port. Vol. i. N. Y., 1901. Q. (N. Y. Gen. & Biog. Soc. Coll. Vol. ii.) No. 54 of 100 copies.

HK—N491

———— Compiler. See: FRENCH Protestant Hospital-Library. Bi-bliotheque de la Providence. Catalogue: with an Introduction by A. G. Browning. London, 1887 & 1890. Q. & O. (3 vols.)

HK—L84—L84.1—L84.111

FAIRBANKS, George Rainsford. History and antiquities of the city of St. Augustine, Florida, founded A. D. 1565. N. Y., 1858. 200 pp., plates, portrait, maps. O.

HE—F15

FAIRCHILD Helen Lincklaen, Editor. See: LINCKLAEN, John. Travels in the years 1791 and 1792 in Pennsylvania, New York and Vermont. Journals of J. L., agent of the Holland Land Company. With a biographical sketch and notes. 1 p. iv, 1-4, v-xi, 1-162 pp., 1 fac-sim., 1 pl., 1 port., 2 maps, & 1 map folded in pocket. O. New York, 1897.

HI—L63

———— Editor. See: van der KEMP, Francis Adrian. 1752-1829. An autobiography . . . edited, with an historical sketch by H. L. F. N. Y., 1903.

FAIRFIELD, Conn., 1779-1879. Centennial commemoration of the burning of Fairfield, Conn., by the British troops under Gov. Tryon. July 8, 1779. 104 pp. O. N. Y., 1879.

HE—Z3

———— See: HURD, D. H., Compiler. History of Fairfield, Conn. . . . Q. Philadelphia, 1881.

HE—H93

———— See: SCHENCK, Mrs. E. H. History of Fairfield, Fairfield County, Conn. . . . 1639-1818. V. I. O. N. Y., 1889. 1 V.

HE—Sch2

FAMILY (A) History. 3 pl., 5-44 pp. O. Taneytown, Md., 1909.

HH—A54

FAVRE, Rev. Robert. Present condition of the French-American Committee of Evangelization, Paris. (Huguenot Soc. of America. Proceedings, 1894. Vol. iii, pp. 92-95.)

HK—H871

FEEN, B. VAN DER, Genealogie de dieu. 8 pp. O. No place. 1895.
Reprint: Maandblad van het Geneal-herald. genootschap "De Nederlansche Leeuw," 1895. HH—W66

FELICE, G. DE. Histoire des protestants de France, depuis l'origine de la réformation jusqu'au temps présent, Deuxième édition. Paris, 1851. 655 pp. O. HA—F33

——— Histoire des Synodes nationaux des Eglises réformées de France. 2 leaves, 324 pp. D. Paris, 1864. HA—F33S

FELICE, PAUL DE. "Comment l'Edit de Nantes fut observe." (HUGUENOT Society of America. Publications. (Tercentenary Volume.) 1900. Translated by F. F. Du Fais. HK—H87

——— Mer (Loir et Cher) son église réformée; établissement, vie intérieure, décadence, restauration. Paris, 1885. 301 pp., map. O.
HA—F332

——— La Reforme en Blaisois: documents inédits. Registre du consistoire. (1665-1677.) LXI. 111 pp. D. Orleans, 1885.
HA—F 332 R

——— See: FRANCE, H. de. Les Montalbanais & le refuge. . . .
1887. HG—F84

FERET, P., ABBE. Un curé de Charenton au XVIIe siècle, [François Veron]. Paris, 1881. 3 leaves, IV, 5-160 pp. S. HG—F37
Author's autograph letter inserted.

FERGUSON, HENRY. Sir Edmund Andros. 32 pp. O. No place.
no date. HG—Mis68
Address delivered before the Westchester Co. Historical Society, October 28, 1892.

FERGUSSON, THOMAS COLYER. See: COLYER-FERGUSSON, Thomas.

FERNOW, BERTHOLD. Albany and its place in the history of the U. S. A memorial sketch written for the 200th anniversary of its birthday as a city. Albany, 1886. 98 pp. O. HE—F39

——— Editor & Compiler. Calendar of Wills . . . 1626-1836. Q. New York, 1896. (COLONIAL Dames, state of New York)
HK—C71

——— Minutes (The) of the Orphanmasters of New Amsterdam, 1655-1663. 1 p. l., VIII, 259 pp. Square O. New York, 1902. (COLONIAL Dames, State of N. Y., Vol. I.) One of 300 copies.
HK—C71.1—Vol. I

——— Editor. See: NEW AMSTERDAM. The Records of New Amsterdam . . . 1653-1674. 7 Vols. New York, 1897. Folio.
HE—N42

FERREE, BARR. Sentiment as a National asset. Oration delivered at the Fourth of July Celebration in Tenafly, N. J. . . . 13 pp. New York, 1908. HE—A512

FERRIERE, HECTOR DE LA. See: DE LA FERRIERE, Hector.

[FETIZON, PAUL.] Apologie pour les réforméz; où, On voit la juste idée des guerres civiles de France, et les vrais fondements de l'Edit de Nantes entretiens curieux, entre un protestant et un catholique. La Haye, 1683. 250 pp. TT.   HA—F43

FEW (A) plain facts by "Justice" concerning the plagiarisms . . . of the Merchant prince of Cornville: an original drama by Capt. Samuel Eberly Gross. . . . N. Y., 1910. xxxv pp. D.   HO—Pamphlet

FILLEAU. See: BEAUCHET-FILLEAU.

FIRST Reformed Church of Tarrytown, N. Y. First record book of the "Old Dutch Church of Sleepy Hollow," organized in 1697, and now the First Reformed Church of Tarrytown, N. Y. An original translation of its brief historical matter, and a copy . . . of its four registers . . . from its organization to 1791, by Rev. D. COLE, D.D., Yonkers, N. Y., 1901. vii, 2 leaves, 257 pp., 1 leaf, 51 facsim., 5 pl.   HH—F44
No. 122 of 500 copies printed.

FISHER, E. T., Translator. Report of a French Protestant refugee, in Boston, 1687 . . . 1868.   HB—R29

FISHER, GEORGE PARKE. History of the Christian Church. N. Y., 1887. 701 pp., maps. O.   HC—F53

FISHKILL, New York. Original deed of partition of land in the vicinity of Fish Kill, New York, between James Bontineau, Gillam Phillips and John Jones. 1751. MS.   HJ

FISKE, JOHN. Beginnings of New England, or, the Puritan theocracy in its relations to civil and religious liberty. 296 pp., map. Boston, 1889. O.   HE—A512

IRVING, WASHINGTON, Abridger. See: Washington and his Country. 1887.

FISKE, WILLARD. Lost (The) MS. of the Rev. Lewis Rou's "Critical remarks upon the letter to the craftsman on the game of chess" written in 1734 and dedicated to his Excellency William Cosby, Gov. of N. Y. (Signed W. F., i. e., Willard Fiske.) 18 pp. O. Florence (Italy), 1902.   HG—Pamphlet
Reprint: Notes and Queries, July 19, 1902, with additions.

FITCH, WILLIAM EDWARD. The First founders in America, with facts to prove that Sir Walter Raleigh's lost Colony was not lost. Paper read at a meeting of the N. Y. Society of the Order of the Founders & Patriots of America. . . . 40 pp., 1 map, folded. New York, 1913. O.   HE—A512

FLATBUSH Dutch Church, Flatbush, Long Island, N. Y. Records: Marriages, 1677, October 14th, 1757, November 5th.
Baptisms, 1677, September 16th, 1754, December 29th.
(HOLLAND Society of New York, Year-book, 1898. pp. 87-152.)   HK—H711

FLETCHER, CHARLES ROBERT LESLIE. Gustavus Adolphus and the struggle of Protestantism for existence. XVIII, 316 pp., 12 pl., 13 port., 3 maps, 1 table. O. New York, 1890. (Heroes of the nations.)　　　　　　　　　　　　　　　　　　　　　　　　HF—F62
No. 139 of 250 copies printed.

FLORIDA. See: SIMMS, W. G. LILY (The) and the totem, or, the Huguenots in Florida.　　　　　　　　　　　　　　　　　HB—Si4

FLORIDE Française. See: GAFFAREL, Paul. Histoiré de la Floride Française. Paris, 1875. O.　　　　　　　　　　　　　　HE—G12

FLOURNOIS, JACQUES. Extraits contenans tout ce qu'ily a d'important dans les registres publics de Geneve. Des l'an 1532 à 1536. I-CCIX pp., 3 leaves. Bound with: FROMMENT, Anthoine. Les actes et gestes merveilleux de la cité de Geneve . . . en fourme de Chroniques annales ou hystoyres commençant l'an MDXXXII. Mis en lumiere par G. Revilliod. O. Geneve, 1854.　　　HA—F922

FLUDD, MRS. ELIZA C. K. Biographical sketches of the Huguenot, Solomon Legare, & of his family . . . also reminiscences of the Revolutionary struggle with Great Britain. 142 pp. O. Charleston, S. C. 1886.　　　　　　　　　　　　　　　　　　　HH—L53

FONTAINE, FRANCIS. The exile: a tale of St. Augustine. N. Y. 1878. 114 pp. Square D.　　　　　　　　　　　　　　　HN—F73

FONTAINE, REV. JAMES. Born 1658. Memoirs of a Huguenot family, translated and compiled from the original autobiography and other family manuscripts, comprising an original journal of travels in Virginia, New York, etc., in 1715 and 1716, by Ann Maury, with an appendix containing a translation of the Edict of Nantes. N. Y. 1853. 512 pp., portraits. D.　　　　　　　　　　　HG—F73

FOOTE, WILLIAM HENRY. Huguenots; or, Reformed French Church; their principles delineated; their character illustrated; their sufferings and successes recorded. Richmond [Va. 1870]. 627 pp. O.
　　　　　　　　　　　　　　　　　　　　　　　　　HA—F73

FORD, PAUL LEICESTER, Compiler. Partial bibliography of the published works of members of the American historical association. (AMERICAN Hist. Association. Annual Report. 1890. pp. 163-386.)　　　　　　　　　　　　　　　　　　　HK—Am3—1890

———— & Clark, A. H., Compilers. Bibliography of the writings of the members of the American Historical Association for . . . 1890. (AMERICAN Hist. Association. Annual report. 1891. pp. 117-160.)　　　　　　　　　　　　　　　　　　　HK—Am3—1891

FORD, WORTHINGTON CHAUNCEY, Compiler. List of the Benjamin Franklin Papers in the Library of Congress. 322 pp. Washington, D. C., 1905. Square Q.　　　　　　　　　　　HE—F711

———— List of the Vernon-Wager MSS.: in the Library of Congress. With fac-simile of Letter of Admiral Charles Wager. 4 fac-sim., 148 pp. Washington, D. C., 1904. Q.　　　　　HF—F711v-w

———— Papers of James Monroe listed in chronological order from the original MSS.: in the Library of Congress. 6 fac-sim., 114 pp. Washington, D. C., 1904. Q. (The fac-sim. is the Purchase of Louisiana.)　　　　　　　　　　　　　　　　　HE—F711m

FORD, William F. Industrial interests of Newark, N. J., containing an historical sketch of the city. . . . 271 pp., illus., 1 map. O. N. Y., 1874.   HE—Z8

FORDHAM, New York. See: WALDRON, William Watson. Huguenots of Westchester and parish of Fordham. N. Y., 1864. S.   HB—W14

FORGUES, The Abbe Michel. Genealogy of the families of the Island of Orleans. 360 pp. O. (Appendix A; part II, Canadian Archives.)   HF—C213

FORMAN, Samuel S. Narrative of a journey down the Ohio & Mississippi in 1789-90; with a memoir and . . . notes by Lyman C. Draper. 67 pp. D. Cincin., 1888.   HI—F76

FOSDICK, Lucian J. French (The) blood in America. 4 leaves, 7-448 pp., 8 groups, 20 pl., 4 port. New York, cop. 1906. O.   HB—F74

FRANCE, H. de. Les Montalbanais et le refuge, augmenté des notes recueillies dans les archives de Berlin par Paul de Félice. Montauban, 1887. 553 pp. O.   HG—F84

FRANCKE, Rudolf. Die Franzosische colonie in Karlshafen. 16 pp. O. Magdeburg, 1892. (Der DEUTSCHE Hugenotten-Verein. Geschichtsblätter, 1892. V. 9.)   HK—D49

FRANKLIN, Alfred Louis Auguste. Les grandes scènes historiques du XVIe siècle, reproduction fac-similé du recueil de J. Tortorel et J. Perrisson. Paris, 1886. Illust., port., folio, half morocco.   HA—F85

FRANKLIN, Benjamin. List of the Benjamin Franklin Papers in Library of Congress. Washington, D. C., 1905. 322 pp. Edited by W. C. FORD. Square Q.   HF—F711F

FRANZOSISCHE Colonie. Zeitschrift für Vergangenheit und Gegenwart der Französische reformirten Gemeinden Deutschlands. Organ des Deutschen Hugenotten-Vereins. Hrsg. von R. BERINGUIER. Vols. 9-10, 11, 9-12, 12, 2-12, 13-14, 15, 1-11, 16; 2-5, 8-11. Berlin, 1895-1902. Q.   HK—D49.1

All of these bound into 3 volumes: Vols. 9-10, 13-14 are complete.

Largely composed of Huguenot history and genealogy, and the French Huguenot families whose genealogies in part or in whole are found therein are under "Family Genealogies" in our Bibliography.

FREDERIKS, J. G. De familie Vorsterman to Amsterdam. 8 pp. n.p., 1895. O.   HH—W66
Reprint: Maanblad . . . Geneal-herald. genootschap "De Nederlandsche Leeuw," 1895.

FREELAND, Mary de Witt. The records of Oxford, Mass. Including chapters of Nipmuck, Huguenot and English history from . . . 1630. . . . Square Q. 2 p. l., 429 pp. Albany, N. Y., 1894. (Munsell's Historical Series No. 22.)   HE—F87

FRENCH (The) blood in AMERICA. By L. J. FOSDICK. New York, 1906. O. HB—F74

FRENCH Church: The Hague, Holland. Trouwboek waalsche Gemeente, 15 April, 1691-27 December, 1699. HJ—H12W MS. A true copy of the entrances of Marriage made and presented to the Society by M. G. Wildeman.

FRENCH Church: New Paltz, New York. Copy and translation of the First Record Book, 1683-1704. MS. 19 pp., folio. Philadelphia, 1846. Translated by William E. DuBOIS, and Indexed by Mrs. E. M. C. A. Lawton. HJ—N558

FRENCH CHURCH du Saint Esprit, New York City. Historical sketches of the first and second edifaces, with wood-cut illustrations. (In: NEW YORK MIRROR, Vol. VIII, No. 2, page 9; Vol. XII, No. 22, page 168; No. 23, page 176; No. 24, page 148. New York, 1830-1835. Square folio. HL—N48

FRENCH colonists & exiles in the United States. Philadelphia, 1907. By J. G. ROSENGARTEN. HB—R71

FRENCH (The) Protestant Church . . . City of Charleston: "The Huguenot Church." A brief history of the Church, and two addresses delivered on the 225th Anniversary . . . April 14th, 1812. 1 pl., 38 pp. Charleston, S. C., 1912. Square O. HB—H875

———— 23 pp., 2 pl. Charleston, S. C., 1898. O. HB—F875 "Fr. Prot. Ch. in Charleston, S. C."

FRENCH PROTESTANT (HUGUENOT) CHURCH in the City of CHARLESTON, S. C. Historical notes: a Biographical list of Mural tablets in the . . . Church and Rules of the Fr. Prot. Ch. . . . adopted after revision, March 7, 1869. Square O. Charleston, 1898. 2-23 pp., 2 pl. O. HB—F875

———— Mural tablets in the Church, commemorating Huguenot ancestors. Biographical list. HB—F875

FRENCH PROTESTANT CHURCH. Liturgy; or, Forms of divine service. Translated from the Liturgy of the Church of Neufchatel and Vallagin, the whole adapted to public worship in the United States of America. Third edition. N. Y. [1853]. 228 pp. D. cloth.

———— In Memoriam William Ravenel and Peter Charles Gaillard. 16 pp. Charleston, 1889. O. HG—Mem51

FRENCH Protestant Hospital, London, England. Bibliotheque de la Providence. Catalogue of the Library, compiled by R. G. FABER, with an introduction by A. G. BROWNING. London, 1887, & 1890. (1st & later editions.) Q. & O.
HK—L84—L84.1—L84.1.1

———— Charter and By-laws of the Corporation of the Hospital for poor French Protestants . . . residing in Great Britain. XXVI, 65 pp., 2 plans, 3 plates. London, 1892. O. HB—F89

FRENCH Refugees. Letter to the French refugees, concerning their behavior to the government. . . . 24 pp. S. London, 1711. HA—B88

FRENCH settlement of the Mississippi Valley. By HAMILTON, Peter J. pp. 136-147. (Extract Amer. Hist. Mag. Vol. VII. No. 2.) O. HE—N533

FRENEAU, PHILIP. Poems relating to the American revolution, with an introductory memoir and notes by E. A. Duyckinck. N. Y., 1865. 288 pp., portrait, fac-sim. Q. HN—F88

FRIEDRICHSDORF: Colonie Reformee Francaise. Chronique de la Colonie . . . suivie de documents et pieces explicatives. Hambourg-es-Monts, 1887. VIII, 190 pp., 5 pl., 1 colored plate, 2 port. O. HC—F81

FROMMENT, ANTHOINE. Les actes et gestes merveilleux de la cite de Geneve . . . en fourme de Chronique annales ou hystoyres commencant l'an MDXXXII. Mis en lumiere par G. Revilliod. XXXI, 250 pp., 1 leaf, I-CCIX pp., 3 leaves, 36 pl., 4 port. O. Geneve, 1854. pp. I-CCIX, 3 leaves, are: FLOURNOIS, Jacques. Extraits . . . registers publics de Geneve. Des l'an 1532 a 1536. HA—F922

FROSSARD, CHARLES LOUIS. L'église sous la Croix pendant la domination Espagnole, chronique de l'église réformée de Lille. Paris, 1857. 336 pp., illust. O. HA—F921

——Numismatique protestante. Description de quarante et un méreaux de la communion réformée. Paris, 1872. 19 pp. O. HA—B645

—————— La réforme dans le Cambrésis au XVIe siècle (1566). Paris, 1855. 47 pp. O. (Bulletin de la Société de l'histoire du protestantisme français.) HA—B645

FROUDE, JAMES ANTHONY. Divorce of Catherine of Aragon . . . a supplementary volume to . . . Froude's "History of England." 476 pp. New York, 1891. O. HF—F93

FURNAS, ROBERT W., Editor. NEBRASKA State Historical Society. Transactions & reports. 1885. HK—N27

GAFFAREL, PAUL. Histoire du Brésil français au 16e siècle. Paris, 1878. 512 pp., map. O. HF—G12

—————— Histoire de la Floride française. Paris, 1875. 522 pp., map. O. HE—G12

GAILLARD, THOMAS. History of the reformation in the church of Christ, continued from close of the 15th century. N. Y. 1847. 557 pp. O. HC—G12

—————— Names of French Refugees who emigrated to South Carolina. (HUGUENOT Society of America. Proceedings. New York, 1884. Vol. I, part 1. pp. 53-54. Q.) HK—H87.1

GALERIES Historiques de Versailles. See: [GAVARD, J. D. C.]

GALLAND, J. A.   Essai sur l'histoire du Protestantisme à Caen et en Basse-Normandie, de l'Edit de Nantes a la Révolution (1598-1791). Thèse pour le dicotrat présentée à la Faculté des Lettres de l'Université de Paris.   3 leaves, xxxviii, 550 pp., 1 leaf, 1 map.   Q.   Paris, 1898.   HA—G13

GALLAUDET, Edward M., LL.D.   The family of Priuli, also called Prioli, Priolo, Prioleau.   (HUGUENOT Society of America. Proceedings, 1891.   Vol. ii.   pp. 299-321.)   HK—H87.1

GARRETT, W. R.   History of the South Carolina cession and the northern boundary of Tennessee.   Nashville, 1884.   32 pp.   O. (Tennessee Historical Society.   Papers.)   HE—Pamphlet

GAUDET, Placide.   Acadian genealogy and notes.   i-xxxiv, 372 pp. O.   (Appendix A, Part iii.   Canadian Archives.   Vol. ii.)   HF—C213

GAULLIEUR, Ernest.   Histoire de la réformation à Bordeaux, et dans le ressort du parlement de Guyenne.   Bordeaux, 1884.   Vol. i, O.   HA—G23

[GAVARD, Jacques Dominique Charles.]   GALERIES historiques de Versailles [text].   2 vols. in 1, folio, half morocco.   HO—G24

GENEALOGICAL (The) Advertiser.   A quarterly magazine of family history.   Vols. i-iv.   Cambridge, Mass., 1898.   4 vols. in 3.   Edited by L. H. Greenlaw.   HH—G32

GENEALOGICAL Queries and memoranda.   A quarterly magazine devoted to genealogy, family history, heraldry and topography.   Edited by G. F. T. Sherwood.   V. i.   Nos. 1-3, 8-10.   O.   London, 1896-'98.   HH—Pamphlet Box

GENEALOGIES: Reprints of N. Y. Gen. & Biog. Record.   Collected and bound together, representing 18 families.   n. t. p.   N. Y., 1863-97.   O.   HH—V42G

GENEALOGY of the Hoffman family, descendants of Martin Hoffman, with biographical notes.   By the Very Rev. Eugene Augustus Hoffman, D.D., New York, 1899.   O.   HH—H65 No. 7 of 250 copies.

GERARD, James Watson.   The old stadt Huys of New Amsterdam; a Paper read before the New York Historical Society, June 15, 1875. 59 pp.   O.   N. Y., 1875.   HE—Z3

——— The old streets of New York under the Dutch; a Paper read before the New York Historical Society, June 2, 1874.   65 pp.   O. N. Y., 1874.   HE—Z3 No. 5 of a vol. of pamphlets.

——— Retribution of Louis XIV.   (Huguenot Society of America. Proceedings.   1891.   Vol. ii., pp. 155-175.)   HK—H87.1

GEROULD, Samuel L.   Genealogy of the family of Gamaliel Gerould, son of Dr. Jacques (or James) Jerould of the province of Languedoc, France.   Bristol, N. H., 1885.   84 pp.   O.   HH—G31

GESLACHT: Register der oude Kaapsche familien. Gecompileerd door Christoffel Coetzee de Villiers. In 3 Vols. Vols. I-III. Square O. Kaapstad, 1894.
                                                                   HH—G33
Deel 1. A tot J.
  " 2. K " O.
  " 3. P " Z.

GESLACHTLIJST der familie deComte later genaamd Voute. 1 p. l., 11 pp., 1 pl. Square folio. 's-Gravenhage, 1893.   HH—V97 Behoort bij No. 2, van het algemeen Nederlandsch Familieblad, 10e jaargang.

GENEVE: See: Fromment, Anthoine. Les actes et gestes merceilleux de la cité of Geneve. . . . [Together with: FLOURNOIS, J., Extraits . . . registres publics de Geneve. Des l'an 1532 à 1536. O. Geneve, 1854.]   HA—F922

GIGLIOTTI, NICOLA. Cor Mundi. The Heart of the World. A contribution to the Mission of the United States of America in the modern war. 2 leaves, 684 pp., 1 leaf. [Erie, Pa., 1918.] O.
                                               HF—Pamphlet

GILLE TILLEMAN et les siens; ou, La Bible aux Pays-Bas sous la domination espagnole: drame historique en cinq actes. Par un Huguenot. 88 pp. Bruxelles, 1896. D.   HN—AH8

GILLETT, WILLIAM KENDALL. See: JACKSON, Samuel Macauley. Edict of Nantes: with a translation of the Edict, together with that of the Revocation of the Edict . . . revised by W. K. G. [New York, 1898.] O.   HA—N19

GILLIS, PETRUM. Kerckelijck Historie van de Gereformeerde Kercken . . . uyt het Frans in 'tNederduyts vertaalt door Gillis van Breen. 24, 496, 44 pp. Amsterdam, 1657. D.

GILMAN, THEODORE. Huguenots as founders and patriots. An Address . . . before the N. Y. Society, Order of Founders & Patriots of America . . . March 27, 1913. 16 pp. New York, 1913. O.
                                             HB—B88

GODET, FRÉDÉRIC. Histoire de la réformation et du refuge dans le pays de Neuchatel, conférences tenues à Neuchatel. Neuchatel, 1859. 302 pp. D.   HB—G54

GODFRAY, HUMPHREY MARETT, Editor. Registre des baptesmes, mariages et morts, et jeusnes de l'église Wallonne et des isles de Jersey, Guernesey . . . etc., établie à Southampton par patente du roy Edouard sixe et la reine Elizabeth. 172 pp. Q. Lymington, 1890. (HUGUENOT Society of London. Publications, 1890. Vol. IV.)
                                  HK—H875—Vol. IV

GOLDSMITH, OLIVER, Translator. MARTEILHE, Jean. Huguenot galley-slave, being the autobiography of a French Protestant condemned . . . for . . . his religion. Translated from the French. xv, 24 pp. N. Y., 1867. D.   HA—M36

GOODE, George Brown. Origin of the national scientific & educational institutions of the United States. (AMERICAN Historical Association. Annual Report, 1890. pp. 53-161.)

HK—Am3—1889

——— Virginia cousins; a study of the ancestry & posterity of John Goode of Whitby . . . with notes upon related families, a key to Southern genealogy & a history of the English surname Gode, Goad, Goode or Good from 1148-1887 with a preface by R. A. Brock. xxxvi, & 526 pp., illus., port., pl. Q. Richmond, Va. 1887. Copy No. 139.

HH—G54

GOSS, Elbridge Henry. Life of Col. Paul Revere. 2 Vols., illus., port., pl., fac-sim. Boston, 1891. O.

HG—R32

GOULART, Simon. See: CRESPIN, Jean, et GOULART, S. Histoire des martyrs. . . . Avec deux indices. . . . 8 p.l., 1526 pp., folio, no place. 1597.

HG—C86

——— Ed. nouvelle, en 3 tomes. Q. Toulouse, 1885-'89.

HG—C86.2

GOUTTEPAGNON, Maurice de. See: BEAUCHET-FILLEAU, Henri & Paul. Dictionnaire . . . des familles du Poitou . . . 2 ed. Poitiers, 1891-continuing.

HG—B38

GRAVES, Horace. Huguenot (The) in New England. No place, no date.

HB—H89

Volume entitled: "Huguenot Essays."

GRAYSON, William J. James Louis Petigru, a biographical sketch. 178 pp., 1 port. New York, 1866. D.

HG—P44

GREEN, Frank Bertangue. History of Rockland county [New York]. N. Y., 1886. 444 pp., map, 4to.

HE—G82

GREEN, Thomas Marshall. Historic families of Kentucky, with special reference to stocks derived from the valley of Virginia. First series. Cincinnati, 1889. 304 pp., port., 8vo.

HH—G82

GREENLAW, Lucy Hall, Editor. Genealogical (The) Advertiser. A quarterly magazine of family history. Vol. i-iv. Cambridge, Mass. 1898-1901. 4 Vol. in 3 Vol. O.

HH—G32

GRIFFIN, Appleton Prentiss Clark, Compiler. Bibliography of the historical societies of the U. S. (AMERICAN Hist. Assoc. Annual report. 1891. pp. 161-267.)

HK—Am3—1891

GRIFFIN, George Butler, Ed. & Tr. Documents from the Sutro collection. 213 pp., 1 fac-sim. O. Los Angeles, 1891. (SOUTHERN Cal. Hist. Soc. Publications. 1891. Vol. ii, part 1.)

HK—C13

Spanish text with English translation.

GRIFFITH, Thomas W. Sketches of the early history of Maryland. 76 pp., 1 leaf, 1 pl. Baltimore, 1821. O.

HE—G854

GRIGSBY, Hugh Blair. History of the Virginia federal convention of 1788 . . . with a . . . sketch of the author & . . . notes by R. A. Brock. Vol. i-ii. O. Richmond, Va., 1890-91. (Virginia hist. soc. Coll. New ser. Vol. ix-x.)   HK—V81—V.9
Vol. ii. contains accounts of the Virginians who were members of the convention.

GROSE, G. Address on Huguenot influence upon our early Colonial life. (HUGUENOT Society of America. Proceedings. New York, 1906. Vol. v. pp. 51-56. Q.)   HK—H87.1

GUILLE Alles Library & Museum. Encyclopædic catalogue of the lending department, compiled under the direction of A. Cotgreave, assisted by H. Boland. 1 p.l., xlvii, 1220 pp. S. Guernsey, 1891.   HK—C94
Bound with: Bibliotheque Guille-Alles . . . section française . . . par Henri Boland. 4 p.l., 273 pp. S. Londres, 1889.

GUIZOT, François Pierre Guillaume. History of France from the earliest times to 1848; by Guizot and Madame Guizot de Witt. Translated by Robert Black. N. Y., 1887. 8 vols. port., pl. D.
HD—G94

GUMBEL, Theodore. Die Wallonisch-französische fremdengemeinde in St. Lambrecht-Grevenhausen. 21 pp. O. Magdeburg, 1893. (DEUTSCHE Huguenotten Verein. Geschichtsblätter, 1893. No. 10, pt. 2.)   HB—T57

GUNITZ, E., Editor. See: BEZE, Theodore de. Histoire ecclesiastique des eglises reformees au royaumè de France. . . . 1833-'89.
HA—B46

GUSTAVUS, Adolphus, and the struggle of Protestantism for existence, by C. R. L. Fletcher. N. Y., 1890. O.   HF—F62

GUYOT, Henri Daniel. Deux (Les) compagnie de francais refugies a Groningue . . . 15 pp. O. Groninque, 189. No title page. Bound with: VERMILYE, A. G. Huguenot element among the Dutch.   HB—A2H

——— Episode de la Revocation de l'edit de Nantes. 23 pp. O. Groningue, 1907.   HA—N19

——— Genealogie de la famille Guyot avec piejes justificatives. 38 pp. 1 ed. O. Groninque, 1892.   HH—Var4

——— 40 pp., 2 ed. O. Groninque, 1900.   HH—Var4

——— Marquis de Venours, protecteur des victimes de l'intolérance de Louis XIV. 31 pp. O. Groninque, 1906.   HG—S33
Volume .?.. "Biographical & Historical Essays."

HAAG, Emile. See: HAAG, Eugène & Emile. La France protestante. . . .   HG—H11

HAAG, Eugène & Emile.   La France protestante.   Deuxième édition
publiée sous les auspices de la Société de l'histoire du protestantisme
français et sous la direction de Henri Bordier.   Paris, 1877-88.   O.
Vols. I-VI.   HG—H11
A—Gas.

HACKENSACK, New Jersey.   See: ROMEYN, Rev. T. B.   Historical discourse. . . . First Reformed (Dutch) Church.   N. J.,
1870.   O.   HC—R66

HAGUE, William.   Old Pelham and New Rochelle.   1882.   Por-
trait.   O.   HB—H12
From the *Magazine of American History*, 1882, vol VIII.

HAGUE (The) Holland.   See: ENGLISH (The) Church in the
Hague.   The oldest Church-book . . . a transcript by M. G. Wildeman.   O.   The Hague, 1906.   HB—W67E

———— French Church; Trouwboek waalsche Gemeente, 14 April,
1691-27 December, 1699.   Folio.   HJ—H12W
MS.   Copy of the entrances of Marriage, made by M. G. Wilde-
man, in A.D., 1895.   Original Registers . . . at the Town House,
(Record Office.)

HALE, John P.   Trans-Allegheny pioneers: historical sketches of the
first white settlements west of the Alleghenies.   1748 and after.
Cincinnati [1886.]   330 pp., illus., port., fac-sim., cloth.   D.
                                                                              HE—H13

HALL, Rev. Edwin, Compiler.   Ancient historical records of Norwalk, Conn., with a plan of the ancient settlement, and of the town
in 1847.   (And the Genealogical register of marriages, births and
deaths.)   320 pp., 1 map.   D., Norwalk, Conn., 1847.   Contains
Autograph of the compiler.   HE—N83h

HALL, Rev. Thomas Cuming, D.D.   The inner spirit of the Calvinistic Puritan State.   (In: UNION Theo. Seminary.   Three addresses delivered at a Service in commemoration of the 400th Anniversary of the birth of John Calvin.)   New York, 1909.   47 pp.
O.   pp. 36-47.   HM—Pamphlet

HAMILTON, Frank Hastings, M.D., 1813-86.   Eulogy on the life
and character of Theodric Romeyn Beck, M.D., delivered before the
Medical Society of the State of New York.   90 pp., 1 port.   O.
Albany, 1856.   HE—Z1

HAMILTON, Peter J.   French (The) settlement of the Mississippi
Valley.   (pp. 136-147.   Amer. Hist. Mag. Vol. VII, No. 2.)   O.
                                                                              HE—N533

HANNA, William.   Wars of the Huguenots.   N. Y. 1882.   344 pp.
plates.   D.   HA—H19

HANOTAUX, Gabriel.   Etudes historiques sur le 16e et le 17e siècle
en France.   Paris, 1886.   350 pp.   D.   HD—H19

HANOVER, Mass. A copy of the records of births, marriages and deaths . . . of the town of Hanover, Mass. 1727-1857. Prepared under . . . direction of . . . a committee appointed by said town. VI, 319 pp. O. Rockland, 1898. HH—H19

HARLEM, New York. See: TILTON, Rev. Edgar, Jr., D.D. Reformed Low Dutch Church of Harlem, organized 1660. Historical sketch. New York, 1910. O. HC—T58

HARPER, LILLIE DuPUY VanCULIN, Editor. Colonial men and times. Containing the Journal of Col. Daniel Trabue, some account of his ancestry, life and travels in Virginia and Kentucky during the Revolutionary period: The Huguenots: Genealogy, with brief sketches of the allied families. 6 p. l., 3-624 pp., 2 groups, 36 pl., 15 port. Philadelphia, 1916. Q. HH—H294

HARPER'S New Monthly Magazine. No. LXXXIII, April, 1857. Vol. XIV. New York, 1857. H·N—C77

HARRISON, Westchester County, New York. See: BAIRD, C. W. History of Rye . . . 1660-1870. . . . Harrison, and the White Plains, till 1788. O. N. Y., 1871. HE—B16

HART, GERALD E. Fall of New France, 1755-1760. Montreal, 1888. 175 pp., port., pl., fac-sim. O. HE—H25

HARTLEY, REV. ISAAC SMITHSON, D.D. Historical discourse delivered on the occasion of the semi-centennial year of the Reformed Church, Utica, N. Y., Jan., 1880. 68 pp., 2 pl. Utica, 1880. HE—Z1

——— Editor. See: HARTLEY, Robert Milham. Memorial. . . . Utica, 1882. O. HG—H25

HARTLEY, ROBERT MILHAM. 1796-1881. Memorial of R. M. H., edited by his son, I. S. Hartley, D.D. 549 pp., portrait and plate. (Extracts from his diary, and other writings included.) Utica, 1882. O. HG—H25

HARVEY, CORNELIUS BURNHAM, Editor. Genealogical history of Hudson and Bergen counties, New Jersey. 2 p. l., 617 pp., 51, 1 map. New York, 1900. Q. HE—H26

HASBROUCK. Historical facts and Chronological table of Hasbrouck family. Compiled by H. C. Colver. 12 pp. Seattle, Wash., 1904?. O. HH—A54

HASTINGS, HUGH, Compiler & Editor. Military minutes of the Council of Appointment of the State of New York, 1783-1821. 4 Vols. O. Albany, N. Y., 1901-02. HE—H27

HAWKS, JOHN, MAJOR. Orderly book and journal, on the Ticonderoga-Crown Point campaign, under General Jeffrey. Amherst, 1759-1760. Introduction by Hon. Hugh Hastings. New York, 1911. XII, 92 pp. O. HK—CW 712 N

HAYDEN, REV. HORACE EDWIN. Oliver genealogy.

HAZARD, WILLIS P. See: WATSON, J. F. Annals of Philadelphia, and Pennsylvania, in the olden time. . . . Illus., 3 vols. O. Phila., 1891.　　　　　　　　　　　　　　　　HE—WATS.33

HEIRESS (The). A Comedy in five acts, by Sir John BURGOYNE. With Prologue by the Right Hon. Richard Fitzpatrick. Also gives Dramatis personae. Hertford-Street, Feb. 1st, 1786. D.　HN—B957

HELFFENSTEIN, ABRAHAM ERNEST. Pierre Fauconnier, and his descendants; with some account of the allied Valleaus. 4 p. l., VII-IX, 226 pp., 2 col. pl., 6 pl., 20 port. Philadelphia, 1911. Q.
　　　　　　　　　　　　　　　　　　　　　　　　HH—F25

HENRY IV. Job le bon Roy Henry. 48 pp., colored plates. Tours, [1894?]. Oblong O. Hermant A.　　　　　　　　　　HD—H55

HENRY, WILLIAM WIRT. Oration on the 100th anniversary of the introduction of the "Resolutions respecting independency," delivered on June 7, 1876, at . . . Philadelphia. . . . 31 pp. Q. Phil., 1876.　　　　　　　　　　　　　　　　　　　　　　HE—Z9

HENRY CLAY PAYNE. A life. [By William W. Wight.] 3 l., 196 pp., 1 port. Milwaukee, 1907. Q.　　　　　　HG—P346

HENTY, G. A. St. Bartholomew's Eve. A Tale of the Huguenot wars. 384 pp., 12 pl., 1 map. D. New York, 1893.　　HN—H

HERALDRY. See: LANNOY, Mortimer Delano. Bibliography of American Heraldry. 12 pp. D. New York, 1896.　　HH—D37

HERALDRY. See: Volume III of LeLABOUREUR, J. Memoires de Messire Michel de Castelnau . . . avec . . . genealogies de plusieurs maisons illustres alliees a celle de Castelnau. Nouvelle ed. Tome I-III. Bruxelles, 1731. F.　　　　　　　HG—L53

HERALDRY illustrated . . . with directions for drawing & painting coats-of-arms. . . . By W. H. ABBOTT. New York, cop. 1897. O.　　　　　　　　　　　　　　　　HH—A2

HERBERT, HENRY WILLIAM, Translator. See. WEISS, Charles. History of the French Protestant refugees. 1854.　HA—W43

HERMANT A. Job le bon Roy Henry. 48 pp., colored plates. Tours, 1894? Oblong O. [Bordier L., Illustrator.]　　HD—H55

HERRICK, JEDEDIAH. Herrick genealogy, genealogical register of the name and family of Herrick from the settlement of Henerie Hericke, in Salem, Mass., 1629-1846, with a concise notice of their English ancestry. Revised, augmented and brought down to 1885, by Lucius C. Herrick. Columbus, Ohio, 1885. 516 pp., illus., port. O.
　　　　　　　　　　　　　　　　　　　　　　　　HH—H43

HERRICK, LUCIUS C., Editor. See. HERRICK, Jedediah. Herrick genealogy . . . 1885.　　　　　　　　　　　HH—H43

HESTER, REV. ST.CLAIR, D.D. Lafayette, the Apostle of Liberty. Sermon preached in the Church of the Messiah . . . Brooklyn, N. Y., May 13, 1917. . . . Brooklyn, 1917. 6 l., 1 pl. O. Illustrated cover.　　　　　　　　　　　　　　HG—Pamphlet

HIGGINSON, Thomas Wentworth. French voyageurs. 1883.
Illustrated. O.   HB—H12
From *Harper's Magazine,* 1883, vol. 66.

HILL, Hamilton Andrews. History of the Old South Church,
(Third Church), Boston, 1669-1884. 2 vols., port., pl., fac-sim.
Boston, 1890.   HC—H55

HILL, William G., Compiler. Family record of . . . James W.
Converse and Elisha S. Converse, including some of the descendants
of Roger de Coigneries . . . Edward Converse . . . Robert Wheaton . . . William Edmonds . . . John Coolidge. . . . IV, 241 pp.,
19 port., 8 pl. O. Boston, 1887.   HH—Con74
Privately printed.

HISTOIRE, de l'Edit de Nantes. 1693-95. BENOIT, Elie. 5 tomes,
pl. Delft, 1693-95. Q.   HA—B44

HISTOIRE des martyrs persécutez et mis à mort pour la vérité de
l'Evâgile depuis le temps des Apostres insques à l'an 1597. . . .
Avec deux indices . . . par Jean CRESPIN et Simon GOULART.
8 leaves, 1526 pp., folio, no place, 1597. Vélin blanc ancien aux
armes frappées en or sur les plats et au dos de la ville d'Amsterdam.   HG—C86

———— Edition nouvelle. En 3 tomes. Q. Toulouse, 1885.   HG—C86.2
Gift of The French Society.

HISTOIRE des plus favoris anciens et modernes, recueillie par feu
. . . P. du Puy. Avec un journal de ce qui s'est passé à la mort du
mareschal d'Ancre. Square O. Leide, 1659.   HG—D92

HISTOIRE des souffrances du bienheureux martyr Louis de Marolles.
1883. Par MAROLLES, de., fils.   HG—M34

HISTORICAL SOCIETY Newburgh & The Highlands. Historical
Papers. Newburgh, N. Y., 1894-1901. 2 Nos. O. Number for
1894: The Huguenots of Ulster Co., N. Y., by R. LeFevre. No.
VIII for 1901: M. E. Church, Newburgh, N. Y. Record of Births
and Marriages, 1789-1835.   HE—N533
In Pamphlet Volume.

———— Same, in another Pamphlet Volume.   HE—H62V

HISTORY of the Protestant reformation in France. O. 2 Vols. By
Mrs. A. Marsh. London, 1849.   HA—M35

HITCHCOCK, Roswell Dwight. Life and writings of Edward
Robinson. . . . 100 pp. New York, 1863. D.   HG—R56

HOES, Rev. Roswell Randall. Baptismal and marriage registers
of the Old Dutch Church of Kingston, Ulster County, N. Y., (formerly named Wiltwyck, and often familiarly called Esopus or
'Sopus), for 150 years from their commencement in 1660. 795 pp.
New York, 1891. Folio.   HC—Hoes67

HOFFMAN, CHARLES FENNE. The Pioneers of New York. Anniversary discourse before St. Nicholas Society of Manhattan, Dec. 6, 1847. 55 pp. O. N. Y., 1848. HE—A512
(Reprint, January, 1915.)
No. 1, of Pamphlet Volume "Americana."

HOFFMAN, VERY REV. EUGENE AUGUSTUS, D.D., Genealogy of the Hoffman family, descendants of Martin Hoffman, with biographical notes, v-x, 1 leaf, 545 pp., 1 fac-sim., 3 pl., 14 port. O. New York, 1899. HH—H65
No. 7, of 250 copies.

HOLDEN, JAMES AUSTIN. State Historian. The Centenary of the Battle of Plattsburg, 1814-September 11, 1914, at Plattsburg, N. Y., Sept. 6-11, 1914. 98 pp., 1 fac-sim. Albany, N. Y., 1914. O. (University State N. Y.) HE
Fully illustrated: plates paged.

HOLGATE, JEROME B. American genealogy . . . some of the early settlers of North America and their descendants, their intermarriages and collateral branches, with genealogical tables. 3 pl., 244 pp. Albany, 1848. Square folio. HH—H731

HOLLAND Society of New York. Annual dinner, 1886. Port., pl. New York, 1886. Q. HK—H711
Subsequent Annual Dinners bound with the Year Book.
Volume lettered: "First Annual Dinner."

———— Collections. Vols. I & III. 2 Vols. in 3. New York, 1891, 1896. HK
Vol. I, part 1, Records. Reformed Dutch Church of Hackensack, N. J. 1891.
Vol. I, part 2, Records. Reformed Dutch Church of Schraelenburgh, N. J. 1891.
Vol. III. Records. Reformed Dutch Church of New Paltz, New York. 1896.

———— Constitution, by-laws, officers and members. 1891-1894. 3 vols. New York, 1891-'94. HK—H71

———— Constitution, by-laws, officers and members. New York, 1891-'94. 3 Vols. HK—H71
Gift of the Society.

———— Report on a Tablet commemorative of the services rendered by Baron Joan Derck van Calellen Tot den Pol, of Overyssel, Holland, on behalf of the North American Colonies in . . . the Revolution . . . June 6, 1908. New York, 1909. 33 pp., 6 pl. O.
Gift of Mr. J. R. Van Wormer. HK—ReH711.van

———— Year Book, 1886-'89, 1894-1900, 1902-1907, 1913-1914, 1917. New York, 1886-1917. 19 Vols. Q.
Illustrated with portraits and plates.
Earlier Volumes are the Gift of the late Theodore M. Banta; later Volumes are the Gift of the Society.
These Volumes are catalogued separately by Title or Author entry, in Class HK; also by cross-reference entries.

HOLLANDSCH-AMERIKAANSCH almanak en jaarboekje. N. Y. 1883. 12mo. HO—Pamphlet

HOLMDEN, ANNIE HARWOOD, Translator. See: BERSIER, Eugene. Coligny: the earlier life of the great Huguenot. . . . 1886. HG—C68

HOLMES, OLIVER WENDELL. Our hundred days in Europe. Boston, 1887. 329 pp. 12 mo. HI—H73

HOMESTEAD (The) of a Colonial Dame. A Monograph. By Alice Cary Sutcliffe. Poughkeepsie, N. Y., 1909. Illus. O. HH—A54

HOOD, JENNINGS, & YOUNG, C. J., Compilers. American Orders and their decorations. The objects of the military and naval orders. Commemorative and patriotic societies of the United States and the requirements for membership therein. 107 pp., 18 colored plates. O. Philadelphia, cop. 1917. HK—A5

HOOGSTRATEN, JOHN VAN. Afscheidsgroete, aan den heeren . . . diaconen der Walsche gereformeerde kerke in 's Graavenhaage. 3 pp. No title page. 1780. O. HH—W66

HOPITAL (L') pour les Pauvres Française Protestants. Ordre a Suivre au Culte Divin a l'occasion de l'Anniversaire. London, no date. 8 pp. Small square O. HM—L78.1
Bound with Eglise Protestant Française de Canterbéry.
Service du Culte Divin pour les Solennites de l'Eglise Française et autres occasions speciales.

HORSFORD, EBEN NORTON. Defences of Norumbega and a review of the reconnaissances of T. W. Higginson, Henry W. Haynes . . . & others . . . 4-84 pp., illus., pl., maps. Boston, 1891. HE—H782

——— Discovery of America by Northmen; Address at the unveiling of the statue of Leif Eriksen delivered, Oct. 29, 1887. 113 pp., illus., pl., maps. Boston, 1888. HE—H78

——— Discovery of the ancient city of Norumbega; a Communication to the . . . American Geographical Society. Nov. 21, 1889. 55 pp., pl., maps. Boston, 1890. HE—H781

HOTTEN, JOHN CAMDEN, Editor. The original lists of persons of quality, emigrants, religious exiles, political rebels, and others who went from Great Britain to the American plantations, 1600-1700. With . . . other interesting particulars. From MSS. preserved in the State Paper Dept., of Her Majesty's Public Record Office, England. 2d edition. XXXII, 33-580 pp. Q. New York, 1880. HH—H79

HOUGHTON, LOUISE SEYMOUR. Idealism of the French people. 3 leaves, 7-80 pp. Boston. [Cop. 1918.] O.

HOUSE (The) of the Wolf. By Stanley J. WEYMAN. Philadelphia, [1898?]. S. HN—W54

HOUSTON, Florence Amelia Wilson. Blaine, L. C., & Mellette, E. D. Maxwell history and genealogy, including the allied families. Also Baptismal record of the Rev. John Craig, D.D., of Augusta County, Virginia, 1740-1749. 8 p. l., 642 pp., 7 pl., 4 groups, 34 port. O. Indianapolis, Ind., [cop. 1916.]   HH—M465

HOVENDEN, Robert, Editor. Registers of the Wallon or Strangers' Church in Canterbury. Lymington, 1891. (HUGUENOT Society of London. Publications. 1891. Vol. v, parts 1-3. 1 vol. in 3.)   HK—H87

HOWARD, Charles Wallace. Sermon at the re-opening and dedication of the French Protestant Church of Charleston, S. C., 11 May, 1845. Charleston, 1845. 24 pp. 8vo.

HOWARD, George Elliotte. Introduction to the local Constitutional History of the United States. Baltimore, 1889. O. (JOHNS Hopkins University Studies in Hist. & Pol. Science. Extra Volumes. No. 4.)   HE—H83
Vol. i. Development of the Township, Hundred, and Shire.

HOWE, Henry. The sad, heart-touching, but ennobling history of Captain Nathan Hale, the hero-martyr of the American Revolution. . . . 21 pp., illus. New Haven, Conn., 1881.   HE—Z2

HOWE, Rt. Rev. William Bell White, Bishop of the Diocese of S. C. Sermon preached in St. Philip's Church, Charleston, S. C., May 12, 1875. (Charleston, S. C., St. Philip's Church, Special services . . . 1876. . . . pp. 51-76.)   HC—C38

HUDSON County, New Jersey. See: HARVEY, C. B. Genealogical history of Hudson & Bergen Counties. New York, 1900. Q.
          HE—H26

——— See: WINFIELD, C. H. History of the County of Hudson. New York, 1874. O.   HE—W72

HUGHES, Thomas P. American ancestry: giving the name and descent in the male line of Americans whose ancestors settled in the United States previous to the Declaration of Independence, A.D. 1776. Albany, 1887. Vols, i, ii and iii, part 1, illustrated, 4to, boards.   HH—H87
Vol. i. City of Albany, N. Y.
Vol. ii. Columbia Co., N. Y.
Vol. iii. Embracing lineages from the whole of the U. S.

HUGUENOT Seminary, Wellington, South Africa. Catalogue. Cape Town, 1882, also later pamphlets.   HO—Pamphlet

HUGUENOT (A). Pseudonym. Gilleman et les siens; ou, la Bible aux Pays-Bas sous la domination espagnole: drame historique en cinq actes. Bruxelles, 1896. 88 pp. D.   HN—AH8

HUGUENOT element in Charleston's pronunciation. By S. PRIMER, Ph. D., Charleston, S. C., 1889. pp. 214-244. O.   HB—H89
Volume—"Huguenot Essays."

HUGUENOT Essays: (Collection of Papers & Essays bound in one Volume.) HB—H89

HUGUENOT exiles, or the Times of Louis XIV. A historical novel by Eliza A. Du Puy. New York, 1856. D. HN—D94

HUGUENOT families in America. By Charles Weiss. Boston, 1862. (Continental (The) Monthly. Vol. I, Nos. 2-4. pp. 231, 151-155, 298-302, 461-465.) O. HB—H897

HUGUENOT galley-slave: autobiography of a French Protestant. . . . By Jean Marteilhe. Translated from the French. New York, 1867. HA—M36

HUGUENOT Garland. Compiled by Julia H. L. De Vaynes. 1890. HA—D49

HUGUENOT lovers: a Tale of the Old Dominion. By C. P. E. Bourgwyn. Richmond, Va., 1889. S. HN—B95

HUGUENOT (The) in New England. By Horace Graves. No place, no date. pp. 497-503. HB—H89
(Volume "Huguenot Essays.")

HUGUENOT memorials of the Refugees who came to America before and after the Revocation of the Edict of Nantes, 1685. HB—B88

HUGUENOT (The) refugee. Song written by Dr. Byles, with music by W. Ryves. 6 pp. No place, no date. Q. HO—Pamphlet

HUGUENOT refugees in England, Ireland, Holland, and America, 1514-1900. Compiled by Mrs. F. J. P. Scott. Rochester, N. Y., 1905. Oblong folio. HH—S425

HUGUENOT (The), a Tale of the French Protestants. By G. P. R. James. New York, 1839. 2 Vols. D. HN—Hug. 87

HUGUENOT'S (A) ride. Copied from Todd's History of New York, and read before the Society by Mrs. Sanford Bissell, at a Meeting held April 14, 1915. (HUGUENOT Society of America. Publications. Vol. IV, pp. 165-166. 1915.)
HK—H87

HUGUENOTS (The). See: GEROULD, S. L., Compiler. Genealogy of the Gerould family. Bristol, 1885. pp. 68-72. HH—G31

HUGUENOTS (The): an Account of their persecution in France, emigration to America, and settlement, particularly Bartholomew Du Puy and his descendants. (See: HARPER, L. DuP. Van C., Editor.) Colonial men and times. Philadelphia, 1916. Part 2. Q. HH—H294

HUGUENOTS in France and America. By Mrs. H. F. (Sawyer) Lee. 1843. HA—L51

HUGUENOT Society of America. Collections. Rev. Alfred V. Wittmeyer, Editor. Registers of the births, marriages and deaths of the "Eglise François à la Nouvelle York," from 1688-1804; and historical documents relating to the French protestants in New York during the same period. N. Y., 1886. 431 pp., plates, fac-simile.

HK—H87.3

–––––– Proceedings. May 29th, 1883-June 15th, 1914. Vols. i-viii. New York, 1884-1915. 8 vols. in 5 vols. O.   HK—H87.1
Vol. i, Part 1, reprinted, December, 1889.
Vol. vi, Reprinted June, 1914.

A complete set of the Proceedings, including the two reprints and the separate volume of "Huguenot Ancestry," Vol. vii (that was also issued bound with reprint of Vol. vi), together with copies of the several editions of the Constitution, By-laws, and list of Members, are beautifully bound in half-morocco, actually comprise eleven volumes bound in five.

–––––– Publications. New York, 1885-1915. 4 vols. Q.   HK—H87
Vol. i.   Commemoration of the Bi-Centenary of the Revocation of the Edict of Nantes, October 22nd, 1885, at New York. 86 pp. New York, 1886. Q. Half-morocco.
Vol. ii.   Catalogue of the books, pamphlets, and MSS. belonging to the Huguenot Society of America. Compiled by Elizabeth G. Baldwin. x, 107 pp. New York, 1890. Q.
Vol. iii. Ter-Centenary Celebration of the Promulgation of the Edict of Nantes, April 13th, 1598. 2 p.l., lxiii, 464 pp., 1 fac-sim. (1st and last pages of the Edict), 7 pl., 28 port. New York, 1900. Q. Blue morocco.
Vol. iv.   Addresses read before the Society. iv, 175 pp. New York, 1915. Q. Half morocco.

Contents of Proceedings and Publications entered under author or title, or both, with any necessary cross-reference, in Class K (Societies), and in this part of the Catalogue also.

Collective contents may be found in the individual volumes.

HUGUENOT Society of London. Proceedings. Vols. i-vi, vii, viii, xi. London, 1885-1918. 11 vols. Illustrations, portraits. O.
Bound in half-morocco.   HK—H87.6
Genealogies herein contained entered under the family name in Section 2 of Class H (Genealogy).

–––––– Publications. Vols. i-xxiii. Lymington, 1887-1916. Vols. i-xxiii. — vols. in —.   HK—H87.5
For Contents see Class K (Societies).
Also entered separately under author or title, with cross-references where necessary, in both Parts of this Catalogue.

–––––– Royal Institute of Painters in water colours, Piccadilly. Conversazione, on Wednesday, May 22nd, 1895. Programme of Music, Etc. (Words and music.) 16 pp. London, 1895. Square O. Privately printed.

HUGUENOT Society of South Carolina. Transactions. Nos. 1-23. Charleston, S. C., 1889-1917. Nos. 1-22, bound in 4 volumes. Illustrated. O. HK—H87.8
Binder's title—"Proceedings."

HUGUES, Edmond. Histoire de la restauration du protestantisme en France au XVIIIᵉ siècle. Antoine Court d'après des documents inédits. Quatrième édition. Paris, 1875. 2 vols. O. HA—H87

——— Inauguration du Musee du Desert. . . . 24 Sept., 1911. Allocution de . . . E. H. . . . Cevennes, 1912. O. (pp. 27-43.)
HA—M986

——— Synodes de desert, actes et reglements des synodes nationaux & provinciaux tenus au desert de France de l'an 1715-1793. . . . 3 vols. por., pl., fac-sim. Q. P. 1885-'86. HA—H871

——— ARNAUD, Eugene. Supplement aux synodes de desert. . . . Square Q. Paris, 1892. HA—H871A

HUIDEKOPER, Frederic Louis. Sieges of Louisbourg in 1745 and 1758. Address . . . before Soc. Colonial Wars, D. C. . . . February 12th, 1914. 21; 3-18 pp.; plans & maps, fld.; 1 view, fld. Wash., D. C., 1914. (Hist. papers. Soc. Col. Wars, D. C. No. 8. "Some important military operations.") HE—A512

——— Struggle (The) between the French and English for the Valley of the Ohio, 1749-1758. Address delivered before the Soc. Col. Wars, D. C. . . . Mch. 5th, 1914. 21, 3-43 pp.; 4 plans folded, 2 maps folded, 1 view folded. Wash., D. C., 1914. O. (Hist. papers. Soc. Col. Wars, D. C. No. 8. "Some important military operations.") HE—A512

HUISSEAU, J. d'. Discipline (La) des églises reformées de France; ou, l'Ordre lequel elles sont conduites & gouvernées. . . . New ed. Genève, 1666. 245 pp. O. HA—H875

HUNNEWELL, James F. Historical monuments of France. Boston, 1884. 336 pp., plates. O. HI—H89

HUNTINGTON, Rev. William Reed, D.D. Address commemorative of Eugene Augustus Hoffman. 28 pp., 1 port. New York, 1903. HG—Mem512
Read before the N. Y. Historical Society, Dec. 2, 1902.

——— The Puritan strain. Sermon preached in Grace Church before the New England Society of the City of New York, on Sunday, March 10, 1901 19 pp. N. Y., 1901. HE—W885

HURD, D. Hamilton, Compiler. History of Fairfield county, Conn., with illustrations and biographical sketches of its prominent men and pioneers. Philadelphia, 1881. 878 pp., illustrated, portraits. Q.
HE—H93

HURLBUT, Henry Higgins. Hurlbut genealogy; or, Record of the descendants of Thomas Hurlbut, of Saybrook & Wethersfield, Connecticut. 545 pp., illus. port. Albany, 1888. O. HH—H93

HYMNAL Companion to the Book of Common Prayer, of the Church of England. Edited by the Rev. E. C. Bickersteth. Title page missing. III-VII pp., remainder unpaged; hymns numbered 1-550, 11 leaves ff. S. HM—HB99

IKEN, J. FR. Wallonisch-französische fremdengemeinde in Bremen. Magdeburg, 1892. 24 pp. O. (DEUTSCHE Hugenotten-Verein. Geschichtsblätter. 1892. Vol. VIII.) HK—D49

INDEX to American genealogies and to genealogical material contained in all works. . . . 282 pp. 4th ed. O. Albany, N. Y.: J. Munsell & Sons, 1895. HH—M96
Supplement, 1900-1908. Q. Albany, 1908.

INDEX to . . . Bishop Meade's Old Churches, ministers and families of Virginia. Compiled by J. M. Toner. Washington, 1898. O. HC—M461

INVENTAIRE-sommaire des archives départementales antérieures à 1790 Charente-inferieure . . . par L. M. M[eschinet] de Richemond. HD—M56

IPSWICH, Mass. The ancient records of the town of Ipswich, Mass. Edited by G. A. Schofield. 1 vol. O. Vol. I, 1899. HE—I 6
Vol. I. From 1634-1650.

IRVING, WASHINGTON. 1783-1859. Washington & his Country; being Irving's "Life of Washington" abridged by John Fiske. 618 pp., 15 maps. Boston, 1887. D. HG—W272

ISLAND of Orleans. See: Genealogy of the families of the Island of Orleans, by the Abbé Michel. 360 pp. O. (Appendix A, Part II, Canadian Archives.) Forgues. Vol. II. HF—C213

JACCARD, E. L'Eglise Française de Zurich. Une page de l'histoire du grand refuge. 425 pp. Zurich, 1889. D. HA—J11

——— Trois homes de grand refuge: Reboulet, Corteiz, Sagnol. . . . 152 pp. O. Lausanne, 1900. HG—B83
In volume: "Etude Biographique."

JACKSON, SAMUEL MACAULEY. The Edict of Nantes; its scope and its place in the development of religious toleration. With a complete translation of the Edict . . . together with that of the Revocation of the Edict . . . revised by W. E. Gillette. New York, 1898. pp. 51-104, 6 pp. O. HA—N19
With the exception of the translation of the Revocation, this is a Reprint from the Ter-Centenary Volume of The Huguenot Society of America.

——— & SCHAFF, REV. PHILIP, Editors. Encyclopedia of living divines. 1887. HG—Sch1

JAL, A. Abraham Du Quesne et la marine de son temps. Vols. I-II. 2 tomes. Paris, 1873. Q. HG—J21

JAMES, EDMUND J. The Stites and James Genealogy. 6 pp. O.
New York, 1898. HH
Reprint: N. Y. Gen. & Biog. Record, April, 1898, and cont. . . .
from Record for Oct., 1897.

JAQUELOT, ISAAC. 1647-1708. Sermons sur divers textes prononcéz
dans la Chapelle royale en présence de sa Majesté le roi de Prusse.
Amsterdam, 1710. Tome 2. S. HM—J27

JAUCOURT, ARNAIL FRANÇOIS. Marquis de. Discours . . . 17
juillet 1889 pour l'inauguration du monument de l'amiral Coligny,
par . . . J. et par E. Bersier. 22 pp., 1 pl. D. Paris, 1889.

JAY, JOHN. The American foreign service. pp. 419-433. Square O.
1877. From the International review, May, 1877. HE—Z6

——— Battle of Harlem Plains; oration before the New York His-
torical Society, Sept. 16, 1876. (NEW YORK Historical Society.
Commemoration of the battle of Harlem Plains. 1876. pp. 5-38.)
HE—Z5

——— Battle of Harlem Plains; oration before the N. Y. Historical
Society, Sept. 16, 1876. (N. Y. Historical Society. Commemoration of the battle of Harlem Plains. 1876. pp. 7-38.) HE—Z3

——— Columbia college; her honourable record in the past, with a
glance at her opportunities in the future, a centennial discourse delivered before the association of the alumni, Dec. 21st, 1876. 48 pp.
O. N. Y., 1876. HE—Z1

JAY, HON. JOHN. Demand for education in American history.
(AMERICAN Hist. Assoc. Annual Report. 1891.)
HK—Am3—1890

——— Huguenot Society of America and Columbia College.
(HUGUENOT Society of America. Proceedings. New York,
1891. Vol. II, Part 1, pp. 1-7.) HK—H87.1

——— Introductory remarks at the First Public Meeting of the Society in the French Church du Saint Esprit, New York, November 15th, 1883. (pp. 5-7. Proceedings, Vol. I, No. 1. ("Abstract of Proceedings,") HUGUENOT Society of America.)
HK—H87.1

——— The President's Annual Address to the Society on April 13th,
1893. (HUGUENOT Society of America. Proceedings. New
York, 1894. Vol. II, Part 2, pp. 246-251.) HK—H871

JENKS, WILLIAM. Eulogy . . . of Hon. James Bowdoin, with notices of his family; pronounced in Brunswick, Maine, at the request
of the Trustees . . . of Bowdoin College. Sept. 2, 1812. 40 pp.
Boston, 1812. HG—B67

JOHNS HOPKINS University Studies in History & Political Science;
Extra volumes. Baltimore, 1889. Edited by H. B. Adams.
No. 4: HOWARD, G. E. Introduction to the local Constitutional
History of the United States.

JOHNSON, Ellen Terry. The House of Hope of the first Connecticut settlers. Paper read before the Connecticut Society of Holland Dames . . . November 19, 1895. . . . 46 pp. Hartford, Conn., 1896. HE—A512

JOHNSTON, Elizabeth Bryant. Original portraits of Washington including statues, monuments and medals. . . . 22-257 pp., illus., 32 pl. Square folio. Boston, 1882. HG—W271

JONES, Henry R. Sketches of the people and places of New Hartford, Connecticut, in the past and present. 33 pp. Hartford, Conn., 1883. HE—A512

JONES, Thomas. History of New York during the Revolutionary War, and of the leading Events in the other Colonies at that period. Edited by Edward Floyd de Lancey, with notes, contemporary documents, maps, and portraits. In 2 vols. New York, 1879. Q. (N. Y. Hist. Soc'y. John D. Jones Fund Series of Histories & Memoirs.) HE—J72

JOURNAL (The) of American History. Vol. xi, Nos. 1-3. Greenfield, Ind., 1917. Fully illustrated. HL—J86—Unbound

JUBILE, de M. Aimé—Louis Herminjard, docteur ès lettres et en théologie, professeur honoraire de l'universite de Lausanne, editeur de la Correspondance des réformateurs dans les pays de langue française. 7 Novembre, 1896. 119 pp., 1 port. Square Q. (Lausanne, 1896?.) HG—H55

JULIEN, Rev. Matthew Cantine. Harvest (The) of Life. A thought for the New Year. 12 pp. D. New Bedford, Mass., January 7, 1906. HM—Pamphlet

——— Huguenots of old Boston. (HUGUENOT Society of America. Proceedings, 1894. Vol. iii, Part 1, pp. 52-72.) HK—H87.1

——— Preliminary (A) statement of the Cantine genealogy, or, The descendants in America of the Huguenot refugee Moses Cantine. 14 pp. O. Boston?, 1903. HH—A54

——— Reason in Religion. 12 pp. New Bedford, Mass., 1907.
HM—Pamphlet

KAHN, Otto H. When the tide turned. The American attack at Château-Thierry and Belleau Wood in 1st week of June, 1918. Address at the meeting of the Boston Athletic Association. 18 pp. [Boston], 1918. O. HF—Pamphlet

KANSAS State Historical Society. Biennial report (8th) for 1890-1892. Topeka, 1892. O. HK—H62V

KEIM, DeBenneville Randolph, Editor. Keim (The) and allied families. Harrisburg, Pa., 1898-1900. HH—K27

KEIM (The) and allied families in America and Europe. A monthly serial of history, biography, genealogy and folklore, of the German, French, and Swiss emigrations to America from the 17th century. Edited by DeB. R. Keim. Harrisburg, Pa., 1898-1900. Vols. I-II, Nos. 1-23. O. HH—K27

KELLY, [———] Rev., Translator. See: CASTELNAU, Michel de. Memoirs of the reigns of Francis II and Charles IX of France.

KERLING, J. B. J., & Dozy, R. B., Compilers. Catalogue de pamphlets et d'estampes concernant les Traites de paix, conclus avec les Pay-Bas depuis 1576-1815. 40 pp., 6 pl. Square Q. HA—Pamphlet

KERSHAW, S. W. Protestants from France in their English home. XII, 170 pp., 1 leaf, 1 fac-sim., 1 pl., 1 port. London, 1885. D. HB—K47

KETCHAM, Rev. William E. Memoir of J. B. Wakeley. (In: WAKELEY, J. B. Lost chapters of American Methodism. cop. 1889. pp. 597-635.) HC—W13

KEY to the Roll of the Huguenots. See: de CRESPIGNY, Mrs. Philip Champion.

KIDDER, Frederic. Beaufort District,—past, present, and future. pp. 381-388. Boston, 1862. O. (Continental (The) Monthly, Vol. I, Nos. II-IV.) HB—H897

KINGS County Historical Society Magazine. Special Year-book and program of the Festival given by the Society in Commemoration of the Long Island Tercentenary. Vol. II, November, 1914. 24 pp. O. HK—Pamphlet

KINGS County, Long Island, New York. See: BERGEN, Teunis G. Register . . . of the early settlers . . . to 1700. . . . New York, 1881. O. HH—B35

——— See: DITMAS, Charles Andrew, Compiler. Historic homesteads of Kings County. HE—D615K

KINGSBURY, J. D. Memorial History of Bradford, Massachusetts, from the earliest period to the close of 1882. Including Addresses at the 200th Anniversary of the First Church of Bradford, Dec. 27, 1882. XII, 192 pp. Haverhill, Mass., 1883. O. HE—B73K

KINGSTON, New York, Records, 1660-1809. See: HOES, Rev. R. R. Baptismal and marriage registers of the Old Dutch Church. . . .

KIRK, Ernest F. See: KIRK, R. E. G., & Kirk, E. F. Returns of aliens dwelling in . . . London. . . . (Huguenot Society of London. Publications. 1900-1908. Vol. x.) HK—H875

KIRK, R. E. G., & Kirk, E. F., Editors. Returns of aliens dwelling in the city and suburbs of London from . . . Henry VIII to . . . James I. 1 vol. in 4 parts. Q. Aberdeen, 1900-1908. (Huguenot Society of London. Publications. Vol. x.) HK—H875
450 copies printed. Nos. 392, 422, 420, & 427.

KNECHT, J. Wallonische gemeinde zu Otterberg. 21 pp. O. Magdeburg, 1892. (Deutsche Hugenotten-verein. Geschichtsblätter, 1892. Vol. VII.) HB—T57

KURTZ, JOHN HENRY. Text-book of Church history. 2 vols. in 1. Philadelphia, 1876. O. HC—K96

LACHERET, E. Sermon . . . prononce le 27 Septembre, 1891. (In: BOURLIER, E. Souvenir du troisieme centenaire de l'eglise Wallonne de La Haye. . . . La Haye, 1891. O. HC—B66

LACURNE DE SAINTE-PALAYE. Dictionnaire historique de l'ancien langage Francois; ou, Glossaire de la langue Francoise depuis son origine jusqu'au siecle de Louis XIV. . . . A-Z. Vols. I-X. Square Q. 10 vols. Niort, [187?]-1882. HO—Pal.18.Z

LAFON, MARY. Histoire d'uno ville Protestante Montaubon. xv, 316 pp. O. Paris, 1862. HA—L132

LAGARD, ALPHONSE. Chronique des églises réformées de l'Agenais. Toulouse, 1870. 340 pp. 12mo. (Société des livres religieux de Toulouse.) HA—L13

LAKE CHAMPLAIN Association & The Ter-Centenary Commissions of New York & Vermont. Banquet given to the Delegation from the People of France presenting a bronze bust of La France to the People of the United States of America. New York, 1914. A brochure of 4 leaves and 4 plates, mounted. Square Q. HK—Pamphlet

LALOT, J. A. Devant la statue de l'amiral Coligny. Ed. 3. 69 pp., 1 pl. D. Paris, pref. 1890. HG—C683

LAMB. Mrs. Martha J[oan Reade Nash]. Career and times of Nicholas Bayard, son of an exiled Huguenot. (Huguenot Society of America. Proceedings. 1891. Vol. II. pp. 27-57.) HK—H871

———— History of the City of New York; its origin, rise and progress. 2 vols. port., pl., maps. New York, 1877-80. Q. HE—L16
Vol. I. Period prior to the Revolution, closing in 1774.
Vol. II. Embracing the Century of National Independence, closing in 1876.

———— Souvenir of the centennial anniversary of Washington's inauguration, April 30. 1789, with the program of ceremonies. N. Y., 1889. 86 pp., illustrated, portraits. 8vo. HE—L16.1
From the *Magazine of American History,* Dec. 1888, Feb. and March, 1889.

LANCASTER, Massachusetts. Birth, Marriages and death register, Church records and epitaphs. 1643-1850. Edited by H. S. Nourse. 508 pp. O. Lancaster, 1890. HH—L22

LANIER, J. F. D. Born 1800. Sketch of the life of J. F. D. Lanier. N. Y., 1871. 62 pp., portrait. O. HG—L27
Printed for the use of his family only.

LANNOY, Mortimer Delano de. Bibliography of American heraldry. New York, 1896. 12 pp., illus. D.   HH—D37
Inserted in his "History and Genealogy of Delano and Lannoy."

DELANO, Major J. A. See: Genealogy . . . of the American house of Delano, 1621-1899. With the history and heraldry of the Maison de Franchimont and de Lannoy to Delano, 1096-1621. . . . New York, 1899. Q.   HH—D37
One of 400 copies published.

La PLACETTE, Jean de. La Communion dévote; ou, la Manière de participer saintement & utilement à l'Eucaristie. Ed. 4. 2 parts in 1 vol. Amsterdam, 1699. S. n.t.p.   HM—L31
Note:—Edition 4 is enlarged by Part 2. First edition printed in 1695. The title page for this copy of the fourth edition has been supplied evidently from that of the *first* edition: the date of the *fourth* edition is as given—1699.

LARPENT, Frederick DeH. Note concerning the family of Larpent settled between 1695-1705 in Denmark and Norway. 7 pp. Square O. London, 1916.   HH—A54

La ROCHELLE. See: BLANCHON, Pierre. Jean Guiton et le Siege de La Rochelle. La Rochelle, 1911. Square D.   HG—G968

LART, Charles Edmund, Editor. Registers of the French Churches of Bristol, Stonehouse and Plymouth. xxviii, 156 pp. Q. London, 1912.   HK—H875
Bound with: WALLER, W. C., Editor. Register . . . French Church at Thorpe-le-Soken in Essex. . . . (HUGUENOT Society of London. Publications. 1912. Vol. xx.)
450 copies printed: No. 414.

———— Registers of the Protestant Church at Caen, Normandy. Vol. i. Vannes, 1907. Q. xxiv, 712 pp.   HH—L33
Vol. i.   Baptêmes et Mariages, 1560-1572.

———— Registers of the Protestant Church at Loudun, 1566 to 1582. Vol. i. Lymington, 1905. O. x, 69 pp.   HH—L33L
Vol. i.   Baptêmes, 1566-1577.

La TOUCHE, John James Digges, Editor. Registers of the French conformed Churches of St. Patrick and St. Mary, Dublin. 312 pp. Q. Dublin, 1893. (HUGUENOT Society of London. Publications. Vol. vii.)   HK—H875
No. 38 of 500 copies printed.

LATROBE, John Hazlehurst. Boneval. . . . A lost chapter in the history of the steamboat. 44 pp. O. Baltimore, 1871.   HE—Z2

LAUX, James B. Huguenot element in Pennsylvania. (HUGUENOT Society of America. Proceedings, 1894. Vol. iii. pp. 96-116.)   HK—H871

LAWRENCE, Eugene. Historical studies. N. Y., 1876. 508 pp. O.   HC—L43

LAWTON, ELIZA MACINTOSH CLINCH ANDERSON. Abstract of report of . . . visit abroad as the representative of the Society. (HUGUENOT Society of America. Proceedings. Vol. III. pp. 73-79.) Read before The Society, Nov. 26th, 1895.   HK—H87.1

—— The Emblematic flower and distinguishing colour of the Huguenots. (HUGUENOT Society of America. Proceedings. 1891. Vol. II. pp. 237-260.)   HK—H87.1
Read before the Society, April 13th, 1893.

—— Societe de l'Histoire de Protestantisme Francais. Extracts . . . account of Meeting . . . at La Rochelle and Sainte Martin-en-Ré. . . . A translation. (HUGUENOT Society of America. Proceedings, 1894. Vol. III. pp. 121-124.)   HK—H87.1

—— Compiler. Index to Flatbush Dutch Church Marriage Records. Typewritten MS.   HK—H71.1.L
Gift of the Compiler.
(The Records are in: HOLLAND Society Year Book, for 1898.)

—— Translator. See: EGLISE de Narragansett. Papier du Consistoire de l'Eglise de Narragansett, A.D. 1687. A typewritten MS., copy in French from the original MS., with an English translation by E. M. C. A. L. 2 leaves, 47, 49, XI leaves. New York, 1896. Square O.   HJ—N23.1.L

LAYARD, SIR HENRY. Despatches of Michele Suriano and Marc Antonio Barbaro, Venetian ambassadors at the Court of France. 1560-1563. XII, 107, CLVI pp. Q. Lymington, 1891. (Huguenot Society of London. Publications. Vol. VI.)   HK—H875
500 copies printed. No. 366.

LAYARD, IDA L. H. Huguenot (A) miniaturist at home. Paper read before the Society at the Annual Meeting of April 14th, 1913. Huguenot Society of America. Publications. Vol. IV. pp. 67-87. New York, 1915.   HK—H87

—— Martyrs (The) of Salies. Paper read before the Annual Meeting, April 13th, 1903. Huguenot Society of America. Proceedings. pp. 55-67. Also an Appendix—Piéces justificatives. pp. 68-77. Vol. IV. New York, 1904.   HK—H87.1

LEACH, JOSIAS GRANVILLE, Editor. See: ROEBLING, EMILY WARREN. Journal of the Rev. Silas Constant . . . Presbyterian Church at Yorktown, N. Y. . . . Records of the Church. . . . Notes on families mentioned. . . . Philadelphia, 1903. O.   HH—C758

LECLERCQ, J. B. Une église réformée au 17e siècle; ou, Histoire de l'église wallonne de Hanau, depuis sa fondation jusqu'à l'arrivée dans son sein des réfugiés français. Hanau, 1868. 293 pp. O.   HB—L49

LEE, MRS. HANNAH F. (SAWYER). Huguenots in France and America. Cambridge, [Mass.], 1843. Vol. II. D.   HA—L51

LEE, William, Compiler. John Leigh of Agawam (Ipswich), Mass., 1634-1671, and his descendants of the name of Lee. . . . 999 pp., 1 map, illus. Albany, N. Y., 1888. O. HH—L51

Le FANU, Thomas Philip, Editor. Registers of the French Church of Portarlington, Ireland. xix, 176 pp. Q. London, 1908. (Huguenot Society of London. Publications. Vol. xix. 1908.) 450 copies printed. No. 411. HK—H875

—— Registers of the Nonconformist Churches of Lucy Lane and Peter Street, Dublin. xiv, 167 pp. Q. Aberdeen, 1901. (Huguenot Society of London. Publications. Vol. xiv. 1901.) HK—H875

Le FEVRE, Rev. James, D.D. Huguenot patentees of New Paltz, New York. HUGUENOT Society of America. Proceedings. New York, 1894. Vol. iii, Part 1, pp. 80-95. HK—H871

LeFEVRE, Ralph. History of New Paltz, New York, and its old families. (From 1678-1820.) Including the Huguenot pioneers and others who settled in New Paltz previous to the Revolution. iii-xiv, 593 pp., 1 port., illus. Q. Albany, N. Y., 1903. HE—L52

—— [New Paltz and its old families.] Appendix giving additional information concerning the Revolutionary Period: likewise the Wills of a number of the Patentees and their sons . . . notice of those who moved from New Paltz in the early days, and other matter. vi, 208 pp. Illustrated. New Paltz, N. Y., 1918? O.
HE—L52A—Vol. ii

—— Huguenots of Ulster County, New York. In: Historical Society Newburgh Bay & The Highlands. pp. 41-55. Newburgh, N. Y., 1894. O. HK—H62V

LEGENDRE, Philippe. Histoire de la persécution faite à l'église de Rouen sur la fin du dernier siècle, précédée d'une notice historique et bibliographique par Emile Lesens. Rouen, 1874. 185 pp., plates. Square O. HA—L52

LE HARDY, Gaston. Histoire du protestantisme en Normandie depuis son origine jusqu'à la publication de l'Edit de Nantes. Caen, 1869. 456 pp. O. HA—L522

LeLABOUREUR, J. Mémoires de Messire Michel de Castelnau, seigneur de Mauvissière . . . avec . . . l'histoire genealogique de la maison de Castelnau, et les genealogies de plusieurs maisons illustres alliées à celle de Castelnau. Nouvelle ed. Tomes i-iii. Bruxelles, 1731. 3 vols. Folio. HG—L53

LELIEVRE, Matthieu. See: CRESPIN, Jean. Histoire des martyrs . . . introduction par D. Benoit . . . [et notes par M. L.]. Edition nouvelle. Toulouse, 1885-1889. 3 tomes. Q. HG—C86.2

LeMERCIER, Rev. André. MS. Sermons (French) Preached at the French Church in Boston, Mass. Dated, 1714-1719. Square O. HJ—L54

—— Treatise on detraction. Boston, 1733. 303 pp. D. HM—L54

Le MONTRESOR. See: MONTRESOR.

[LENNOX, Mrs. C. R.], Translator. See: SULLY, Maximilian
de Bethune duc de Memoirs . . . 1763.   HD—Su5

LEROUX, Alfred. Histoire de la Réforme dans la Marche et le
Limousin (Creuse, Haute-Vienne, Corréze). xlvii, 391 pp. O.
Limoges, 1888.   HA—L56

LESCARBOT, Marc. Histoire de la Nouvelle-France, contenant les
navigations, découvertes et habitations faites par les Français ès Indes
occidentales et Nouvelle-France; suivi des muses de la Nouvelle-
France. Nouvelle édition, publiée par Edwin Tross. Paris, 1866.
3 vols., maps. O.   HE—L56

LESENS, Emile, Editor. See: BIANQUIS, J. La revocation de
l'edit de Nantes . . . à Rouen. 1885.   HA—B47

———— DAVAL, Gu. & Jean. Histoire de la reformation à Dieppe,
1557-1657. . . . 1878-'79.   HA—D27
(Soc. Rouennaise de bibliophiles.)

———— LEGENDRE, Ph. Histoire de la persecution faite a l'église de
Rouen. 1874.   HA—L52

LESTER, Henry M. New Rochelle's 221st Anniversary. (In: Westchester Co. Magazine, No. 4, pp. 13-15.) O.   HE—N533

LETTER of commendation given to Antoine Trabue, dated 1687.   HJ

LETTER to the French refugees concerning their behavior to the government. London, 1711. 24 pp. S.   HB—L56

LETTERS & papers relating . . . to the . . . history of Pennsylvania,
1855. By Thomas Balch.   HE—B18P

LIEVE, Auguste François. Histoire des protestants et des églises
réformées du Poitou. Paris, 1856-60. 3 vols., maps. O.   HA—L62

LILY (The) and the totem, by SIMMS, William Gillmore.
1850.   HB—S14

LINCKLAEN, John. Travels in the years 1791 and 1792 in Pennsylvania, New York, and Vermont. Journals of J. L., agent of the
Holland Land Company. With a biographical sketch and notes by
H. L. Fairchild. iv, 1-4, v-xi, 1-162 pp., 1 fac-sim., 1 pl., 1 port., 2
maps, & 1 map folded in pocket. O. New York, 1897.   HI—L63

LINCOLN, Charles Henry, Compiler. Naval records of the American Revolution, 1775-1788. Prepared from the originals in the
Library of Congress. 3-54 pp. Washington, 1906. Q.   HE—L737

LINN, James B., & EGLE, W. H., M.D., Editors. See: PENN-
SYLVANIA Archives. Vols. viii & ix. Harrisburg, Pa., 1895-
'96.   HC—Pa.11

LISTS of passengers, 1657-1664, and of owners of houses and lots in
New Amsterdam about 1674. . . . (In: HOLLAND Society Year-
Book, 1896.)   HK—H711

LISTS of persons who went from Great Britain to America, from 1600-
1700. See: HOTTEN, J. C., Editor. Original lists. . . . 2nd
edition. New York, 1880. Q.   HH—H79

LISTS of professors and students in France in the 16th & 17 centuries.
See: BOURCHENIN, D. Etude sur les academies Protestants
in France au XVIᵉ & XVIIᵉ siècle. Paris, 1882. O.   HA—B66

LITTLE (The) Huguenot. A Romance of Fontainebleau. N. Y.,
1895. By Max PEMBERTON.   HN—P37

LITURGIE pour les protestans de France ou prieres pour les familles
des fidelés privés de l'exercice public de leur religion. Avec un
discourse Préliminaire *sur quelques Matieres intéressantes.* A Amsterdam, Chez Marc-Michel Rey, 1758. O. pp. 294.   HM—L73

LITURGY; or, Forms of divine service. Translated from the liturgy
of the church of Neufchatel and Vallagin, the whole adapted to
public worship in the United States of America. Third edition.
N. Y., [1853]. 228 pp. O.   HM—L53

———— Same. Fourth edition. Charleston, S. C., 1886. xxiv, 230 pp.
O. (Contains as Additional Canticles, the Nunc Dimittis and the
Magnificat.) Inside of front cover is "This Edition of the Liturgy
of the French Protestant Church of Charleston, South Carolina,
is presented to the Church by William Ravenel, Esq. 1886."
                                                           HM—L53R

LIVRE des prières publiques de l'administration des sacremens et des
autres rites et cérémonies de l'église, selon l'usage de L'EGLISE
PROTESTANT EPISCOPALE dans les Etats-Unis d'Amérique
avec le psautier. Nouvelle édition. N. Y., 1831. 464 pp. Q.
                                                           HM—L782F

LOMBARD, Alexandre. Pulicens, Bulgares, et bonshommes en
Orient et en Occident, étude sur quelques sectes du moyen age.
Genève, 1879. 319 pp., fac-simile. D.   HA—L83

LONG ISLAND Historical Bulletin. Vol. i, Nos. 1-4. Brooklyn,
N. Y., 1913. Published and copyrighted by Chas. A. Ditmas.
                                                      HL—Unbound
This volume contains articles in reference to the Works of Daniel
M. Tredwell, and is largely composed of his historical sketches
about Long Island.

LONG ISLAND Historical Society. Catalogue of the Library
. . . 1863-1893. 801 pp. Brooklyn, N. Y., 1896. Q.   HK—L861

———— Memoirs. Volume i. plates, map. Brooklyn, New York,
1867. O.   HK—L86

LONG ISLAND, New York. See: MATHER, F. G. Refugees of 1776 from Long Island to Connecticut.   HE—M42.7

—— See: RIKER, JAMES. Annals of Newtown.   HE—R44N

—— See: TREDWELL, DANIEL M. Personal reminiscences. Brooklyn, N. Y., 1912 & 1917. Q. 2 vols.   HE—T78

LORD, REV. CHARLES E., Compiler. MS., list of Huguenots who settled in various parts of the United States. 33 leaves. D.   HJ

LORRAINE, CHARLES IV, DUC DE. 1604-75. Histoire de l'emprisonnement de Charles IV, Duc de Lorraine. By Nicolas Du Bois de Riacourt. Cologne, 1688. 132 pp. S.   HD—B38
Bound with *Beauvau, Henri, Marquis de, Memoires.*

LOST MS. of the Rev. Lewis Rou's "Critical remarks upon the letter to the craftsman on the game of chess," written in 1734 and dedicated to . . . William Cosby, Gov. of N. Y. Signed W. F., i.e., Willard Fiske. 18 pp. Florence, 1902.   HG—Pamphlet
Reprint: Notes & Queries, July 19, 1902. With additions.

LOUDON; Registers of the Protestant, 1566-1582. Vol. I. Edited by C. E. LART. 1 vol.   HH—L33L

LOUIS XIV, King of France, 1638-1715. Original decree of Louis XIV in relation to the Temple (protestant church) of Bergerac, with an English translation by Rev. Alfred V. Wittmeyer. Fontainebleau, 1679. See: MENESTRIER, C. F., Compiler. Histoire du roy Louis le Grand par les medailles, emblems . . . armoires et autres monumens publics. . . . Paris, 1691.   HJ

LOUIS, ROY DE FRANCE. Arrest de reglement de la cour de Parlement de Toulouse: sur les choses qui doivent estre observées par ceux de la Religion Pretenduë Reformée. . . . Toulouse, 1682. 6 pp., [1 leaf]. Square O.   HA—L888

—— Declaration de Roy concernant les pensions sur les Benefices, cures et prebandes. Verifiee & Enregistrée au Parlement de Bourdeaux le treisiéme Aoust, 1671. Saintes, 1671. 8 pp. Square S.   HA—L888

—— Declaration. . . . Contreceux qui s'étant convertis. fortiront de Royaume sans permission du Roy. . . . Paris, 1686. 4 pp. Square O.   HA—L888

—— Declaration du Roy, portant defences aux Ministres, et aux consitoires de recevoir les relaps, et apostats, sur paine de desobeissence de suppression des Consistoires, & d'interdiction des Ministres. Toulouse, 1679. 7 pp. Square O.   HA—L888

—— Declaration du Roy, portant interdiction de l'Exercise de la Religion P. R. & démolition des Temples où il aura esté fait des mariages entre personnes (Roman) Catholiques & de ladite R. P. R. . . . Toulouse, 1685. — pp. Square O.   HA—L888

LOUIS, Roy de France. Declaration du Roy, portant, que ceux de la R. P. R. ne pourront tenir leurs Consistoires qu'une fois en quinze jours, & en presence d'un Iuge Royal. . . . Toulouse, 1685. 7 pp. Square O. HA—L888

————— Déclaration du Roy, qui défend aux Sujets de la Religion prétendue Reformée, de vendre aucuns biens sans permission de sa Majesté, pendant le temps detrois ans. Paris, 1723. 3 pp. Square O. HA—L888

————— Declaration du Roy, portant que l'exercice de la R. P. R. ne pourra estre fait dans les lieux où il y aura moins dix familles de ladite R. P. R. sans comprendre celle du Ministre. . . . Toulouse, 1685. 6 pp. Square O.

————— Déclaration du Roy, portant que les Ministres de la R. P. R. ne pourront exercer leur Ministere plus de trois ans en un même lieu d'Exercice, soit réel ou personnel. Toulouse, 1685. 4 pp. Square O. HA—L888

————— Déclaration . . . portant que les Ministres de la R. P. R. ne pourront demeurer plus prés que de six lieues des endroits où l'Exercice de ladite Religion ne se fait plus. . . . Toulouse, 1685. 4 pp. Square O. HA—L888

————— Declaration du Roy, portant qu'il sera marquéun lieu dans les Temples de ceux de la R. P. R. pour les (Roman) Catholiques qui y voudront aller. . . . Toulouse, 1683. 4 pp. Square O. HA—L888

————— Declaration . . . pour changer la peine des Galeres en celle de mort, contre ceux qui favori-seront l'évasion des nouveaux Catholiques hors du Royaume. Paris, 1687. 4 pp. Square O. HA—L888

————— portant défenses de faire, aucun Exercice public de la R. P. R. dans son Royaume. . . . [Toulouse?], 1685. 4 pp. Square O. HH—L888

————— Edict du Roy d'abolition en faveur de ses subjets de la Religion prétendue reformée qui s'estoient sousleues en armes contre son service. Castres, 1630. 16 pp. O. HH—L888

————— Lettres patentes du Roi, portant défenses aux personnes qui ont fait profession de la Religion Prétendue Réformée, de vendre leurs biens, & l'universalité de leurs meubles, sans la permission du Roi. Paris, 1757. 3 pp. Square Q. HH—L888

————— Ordonnance du Roy pour empescher les Assemblées des Nouveaux Convertis dans les Provinces de son Royaume. . . . Toulouse, 1689. 4 pp. Square O. HH—L888

————— Ordonnance . . . portant exemption delogement de Gens de Guerre & Contributions à iceux pendant deux ans, en faveur de ceux qui estans de la R. P. R. . . . se sont convertis & faits Catholiques, depuis le premier Janvier dernier, & qui se convertiront cyoprés. . . . Paris, 1681. 7 pp. Square O. HH—L888

LOUISIANA: Purchase of Louisiana. Monroe's Journals of Negotiations, 1803. Fac-simile on 6 pp. of List of "Papers of James Monroe . . . in Chronological order from original MSS., in the Lib'y of Congress." Washington, D. C., 1904. Q. Compiled by W. C. Ford.   HE—F711M

LOWER Norfolk County Virginia Antiquary. Edited by E. W. James. Vols. I-II, III, Nos. 1, 2, and IV, V, Nos. 1, 2, & 3. Richmond, Va., cop. 1895-1905. O.   HH—J28

LOWER Wall Street Business Men's Association. 1914. New York's Commercial Tercentenary. . . . A few Historical events as given by historians compared with their actual occurrence. By A. Wakeman, Secretary. 40 pp. Square Q. New York, 1914. (2 mounted illustrations paged in.)   HE—N483

——— Unveiling of Commemorative Tablet on the site of the Merchants' Coffee House. (The "Birthplace of our Union,") Southeast corner of Wall and Water Streets, New York City. 4 leaves, illustrated. Square Q. New York, 1914.   HE—N485

LUCANUS, MARCUS ANNÆUS. Pharsalia; sive, De bello civili, libri decem, ad fidem editionis Oudendorpianæ, re-editi, cum supplemento Thomæ Maii. London, 1815. 206 pp. T.   HN—L96

LUCAS, FREDERICK W. Appendiculæ historicæ; or, Shreds of history hung on a horn. 216 pp., 1 pl., maps. Q. London, 1891. (Contains an account of the discovery, settlement & Anglo-French wars of America.)   HE—L96

LUTHERAN Church, New York City. See: ST. MATTHEW'S Lutheran Church, New York City.

LUTTEROTH, HENRI. La réformation en France pendant sa première période. Paris, 1859. 233 pp. O.   HA—L97

LYLE, MARIA CATHERINE NOURSE, Compiler. James Nourse and his descendants. 138 pp., 4 pl., 6 port., 4 group port., 1 fac-sim., 1 table. Lexington, Ky., 1897. Q. (Printed by request.)   HH—N85

MAANDBLAD van het Genealogisch-heraldiek genootschap. . . . De Nedersche Leeuw." XIIIe Jaargang, 1895. Nos. 1-12, & Index. s'Gravenhage, 1895. Square Q.   HH—V97
Illustrated with coats-of-arms, and 2 heraldry plates paged.
Bound with: VOUTE family genealogy.

McALLISTER, JAMES GRAY. Family records: compiled for the descendants of Abraham Addams McAllister and his wife Julia Ellen (Stratton) McAllister, of Covington, Virginia. Containing a sketch of A. A. McAllister. 2 p.l., 5-88 pp., 1 port. O. Easton, Pa., 1912. Illustrated.   HH—A54

MACAULAY, THOMAS BABINGTON. (Macaulay, 1st Baron, 1800-59.) History of England. 5 vols. in 1 vol. Philadelphia, no date. 1 port. O. Volume V edited by Lady Treveylan.   HF—M1.1

McCRADY, EDWARD. The history of South Carolina under the proprietary government, 1670-1719. O. IX, 762 pp., 1 map. New York, 1897. HE—M13

McPIKE, EUGENE F., Editor. Tales of our forefathers and Biographical annals of families allied to those of McPike, Guest and Dumont. . . . Square Q. 181 pp. Albany, N. Y., 1898. HG—M17

MacSPARRAN, JAMES, D.D. America dissected . . . in sundry letters from a Clergyman there. (See: UPDIKE, WILKINS. History of the Episcopal Church in Narragansett, R. I. . . . With an appendix . . . reprint of a work now extremely rare . . . "America dissected." New York, 1847. pp. 483-533. O. HC—Up1

MADELIN, LOUIS. Victory of the Marne. The enemy's onslaught: Order to stand firm: The Battle: Immediate results: Historic consequences. Translated by Lilly M. Grove. 64 pp., 2 maps folded. Paris, 1917. O. (Studies & Doc. on the War.)

MAGAZINE of American History, with notes and queries, edited by Mrs. Martha J. Lamb. N. Y., 1885-89. Vols. XIII-XXII, illustrated. Square O. Half roan. HL—M27

MAGAZINE of the Daughters of the Revolution. New York, 1893. Vol. I, No. 1. O. HH—Pamphlet

MAGDEBURG. See: TOLLIN, HENRI. Geschichte der französischen Colonie zu Magdeburg. . . .

MAIMBOURG, [LOUIS]. Histoire de Calvinisme. New edition. XXI, 1-514, 26 pp. T. Paris, 1682. HM—M28

MAINE Historical & Genealogical Recorder. Vols. I-VI. Edited by S. M. Watson. Portland, Me., 1884-1889. 6 Vols. Square O. HH—M28

MALLERY, REV. CHARLES PAYSON. Ancient families of Bohemia Manor; their homes and their graves. 2 leaves, 74 pp. O. Wilmington, Del., 1888. (Papers of the Hist. Soc. of Delaware. No. 7.) HH—M253

[MALLET, EDMOND, ABBÉ.] Négociations de le comte d'Avaux en Hollande depuis 1679 jusqu'en 1684. Paris, 1754. 6 Vols. in 2. S. HF—M29

MALTBIE, JONATHAN, of the United States Revolutionary Army. A brief sketch of Jonathan Maltbie, who was in the Service of the U. S., during the Revolution, compiled from the Archives in the State Department. Washington, D. C., 1883. MS. HJ

MANDELOT, SIEUR DE, GOUVERNEUR DE LYON. Correspondance du Roi Charles IX, et du . . . gouverneur de Lyon, pendant l'année 1572, epoque du massacre de la Saint-Barthélemy. [Edited by P. Paris.] D. Paris, 1830. (Monumens inedits de l'histoire de France. Pt. 1, pp. 1-103.) HD—M815

MANN, FLORIAN A. Story of the Huguenots. A sixteenth century narrative wherein the French, Spaniards, and Indians were the actors. St. Augustine, Fla. 197 pp. 1898. HN—M13

MARIE ANTOINETTE, Queen of France. 1755-1793. See CAMPIN, Mme. J. L. H. G. Memoires sur le vie de Marie Antoinette. 488 pp. Paris, 1849. Also see WEBER, Joseph, Memoires de Weber, frere de lait de Marie Antoinette. Ascribed also to Marquis LALLY-TOLLENDAL. HG—B27
Both Memoires In: BARRIERE, J. F., Editor. Bibliotheque des Memoires relatifs a l'histoire de France. 1849. Vol. x.

MAROLLES, LOUIS DE. 1629-92. Histoire des souffrances du bienheureux martyr Louis de Marolles, réimprimée sur la seconde édition avec une préface et des notes par Jules Bonnet. Paris, 1883. 132 pp. D. HG—M34

MAROT, CLEMENT, Translator. Les Pseaumes de David. 1652. HM—P95

MARQUAND, PROF. ALLAN. Huguenot Industries in America. Read before the Society, April 20th, 1888. (HUGUENOT Society of America. Proceedings. pp. 87-96. Vol. I. No. 2.) HK—H871

MARRIAGE notices, 1785-1794, for the whole U. S. See: BOLTON, Charles Knowles. HH—B69

MARSELLOIS Hymn: words and music. (In NEW YORK Mirror, Vol. VIII, No. 13, pp. 103-104. New York, 1830. Square folio. With notes on the author (Rouget) and the composer of the music, its origin, etc. HL—N48

MARSH, MRS. ANNE. History of the Protestant Reformation in France. 2 Vols. O. New ed. London, 1849. HA—M35

MARSH, REV. DWIGHT W., Editor. MARSH, L. B., Compiler. Genealogy of John Marsh of Salem. HH—M35

MARSH, LUCIUS B., Compiler. Genealogy of John Marsh of Salem & his descendants 1633-1888, revised & edited by Rev. D. W. Marsh. 283 pp. O. Amherst, Mass. 1888. HH—M35

MARSH, LUTHER R[AWSON]. Oration before the Society of the Army of the Potomac, at Burlington, Vermont, June 16, 1880. 29 pp. O. No title-page. HE—Z1

MARSHALL, EDWARD CHAUNCEY, Ancestry of General Grant, & their contemporaries. 186 pp. N. Y. 1869. O. HH—G76

MARSHALL, REV. JAMES. The Lebanon Club; an Address before the Lebanon Club for workingmen . . . Dec. 13, 1878. 31 pp. N. Y. 1879. HE—Z7

MARTEILHE, JEAN. Huguenot galley-slave: being the autobiography of a French protestant condemned to the galleys for the sake of his religion. Translated from the French. N. Y. 1867. 241 pp. D.
HA—M36

MARTIN, ALPHONSE. Notice historique sur Sanvic et le Protestantisme. Dans cette Paroisse au Havre et dans les Environs. (XVIe et XVIIe siècles.). . . . X, 407 pp., 5 leaves, 2 pl. D. Fécamp, 1877.
HA—M362

MARTIN, E. K. The Mennonites. Philadelphia, 1883. 17 pp. O.
HF—M36

MARTIN, HENRI. Les cinq étudiants de l'académie de Lausanne brulés vifs à Lyon sur la Place des Terreaux, le 16 Mai, 1553, étude historique. Lausanne, 1863. 62 pp. S. ("French Church History.")
HA—M361

MARTIN, REV. J. A., Compiler. See EGLISE l' Francaise de Cantorbery. Livre du Sanctuaire.

MARTIN, REV. J. H. Dominic De Gourgues, a poem. 1883. MS.
HJ

———— Translator. See LOUIS XIV. King of France. Original decree of Louis XIV. in relation to the Temple (Protestant Church) of Bergerac. A. D., 1679. MS.
HJ

MARTYN, REV. W[ILLIAM] CARLOS. History of the Huguenots. 528 pp. D. New York, [1866].
HA—M364

MARY, QUEEN OF SCOTS. A study. By "Anchor." 144 pp. New York, 1882. O.
HF—D419

———— 1542-1547. See de PEYSTER, John Watts, Maj. Gen., U. S. A. (In his "Works on Mary Stuart," bound in de Peyster Volume.)
HF—D419

MARYLAND. See: GRIFFITH, Thomas W. Sketches of the early history of Maryland. Baltimore, 1821. O.
HE—G854

MARYLAND Association of the Freeman of Maryland. By Col. C. Chaille Long. (In: Republic Magazine. Vol. No. 1. N. Y., 1890. Q. pp. 42-48.)
HE—Cha35

MARYLAND HISTORICAL SOCIETY. . . . Proceedings in connection with the celebration of the 150th anniversary of the settlement of Baltimore. 123 pp., illust. Baltimore, 1880. O.
HE—Z4

MASSACHUSETTS. Report by the commissioners upon the condition of the records, files, papers and documents in the secretary's department. Boston, 1885. 42 pp. 8vo.
HE—Q4
Inserted in Volume.

MASSACHUSETTS of today. A memorial of the State; historical & biographical; issued for the World's Columbian Exposition at Chicago. Edited by T. C. Quinn. Illust. 619 pp. Folio. Boston, 1892. HE—Q4

MASSON, Gustave. The Huguenots: a sketch of their history from the beginning of the reformation to the death of Louis XIV. . . . 192 pp. London. [1881.] S. HA—M38

MATHER, Frederic Gregory. The Refugees of 1776 from Long Island to Connecticut. Albany, N. Y., 1913. 1204 pp., 1 port., fully illustrated throughout. Square O. HE—M427

Part 1. Historical: I. Division; Short story of the Revolutionary War. II. Division; Military & Civil service. III. Division; Effects of the Battle of Long Island—The Refugees. IV. Division; Local conduct of the War.

Part 2. Biographical. I. Division; Captains & Masters of Ships. II. Division; Refugees from Long Island to Connecticut. III. Division; Refugees from Canada & Nova Scotia. III. Division; Refugees from New York City.

Part 3. Documentary.

With an etched plate of Sylvester Manor, inserted.

MAURY, Ann, Editor. See: FONTAINE, Rev. James. Memoirs of a Huguenot family . . . 1853. HG—F73

MAURY, Col. Richard L. Huguenot (The) Martyrs of Meaux, commonly called the Fourteen of Meaux. In: Huguenot Society of America. Proceedings. Vol. iii, Part 2. pp. 149-166. New York, 1903. HK—HE71

———— Huguenots in Virginia. (HUGUENOT Society of America. Publications. Vol. iii. 1900.) HK—H87

MAY, Thomas. Supplementum Lucani. (In Lucanus, M. A. Pharsalia.) HN—L96

MEADE, Rt. Rev. William, D.D. Bishop of Vermont. Old Churches, Ministers, and families of Virginia. Philadelphia, 1900. 2 Vols. Q. HC—M46

Index by J. M. Toner, bound separately and published by the Southern Historical Assoc., as Extra Vol. i. HC—M461

MEADS, Orlando. Annual address before the Albany Institute delivered May 25, 1871. . . . 36 pp. O. Albany, 1871. HE—Z1

MEE, Isaac du. Oprechte uitboezeming aan den . . . diaconen der Walsche gereformeerde kerke in 'sGraayenhaage. . . . 3 pp. O. n. p., 1780. HH—W66

MEEKER, Mary Falconer Perrin. See: PERRIN, Anna Fauconnier, & Meeker, M. F. P. Allied families of Purdy, Fauconnier, Archer, Perrin. New York, cop. 1911. O.   HH—P458
No. 36, of 79 copies.

MEGE, Salvadore, Artist. The great painting: The massacre of the Huguenots, in Paris, on Saint Bartholomew's Day, August 24th, 1572. 15 pp. N. Y., 1888. O.   HA—Pamphlet
MS. description by J. O'Donoghoe inserted.

MEILLE, W. Le reveil de 1825 dans les vallees vaudoises Piemont raconte a la génération actuelle. 105 pp. 1 port. O. Turin, 1893.
Volume titled "French Church History."   HA—R67

MEILLEUR, J. B. Mémorial de l'éducation du Bas-Canada, 1615-1855. Montreal, 1860. 389 pp. S.   HF—M47

MELLETTE, Ella Dunn. Houston, Florence A. Wilson, Blaine, L. C. & Mellette, E. D. Maxwell history & genealogy, including the allied families. . . . Also Baptismal record of Rev. J. Craig, D.D., of Augusta Co., Va., 1740-1749. O. Indianapolis, Ind., [Cop. 1916.]   HH—M465

MELLICK, Andrew D., Jr. Story of an old farm Bedminster, Somerset Co., N. J., or, Life in New Jersey in the 18th century; with a genealogical appendix. 743 pp., pl. Q. Somerville, N. J., 1889.
Bibliography, pp. 714-720.   HE—M48

MELLY, Charles Du Bois. See Du Bois-Melly, Charles.

MEMOIRES concernant la Pucelle d'Orléans. XVe siècle par Denys Godefroy. pp. 1-222. (Coll. Univ. Mem. . . . relatifs à l'hist. France., tome vii.) Paris, 1785. D.   HD—C696

MEMORIAL of Fitz-Greene Halleck; a description of the dedication of the monument erected to his memory at Guilford, Conn., and of the proceedings connected with the unveiling of the poet's statue in the Central Park, N. Y. 72 pp., 2 pl. Q. N. Y., 1877.   HE—Z9

MENESTRIER, Claude Francois, Compiler. Histoire du roy Louis le Grand par les médailles, emblêms . . . armoiries and autres monumens publics . . . 64 pp., illus., pl. Paris, 1691. Folio.
          HG—L92

MERCHANTS' (The) Coffee House, N. Y. City. See: Lower Wall Street Business Men's Association.

MERLE D'AUBIGNE, Jean Henri. Histoire de la réformation en Europe au temps de Calvin. Paris, 1863-66. 4 Vols. O.   HC—M54

———— History of the reformation in the 16th century, translated by David Dundas Scott and H. White. Lancaster, Pa. [No date.] 2 Vols., illust., port. Q.   HC—M541

MESCHINET DE RICHEMOND, [LOUIS MARIE.] Don fait par Louis XIII, pendant le siège de la Rochelle. 30 Octobre, 1627. Paris, 1901. 8 pp. O.   HG—S33
Reprint: Bull. Hist. et Philologique, 1900.

———— Inventaire-sommaire des archives départementales antérieures à 1790. Charente inférieure, archives civiles et ecclésiastiques. Séries C. D. G. et H. Paris, 1877. Vol. 2, folio, morocco.   HD—M56

———— List of books, dated at La Rochelle, 29 Mars, 1909. A bibliography of his books and writings, in letter form to E. M. C. L., Secretary of the Huguenot Society of America. 6 letter sheets, closely written on both sides, closing with the Author's signature. Octavo. MS., inserted in a volume of his pamphlets.   HD—M56.1

———— Medecin (Le) Pierre Chaille de la Tremblade et sa famille, 1693-1775. pp. 39-42. O. Paris, 1895.   HH—C434
Contains insert; MS. Genealogy of Chaille family.
Bound with: Weiss, N. Independance des Etats d'Amerique et Pierre Chaille. . . .

———— Origine et progrès de la réformation à La Rochelle, précédé d'une notice sur Philippe Vincent. Deuxième édition. Paris, 1872. 128 pp. D.   HA—R67

———— Rapport de l'archiviste du département. [Charente-Inférieure] 1885. 19 pp. O.   HD—M56.1

———— Relations inédites et autographes des voyages, dans l'Europe centrale de Jean Godeffroy, d'Orléans (de 1568-1571), et de Jacques Esprinchard, sieur du Plomp, Rochelois (de 1593-1598). Paris, 1882. 9 pp. O.   HD—M56.1
Reprint from Association française pour l'avancement des sciences. Congrès de la Rochelle. 1882.

———— Une famille d'ingénieurs, geographes, Claude Masse (1650-1737) sa vie et ses œuvres. Rochefort, 1882. 20 pp. O.   HD—M56.1
Reprint from Société de Géographie de Rochefort. Bulletin, 1882, Vol. III.

———— Voyage a le cité souterraine; le dernier explorateur des catacombes de Rome. Rochefort, 1882.   HD—M56.1
Reprint from Société de Géographie de Rochefort. Bulletin, 1882, Vol. III.

METHODIST Episcopal Church. Record of Baptisms & Marriages, copied from and compared with the original entries in Stewards' Book, Newburgh, N. Y., circuit . . . 1789-1835, by A. Leslie, & Mrs. W. Vanamee. (Hist. Soc. Newburgh Bay & The Highlands, Hist. Papers, No. 8, 1901.) O. pp. 7-35.   HE—N533

MICHEL, ADOLPHE. Louvois et les protestants. Paris. [No date.] 350 pp. D.   HA—M58

MICKLEY, Minnie Fogel. Genealogy of the Mickley family of America . . . with a . . . record of the Michelet family of Metz, and some . . . biographical . . . and historical memorabilia. 182 pp., 3 leaves, 2 port. O. Mickleys, Pa., 1893.　　HH—M62

Additional items inserted in volume, Oct., 1917, regarding the Unveiling of the Huguenot and Revolutionary Memorial of the Mickley family by the Michelet Chapter, N. S. D. A. R.

MIGAULT, Jean. Journal de Jean Migault, maitre d'ecole (1681-1688). Publie pour la premiere fois d'apres le texte original avec une introduction et des notes par N. Weiss & H. Clouzot. 302 pp. 3 fac-sim., 1 map, folded, 19 pl., 3 port. D. Paris, 1910.　HA—M634

MINET, Susan. See: MINET, William, & Minet, S. Livre des Conversions et des Reconnoissances faites a l'Eglises Françoise de la Savoye. . . .

——— See: MINET, William, & Minet, S. Livre des tesmoignages de l'Eglise de Threadneedle Street. . . .

MINET, William, Compiler. Some account of the Huguenot family of Minet from their coming out of France at the Revocation of the Edict of Nantes, 1686; founded on Isaac Minet's "Relation of Our Family." 7 & 240 pp., illust., fac-sim., tab. Square F. London, 1892.　　HH—M63

250 large paper copies privately printed.

——— and Minet, Susan, Editors. Livre des Conversions et des Reconnoissances faites à l'Eglise François de la Savoye. 1684-1702 . . . xxxvi, 42 pp. Q. London, 1914. (Huguenot Society of London, Publications. Vol. xxii.)　　HK—H875

450 copies printed. No. 379.

——— and Waller, W. C., Editors. Registers of the Church known as La Patente, in Spittlefields, from 1689-1785. xxvi, 254 pp. Q. Lymington, 1898. (Huguenot Society of London, Publications. Vol. ii.)　　HK—H875

450 copies printed. No. 427.

——— Transcript of the Registers of the Protestant Church at Guisnes from 1668-1685 . . . vii, 329 pp., 1 p., 1 map. Q. Lymington, 1891. (Huguenot Society of London. Publications. Vol. iii.)

500 copies printed. No. 359.　　HK—H875

Vol. ii. & iii. bound in one volume.

MINNICH, Michael Reed. Some data of the Hillegas family. (In: The American Historical Register, Philadelphia, 1894. No. 1.)　　HH—Pamphlet

MISER'S (The) curse. A veritable ghost story. By Eliza A. Du Puy. (Harper's New Monthly Magazine. April, 1857. pp. 641-646.) O. N. Y., 1857.　　HN—C77

MOENS, WILLIAM JOHN CHARLES, Editor. Marriage, baptismal and burial registers, 1571-1874, and monumental inscriptions in the Dutch reformed church, Austin Friars, London, and a short account of the strangers and their churches. Lymington, 1884. 227 pp., illust. Q.   HH—M72

—— Editor. Register of Baptisms in the Dutch Church at Colchester, from 1645-1728 . . . XLIII, 177 pp. Q. Lymington, 1905. (Huguenot Society of London. Publications. 1905. Vol. XII.) 450 copies printed. No. 363.   HK—H875

—— Registers of The French Church, Threadneedle Street, London. Vol. I. VI, 364 pp. Q. Lymington, 1896. (Huguenot Society of London. Publications. 1896. Vol. IX.)   HK—H875 450 copies printed. No. 402.

—— Walloons and their Church at Norwich: their history and registers. 1565-1832. 2 parts in 1 vol. Q. Lymington, 1887-1888. (Huguenot Society of London. Publications. 1887-'88. Vol. I.) Only 309 copies printed.   HK—H875

MOERIKOFER, J. C. Histoire des réfugiés de la réforme en Suisse. Traduit de l'allemand et illustré par G. Roux. Paris, 1878. 432 pp., illust. O.   HB—M72

MONASTIER, ANTOINE. Histoire de l'église Vaudois depuis son origine et des Vaudois du Piémont jusqu'a nos jours. Paris, 1847. 2 vols. in 1, portrait, map. O.   HA—M74

MONMOUTH County, New Jersey. See: SALTER, EDWIN. A History of Monmouth and Ocean Counties. O. Bayonne, N. J., 1890.   HE—S27.7

MONNETTE, ORRA EUGENE, Compiler. Monnet family genealogy: an emphasis of a noble Huguenot heritage. Somewhat of the first immigrants, Isaac and Pierre Monnet: being a presentation of those in America bearing the name as variously spelled . . . and . . . short account of . . . families connecting with the ancestral lines. Los Angeles, Cal., 1911. Q.   HH—M748 Illustrations paged in.

MONNIER, MARC. Histoire de la littérature moderne; la réforme, de Luther à Shakespeare. Paris, 1885. 495 pp. D.   HN—M75

MONOGRAPH of the Anderson, Clark, Marshall & McArthur connection. 36 pp., 1 chart folded. Portland, Ore. By Brig. Gen. Thomas McArthur Anderson.   HH—A54

MONROE, JAMES. 4th President, U. S. A. Papers . . . listed in chronological order from the original MSS.; in the Library of Congress. (Also Purchase of Louisiana, Fac-simile from his Journals of Negotiation, 1803.) Compiled by W. C. Ford. 1 leaf, 6 fac-sim., 114 pp. Washington, D. C., 1904. Q.   HE—F711M

MONTAUBON. See: LAFON, MARY. Histoire d'une ville Protestante. XV, 316 pp. O. Paris, 1862.   HA—L132

MONUMENS inédits de l'histoire de France. I. Correspondance du Roi Charles XI et du Sieur de Mandelot, gouverneur de Lyon, pendant l'année 1572, époque de massacre de la Saint-Barthelemy. II. Lettre des seize au Roi d'Espagne Philippe II année 1591. [Edited by P. Paris.] 2 en 1 tome. Paris, 1830. VII-XVI, 128 pp. D.   HD—M815

MORAVIAN Church: Staten Island, New York. See: NEW YORK Genealogical & Biographical Society. Collections. Vol IV. WRIGHT, TOBIAS ALEXANDER, Editor. Records. . . .   HK—N49.1

MORGAN, CHRISTOPHER, Editor. N. Y. (State) State Dept. Documentary history of the State. 1849-51. 3 vols.   HE—N48

MORRIS, ANNE CARY, Editor. Diary and letters of Gouverneur Morris, Minister of the United States to France. . . . 2 vols., 2 port. New York, 1888. O.   HG—M83

MORRIS, GOUVERNEUR. 1752-1816. Diary and letters, edited by Anne Cary Morris. 2 vols., 2 port. New York, 1888. O.   HG—M83

MORRIS, JOHN E., Compiler. Ancestry of Daniel Bontecou, of Springfield, Mass. Hartford, 1887. 29 pp. O.   HH—Var4

———— Bontecou genealogy; a record of the descendants of Pierre Bontecou, a Huguenot refugee from France, in the lines of his sons. 271 pp. O. Hartford, 1885.   HH—B64

———— The Felt genealogy. A record of the descendants of George Felt of Casco Bay. 568 pp. O. Hartford, Conn., 1893. HH—F36

———— Resseguie family, an historical and genealogical record of Alex. Resseguie of Norwalk, Conn., and four generations of his descendants. 99 pp. O. Hartford, 1888.   HH—R31

MORRIS, REV. WILLIAM, Translator. See: VERREN, REV. ANTOINE. The Huguenots in this Country. 1862.

MORRISON, HUGH ALEXANDER. American almanacs, 1639-1800: A preliminary check list. 160 pp. Washington, D. C., 1907. Square Q. (Library of Congress.)   HE—M879

———— See: TONER, J. M., M.D. Index to . . . Meade's Old Churches . . . of Virginia. Revised by H. A. M.

MOUTARDE, E. La Reformé en Saintonge: les églises reformées de Saujon et de la presquile d'Arvert. . . . VII, 215 pp., fac-sim. O. Paris, 1892.   HA—M86

MUELEN, J. C. VAN DER. Kwartierstaten betreffende het geslacht Martini. 14 pp. O. n.p., 1895.   HH—W66
Reprint: Maandblad van het Geneal.-herald. genootschap "De Nederlandsche Leeuw," 1895.

MUHLENBECK, Eugene. See: ROUGET, Claude. Une Eglise Calviniste au XVIᵉ Siècle 1550-1581. Histoire de la comminaute reformée de Sainte-Marie-aux-Mines (Alsace). Publiée . . . avec notes et commentaries par E. M. xiv, 515 pl. Q. Paris, 1881.
HA—R75

MULFORD, William Remsen. Genealogy of the family of Mulford. 12 pp. O. Boston, 1880. HE—Z2
No. 7 of a vol. of pamphlets.

MUNSELL'S [Joel] Sons. Supplement, 1900-1908. Being supplement to the Index to Genealogies published in 1900. 207 pp. Albany, N. Y., 1908. Q. HH—M96

———— Same. 4th edition. 1885.

MURPHY, Henry Crude. Voyage of Verrazzano; a chapter in the early history of maritime discovery in America. 198 pp., illus., 4 maps. O. N. Y., 1875. HE—Z5
No. 14 of a vol. of pamphlets.

———— Editor. See: DANKERS, Jasper, & Sluyter, P. Journal of a voyage to New York. . . . HK—L86

MURRAY, Rev. Andrew. De Hugenoten-school; verslag over de jaren van Januari, 1874, tot December, 1878. [No date.] 7 pp. O.

MUSEE de Desert. Inauguration de Musée de Desert le Dimanche 24 Sèptembre 1911. Allocutions de F. Praux, . . . E. Hugues (et) C. Babut. en Cevennes, 1912. 60 pp., 4 pl. O. HA—M98

MUSICK, John R. Saint Augustine. A story of the Huguenots in America. vi, 309 pp., 8 pl. D. New York, 1892. HN—M9

MUSS, Nicolas. See: DU BOIS-MELLY, C. De recit de Nicolas Muss, serviteur de Mr. l'Amiral, episode de la Saint-Barthelemy . . . 1878. HA—D85

MY FLAG. A brochure of 10 leaves with colour illustrations. Philadelphia, 1917. O. By Jervis A. Wood. HE—Pamphlet

NAEF, F. Réforme en Bourgogne: notice sur les Eglise réformees de la Bourgogne avant la Révocation de l'Edit de Nantes. Editée . . . par R. Claparède. 258 pp., 5 pl., 1 port., 1 map. D. Paris, 1901. HA—N12

NAMES of about 8000 persons a small portion of the number confined on board the British prison ships during the War of the Revolution. 61 pp. Brooklyn, N. Y., 1888. (Society of Old Brooklynites.)
HK—B '9

NARRAGANSETT, Rhode Island. See: EGLISE de Narragansett. Papier du Consistoire, 1687. MS., et Translation. HJ

———— See: POTTER, Elisha Reynolds, Jr. Early history of Narragansett. . . . Providence, 1835. 2nd edition. O. (Collections. R. I. Historical Soc'y. Vol. iii.) HK—P€ 'N

———— 2nd copy. HE—P€ 'N

NATIONAL HISTORICAL SOCIETY. Journal of American History. Produced in Quarterly editions. Vol. XI, Nos. 2-4. Greenfield, Ind., Cop. 1917. Q. HK—N277

NATURALIZATIONS and names. See: AGNEW, REV. DAVID C. A. Protestant exiles from France in the reign of Louis XIV, or, Huguenot refugees . . . in Great Britain and Ireland. 2 vols. London, 1871. Square O. HB—A273

NAVAL records of the American Revolution, 1775-1788. Prepared from the originals in the Library of Congress, by C. H. Lincoln. 3-549 pp. Washington, 1906. Q. HE—L737

NEBRASKA STATE HISTORICAL SOCIETY. Transactions and reports, edited by R. W. Furnas. Lincoln, 1885. Vol. I. O. HK—N27

NEDERDUITSCHE GEREFORMEERDE KERK IN ZUID-AFRIKA. Almanak. Kaapstad, 1886. Vol. XXXVII. HB—H87SA

"NEDERLANDSCHE (De) Leeuw." See: MAANDBLAD van het Genealogisch-heraldiek genootschap.

NEGOCIATIONS de M. le comte d' Avaux en Hollande. . . . 1754. Mallet, Edme. l'abbe. HF—M29

NEGRE, LÉOPOLD. Vie et ministère de Claude Brousson, 1647-1698. . . . 230 pp. Paris, 1878. O. HG—B83

NEILL, EDWARD DUFFIELD. History of the Virginia company of London, with letters to and from the first colony, never before printed. Albany, 1869. 432 pp., portrait. Square Q. HE—N31

NEUCHATELOIS. See: VIVIEN, LOUIS. Les familles du refuge en pays Neuchatelois. Paris, 1899. O. HH—V861

NEW YORK. See: HOFFMAN, C. F. Pioneers (The) of New York. An Anniversary discourse . . . Dec. 6, 1847. O. N. Y., 1848. HE—A512

NEW YORK. See: PELLETREAU, WILLIAM S. Historic homes . . . Genealogical and family history of New York. 4 vols. Illustrated. New York, 1907. Q. HH—P36 (Index in Vol. IV.)

NEW AMSTERDAM GAZETTE. Historical sketches and reminiscences of the Dutch régime of New Amsterdam and the New Netherlands: History of the early Churches: Dutch progress in later years in Holland and America: Views of Holland and other illustrations. Edited by Morris Coster. Vols. I-VII. New York, 1883-1893. 7 vols. in 4. Square Q. HL—L421

———— Records of New Amsterdam from 1653-1674, anno Domini. Edited by B. Fernow. Vols. I-VII. New York, 1897. 7 vols. F. Index in Vol. VII. HE—N42

———— Year Book. Vol. I, Nos. 1-3, 1897-1899. Edited by Morris Coster. New York, 1897-'99. O. HL—N421.1 Publication discontinued.

NEW AMSTERDAM, New Orange, New York, with chronological data. By C. W. DARLING. Utica, 1889. HK—H62V

NEW AMSTERDAM. See: COLONIAL Dames, State of New York. Minutes of the Orphanmasters. . . .

NEW AMSTERDAM. See also NEW YORK.

NEW ENGLAND HISTORIC GENEALOGICAL SOCIETY. Memorial biographies. Volume IV. Boston, 1885. O. HK—NR44

———— Proceedings, 1887, 1894, & 1901, unbound; 1908-1916, bound in two volumes. HK—NR44

———— Historical and Genealogical Register. Vols. I-v, 66-71, portraits & plates. Boston, 1847-1917. 12 vols. O. HK—NR44

———— Index to genealogies and pedigrees in the . . . Register for 50 years. From January, 1847, Vol. I—October, 1896, Vol. L. Compiled by W. W. Wight. O. Boston, 1896. Reprint: N. E. Hist. & Gen. Register, Oct. 1896. HK—NR44—Index

NEW ENGLAND SOCIETY. Ninety-seventh Anniversary Celebration of the . . . Society, in the City of New York, . . . December 22, 1902. 136 pp. New York, 1902. O. HK—Pamphlet

NEW ENGLAND. SAVAGE, JAMES. Genealogical dictionary of the first settlers. . . . Boston, 1860-'62. 4 vols. O. HH—Sa9

NEW HARTFORD, Connecticut. See: JONES, HENRY R. Sketches of the people and places of New Hartford in the past and present. Hartford, Conn., 1883. O. HE—A512

NEW HAVEN (CONN.) COLONY HISTORICAL SOCIETY. Papers. New Haven, 1865-88. 4 vols. O. HK—N45

———— Proceedings in commemoration of the settlement of the town of New Haven. [New Haven], 1888. 68 pp. O.

NEW JERSEY. See: CHAMBERS, THEO. F. Early Germans of New Jersey, their history, churches, & genealogies. Dover, 1895. Q. HE—C445

———— Colonial history. See: SMITH, Samuel. History of the Colony of Nova-Cæsaria, or, New Jersey. Trenton, N. J., 1890. (A reprint of edition of Burlington, N. J., 1765.) HE—N46S

NEW NETHERLANDS: Early immigrants to New Netherland. A bibliographical sketch "concerning . . . names, etc., of early settlers." . . . In: HOLLAND Society Year-Book, 1896. pp. 124-129. HK—H711

NEW NETHERLANDS: Passengers to New Netherland. List of passengers, 1654-1664. From New York Colonial MSS., Vol. xiv, pp. 83-123. In: HOLLAND Society Year-Book, 1902. pp. 1-37.
HK—H711

NEW NETHERLANDS: Register. See: O'CALLAGHAN, E. B. Register of New Netherlands, 1626-1674. Q. Albany, 1865.
HE—Oc.1

NEW PALTZ, N. Y. See: LE FEVRE, Ralph. New Paltz and its old families. 2 vols. O.

NEW PALTZ, (N. Y.) French Church. Copy of the first record book of the French Church at New Paltz, Ulster Co., N. Y., 1683-1702, with an English translation by William Ewing Du Bois. 1846.
HJ—N558

—— See: Reformed Dutch Church Records. In: HOLLAND Society of New York Collections. Vol. iii.

—— VENNEMA, Rev. Ame. See also: Reformed Church . . . History . . . 1683-1883.

—— LE FEVRE, Ralph. See also: History of New Paltz, N. Y., and its old families (1678-1820) including the Huguenot pioneers. Q. Albany, N. Y., 1903.
HE—L52

NEW ROCHELLE, New York. Photographs of houses built by Huguenot settlers at New Rochelle, N. Y. 23 photographs with names of original and present owners. Square folio. Half morocco.
HB—P56

—— See: AUGUR, C. H. New Rochelle through seven generations. 65 pp., illus. New Rochelle, N. Y., cop. 1908. Square D.
HB—Au4

NEW ROCHELLE on the Sound. Illustrated by Joseph Rösch. A brochure of 48 pp. White Plains, N. Y., cop. New York, 1903.
HB—Pamphlet

NEW ROCHELLE Press Almanac. New Rochelle, 1879-84. Vols. i-vi. D. & S.
HE—NR.87.S.

NEW SOUTH WALES. See: BARRINGTON, George. Voyage to New South Wales, with a description of the Country, the manners, customs, religion, etc., in the vicinity of Botany Bay. Philadelphia, 1796. Narrow S.
HI—B276

NEW YORK (City)—Common Council. Manual of corporation. 1853-70. 17 vols., illustrated, portraits, maps, fac-similes. D. Cloth.
HE—N481

Note:—These Volumes are best known as "Valentine's Manuals of the City of New York."

Volumes prior to 1853 would be acceptable for our Collection, and any other volumes, as they are no longer obtainable.

N. Y. (CITY)—Reformed Protestant Dutch Church. Celebration of the quarter-millennial anniversary of the Reformed protestant Dutch church of the city of N. Y. Nov. 21st, 1878. 104 pp. O. N. Y., 1878.   HE—Z8

NEW YORK City. DE WITT, REV. THOMAS. Discourse delivered . . . North Reformed Dutch (Collegiate) Church . . . August, 1856. N. Y., 1857.   HC—D51

NEW YORK: Colony and State. Civil list and Constitutional history of the Colony and State of New York, by E. A. Werner. III-VII, 663 pp., 16 pl. Albany, 1886. O.   HE—W5

NEW YORK: Executive Council of the Province. Minutes. Administration of Francis Lovelace, 1668-1673. Edited by Victor H. Paltsits, State Librarian. Vols. I-II. Albany, 1910. 2 vols. Q.   HE—N46

Vol. I.   Minutes. Collateral and illustrative Documents, I-XIX.

Vol. II. Collateral and illustrative Documents, XX-XCVIII. Facsimiles, plan, portrait, 2 maps, folded in pockets.

NEW YORK, Fishkill Village, Dutchess County. See: VAN VOORHIS, E. W., Compiler. Tombstone inscriptions . . . of the First Reformed Dutch Church. O. N. Y., [pref. 1882].   HH—V37

NEW YORK GENEALOGICAL & BIOGRAPHICAL SOCIETY. By-laws. 16 pp. N. Y., 1882.   HE—Z7

—— Collections. Vols. I-IV. Q. New York, 1890-1909.   HK—N49.1
Vol. I.   PURPLE, S. S., Editor. Records . . . Ref. Dutch Ch. in New Amsterdam & New York. Marriages . . . 1639-1801. 1890.

"   II.   EVANS, T. G., Editor. Records . . . Ref. Dutch Ch., New Amsterdam & New York. Baptisms . . . 1639-1730. Vol. I.

"   III. WRIGHT, T. A., Editor. Records . . . Ref. Dutch Ch., New Amsterdam & New York. Baptisms . . . 1731-1800. Vol. II.

"   IV.   —— Staten Island Church Records. Dutch Ref. Ch., Port Richmond, S. I., Baptisms, 1696-1772. Moravian Ch., S. I., Births & Baptisms, 1749-1853: Marriages, 1764-1863: Deaths & Burials, 1758-1828. St. Andrew's Ch., Richmond, S. I., Births & Baptisms, 1752-1795: Marriages, 1754-1808. 1909.

—— Officers, Committees, By-Laws, Members. New York, 1900, '02, '06, '08, '10, '15. 5 vols. 1900-1915. D.   HK—N49.1

NEW YORK Historical Society. Charter & By-laws, revised Jan. 1858, with the amendments and a list of resident members. 39 pp. N. Y., 1870. HE—Z1

—— Collections, for the years 1868-1918. Vols. i-li. New York, 1868-1918. 51 vols. O. HK—N53.2
Perpetual Gift of Mrs. Jas. M. Lawton.

—— Commemoration of the Battle of Harlem Plains on its 100th Anniversary. 98 pp. N. Y., 1876. HE—Z5

—— Same. 52 pp. N. Y., 1876. HE—Z3

—— John D. Jones Fund Series of Histories & Memoirs. See: JONES, Thomas. History of New York, 1879.

—— Semi-centennial celebration; 50th Anniversary of the Founding of the New York Historical Society . . . Nov. 20th, 1854. 96 pp. N. Y., 1854. HE—Z3
No. 2 of a Volume of Pamphlets.

NEW YORK MARRIAGES. Names of persons for whom Marriage licenses were issued by the Secretary of the Province of N. Y., previous to 1784. 480 pp. Albany, 1860. O. HH—N42

—— Supplementary list of Marriage licenses; years 1752-1753, 1755-1756, & 1758. Albany, 1898. O. (University of N. Y., State Library Bulletin History, No. 1.) HH—N42—Supplement

NEW YORK Mirror and Ladies' Literary Gazette. N. Y., 1831-35. Vols. viii & xii, illustrated. Square F. HL—N48

NEW YORK: Need of a history of New York. 55 pp., 1 port. N. Y., 1915. O. (United Historical & Patriotic Soc'y & Assoc., of N. Y.) HE—H726
Bound with: HOLDEN, J. A. Centenary . . . Battle of Plattsburg. . . .

NEW YORK (State) Commissioners of the correct Arms of the State of New York. Report transmitted to the Senate, April 13, 1881. 31 pp., 4 pl. Albany, 1881. HE—Z7
No. 8 of a Volume of Pamphlets.

—— Ecclesiastical records. Vol. iii. Index, compiled by Rev. E. T. Corwin, D.D. Albany, 1816. O. HC—C832

—— State Historical Association. Proceedings, Vols. ii & iii. Annual Meeting, with Constitution & By-laws and List of Members. pl., port. New York, 1901-'02. 2 vols. Q. HK—N42
Note:—Proceedings of First Annual Meeting not published.

—— (Legislature.) Documents relative to the colonial history of the state, procured in Holland, England and France by John Romeyn Brodhead. Edited by E. B. O'Callaghan. Albany, 1856-61. 11 vols., maps. Square Q. HE—N482

NEW YORK Military Minutes of the Council of Appointment. 1783-
1821. 4 vols. O. Edited by Hugh Hastings.　　　　HE—N482.2

———— Regiment. (VIIth.) The Veteran's room, Seventh Regiment,
National Guard, State of New York, Armory. N. Y., 1881. 24
pp.　　　　　　　　　　　　　　　　　　　　　　HE—Z7

———— Documentary history of the State, arranged under the direction of Christopher Morgan by E. B. O'Callaghan. Albany, 1849-
51. 3 vols., illustrated, portraits, maps. O. Cloth.　　HE—N48

NEWBERRY, JOHN STRONG. Geological history of New York Island
and Harbor. 20 pp., illustrated. No title page.　　　　HE—Z2

NEWBURGH, New York. See: METHODIST Episcopal Church.
Record of Baptisms & Marriages; copied from the original entries
in Stewards' Book, . . . circuit of the M. E. Church, 1789-1835, by
A. Leslie. (Hist. Soc., N. B. & H.) Newburgh, 1901. O
　　　　　　　　　　　　　　　　　　　　　　　　HE—N533

NEWPORT (R. I.) HISTORICAL SOCIETY. Annual report. Newport,
1886. Vol. I. O.　　　　　　　　　　　　　　HK—H62V

NICHOLE, P. De l'unité de l'église; ou, Refutation du nouveau sys-
têne de M. Jurieu. Paris, 1687. 484 pp. S.　　　HM—N51

NICOLAS, MICHEL. Histoire de l'ancienne académie protestante de
Montauban (1598-1659), et de Puylaurens (1660-1685). Montauban, 1885. 440 pp. O.　　　　　　　　　　　　HA—N54

NOBLE, JOHN. De geschiedenis der Hugenoten in Zuid Afrika. 1860.
41 pp. S.　　　　　　　　　　　　　　　HB—H87.S.A.

NOIR, PHILIPPE, SIEUR DE. See: CREVAIN, PHILIPPE LE NOIR,
SIEUR DE.

NORTH AMERICAN Colonies. See: HOLLAND Society of New
York. Report . . . on a Tablet commemorative of . . . services
rendered . . . on behalf of the No. American Colonies in . . . the
Revolution. . . . New York, 1909. 33 pp., 6 plates. O.
　　　　　　　　　　　　　　　　　　　HK—H711—Van

NORTH CAROLINA Huguenots. See: RAND, JAMES HALL. Indians of N. C., and their relations with the settlers.　HK—Pamphlet

NORWALK, Connecticut. 1648-1800. See: HALL, REV. EDWIN,
Compiler. Ancient historical records . . . and the Genealogical reg-
ister of marriages, births and deaths. D. Norwalk, Conn., 1847.
　　　　　　　　　　　　　　　　　　　　　　　HE—N83H

NORWICH, Connecticut. 1660-1800. See: PERKINS, MARY E.
Old houses of the antient town of Norwich. Norwich, Conn., 1895.
Square O.　　　　　　　　　　　　　　　　　HE—P41

NORWOOD, Andrew Sickles, Deponent. Deposition relating to various historical facts "in New York City during the period of our Revolutionary history." Sworn to before F. E. Westbrook, Comm'r of Deeds, 20th of May, 1854. 3 leaves. A typewritten MS. New York, 1854. HE—Pamphlet

NOTES & QUERIES: a Medium of intercommunication for literary men. . . . No. 238 (9th Ser.) Sat. July 19, 1902, containing article: "The 'craftsman' on chess: L. Rou." Signed W. F., i. e., Willard Fiske. HG—Pamphlet
SEE entry under Author for reprint with additions & comments. See also: ROU, Rev. Louis.

NOTES upon the ancestry of Ebenzer Greenough and wife . . . Abigail Israel . . . also a list of their descendants. HH—P69 Compiled by F. Platt. Philadelphia, 1895. O.

NOTICE sur la vie et les oeuvres de William Beach Lawrence. 74 pp. Gand, 1876. HE—Z1

NOURSE, Henry Stedman, Editor. Lancaster, Massachusetts. Birth, marriage, and death register, Church records and epitaphs, 1643-1850. 508 pp. Lancaster, 1890. O. HH—L22

NOUVEAU TESTAMENT, c'est-a-dire, la nouvelle alliance de notre Seigneur Jesus Christ. Amsterdam, 1770. S. Russia leather.
HM—N85

——— Revu sur les originaux par David Martin. New York, 1846. S. HM—N85.1

——— Texte grec, Vulgate et traduction latine avec notes, de Theodore de Bèze. Cinquiéme Edition. Dédidace de Ch. de Bèze à Louis de Bourbon, 1565. Dédidace de Loselerius Villerius à henri d'Hastings, 1573. L'Imprimeur au Lecteur. Exhortation à la lecture de Nouveay Testament (h'Etienne). (Deux parties en un volume.) Londres: Loselerius Villerius, 1574. O. HM—N85.1

O'CALLAGHAN, Edmund Burke. Register of New Netherlands, 1626-1674. Albany, 1865. 198 pp. HE—Oc1

——— Editor. NEW York (State) State Department. Documentary history of the State of New York. 1849-1851. HE—N48

——— Editor. NEW YORK (State) Legislature. Documents relative to the Colonial history of New York. 1856-1861. HE—N482

OCEAN COUNTY, New Jersey. See: SALTER, Edwin. A history of Monmouth and Ocean Counties. . . . O. Bayonne, N. J., 1890. HE—S277

ŒUVRES (Les) du protestantisme français au XIXe siècle. Edited by F. Puaux. Paris, 1893. Folio. HA—P96

OGILVY, Gabriel, Compiler. French families in England. List of marriages at the foreign churches in London, from 1688-1740, with the names, dates, professions, places in France whence they came; consisting of thousands of names taken from the original registers now in Somerset House. 4 vols. in 2 vols. [MSS.] Square D. [No place, no date.]   HJ—Og4

——— Nobiliaire de Normandie. Proces-verbaux . . . 1463 . . . 1727. . . . Origines et genealogies des familles et existantes jusqu'a 1789. (HUGUENOT Society of America. Publications. Vol. IV, pp. 45-66. New York, 1915.)   HK—H87

OHIO. See: RYAN, D. J. History of Ohio, with biographical sketches of her governors and the ordinance of 1787. Columbus, O., 1888. O.   HE—R95

OHIO State Archæological & Historical Society. 8th Annual Report. Columbus, 1892. O.   HK—H62V

OHIO Society of New York. Eighteenth annual banquet given for the Hon. William Howard Taft, Secretary of War, at the Waldorf-Astoria . . . March 5th, 1904. . . . Full page illustrations of the American Battles with portraits of their Commanding Officers. A brochure designed and executed by Thomas A. Sindelar. 4 leaves, 16 plates, 4 portraits, 2 groups of portraits.   HE—Pamphlet

"OLD Dutch Church of Sleepy Hollow." The First Reformed Church of Tarrytown, New York. First Record Book, . . . a copy . . . by Rev. D. Cole. Yonkers, N. Y., 1901. Q.   HH—F44

OLD First Presbyterian Church, New York City. Dedication of the Huguenot Window, given by Dr. Benjamin G. Demarest as a Memorial to his Mother, in the Church, on Sunday, December 19th, 1915. New York, Huguenot Society of America, 1916. 2 plates, 25 pp. Square Q.   HC—Pamphlet

"OLD NORTHWEST" Genealogical Quarterly. Columbus, Ohio, 1898-1900. Vol. I, complete; Vol. II, No. 5, and Index; Vol. III, Nos. 1 & 2.   HH—Unbound

OLD PELHAM & NEW ROCHELLE. See: HAGUE, W. O. No title-page. 1882. pp. 521-537. Magazine of Amer. Hist., 1882. Vol. VIII.   HB—H12

OLIVIER, Daniel Josias. Memoirs of the ancient and worthy family, D'Olivier and their alliances, 1520-1803. Also a family table. (HUGUENOT Society of America. Publications. Vol. IV, pp. 88-161.) New York, 1915.   HK—H87

OLLIER, Daniel. Guy de Brès, étude historique sur la réforme au pays Wallon (1522-1567). Paris, 1883. 200 pp. O.   HB—Ol4

OLNEY, Hon. Peter B. Huguenot Settlement at Oxford, Massachusetts, its Park, Monuments, etc. A Paper read at the Meeting held at New Rochelle, August 14, 1885. (HUGUENOT Society of America. Proceedings. Vol. I, Part 2, pp. 56-64.)   HK—H871

OPDYCK, Gysbert. See: JOHNSON, Ellen Terry. The House of Hope of the first Connecticut settlers. . . . HE—A512

ORDERLY Book and Journal of Major John Hawks on the Ticonderoga-Crown Point Campaign, under General Jeffrey Amherst, 1759-1760. N. Y., 1911. 92 pp. (Society Colonial Wars. N. Y., Publication No. 15.) HK

ORIGINE & progres de la reformation a La Rochelle. 1872. See: MESCHINET de Richemond, Louis. HA—R67

OSGOOD, Rev. Samuel. 1812-80. Thomas Crawford and art in America; address before the New York Historical Society . . . April 6, 1875. . . . 40 pp. O. N. Y., 1875. HE—Z2

OSWEGO Historical Society. Publication No. 1. 1899. Oswego, N. Y., 1899. 1 vol. O. HK—Os8

OUDIN, Antonin. Curiositez françoises. . . . See: LA CURNE de Sainte-Palaye. Dictionaire historique de l'ancien langage François. . . . Square Q. Niort, [187?]-1882. A-Z. Tomes 1-10. HO—Pal 18z

OXFORD, Massachusetts. See: DANIELS, D. F. Huguenots in the Nipmuck Country; or, Oxford prior to 1713. . . . Boston, Mass. O. HB—D22

—— See: FREELAND, Mary de Witt. Records of Oxford, Mass. Square O. Albany, N. Y., 1894. (Massachusetts Historical Series, No. 22.) HE—F87

—— See: OLNEY, Peter B. Huguenot Settlement at Oxford, Mass. (In: HUGUENOT Soc'y of America. Proceedings. Vol. i, Part 2, pp. 56-64.) HK—H87.1

—— See: OLNEY, Hon. Peter B. The Huguenot Settlement at Oxford, Mass., its Park, Monuments, etc. (HUGUENOT Society of America. Proceedings. Vol. i, Part 2, pp. 56-67.) HK—H871

PAGE, William, Editor. Letters of denization and Acts of Naturalization for aliens in England. 1509-1603. liii, 1, 258 pp. Q. Lymington, 1893. HUGUENOT Society of London. Publications. 1893. Vol. viii.) H875

PALISSY, the Huguenot potter. A true tale. 204 pp., 18 pl. Philadelphia, cop. 1864. S. HG—P16

PALTSITS, Victor Hugo. The Function of State Historian of New York. Read before The N. Y. State Hist. Assoc. . . . at its Annual Meeting . . . 1908. 14 pp. O. Albany, N. Y., 1909. HE—A512 (Title of volume: "Americana.")

—— Editor. See: New York: Executive Council of the Province . . . Minutes. Administration of Francis Lovelace, 1668-1673. Vol. i. Albany, 1910-. v. Q. HE—N48
Vol. i. Minutes. Collateral & illustrative Documents, i-xix.
Vol. ii. Minutes. Collateral & illustrative Documents, xx-xcviii.

PANNIER, Jacques. Etudes historiques sur la reforme dans l'Arrandissement de Corbeil. 1. Le prieure et la seigneurie de Longjumeau au milieu de XVIᵉ siècle. Theodore de Beze et Michel Gaillard. Paris, 1898. 20 pp., illustrated. Q.   HA—D74

PARIS, P., Editor. See: Monumens inedits de l'histoire de France. Paris, 1830. D.

PARIS-Académie royale des médailles et des inscriptions. Médailles sur les principaux evenements du regne de Louis le Grand; avec des explications historiques. Paris, 1702. 286 leaves, illustrated. Folio.   HD—L888.1

PARIS (The) memorial. Re-interment of Col. Isaac Paris. O. 32 pp. 1880.   HE—Z7

PARISET, Georges. L'état et les Eglises en Prusse sous Frederic-Guillaume Iᵉʳ. (1713-1740.) These pour le doctorat presentee à la faculte des lettres de Paris. xx, 990 pp. O. Paris, 1896.   HB—P21

PARKHURST, Rev. Charles Henry. Madison Square Presbyterian Church to its first Pastor the Rev. William Adams, a tribute; a sermon by the pastor . . . Nov. 7th, 1880. 23 pp. N. Y., 1880.
                                             HE—Z1

———— Sermon preached on Sabbath morning following the death of President James A. Garfield (Sept. 25, 1881), at the Madison Square presbyterian church. . . . 16 pp. D. N. Y., 1881.   HE—Z7

PARKMAN, Francis. Conspiracy of Pontiac and the Indian war after the conquest of Canada. Tenth edition, enlarged. Boston, 1882. 2 vols., maps. D.   HE—P23

———— Count Frontenac and New France under Louis XIV. Tenth edition. Boston, 1882. 463 pp., maps. D. (France and England in North America, Vol. v.)   HE—P231

———— Jesuits in North America in the 17th century. Sixteenth edition. Boston, 1882. 463 pp., maps. D. (France and England in North America, Vol. ii.)   HE—P232

———— La Salle and the discovery of the great west. Twelfth edition, enlarged. Boston, 1882. 483 pp., maps. D. (France and England in North America, Vol. iii.)   HE—P233

———— Old régime in Canada. Eleventh edition. Boston, 1882. 448 pp., map. D. (France and England in North America, Vol. iv.)   HE—P234

———— Oregon trail, sketches of prairie and Rocky Mountain life. Eighth edition. Boston, 1882. 381 pp. D.   HE—P235

———— Pioneers of France in the new world. Nineteenth edition. Boston, 1882. 427 pp., portrait, maps. D. (France and England in North America, Vol. i.)   HE—P236

PARMENTER, C. O. History of Pelham, Mass., from 1738-1898, including the early history of Prescott. . . . vi, 531 pp., 8 port., 35 pl., 1 fac-sim. O. Amherst, Mass., 1898.   HE—P21

PASCAL, César. La révocation de l'Edit de Nantes et Mme. de Maintenon, sa vie, son caractère, son influence. Deuxième édition. Paris, 1885. 108 pp. D.   HA—P26

PAXTON, William McClung. Marshall family; genealogical chart of the descendants of John Marshall and his wife . . . and notices of families connected with them. 415 pp., 1 port., 1 pl. Cincinnati, 1885. O.   HH—M351

PEARSON, Jonathan, Translator. See: Albany, N. Y. Early records of the city and county of Albany and Colony of Rensselaerswyck. Revised and edited by A. J. F. vanLaer. Albany, 1916-1919. Vols. ii-iv. Q. 3 vols. Univ. State N. Y. N. Y. State Lib'y Hist. Bull. No. 11.   HE—A326

PEET, Henry, Editor. Register of Baptisms of the French Protestant refugees settled at Thorney, Cambridgeshire. 1654-1727. xvi, 138 pp., 1 fac-sim., 1 leaf. Q. Aberdeen, 1903. (HUGUENOT Society of London. Publications. Vol. xvii.)   HK—H875

PELHAM, Massachusetts. See: PARMENTER, C. O. History of Pelham, 1738-1898, including the early history of Prescott. Amherst, Mass., 1898. O.   HE—P21

PELHAM and New Rochelle. See: HAGUE, W. N. Y., 1882. O.   HB—H12

PELLETREAU, William S. Historic homes and institutions, and genealogical and family history of New York. Vols. i-iv. New York, 1907. 4 vols. Illus., pl., port., fac-sim. Q.   HH—P36
Note:—In Volume iii is inserted a "Photograph of Register in the old Family Bible which belonged to Benjamin L'Hommedieu, Jr., of Southold, son of Benjamin L'Hommedieu the Emigrant from La Rochelle, France, after the Revocation of the Edict of Nantes. This Bible belongs to Katherine Ward Lane of Boston, who also owns the portrait by Earle of her great-great-grandfather, Ezra L'Hommedieu, of Southold, who was for over 40 years in the service of his Country." This Photograph faces page 194 in Vol. iii.

——— Huguenot (The) Church Lot and its neighbors. Read at the Unveiling of the Commemorative Tablet, marking the Site of the First French Church in New York, at the N. Y. Produce Exchange, May 10, 1902. (HUGUENOT Society of America. Proceedings. Vol. iv. pp. 53-54. See also page 8.) New York, 1904.
                                                                        HK—H871

PEMBERTON, Max. "The little Huguenot." A romance of Fontainebleau. 177 pp., 1 port. S. New York, 1895.   HN—P37

PENNSYLVANIA archives. Vols. VIII and IX. Edited by J. B. Linn & W. H. Egle, M.D. Harrisburg, Pa., 1895-'96. O. 2nd series. HC—Pa.11

―――― Historical items in: LETTERS and papers relating . . . to the . . . history of Pennsylvania, 1855. By Thomas Balch. HE—B18P

―――― HUGUENOTS. See: Stapleton, Rev. A. "Huguenota Pennsylvanianica." Articles . . . clippings from newspapers, etc., mounted in blank book. Square O. Lewisburg, Pa., 1898-'01. HB—S794.1

―――― Marriages, prior to 1810. See: PENNSYLVANIA Archives. Harrisburg, Pa., 1895-'96. Vols. VIII & IX. 2nd series. O.

PENNSYLVANIA SOCIETY OF NEW YORK. First Annual Dinner, 1899. 54 pp. New York, 1899. O. HK—P37 Subsequent Annual Dinners bound with Year Book.

―――― Year Book, 1901-'03. 3 vols. Port., pl., maps. New York, 1901-'03. O. HK—P371

PEPPERELLBOUROUGH, Massachusetts. First Book of Records of the Pepperellbourough, now the City of Saco. Printed by vote of the City Council, March 18, 1895. 299 pp. Portland, Me., 1896. O. HE—Sa.1

PERINE. See: PERRIN and PERRINE.

PERKINS, MARY E. Old houses of the antient town of Norwich, Connecticut, 1660-1800. Norwich, Conn., 1895. XVIII, 62 pp., 23 port., 8 group port., 3 pl., 3 maps, 2 plans. Square O. HE—P41

PERRENOUD, HENRI. Etude historique sur les progrès de protestantisme en France au point de vue statistique, 1802-1888. Paris, 1889. 253 pp. Q. HA—P42

PERRIN, ANNA FALCONER, & Meeker, M. F. P. Allied families of Purdy, Fauconnier, Archer, Perrin. 9 p.l., 15-114 pp., 2 charts, folded, 9 pl., 8 port., 2 maps. New York, [cop. 1911]. O. HH—P458

PERRINE, HOWLAND DELANO. Daniel Perrin, "The Huguenot," and his descendants in America, of the surnames Perrine, Perine, and Prine, 1665-1910. 4 p.l., 547 pp., 1 fac-sim., 11 groups, 25 part., 5 pl., 3 maps. Q. South Orange, N. J., 1910. HH—P458.1

PERRISSON, J. See: FRANKLIN, ALFRED LOUIS AUGUSTE. Grandes scènes historiques de XVIe siècle, reproduction facsimilé du recuiel de J. Tortorel & J. P. Illustrated, portrait. Folio. Paris, 1886. Half morocco. HA—F85

PERRY, AMOS. Memorial of Zachariah Allen, 1795-1882. 108 pp. port. Cambridge, 1883. O. HG—Al.5

PERRY, RIGHT REV. WILLIAM STEVENS, D.D., LL.D. Bishop of Iowa. History of the American Episcopal Church. 1587-1883. Boston, 1885. 2 Vols. Square quarto. **HC—P43**

Vol. I. The planting and growth of the American Colonial Church, 1587-1783.

Vol. II. The organization and progress of the American Church, 1783-1883.

PEYRAT, NAPOL. Historie des pasteurs du desert: depuis la Révocation de l'Edit de Nantes: jusqua la Revolution française. 1685-1789. 2 Vols. Paris, 1842. O. **HG—P45**

PHILIP II, KING OF SPAIN.
{ HJ
Autograph
Letters

1. Letter signed in French. Dated 15 March, 1578.
2. Letter. 1 page, folio. Dated February 9, 1579.
3. Letter signed in French. 6 pages, folio. Dated 1577.
4. Letter. 1 page, folio. Dated 1579.
5. An official copy of the King's Orders. Dated 1578.

PHILIP II. Lettre envoyée au Roi d'Espagne . . . par le Conseil des Seize, en 1591, pendant le siege de Paris. [Edited by P. Paris.] D. Paris, 1830. (Monumens inedits de l'histoire de France. Part 2.) **HD—M815**

PHILADELPHIA. See: WATSON, J. F. Annals of Philadelphia, Pennsylvania, in the olden time. 3 vols. O. Phila., 1891. **HE—WATS.33**

——— See: WOOLSEY, SUSAN C. Short history of the city of Philadelphia. 1887. **HE—W88**

PHŒNIX, STEPHEN WHITNEY. Whitney family of Connecticut and its affiliations; being an attempt to trace the descendants . . . of Henry Whitney from 1649-1878 . . . with some account of the Whitneys of England. 3 Vols. pl., table. New York, 1878. Q **HH—W61**

PICHEREL-DARDIER, MME. A. See: RABAUT, PAUL. Lettres à Antoine Court, 1739-1755. No date. **HG—R11**

PIERCE, FREDERICK CLIFTON. Field genealogy, being the record of all the Field family in America, whose ancestors were in this country prior to 1700. . . . All descendants of the Fields of England, whose ancestor, Hurbutus De la Field, was from Alsace-Lorraine. 2 vols., pl., port. Chicago, Ill., 1901. Q. **HH—F45**

PIERRE and his family, or, a Story of the Waldenses. VI, 7-214 pp., 4 pl. Philadelphia, [1842]. S. Rev. ed. **HN—P81**

PIERREFLEUR, Pierre de. Mémoires de Pierrefleur grand banderet d'Orbe où sont contenus les commencements de la réforme dans la ville d'Orbe et au pays de Vaud (1530-61), publiés [avec] de notes historiques par A. Verdeil. Lausanne, 1856. 412 pp. O. HB—P61

[PILATTE, Leon.] Edits, déclarations, et arrests concernans la réligion p. réformée, 1662-1751, précédés de l'Edit de Nantes, réimprimés pour le deuxième centenaire de la révocation de l'Edit de Nantes. Paris, 1885. 660 pp. D. HA—P64

PILGRIM (The) of old France, or, the Huguenots on the Hudson, 1613-'14 . . . and other pieces of verse; by Rev. B. F. DeCOSTA, D.D. 2nd ed. New York, 1893. T. HN—D35

PITHOU, Nicolas. Le protestantisme en Champagne; ou, Récits extraits d'un manuscrit concernant l'histoire de la fondation et du développement de l'église réformée de Troyes dès 1539-95. Par C. L. B. Recordon. Paris, 1863. 259 pp. O. HA—P68

PLAINTES des protestans cruellement opprimez dans le royaume de France. [Par CLAUDE, Jean.] Edition nouvelle avec commentaires par Frank Puaux. Paris, 1885. Square O. HA—C571

PLATT, Franklin, Compiler. Notes upon the ancestry of Ebenezer Greenough . . . and of his wife . . . Abigail Israel . . . also a list of their descendants. 38 pp., 4 leaves. Philadelphia, 1895. O. HH—P69

PLATTSBURG, New York. See: HOLDEN, James Austin. Centenary (The) of the Battle of Plattsburg, 1814. September 11, 1914. Albany, 1914. O. HE—H726

PLEINE, J. N. Französische reformirte kirche in Emden. O. Magdeburg, 1890. (In: DEUTSCHE Hugennoten Vereins. Geschichtsblätter. 1890. Vol. ii.) HK—D49

PLYMOUTH, Massachusetts. Records of the Town of Plymouth. Plymouth, 1889. Vol. i. 1636-1705. O. HE—P74

POESIES Huguenotes du 16ᵉ siècle. Edited by [SCHMIDT, Charles Guillaume Adolphe]. 44 pp. Strasbourg, 1882. D.

POITOU: familles du. See: BEAUCHET-FILLEAU, Henri & Paul. Dictionnaire historique et genealogique. . . . 2nd ed. Tomes i-iv. Poiters, 1891-1901. HG—B38

POOLE, Reginald Lane. History of the Huguenots; of the dispersion at the recall of the Edict of Nantes. London, 1880. 208 pp. D. HA—P78
Lothian essay. 1879.

PORCHER, Frederick A. Historical and social sketch of Craven co. South Carolina. (In: DUBOSE, S. Contribution to the history of the Huguenots of South Carolina.) HB—D85

——— Same. HB—F87.5

PORTER, Rev. Noah. 1781-1866. Half century discourse, on occasion of the 50th anniversary of his ordination as Pastor of the First Church in Farmington, Conn., delivered Nov. 12th, 1856. 54 pp. O. Farmington, 1857. HE—Z1

PORTSMOUTH, New Hampshire. See: BREWSTER, C. W. Rambles about Portsmouth. . . . Portsmouth, 1859. O. HE—P83B

POPE, Joseph. Jacques Cartier; his life and voyages. 168 pp., 1 pl. Ottawa, 1889. D. HG—C24

POTTER, Charles Edward, Editor. Genealogies of some old families of Concord, Mass., and their descendants in part to the present generation. . . . 14 port., 1 pl., 3 leaves, 5-143 pp. Vol. i. Boston, 1887. Square Q. HH—P85

POTTER, Elisha Reynolds, Jr. Early (The) History of Narragansett; with an appendix of original documents, many of which are now for the first time published. xix, 423 pp. 2nd ed. Providence, 1835. O. (RHODE ISLAND Historical Society. Collections. Vol. iii.) HK—P85

——— Same. HE—P85N

——— Memoir concerning the French settlements and French settlers in the colony of Rhode Island. Providence, 1879. 138 pp., 2 maps. 8vo. (Rhode Island historical tracts. No. 5.) HE—P85R

PRESCOTT, Massachusetts. See: PARMENTER, C. O. History of Pelham, . . . 1738-1898, including the early history of Prescott. . . . Amherst, Mass. O. HE—P21

PRETENDUE (La) trahison de Coligny. [By N. Weiss.] 11 pp. 1900. HG—S33
Reprint: Bull. Soc. Hist. Prot. Fr.
Bound in Volume, "Biographical & Historical Essays."

PRIEST and Huguenot; or, Persecution in the Age of Louis XV. By Laurence Louis Felix BUNGENER. Translated from the French. Boston, 1854. 2 Vols. D. HN—B88

PRIME, Temple. Some account of the Bowdoin family, with notes on the families of Pordage, Lynde, Newgate, Erving. 52 pp. 2d ed. O. New York, 1894. HH—A54

PRIMER, Sylvester, Ph.D. The Huguenot element in Charleston's pronunciation. pp 214-244. Charleston, S. C., 1889. O. Volume entitled: "Huguenot Essays." HB—H69

PRINE. See: PERRIN.

PROTESTANT Church at Loudin. See: Loudin: Registers of the Protestant Church.

PROTESTANTISME (Le) refute par luimeme; Response aux ministres du canton de Sainte-Foy. 2 leaves, 5-224 pp. Bordeaux, 1838. O. HM—P96

PROTESTANTS from France, in their English home. By S. W. KERSHAW. London, 1885. D. HB—K47

PROVOST, Rev. J. See: EGLISES Evangelique Françaises des Etats-Unis. Confession de foi et liturgie.

PSEAUMES DE DAVID. Mis en rime Françoise. Par Clement Marot et Theodore de Beze. Paris: Pierre Des-Hayes, 1652. O. Aussi:
Les Dix commandemens.
Le catechisme.
Confession de foi faite d'un commun accord par les églises réformées du royaume de France.
La forme des prieres ecclesiastiques. HM—P95

———— Mis en Vers François. Revus et approuves par les Pasteurs et Professeurs de l'Eglise et de l'Académie de Genève. Nouvelle Edition. A Genève, Chez Pierre-Isaac Faber, 1790. D. pp. 652. CANTIQUES SACRES POUR LES PRINCIPALES SOLENNITES DES CHRETIENS, et sur autres sujets. Nouvelle Edition, augmentée de plusieurs Cantiques et prières. A Niort, Chez Jean-Baptiste Lefranc-Elies, Imprimeur-Libraire, 1790. D. pp. 313. (Both works bound in one volume.) HM—P95.2

————Mis en Vers François, revus et approuvez par le synode Walon des Provinces-Unies. 269 pp. Amsterdam, 1770. S. HM—N85 (Bound with: (Le) NOUVEAU Testament, 1770.)

PUAUX, Frank. Le Baron Fernand de Schickler. Discours prononce à la Assemblée Générale de la Société de l'Histoire de protestantisme français, le 28 avril, 1910. 18 pp. Paris, 1910. O. HG—S33 (Volume of Biographical & Historical Essays, in French.)

———— Défence de la Réformation. Conférence faite à Saint-Jean-du-Gard. Le 25 Septembre, 1910. 31 pp. [Paris, 1910.] O. HA—R67

———— Histoire de l'établishment des protestants français Suède. 212 pp. Paris, 1892. O. HA—P961

———— Inauguration de Musée de Désert . . . 24 Sept., 1911. Allocutions de F. Puaux, E. Hugues et C. Babut. Cévennes, 1912. pp. 19-26. O. HA—M986

———— Editor. Oeuvres du protestantisme française au XIXe siècle. Paris, 1893. xxxiv, 480 pp., 18 port. Folio. HA—P96

———— Editor. Plaintes (Les) des protestants cruellement opprimez dans le royaume de France. Par Jean Claude, 1885. (Classiques du protestantisme français, XVIe, XVIIe, XVIIIe siècle.) HA—C571

PUMPELLY, Josiah Collins. Historical sketches of the Hampton Settlements on Long Island. pp. 217-236, 1 port., 5 pl., n. p., 1911. O. (In: Americana, March, 1911.) HE—A512

—— Historical addresses and papers. HB—P87
Contents:
I. Huguenot builders of New Jersey. pp. 49-60, 1 port.
II. Incidents in the early history of Berkshire County, Mass., and the Pumpelly, Pixley, Paterson, and Avery families. pp. 65-72, 1 pl. (N. Y. Gen. & Biographical Record, April, 1893, & April, 1896.)
III. Mahlon Dickerson, industrial pioneer and old time patriot. 26 pp. 1892. O.

—— Huguenot settlement in New Jersey. (HUGUENOT Society of America. Publications. Vol. iii. 1900.) HK—H87

—— Our French Allies in the Revolution and other addresses, Morristown, pref. 1889. 64 pp. D. HE—Pu986

PURPLE, Samuel Smith, M.D., Editor. Records of the Reformed Dutch Church in New Amsterdam and New York. Marriages from 11 December, 1639, to 26 August, 1801. xii, 9-351 pp., 1 fac-sim., 1 pl. New York, 1890. Q. (New York Genealogical & Biographical Collections. Vol. i.) HK—N491

PUTNAM, Eben., Editor. Salem Press Historical & Genealogical. Record. Vol. i, No. 1, Vol. ii, No. 3. Salem, Mass., 1890-92. HH—Sal

PUTNAM, Eleanor, pseudonym. See: BATES, Mrs. Harriet L. Vose.

PUTNAM, Ruth. William the Silent, Prince of Orange, the moderate man of the XVIth century. The story of his life. 2 vols. 2nd ed., pl., tables. New York, 1898. O. HG—P98

QUATREFAGES de Breau, J. L., Armand, de., La Rochelle et ses environs avec un precis historique . . . 385 pp., 1 pl., 1 map. D. La Rochelle, 1866. HA—Qu2

QUELQUES femmes de la réforme, recueil biographique. Seconde édition. Lausanne, 1865. D. HG—Qu3

QUINN, Thomas C., Editor. See: MASSACHUSETTS of today. A memorial of the State, historical and biographical. . . . Boston, 1892. Folio. HE—Qu4

QUICK, John, Compiler. Synodicon in Gallia reformata; or, the Acts, decisions, decrees, and canons of those famous national councils of the reformed churches in France collected and composed out of those renowned synods. A work never before extant in any language. London, 1692. 2 vols., folio, half calf. HA—Qu4

RABAUD, Camille. Histoire du protestantisme dans l'Albigeois et le Lauragais, depuis son origine jusqu'à la révocation de l'Edit de Nantes (1685). Paris, 1873. 514 pp. O. HA—R11

RABAUT, Paul. 1718-94. Lettres à Antoine Court (1739-1755). Dix-sept ans de la vie d'un apôtre du désert, avec notes, portrait et autographe par A. Picheral-Dardier, et une préface par Ch. Dardier. Paris [1884.] 2 Vols., port., fac-sim. O.　　　　　HG—R11

———— Biographie de Paul Rabaut, pasteur du désert et de ses trois fils. By Abraham Borrel. Nîmes, 1854. 168 pp. D.　　　HG—R11.1

RAHLENBECK, Charles. Expositions (Les) Belges a la cour d' Elizabeth. 1558-1603. (Extrait de la Revue de Belgique.) 16 pp. Bruxelles, 1880. O.　　　　　　　　　　　　HG—S3.3
Biographical & Historical Essays, in French.

RAMBAUD, Alfred. Histoire de la civilisation contemporaine en France. Paris, 1888. 750 pp. D.　　　　　　　　　HD—R14

RAMSAY, David. Memoirs of the life of Martha Laurens Ramsay, with an appendix containing extracts from her diary, letters and other private papers. Fourth edition. Boston, 1814. 219 pp. TT.
　　　　　　　　　　　　　　　　　　　　　　　HG—R14

RAVENEL, Daniel, Compiler. "Liste des François et Suisses." From an old manuscript list of French and Swiss protestants settled in Charleston, on the Santee, and at the Orange Quarter in Carolina, who desired naturalization. Prepared about 1695-6. N. Y. 1888. 77 pp., map. O.　　　　　　　　　　　　　　HB—R19

RAVENEL, Henry Edmund. Ravenel records. A history of gene-alogy of the Huguenot family of Ravenel, of South Carolina; with some . . . account of the parish of St. John's, Berkeley, which was their principal location. V. 279 pp., 9 pl., 2 port. Atlanta, Ga., 1898. O.　　　　　　　　　　　　　　　　HH—R11

RAND, James Hall. Indians (The) of North Carolina and their re-lations with the settlers. 41 pp. O. (Univ. of No. Carolina, The James Sprunt Hist. Pub. Vol. xii., No. 2.) Chapel Hill, N. C., 1913.　　　　　　　　　　　　　　　　　HK—Pamphlet
Contains references to North Carolina Huguenots, pp. 22, 23 & 35.

READ, Charles, Editor. See: SATYRE Menipee. 1876.　　HN—Sa8

READ, Charles, & WADDINGTON, Francis. Mémoires inédits de Dumont de Bostaquet, gentilhomme Normand. Sur les temps qui ont précédé et suivi la Révocation de l'Edit de Nantes, sur le refuge et les expéditions de Guillaume III. en Angleterre et en Irlande. Et précédés d'une introduction historique. xlvi, 376 pp. Paris, 1864. O.　　　　　　　　　　　　　　　　　　HG—R22

RECORD (The) of births, marriages, and deaths . . . in the town of Stoughton . . . 1727 to 1800, and . . . Canton . . . 1797 to 1845, preceded by . . . records of the south precinct of Dorchester . . . 1715 to 1727. Ed. by F. Endicott. vii, 317 pp. O. Canton, Mass., 1896.　　　　　　　　　　　　　　　　　　HHn—St6

RECORDON, Ch. L. B., Editor. See: PITHOU, N. Le Protestan-tisme en Champagne. 1863.　　　　　　　　　　HA—P68

REFORMED DUTCH CHURCH; Albany, New York. Records.
1683-1764. Vols. I-IV. Q. (HOLLAND Society, New York.
Year book, 1904-1907.) 4 Vols. Albany Book, Nos. 1, 2, 3 & 4.
HK—H71.1

———— Hackensack and Schraalenburg, New Jersey. Records of the
Churches . . . with the Registers . . . and the Consistories to the
beginning of the 19th century. (HOLLAND Society, New York.
Collections. Vol. I, 2 Vols. in 1. 1891.) HK—H71

———— New Amsterdam and New York. Records. Q. 3 Vols. New
York, 1890, 1901-'02. HK—N491
Marriages, Dec. 11, 1639-August 26, 1801. PURPLE, S. S., Editor.
Baptisms, Dec. 25, 1636-Dec. 27, 1730. Vol. I. EVANS, T. G.,
Editor.
Baptisms, Jan. 1, 1731-Dec. 29, 1800. Vol. II. WRIGHT, T. A.,
Editor.
(N. Y. Gen. & Biog. Soc'y. Collections, Vols. I, II, III, & IV.)

———— New Paltz, New York. Records: containing an account of the
Church, and Registers of Consistories, Members and Baptisms.
(HOLLAND Society of New York. Collections. Vol. III. 1891.
O.) HK—H71H

———— Port Richmond, Staten Island, New York. Records of the
Baptisms from 1692 to 1772. Edited by T. A. WRIGHT. (N. Y.
Gen. & Biog. Soc'y. Collections. Vol. IV. 1909. Q. HK—N49.1

———— North America. List . . . Ministers . . . from 1763-1800.
(In: DE WITT, T. Discourse delivered . . . August, 1856. . . .
N. Y., 1857. pp. 71-79. O.) HC—D51

———— (First) Dutch Church: Hackensack, N. J. Register of the
members. 1686-1870. (In: ROMEYN, Rev. T. B. Historical
discourse. . . . New Jersey, 1870. O. pp. 1-23. Appendix.)
HC—R66

———— Low Dutch Church of Harlem. Organized 1660. Historical
Sketch by Rev. Edgar Tilton, Jr., D.D., New York, 1910. 181
pp., 1 colored plate, other plates paged in. HC—T58

———— Protestant Dutch Church, Albany, New York. Register of
members of the . . . Church, 1683-1700?. In: ROGERS, Rev.
E. P. Historical discourse . . . Nov. 26, 1857 . . . pp. 67-80. N.
Y., 1858. O. HC—R63

———— Bergen, New Jersey. Bergen Church Records. Vols. I-II. 2
Vols. Q. HK—H71.1
Vol. I. Baptisms, 1666-1788.
Vol. II. Marriages, 1665-1788, & Register of Members. (HOL-
LAND Society of New York, Year Book. 1913, & 1914.)

———— New York City: Celebration of the quarter-millennial anniversary, Nov. 21, 1878. 104 pp. N. Y., 1878?. O. HC—N48

———— Year book of Collegiate Reformed Protestant Dutch Church.
N. Y., 1882. D. HC—Pamphlet

REFUGEES (The) : a tale of two Continents. By A. C. Doyle. N. Y.,
1893. D.   HN—D77

RENSSELAERSWYCK, New York. See: Albany, N. Y.

———— Settlers from 1630-1646, compiled from the books of monthly
wages and other MSS. From O'Callaghan's "History of New Netherlands." pp. 430-441. (In: HOLLAND Society Year Book, 1896.
pp. 130-140.)   HK—H711
NOTE:—Also; Passenger Lists, 1657-1664. From "Doc. Hist. of
New York." Vol. II. pp. 52-63. See: pp. 141-166 in this Vol.

REPORT of a French protestant refugee in Boston, 1687. Translated
from the French by E. T. Fisher. Brooklyn, N. Y. 1868. 42 pp.
Square O.   HB—R29

REPUBLIC Magazine. Vol. I, No. 1. N. Y., 1890. Q.
See: CHAILLE-LONG, Col. Charles.

REQUA, REV. AMOS CONKLIN. The family of Requa. 1678-1898.
XXXVIII, 1-63 pp., 18 port., 1 pl. O. Peekskill, New York, 1898.
                                                       HH—Rq31

REUSS, RODOLPHE. Pierre Brully: ancient Dominicain de Metz, ministre de l'Eglise française de Strasbourg, 1539-1545.   HG—B83
Volume "Etude Biographique."

REVEILLAUD, EUGENE. l'Etablissement d'une Colonie de Vaudois
français en Algerie; publie sous les auspices de le Societe Coligny.
118 pp., 4 l., 4 pl., 1 map folded. Paris, 1893. S.   HB—R32

REVILLIOD, GUSTAVE. Fromment, Anthoine. Les actes et gestes
merceilleux de la cite de Geneve. . . . O. Geneve, 1854. HA—F922

REVEREND LOUIS ROU, Pastor, French Protestant Church, N. Y.
City, and the missing MS., of his tract . . . (1734) entitled: Critical remarks on the game of chess, occasioned by his paper of . . .
15th Sept., 1733, and dated from Slaughter's Coffee-house, Sept. 21.
Florence (Italy), 1902. 14 pp. D.   HG—Pamphlet

REVOCATION de l'Edit de Nantes, d'après des documents inédits par
E. O. DOUEN. Paris, 1894. 3 Vols. Q.   HA—R32

———— de l'Edit de Nantes; discours prononcés à l'occasion du deuxième anniversaire det événement. Montreal, 1885. 157 pp. O.
                                                       HA—N19

RHODE ISLAND HISTORICAL SOCIETY. Collections. Vol. III. Providence, R. I., 1835. O.   HK—P85
Vol. III. POTTER, E. R. Early history of Narragansett.

———— A second copy.   HE—P85N

RHODE ISLAND HISTORICAL TRACTS. No. 5. Memoir concerning
the French . . . settlers in . . . Rhode Island. By Elisha Reynolds
Potter. Providence, 1879. Square O.   HE—P85

RHODE ISLAND. See: AUSTIN, John Osborne. Genealogical dictionary of three generations . . . before 1690. Albany, N. Y., 1887. Square folio.   HH—A93

RIBARD, CLEMENT. Notes d'histoire Cévenole d'après des documens la plupart inédits. 344 pp. O. SeVend, [190?].   HD—R35

RICE, FRANKLIN P., Editor. Worcester town records, from 1753-1783. 472 pp. Worcester, Mass., 1882. O. (Worcester Society of Antiquity. Collections, Vol. IV.)   HE—W89

RICHEMOND, LOUIS MARIE DE. See: MESCHINET de RICHE-MOND, Louis Marie.

RIKER, JAMES. Annals of Newtown, in Queens County, New York: containing its history from its first settlement . . . also, a particular account of numerous Long Island families now spread over this and various other States. New York, 1852. 437 pp., 2 maps. O.
                                                              HE—R44N

——— "Evacuation Day," 1783 . . . with recollections of Captain John Van Arsdale . . . by whose efforts on that day . . . the American Flag successfully raised on the Battery (New York City). 56 pp. N. Y., 1883. O.   HE—A51.2

——— Harlem (City of N. Y.): its origin and early annals, prefaced by home scenes in the fatherlands; or, Notices of its founders before emigration; also sketches of numerous families, and the recovered history of the land-titles. N. Y. 1881. 636 pp., illust., maps. O.
                                                              HE—R44

RILLIET, ALBERT. Notice fur le premier séjour de Calvin à Genève. (In: CALVIN, John. Le catéchisme français de Calvin, publié en 1537.)   HM—C13

ROBERT, PFARRER, & DITTMAR, W. Waldenser (Die) und ihre Colonie Walldorf. 23 pp. O. Magdeburg, 1891. (In: DEUTSCHE Hugenotten Verein. Geschichtsblätter. 1891. Vol. III.)   HK—D49

ROBERT-LABARTHE, U. de., pasteur. Histoire du protestantisme dans le Haut-Languedoc, le Bas-Quercy et le comte de Foix de 1685-1789. D'apres des documents pour la plupart inedits par . . . pasteur. 2 v. O. Paris, 1896.   HA—R54
Vol. I. 1685-1715.
Vol. II. 1715-1789.

ROBERTSON, CHARLES FRANKLIN. Historical Societies in their relation to local historical interest. An address . . . before the Missouri Historical Society, September 19, 1883. 16 pp. St. Louis, 1883. O.   HK—H62V

ROBERTSON, WYNDHAM. Pocahontas, alias Matoaka, and her descendants through her marriage . . . with John Rolfe . . . with . . . notes by R. A. Brock. 7 & 84 pp. 1 port. O. Richmond, Va. 1887.   HH—P75

ROBINSON, Conway, Compiler. Abstract of the proceedings of the Virginia Company of London, 1619-1624. . . . Edited by R. A. BROCK. 2 Vols. O. Richmond, 1888-'89. (VIRGINIA Historical Society. Collections. New Series. 1888-'89. Vols. VII-VIII.)   HK—V81

ROBINSON, Mrs. Ida May. Items of ancestry, by a descendant. 93 pp. O. Boston, 1894.   HH—Rob56
Privately printed.

ROBISON, Jeannie Floyd-Jones, & Bartlett, H. C., Editors. Genealogical records. Manuscript entries of births, deaths, and marriages, taken from family Bibles, 1581-1917. xv, 331 pp., 3 fac-sim., 7 pl., 6 port. New York, 1917. Square O. (COLONIAL Dames, State of New York.)   HK—C711
200 copies. No. 85.

ROCKLAND County, New York. See: GREEN, F. B. History of Rockland County. N. Y., 1886. Q.   HE—G82

ROCKWELL, William Walker. S. T. B., Lic. Th. Calvin and the Reformation. (In: UNION Theo. Seminary. Three addresses delivered by Professors in the Seminary, at a Service in commemoration of the 400th Anniversary of the birth of John Calvin.) New York, 1909. 47 pp. O. pp. 5-19.   HM—Pamphlet.

RODOCANACHI, E. Une protectrice de la Réforme en Italie et en France. Renée de France, duchesse de Ferrare. 573 pp., 1 port. Paris, 1896. O.   HG—R29

ROE, Francis Asbury, Rear Admiral, U. S. N. American sea Captain of Colonial times. A paper read before Soc. Colonial Wars, D. C., March 12, 1900. 11 pp. O. (No. 2, Hist. Papers, Soc. Col. Wars, D. C., 1900.)   HG—Mem512

—— Huguenots (The). Some account of their persecution, sufferings, wanderings, and achievements, together with an estimate of their character and influence in America. HUGUENOT Society of America, Publications. Vol. IV. pp. 1-7. New York, 1915.   HK—H87

ROEBLING, Emily Warren. Journal of the Rev. Silas Constant . . . Presbyterian Church at Yorktown, N. Y. . . . Records of the Church . . . list of marriages, 1784-1825 . . . notes on families mentioned. Edited by J. Gleach. 561 pp., 1 chart, 3 fac-sim., 5 groups, 15 plates, 11 port. Philadelphia, 1903. O.   HH—C788

ROGER Williams (The) Calendar. Compiled by J. O. Austin. Central Falls, R. I. 1897. D.   HO—C13

ROGERS, Rev. Ebenezer Platt, 1871-81. The Glory of New York; a discourse delivered in the South Reformed Church on Thanksgiving Day, Nov. 26th, 1874. . . . 18 pp. O. N. Y., 1874.   HE—Z1

—— Historical discourse on the Reformed Protestant Dutch Church of Albany, Nov. 26, 1857, delivered in the North Dutch church. N. Y. 1858. 120 pp., illust., pl. O.   HC—R63

ROGERS, S. H. Tradition of the "Betrothal Medal," supposed to have been brought to South Carolina from Holland, by the Ioor family, Huguenot refugees from France, with a copy of the "Medal" taken from the original.   HJ—& Medal

ROISSELET DE SAUELIERES, FILS. Histoire de Protestantisme en France, precedee de la Refutation d'un libelle de E. B. D. Fressard . . . intitule: Evenemens de Nismes. . . . Vol. I. v-xlviii, 415 pp. O. Nismes, 1836. (Imprint on cover: Montpellier, 1837.)   HM—P96 Bound with "Protestantisme (Le) refute. . . ."

ROMAN forgeries, or a True account of false records discovering the impostures and counterfeit antiquities of the Church of Rome. By a Faithful Son of the Church of England, i. e.; T. TRAHERNE. London, 1673.   HM—E9

ROMEYN, REV. THEODORE BAYARD. Historical discourse delivered on the occasion of the re-opening and dedication of the First Reformed (Dutch) church at Hackensack, N. J., May 2, 1869. N. Y. 1870. 131 pp., pl., fac-sim. O.   HC—R66

ROSENGARTEN, JOSEPH GEORGE. French colonists and exiles in the United States. 234 pp. O. Philadelphia, 1907.   HB—R71

——— The German soldier in the Wars of United States. 2nd edition, enlarged. 298 pp. Philadelphia, 1890. (Cop. 1886.)   HE—R72

——— Reynolds Memorial address. March 8th, 1880. 34 pp. Philadelphia, 1880. O.   HE—A512

ROSER, FRANCIS M. Memorial of Adrian Oliver Iselin. [N. Y. 1885.] 34 pp. O.   HG—Mem.51

ROSSIER, L. Histoire des protestants de Picardie particulièrement de ceux du département de la Somme d'après de documents pour la plupart inédits. Paris, 1861. 328 pp. D.   HA—R73

ROU, JEAN. 1638-1711. Mémoires inédits et ospuscules (1638-1711). Publiés pour la Société de l'histoire du protestantisme français, d'après le manuscrit conservé aux archives de l'état à La Haye, par Francis Waddington. Paris, 1857. 2 vols., table. O.   HG—R75

ROUGET, CLAUDE. Une Eglise Calviniste au XVIme siècle, 1550-1581. Histoire de la communauté réformée de Sainte-Marie-du-Mines (Alsace). Publiée pour la première fois avec notes et commentaires par E. Muhlenbeck. xiv, 515 pp., 1 leaf. Paris, 1881. Q.   HA—R75

ROUX, G., Translator. See: Moerikofer, J. C. Histoire des réfugiés de la réformé en Suisse. 1878.   HB—M72

ROXBURY CHURCH. Records relating to Brookline. (Brookline Hist. Pub. Society Publications, No. 5, pp. 55-57.) A reprint, Vol. VI. Reports of Record Commissioners of Boston, 2d edition, 1884.   HH—Pamphlet

ROY, Joseph E.   Manual of the principles, doctrines and usages of
congregational churches.   Revised edition.   Boston, no date.   48 pp.
D.   HM—Pamphlet

ROYAL (The) descent and Colonial ancestry of Mrs. Harley Calvin
Gage.   32 pp.   O.   n. p., cop. 1910.   HH—A54

RUBLE, Alphonse, le baron de, Editor.   See: AUBIGNE, Theodore.   Agrippa d'Histoire universelle . . . 1886.   HF—Av.1

RUPP, I. Daniel, prof.   A collection of . . . thirty thousand names
of German, Swiss, Dutch, French, and other immigrants in Pennsylvania, from 1727 to 1776. . . . With . . . historical and other
notes, also, an appendix containing lists of more than one thousand
German and French names in New York prior to 1712.   495 pp.
Philadelphia, 1880.   2d ed., revised . . . with German translations.
D.   HH—R82

RYAN, Daniel J.   History of Ohio, with biographical sketches of her
governors, and the ordinance of 1787.   Columbus, 1888.   210 pp.,
port.   O.   HE—R95

RYE, New York.   See: BAIRD, C. W.   History of Rye . . . 1660-
1870.   New York, 1871.   O.   HE—B16

RYVES, Windham.   The Huguenot refugee.   Song.   (With chorus.)
Words by Dr. Byles.   Q.   6 pp.   n. p., n. d.   HO—Pamphlet

SACO, Massachusetts.   See: PEPPERELLBOROUGH,   Mass.
First book of records of the town. . . . Portland, Me., 1896.   HE—SA.1

SAGARD-THEODAT, Gabriel.   Histoire du Canada et voyages que
les frères mineurs recollects y ont faicts pour la conversion des infidèles depuis l'an 1615, avec un dictionnaire de la langue huronne.
Nouvelle édition publiée par Edwin Tross.   Paris, 1866.   4 Vols.
O.   HF—Sa.1

SAINT ANDRE Du PIN de.   See: DUPIN DE SAINT ANDRE,
Armand.

ST. ANDREW'S (Episcopal) Church, Richmond, Staten Island, New
York.   Births and Baptisms from 1752-1795.   Marriages from
1754-1808.   Edited by T. A. WRIGHT.   (N. Y. GEN. & BIOG.
Soc'y.   Collections.   Vol. iv.   1909.   Q.)   HK—N491

SAINT Augustine: a story of the Huguenots in America.   By J. R.
MUSICK.   New York, 1892.   D.   HN—M97

SAINT Bartholomew's eve.   A tale of the Huguenot wars; by G. A.
HENTY.   New York, 1893.   D.   HN—H38

ST. BRIS, Thomas de.   See: De St. BRIS, Thomas.

ST. DUNSTAN'S, Stepney, England. Marriage registers. Edited by
Thomas COLYER-FERGUSSON. 3 vols. Canterbury, 1898.
1902. Q.   HH—F38
Vol. i. 1568-1639.
Vol. ii. 1640-1696.
Vol. iii. 1697-1719.

ST. GEORGE'S Society of New York. History of St. George's Society of New York from 1770-1913. 389 pp., 1 col. pl. New York,
1913. O. (Also port., etc., paged in.)   HK—G23
No. 176 of 1,000 copies printed.

ST. JACOBSKERK. Grafboeken der Groote of St. Jacobskerk, te
s'Gravenhage, 1620-1830. Bewerkt door M. G. WILDEMAN.
2 p. l., 209 pp., 8 leaves. Square folio. s'Hertogenbosch, 1898.
                                                            HB—W67

SAINT MARK'S Church-in-the-Bowerie. Services in commemoration
of the 100th Anniversary of the Consecration of the Church, on May
9th, 1899. New York, 1899. 4 leaves. Square Q.   HC—Pamphlet

ST. MATTHEW'S Evangelical Lutheran Church, New York City.
Some early records of the Lutheran Church (Broome Street) New
York. Marriages prior to the Revolution, and the earlier Baptisms.
September 14, 1704-1723. (In: HOLLAND Society, N. Y., Year
Book. 1903. pp. 1-118.)   HK—H711

SAINT MICHAEL'S Church, Charleston, S. C. See: BEESLEY,
C. N. Illustrated guide to St. Michael's. . . .

ST. NICHOLAS Society of New York. Genealogical record, containing the lines of descent of members of the Society . . . to July 1,
1916. Vols. i-ii. New York, 1905, 1916. 2 Vols. Q.   HK—N48

——— Record of the Semi-centennial Anniversary, February 28, 1885.
42 pp., 1 leaf. New York, 1885. O.   HK—N481A

SALEM (The) Book: records of the past and glimpses of the present.
Prepared for publication by a group of Salem's sons and daughters.
2 p.l., 250, 8 pp., 1 port., 5 pl. Salem, N. Y., 1890. O.   HE—Sa3

SALEM, New York. See: SALEM (The) Book: records of the past
and glimpses of the present. . . . Salem, N. Y., 1896. O.

SALEM: Old Salem, by Mrs. Harriet L. Vose BATES. Edited
by Arlo Bates. 120 pp. Boston, 1886. S.   HI—B276

SALEM PRESS Historical & Genealogical Record. No. 1, Vol. i,
No. 3, Vol. ii. Salem, Mass., 1890-1892.   HH—Sa1

SALISBURY, Edward Elbridge, & Salisbury, E. McC., Family Histories and genealogies; a series of genealogical and biographical monographs. . . . With 29 pedigree-charts and 2 charts of combined descents (in a supplement separately bound). 3 vols. in 5 vols., pl.,
charts. New Haven, 1892. Folio.   HH—Sa3H

SALISBURY, Edward Elbridge. Family memorials. A series of
genealogical and biographical monographs. . . . With 15 pedigrees
and an appendix. 2 Vols. Square folio. New Haven, 1885.
HH—Sa3M

SALTER, Edwin. A history of Monmouth and Ocean counties . . .
a genealogical record of earliest settlers . . . and their descendants.
4 p.l., iii-xiii, 442, 80 pp., 1 pl., 2 port. Bayonne, N. J., 1890.
O.   HE—S277

SANXAY, Theodore Frederic. The Sanxay family, and descendants
of Rev. Jacques Sanxay, Huguenot refugee to England in sixteen
hundred and eighty-five. . . . 217 p. Square O. New York,
printed privately. 1907.   HH—Sa5

SATYRE Ménippée; ou, La vertu du catholicon selon l'édition princeps
de 1594, avec introduction et éclaircissements par Charles Read. Edition nouvelle. Paris, 1876. 322 pp. T.   HN—Sa8

SAVAGE, James. Genealogical dictionary of the first settlers of New
England, showing three generations of those who came before May,
1692, on the basis of Farmer's Register. Vols. i-iv. Boston, 1860-
1862. 4 Vols. O.   HH—Sa9

SCHAEFFER, Adolphe. Les Huguenots du seizième siècle. Paris,
1870. 331 pp. O.   HA—Sch1

SCHAFF, Rev. Philip. History of the Edict of Nantes. (HUGUE-
NOT Society of America. Proceedings. 1891. Vol. ii. pp. 85-
114.)   HK—H87

———— and Rev. Samuel Macauley Jackson, M.A., Editors. Encyclopedia of living divines and Christian workers of all denominations in Europe and America. N. Y. 1887. 271 pp.   HG—Sch1

SELLAR, Robert. History of the county of Huntingdon and of the
seigniories of Chateaugay and Beauharnois from their first settlement
to 1838. Huntingdon, Quebec, 1888. 584 pp. O.   HE—Se4

SELLEW, Philip. Genealogical sketch of the Sellew family.   HJ

SENTER, Oramel S. Civic and scenic New England. Newport in
1877. p. 1-15, illust. O. 1877. From Potter's American monthly.
1877. Vol. ix.   HE—Z6

SEYMOUR, Horatio. Address before the New York state agricultural society, at the annual meeting . . . Jan. 21, 1880. . . . 37 p.
1 map. O. Albany, 1880.   HE—Z4

———— Address at Wells Female College, Aurora, N. Y., June 16,
1880.   HE—Z4

———— History and topography of New York; a lecture at Cornell University, June 30th, 1870. 32 pp. O. Utica, 1870.   HE—Z2

———— Influence of New York on American jurisprudence. pp. 217-
230. Square O. 1879. From Magazine of American history.
1879. Vol. iii, No. 4.   HE—Z6

SHARP (The) Papers in the Brookline Public Library. (BROOK-LINE Historical Society. Publications. No. 2. pp. 7-14.)
HK—Pamphlet

SHAW, WILLIAM A., Editor. Letters of denization and acts of naturalization for aliens in England and Ireland. 1603-1700. xxxvi, 413 pp. Q. Lymington, 1911. (HUGUENOT Society of London. Publications. 1911. Vol. xviii.) HK—H87.5
450 copies printed. No. 405.

SHEPHERD, WILLIAM R. Story (The) of New Amsterdam. (HOLLAND Society of New York. Year Book, 1917. pp. 1-111.)
HK—H71.1

SHERMAN, REV. HENRY BEERS. These three. A sermon preached at Woodbury, Conn.; on occasion of its Bi-centennial celebration, July 5, 1859. 18 pp. O. (In: COTHREN, (W), editor. Second centennial . . . Woodbury . . . pp. 107-125.) HE—W885
(Volume "Ancient Woodbury.")

SHERWOOD, GEORGE F. TUDOR, Editor. Genealogical Queries and memoranda. A quarterly magazine. . . . London, 1896 to '98.
HH—Pamphlet

SIMMS, WILLIAM GILMORE. Life of Francis Marion. HG—M33

———— Lily (The) and the totem; or, Huguenots in Florida. 1562-1570. Second edition, N. Y., 1850. 470 pp. D. HB—Si4

SLUYTER, PETER, and DANKERS, JASPAR. Journal of a voyage to N. Y. 1679-80. (Long Island Historical Society. Memoirs, Vol. I.) HK—L86

SCHENCK, ALEXANDER DU BOIS, Compiler. Rev. William Schenck, his ancestry and descendants. Washington, 1883. 163 pp., plate, table. O. HH—Sch2

SCHENCK, H. J., Compiler. Rev. W. Schenck, his ancestry and descendants. . . . 163 p., pl., tab. O. Washington, 1883. HH—Sch2

SCHENCK, MRS. ELIZABETH HUBBELL. History of Fairfield, Fairfield Co., Conn., from 1639-1818. N. Y. 1889. Vol. I, map. O. *Genealogies of Fairfield*, pp. 347-423. HE—Sch2

SCHICKLER, FERNAND, BARON DE. Les eglises du refuge en Angleterre. 3 vols., fac-sim. Paris, 1892. Q. HB—Sch3
Contents:
Vol. I. Edouard VI-Jacques I. 1547-1625.
Vol. II. Charles I-Jacques II. 1625-1685.
Les églises réformées des Iles de la manche.
Vol. III. Pièces justificatives et complementaires du tome I et du tome II.
Table generale alphabetique.

SCHMIDT, Charles, Editor. Les libertins spirituels, traités mystiques écrits dans les années 1547-1549. Publiés d'après le manuscrit original. Bale, 1876. 251 pp. D.   HM—Sch5

———— Charles Guillaume Adolphe, Editor. Poésies huguenotes du 16e siècle. Strasbourg, 1882. 44 pp. D.

SCHOFIELD, George A., Editor. See: IPSWICH, Mass., The Ancient Records. . . . Vol. i. 1899. O.   HE—I6

SCHOUTEN, H. J. De Hollandsche tak van het Schotschegeslacht Craffort of Crawfurd. 13 pp. O. n. p. 1895.   HH—W66
Reprint: Maandblad van het Geneal.-herald. genootschap "De Nederlandsche Leeuw," 1894.   HH—W66

SCHUYLER, Montgomery. Sermon on the 25th anniversary of his rectorship, Christ Church, Oct. 5, 1879. St. Louis, 1879. 26 pp. O.   **HM—Pamphlet**

SCOTT, David Dundas, Translator. See: MERLE d'AUBIGNE, Jean Henri. History of the Reformation in the XVI. century.

SCOTT, Mrs. Fannie J. Platt. French Protestant exiles in England and Sweden. Reproduced from recognized authorities, from privately printed family histories, and . . . MS., pedigrees. Rochester, N. Y., 1909. 11 leaves. Square Q.   HH—S425
Typewritten MS., in Swedish with English translation.

———— Miscellaneous genealogies of the Huguenot refugees in England, Ireland, Holland, and America, 1514-1900. 47 leaves, oblong folio. Rochester, N. Y., 1905.   HH—S425
MS. typewritten, presentation page engrossed.

SCOTT, Mrs. Jacob de la Barre. See: SCOTT, Fannie J. Platt.

SCULL, G. D.. Editor. Montresor (The) Journals. xii, 578 pp., 2 port. O. New York, 1881. (New York Hist. Soc'y. Collections. Vol. xiv.)   HK—N532

SMEDLEY, Rev. Edward. History of the reformed religion of France. N. Y., 1834. 3 vols., portraits.   HA—Sm3

———— History of the reformed religion of France. London, 1832-34. 3 vols., portraits. S.   HA—Sm31

SMILES, Samuel. Les Huguenots: leurs colonies, leurs industries, leurs Eglises, en Angleterre et en Irlande. Traduction autorisée par l'auteur, avec une préface par A. Coquerol, fils. 2 p.l., xvi, 464 pp. O. Paris, 1870.   HA—Sm4.F

———— The Huguenots: their settlements, churches and industries in England & Ireland, with an Appendix relating to the Huguenots in America, by G. P. Disosway. 448 pp. N. Y., 1868. O.
     HA—Sm4.E
List of Huguenot refugees & their descendants on pp. 397-426.

SMITH, HENRY B. Remarks on the announcement of the death of Dr. Robinson. (In: HITCHCOCK, R. D. Life of Edward Robinson.) 1863. pp. 3-16. HG—R56

SMITH, J. J. PRINGLE. Address in St. Philip's Church, Charleston, May 13th, 1875. (In: CHARLESTON, S. C., St. Philip's Church. Special services . . . 1876. pp. 77-127.) HC—C38

SMITH, SAMUEL. History of the Colony of Nova-Cæsaria, or New Jersey: . . . an account of its first settlement, . . . and other events to the year 1721. With . . . a view of its present state. XIV, 613 pp., 4 maps folded. O. Burlington, N. J., 1765. Repr., Trenton, N. J., 1890. HE—S759

SMITH, REV. SAMUEL FRANCIS. Discourse in Memory of William Hague. Boston, 1889. 67 pp., 1 port. O. HG—H12

SMITH, WILSON CARY. The Roger Morris house, Washington's Headquarters on Harlem Heights. pp. 89-104, illus., 1 pl. O. 1881. (From Magazine of American history, Feb., 1881.) HE—Z6

SNITZLER, MARIE GRAHAM. Biographical sketch of Dr. Jacques L. Laborie. (Dr. James Labaree.) (HUGUENOT Society of America. Publications. Vol. IV, pp. 8-11.) HK—H87

SOCIETE DE L'HISTOIRE DE FRANCE. See: AUBIGNE, [THEODORE] AGRIPPA D'. Histoire universelle. 1886. HF—Av.1

SOCIETE DE L'HISTOIRE DU PROTESTANTISME FRANÇAIS. Bulletin, historique et litteraire. Vols. I-LXVII. Series 1-5. Illustrated. Paris, 1853-1918. O. HK—So.1
Vols. I-XIV, title, "Doc. Hist. inedits et originaux."

——— Tab. generale des matieres de la 1e ser. Vols. I-XIV. HK—So.1

——— Commemoration de l'Enregistrement de l'Edict de Nantes par le Parlement de Paris (25 fevrier 1599). Paris, 1899. 87 pp., 1 plan. HK—So.1.N
Bound with: Troisieme centenaire de l'Edict de Nantes.

——— Jubile cinquantenaire de la Societe . . . (25 mai au 4 juin 1902). IV, 240 pp. O. Paris, 1902. HK—So.1—1902
Extr. Bull. Soc. Hist. Prot. Fran., Sept., 1902.

——— Notice sur la Societe . . . 1852-1872. 195 pp. Paris, 1874. S. HK—So.1.N

——— Quarante-deuxieme assemblee generale tenue a la Rochelle et a Saint-Martin-en-Re les 18, 19 en 20 juin 1895. 172 pp. Paris, 1895. O. HK—So.1.R

——— Troisieme centenaire de l'Edict de Nantes en Amerique et en France. 224 pp., 1 fac-sim. Paris, 1898. O. (Illus., pl., port., paged in.) HK—So.1.N
Bound with: Commemoration l'Enregistrement de l'Edict de Nantes.

SOCIETE D'HISTOIRE VAUDOISE. Bulletin. Nos. 1-26, bound in 8 volumes. Pignerol, & Aplina, 1884-1912. Port., illus. O.   HK—V46

Title of No. 6, "Bulletin de bi-centenaire de la glorieuse rentree, 1689-1889." 158, 1 pp., illus. O. Turin, 1889.

Title of No. 15, "Bollettino del cinquatenario della emancipazione." 1848-1898. VIII, 176 pp., illus., pl. O. Torino, 1898.

SOCIETE DES LIURES RELIGIEUX DE TOULOUSE. Lagarde. Chronique des églises reforme de l'Agennais.   HA—L13

SOCIETY OF AMERICAN WARS. Commandery of the State of New York. Book of the Society. Vols. I-II. New York, 1911-1917. 2 vols. O.   HK—A51

SOCIETY OF COLONIAL WARS. Commonwealth of Massachusetts. Publication. No. 8. 1 vol. Boston, 1906. O.   HK—CW712M

SOCIETY OF COLONIAL WARS, D. C. Historical papers. Nos. 3 & 8. Washington, 1901-1914.   HE—A512

No. 3. Thompson (Gilbert) Historical military powder horns.

No. 8. Huidekoper (Frederic Louis). Some important military operations.

—— Memorial papers, Nos. 2-4. 1902-'03.   HG—Mem512

—— District of Columbia Register for 1904. Port., pl. Washington City, 1904. 1 vol. O.   HK—CW.712.D.C.

—— State of New York. Publications. Nos. 16-28. 4 vols. O. New York, 1911-1916. (Addresses and Year Book.)   HK—CW712

SOCIETY OF DAUGHTERS OF HOLLAND DAMES. Descendants of the Ancient and Honourable families of New Netherland. Second Record Book. New York, 1913. O.   HK—H7

SOCIETY OF OLD BROOKLYNITES. Names of about 8000 persons, a small portion of the number confined on board the British prison ships during the War of the Revolution. 61 pp. Brooklyn, New York, 1888. O.   H—Br79

SOCIETY FOR PROPAGATING THE GOSPEL AMONG THE INDIANS. Historical sketches of the Society by James F. Hunnewell and Rev. Peter Thacher; list of officers & members; by-laws adopted May 26, 1887. 52 pp., 1 pl. Square O. [Boston?], 1887.   HK—P 956 I

SOCIETY FOR THE PROPAGATION OF THE GOSPEL IN FOREIGN PARTS. Classified digest of the Records, . . . 1701-1892. (With much supplementary information.) XVI, 980 pp. London, 1893. O. Port. & group port., paged in.   HK—P956F

SOCIETY of Sons of the Revolution. Constitution, by-laws, membership. 87 pp. New York, 1890. O. HK—So.32

—— 282 pp., illus., port., pl. New York, 1892. Q. HK—So.32

—— Year book, 1899, and Supplement to Year book of 1899. 2 vols. New York, 1899 & 1903. Q. Fac-sim., port., pl. HK—So32.1 Gift of the Society.

SOULICE, Louis. L'intendant Foucault et la révocation en Béarn. Pau, 1885. 151 pp. O. (In: Documents pour l'histoire du protestantisme en Béarn, Vol. iii.) HA—So8

SOULIER. Explication (L') de l'Edit de Nantes, de M. Bernard. Avec de nouvelles observations, et les Nouveaux Edits, Declarations et Arrests donnez jusqu'a present, touchant la Religion pretendue reformee. Paris, 1683. 13 leaves, 566 pp. D. HM—S723

SOUTH AFRICA. See: CAPE COLONY.

—— See: VILLIERS (de). Brief notices of the Huguenot families who sought refuge in Cape Colony. MS. HJ—D494

—— Huguenot refugees. See: Volume of 8 Pamphlets. HB—H87S.A

SOUTH CAROLINA, 1680-84. See: CLUTE, R. F. Annals & parish register of St. Thomas' & St. Denis' parish. . . . O. Charleston, 1884. HB—C62

—— 1670-1719. See: McCRADY, E. History of S. C., under the proprietary government. . . . O. N. Y., 1897. HE—M13

—— 1695-96. See: RAVENEL, D., Compiler. "Liste des François et Suisses." . . . O. N. Y., 1888. HB—R19

SOUTH CAROLINA Society. Transactions, upon the occasion of the Centennial Celebration, July 25, 1904, of the Occupancy of the Society's Hall on . . . Meeting Street . . . in the City of Charleston, S. C. Charleston, 1905. 22 pp., 5 pl., 7 group port. D.
HK—Pamphlet

SOUTHERN California Historical Society. Annual publication, 1888-'91. 3 vols. in 2. San Francisco, 1889-'91. O. HK—C131 Vol. for 1888-'89 bound separately.

—— Publications. Vol. ii, Part 1. 1 fac-sim. O. Los Angeles, 1891. HK—C131 Vol. ii, Part 1: GRIFFIN, G. B., Editor and Translator. Documents from the Sutro collection.
Bound with: Annual publications, 1890-'91.

SPARKS, Jared. Life of George Washington. 562 pp., pl. O. Title page wanting. HG—W273

SPRINGFIELD, Mass. French protestant college. Annual report. (6th & 7th.) O. Springfield, 1892. HO—Pamphlet

STANARD, Mary Newton, & W. G., Compilers. See: Colonial (The) VIRGINIA Register.

STANARD, William G., & M. N., Compilers. See: COLONIAL (The) VIRGINIA Register. Albany, 1902.   HH—V817

STAPLETON, Rev. Ammon. Memorial of the Huguenots in America, with special reference to their emigration to Pennsylvania. ix, 164 pp., 1 fac-sim., 7 pl., 6 port. Carlisle, Pa., 1901. O.   HB—S794

——— "Huguenota Pennsylvanianica." Series of Articles; clippings from newspapers, etc., in which they were published; mounted in blank book. 75 leaves, 1 port. Square O. Lewisburg, Pa., 1898-1901.   HB—S794.1

STATE Historical Society of Wisconsin. Annotated catalogue of Newspaper files in the Library of the Society. Prepared by E. H. Blair. xii, 375 pp. O. Madison, Wis., 1898.   HK—W.75

——— Proceedings. Nos. 37-41, and 45. Also Annual Report of 1886. Madison, 1886, 1890-'98. O.   HK—W75

STATEN ISLAND Church Records. See: WRIGHT, Tobias A. Records. . . . (N. Y. Gen. & Biog. Society. Collections. Vol. iv.)

STEELE, Richard. Christian (The) hero: an Argument proving principles of religion sufficient to make a great man. London, 1727. 8th edition. S.   HM—S814

STEVENS, John Austin. The Burgoyne campaign, an address delivered on the battle-field, on the 100th celebration of the Battle of Bemis Heights, Sept. 19, 1877. 43 pp. N. Y., 1877.   HE—Z2

——— New York in the continental congress. pp. 151-159. (From the Galaxy 1876. Vol. ii.)   HE—Z2

——— Progress of New York in a century, 1776-1876, an address delivered before the New York Historical Society Dec. 7, 1875. 66 pp. O. N. Y., 1876.   HE—Z2

STEVENS, The Rev. William Bacon, M.D., D.D. History of Georgia, from its first discovery by Europeans to the adoption of the present Constitution in MDCCXCVIII. 2 vols. New York, 1847, Vol. i. Philadelphia, 1859, Vol. ii. O.   HE—S843

STILES, Henry R., M.D. History and genealogies of ancient Windsor, Connecticut; including East Windsor, South Windsor, Bloomfield, Windsor Locks, and Ellington. 1635-1891. 2 vols., fac-sim., maps, pl., port. Q. Hartford, Conn., 1891-'92.   HH—Sti 5
Vol. i. History.
Vol. ii. Genealogy & Biography. Vol. ii revised & enlarged edition.

STONE, WILLIAM L. Biographical sketch of Brev. Maj. Gen. J. W. dePeyster. New York, 1894. 16 pp. Square Q.　　HF—D419W
Bound with: dePeyster, J. W. Authorities cited. . . . Waterloo, N. Y., 1894.

STONE, WILLIAM LEETE. 1792-1844. George Clinton. pp. 329-354. Square O. 1879. (From Magazine of American history. 1879. Vol. III, No. 6.)　　HE—Z6

———— 1835- ed. Memoir of the Centennial Celebration of Burgoyne's Surrender, held at Schuylerville, N. Y., under the auspices of the Saratoga Monument Association, on the 17th of Oct., 1877. 189 pp., 1 pl. Albany, 1878. O.　　HE—Z2

STORY (The) of a Huguenot's sword. By John Esten Cooke. New York, [1857?]. O. (Harper's New Monthly Magazine. April, 1857.)　　HN—C77

STORY of the Huguenots: a Sixteenth Century narrative wherein the French, Spaniards, and Indians were the actors. By Florian A. Mann. St. Augustine, Fla., 1898. Tt.　　HN—M13

STOUDT, JOHN BAER. Rev. Michael Schlatter in the Lehigh Valley. June 24-July 2, 1747. n.p., n.d. 15 pp. O.　　HC—Pamphlet
Reprint: The Reformed Church Review, Vol. xx, No. 1, Jan., 1916.

STOUGHTON, Massachusetts. See: RECORD of births, marriages and deaths . . . 1727-1800. . . . Edited by F. Endicott. Canton, Mass., 1896. O.　　HH—St.6

STOUPPE, REV. PIERRE. MS. Sermons (in French) preached in the Huguenot Church in New Rochelle, New York, A.D. 1724-1740. Also one dated Charleston, S. C., 1720. Square O.　　HJ—S88

STURSBURG, JOHANNES. Die franzosische-reformirte gemeinde in Erlanger. 27 pp. O. Magdeburg, 1892. (In: Der DEUTSCHE hugenotten-Verein. Geschichtsblätter. 1892. Vol. VI.)　　HB—T57

SULLY, MAXIMILIEN DE BÉTHUNE, DUC DE. Autograph letter signed. 1 page, folio.　　HJ

———— Memoirs containing history of the life and reign of [Henry the Great] translated from the French [by Mrs. C. R. Lennox] with tryal of Ravaillac. Fourth edition. London, 1763. 6 vols., map. D.　　HD—Su5

SURIANO, MICHELE. Fl. 1560. Dispacci di Michele Suriano estratti dal cod. MXLV, classe VII dei MSS. Italiani della r. biblioteca Marciana di Venezia. (HUGUENOT Society of London. Publications. 1891. Vol. VI, Appendix, pp. 1-57.)　　HK—H875
Preceded by an English translation.

SUTCLIFFE, ALICE CRARY. Homestead (The) of a Colonial dame. A monograph. 3 p.l., 5-57 pp., 1 map. 8 pl., 5 port. Poughkeepsie, New York, 1909. O.　　HH—A54

SWIFT, JOSEPH GARDNER. Memoirs of Gen. Joseph Gardner Swift, first graduate of the U. S. Military Academy, West Point . . . with a genealogy of the family of Thomas Swift . . . 1634, by H. Ellery. 292, 58, 21 pp., illus., port., 1 pl. Worcester, Mass., 1890. Square Q. (Privately printed.) HG—Sw5

SWOPE, GILBERT ERNEST, Compiler. History of the Swope family and their connections. 1678-1896. 390 pp., 3 fac-sim., 18 group port., 42 port., 7 pl., 1 table. Lancaster, Pa., 1896. Q. HH—Sw7

SWORDS'S pocket almanack, Christian's. Calendar and Ecclesiastical Register. N. Y., 1829-59. 12 vols. bound in 3 vols. S. & D.

TALES of our forefathers, and Biographical annals of families allied to those of McPike, Guest & Dumont. . . . Edited by Eugene F. McPike. 181 pp. Albany, N. Y., 1898. Square Q. HG—M17

TARRYTOWN, N. Y., First (The) Reformed Church. . . . First record book of the "Old Dutch Church of Sleepy Hollow" . . . a copy . . . by Rev. D. Cole. . . . Q. Yonkers, N. Y., 1901. HH—F44

TENNESSEE HISTORICAL SOCIETY. Papers. GARRETT, History of the South Carolina cession, 1889. HK—Pamphlet

THEAL, GEORGE McCALL. Boers and Bantu; a history of the wanderings and wars of the emigrant farmers from their leaving the Cape Colony to the overthrow of Dingan. 1 p.l., 128 pp. Cape Town, 1886. S. Reprint: "So. African Ill. News." HB—H87SA

———— Compiler. Chronicles of Cape commanders; or, An abstract of original manuscripts in the archives of the Cape Colony, 1651-91. Compiled with printed accounts of the settlement. Cape Town, 1882. 428 pp., maps. O. HF—T34

———— The Republic of Natal . . . Imperial treaties with Panda, and establishment of the colony of Natal. 1 p.l., 69 pp. Cape Town, 1886. Reprint: "Cape Mercantile Advertiser." HB—H87SA

THOMAS, THEODORE GAILLARD, M.D. Short sketch of two South Carolina Huguenots of the fourth generation. Read before the Society's Annual Meeting, April 13, 1904. (In: HUGUENOT Society of America. Proceedings. Vol. IV. New York, 1904. pp. 78-82.) HK—H87

———— Editor. See: DUBOSE, SAMUEL. Contributions to the history of the Huguenots of South Carolina. . . . 1887.

———— Same, in Volume entitled "FRENCH Protestant Church in Charleston, S. C." HB—F875

THOMPSON, GILBERT. Historical military powder-horns. 16 pp., 3 plans, 6 pl., 2 maps. [Washington], 1901. O. HE—A512
No. 12 of Pamphlet Volume, "Americana."

THREADNEEDLE Street French Church. **Registers.** London, 1599-
1840. 4 vols. (HUGUENOT Society of London. Publications.
Vol. I is Vol. IX of Publications; Vol. II is Vol. XIII; Vol. III is Vol.
XVI; Vol. IV is Vol. XXIII.)   HK—H875

TICONDEROGA Historical Society. Memorial (A) tablet at
Ticonderoga. A corporation's gift to history. 2 p.l., 7-30 pp., 1 pl.
Cambridge, 1911. O. Reprinted by the Ticonderoga Pulp & Paper
Co.   HE—H726

TILLEY, Risbrough Hammett. Huguenots (The) of Rhode Island.
(HUGUENOT Society of America. Proceedings. Vol. III,
Part 1, pp. 144-149.)   HK—H871

TILTON, Rev. Edgar, Jr., D.D. REFORMED Low Dutch Church
of Harlem, organized 1660. Historical sketch. New York, 1910.
181 pp.. 1 colored plate, 19 pl., 6 port., 1 plan, paged in. O. HC—T58

TOLLIN, Henri Wilhelm Nathanael, 1833-1902. Deutschen
Hugenotten-Vereins Würdigung durch das Hugenottische Ausland.
15 pp. O. Berlin, 1895.   HK—D491
Reprint of, and Bound with: FRANZOSISCHE Colonie, Vol.
1895-'96.

————— Geschichte der französischen colonie von Halberstadt. (In:
Deutsche Huguenotten Verein. Geschichtsblätter. 1893. No. 10,
part 3.)   HK—D49

————— Geschichte der französischen colonie zu Magdeburg, jubilaus-
schrift. Vols. I-III in 5 vols. Halle (Vol. III, Magdeburg), 1886-
1894. Port. pl., 3 vols. in 5.   HB—T57
Vol. I. Buch 1, Die Huguenotten in Frankreich. Buch 2, Das
  Refuge.
Vol. II. Buch 3, Die Französischen Colonieen in der Provinz Sachsen.
Vol. III. Abtheilung 1, A. Der kampf der hugenottischen glaubens-
  fluchtlinge inbesondere in Magdeburg.
Vol. III. Abtheilung 2, B. Vom nutzen des refuge inbesondere in
  Magdeburg.
Vol. III. Abtheilung 3, C. Kirche des Refuge insondere in Magde-
  burg.

————— Huguenotten (Die) in Magdeburg. (In: Deutsche Huguenotten
Verein. Geschichtsblätter. 1890. Vol. I. pp. 9-40.)   HK—D49

————— Johann Duraeus. Magdeburg, 1898. 2 v. in 1. pp. 227-285,
26-81. No title page.   HG—D947
Gift of the Author.

————— Ueber den Namen "Hugenotten." Erlangen, 1899. pp. 387-
415. Q. (Reformirte Kirchen-Beitung. Nos. 49-52.)   HB—T571
Gift of the Author.

————— & Béringuier, Richard. Französische colonie in Berlin. 42 pp.
O. Magdeburg, 1891. (In: Deutsche Huguenotten Verein. Geschichtsblätter. 1891. Vol. IV.)   HK—D49

TONER, JAMES MEREDITH. Index to names of persons and Churches in Bishop Meade's "Old Churches, Ministers and Families of Virginia." Washington, D. C., 1898. 63 pp. O. (Southern Hist. Assoc., Pub. Supplement to Vol. II, No. 4, No. 1.)   HC—M461

TORTOREL, J. See: FRANKLIN, Alfred L. A. Les grandes scènes historique du XVIᵉ siècle. 1886.   HA—F85

TOURTELLOT, JESSE STEERE, Compiler. Genealogy of the Tourtellot family. 1854. 1 p. Q.   HH—S425
(Inserted in volume.)

TOWER of Constance. See: CYR, Narcisse. Heroism of Huguenot women. . . .   HG—Qu3

TOWNSHEND, CHARLES HERVEY. The British invasion of New Haven, Conn. . . . with some account of their landing and burning the towns of Fairfield and Norwalk, July, 1779. 112 pp. 5 pl. O. New Haven, 1879.   HE—Z1
No. 15 of a volume of pamphlets.

TRABUE, ANTOINE. Letter of commendation given to Antoine Trabue. Dated 1687. MS.   HJ

TRAHERNE, THOMAS, B.D. Roman forgeries, or a True account of false records discovering the impostures and counterfeit antiquities of the Church of Rome. By a Faithful Son of the Church of England. 17 leaves, 316 pp. London, 1673. S.   HM—E9

TRAICTE d'Association faice par Monseigneur le Prince de Condé avec les Princes, Chevaliers de l'Ordre, Seigneurs, Capitaines, Gantilshommes, et aultres de tous estats, qui sont entrez ou entreront cy apres en la dicte association pour mantenir, l'honneur de Dieu, le repos de ce Royaume, et l'estat et libetté de Roy sous le gouvernemét de la Roine sa mere, auctorisee et establie par les Estats. Orleans, 1562. 7 leaves. T.   HA—L888

TRAITES de paix: Catalogue de pamphlets et d'estampes concernant . . . conclus avec les Pays-Bas, depuis 1576-1815. La Haye, 1913. 2 l., 40 pp., 6 pl. Square O. Kerling, J. B. J. & Dozy, R. B.
   HA—Pamphlet

TRAITS and stories of the Huguenots. pp. 185-190. n. p., n. d. (Volume "Huguenot Essays.")   HB—H89

TRAVELS in . . . 1791 and 1792 in Pennsylvania, New York, and Vermont. Journals of John LINCKLAEN. With a biographical sketch, by Helen L. Fairchild. New York, 1897. O.   HI—L63

TREDWELL, DANIEL M. Personal reminiscences of men and things on Long Island. One Volume in two parts, paged consecutively. Brooklyn, N. Y., 1912, Part 1; 1917, Part 2. Q.   HE—T78
Part I: 182 pp., 1 map, 1 port.
Part II: 4 p. l., 197-250 pp., 1 fac-sim., 1 map, 4 pl., 1 port.
No. 176 of 500 copies.

TREE PLANTING ASSOCIATION, and The Washington Square Association, N. Y. City. In memoriam Cornelius Berrien Mitchell. Minutes and Resolution. . . . 5 leaves. S. New York, 1902.
HG—Mem512

TREVEYLAN, Lady Hannah More Macaulay, Editor. See: Macaulay, T. B. M. 1st baron. 1800-59. History of England. Vol. V. HF—M.11

TRIQUETI, Henri, Baron de. Les premiers jours du protestantisme en France, depuis son origine jusqu'au premier synode national de 1559. Paris, 1859. 300 pp. D. HA—T73
Ouvrage publié à l'occasion du 3e jubilé, séculaire de ce synode.

TROSS, Edwin, Editor. See: LESCARBOT, Marc. Histoire de la Nouvelle-France . . . 1866. HF—L56

——— Editor. See: SAGARD-THEODAT, Gabriel. Histoire du Canada . . . 1866. HF—Sa11

TUCKER, Gideon J., Compiler. See: UNIVERSITY State of New York. Supplementary list of Marriage licenses. (State Library Bulletin, History, No. 1.)

TURRETTINI, Jean-Alphonse. Lettres inedites adressee de 1686 à 1737 à J.-A. T., theologien Genevois. Publiees et annotees par E. de Bude. Vols. i-iii. Paris, 1887. 3 Vols. D. HM—T86

UBERSICHT der wanderungen und niederlassungen französischer, savoyischer und niederländischer religionsflüchtlinge besonders nach und in Deutschland. Karlsruhe, 1854. 130 pp. O. HA—Ub3

ULLMAN, Percival Glenroy, Compiler. The Coursens from 1612-1917: compiled from ancient and modern records, with the Staten Island branch. 88 pp., 2 pl., 1 port. New York, 1888. O.
HH—C86.1

ULSTER COUNTY, New York. See: ANJOU, Gustav.

UNION Theological Seminary. Three addresses delivered by Professors . . . at a Service in commemoration of the 400th Anniversary of the birth of John Calvin, in the Adams Chapel, third of May, 1909. New York, 1909. 47 pp. O. HM—Pamphlet

i. Calvin and the Reformation. Prof. Wm. W. ROCKWELL, S. T. B., Lic.

ii. Calvin's Influence upon Theology. Prof. Wm. A. BROWN, Ph.D.

iii. Inner (The) spirit of the Calvinistic Puritan State. Prof. Thos. C. HALL, D.D.

UNITE (De l') de l'Eglise. 1678. By P. NICHOLE. HM—N51

UNITED Brethren Congregation. See: MORAVIAN Church.

UNITED Historical & Patriotic Societies of New York. The need of a history of New York. 55 pp., 1 port. New York, 1915. O. Bound with: HOLDEN, J. A. Centenary . . . Battle of Platts- burg. . . .   HE—H726

U. S. Congress. Congressional directory . . . 2d ed., corrected to Jan. 21, 1881. 167 pp., 4 pl. O. Washington, 1881.   HE—Z5

UNITED STATES State Dept. Letter from the secretary transmitting a report of Theodore F. Dwight on the papers of Benjamin Franklin offered for sale by Henry Stevens, & recommending their purchase by Congress. 99 pp. O. Wash., 1882. No title-page.   HE—Z7

UNIVERSITY State of New York. Supplementary list of Marriage licenses, year 1752-'53, 1755-'56, & 1758. Albany, 1898. O. (State Library Bulletin. History, No. 1.) G. J. TUCKER, Com- piler.   HH—N42—Supplement

UPDIKE, WILKINS. History of the Episcopal Church in Narragansett, Rhode-Island; including . . . other Episcopal Churches in the State; with an Appendix containing a reprint . . . entitled, "America dis- sected," by the Rev. J. MacSPARRAN, D.D. With . . . gene- alogical and biographical accounts. . . . xxxiii, 34-533 pp., 1 port. New York, 1847. O.

UTICA (N. Y.) Manufacturing and Mercantile Association. Consti- tution and a commercial history of Utica. 44 pp. O. 1880. No title-page.   HE—Z4

VERNEDE, JEAN SCIPION, Translator. See: DODDRIDGE, Philip. Commencemens (Les) de la vraie piete. 1751.   HM—D66

VERNON, EDWARD, VICE-ADMIRAL. List of the Vernon-Wager MSS., in the Library of Congress. With fac-sim. 148 pp. Washington, D. C., 1904. Q.   HF—F711V-W

VERREN, REV. ANTOINE. The Huguenots in this country, in Pine, Franklin and West 22d Sts.; or, A discourse delivered June 26, 1862, on the occasion of laying the corner-stone of their new temple. Translated from the French by Rev. William Morris. N. Y. 1862. 24 pp. O.   HB—A2H

VERSTEEG, DINGMAN, Editor. See: REFORMED Dutch Church Records. 2 Vols. 1666-1788. Q. (HOLLAND Society, New York. Year Book. 1913 & 1914.)   HK—H71.1

VIE D' JEAN FRÉDÉRIC OBERLIN, Pasteur au Ban de la Roche. Tou- louse, 1854. 223 pp. D.   HG—Ob2

VIE de Pierre du Bosc. Enrichie de lettres, harangues, dissertations et autres pieces importantes. Rotterdam, 1694. 610 pp. O. Vellum.   HG—D85

VILLIERS, DE. Manuscript containing brief notices of the Huguenot families who sought refuge in Cape Colony, South Africa. Folio.   HJ—V71

VILLIERS, Christopher C. de. Aankondiging; iets belangrijks voor onze oude Afrikaansche familien. Kaapstad, 1885. 8 pp. O.

HB—H87SA

Reprint from *Ned. Geref. kerk-almanak.*

VINCENT, Rev. John Hey, D.D. Centennial souvenir of John Himrod Vincent, born in Milton, Pa., April 20, 1798. No place, 1898. D.

HG—Mem512

One of very few copies printed.

VINET, A. Histoire de la prédication parmi les réformés de France au dix-septieme siècle. 2 leaves, v-viii, 718 pp., 1 leaf. Paris, 1860. O.

HA—V783

VIRGINIA: Colonial History. See: Colonial Virginia Register.

HE—V817

VIRGINIA cousins. By G. B. GOODE.

HH—G54

VAIL, Charles Montgomery. Vail and Armstrong. A short record of my ancestors beginning with John Vail, Southold, Long Island, 1670-1760. Francis Armstrong (from Ireland) 1727. With a reference to the L'Hommedieu family. 57 pp., 1 pl., 1 fac-sim. Goshen, N. Y., 1894. O.

HH—V19

VALENTINE, David Thomas. History of the city of New York. N. Y., 1853. 404 pp., plates, maps. O.

HE—V23

——— Editor. See: New York City Common Council Manual of Corporations, 1853-'70. 17 vols. D.

Note:—These volumes are best known as "Valentine's Manuals."

VAN DER KEMP, Francis Adrian. 1752-1829. An autobiography, together with extracts from his correspondence. Edited, with an historical sketch by H. L. Fairchild. xii, 230 pp., 3 fac-sim., 8 port. New York, 1903. O.

HG—V28

VAN DYKE, Rev. Paul, prof. Huguenots (The) and the Beggars. (HUGUENOT Society of America. Proceedings. 1894. Vol. ii. pp. 210-223.) New York.

HK—H871

VAN LAER, A. F., Editor. Early records of the city and county of Albany and colony of Rensselaerswyck. Translated from the original Dutch by J. Pearson. Vols. ii-iv, Albany, 1916-'19. 3 vols. Q. Univ. State N. Y., N. Y. State Lib'y Hist. Bull. 9.

HE—A326

VAN NEST, Rev. Abraham Rynier. Memoir of Rev. George W. Bethune. vi, 446 pp., 3 port., pl. New York, 1867. D.

HG—B46

VAN RENSSELAER, Rev. Maunsell. Annals of the Van Rensselaers in the United States, especially as they relate to the family of Killian K. Van Rensselaer. 241 pp., port., fac-sim. Albany, N. Y., 1888. O.

HG—V35

VAN RENSSELAER, Mrs. Sarah. Ancestral sketches and records of olden times. . . . 375 pp. Square Q. New York, 1882.

HG—V351

VAN SLYKE, Rev. J. G., D.D. Huguenots (The) of Ulster County.
(HUGUENOT Society of America. Proceedings. New York,
1894. Vol. ii., pp. 224-236.)   HK—H871

VAN VOORHIS, E. W., Compiler. Tombstone inscriptions from the
church-yard of the First reformed Dutch church of Fishkill Village,
Dutchess Co., N. Y. N. Y. [1882.] 229 pp., plate. O.   HH—V37

VAUDOIS du Dauphine. See: ARNAUD, Eugene. Memoirs historiques.   HA—Ar6
A collection of 6 pamphlets (in French) by E. Arnaud.

                                                        HA—Ar6

VAUDOIS (Les). Leur histoire sur les deux versants des Alpes de
IVᵉ siècle au XVIIIᵉ. Par BERARD, Alexandre. Lyon. 1892.
O.   HA—B461

VAURIGAUD, Benjamin. Essai sur l'histoire des églises réformées
de Bretagne, 1535-1808. Paris, 1870. 3 vols. O.   HA—V461

———— Histoire de l'église réformée de Nantes, depuis l'origine jusqu'au
temps présent. Paris, 1880. 377 pp. O.   HA—V46

———— Editor. See: CREUAIN, Philippe le Noir, Sieur de. Histoire
ecclésiastique de Bretagne. 1851.   HA—C86

VEDDER, Rev. Charles S., D.D., LL.D. Historical address, 225th
anniversary, April 14th, 1912. The Huguenot Church. pp. 12-22.
(FRENCH Protestant Church, Charleston, S. C., 1912).   HB—F875

———— Holland. A poem written for the anniversary of the Holland
Society of New York, 1892. Square O. New York, 1898.
(1 of 300 copies.)   HO—Pamphlet

———— Huguenot church of Charleston, S. C. Two discourses preached
May, 1879, and 1880. Charleston, S. C. 1880. 32 pp. O.

———— Huguenots (The) of South Carolina and their Churches.
(HUGUENOT Society of America. Proceedings. Vol. i, part 1.
New York, 1884. pp. 31-48. O.)   HK—H87.1

———— Poem: read at the celebration by the Huguenot Society of
Charleston, S. C., April 14, 1890, of the Promulgation of the Edict
of Nantes, 1598. Charleston, 1890. S. Oblong. 21 leaves. Privately printed.   HO—Pamphlet.

———— "This day shall be unto you for a memorial." Sermon preached
in the Huguenot church, Charleston, S. C., May 11, 1873, the 28th
anniversary of the dedication of the present edifice. Charleston, S.
C., 1873. 15 pp. O.

VENNEMA, Rev. Ame. History of the Reformed Church of New
Paltz, Ulster Co., N. Y., 1683-1883. Rondout, N. Y., 1884. 40
pp. D.   HC—V56

VERDEIL, A., Editor. See: PIERREFLEUR, Pierre. Memoirs
. . . 1856.   HB—P61

VERMILYE, Rev. Ashbel Green, D.D. Huguenot element among
the Dutch. Schenectady, N. Y., 18? 23 pp. O.   HK—A2H

―――― A second copy in HB.

―――― Mingling of the Huguenots and Dutch in Early New York.
(HUGUENOT Society of America. Proceedings. New York,
1884. pp. 24-31.)   HK—H871

―――― Memorial sketch of the Honorable John Jay, First President of
the Huguenot Society of America, 1883-1894. (Huguenot Society of
America. Proceedings. New York, 1896. pp. 22-36.)   HK—H871

―――― Patriot (The) clergy and the New York city chaplains in the
War of the Revolution. An address before the N. Y. Hist. Soc.
28 pp. O. New York, 1895.   HE—A512

VERSTEEG, Dingman, Editor. See: REFORMED Dutch Church
Records. 1666-1788. 2 Vols. Q. (HOLLAND Society, New
York. Year Book. 1913, 1914.)   HK—H71.1

VIRGINIA Historical Society. Catalogue of the MSS. in the Collection of the Society, and also of some printed papers. Richmond,
1901. 120 pp. O.   HK—V81
Supplement to the VIRGINIA Magazine of History & Biography.

―――― Collections. New Series. Richmond, 1886-1891. O. Vols.
v-x.   HK—V81
Vol. v. BROCK, R. A., Editor. Huguenot emigration to Virginia.
Vol. vi. BROCK, R. A., Editor. Miscellaneous papers, 1672-
1865.
Vols. vii-viii. ROBINSON, C., Compiler. Virginia Company,
1619-1624.
Vols. ix-x. BRIGSBY, H. B. History of the Virginia Federal Convention of 1788.
Volumes v, vi, & vii, Gift of the Society. Volume viii, (Another
copy) viii, ix, & x.

―――― Proceedings of the Society at its Annual Meeting. Richmond,
1894, 1898, 1903-'04, 1914-'17. O.   HK—V81
Proceedings are bound with the Virginia Magazine of History &
Biography.

―――― VIRGINIA Magazine of History & Biography. Vols. ii, vi,
xi-xii, xxii-xxv, Richmond, Va., 1894-1918. 8 Vols. O.   HK—V81
Also unbound numbers: Vol. iv, No. 2, xix, No. 2, xx, No. 2.
Note: Numbers to complete our file would be acceptable.

VIRGINIA Magazine of History and Biography. See: VIRGINIA
HISTORICAL Society.

VIVIEN, Louis. Familles (les) du refuge en pays Neuchatelois. . . .
2-4 pp. O. Paris, 1899.   HH—V861
Note: pp. Illustrated with portraits and crests.

VOLTAIRE, François Marie Arouet de. Lettres de Voltaire à
Louis Necker de Germany. 13 pp. O. [Genève, 1882.] (Ext.
Bulletin de la Soc. d'hist. et d'archeologie de Geneve, tome I, livre
2.)   HO—Nec28

VOS, P. D. De. De Grafschriften der voormalige St. Lievens-Mons-
terkerk te Zierikzee. 46 pp. O. n. p., 1895.   HH—W66
Reprint: Maandblad Geneal.-herald. genootschap "De Nederl.
Leeuw." 1895.   HH—W66

VOSSION, Louis. Constitution (La) Americaine et ses amende-
ments texte, notice historique et commentaire. Avec une preface par
J. Chailley. . . . 2 p. l., v-xxiv, 74 pp., 3 port. Paris, 1889. O.
Fac-sim. paged in.   HE—V97

VREELAND, Helen Kearny, Editor. See: AUSTIN, M. S.
Philip Freneau, the poet of the Revolution: A history of his life and
times. 1901.   HG—F88A

WACE, The Very Rev. Henry, D.D. John Calvin. 10 pp. O.
London, 1909.   HG—Mem512
Reprinted, after revision by the Author, from "The Churchman,"
for July, 1909.

WADDINGTON, Francis. Le Protestantisme en Normandie depuis
la Révocation de l'Edit de Nantes Jusqu'a la fin du dix-huitieme
siècle. (1685-1797.) VII, 140 pp. Paris, 1862. Q.   HA—W11

——— See: ROU, Jean. Memoires inedits et opuscules. 1857.
                                                         HG—R75

——— & READ, C. Mémoires inédits de Dumont de Bostaquet, gentilhomme Normand. . . . XLVI, 376 pp. O. Paris, 1864.   R22

WAGER, Charles, Admiral. List of the Vernon-Wager MSS.; in
the Library of Congress. Compiled by W. C. FORD. With fac-
sims. 148 pp. Washington, D. C., 1904. Q.   HE—F711

WAGER, Daniel E. Col. Marinus Willett, the hero of Mohawk Valley; an Address before The Oneida Historical Society, Utica, N. Y.,
1891. 50 pp. O.   HG—Mis68

WAKELEY, Joseph B. Lost chapters recovered from the early history
of American Methodism, with a memoir of the author by Rev. W.
E. Ketcham. . . . 635 pp., port., pl., fac-sim. New York, cop.,
1889. O.   HC—W13

WAKEFIELD, Edward. Waifs and strays of American History.
(HUGUENOT Society of America. Proceedings. 1891. Vol. II.
pp. 115-134.)   HK—H87

WAKEMAN, ABRAM. New York's Commercial Tercentenary. . . . A few Historical events as given by historians compared with their actual occurrence. 40 pp. Square Q. New York, 1914.   HE—N485

WALDRON, WILLIAM WATSON. Huguenots of Westchester and Parish of Fordham . . . with introduction by Rev. S. H. Tyng, Jr. 126 pp., 1 pl. New York, 1864. S.   HB—W14

WALLACE, JOHN WILLIAM, 1815-84. Discourse pronounced on the inauguration of the new hall, March 11, 1872, of the Historical Society of Pennsylvania. . . . 66 pp. O. Philadelphia, 1872.   HE—Z4

WALLER, WILLIAM CHAPMAN, Editor. Register of the French Church at Thorpe-le-Soken in Essex. 1684-1726. x, 27 pp. Q. London, 1912.   HK—H875
Bound with: LART, C. E. Registers . . . French Churches . . . Bristol, Stonehouse, & Plymouth. (HUGUENOT Society of London. Publications. 1912. Vol. xx.)

———— & Minot, William, Editors. Registers of the Church known as La Patente in Spittlefields, from 1689-1785. (HUGUENOT Society of London. Publications. Vol. xi. 1898.)   HK—H875
450 copies printed. No. 427.

———— Transcript of the Registers of the Protestant Church at Guisnes from 1668-1685. (HUGUENOT Society of London. Publications. Vol. iii. 1891.)   HK—HK

WALLOON (A) family in America: Lockwood deForest and his forbears. Together with a Voyage to Guiana: the Journal of Jesse deForest and his colonists. By Emily Johnston DE FOREST. Vols. i-ii. Boston, 1914. 2 Vols. O.   HH—D315
Both volumes beautifully illustrated.

WALTER, JAMES. Memorials of Washington and of Mary, his mother, and Martha, his wife, from letters and papers of Robert Cary and James Sharples. . . . 362 pp., illust., port., New York. 1887. Q.   HG—W27

WASHBURNE, ELIHU BENJAMIN. Recollections of a Minister to France, 1869-77. N. Y. 1887. 2 vols., illust., port., fac-sims. O.
     HD—W27

WASHINGTON, GEORGE. 1732-1799. Journal, from the original MS., in the Library of the Department of State at Washington, May to August, 1781. pp. 108-125.   HE—Z6
From Magazine of American History, February, 1881.

———— Letters, 1754-1777. pp. 125-240.   HE—Z6
From Magazine of American History, February, 1881. No. 10 of a Vol. of Pamphlets.

WASHINGTON'S Headquarters, New York. Sketch of the Morris Mansion (or Jumel Mansion) used by Washington as his Headquarters in 1776. By R. P. Bolton. 2 leaves, 1 pl., 1 port., 3-40 pp. New York, 1903. S.   HE—A512

WATERMAN, Rev. Elijah. A Century sermon, preached before the First Church in Windham, December 10, A.D., 1800, in commemoration of its institution, December 10, A.D., 1700. Containing historical facts. . . . 43 pp. Windham, 1801. O.　　　　HE—W885
"Ancient Woodbury."

WATERS, Edward Stanley. Notes on some Huguenot families: Vincent, Magny (Many), Aymar, Erouard (Harway), and others. (HUGUENOT Society of America. Proceedings. New York, 1903. Vol. III, Part 2. pp. 245-271.)　　　　HK—H871

WATERS, Henry F. Genealogical gleanings in England. 2 Vols. Boston, 1901. O.　　　　HH—W31
Index of persons and places in Vol. II.

WATSON, John Fanning. Annals of Philadelphia, and Pennsylvania, in the olden time; being a collection of memoirs, anecdotes, and incidents of the City and its inhabitants, and of the earliest settlements of the inland part of Pennsylvania. . . . Enlarged and revised by W. P. Hazard. Vols. I-III. Philadelphia, 1891. 3 vols. O.　　　　HE—WATS33

――― Olden time researches & reminiscences of New York City, [1828]. 78 pp. O. No place, no date.　　　　HE—Z7

WATSON, Stephen Marion, Editor. See: MAINE Historical & Genealogical Recorder. Vols. I-VI. Portland, Me., 1884-1889. 6 Vols. Square O.　　　　HH—M28

WEAVER, Ethan Allen. William Herman Wilhelm. 9 pp., 1 port. Washington, D. C., 1902. O. (Soc. Col. Wars, D. C., Mem. Papers, No. 3.)　　　　HG—Mem512

WEISS, Charles. History of the French protestant refugees, from the revocation of the Edict of Nantes to our own days. Translated from the French by Henry William Herbert. N. Y. 1854. 2 Vols. port. D.　　　　HA—W43

――― Second copy. 2 Vols.　　　　HA—W43

――― Huguenot families in America. (In: The Continental Monthly, Vol. I, Nos. 2-4, pp. 231-232, 151-155, 298-302, 461-465.) Boston, 1862. O.　　　　HB—H897

WEISS, Nathanël. La chambre ardente; étude sur la liberté de conscience en France sous François Ier et Henri II; suivie d'environ 500 arrêts inédits, rendus par le Parlement de Paris, 1547-1550. Publié pour le premier centenaire de la liberté de conscience sous les auspices de la Société de l'histoire du protestantisme français. Paris, 1889. 432 pp., plates. D.　　　　HA—W432

――― Ennemis (Les) de l'Edit de Nantes. (HUGUENOT Society of America. Publications. Vol. III. 1900.)　　　　HK—H87

WEISS, NATHANËL. Indépendance das Etats d'Amerique et Pierre Chaillé, fils du Médecin de la Tremblade, prisonnier pour la foi, 1693-1775. [Paris, 1895.] 22 pp. O.   HH—C434
(Extract: Bulletin Soc'y Prot. Français. Juin, 1895.)
Bound with: MESCHINET de RICHEMOND, L. M. Médecin (Le) Pierre Chaillé.

――― Pretendue trahison de Coligny. [Paris?] 1900. 11 pp. O. Reprint: Bull. Soc. Hist. Prot. Fr.   HG—S33
(Volume lettered—Biographical & Historical Essays.)

――― Editor. See: MIGAULT, Jean. Journal de Jean Migault, mitre d'école, 1681-1688. Publié pour la première fois d'après le texte original avec une introduction et des notes. Paris, 1910. D.   HA—M634

WEISSE, MRS. JOHN A., Translator. See: DUCHESNE, André. History of the Bethune family. 1884.   HG—B67

WELLES, THEODORE W., D.D. Hardenbergh. Leaves out of ancestral tablets, from Colonial days to the present era. 1 pl., 79-176 pp. No place, no date. O.   HH—H25

WERNER, EDGAR A. Civil list and Constitutional history of the Colony and State of New York. 2 p. l., III-VII, 3-663 pp.. 16 pl. Albany, 1886. O.   HE—W5

WESTCHESTER County Magazine. Vol. III, No. 4, & Vol. IV, No. 2. White Plains, New York, July & November, 1909. O.   HE—N533

WESTCHESTER, New York. See: WALDRON, Wm. Watson, Huguenots of Westchester and Parish of Fordham. New York, 1864. S.   HB—W14

WESTPHAL-CASTELNAU. Yesterday and today; or, The activities of French protestants since the commencement of this century, with an introduction and notes by Rev. A. F. Beard. Translated by permission. Paris, 1885. 48 pp. O.   HB—A.2.H

WETMORE, JAMES CARNAHAN. Wetmore family of America and its collateral branches. x, 2-670 pp. Albany, 1861. Q.   HH—W53

WEYMAN, STANLEY JOHN. Count Hannibal. A Romance of the Court of France. New York, 1901. VI, 403 pp., 1 pl., D.   HN—W54

――― House (The) of the wolf. 234 pp., 1 port. Philadelphia, [1898.] S. .   HN—W54H

WHITE, H., Translator. See: MERLE d'AUBIGNE, Jean Henri. History of the Reformation in the XIVth century.   HC—M541

WHITE Plains, Westchester County, New York. See: BAIRD, C. W. History of Rye . . . 1660-1870 . . . including . . . White Plains till 1788. O. New York, 1871.   HE—B16

WHITMORE, WILLIAM HENRY, Compiler. Graveyards of Boston.
Albany, 1878. Vol. I, illust. O.   HH—W59
Vol. I, *Copp's Hill epitaphs.*

—— The Massachusetts civil list for the Colonial and Provincial
periods, 1630-1774. Being a list of the names . . . of all the civil
officers. . . . 172 pp. O. Albany, 1870.   HE—W61

WHITTEMORE, HENRY, Compiler. History of the Sage and Slocum
families of England and America, including the allied families of
. . . Jermain or Germain . . . Hon. Russell Sage and Margaret
Olivia (Slocum) Sage. . . . 27, XIX, 29-44, 1-50 pp., 4 plates, 5 port.
New York, 1908. Square folio.   HH—S12

WHY is history read so little? DENHAM, Edward.   HE—Z7

[WIGHT, WILLIAM W.] Henry Clay Paine. A life. 196 pp., 1
port. Milwaukee, 1907. Q.   HG—P346

—— Compiler. See: NEW ENGLAND Historical & Genealogical
Register. Index to genealogies and pedigrees in the Register. . . .
Vol. II-Vol. L. Boston, 1896. 11 pp. O.   HK—NR44
Reprint: N. E. Hist. & Gen. Register, October, 1896.

WILDEMAN, MARINUS GODEFRIDUS. Aanteekeningen van Benck-
endorff en Crommelin. 11 pp., n. p., 1899. O.   HH—W673N
Overgedrukt . . . Maandb. . . . Geneal.-her. genoots. de Nederl.
Leeuw. 1899.

—— Archaeography of Delft curiosities. Delft, 1903. 74 pp., 16
pl., 1 map. D.   HI—W673
Bound with his: Itineraire archeologique de Delft.

—— Delfsche poorters. 10 pp., n. p. 1896. O.   HH—W673N
Reprint: Maandblad . . . Geneal.-herald. genootschap "De Nederl.
Leeuw." 1896.

—— Doodsberichten 1597-1743, rakende de geslach ten: v. Arnhem,
v. Balveren, v. Boelzelaar, v. d. Bongert, v. Brederode, Cloeck,
Cock, v. Delen, v. Essen, v. Harften, v. Langen, de Lannoy, v. Lyn-
den, v. Matenesse, Pieck, v. Randwyck, v. Rechteren, v. Reede, v.
Spuelde, v. Tellicht Vygh, v. Welderen, v. Wyhe, ea n. p., n. d.,
n. t. p.   HH—W66

—— Eenige kwartierborden der Wassenaer's zovals zij indertijd aanwezig waven in de kerken van Giessen, Warmond, Leiden en Leiderdorp. n. p. 1895. 13 pp. O.   HH—W66
Reprint: Maandblad . . . Geneal.-herald. . . . "Nederlandsche
Leeuw." 1894.

—— The Eldest Church-book of the English congregation in the
Hague. . . . A transcript. I-IV, 84 pp. The Hague, 1906. O.
                                                                    HB—67E

—— Familie-aanteekeningen Gerlings. 12 pp. O. n. p. 1897.
Rept. Maandblad . . . Geneal.-herald. . . . 1897.   HH—W673N

WILDEMAN, Marinus Godefridus. Genealische kwartierstaten van Nederlandsche Geslachten samengesesteld en byeengebrachtdoor . . . 'sGravenhage, 1894. Square folio.　　　　　　HH—W673
This is the Author's family chart, cut and bound in 7 leaves. Also his portrait and autograph, and a card showing his connections and standing in many historical and genealogical societies, the latter having been collected and added to his chart, by H. S. of A.

———— Geslacht Brandwijk van Blokland. 20 pp. n. p. 1896. O.
Reprint: Maandblad van het Geneal.-herald. . . .　　　HH—W66

———— Het geslacht Goekoop. 3 p. l., 57 l., 1 pl. 'sGravenhage, 1914.
Q.　　　　　　　　　　　　　　　　　　　　　　　　　　　HH—G59

———— Compiler. Grafboeken (De) der Groote of St. Jacobskerk te s'Gravenhage, 1620-1830. 2 p. l., 209 pp., 8 leaves. s'Hertogengosch, 1898. Square folio.　　　　　　　　　　　　HB—67

———— Itinéraire archéologique de Delft. 2d ed., revue, corrigée et augmentée. 96 pp., 19 pl. Delft, 1906. D.　　　　　HI—W673
Bound with his English edition.

———— Namen der . . . burgemeesteren, Schepenen, Vroddschappen en tresoriers can 's Gravenhage die sedert . . . 1738 tot 1794. . . . Een vervolg op de lijst can J. DeRiemer. . . . No place, 1896. 32 pp. O.　　　　　　　　　　　　　　　　　　　　　　HH—W66
Reprint: Maandblad . . . Gen.-Herald. . . .1896.

———— Nassau en Oranje—Nassau te Haarlem. (1515-1897.) Archivalia. 124 pp. Haarlem, 1898. O.　　　　　　HH—W673N

———— Ontwerp van een Wapen voor H. M. de Koningen. 14 pp. 1 pl. No place. 1897. O.　　　　　　　　　　　HH—W673N
Reprint, het Maandblad . . . Genealogisch-heraldiek . . . "Nederlandsche." 1897.

———— Prins Willem I. (fragment) 1535-1558. 29 pp. 1 port. No place. 1898.　　　　　　　　　　　　　　　HH—W673N

———— Walloon Church of Haarlem. (HUGUENOT Society of America. Publications. Vol. iii. 1900. pp. 201.　　　HK—H87

———— Worbert (Les) comtes van Wassenaer-Starrenburg devant le tribunal de l'histoire. 3 p. l., 49 pp. Amersfoort, 1899. O.
　　　　　　　　　　　　　　　　　　　　　　　　　　HH—W673N

WILLIAM the Silent, prince of Orange. The story of his life. By Ruth Putnam. New York, 1898. 2 vols., 2d ed. O.　　HG—P98

WILLIAMS, Rev. J. N. Our debt to the Huguenots; or, What we owe to French protestantism. 1882. O.　　　　　HB—H12

WILLIAMS, Rev. Solomon. Historical sketch of Northampton, from its first settlement: in a sermon, delivered on the National Thanksgiving, April 13, 1815. 24 pp. O. Northampton, 1815. HE—W885
Volume "Ancient Woodbury."

WILSON, GEN JAMES GRANT, U. S. A. Bayard family of America and Judge Bayard's London diary of 1795-'96. (HUGUENOT Society of America. Proceedings. New York, 1891. Vol. II. pp. 135-154.) HK—H871

—— Memorial of Col. John Bayard; read before the New Jersey historical society . . . May 16th, 1878. O. pp. 141-160. HE—Z7

WILSON, THOMAS WOODROW, PRES. U. S. A. President Wilson's War Address to Congress and Proclamation, together with joint Resolution of House and Senate, giving names of those voting for and against the measure. Illust. cover. 61; 1 pl., 1 port. Q. New York, 1917. HE—Pamphlet

WILSON, REV. WILLIAM T. The death of President Lincoln. A sermon preached in St. Peter's Church, Albany, 1865. 25 pp. Albany, 1865. O. HG—Mem512

WINCHESTER, REV. ELHANAN, Translator. See: DE BENNE-VILLE, George. 1703-1793. Some remarkable passages in the life of Dr. George de Benneville. 1890. HG—D35

WINFIELD, CHARLES HARDENBERGH. History of the county of Hudson, New Jersey. VII, 568 pp., illust., port., pl. New York, 1874. O. HE—W72

WINSOR, JUSTIN. A history of the town of Duxbury, Mass., with genealogical registers. VIII, 9-36 pp., 1 port. O. Boston, 1849. Autograph of Author. HE—W721

WINTHROP, ROBERT CHARLES. Life of James Bowdoin. 2d ed., 50 pp. Boston, 1876. O. Privately printed. HG—B67

WISCONSIN HISTORICAL SOCIETY. Annual report. 1886. O. HK—Pamphlet

WITT, MME. PAULINE GUIZOT DE. See: GUIZOT, François P. Guillaume. History of France . . . 1887. HD—G94

WITTMEYER, REV. ALFRED VINTMOIRE, Compiler. Genealogy of the Fresneau family, copied from an old family Bible. HJ

—— Historical sketch of the "Eglise François à la Nouvelle York," from 1688-1804. N. Y., 1886. 82 pp., plate. Q. HB—Wit77 Reprint from the HUGUENOT Society of America. Collections, Vol. I.

—— "Registers of the births, marriages and deaths of the Eglise Françoise à la Nouvelle York," from 1688-1804, and historical documents relating to the French Protestants in New York during the same period. LXXXVIII, 431, 42 pp., fac-sim., plates. Q. New York, 1886. (HUGUENOT Society of America. Collections. Vol. I.) HK—H87.3

—— Translator. See: LOUIS XIV. King of France. Original decree of Louis XIV. in relation to the Temple (Protestant Church) of Bergerac. A.D., 1679. HJ

342

WONDERFUL instance of God's appearance for, and presence with his people in a day of suffering. HG—R33

WOOD, JERVIS A. My Flag. 101 pp. with color illus. O. Philadelphia, 1917. Gift of John Wanamaker. HE—Pamphlet

WOODBURY, Connecticut. See: COTHREN, W. Second centennial celebration . . . of ancient Woodbury . . . July 4 and 5, 1859. Woodbury, 1859. O. HE—W885

WOODRUFF, FRANCIS E. Coursens (The) of Sussex County, New Jersey. A reprint from "The Woodruffs of New Jersey." 2 p. l., 5-123 pp. New York, 1909. O. HH—C86

WOOLSEY, SARAH CHAUNCEY (Susan Coolidge). Short history of the city of Philadelphia from its foundation to the present time, by Susan Coolidge. Boston, 1887. 288 pp. D. HE—W88

WORCESTER, Massachusetts. See: WORCESTER Society of Antiquity. Collections. Vol. IV. O. Worcester, Mass. 1882.
HE—W89

WORCESTER Society of Antiquity. Collections. Vol. IV. O. Worcester, Mass. 1882. HE—W89

WORTHINGTON, ERASTUS. The history of Dedham, Mass., from the beginning of its settlement in September, 1635, to May, 1827. 146 pp. O. Boston, 1827. HE—Ded36

WRIGHT, TOBIAS ALEXANDER, Editor. Records of the Dutch REFORMED Church of Port Richmond, Staten Island. Baptisms from 1696-1772. UNITED Brethren Congregation, commonly called MORAVIAN Church, Staten Island. Births and Baptisms: 1749-1853. Marriages: 1764-1863. Deaths and Burials: 1758-1828. St. ANDREW'S Church, Richmond, Staten Island: Births and Baptisms from 1752-1795: Marriages from 1754-1808. IX, 335 pp., 3 pl., 1 port. Q. New York, 1909. (New York Gen. & Biog. Society. Collections. Vol. IV. 1909.) HK—N491

——— Records of the REFORMED Dutch Church in New Amsterdam and New York. Baptisms from January 1, 1731-December 29, 1800. 634 pp., 1 port. New York, 1902. Q. (New York Gen. & Biog. Society. Collections. Vol. III.) HK—N491

YORKTOWN, New York Presby. Ch. Records. See: Roebling, Emily Warren. Journal of the Rev. Silas Constant . . . with . . . Records. . . . List of marriages, 1784-1825. O. Philadelphia, 1903.
HH—C758

ZACHOS, JOHN CELIVERGOS. 1820 ed. Cooper, Peter. 1791-1883. Political and financial opinions. 1877. HE—Z2

ZEISBERGER, David. 1721-1808. Diary of David Zeisberger, a Moravian missionary among the Indians of Ohio. Translated from the original German manuscript and edited by E. F. Bliss. Cincinnati, 1885. Vol. I. O.   HG—Ze5

ZEITSCHRIFT fur kirchengeschichte, in verbindung mit W. Gass, H. Reuter, und A. Ritschl, herausgegeben von Theodor Brieger. Gotha, 1877-82. Vol. I-II, & v. O.   HC—Ze3

ZIEBER, Eugene. Rules for the proper usage of heraldry in the United States, and other extracts from the popular authority, "Heraldry in America." 34 pp. S. Philadelphia, Pa. 1900.
                                                                    HH—Pamphlet

ADDENDA TO DICTIONARY

GROVE, Lilly M., Translator. See: MADELIN, Louis. Victory (The) of the Marne. Paris, 1917. O.

NEW YORK Genealogical and Biographical Record. Devoted to the interests of American Genealogy and Biography. Vols. i-xlix. New York, 1870-1919. 49 vols. Illustrations, portraits, fac-similes, coats-of-arms. Q.   HK—N49

NEW YORK Genealogical and Biographical Society. See: NEW YORK Genealogical and Biographical Record. Published Quarterly by the Society.   HK—N49

POLLARD, Eliza F. King's (The) Signet, or, the Story of a Huguenot family. 1 leaf, v-vi, 1 leaf, 9-288 pp. London, 1900. O.
                                                         HN—P91

ADDENDA

HOUGHTON, Louise Seymour. Idealism of the French people. 3 leaves, 7-80 pp. Boston, cop. 1918. O.   HD—H81

PIERRE and his family; or, a Story of the Waldenses. vi, 7-214 pp., 4 pl. Revised edition. Philadelphia, 1842. S.   HN—P81

GENEALOGICAL and family history of Southern New York and the Hudson River Valley. A Record of the achievements of her people in the making of a Commonwealth and the building of a Nation. Edited by Cuyler Reynolds. Vols. i-iii. Illustrated. 3 vols. Q.   HH—R46
Gift of Mrs. James M. Lawton.
> Note: These volumes are profusely illustrated with full-page portraits of members of the numerous families whose genealogies are published herein. A complete index to family names is found in Volume iii. Amongst these are many Huguenot names:—Bayard, Clarkson, de Forest, Delafield, Delano, De La Vergne, de Peyster, Hasbrouck, van Rensselaer, van Santvoord, etc. Also portraits and interesting data of the Anderson, Lawton, Roe and other families.

REYNOLDS, CUYLER, Editor. See: GENEALOGICAL and family
history of Southern New York and the Hudson River Valley. . . .
Vols. I-III. Illustrated. 3 vols. Q. New York, 1914. HH—R46

GEOGRAPHICAL REFERENCE ADDENDA

AIGUES-MORTES, South of France. See: CRY, N. Heroism of Huguenot women imprisoned for life in the Tower of Constance. Springfield, Mass., 1894. HG—Qu3

ALBANY, New York and its place in the United States. See: FERNOW, BERTHOLD. Albany, N. Y., 1886. HE—F39

ALBANY, New York. See: VAN LAER, A. J. F., Editor. Early Records of . . . Albany and Colony of Rensselaerswyck. 3 vols. Albany, 1916-1919. Q. (UNIV. STATE N. Y. N. Y. State Lib'y Hist. Bull. 9-11.) HE—A326

AMERICAN Battles: famous in History of Army and Navy. Full-page illustrations. See: OHIO SOC. OF N. Y. 1904. HE—Pamphlet

BERGEN County, New Jersey. See: HARVEY, C. B. Genealogical history of Hudson & Bergen Counties, New Jersey, N. Y., 1900. HE—H26

BRADFORD, Massachusetts. See: KINGSBURY, J. D. Memorial history of Bradford. . . . Haverhill, Mass., 1883. HE—B73K

CONCORD, Massachusetts. See: POTTER, CHAS. EDW., Editor. Genealogies of old families . . . and their descendants. . . . Vol. I. Boston, 1887. HH—P85

DEDHAM, Massachusetts. See: WORTHINGTON, E. History of Dedham. . . . Boston, 1827. HE—Ded36

DUXBURY, Massachusetts. See: WINSOR, JUSTIN. History of Duxbury . . . with genealogical registers. Boston, 1849. HE—W721

ETHERIDGE, GEORGE. See: DUXBURY, Mass. Copy of the old records . . . 1642-1770. Plymouth, Mass., 1893. HE—D95

FAIRFIELD, Connecticut. See: HURD, D. H., Comp. History of Fairfield, Conn. . . . Philadelphia, 1881. HE—H93

———— See: SCHENCK, MRS. E. H. History of Fairfield, Fairfield County, Conn. . . . 1639-1818. Vol. I. N. Y., 1889. 1 vol. HE—Sch2

FLORIDE Française. See: GAFFAREL, PAUL. Histoire de la Floride Française. Paris, 1875. HE—G12

HARRISON, Westchester County, New York. See: BAIRD, C. W. History of Rye . . . 1660-1870, . . . Harrison, and the White Plains till 1788. N. Y., 1871.   HE—B16

HUDSON County, New Jersey. See: HARVEY, C. B. Genealogical History of Hudson & Bergen Counties. New York, 1900.   HE—H26

—— See: WINFIELD, C. H. History of the county of Hudson. New York, 1874.   HE—W72

KINGS County, Long Island, New York. See: BERGEN, Teunis G. Register . . . of the early settlers . . . to 1700. . . . New York, 1881.   HH—B35

—— See: DITMAS, Charles Andrew, Compiler. Historic home-steads of Kings County.   HE—D615K

LaROCHELLE. See: BLANCHON, Pierre. Jean Guiton et le Siege de LaRochelle. LaRochelle, 1911.   HG—G968

LONG ISLAND, New York. See: MATHER, F. G. Refugees of 1776 from Long Island to Connecticut.

—— See: TREDWELL, Daniel M. Personal reminiscences. . . . Brooklyn, N. Y., 1912, 1917. 2 vols.   HE—T78

MARYLAND. See: GRIFFITH, Thomas W. Sketches of the early history of Maryland. Baltimore, 1821.   HE—G58

MONMOUTH County, New Jersey. See: SALTER, Edwin. His-tory of Monmouth and Ocean Counties. . . . Bayonne, N. J., 1890.   HE—S27

NEW AMSTERDAM. See: New York.

NEW ENGLAND. See: SAVAGE, James. Genealogical dictionary of first settlers. . . . 4 vols. Boston, 1860-'62.   HH—Sa9

—— See: Senter, Oramel S. Civic and scenic New England. New-port in 1877. Illustrated.   HE—Z6

NEW HARTFORD, Connecticut. See: JONES, Henry R. Sketches of . . . New Hartford in the past and present. Hartford, Conn., 1883.   HE—A512

NEW JERSEY. See: CHAMBERS, Theo. F. Early Germans of New Jersey, their history, churches, & genealogies. Dover, N. J., 1895.   HE—C445

—— Colonial history. See: SMITH, S. History of the Colony of Nova-Cæsaria, or, New Jersey. Burlington, N. J., 1765. A reprint.   HE—N46S

NEW NETHERLANDS. See: O'CALLAGHAN, E. B. Register of New Netherlands, 1626-1674. Albany, 1865. HE—Oc.1

NEW PALTZ, New York. See: LeFEVRE, Ralph. History of New Paltz, N. Y. . . . 1670-1820. Albany, N. Y., 1903-[18]. 2 vols. HE—L52 & L52A

———— See: Vennema, Rev. Ame. History of the Reformed Church—1683-1883. HC—V56

NEW ROCHELLE, N. Y. See: WINTER, Clare B. Huguenots in other Countries.

NEW YORK. See: HOFFMAN, C. F. Pioneers of New York. An Anniversary discourse . . . Dec. 6, 1847. N. Y., 1848. HE—A512

———— See: PELLETREAU, William S. Historic homes . . . genealogical and family history of N. Y. 4 vols. N. Y., 1907. HH—P36

NEW YORK CITY, N. Y. See: DeWITT, Rev. Thomas. Discourse . . . North Reformed Dutch (collegiate) Church . . . 1856. HC—D51

———— Also see 9 Volumes of Pamphlets. HE—Z1—Z9

NEW YORK, Fishkill Village, Dutchess County. See: VAN VOORHIS, E. W., Compiler. Tombstone inscriptions First Reformed Dutch Church. . . . N. Y. pref. 1882. HH—V37

NEWBURGH, New York. See: METHODIST Episcopal Church. Record of Baptisms & Marriages. 1789-1835. HE—N533

NORWALK, Connecticut. 1648-1800. See: HALL, Rev. Edwin, Compiler. Ancient historical records . . . and the Genealogical register of marriages, births and deaths. Norwalk, Conn., 1847. HE—N83H

NORWICH, Connecticut. 1660-1800. See: PERKINS, M. E. Old houses of the antient town of Norwich. Norwich, Conn., 1895. HE—P41

OCEAN County, New Jersey. See: SALTER, Edwin. History of Monmouth and Ocean Counties. . . . Bayonne, N. J., 1890. HE—S277

OHIO. See: RYAN, D. J. History of Ohio . . . with biographical sketches of her governors & the ordinance of 1787. Columbus, O., 1888. HE—R95

OXFORD, Massachusetts. See: entries in Dictionary Section of this Catalogue.

PELHAM, Massachusetts. See: PARMENTER, C. O. History of N. Y.: Pelham . . . 1738-1898, including the early history of Prescott. Amherst, Mass., 1898. HE—P21

—— See: HAGUE, W. Old Pelham and New Rochelle. 1882. O. HB—H12

PHILADELPHIA. See: WATSON, J. F. Annals of Philadelphia, Pennsylvania, in the olden time. . . . 3 vols. Philadelphia, 1891. HE—WATS33

—— See: WOOLSEY, SUSAN C. Short history of the city of Philadelphia. 1887. HE—W88

PLATTSBURG, New York. See: HOLDEN, JAMES AUSTIN. Centenary of the Battle of Plattsburg. 1814. Albany, 1914. HE—H726

PORTSMOUTH, New Hampshire. See: BREWSTER, C. W. Rambles about Portsmouth. . . . Portsmouth, 1859. HE—P83B

PRESCOTT, Massachusetts. See: PARMENTER, C. O. History of Pelham, . . . 1738-1898, including the early history of Prescott. . . . Amherst, Mass. HE—P21

RENSSELAERSWYCK, New York. See: VAN LAER, A. J. F., Editor. Early records of the City and County of Albany and Colony of Rensselaerswyck. 3 vols. Albany, 1916-1918. Q. (Univ. State N. Y. N. Y. State Lib'y Hist. Bull., Nos. 9-11.) HE—A326

ROCKLAND County, New York. See: GREEN, F. B. History of Rockland County. N. Y., 1886. HE—G82

RYE, New York. See: BAIRD, C. W. History of Rye . . . 1660-1870. New York, 1871. HE—B16

SACO, Massachusetts. See: PEPPERELLBOROUGH, Mass. First book of records. Portland, Me., 1896. HE—SA1

SALEM, New York. See: SALEM Book: records of the past and glimpses of the present. . . . Salem, N. Y., 1896.

SOUTH AFRICA: Huguenot refugees. See: A Volume of 8 Pamphlets on South Africa. HB—H87S.A

SOUTH CAROLINA. 1670-1719. See: McCRADY, E. History of South Carolina under the Proprietary Government. . . . N. Y., 1897. HE—M13

STOUGHTON, Massachusetts. See: RECORD of births, Marriages and deaths . . . 1727-1800. . . . Ed. by F. Endicott. Canton, Mass., 1896. HH

TOWER of Constance. See: CRY, N. Heroism of Huguenot women imprisoned for life in the Tower of Constance. HC—Qu3

UNITED Brethren Congregation. See: MORAVIAN Church.

WHITE PLAINS, Westchester County, New York. See: BAIRD, C. W. History of Rye . . . 1660-1870 . . . including . . . White Plains till 1788. New York, 1871.   HE—B16

WOODBURY, Connecticut. See: COTHREN, W. Second Centennial Celebration . . . of ancient Woodbury. Woodbury, 1859.
                                                                                HE—W885

WORCESTER, Massachusetts. See: WORCESTER Soc. of Antiquity. Collections. Vol. IV. Worcester, Mass., 1882.   HE—W89

www.ingramcontent.com/pod-product-compliance
Lightning Source LLC
Chambersburg PA
CBHW060137280326
41932CB00012B/1549